THE MAKING OF
ROUMANIA

OXFORD UNIVERSITY PRESS
AMEN HOUSE, E.C. 4
LONDON EDINBURGH GLASGOW
LEIPZIG NEW YORK TORONTO
MELBOURNE CAPETOWN BOMBAY
CALCUTTA MADRAS SHANGHAI
HUMPHREY MILFORD
PUBLISHER TO THE
UNIVERSITY

PRINTED IN GREAT BRITAIN AT THE UNIVERSITY PRESS, OXFORD
BY JOHN JOHNSON, PRINTER TO THE UNIVERSITY

THE MAKING OF
ROUMANIA

A STUDY OF AN INTERNATIONAL
PROBLEM, 1856–1866

BY /

T. W. RIKER, B.LITT. OXON

Professor of Modern European History in the
University of Texas

OXFORD UNIVERSITY PRESS
LONDON : HUMPHREY MILFORD
1931

TO MY MOTHER

LOUISE D. RIKER

TO WHOSE LOVE AND SELF-SACRIFICE

I FEEL THAT I OWE MY WHOLE LIFE-WORK

THIS BOOK IS DEDICATED WITH

THOUGHTS TOO DEEP TO

FIND EXPRESSION

PREFACE

THE making of Roumania is a study of a more or less fortuitous experiment in international polity. The efforts of the Concert of Europe to direct the destinies of a nationality in an age when nationalism was coming gradually to awaken to its own inherent power gives us the essence of our problem. In my attempt to sketch these ten formative years of the Roumanian nation I concern myself with domestic history only so far as may be necessary to show the nationalist reaction to an intrusive internationalism. My interest is rather external—looking in from without and outward from within. Since comparatively little has been published on this phase of history, the work is based for the most part on archival evidence. It is from such sources that one is best able to follow the tortuous ways of Europe's diplomats and to learn the nature of the reports from her consular representatives, which provided the lens through which this problem was surveyed. These agents at Bucharest and Jassy were, in a sense, the pillars of the European protectorate; and there were certainly no keener observers of this nation in the making.

It is sometimes hard to be consistent in the spelling of foreign proper names. I have tried to adopt consistently the French spelling, though, as Cogalnitchano is spelled in various ways by the French themselves, I decided to follow the form which I found in a letter written in French by a contemporary Roumanian, John Ghika.

Though the expense of this undertaking has been largely my own, I am happy to acknowledge a subsidy from the Social Science Research Council, which enabled me to make a second trip to Europe to finish my investigations, and also a large grant from the Social Research Fund of the University of Texas, as well as an additional grant from that University to defray the cost of transcribing documents. The gratitude which I feel to certain of my colleagues, who in some ways fathered this work, is a very small return for so much generous interest. It is a pleasure also to testify my appreciation to Dr. Johann Sass of the Reichsarchiv, Berlin, and to Dr. Lothar Gross of the Staatsarchiv, Vienna, for their very kindly courtesies; and, indeed, the foreign scholar cannot but appreciate the privileges which are accorded him of using the dispatches of the Public Record Office, the Archives du Ministère des Affaires Étrangères, the Reichsarchiv at Berlin, the

Staatsarchiv and Kriegsarchiv at Vienna, as well as the great libraries like the British Museum and the Bibliothèque Nationale. It is also a pleasure to acknowledge the debt that I owe Professor Max S. Handman of the University of Texas for placing his Roumanian works at my disposal as well as giving me so freely of his time in the discussion of economic phases of my problem. Professor E. R. Adair of McGill University and Professor Bernadotte E. Schmitt of the University of Chicago were kind enough to give me some valuable suggestions; Professor Herbert C. Bell of Wesleyan University generously allowed me to use some of the material which he had gathered for his study of Palmerston; and the co-operation of my wife throughout the undertaking has been nothing less than indispensable. To Professor A. F. Pribram, Principal C. Grant Robertson, Professor R. W. Seton-Watson, Sir Bernard Pares, and Dr. Louis Eisenmann I am grateful for help along the path of my labours, and I owe much to the sound historical judgement of my friend, Dr. Margarete Merores of Vienna. And, finally, the Roumanians whom I have met have done much to sustain my enthusiasm for pursuing this study of their interesting country. It has been impossible not to feel a certain partisan sympathy for their fathers and grandfathers who represented the national hopes in the making of Roumania.

T. W. R.

Austin, Texas, August 1931.

POSTSCRIPT

The publication of M. Paul Henry's work, *L'Abdication du Prince Cuza et l'avènement de la dynastie de Hohenzollern au trône de Roumanie*, though it contains some interesting excerpts from Couza's private papers, did not appear soon enough for me to utilize it in the preparation of my book, then far advanced in proof. I note chiefly a dispatch of Alexandri's, revealing a studied effort on Couza's part to mollify the French and British governments after his *coup d'état* and the reproduction, in part, of his last appeal to Napoleon, October 1, 1865 (to which I refer on p. 482). The documents, which are drawn from the French and Austrian archives, were, of course, available to me.

T. W. R.

CONTENTS

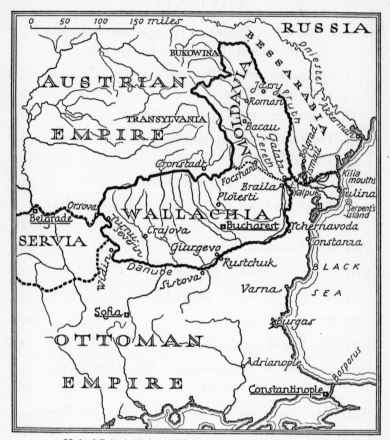

United Principalities of Moldavia and Wallachia in 1866

part of the life of the Near East, but hardly even an outpost of Europe. It is true that silent forces were already operating to bring them within the pale of Western civilization. But, without depreciating the traces of French influence, which certain incidents of history had implanted in these lands, and without ignoring the traffic in *articles de luxe* which Austrian merchants brought by steamer from Vienna, the Danubian Principalities had scarcely as yet emerged from their historic and geographical isolation. Even after the Peace of Adrianople in 1829 had opened the Black Sea to Western trade, and had restored to the Principalities their economic autonomy (and this did not prevent Russia from imposing tariffs in the Danube delta)[1], the new direction which commerce should take was clearly a matter of slow adjustment. Politically, socially, economically, the Danubian Principalities were before the middle of the nineteenth century like a child just beginning to learn its letters. The Frenchman, Vaillant, writing in 1844, expressed his belief that, if these provinces were united under a single head, with Focshani (close to the frontier which divides them) as their common capital, they would become one of the most important centres of the East; 'that', he said, 'is my dream'.[2] With greater vision his contemporary, Ubicini, pleaded for Europe's aid in preparing these people—once the rampart of the Roman Empire against barbarian invaders from the East—to play an integral role in her affairs.[3] It was Europe's destiny to help realize the dream of union, but the greatest of her services were to come of contacts more gradual and pervasive.

Certainly the intrinsic value of these lands was no criterion of the fluid wealth of their inhabitants. The time had yet to come when modern capital and modern science would tap the mines, utilize the water-power, and glean full value from the richness of the soil. The great mass of the population—estimated by Ubicini in 1840 as 3,754,000[3]—was still agrarian, and even the larger towns were little more than greatly extended villages, the largest of all being a sort of *maison de luxe*, ministering to the wants of some fifteen thousand absentee proprietors. In the middle of the nineteenth century Bucharest was a city of somewhat over 100,000 souls. Squalid and poorly paved, more conspicuous for its church spires than for its public monuments, with most of its business in the hands of Greeks and Jews, the Wallachian capital had few of the graces of a metropolitan city. Jassy, with less than half of the population of Bucharest, had much the same character as the sister

[1] Vaillant, *La Romanie*, vol. iii, p. 63.   [2] *Ibid.*
[3] Ubicini, 'Provinces d'origine roumaine', pp. 217–18 in Chopin and Ubicini, *Provinces danubiennes*. A detailed French *mémoire* of 1850 gives the figures ('not perhaps absolutely exact but approximate') as 2,722,000 for Wallachia and 1,370,500 for Moldavia: *Aff. étr., Mém. et doc., Turquie*, vol. 55, no. 4.

INTRODUCTION

THE DANUBIAN PRINCIPALITIES AND THE POLITICAL ASPIRATIONS: UNION AND A FOREIGN PRINCE

'ARTIST, student, poet, or man of affairs, traversing the Danube country—what traveller has not been struck wit rich natural resources of the Roumanian principalities! Abun rivers, fertile soil, huge mountains concealing their treasur temperate climate, a blue and limpid sky! These count granaries for a host of people, and which the Turks in t picturesque language called "the garden of Stamboul", have the like in Europe, and must only be analogous to what the va of the Mississippi is to America.'[1] Thus wrote Nicolas Balces one of the pioneer reformers of Wallachia, who prefaced in t way his study of the economic distress of a people whom Natu had endowed so generously with her gifts. There is not mu exaggeration in this ecstasy over the orographical assets of t Danubian Principalities. Traversed by a long stretch of plain, i soil enriched by the black earth which one associates with souther Russia, and freshened by a score of turbulent streams, dancing down the mountain slopes to empty into the great river which is central Europe's highway to the East, a richly carpeted vestibule between the mountains and that great sea which opens the treasures of the East to the markets of the West, Moldavia and Wallachia were lands which must in time support a strong and prosperous nation.[2] But our study of the making of Roumania brings our recollection back to a time when the Danubian Principalities were a little-known appendage of the Ottoman Empire, visited now and again by Frenchmen who recorded their observations, described by a British consul who was struck with their commercial possi- bilities, but only gradually emerging from a state of economic servitude to Turkey, and still sending the bulk of their cattle and hides across the mountains to Hungary,[3] or emptying their store of wheat into Greek or Turkish merchantmen[4]—in short, an integral

---

[1] Balcescu, 'Question économique des principautés danubiennes' in *Acte și legiuiri privitoare la chestia tărăneasca*, seria i, vol. iv, p. 45.

[2] 'The vast and fertile plains washed by the Danube are succeeded by a middle district of undulating country, partly clothed with woods and extending in pastures which feed immense herds of horses and cattle' : Forester, *The Danube and the Black Sea*, p. 84.

[3] Cioriceanu, *La Roumanie économique*, pp. 152, 159. The figures which are here given show that in 1862 considerably more than half the animals and hides were exported to the Austrian Empire. It is reasonable to suppose that a much greater proportion had been sent thither before the growth of commercial inter- course with the West. [4] Vaillant, *La Romanie*, vol. iii, p. 62.

B

capital on a smaller scale.[1] It is a common mistake to judge a
country by its cities, and neither of these centres of urban life was
conspicuously interesting. Yet Bucharest had a certain flare.
There was a good deal of gaiety during the winter months, when
the landed nobility left their lonely estates and gathered to spend
their substance. Vice flourished on a large scale, and there was
much tawdry extravagance. A French writer, who enjoyed a long
sojourn in the Principalities, found in the social life of this capital
a hollow pretentiousness, as though its people aped a culture which
they had not yet assimilated. 'A prince without a palace, a clergy
without morals, an academy without members, immense streets
without homes, a library without readers, splendid dwellings and
vile cottages, magnificent promenades and filthy dumps'[2]—one
need not continue his catalogue of contradictions. A friendlier pen
than this wrote with some astonishment of the broad avenues and
'some houses which are not surpassed by the finest in Paris',[3] and,
if the dust or mud was quite intolerable, there was something
individual in the thousands of equipages which the condition of
the streets rendered necessary. Flecked, as it were, by certain
evidences of comfort or luxury, the Danubian Principalities were,
after all, merely oriental lands, straining to taste the seductive
culture of the Occident.[4] Such exotic manifestations as one found
were largely due to influences from Paris which mingled with the
habits cultivated during Phanariot days. Yet Bucharest was not
the core of the Principalities, and the bulk of the population,
whose life was strictly rural, was quite immune from such distrac-
tions. It was on the basis of the poverty of the many that the few
were able to spend their modest fortunes.

The time had not yet come when peasant and lord would seek
in their economic interdependence a mutually profitable relationship, or when a vigorous middle class would constitute the avenue
to foreign capital, so sorely needed. Thouvenel epitomized the
social structure of the Principalities when he wrote, 'In Wallachia
the sultan weighed on the prince, the prince on the *boyards*, and the
boyards on the peasants; there existed a hierarchal tyranny, of
which the head alone has been destroyed.'[5] The leaders of the

---

[1] A German sojourner remarked that it was 'a hideous city', having partly the
characteristics of a Russian provincial city, partly those of a Levantine town:
Sayn-Wittgenstein, *Souvenirs et correspondance*, vol. i, p. 373. The British consul,
Wilkinson, on the other hand, thought it rather more attractive than Bucharest:
An Account of the Principalities of Wallachia and Moldavia, p. 88.

[2] Le Cler, *La Moldo-Valachie*, p. 307. Le Cler wrote in 1866.

[3] Thouvenel, 'La Valachie en 1839', *Revue des deux mondes*, nouv. sér., vol.
xviii, p. 568.

[4] 'Bucharest, composed of a great collection of villages, in the midst of which
rise some houses of fine appearance, is only an oriental city, perhaps inferior to the
great cities of Slavic Turkey': Desprez, 'La Moldavie et le mouvement roumain',
Revue des deux mondes, nouv. sér., vol. xxi, p. 112.   [5] Thouvenel, *op. cit.*, p. 570.

national life, in so far as leadership was apparent, were to be found among the landed aristocracy, or *boyards*, as they were called, legally immune from taxation, and enjoying still, by the grace of Russia, a political ascendancy. The larger proprietors, or greater *boyards*, were not even of native extraction, most of them coming of families who had been imported with the Greek princes or *phanariots*, who had ruled the Principalities during the period of greatest oppression. Though originally land had been given by the native princes to their warrior chiefs as a suitable reward for military service, the *boyards* became recruited in course of time from the members of the phanariot bureaucracy; hence the term, *ciocoi*, or *parvenus* (literally, 'dogs'), which their enemies had given them.[1] Some few members of the *boyarie* had grown accustomed to send their sons to Paris, and had acquired a certain veneer of Gallic culture, but the great majority remained content to spend their lives as humble magnates who were too poor or too indolent to become successful cultivators, and were chiefly noted for their skill in gambling. Saint-Marc-Girardin[2] found the *boyards* of Moldavia more proud and independent than the members of the same class in Wallachia—a fact which may account both for the particularism which they manifested at a later day as well as for the zest with which the younger *boyards* strove at the same time against the régime which Europe then ordained. It is hard to make distinctions between backward provinces, but one gathers that Moldavia was in general rather more prosperous than Wallachia.[3] A British observer noted that the Moldavian *boyards* were much inclined to stay at home to manage—or mismanage—their estates, but their Wallachian brothers could not resist the lure of Bucharest.

'Almost without exception,' he writes, '[they] spend the greatest part of the year in the capital, and farm out their lands chiefly to Greeks, who pay so much to the proprietor, and make what they can out of the property; the term of lease is in such cases for five years, three of which are paid [for] in advance. But, as no regulations are entered into to provide for the proper cultivation of the soil, and the leases are in themselves so brief, estates under this method do not improve, and the landlords, indolent, luxurious, and extravagant are generally deeply involved in debt.'[4]

Time-servers, who lived solely by exploiting their tenants, and always harassed by creditors, the *boyards* of the Principalities formed a class which only the rough hand of Time would mould

---

[1] Castille, *Portraits politiques*, p. 47.

[2] Saint-Marc-Girardin, *Souvenirs de voyage*, pp. 262–3.

[3] Colquhoun to F.O., Sept. 9, 1836, F.O. 195/78; Poujade to Tocqueville, no. 2, July 23, 1849, *Aff. étr., Turquie, Bucharest*, vol. vii. Moldavia was represented as richer by reason of its greater natural resources.

[4] Bulwer to Clarendon, no. 423, Feb. 6, 1858, enc., F.O. 78/1374.

into a vigorous force, capable of leading or sustaining the national growth. For the present they were but dimly aware of their opportunities.

Unquestionably it was the social order which most distinguished the Danubian Principalities from the Western world, and gave them a character somewhat medieval in politics and economy. The poverty of a land so blessed with natural resources might be partly ascribed to oriental lethargy, but was mainly the result of history. The Industrial Revolution had not yet come down the Danube, and agriculture was not only primitive in its methods but based on that medieval social system which divided most of mankind into the privileged and unprivileged. Generally speaking it was the *boyard* who reaped what the peasant sowed. On the toil of the two million and a half peasants rested the economic life of the country. Though no longer legally a serf since the middle of the eighteenth century, the peasant had long since ceased to be a freeholder. He had the usufruct of a certain tract of land on the lord's estate, two-thirds of which must by law be placed at the disposal of the tenantry. For this service he must work a certain number of days out of each year, and pay an annual tax in kind in addition to the fee which he was charged for the use of the grazing land or for other privileges (reminding one of the *banalités* of France of the old régime). Finally, since the *boyard* had obtained immunity from taxation when serfdom was abolished, he had to bear the chief weight of the State's support. As the manorial exactions (often but not always sanctioned by law) were continually on the increase, the poverty of these children of the soil—compelled to subsist for the most part on carrots and maize, and always in debt to the village usurer—may well have been as dire as Balcescu paints it. With no government strong enough to challenge their oppressors, one wonders that they were not driven by sheer despair to attempt a *jacquerie*. Perhaps the answer may be found in a British consul's comment:

'There does not, perhaps, exist a people labouring under a greater degree of oppression from the effect of despotic power and more heavily burthened with impositions and taxes than the peasants of Wallachia and Moldavia, nor any who would bear half their weight with the same patience and seeming resignation. Accustomed, however, to that state of servitude which to others might appear intolerable, they are unable to form hopes for a better condition. The habitual depression of their minds has become a sort of natural stupor and apathy, which renders them equally indifferent to the enjoyments of life and insensible to happiness as to the pangs of anguish and affliction.'[1]

---

[1] Wilkinson, *An Account of the Principalities of Wallachia and Moldavia and Various Political Observations relating to them*, p. 155.

Perhaps, after all, in their vampires and evil spirits, no less than in their quaint marriage customs and scrupulous observance of church fêtes, they found a little relief from the sheer monotony of living. In any event, the Russian occupation in 1829 was followed by General Kisseleff's gallant efforts to relieve the inhabitants in his charge. The *Règlement organique* (of which mention will be made again) fixed in definite categories the privileged and un-privileged, and regulated with meticulous thoroughness the rela-tions of landlord and peasant. The customary dues to the landlord were confirmed, and the economic position of the peasant so restricted as to amount practically to a restoration of serfdom. True, the very precision of the statute gave promise of an end of arbitrary exactions, but, on the other hand, the hated *corvées* were so extended that about half the peasant's time was at the disposal of the lord.[1] In short, the result of such a system as we have out-lined was to depress the class, which, nearest the soil, was the most fundamental element in the national economy. Compelled to give the best days of the harvest period to the lord, tilling his own land when the weather was least propitious,[2] he had also to work under the physical disabilities that come of an unnutritious diet,[3] not to mention the moral depression which is the lot of the exploited. Manifestly, the agrarian problem was more aggravated than solved. Kisseleff, who had really hoped to relieve the peasant, was by no means satisfied with the reform which he had instituted, but the callous selfishness of the *boyards*, whose favour was necessary to the Russians, prevented any real measure of relief.[4] In truth, the *boyards* had by this time come to know the luxuries of the West, and, now that the Black Sea was open to merchantmen, they found for the first time a profitable market for their wheat; hence, by driving the peasants to greater exertions they might hope to achieve for themselves a higher standard of living.[5] The more *corvées*, the more wheat; the more wheat, the more French wines

[1] Evans, *The Agrarian Revolution in Roumania*, pp. 30–2. In view of this fact it does not seem to me that Mr. Evans's palliation of the effects of the *Règlement* is very convincing. Moreover, when the manorial estates were administered by overseers or leasers, as was becoming more and more the case, the drafting of the peasants' time was so much the more serious.

[2] Balcescu, *op. cit.*, p. 77.

[3] Arion, *La Situation économique et sociale du paysan en Roumanie*, p. 17.

[4] A law of 1851 allowed the peasant to bargain with the landowner for addi-tional land, if any were available, but obviously few of such arrangements between exploiters and exploited would be satisfactory to the latter.

[5] Xénopol, *Histoire des Roumains de la Dacie Trajane depuis les origines jusqu'à l'union des principautés en 1859*, vol. ii, pp. 418, 459. According to a carefully prepared *mémoire* of the French consul, Botmiliau, in 1850, some of the peasants were debased by a common practice on the part of the *boyards* of establishing distilleries and taverns on their estates, farming the business out to Jews, who sold liquor to the peasants at an exorbitant price: *Aff. étr., Mém. et doc., Turquie*, vol. 55, no. 4.

and British waistcoats! Yet it is a fact that the *boyards* were not, in general, efficient managers, and many of their estates were heavily mortgaged. Only by the introduction of a more modern technique and the social amelioration of the tillers of the soil would agriculture begin to gain the reward which Nature had ordained.

As a medium for promoting social progress the Orthodox Church ought naturally have been in the forefront. But, however great its influence with the masses, it would appear from all accounts that this ancient institution was now distinctly moribund (perhaps the very prevalence of divorce attests to that),[1] and, as far as its upper circles are concerned, reputedly corrupt, like the judiciary. Though some of the monasteries still occupied themselves with the social needs of the inhabitants, a considerable number of charitable institutions were endowed by wealthy *boyards* or founded and supported by the public authority. Until the *Règlement organique* made some degree of schooling obligatory for the clergy, the parish priests were as ignorant as they were indigent, and remind one of the miserable *curés* of pre-Revolutionary France. In fact the Church in the Principalities was not an educative force. It is a tribute to the public spirit in the Principalities that so many schools had been provided for the needs of the inhabitants, and, while the proportion of illiterates was no doubt very high, Thouvenel was able to write in 1839: 'Public instruction has made immense progress.'[2]

No doubt the inspiration was partly of native origin. The passing of the Phanariots and the lessening of Turkish *ingérance* served to liberate the national soul and to engender self-confidence. It is also true that the tradition of French influence gave to Paris a certain attractive force. Undoubtedly the means of further enlightenment must come, as was said, from greater intercourse with the West; and it is equally clear that the impulse must come from the Principalities themselves. Before 1868 there were no railroads in these lands, and communication was either by the Danube to Orsova, by water to the ports of Braila or Galatz, or, less frequently, by the roads through the passes in the Carpathians. The principal highway was the route taken by the post, which arrived from Austria via Orsova twice a week. With few exceptions the roads which traversed the country were wretched in the extreme, bridges were few, and the rivers frequently impassable. Under these circumstances travelling by diligence was too uncomfortable to attract many tourists,[3] and, as commerce was only just beginning to find

[1] Le Cler, *op. cit.*, p. 279. One traveller seemed more impressed with the prevalence of divorce than any observation that he made: Schickler, *En Orient; Souvenirs de voyage*, p. 10. Wilkinson and St.-Marc-Girardin discuss it at length.

[2] Thouvenel, *op. cit.*, pp. 577–8.   [3] Cioriceanu, *op. cit.*, pp. 122–3.

its new channels, foreign visitors to the Principalities were certainly not numerous. For the most part the development of the national culture was the work of certain native enthusiasts who had drawn their inspiration from their wanderings abroad, and whose tireless efforts can hardly be overpraised.

'The progress of the Rouman states', writes Xénopol, 'was the work of some individuals, who strove to triumph over all obstacles. They wished to improvise everything: schools without professors, without books, without premises; a theatre without scenery, without actors, without repertory; a national development and patriotic revival without the necessary liberty for its manifestation. A gigantic struggle was inaugurated between some *natures d'élite* and the darkness which everywhere obscured the horizon.'[1]

Little by little these dreams took more substantial shape; the process of national education began to unfold and show results. During the first half of the nineteenth century an increasing number of elementary schools had been founded, as well as an academy at Jassy and a college at Bucharest; and, though the higher courses of instruction were suppressed for a time by Russian influence, the movement underwent only a casual interruption. While it can hardly be said that complete freedom of opinion was as yet permitted, both the capitals possessed newspapers, and already a national literature had come into being—in itself a powerful generator of nationalism. At the same time the prevalence of the French language in the upper circles was a fair indication that Western ideas were in the process of infiltration. Meanwhile at Paris itself the romantic movement of the nineteenth century—the same impulse which had driven Byron to Greece and Shelley to Italy—had interested such men as Michelet, the historian, Quinet, the philosopher, and a host of lesser lights in this people of Romanic tongue, whom ill-fate had subjugated to Mohammedans and Slavs. Doubtless it was the unquenchable vitality of this period that was now stirring the Moldo-Wallachians themselves into something like a national consciousness.

Though in essence a single nationality, the Roumans had never—except during a brief interval under Michael the Brave—been united under a single sceptre. That portion which dwelt in Transylvania had fallen long ago under the sway of Hungary, while in 1779 the northernmost tip of Moldavia, known as Bukovina, had been ceded by Turkey to Austria. In later history these 'ultramontanes' became somewhat more enlightened than their brothers on the Danube. If oppressed by Magyars they at least suffered less from invasions, and their contacts were rather with the Occident than with the Orient; perhaps because their alien domination had been more

[1] Xénopol, *op. cit.*, vol. i, p. 465.

evident, and partly because their clergy were better educated, the nationalist feeling was first to germinate among these outlanders. There is plenty of evidence that their activities gave stimulus to the movement in 'Moldo-Wallachia', and when in 1848 the Transylvanian peasant finally achieved his economic freedom a standard was set which could not fail to mark a lesson for his less fortunate kinsmen. Quickened by influences that came from the West the cultural development of these people was, in short, appreciably higher than that of the Moldo-Wallachians.[1]

Moldavia and Wallachia, the two political entities with which our study is concerned, had an exceptionally chequered history. We shall not take the space to inquire into the origins of these people of Romanic speech or to follow their successive struggles to preserve their freedom against the hordes of invaders who poured from Asia into southern Europe. Geographically so situated as to be a natural highway from the north and east, the two little principalities of Moldavia and Wallachia had often the misfortune of being a shuttle-cock between contending neighbours. In the fifteenth century Wallachia and in the sixteenth Moldavia succumbed to that wave of Ottoman expansion which had previously swamped the Christian nations further south. Yet the imposition of the Sultan's suzerainty meant at first but little diminution of the independence enjoyed by the native *voivodes* or hospodars. Certain capitulations signed by the Porte acknowledged the ancient sovereignty of both principalities, save for the payment of annual tribute—the usual symbol of subjection to an oriental overlord. In 1571 a treaty or capitulation with Moldavia provided that Turkey must defend that country against invasion, while in return the Moldavian prince was to furnish a contingent in the Sultan's army. This, however, was more like a defensive alliance than an unequal contract between suzerain and vassal. Moreover, it was explicitly stated that no Turk should own land in Moldavia—a concession which had already been granted to Wallachia. If the Danubian Principalities had been spared external struggles, and if these early treaties had been scrupulously observed, the future course of their history would have flowed towards independence.

But the autonomy of the Danubian Principalities was more apparent than real, for the Sultans were able to subject them to an economic spoliation[2] more deadly in its effect than any immediate interference in governmental affairs. From the time of Solyman the Magnificent shipments of grain and sheep were sent regularly to Turkey (the Porte having a right of pre-emption in the native

---

[1] For an interesting account of cultural development among the Roumans of Transylvania see Iorga, *Geschichte des rumänischen Volkes*, vol. ii, part 7, chap. i.

[2] The subject is fully discussed in Xénopol, *op. cit.*, vol. i, pp. 426–33.

market), and, while sometimes these were paid for, more often they had the character of gratuitous requisitions. Such exactions, moreover, were additional to tribute, which, as time went on, became steadily augmented. And when finally the Porte, in consequence of native quarrels, was able to influence directly the choice of hospodars, another avenue of extortion was opened to the exploiters. As the Ottoman Empire shrank in size with its continuous decline, the burden on its Christian provinces became steadily more onerous. The Principalities became to a large extent the granary of the Empire; but the absence of a free market, together with the extortion of the hospodars who sought to recoup themselves for the bribes which they had to send to Constantinople, kept these lands in a state of material stagnation. Conditions were at their worst during the Phanariot régime, and this economic servitude was not ended till the Peace of Adrianople in 1829 prohibited the shipments of produce which the two lands were 'formerly required to furnish'.[1] Yet the opening of their markets to foreign competitors forged, strangely enough, a new link which bound them to the Empire.

The privileged position of foreigners in the Ottoman Empire was the logical outgrowth of the establishment of an oriental state in a position which rendered it attractive to Western trade. We shall not recount the familiar story of the successful efforts by which foreign Powers acquired the privilege of trading with the Ottoman dominions and secured for their nationals special rights of immunity from Turkish law and administration. These rights were registered in a series of 'capitulations', signed between Turkey and the several Powers who entered into commercial relations with her, and, as they were supposed to apply to all the Ottoman dominions, they were naturally extended to the Danubian Principalities. While there were some slight variations in the capitulations, as obtained by different Powers, fundamentally the privileges accorded were the same. In the application of these rights of exterritoriality the consular representatives of foreign Powers had the position of exercising certain rights of sovereignty.[2] Not only were the consulate and its archives inviolable, and its shipments from abroad duty-free, the consul had jurisdiction over all suits, civil and criminal, between the nationals whose interests he represented, such cases being tried in the consular court in accordance with the law of the metropolis. To that extent a foreign community enjoyed the sovereignty of the government of which it was subject. But a more vital encroachment on Turkish

[1] Hertslet, *The Map of Europe by Treaty*, vol. ii, no. 145.
[2] Formerly the ambassador also had some jurisdiction. See e.g. the British Capitulations of 1675, art. 10: Noradounghian, *Recueil d'actes internationaux de l'empire ottoman*, vol. i, p. 149.

sovereignty was the consul's connexion with cases, civil and criminal, in which his nationals were involved with the hospodar's own subjects. While such cases came within the competence of the native courts and the native law, no suit could be heard or trial held or judgement rendered without the presence of the consul or his dragoman, and it became more and more the established usage that the formal assent of this foreign representative was neccessary for the validity of the verdict.[1] Furthermore, as the inviolability of the foreigner's domicile was another privilege recognized by treaty, it was necessary for the public authority to apply to the consul for the execution of the sentence. In case some foreigner was a notoriously undesirable resident, his consul had the legal right to expel him, but no such right adhered to the native government unless the consul's concurrence were obtained. These judicial immunities, established and again and again confirmed by the numerous capitulations, were based on the assumption that Moslem law was inapplicable to a Christian population, and that, hence, justice could not be procured from the native tribunals. When the theory was applied to Christian provinces, which like the Principalities were backward in civilization, the reasoning at least was the same, even where the premise had no validity. The foreign resident in the Principalities was thus to some extent a privileged person, subject primarily to the sovereignty of the country to which he belonged. Since he was practically immune from the native jurisdiction he could not legally—or logically— own land, but, on the other hand, he was expressly exempted from all personal taxes, and thus subject only to the tariffs which were fixed by treaties between his government and the Porte. The granting of such concessions was not a derogation of dignity in the oriental mind, since in Turkey, for example, law is funda- mentally based on religion, and already the non-Moslem subjects of the Sultan were, 'as far as their personal status was concerned, subject to their own personal law'.[2] One can readily surmise, however, that, when a Christian community, like the Principalities, should come to be nation-conscious and to want to make the most of its autonomy, the vested rights of foreign residents would be regarded as the expression of an alien interference, not only obsolete but incongruous and unnecessary.

But the number of foreign residents in the Principalities was not considerable until the nineteenth century, and for some time it was not the foreigner but the Turk who was looked upon as inimical to the national autonomy. Taking advantage of local quarrels, the suzerain Power had usurped the right of passing

[1] Pélissié du Rousas, *Le Régime des Capitulations dans l'Empire ottoman*, vol. i, pp. 439–40. [2] *Ibid.*, vol. i, p. 421.

favourably or otherwise upon the election of hospodars, and through these instruments of her favour had fastened an ever-tightening hold upon the Principalities. In the eighteenth century had begun the Phanariot régime—politically the darkest page in Roumanian history—when hospodars of Greek extraction were chosen from the Phanar district of Constantinople to rule at Bucharest or Jassy. Obtaining their crowns by bribery and usually displaced in a year or two to make possible another auctioning of the spoil, the Phanariot took occasion to make hay while the crescent shone in his favour, and it was at this period that the *boyarie* was so largely recruited from the henchmen of these foreign interlopers. It was not until relief came from the north that this period of exploitation—which lasted from 1711 to 1821—came to an end.

The advance of Russia towards the south affected the fate of the Principalities as well as every other Balkan state. Whether Russia ever meditated annexing them is a mooted question; she had certainly the opportunity in 1774, and either deliberately or by dint of better judgement threw it away. But with her eyes steadily fixed on Constantinople she could not but see the importance of making her influence paramount on both sides of the Danube; and little by little, without at first encroaching on the autonomy of the Principalities, she assumed a sort of unwritten protectorate over these lands. By the Treaty of Kutchuk Kainardji in 1774 she had obtained the right to intercede in their interest at Constantinople. By subsequent treaties she limited that Porte's right to dispossess a hospodar, and prohibited the Turks from owning land in the Principalities—the renewal of their earlier privilege which evidently had been broken. Yet Russia was not wholly disinterested in her treatment of the Roumans. She acquired Bessarabia from Moldavia in 1812, and restored only a part of it (and that, too, under compulsion) by the Treaty of Paris in 1856. Moreover, her consul acquired an influence which easily arose from the native sympathy with a Power, who in the name of a common religion was ever ready to intervene to protect her little protégés from Mussulman oppression. When the insurrection of the Phanariot, Ypsilanti, had been ruthlessly suppressed by the Turks, who visited their wrath on the helpless population, the government of St. Petersburg, though unwilling to allow the Moldavians to remodel their form of government, was equally determined to end the period of Turkish interference. By the Convention of Akkerman in 1827 all the privileges which the Principalities had previously enjoyed were formally confirmed 'under the tutelary influence of the cabinet of St. Petersburg'. Henceforth the hospodars were to be elected by the native assemblies or divans for a period of seven years, and no election of a hospodar could be vetoed by the Porte without the consent of Russia. Thus, by treaty, was confirmed what had already taken place through revolution: the end of the Phanariot régime. Two years later, by the Peace of Adrianople (which terminated the Russo-Turkish War), the autonomy of the Principalities was fully recognized. Apart from treaty relations with foreign Powers, affecting the Empire as a whole, the Sultan's authority was practically limited to that of receiving annual tribute and in addition—as compensation for the abolition of requisitions of produce, mentioned above— a fixed sum on the election of every hospodar, who was henceforth to be invested with his dignity for life. Not only were the Turks prohibited from keeping a garrison at any point in either land, but each of the Principalities was allowed a native militia, which should enable it to keep order and thus dispense the suzerain Power from any excuse to intervene. Finally, the Porte agreed to accept a constitution, which had been adopted in principle in the Akkerman convention, and the operation of which was to be confided to Russian consuls. Thus, little by little, the sovereignty of Turkey had been limited not only by the restoration of the national autonomy but by a subtle invasion of that autonomy by the new protecting Power. The terms by which that new relationship was variously defined[1] is relatively unimportant. The right of control which Russia exercised from 1827 to 1856 may be fitly designated as a 'protectorate'.

The gauge of Russia's intentions was clearly revealed by her conduct in the Principalities, after her armies had taken possession in 1828. This military occupation lasted for six years, and though it appears that ultimate annexation was seriously considered[2] the government of St. Petersburg was satisfied, for the moment, with exercising 'protection'. During the period of occupation the administration of the Principalities was vested, as an extraordinary measure, in a Russian officer, General Kisseleff, an enlightened and energetic man who proceeded to institute reforms with a celerity and profusion that is only possible when despotism acts. Though the task of reorganization had been confided to a commission of native *boyards*, actually the *Règlement organique* was—in general character, at least—the work of Kisseleff himself. Consisting of two almost identical documents—a *règlement* for each principality[3]—it was more comprehensive than the con-

[1] The Treaty of Adrianople had used the term 'guarantor', just as the Convention of Akkerman had employed the word 'tutelage'. By the *Règlement organique* Russia was designated as the 'protecting court'. Considering the role that she actually played in the Principalities during this period, it mattered little that she later objected to the term 'protectorate'.

[2] Iorga, *op. cit.*, vol. ii, p. 255.

[3] The *Règlement organique* for Moldavia is printed in *British and Foreign State Papers*, vol. xxxii, pp. 586 ff.; that of Wallachia is summarized by Blaramberg,

ventional constitution, for it included within its purview such matters as sanitation, the Church, public education, the humanitarian
institutions, and even the status of the peasants. By its political
provisions the organic powers of the hospodars and of the divans,
the nature of the judiciary, the system of administering the country
(through *ispravniks* or prefects for the various districts), and the
organization of the militia were all minutely regulated. Within
the limits of the native autonomy the divan was empowered to
make laws, subject to the sanction of the prince; but, as no initiative
was allowed him in legislation, and as the ministers were little
more than administrative officers, the legislative aspects of the
system were rather weak. As was perhaps natural to a scheme
which emanated from Russia, the chief attention (as far as the
political arrangements were concerned) was given to the elaboration of a bureaucracy. In any case, as the divans were composed
exclusively of *boyards* there was little chance that the Principalities
would become a field for innovations. Finally, as a check (we
may presume) on the hospodars, a maximum was fixed for the
size of each militia: 4,665 for Wallachia[1] and 2,270 for Moldavia[2]—
a body of troops, which, even when frontier and local guards are
added to these figures, was, as Vaillant observes, decidedly dispro-
portionate to the size of the population.[3] But the gifts of a protecting Power must not be scrutinized too critically. As a parting
act of her authority Russia dictated the choice of the two hospodars,
Michael Sturdza for Moldavia and Alexander Ghika for Wallachia.

There was, of course, but little interest manifested by the West
in these events. The Principalities were still a remote corner of
a remote empire, which itself was still outside the existing
comity of nations. But in one respect the ascendancy of Russia
weighed heavily on foreigners. It was in order to get a ready
outlet for her people in Bessarabia that she had been so anxious
to free the principal mouth of the Danube;[4] but, when she found
that Austrian merchants were quick to derive profit from the long-
desired opening of the river, and that others from the more
industrial West were busily engaged in establishing agencies at
Galatz and Braila, the 'protecting Power' used her position
deliberately to hamper her competitors. One finds interesting
reports from the British consuls, complaining of the quarantines

Essai comparé sur les institutions et les lois de la Roumanie. An excellent critique
of the *Règlement organique* is Filitti, *Les Principautés roumaines sous l'occupation
russe: Le Règlement organique.* Filitti feels that the *Règlement* gave the Principalities a stable order, and greatly extended the facilities for internal trade.

[1] This is the number specified in Blaramberg's summary.
[2] The number is computed from the data given in the *Règlement*.
[3] Vaillant, *op. cit.*, vol. iii, p. 76.
[4] The Kilia mouth, which touched Russia, was too shallow for any but very
small vessels.

which Russia had established—more as a means to delay shipping than for any practical purpose;[1] and during the early years of her dominance she even exacted tribute from the merchantmen which entered the Sulina mouth, some being 'stopped no less than eight times by as many different commanders'.[2] But such difficulties only slightly touched the interests of the Principalities—for the chief sufferers were foreign merchants—though it helps us to understand why the freedom of the Danube became an object of the Congress of Paris. Russia's hold on the Principalities was rather more political and moral than economic. She had given them a government; she had raised the level of much of their national life; and, if they did not show continuous satisfaction, her Cossacks were ever ready to march on an instant's notice. It was a species of invisible autocracy—not the less potent, indeed, because its hold was chiefly moral and its power but seldom exercised.

Yet nothing like public sentiment existed in the Principalities, and little did Russia care if the *boyards* sometimes grumbled over their cards. During the period of occupation many of them had been won, as a recent writer puts it, 'by a generous bestowal of orders, uniforms, and jewelled snuff-boxes and by the protection of their privileges in the new constitution'.[3] True, there was at first some resentment at the reduction of the *corvées*,[4] but it is an evidence of their political importance that they were permitted by the *Règlement* to keep their tenants in bondage, and doubtless in time they learned that their power in this respect was even strengthened. With the exception of a few *boyards* in Moldavia who so resented the Russian yoke that they sold their lands and moved to Bukovina[5] (some were even said to desire Austrian rule),[6] most of the *boyarie* seemed content to bow their necks to the Russian protectorate, and they certainly must have realized that Russia was much too formidable to be trifled with. When the hospodar, Ghika, was deposed by St. Petersburg for wavering in his subservience, the *boyarie* was given a demonstration of the length of Russia's arm; and when, later, some of the younger *boyards* were fain to indulge in revolutionary dreams, the advantage of an aristocratic polity and a quasi-feudal economy, consecrated in a Russian statute, was quite sufficient to keep most of these magnates as docile as could be wished. Much as the new hospodar,

[1] Blutte to Cowley, no. 6, June 4, 1830, F.O. 97/402. The most vigorous attack on her policy was David Urquhart's brochure, *The Mystery of the Danube*.
[2] Gardner to Backhouse, Aug. 3, 1836, F.O. 195/136.
[3] East, *The Union of Moldavia and Wallachia, 1859*, p. 14.
[4] Blutte to Cowley, no. 6, Feb. 5, 1830, F.O. 97/402.
[5] Blutte to Mandeville, Aug. 7, 1833, F.O. 195/136.
[6] Duclos to Bastide, no. 2, June 23, 1848, *Aff. étr., Turquie, Jassy*, vol. 2.

Bibesco, enjoyed the confidence of St. Petersburg, the Wallachian *boyards* were quite free to feed their egoism by cavilling at his policy; for none knew better than the Russians that progress was the one thing the *boyarie* discountenanced. As long as the Principalities revolved within the orbit of the *Règlement organique* there was no need for St. Petersburg to worry. And yet forces were then at work that were gently and insidiously challenging the existing order.

Removed as were the Principalities from the main avenues of Western influence, many of the sons of the wealthier *boyards*, as we have said, found their way to Paris and other places to complete their education. Such persons as the Golesco brothers, John Ghika, Boeresco, and others imbibed in this way the more liberal spirit of the West, while others, who belonged to the earlier school of Héliade, devoted themselves to romantic literature—not without effect on the general quickening of the national spirit. Undoubtedly the interest which certain French savants, notably Quinet, Saint-Marc-Girardin, and Vaillant, had shown in the Roumanian people, had much to do with giving these young patriots a feeling of confidence and pride in their native land. In the salons of Bucharest and Jassy, where only French was spoken, much was thought and said about the future of 'Roumania'. Whether at Berlin, where Cogalnitchano pursued his studies, or at Paris, where Rosetti, the Golescos, and the Bratianos got their inspiration, the germs of a movement were being planted, which, transferred to native soil, might flourish in something closely approximating revolution. Since the Moldo-Wallachian *boyards*, in general, were rather men of leisurely contemplation than men of action there was little effort to quash these vague activities of 'young Roumania'. But Russia's watchful eye was ever on the alert, and through the medium of the hospodars some higher courses of instruction in the academies were suppressed, as were the *internats*, or board schools, where the children of the masses obtained some rudiments of learning. Even a literary society, the Philharmonic, was dissolved, though as often happens when an innocent movement is crushed, it soon reappeared in much more dangerous form as a secret organization. There was undoubtedly a certain ferment and a deep resentment against the meddlesome tutelage of Russia. Yet the number of these intellectuals was small, and nothing might have happened had not Europe entered, almost unconsciously, upon the fateful year 1848.

John Ghika, one of the leaders of the Wallachian liberals, writes in his memoirs that discontent was very rife during the year 1847. There were scandals in high places and friction in the government; and bread was scarce in the towns. Even some of the *boyards* wanted change[1]—perhaps ready to throw themselves into any violent cataclysm. Then came the news of the revolution of February, 1848 in Paris, which electrified so many dismal quarters in old Europe. In Moldavia a group of liberals, numbering, it is said, as many as three thousand, presented the hospodar with a *mémoire* demanding such things as ministerial responsibility, a more representative assembly, and the institution of a national guard. Unhappily Sturdza was in close collusion with the commander of a Russian army, quartered just across the border, and the invasion of these Cossacks put down the revolution almost as soon as it began. In Wallachia things took a livelier turn. A revolutionary committee was constituted, consisting of such men as Héliade, John Ghika, Rosetti, the brothers Bratiano,[2] and César Bolliac. Most of them were youths, who, sure of the truth of their doctrines, conceived an honest contempt for the older *boyards*, and thought they had but to deal with a rickety government.[3] The hospodar, Bibesco, instinctively shunning violence and unwilling, it was said, to avail himself of Russia's offer of aid,[4] accepted without hesitation the constitution that was proffered him, and even allowed himself to be overshadowed by the revolutionary committee, which practically played the role of a provisional government. Though the new constitution embodied even more radical changes than had been demanded in Moldavia, and was far-reaching enough to proclaim free proprietorship of land for the peasants, this movement, unlike the one at Jassy, was directed largely against Russia, whose 'protection' it aimed definitely to abolish.[5] To this end John Ghika was dispatched to Constantinople to place the wishes of Wallachia before the suzerain Power.[6] It might seem as though Turkey had now a chance to recover some of her former hold on the Principalities, but Russia was too quick for her.[7] Bibesco paid for his submission to the revolution by being forced to abdicate, and a Russian army soon put the 'provisional government' rather ignominiously to flight. Russia had said that she would not tolerate any novelties contrary to existing treaties and the *Règlement organique*,[8] and she kept her

---

[1] Chainoi, *L'Occupation des principautés danubiennes*, pp. 80–2.

[2] Rosetti and the two Bratianos were said to have participated in the revolution at Paris: Bibesco, *Le Règne de Bibesco*, vol. ii, p. 399.

[3] Nion to Lamartine, no. 48, Mar. 26, 1848, *Aff. étr.*, *Turquie, Bucharest*, vol. 3.

[4] Bibesco., p. 358. [5] Iorga, *op. cit.*, vol. ii, p. 274. [6] Damé, *op. cit.*, p. 60.

[7] The Porte actually did send a force across the Danube as well as a commissioner to investigate the tumult; but the commissioner was recalled at the request of Russia, and no attempt was made to interfere with the activities of the Russian army, already in occupation.

[8] Nion to Lamartine, no. 49, Apr. 8, *Aff. étr.*, *Turquie, Bucharest*, vol. 3. As a matter of fact, no treaty, as a French publicist pointed out, warranted Russia's military occupation of the Principalities: De Mars, 'L'Occupation russe dans les principautés du Danube', *Revue des deux mondes*, 2nd sér., vol. iv, pp. 596 ff.

word. Though it is possible that Ali Pasha, the grand vizier, might have temporized with the movement,[1] the action of Russia had shown where the real power lay, and in 1849 the Porte subscribed to the Treaty of Balta Liman, whereby the existing assemblies were replaced by others even less representative in character, and the hospodars were to be appointed by the Porte for seven years on condition that the choice had been approved by the Protecting Power. In this manner was a certain degree of punishment inflicted on these lands for playing at revolution.

The revolution of 1848 at Bucharest and Jassy was thus little more than an *opéra bouffe*. At Jassy it lacked not only roots but organization, and could not cope with a man of Sturdza's phlegm. At Bucharest there was much more serious planning, and the point was grasped that its only chance of success lay in some external support—that of France, say, or Turkey—which the orderly character of the movement might be calculated to enlist. But, in general, these zealous patriots took the mistaken course which revolutionists are wont to take. They quarrelled among themselves as to the ultimate objects in view; they showed so little judgement as to appoint as their chief the metropolitan, Neofit, who was notoriously a tool of Russia, and was quick to betray his fellows; and, by trying to rouse the peasants with the promise of free proprietorship, they alienated the *boyards*, already frightened by the *jacquerie* in Galicia two years before. Even despite the certainty of attack no armed resistance was dreamed of;[2] no martyr's blood had hallowed their adventure. In any case, the movement had no chance against Russian bayonets. The chief historical importance of the episode lies in the fact that in this group, this 'young Roumania', one finds the nucleus of a radical party which later made its influence felt at more than one stage in the national evolution; while perhaps, on the other hand, the very failure of these hopes was a useful experience to men such as Couza and Cogalnitchano, both Moldavians, and John Ghika, the Wallachian. Purified somewhat by this baptism of fire, Ghika acquired a moderation

---

[1] The French government had tried in vain through its ambassador at Constantinople to induce the Porte to refrain from any military action but to make a protest to the Powers. At the same time it expressed itself as unwilling to interfere 'in the presence of the uncertain state of Europe . . . and when it is a question of a government [the Porte was meant] whose constancy and energy offer so little guarantee' (Bastide to Aupick, no. 7, Aug. 6, 1848, *Aff. étr., Turquie*, vol. 299). In an earlier dispatch the Wallachian revolution was pronounced 'much too premature for the situation and the true interests of the Moldo-Wallachians' (Bastide to Aupick, no. 5, July 17, *ibid.*). Apart from the domestic difficulties of the Second Republic, one must realize that the Moldo-Wallachians were not big enough to be seen behind the figures of the revolting Italians near at hand. Great Britain, whose good offices (as well as those of France and Austria) had been solicited by the provisional government, decided that she could do nothing without the express solicitation of the Porte (see East, *op.cit.*,p.20). [2] Hory to Bastide, no. 41, Nov. 3, *Aff. étr., Turquie, Bucharest*, vol. 4.

that enabled him to keep his reputation from being blasted throughout long years of vicissitudes, and Couza and Cogalnitchano learned
at least to hold their principles in reserve. Only such men as Rosetti,
the Bratianos, and the Golescos scorned the path of opportunism.

It is also true that in such ordeals one often finds the soul of
a nation in the making. While it is clear that the liberalism of the
Paris boulevards was far too strong a dose in 1848 for a country,
cursed with an effete landed aristocracy and oriental traditions,
yet that effervescence of hostility to Russia, however important
had been her services, was an unmistakable sign that nationalism
was alive. With his vigorous pen the youthful Cogalnitchano
deplored the blighting yoke of the Russian protectorate. 'Since
1834,' he wrote, 'what general measure has been adopted in the
state; what law has been proposed in the assembly, confirmed, or
placed in application without receiving the assent of Russia!'[1]
There could be no real autonomy with the Russian sword hanging
over these lands, and russophil hospodars governing these peoples.

It was enmity to Russia which had formed the one bond of
unity in the programme of the Wallachian patriots. Apart from
wanting to see their country rid of this hated protectorate, one
finds no settled plan of the ultimate objects in view. Most of the
party, it is true, disavowed any purpose of severing the tie with
Turkey. Yet some of the extremists talked openly of independence,[2]
and even dreamed of carving out a new kingdom of Dacia, com-
pounded of all the elements of the Rouman nationality. Doubtless
the simultaneous revolt of the Transylvanian brothers—more
vigorous though equally disastrous in results—had some influence
on the Wallachian insurgents. Out of this welter of ideas and
ideals one sees slowly emerge the idea of union—not so much the
union of all Roumans, but the union of that portion of the race
whose language was identical and whose life had flowed more
continuously in common, namely the Moldo-Wallachians.

The origins of the idea of union under a foreign prince are still
obscure. It is an odd fact, however, that Russia, of all Powers,
had been one to stimulate this purpose. In articles 425 and 426
of the *Règlement organique* we find stated:

'The origin, the religion, the usages, and the conformity of language
of the inhabitants in the two principalities, as well as their mutual needs,
contain not only the principle but the elements of an intimate union,
which has been traversed and retarded by fortuitous and secondary

---

[1] Damé, *op. cit.*, p. 57.
[2] John Ghika, who was rather more level-headed than most of these patriots,
once conceived the idea of buying independence of Turkey by paying a sum
equivalent to ten, twelve, or fifteen years' tribute: Colquhoun to Canning, Apr. 6,
1848, F.O. 78/1742. The idea does rather more honour to his talents as a diplomat than as a statesman.

circumstances. The salutary consequences resulting from the union of these two peoples cannot be held in doubt. The elements of the fusion of the Moldo-Wallachian people are already postulated in this *règlement* by the uniformity of the administrative bases of the two states.

Identity of legislation being one of the most efficacious means for consummating this moral union, a mixed commission will be named by the government of the two principalities for the purpose of formulating the civil and penal code of the two states in a single and identical body of Moldo-Wallachian laws. . . .'[1]

Indeed, Kisseleff himself, as a recent writer has pointed out, had been styled 'governor general or viceroy of the United Principalities',[2] and the commission which had assisted him in putting together the *Règlement* had been drawn in equal number from both Principalities. Doubtless Russia felt no apprehension at the thought of uniting two states which were so effectually under her control. If the work of codification was never seriously undertaken, we at least hear of no remonstrance when Bibesco made a *zollverein* of the two Principalities. In the words of Xénopol 'Georges Bibesco took a great step forward towards the fusion of the interests of the Principalities in suppressing the reciprocal duties and in realizing tariff union, the forerunner of their political union.'

Yet the aims of Rouman nationalism were not a foreign importation; nor were they merely the conception of a Wallachian hospodar. It was a Moldavian *boyard*, who, serving on the joint commission which helped to draft the *Règlement*, was himself the author of the article we have noted. He would fain have added the clause that the ruler of 'Moldo-Wallachia' should not be chosen from the dynasty of one of the neighbouring Powers, but such a notion was naturally displeasing to St. Petersburg, and consequently abandoned.[3] We also read of an invitation to Sturdza of Moldavia to become, in addition, hospodar of Wallachia (it was not an uncommon thing for hospodars to be interchanged, though none had held both offices), and even before the revolution of 1848 brochures had appeared, advocating the union of the Principalities. Naturally the revolution gave impetus to the movement. Rosetti, addressing a deputation of Moldavians, had declared, 'The Wallachians and Moldavians are brothers, a single nation.'[4] Cogalnitchano openly advocated the union of the Principalities, and other writers—eloquent, if not numerous—uttered the same plea.[5]

[1] *Brit. and For. State Papers*, vol. xxxii, p. 786.

[2] Blutte to Lamb, no. 7, Feb. 8, 1833, F.O. 97/404, cited by East, *op. cit.*, p. 22.

[3] Le Cler, *op. cit.*, pp. 339–40. Some of the commission, it appears, had talked of drawing up a memorial, petitioning for union under a prince of one of the reigning dynasties of Europe; but, though Kisseleff graciously promised to forward the document to his court (Blutte to Cowley, no. 6, Feb. 5, 1830; F.O. 97/402), we have no positive evidence that it was ever drafted.

[4] Xénopol, *op. cit.*, vol. ii, pp. 545–7.

[5] It is interesting, however, to find that a French consul noted a tendency in

After the *débâcle* of 1848 many of the patriots, now exiled, issued pamphlets from the printing-presses of Paris, calling their country-men at home to the need of resolution for the achievement of Rouman aims. Little by little, union and a foreign prince (the latter to give dignity to a nation aspiring to membership in the European family) became the key-notes of the Rouman nationalist movement.[1]

For the time being—that is since the failure of the revolution—the history of the Principalities maintained a fairly placid course. The two hospodars, Stirbey (elder brother of Bibesco) in Wallachia and Gregory Ghika in Moldavia, had been selected by the Porte in concert with Russia. Both of them, particularly Stirbey, were bitterly attacked by the exiled patriots of 1848[2] who regarded them as instruments of foreign Powers. Yet Stirbey, though reputedly corrupt, had a good deal of practical ability and a talent for mastering detail, however arduous.[3] He succeeded in persuading the Russians to complete their evacuation in 1851, and, though the weight of that occupation had been heavy, he was able by rigorous economy to reduce his state's indebtness. He also improved the army, made some efforts to relieve the peasant, and even forced the *boyards* to contribute a little to the expense of maintaining the highways—the first attempt to invade the im-munity of the privileged classes in taxation. In various other ways he showed that the reform spirit, engendered by the *Règlement* and quickened by the revolution, had not been entirely vain. Ghika applied himself similarly to reform in Moldavia, and showed his interest in the nationalist cause, not only by welcoming back the *émigrés*,[4] but also by granting freedom of the press. Both hospodars withdrew and went to Vienna on the occasion of the Russian occupation which precipitated the Crimean War, but returned to power later when the Austrians replaced the Russians. By that time it was apparent that the doom of the Russian pro-tectorate was sealed; and the Danubian Principalities were flung, as a not-too-welcome ward, at the door-steps of the Powers. The Crimean War had made the case of the Moldo-Wallachians a European problem.

Moldavia to resent being coupled too much with Wallachia, as though they 'feared assimilation': Poujade to Tocqueville, no. 2, July 23, 1849, *Aff. étr.*, *Turquie, Bucharest*, vol. 7.

[1] Writing in 1854, Bois-le-Comte declared that union was the general desire of the people, both of Bucharest and of Jassy. 'To the idea of the union of the two provinces', he added, 'is joined that of putting the government under a foreign prince': Anon., *Les Principautés-unies devant la Conférence*, p. 7.

[2] Notably, Texier, *Appel au congrès au faveur des Roumains*, pp. 16–19. The most severe criticism of Ghika is found in Bataillard, *La Moldo-Valachie dans les manifestations de ses efforts et ses vœux.*

[3] Bulwer to Clarendon, no. 378, Jan. 2, 1858, F.O. 78/1374.

[4] B., *L'Autriche, la Turquie, et les Moldo-Valaques.*

CHAPTER I

EUROPE ASSUMES A PROTECTORATE : THE CONGRESS AND TREATY OF PARIS

THE Concert of Europe has never been an institution—if institution, it could be called—that has commanded the respect of historians. As a prototype of the League of Nations it has, perhaps, played a sorry part. It had its birth in that combination of fear and cupidity which brought Napoleon the Great to his knees, and it strove, with some dexterous and not altogether welcome assistance from Talleyrand, to shape a new Europe, based for the most part on the old, save that territorial boundaries were rectified to suit the interests of the Great Powers (France excepted), which, in essence, formed the Concert. On the Vienna-Paris Settlement of 1814–15 the fabric of Europe was to rest, and permanent peace to be assured. If the energies of the Concert of Europe were misdirected, it was not because it was insincere in desiring peace, but quite the contrary. It had unfortunately the notion that peace must rest on the outworn doctrines of the old régime; that a 'holy alliance' must be formed against the promoters of liberalism and nationalism—those legacies of the Revolution, which History had flung at the triumphant autocrats, knowing full well that Time, whose whole abundant store she would herself appropriate, would call them into new life. Yet the underlying principle of the Concert of Europe is not to be discountenanced. The adjustment of mutual differences, the promotion of common ends, and the guarding of Europe's peace were tasks that could best be undertaken through international congresses. It was something that the slave trade had been condemned by such an instrument; it was equally to the common interest that the principle of freedom of navigation had been adopted for international rivers. Internationalism was, moreover, the necessary rein to place on nationalism or on national ambition. The independence of Belgium, however much the result of accidental circumstances, was, at least, a monument to the docility of the Concert of Europe, already chastened by experience. But it is obvious that so unwieldy a vehicle cannot readily adapt itself to exigencies without and discords within; and unanimity in attaining higher levels of political morality seems humanly—and certainly internationally—impossible. By the middle of the nineteenth century much of their handiwork, so diligently wrought at Vienna, was being systematically undermined, and, paradoxically enough, it might take a war or several wars to overturn the flimsy structure which had been fashioned to preserve peace. It was not, perhaps, unfitting that the rise of another Bonaparte should mark its coming doom.

The role of Louis Napoleon in European history was forecast as soon as the French had granted him a throne. Sensitive, as is every *parvenu* about the reality of his prestige, and legatee of the spirit of *revanche* which had been enkindled by the memories of Moscow, Leipzig, and Waterloo, the Emperor Napoleon III could never have hoped to justify his *quasi*-reincarnation of the past, unless France, under his leadership, were to become once more the leading power of Europe. To him, as well as to her, the Paris-Vienna Settlement was anathema. Peace he wanted, and would have; but it was peace that must be founded on a new Europe, based on the principle which his great predecessor had flouted, the principle of nationality; and it was fitting, perhaps, that France, who had done so much to promote the freedom of mankind, should not only break down her own bars, but lead the little peoples to the Promised Land. Historically, Napoleon III was a higher type of internationalist than either Metternich or Alexander I. The Concert of Europe was worth saving, worth utilizing, but it should enlarge its vision and accept the sacrifices that realism must sometimes make to idealism. Yet Napoleon was not simply a visionary. Though only through a cluster of memories and a platform of abstractions could he have hoped to become emperor of the French, he had owed much of his progress to an adroit opportunism. Now that he was enthroned, he must respond to the national will. He must rehabilitate the France of the Restoration. It mattered not that his country wanted peace, and that he himself was reluctant to make war. The position which he had fore-ordained for France, and which, at least in its beginnings, seemed to require the co-operation of Great Britain, was driving him into a destiny that he could not well escape. Whatever the public demand for peace, however prompt, his assurance that the Empire meant peace, he knew, better than his people themselves realized, how much they really demanded that France should play a shining role. Such, then, was part of that sentiment—though British hatred of Russia was much more the prime cause—that produced the Crimean War. And thus it was an embryonic internationalist and instinctive hater of war who contributed to shatter the long peace which had been inaugurated at Vienna.

It may be argued that all wars are unnecessary, but the Crimean War seems particularly in that class; and, saving its partly unforeseen effect upon the people with whom our story is concerned and its quite accidental effect upon the Italians, few wars have been more barren of desirable results. It is certainly disputable whether the Ottoman Empire was worth saving (Napoleon clearly did not think so), and it may be questioned whether Great Britain's fear of Russia or the unconscious vanity of France was really worth the dose of homicide and cholera with which both countries were rewarded. Indeed, had it not been for the evil genius of Stratford Canning, for whose presence at Constantinople the British government was, of course, responsible,[1] even the play of historical forces might have been robbed of all its strength. We shall not, however, review the causes of the war or describe its course. After the breach had come between Russia and Turkey, and the Russian armies had entered the Principalities, the Western Powers made this occupation a *casus belli*. Three months after the opening of the war, when the Allied fleets had already entered the Black Sea, and the Turks had so far hindered the Tsar's troops from crossing the Danube, Austria took the sudden step of threatening to enter the war unless Russia should immediately withdraw from the Principalities. Incensed at this action on the part of a Power which he had saved from annihilation in 1849, the Tsar recalled his forces, and the evacuation had hardly been completed before an Austrian army took their place. The Vienna government had acted by virtue of a convention with Turkey, June 14, 1854, in which it had promised to guarantee the Principalities against attack, and to restore them to the Porte at the termination of the War;[2] while the suzerain Power, not wholly trusting her new ally, had not only insisted that the 'legal state of things' should be re-established 'as far as possible',[3] but sent a force of its own to occupy certain fortresses on the Wallachian side of the Danube. Six months later, after the invasion of the Crimea had commenced, the Western Powers themselves made an alliance with Austria, according to the terms of which the Austrian occupation was duly sanctioned as a military measure, and it was agreed by the signatories that only after a previous understanding among themselves might any overture from the enemy be received.[4] Since, however, the basis of a negotiation had already been worked out by correspondence between London and Vienna,[5] the Allied Powers presented Russia on December 28 with a memorandum, known as the Four Points, the first of which declared in part that

'it was necessary to abolish the exclusive protectorate exercised by Russia over Moldavia, Wallachia and Servia, and henceforward to place under the collective guarantee of the Five Powers the privileges accorded by the sultans to the[se] principalities'.[6]

It was not this stipulation but the one requiring the neutralization

---

[1] On this point see the excellent discussion by Mr. F. A. Simpson in his *Louis Napoleon and the Recovery of France*, pp. 232–6.

[2] Hertslet, *op. cit.*, vol. ii, pp. 1213–15.

[3] Drouyn de Lhuys to Walewski, no. 132, June 28, 1854, *Aff. étr.*, *Angleterre*, vol. 695.

[4] Hertslet, *op. cit.*, vol. ii, pp. 1216–17.

[5] *Ibid.*, pp. 1222–4.   [6] *Ibid.*, pp. 1225–6

of the Black Sea, which made peace on such terms problematical. While the Tsar was willing, thanks to Austria's ominous neutrality, to negotiate at a conference on the basis of the Four Points, it was certainly with the hope that Austrian ingenuity would furnish a more palatable substitute. If Russia failed to comprehend the contortions of Vienna, she was probably not the only Power at fault.

It was already manifest that Austria's chief interest lay in the question of the Principalities. She, more than any other Power, was anxious to see the end of the Russian protectorate, and, rather than permit Russia to strengthen her hold on these provinces, she would undoubtedly have entered the war. She did not want, however, to become a belligerent, and she had accomplished her chief end by skilful diplomacy. Yet, apart from her vital interest in the question of the freedom of the Danube, she felt herself too important a Power to allow a settlement of the Eastern Question to be reached without being, herself, a participant in the discussions. Should she be able to mediate the final peace, her prestige might be enhanced without the sacrifice of a single soldier. It was, however, an exceedingly delicate problem to keep on good terms with the Power who had accused her of ingratitude and with her two allies who resented her neutrality, and were indisposed to yield an atom of the Four Points. Some of the difficulty, too, which the court of Vienna was to encounter in the pursuit of its objects may be attributed to the Emperor Francis Joseph. He would not wholly trust his minister of foreign affairs, Count Buol-Schauenstein, and in secret gave his confidence to the man whom he had chosen for second plenipotentiary at the conference.[1] It is no small tribute to Buol's patience and resourcefulness that he was able to grasp the initiative in the subsequent negotiations and bring the combatants to terms. But for the present Francis Joseph was very anxious to avoid a breach with St. Petersburg; and Buol, who would have assumed a much stiffer attitude towards Russia,[2] had to bear the risk of being thought disloyal to the common cause. Meanwhile Palmerston was loath to make the slightest concession. Thus the coming conference at Vienna was foredoomed to failure. Its only importance to us is the attention that would be given to the question of the Danubian Principalities.

The Conference of Vienna opened on March 15, 1855. The Powers represented were Great Britain, France, Turkey, Austria, and Russia; and Austria's foreign minister was naturally chosen to preside. At the opening session Buol read a commentary on the Four Points, all of which were then adopted as the basis of negotiation; and, it being then decided to take up the points in numerical

---

[1] Friedjung, *Der Krimkrieg und der österreichische Politik*, pp. 151–2.
[2] Charles-Roux, *Alexandre II, Gortchakoff, et Napoleon III*, p. 16.

order, Baron Prokesch-Osten, the second Austrian plenipotentiary, presented a working plan for the first point.[1] In this manner the question of the Danubian Principalities was opened for discussion by the Concert of Europe.

The release of the Principalities from Russian tutelage had suggested at once that their existing constitution, of Russian authorship, should be subjected to modification or totally abolished. Naturally it was desirable to retain the privileges that Russia had procured for them—such as freedom of worship, commerce, and navigation, and the enjoyment of a limited autonomy, and there was no thought of weakening (indeed, Palmerston would have strengthened)[2] the tie which bound them to the suzerain Power, Turkey. But the status of the hospodars and the character of the assemblies, as well as the means for national order and defence, and above all, the question of uniting the Principalities into a single, homogeneous state—an issue, already raised, as we have seen, in the Principalities themselves—would inevitably furnish material for discussion. How little the sentiments of the Moldo-Wallachians themselves would weigh in the scale of their destinies was only too easy to forecast in an assemblage devoted to the broader question of Europe's peace; yet the lesson of 1848 might not be wholly lost on diplomats whose memories of that upheaval were still vivid. It is interesting to notice that Austria had been anxious that delegates from each of the Principalities, appointed by the respective hospodars, should be sent to the Conference to furnish information on the demand of its members, and to this end had pressed the matter upon the Porte, as well as sounded the French and British governments. Apparently neither Paris nor London was enthusiastic over the plan, doubting especially the wisdom of having the hospodars, rather than the Porte, make the appointments;[3] and, though it was finally decided to invite the hospodars to choose a delegate from three persons to be nominated by the Porte, the selections were made much too late to be of any service for the purpose intended.[4] While it may be doubted if the presence

---

[1] *Actes et documents relatifs à la régénération de la Roumanie* (ed. Sturdza and Petrescu), vol. ii, no. 403, protocol no. 1. The protocols of the Conference of Vienna may also be found in Martens, *Nouveau recueil général de traités*, vol. xv, pp. 633 ff. or in *British and Foreign State Papers*, vol. xlv, pp. 54 ff.

[2] To Russell, Mar. 28: Ashley, *Life of Palmerston*, vol. ii, pp. 84 ff.

[3] Clarendon to Cowley, no. 248, Mar. 7, 1855, F.O. 27/1051; to Westmorland, no. 57, Mar. 8, F.O. 7/446; Cowley to Clarendon, no. 1064, Mar. 7 and no. 1089, Mar. 8, F.O. 27/1064.

[4] Colquhoun to Westmorland, no. 57, June 15, F.O. 480/195. Arsaki, a pro-Russian Greek was chosen for Wallachia—'clever, shrewd, and very dangerous', Colquhoun, the British consul, called him; for Moldavia Ghika sent Costache Negri, a man whose abilities had yet to be recognized, and whom the Austrians distrusted because of his liberal tendencies (Testa to Buol, Apr. 16, telg., Staatsarchiv, xxxviii/103). He had been a 'forty-eighter'.

of these delegates would have had any effect on the decisions of the Conference, the plan deserved a much more serious consideration than it received. Meanwhile Prokesch's memorial, after some amendment, was postponed for further discussion to the next session, that of March 17.[1]

It was to be observed that the idea of uniting the Principalities formed no place in Prokesch's scheme. Of all the Powers, Austria was perhaps most bitterly opposed to the idea of union. Neighbouring on the Principalities, and forced by the course of her great river to extend her influence eastward, she had long been engaged in a sort of economic invasion of these lands, and had unquestionably more capital invested there than any other Power. Already her occupation of the Principalities had been signalized by such enterprises as the construction of new roads across the mountains, a systematic improvement of the navigation of the Danube, and the establishment of telegraphic connexion between Bucharest and Jassy[2]—all of which measures were no doubt designed to further the economic conquest of the region. Whether it were a question of establishing a bank, or constructing a railroad,[3] or promoting navigation on the Danube, she expected a virtual monopoly of the field.[4] Such schemes, of course, entailed a skilful use of opportunities not only at Constantinople but at Bucharest and Jassy. Manifestly it would be easier to manipulate two smaller states than one large one, and the characteristic policy of Vienna was to deal with petty princes, who could be taught the lesson of subservience in the true Metternichian style. To that end a vast network of vice-consuls and *starosts*, under orders from the consul general at Bucharest, constituted what might almost be called a state within a state.[5] Yet it was not so much the economic as the political interests of Austria that impelled her to oppose the union of the Principalities. The awakened consciousness of the Roumans of Transylvania and Bukovina was already an accomplished fact; and, of all the subversive tendencies of the time, nationalism, for the ramshackle Austrian Empire, was the most perilous. One can

[1] Protocol no. 1. [2] Friedjung, *op. cit.*, pp. 184–5.

[3] The 'Feldakten' of the Austrian commanders in the Principalities during the military occupation (found in the Kriegsarchiv) reveal the fact that the Vienna government seriously took up with Prince Stirbey the project of a railway-line from Cronstadt in Hungary to Bucharest and Braila.

[4] That she sought 'the monopoly of railway enterprises and credit institutions' was evidently appreciated at Paris, as evidenced by a memorandum of the foreign office, dated Mar. 16, 1856: *Aff. étr., Mém. et doc., Turquie*, vol. 18, no. 29.

[5] See *L'Autriche et le prince roumain*, p. 26. As far back as 1842, in commenting upon this system, a British consul declared that 'there is exercised over the whole principality an Austrian surveillance as vigorous as that of the Protecting Power': The *starosts*, he went on to say, were originally a border police, but were now spread over these lands, exercising judicial functions: Gardner to Canning, no. 11, Jan. 15, F.O. 195/211. Austria's extention of her extraterritorial rights were a bitter source of complaint.

hardly blame Vienna for fearing a movement that might foster separatist tendencies in Hungary.

Not much less hostile to union was the Sublime Porte, which, mindful of the case of Greece, was apprehensive lest union would so strengthen this subject nationality that, in the end, it might snap the slender ties which bound it to the suzerain Power. Some interesting light on its attitude may be found in the instructions which were given its plenipotentiary at the Conference. Turkey had no objection to placing the Principalities under the joint guarantee of the five Great Powers, and would under certain conditions[1] promise to effectuate reforms, but it was evident that she hoped to retain her present hold over these provinces, if not actually to strengthen it,[2] and she desired that any discussion over changes that should be made might be held, not at Vienna, but at Constantinople. The principle of union was specifically discountenanced, and the Porte affirmed that it would never agree to it. Yet the Turks seemed indisposed to take the lead in the coming conference, for the Ottoman plenipotentiary was merely 'to make known the opinion of the Porte when necessary',[3] and it was doubtless surmised that British diplomacy could, as usual, be relied upon to avert danger from their heads. Great Britain, for her part, solicitous always for the maintenance of the worn-out fabric of Ottoman Power, was hardly less opposed to union than the Porte. There is no doubt, of course, that to her Turkey was always the needed bulwark against the formidable Russian colossus, and a legalistic view of the rights of the suzerain Power, notwithstanding the fact that these rights were founded on conquest, always furnished the British government with a specious— though undoubtedly sincere—argument for the maintenance of the *status quo*. Perhaps, if one had played up the Roumans as sons of Trajan, submerged among Slavs and subjugated by Moslems, one might have enlisted that ready sympathy which British opinion had accorded the Greeks; but Rouman nationalism had done little with its romantic possibilities, and few Englishmen knew anything whatever of these people or their origin. To the French, on the contrary—or, more exactly, perhaps, to the French intellectuals— the Moldo-Wallachian was by no means a stranger. We have already had occasion to observe that several Frenchmen had visited this land, and published their experiences; and the fact that they were a 'Latin people' was something of a claim on Gallic

---

[1] 'She will not consent to alter the present state of the administration of these provinces'—whatever might be meant by that.

[2] It was evidently desired to retain the right of nominating the hospodars· and to recover certain fortresses on the Danube which Turkey had held prior to 1829.

[3] Stratford to Clarendon, no. 250, Mar. 31, 1855, enc., F.O. 78/1075.

sympathies. More important, however, than any romantic interest in the Roumans was the Emperor's attachment to an abstract ideal. It was in consequence of his advocacy of the principle of nationality that France became the most conspicuous champion of union, while, in order to find an argument that would perhaps appeal to the more practical British mind, she took the ground that it was desirable to erect a strong barrier against Russia.[1] Yet the idea met with no favour across the Channel,[2] and the Emperor seems to have decided not to press the point for the present. Strange indeed that Palmerston, so often the daring innovator in foreign politics, was now opposed to union as promising incalculable complications![3]

Oddly enough it was Russia who definitely snatched the honour of succouring the nationalist cause in the Principalities. It may be that Russia wished once more to pose as the Power really interested in their welfare (she it was, as we may remember, who had long ago subscribed to the idea of union), or possibly her diplomats saw an advantage to be gained by approaching the French position and thus forcing a wedge between her two great adversaries. Since, however, the opposition to union was too strong for a frontal attack, Russia devised a flanking movement to secure the desired end. On the 17th, when Prokesch's memorial was again brought up for discussion, Prince Gortchakoff, the leading Russian plenipotentiary at the Conference, introduced a memorandum in which he proposed that it should be agreed to 'consult the wishes of the country as to the maintenance or modification of the act [i.e. the *Règlement organique*] which constitutes the basis of its [the state's] internal reorganization'.[4] Since no decision was taken to consult the spokesmen of the Principalities (though Austria had invited each to send one),[5] one may presume that what was meant was a plebiscite to ascertain the wishes of the inhabitants. As there was apparently no objection to this proposal,[6] a counter-project, based upon the Austrian and Russian schemes, was presented to the same session by the second Russian plenipotentiary, and formed, after some amendment by the Conference, the annex to protocol 3 of the session of March 9.[7] France for the moment seemed satisfied

[1] Walewski to Persigny, no. 38, Feb. 25, *Aff. étr., Angleterre*, vol. 699.
[2] Persigny to Walewski, no. 65, Mar. 14, *ibid.*, vol. 700.
[3] Private letter to Clarendon, Jan. 9.
[4] Wambaugh, *A Monograph on Plebiscites*, appx., pp. 728 ff.
[5] Testa to Buol, Mar. 21, telg., Staatsarchiv, xxxviii/102; Mihanovich to Buol, no. 27, Mar. 26, *ibid.*
[6] We learn from the protocol only that the two texts (Prokesch's and Gortchakoff's) were subjected to a 'discussion approfondie'. The correspondence of the diplomats is silent upon the details, and for that reason it is reasonable to suppose that there was no serious objection to the idea. Buol wrote to the Austrian ambassador at St. Petersburg that on the first point there were only 'light differences': Buol to Esterhazy, Mar. 7, no. 1, *ibid.*, x/28.
[7] See protocol 2, Mar. 17, annex.

with this compromise, though Baron Bourqueney, the French plenipotentiary, had suggested a change of wording in order not to exclude the possibility of union, if it were ever judged desirable.[1] Perhaps none of the Powers was thoroughly convinced as to what the Moldo-Wallachians really wanted.

The more pressing immediate problem was that of providing internal repose in the Principalities now that the Russian protectorate was to be replaced by a European guarantee. It was not astonishing that an Austrian suggestion to submit all disputes between Wallachia and the Porte to a tribunal of the ambassadors at Vienna should have been firmly rejected by Russia.[2] The Court of St. Petersburg had no notion of letting its old protectorate (the Russians objected to the word 'protectorate'[3]) be replaced by anything that savoured of an Austrian preponderance. Likewise the British objected to a provision in Titoff's original draft that any augmentation of the national militia (the chief reliance for national order and defence) should be subject to an arrangement between the *limitrophe* Powers.[4] It is clear that Palmerston and Clarendon suspected a kind of covert understanding between Austria and Russia; and Clarendon, indeed, found fault with almost every feature of Titoff's amended and adopted work.[5] But there was little reason to disapprove of the arrangement that 'no armed intervention could take place on their territory [i.e. the Principalities] without being or becoming the object of a preliminary understanding between the high contracting Powers';[6] and Lord John Russell, the leading British plenipotentiary, assured Clarendon that the collective guarantee (which Clarendon had compared to the Holy Alliance) would be all that was necessary to guard the Principalities against their two dangerous neighbours.[7] Palmerston did not think so;[8] and apparently the British government was very dubious as to the wisdom of a European protectorate.

In the matter of the organic arrangements for the Principalities the disposition of the Conference seemed to be to adjourn the problem to some future entente between the Powers and the Porte. France made some slight efforts at Constantinople to convert the Porte to union, but the argument that such a device was 'the best

---

[1] See protocol 3, Mar. 19, annex.
[2] Russell to Clarendon, no. 25, Mar. 20, F.O. 7/462. [3] Protocol 1.
[4] F.O. to Russell, no. 31, Mar. 28, F.O. 7/461.
[5] Palmerston to Russell, Mar. 28, Ashley, *op. cit.*, vol. ii, pp. 86–7; F.O. to Russell, no. 27, Mar. 28, F.O. 7/461. For Russell's reply, defending his action, see Russell to Clarendon, no. 53, Apr. 1, F.O. 7/464. [6] Annex to protocol 3.
[7] Russell to Clarendon, no. 53, Apr. 1, F.O. 7/462. Mr. East (*op. cit.*, p. 31) remarks that it is significant that the instructions to Russell (*Parliamentary Papers, 1854–5*, vol. lv, p. 265) had contained no mention of a collective guarantee. As a matter of fact Palmerston had pronounced himself against the idea in his private letter of Mar. 15 to Russell.
[8] Palmerston to Russell, Mar. 15, Russell Papers, G. and D. 22/12, Pub. Rec. Off.

check upon Russia' quite failed to carry conviction.[1] Nevertheless, at the session of March 26, Bourqueney asked that a memorandum of his government on the First Point be recorded as an opinion that should be considered in any final settlement. This record—which was annexed to protocol 6—reviewed the arguments in favour of union, and suggested an hereditary prince chosen from some foreign dynasty. Russell then remarked that he reserved his opinion on this question, as he felt that all initiative should proceed from the Sublime Porte.[2] Clarendon's own opinion was much more pronounced. He told Persigny, the French ambassador, that he did not feel that local conditions justified union, and, since it was inadvisable to strengthen Turkey's position as a counterweight to Austria and Russia, he feared that an hereditary prince would find it unnecessary to rely on Turkish influence.[3] To Russell he declared that union was 'inexpedient', and recommended the establishment of a Christian prince in each principality, nominated by the Porte, and holding office for life.[4] Since direct overtures had steadily failed to surmount British prejudice against union, France made no effort at the time to carry her point, though, in reserving her opinion, she had shown that she regarded the question as not settled but only shelved. Much more serious difficulties arose when the other points of the original memorandum came up for discussion; for Russia was not yet prepared to grant the neutralization of the Black Sea, and both France and Great Britain seemed convinced that Austria was playing too equivocal a role to make the continuance of the negotiations practicable.[5] Hence the Conference terminated in June without result. Then the fall of Sebastopol, which made the Tsar more anxious for peace, and the discovery of a secret exchange of views between the courts of Paris and St. Petersburg[6] determined Austria to come to the point of an ultimatum. As Napoleon was now resolved to end the war, it was useless for Palmerston to try to continue the struggle, and, after some modifications in the Austrian draft (to humour British pique), the ultimatum—which was substantially the memorandum of December 28—was presented and accepted. Arrangement was made for a peace congress to open at Paris in February 1856.

As far as the question of the Principalities was concerned, the Conference of Vienna had been of importance only as furnishing an approach to the problem, and as revealing the attitude of the

---

[1] Stratford to Colquhoun, no number, Mar. 24, F.O. 78/1075; cf. Benedetti to Lhuys, no. 95, Mar. 25, *Aff. étr., Turquie*, vol. 319.

[2] Protocol 6, Mar. 26 and annex; Westmorland to Clarendon, no. 146, Mar. 30, F.O. 7/453.

[3] Persigny to Walewski, no. 68, Mar. 24, *Aff. étr., Angleterre*, vol. 700.

[4] Clarendon to Russell, no. 48, Apr. 5, F.O. 7/461.

[5] Clarendon to Cowley, June 2, telg., F.O. 27/1053.

[6] See Friedjung, *op. cit.*, pp. 173–4.

various Powers. So far the only point that seemed really settled
was the termination of the Russian protectorate. But suppose that
Austria, despite her signed agreement with Turkey, should strive
in some way to obtain a permanent hold on these lands! 'We have
the Danubian Principalities in our pockets', boasted Buol to a
friend in September, 1855.[1] We shall note some evidence later
that the idea of placing these lands under some scion of the imperial
house had at least entered the realm of Austrian thoughts, and it is
not impossible that she may have known that Palmerston had once
thought of an exchange by which Sardinia should have Lombardy
and Venetia, and Austria take the Principalities.[2] In any event,
the slippery role which she had played during the late war had
made her thoroughly unpopular, and the Western Powers were
only too ready to suspect her of trying to edge into the position
once occupied by Russia. 'Austria will want as much watching as
Russia,' remarked Palmerston.[3] 'She aims', wrote Clarendon, 'at
transferring to herself the power hitherto exercised by Russia in
the Principalities, or, at least, of sharing this power with Russia.'[4]

Perhaps that is why Clarendon, in particular, was anxious to get
some settlement of this question without delay. In September he
bethought himself of a scheme by which the Porte should propose
to France and Great Britain some plan for the reorganization of the
Principalities,[5] and he believed that by a tripartite agreement the
idea of a European protectorship—for which Austria was suspiciously solicitous—might be avoided. While it will be remembered that this plan had been embodied in the First Point, and
practically assumed as a basis at the Conference of Vienna, the
British statesman now imagined that Austria and Russia might
have 'greater powers of interference in the provinces than have
hitherto been claimed and exercised by Russia alone'.[6] All the
Principalities needed, he felt, was a 'constituent act, emanating from
the Sultan, and seconded by the Allies, which would afford the
best means and most convenient security for the sovereign and
for the people'.[7]

---

[1] Friedjung, *op. cit.*, p. 43.

[2] See East, *op. cit.*, p. 32. Palmerston writes on a later occasion that he dis-
cussed the matter with Walewski when the latter was ambassador at London:
Palmerston to Russell, Nov. 17, 1864, Russell Papers, G. and D. 22/15, Pub.
Rec. Off.

[3] Palmerston to Russell, Mar. 15, Russell Papers.

[4] Cowley to Clarendon, no. 1315, Nov. 13, F.O. 27/1059.

[5] Clarendon to Stratford, no. 720, F.O. 78/1066.

[6] Clarendon to Cowley, no. 1315, Nov. 13, F.O. 27/1059. To Buol he argued
that such security against Turkey was unnecessary, and a guarantee of the
government of the Principalities might lead to dissensions among the Powers:
Clarendon to Seymour, no. 49, Dec. 26, F.O. 7/450.

[7] Clarendon to Stratford, Feb. 13, 1856, F.O. 195/499, cited by East, *op. cit.*,
p. 41.

Of course, the question of whether a system of government, secure against usurpations from both sides, could be satisfactorily worked out was, at least, problematical, and so doctrinaire a view was hardly likely to win converts. Thouvenel, the French ambassador at Constantinople, would have laughed at the idea of leaving the Principalities to the tender mercies of their suzerain. Meanwhile, it was but natural that some detailed study should be expended on the subject before the Congress should meet to bandy generalities. At the request of the British government, the British ambassador to the Porte, Lord Stratford de Redcliffe, submitted a lengthy memorandum to the Foreign Office, conveying the result of his scattered impressions of the Principalities and his views as to the proper point of beginning. While professing to believe that the *Règlement organique* was 'not unacceptable to the leading classes', he recognized that the great majority of the inhabitants of both provinces were 'animated by national feelings', and went so far as to admit that 'the country would probably gain by a single administration'. The international bearings of the problem then evoked the diplomat's 'sober exercise of judgement'. Uniting the Principalities would rouse the spirit of independence, and, consequently, if such a step were taken, both Austria and (especially) Russia would be likely to try a fresh aggression at their expense; so the final advice of the ambassador included the replacing of the *Règlement* by a new constitution, which should assume the separation of the two provinces, the selection of native hospodars, and the continuance of their present connexion with the Porte.[1] Nothing is more illustrative of that contemporary *Realpolitik* which proposed to sacrifice the legitimate interests of a people to the maintenance of European peace.

Whatever might be the ultimate opinion of the British government, the Stratford memorandum furnished useful data on which Clarendon could exercise his intellect, and it was at his instance that the French and British governments decided that an elaboration of the First and Fourth Points should be drawn up by their respective embassies at Constantinople in collaboration with the Turkish ministers. Both points, as a writer has said, 'affected the sovereignty of the Porte',[2] and out of courtesy might in the first instance be treated at Constantinople; but the plan to exclude Austria from the deliberation, especially in view of her prominent part in recent discussions of the First Point, was, to say the least, extraordinary. It is clear that Clarendon intended deliberately to ignore her, believing, no doubt, that in this way the danger of a European guarantee could be avoided. But,

[1] Stratford to Clarendon, no. 976, Dec. 2, 1855, enc., F.O. 78/1903.
[2] East, *op. cit.*, p. 42.

while Walewski, the Emperor's new foreign minister, was at first willing to concur in this arrangement, it seems probable that Napoleon was opposed to snubbing Vienna, for, in the end, on his insistence, the Austrian internuncio, Baron Prokesch, was invited to participate with Thouvenel, Stratford, and the Turkish ministers in the conference at Constantinople.[1]

Stratford, as dean of the ambassadors, had the privilege of convoking the Conference, and to that end he had just sent his secretary, Alison, to Wallachia to gather information that would enable him to formulate his views.[2] If the British ambassador hoped that public sentiment in the Principalities was less favourable to union he was doomed to disappointment. Alison wrote him that Stirbey, when he received him, had emphasized the importance of granting union (his preference naturally was a native prince);[3] and for some months the chief pastime of the *boyards* had been the preparation of *mémoires*, in which the advantages of union were much paraded.[4] Stratford replied to Alison that he was 'not insensible' of these supposed benefits, but that 'under the present circumstances' such a solution was impracticable.[5] For Stirbey the British ambassador had a profound contempt, not so much because he favoured union as because Austria looked upon him as the instrument of her policy in the Principalities.[6]

Whatever the merits of union, it is fairly evident that an attempt to impose it on the Turkish ministers at this time would have so complicated the work of the Conference that its whole task would have probably proved abortive. Such may have been the reason why Napoleon made no effort to get it discussed, and Walewski was reported to have declared that the Emperor had not made up his mind on the subject, though he (Walewski) believed that when the time came for decision he would pronounce definitely for union and a foreign prince.[7] In fact, apart from the substitution of Turkish for Russian control over the Principalities, no proposal of any fundamental change was permitted by the instructions of

---

[1] For the correspondence on this question see Clarendon to Cowley, no. 115, Nov. 15, 1855, F.O. 27/1059 and no. 63, Jan. 11, 1856, F.O. 27/1108 and Cowley to Clarendon, no. 1514, Nov. 20, 1855, F.O. 27/1079 and Jan. 11, 1856, telg., F.O. 27/1121.

[2] Stratford to Alison, no. 2, Jan. 9, F.O. 78/1170.

[3] Alison to Stratford, no. 2, Jan. 11, *ibid.*

[4] See e.g. Testa to Buol, no. 21, Apr. 5, 1855 and no. 22, Apr. 4; Mihanovich to Buol, no. 22, Apr. 14 (enclosing Stirbey's own plan), Staatsarchiv, XXXVIII/103; Russell to Clarendon, Mar. 28, enc., F.O. 7/463 and Colquhoun to Clarendon, no. 41, July 11, enc., F.O. 78/1097.

[5] Stratford to Alison, no. 2, Feb. 16, 1856, F.O. 78/1173.

[6] Colquhoun, the British consul at Bucharest, said that Stirbey wanted the Austrian occupation to be permanent on the ground that it was necessary to repress internal disorder: Colquhoun to Stratford, no. 41, Apr. 16, F.O. 78/1097.

[7] Hübner to Buol, no. 9 D, Jan. 25, Staatsarchiv, IX/51. Walewski told Cowley that, while his government would prefer union, it might be willing to yield on

the ambassadors.[1] Furthermore, when discussion opened, the problem of fixing the exact status of the Principalities, including the degree of control to be exercised by the suzerain and the determination of where power should lie in the provinces themselves, was found to furnish too broad a field for disagreement to make possible anything more than a sketchy outline of an arrangement. Stratford has testified that he would really have favoured union under a foreign prince, if a fortified barrier could have been erected against Russia, and he would fain have seen some degree of representative government instituted in the country;[2] but the establishment of fortresses in Moldavia (desired also by the Turks) would have been too clearly an entering wedge for a Turkish occupation to find favour with his colleagues, and Thouvenel, supported by Prokesch, insisted that representative government was not feasible in the East; besides, neither of these diplomats shared Stratford's confidence in the *boyerie*.[3] At times the British ambassador was very difficult, and the debates were somewhat stormy. 'He is no ambassador; he is a sovereign', complained Prokesch, who declared that it was his (Stratford's) dogma that no one was deemed worthy who did not share his opinion; and he even suspected that his British colleague was trying to curry favour with the Moldo-Wallachians.[4] In the end the Protocol of Constantinople (February 11, 1856) was mainly Thouvenel's composition. The recommendation of chief importance was that of instituting a caimacamie or provisional government during the interval until a new constitution could be put in operation.[5] Nothing was said of a European guarantee; so, thus far, Clarendon's scheme had worked; and he later pronounced the protocol 'the groundwork of a good organization of the Principalities'.[6] Thouvenel, however, set little store by his handiwork,[7] and doubtless reflected that the struggle for union (a reform that would scrap this whole scheme) was yet to come.

It can, of course, be readily appreciated that public opinion in the Principalities, while by no means rebellious, was becoming increasingly nervous, as rumours arrived of some disposition being made of them. When more definite information was received, disappointment seemed general, and took no account of

the matter. Cowley believed, however, that Walewski was simply trying to bargain for something else: Cowley to Clarendon, no. 124, Jan. 23, F.O. 27/1122. Apparently Napoleon had not yet formulated his plans.

[1] Thouvenel to Walewski, Feb. 11, *Actes et docs.*, vol. ii, no. 477.
[2] Stratford to Clarendon, no. 160, Feb. 11, F.O. 78/1172.
[3] Thouvenel to Walewski, no. 477 and annexes.
[4] Prokesch to Buol, no number, Feb. 11, Staatsarchiv, XIII/11.
[5] *Actes et docs.*, vol. ii, no. 476. (The document is here misdated 'January 11').
[6] Clarendon to Stratford, no. 240, Mar. 4, F.O. 78/1160.
[7] Thouvenel to Walewski, Mar. 23, *Actes et docs.*, vol. ii, no. 500.

party differences.[1] It was contended that the making of a constitution should be confided to a national assembly, meeting under
the auspices of commissioners of the Powers, after which it might
be presented to the Porte for final sanction.[2] Moreover, the
position of the suzerain Power, as provided by the protocol, gave
rise to much distrust.[3] But, above all, the failure of the Conference
to adopt the principle of union under a foreign prince was deplored
on all sides.[4] Stirbey, who had been courting Napoleon through
an indirect channel,[5] poured his dissatisfaction into both French
and British ears;[6] while Gregory Ghika sent a *mémoire* of his own
to Walewski, undoubtedly with the hope of directly influencing
the Congress.[7] Naturally the chief hope of the Principalities was
in France, whose sentiments at Vienna had not passed unnoticed.
Princess Ghika, herself a French woman, had even written
a personal letter to the Emperor, invoking his interest in her
adopted country—'sacrificed', she added shrewdly, 'to the reserved
policy of King Louis Philippe'.[8]

The Congress of Paris finally opened its sessions, February 25,
1856.[9] Each Power was represented by two plenipotentiaries,
and after some hesitation Sardinia and Prussia were included as
participants. Since Sardinia had been a belligerent, there could

---

[1] Cartaing to Walewski, no. 13, Feb. 29, *Aff. étr., Turquie, Jassy*, vol. 5;
Colquhoun to Stratford, no. 9, Feb. 24, and to Clarendon, no. 9, Mar. 5, F.O.
78/1199.

[2] Colquhoun to Stratford, no. 6, Feb. 27, F.O. 195/529. An eloquent appeal
for conferring the initiative on the Principalities had been addressed to the
Sultan by the Metropolitan of Moldavia in December: Stratford to Clarendon,
no. 207, Mar. 10, enc., F.O. 78/1175.

[3] Colquhoun to Clarendon, no. 9.

[4] A petition to Ghika from some of the *boyards* declared union to be a 'need
for fulfilling the mission which Providence and the interest of Europe have
indicated at the mouths of the Danube': *Actes et docs.*, vol. ii, no. 489. It was
reported that the Moldavians did not feel that any of their number had the
qualifications needed in 'the chief of a state': Cartaing to Walewski, no. 12, Feb.
15, *Aff. étr., Turquie, Jassy*, vol. v.

[5] Thouvenel, *Trois années de la question d'Orient*, p. 16.

[6] Béclard to Walewski, Mar. 14, *Actes et docs.*, vol. v, no. 1919; Alison to
Stratford, no. 8, Mar. 3, F.O. 78/1171.

[7] *Actes et docs.*, vol. ii, no. 487 and 488. This was mainly a searching criticism
of the Protocol of Constantinople. He contended, like others, that the initiative
in working out a new order should have come from the Principalities, and that
the protocol itself signified a fettering of the national autonomy. Ghika's action
was possibly inspired by a petition (mentioned above) which a group of *boyards*
had presented to him a few days previously, begging him 'not to permit the
rights of the state to be infringed without employing all measures, indicated by
circumstances', and asking that the petition be presented to the Congress.
Another *mémoire* of Ghika's, declaring for union and a foreign prince, was presented
to the Porte, and drew from Stratford a tirade against the 'malignant' principle
of nationality: Prokesch to Buol, no. 23, Mar. 17, Staatsarchiv, XIII/11.

[8] Princess Ghika to Napoleon, Jan. 27, *Aff. étr., Mém. et docs., Turquie*, vol. 54.

[9] The protocols of the Congress will be found in Martens, *op. cit.*, vol. xv,
pp. 700 ff. or *British and Foreign State Papers*, vol. xlvi, or *Actes et docs.*, vol. ii,
no. 490.

be no logic in refusing her admittance, but it was chiefly through
Napoleon's influence, and rather in spite of British sentiments,
that Prussia was invited to take part, and, as Clarendon put it
rather bitingly, her plenipotentiaries arrived 'only in time for
dessert'.[1] Austria was represented by Count Buol and Baron
Hübner (ambassador at Paris), Great Britain by Lords Clarendon
and Cowley (ambassador at Paris), and France by Count Walewski
and Baron Bourqueney (ambassador at Vienna); Cavour, Ali
Pasha, and Count Orloff were the leading representatives of Sardinia,
Turkey, and Russia respectively. Walewski was chosen at the
first session to preside over the Congress. A cousin of the Emperor,
he had been lately elevated to the ministry of foreign affairs from
the embassy at London, and was hailed (rather prematurely) by
Hübner as a friend of Austria.[2] Without much intellect or force,
he merely carried out the will of his master, but generally in
a manner so lacking in assurance that he often defeated his object,
and so equivocal that he seemed always to rouse the distrust of
other diplomats without ever really deceiving them. At the
Congress he was simply the mouthpiece of the Emperor, whom
he consulted, it was said, twice each day.[3] Undoubtedly the most
picturesque figure at the Congress was Orloff, whose long career
as a soldier and diplomat had given him a peculiar distinction,
while his frankness, his good humour, and his studied efforts to
make himself agreeable were undoubtedly responsible for saving
his country from many embarrassments. Conspicuous always on
account of his height and stately bearing, he was the object of
a certain curious admiration wherever he went, and among
fashionable society was distinctly the vogue.[4] The Austrians,
much more than the Russians, were the butts of the Congress.[5]
Cavour was, of course, out for their blood, and Clarendon was
too honest to disguise his attitude towards Austrian rule in Italy.
Napoleon, for his part, did not like either Hübner or Buol,[6] and
the conceit of the latter, no less than his slippery performances,
made him thoroughly unpopular. It was said that Buol and Orloff
did not speak, or even bow, when they met.[7] While the Russians

---

[1] See the interesting narrative in East, *op. cit.*, pp. 45–6.
[2] Hübner, *Neuf ans de souvenirs d'un ambassadeur d'Autriche à Paris*, vol. i, p. 385.
[3] Senior, *Conversations with M. Thiers, M. Guizot, and other Distinguished
Persons during the Second Empire*, vol. ii, p. 72.   [4] Charles-Roux, *op. cit.*, p. 86.
[5] On the occasion of an extravagant statement of Buol's, Orloff was said to
have remarked, in an audible whisper, 'Ma foi, pas mal, M. le Comte, pas si mal!
On dirait que c'est les Autrichiens qui ont pris Sébastopol': *The Times*, Apr.
21, Paris correspondent.
[6] Satow, *An Austrian Diplomatist in the Fifties*, p. 42 and Vitzthum, *St.
Petersburg and London*, vol. i, pp. 292–3, cited by East, *op. cit.*, p. 58; cf. Clarendon's impression in Martin, *op. cit.*, vol. iv, p. 49.
[7] *The Times*, Mar. 13, Paris correspondent; cf. Vielcastel, *Memoirs* (Eng.
trans.), vol. i, p. 232.

were among the earliest to arrive, Lord Clarendon, as the minister of France's leading ally, was the first to be received by the Emperor.[1] He had come to the Congress with great reluctance, fearing that he would bring back an unpopular peace or a breach of Anglo-French relations;[2] but, whatever their disagreement on certain particulars, Clarendon soon became very favourably impressed with the Emperor,[3] and both he and his grave colleague, Lord Cowley, showed a moderation at the Congress that was hardly to be expected. Perhaps, indeed, all the plenipotentiaries felt the atmosphere of *bonhomie* in which the Congress began its sittings, for Paris was in a joyous mood, and peace was in every heart. A host of entertainments was provided for these guests, and Clarendon was reported by his secretary as 'up to the neck in interviews, conferences, tea-parties, and dinners'.[4] The meetings of the Congress were held in the Hall of the Ambassadors at the French ministry of foreign affairs. Sitting about a table in their gilded arm-chairs, with their feet on a carpet of green velvet, these sixteen diplomats matched their wits in the business of liquidating a war to the satisfaction of all.

It is, of course, from a European congress that oppressed peoples will always try to obtain a hearing; and, to this extent, the Concert of Europe had acquired a certain prestige. The efforts of Cavour, as champion of the Italians, is somewhat outside this story. But no people were more active than the Roumans in supporting their nationalist aims. We have already mentioned the memorial that had been sent to the Congress from Moldavia. In Paris itself the Rouman colony totalled, it was said, about two hundred,[5] and easily made up for the smallness of their numbers by the zeal with which they pushed their country's cause. Both of the Golescos had sent Walewski their written views on the needs of the Principalities,[6] and, finally, an address to the Congress was drawn up and signed by all the Roumans resident in Paris. The petition was simply an appeal for union on the ground of complete identity in language, religion, customs, and institutions between the two Principalities. 'The question of their union [so ran the petition] is superior to all others relating to the Principalities.'[7] Nothing was said of a foreign prince, it being felt that such a proposal might lessen the chance of obtaining union.[8] Whether

[1] Gourdon, *Histoire du Congrès de Paris*, p. 426.
[2] *The Later Correspondence of Sir John Russell*, vol. ii, pp. 217–18.
[3] Greville, *Journal of the Reign of Queen Victoria*, vol. ii, p. 24.
[4] Ponsonby to Bloomfield, Feb. 27, Bloomfield Papers, F.O. 356/31.
[5] Bataillard, *La Moldo-Valachie dans les manifestations de ses efforts et ses vœux*, p. 30.   [6] *Les Principautés-unies devant la Conférence*, pp. 9–11.
[7] *Journal des débats*, Mar. 24–5, 1856; likewise printed in *The Times* of Mar. 24.
[8] Bataillard, *op. cit.*, p. 30.

the efforts of these *émigrés* had an influence upon the Emperor's already awakened sympathies is difficult to judge. Clarendon wrote to Stratford that the general feeling of this element was in favour of union under a foreign prince and independence, and 'that the Emperor is not unfavourable to this arrangement, though H. M. admits that it would be attended with many difficulties'.[1] It is perhaps reasonable to suppose that Napoleon meant to get for the Moldo-Wallachians as much as he could.

Meanwhile the question of the Principalities came up at the first session of the Congress, when the First Point, embodying the abolition of the Russian 'protectorate', was formally adopted along with the other three. Since this declaration also declared that the contracting Powers should grant or confirm to them 'an internal organization in conformity with the needs and wishes of the population',[2] the Congress was certainly committing itself at the outset to an impartial work of reconstruction. Whether the union of the Principalities would be in accord with those 'needs and wishes' was, of course, for the Congress to decide. The matter came up again at the second session, February 28, when it was unanimously agreed that a committee should be appointed *dans le sein du congrès*, which should set forth the principles to be adopted for a constitution for the Principalities, leaving the details to be worked out by a second committee, to meet after the conclusion of peace.[3] No hint was given at this session that France intended to propose union as a basis, but Cowley had told Clarendon that he expected him to do so,[4] and we know that Bourqueney had tried to convince Buol that union under a foreign prince would be to Austria's interest, as the Emperor had thought of the Duke of Modena (a scion of the Hapsburg house) for that honour.[5] On the surface it might seem as though the manœuvre was an attempt to sell the Principalities to Austria in return for the furtherance of Italian unification, and we know that Napoleon had seriously proposed such a plan in 1854;[6] but it is not an assured fact that an Austrian prince would have been eventually unacceptable to the Principalities, provided his power were reasonably restricted. Politically progress is generally achieved only through slow and devious treading, and we must bear in mind that Napoleon had already committed himself to a solution of the Italian question. What could be shrewder than to further the union of two nationalities at one stroke?

[1] Clarendon to Stratford, no. 240, Mar. 4, F.O. 78/1160.   [2] Protocol 1, Feb. 26.
[3] Protocol 2, Feb. 28.   [4] Cowley to Clarendon, no. 279, Mar. 5, F.O. 27/1124.
[5] Buol to Francis Joseph, Mar. 9, Staatsarchiv, XII/200.
[6] This indirect overture was declined by Austria. See Ernest of Saxe-Coburg, *Memoirs* (Eng. trans.), vol. iii, pp. 66, 105–6, cited by Simpson, *op. cit.*, p. 301 n. See above, page 32.

As a matter of fact, Napoleon was not the prime mover in this particular scheme. The keenest mind at the Congress, beyond a doubt, belonged to Cavour, who had readily seen in the Emperor's policy an opportunity for gaining the objects so eagerly cherished by his own country. Some months previously he had broached to Napoleon the idea of enlarging Sardinia by finding compensation for Austria in the Principalities, and Napoleon seems to have promised that he would bring the Italian question before the Congress and would propose explicitly that the Duke of Modena should be transferred to the Principalities, the Duchess of Parma being given Modena in exchange, and thus Parma be ceded to Sardinia.[1] We have already noticed that the Emperor had sounded Buol on the subject—an overture, which, however, met with no encouragement.[2] As Clarendon was also cold to the proposal,[3] the wily Italian ordered D'Azeglio (Sardinian minister to London) to seek Palmerston's consent to the designation of the Duchess of Parma to the Principalities on the understanding that she should sacrifice Parma to Sardinia.[4] In the end, however, Cavour seems to have concluded that the opposition to these schemes was insurmountable, and he fell back on the general policy of cultivating Napoleon's friendship by backing his desire for the union of the Principalities. And, after all, if Rouman nationalism were promoted by the Congress, there was no inherent reason why the Italian question should not also be submitted to the wisdom of the Powers. It lies outside the theme of this story to follow the fortunes of all Cavour's tortuous schemes. The important thing is to note that he strove with all his might through D'Azeglio to gain Palmerston's support for the Principalities.[5]

Much less interested in the question was the Court of St. Petersburg, which could look for no immediate gain from any scheme of reorganizing the Principalities. But a chance to win a smile from the magnanimous sovereign who was already willing

[1] Cavour to D'Azeglio, Dec. 8, 1855, and Feb. 26, 1856, *Actes et docs.*, vol. iv, nos. 1383 and 1386. (These and the following letters of Cavour were reprinted from Bianchi, *La Politique de Cavour: Lettres inédites*). Napoleon's recommendation is also found in a note in his own handwriting on a foreign office memorandum in the French archives: *Mém. et docs.*, *Turquie*, vol. 55.

[2] Buol to Francis Joseph, Mar. 9.

[3] Cavour to D'Azeglio, Feb. 28, 1856, *Actes et docs.*, vol. iv, no. 1387.

[4] Cavour to D'Azeglio, Feb. 29, *ibid.*, no. 1388. Cavour did not hint to Napoleon any disapproval of the transference of the Duke of Modena, but, as the Austrians were unpopular in the Principalities, the Duchess of Parma, a Bourbon, would be a better selection, and doubtless one could find her a satisfactory husband.

[5] Cavour to D'Azeglio, Mar. 6, 7, and 18, *ibid.*, nos. 1391, 1392, and 1399. 'For the love of Heaven, persuade Palmerston', wrote Cavour, 'that it would be *un crime de lèse-civilisation*, if he upheld the status quo and opposed the just wishes of the entire Rouman population.'

to efface the memory of the late war could hardly have been lost on the veteran, Orloff, who, as we learn, bestowed such fulsome praise on that sovereign;[1] and the *rapprochment,* as we have noticed during the negotiations of the preceding year, needed only to be clinched in order to procure some indulgence now or later. One knows that it is always wise for the defeated party to court the least vindictive of its enemies. Walewski told Hübner an odd story to the effect that, when Napoleon asked the Russian plenipotentiaries what attitude they proposed to take, they made answer, 'Sire, we shall vote with you for or against union, according to your desire.'[2] Napoleon told Clarendon that Russia favoured union, or at least improved conditions in the Principalities.[3] Thus it can be seen that three Powers (Prussia was not then a member of the Congress) could probably be counted on to support the aspirations of the Roumans.

The attitude of Austria and Turkey, on the other hand, implied a stubborn resistance to the Emperor's project. Buol, as one of the plenipotentiaries remarked, was opposed to union *jusqu'à l'épilepsie,*[4] and, if he had shown sufficient subtlety and resolution, he might well have put a quietus on the question. The tactics of Ali, on the contrary, were characteristically evasive. He had no instructions even to discuss union, and by Fabian strategy he might hope to see the question go by default. According to a newspaper report, the discussion of union at the Congress 'threw the whole official world of Stamboul into a state of excitement', and a protest to Ali was telegraphed that such a discussion was an interference in the internal affairs of the Empire.[5]

With Austria and Turkey bitterly opposed to union, and France, Russia, and Sardinia ranged in its favour, it is obvious that Great Britain held a somewhat pivotal position. We have noticed her prejudices on the subject during the Conference of Vienna, and it is a well-known fact that British policy not only is seldom opportunist, but clings to a tradition (like the strengthening of the Ottoman Empire) with frequently little regard for altered circumstances. Before the Congress, Cowley had written to Clarendon that he himself concurred in Turkey's disapproval of union,[6] and, in view of his former attitude, one can hardly be surprised at Clarendon's own reluctance to second such a scheme. Writing on March 6, Cavour declared that the British statesman was

---

[1] Thouvenel, *Pages de l'histoire du Second Empire,* p. 268.
[2] Hübner to Buol, no. 52 D, June 9, Staatsarchiv, IX/51.
[3] Clarendon to Palmerston, no. 40, Mar. 7, F.O. 27/1164, printed in Martin, *Life of the Prince Concert,* vol. iii, p. 465.
[4] *The Times,* Apr. 23, Paris correspondent.
[5] *Ibid.,* Mar. 25, Constantinople correspondent.
[6] Cowley to Clarendon, no. 255, Feb. 27, F.O. 27/1124.

undecided, but leaned toward the *status quo*.[1] Did he allow himself to be moved by his attraction for Napoleon? We know that he had an interview with the Emperor on the 6th, and that, when the latter declared that 'nothing could satisfy the people of Moldavia and Wallachia but the union of the Principalities under a foreign prince', Clarendon raised many difficulties as to the selection of such a prince, foresaw a strenuous opposition from Austria and Turkey, and considered, himself, that such a measure would be an 'act of spoliation'. Yet withal he had admitted that the plan 'might be the best for the Principalities' and 'well worthy of consideration'.[2] Whether some private hint from Palmerston was responsible for the final plunge is not discoverable in any evidence that is available;[3] nor have we any inkling of the motive beyond a subsequent statement of the Austrian ambassador that the Government's hand was forced by public opinion.[4] If that is true, then it was merely because the British statesmen were loath to borrow future trouble, for British sentiment was at present indifferent to the issue. More plausible, perhaps, was Buol's guess that Clarendon swung to union in order to please France.[5] Oftentimes concessions are made on points, seemingly for the moment trivial, which later turn out to be ghosts to haunt a diplomat's peace of mind. Whether Clarendon merely performed a diplomatic obeisance, the committal of his government was not, as it turned out, a very happy venture.

But it was not long before this important question would be decided in some fashion, for Napoleon was determined to make an effort to win the Congress to his views. 'The great fault committed by the Congress of Vienna', he had told Clarendon, 'was

[1] Cavour to D'Azeglio, Mar. 6, *Actes et docs.*, vol. iv, no. 1391.

[2] Clarendon to Palmerston, no. 40.

[3] Reference to Palmerston's private correspondence with Clarendon (gleanings from which were kindly placed by Professor Bell at my disposal in anticipation of his forthcoming work on Palmerston) does not settle the matter conclusively. Palmerston had been somewhat tempted by Cavour's exchange-project, but finally dismissed the idea as impracticable. On the day *after* the crucial meeting of the Congress he wrote to Clarendon that, while he himself preferred separation, it was probable that the English public would be pleased with union, and that he saw no great objection to it 'if the Emperor presses very much for union' and "Turkey can be induced to consent'. It is possible that Palmerston had given some hint of a change of attitude in a private telegram to Clarendon of which we have no record. (The Queen, it may be remarked, had written him on the 6th that she felt that an hereditary monarchy, being 'the arrangement that will satisfy the people themselves' would be the best barrier against Russian intrigues: *Letters of Queen Victoria, 1837–61*, vol. iii, p. 229). But the simplest conjecture is that Clarendon, rather desirous of pleasing the Emperor and deeming the matter of relative unimportance, simply exercised his own judgement.

[4] Apponyi to Buol, no. 22 C, Sept. 18, Staatsarchiv, viii/45. For Palmerston's comment in this connexion see the preceding note.

[5] Buol to Prokesch, June 28, *ibid.*, xii/58.

that the interests of the sovereigns were consulted, while the interests of their subjects were only neglected, and the present congress ought not to fall into a similar error.' He had told Clarendon definitely that he intended to bring the question before the Congress.[1]

The occasion for the French proposal was the session of March 8, when the question of the organization of the Principalities was scheduled to come up. Walewski, opening the discussion, declared that an answer to the dominant question, union or separation, should be adopted as a basis; for his own part, he believed that the interests of the Principalities demanded union, and he thought that the Congress should proclaim it. Thus France had definitely made the proposal, and Cavour assures us that the minister had expressed himself with warmth. Clarendon took occasion to speak next, and one may well judge with what strained attention his voice was heard. We have no record of his exact words, but the dry recital of the protocol informs us that he endorsed Walewski's stand on the ground that the wishes of the people should be considered. It was a lovely little snare for the Opposition, though the single-minded Clarendon had certainly not so designed it. Ali and Buol at once combatted the idea that union was really desired by the Principalities, Buol arguing that Ali was in a better position to know the truth than Walewski's informants, who, according to the latter's statement, had represented the sentiment for union as unanimous.[2] It was a long debate, and not too amicable. Unwilling to yield an inch, Buol protested that he had no instructions to discuss union, and would not even ask for them, though the milder Hübner suggested that at least discussion was permitted.[3] Bourqueney, Orloff, and Cavour also spoke in turn—Orloff affirming that his government favoured union, and Cavour, according to his own account, supporting it warmly.[4] No final decision was taken at this meeting, but it was evident that Great Britain's vote had turned the scale. Though Clarendon had spoken without enthusiasm, the result was satisfactory to Walewski, who remarked, after a later conversation with the British statesman, that while Great Britain was not *aussi fermement*

---

[1] Clarendon to Palmerston, no. 40. According to Clarendon, who with Cowley had an interview with Walewski on the 7th, 'His Excellency read to us a letter, stating in strong terms that no peace would be solid or durable which did not provide for the union and independence of the Principalities, and urging that an instruction to that effect should be given to the committee of the Conference which was to consider and report on the form of government to be established': Clarendon to Palmerston, no. 39, Mar. 7, F.O. 27/1168. Apparently Napoleon must have subsequently given up his idea of 'independence'.

[2] Protocol 6, Mar. 8.

[3] Hübner, *op. cit.*, vol. i, p. 401.

[4] Cavour to D'Azeglio, Mar, 9, *Actes et docs.*, vol. iv, no. 1394.

résolu que France, he felt convinced that she would support their common policy.[1]

Unqualified acceptance of union was, however, almost as impossible at the present juncture as it had been a year earlier at Vienna; for Austria and Turkey would not have accepted it without a struggle, and a peace congress has too heavy and complex a task to risk the provocation of a rupture. Yet one cannot tell what course France might have taken, if she had known that Buol was very much afraid that Turkey would give way, and was beginning to ponder how, in case a foreign prince were really granted, Austria might manage to get the position for one of her archdukes. The Austrian minister could only urge that Prokesch be instructed to bolster up the courage of the Porte.[2]

When the scene shifted for the moment to Constantinople, it seemed at first that Austria might win a decisive victory. While Stratford and Thouvenel were commanded to urge the Porte to send Ali the instructions to discuss union,[3] Prokesch was ordered to 'bend every effort to prevent it', and to assure the Porte that Austria 'would stand firmly by its side', if it refused to countenance union.[4] Thanks partly, no doubt, to Prokesch's efforts, and quite as much because Stratford privately encouraged the Porte to reject his government's request, the Turkish council declined to send the necessary instructions;[5] but, fortunately for the cause of Rouman nationalism, the two recalcitrant Powers had made the strategic blunder of emphasizing the dissent of the Moldo-Wallachians themselves to the principle of union, and hence the logical rejoinder was a direct appeal to the populations concerned. Thus emerged the entering wedge of the Russian idea of a plebiscite. At the session of March 12, a committee, chosen by virtue of action taken two days previously, and composed of Bourqueney, Buol, and Ali, proposed that, instead of the final status of the Principalities being determined in the treaty of peace, measures should be taken through a popularly elected divan ('divan *ad hoc*',

---

[1] Walewski to Thouvenel, Mar. 29, *Actes et docs.*, vol. ii, no. 502.

[2] Buol to Francis Joseph, Mar. 9.

[3] Walewski to Thouvenel, Mar. 8, telg., *Aff. étr., Turquie*, vol. 325. 'Bend all your efforts', telegraphed Walewski, 'to get the Sultan himself, and as promptly as possible, to authorize Ali Pasha to enter into our views. The Emperor has done enough for Turkey to expect that on this occasion his opinion will be complied with'; F.O. to Stratford, Mar. 10, telg. Stratford stated in a later letter (to Clarendon, no. 6, Feb. 9, 1857, F.O. 78/1279) that 'Ali Pasha had consented to the discussion of the union at Paris'; but this may apply to the discussion of Mar. 8. The fact that Ali had committed this indiscretion was seized upon by his enemy, Reshid Pasha (whom he had supplanted) as ground for attacking him, and led Ali himself, according to Stratford, to assume, in self-defence, an attitude of hostility to union.

[4] Werner to Prokesch, Mar. 9, telg., Staatsarchiv, XII/200.

[5] Thouvenel to Walewski, Mar. 13, *Actes et docs.*, vol. ii, no. 497. Vienna telegraphed the glad news to Buol, Mar. 11: Staatsarchiv, XII/200.

it was called) in each of the Principalities to ascertain the wishes of the Moldo-Wallachians.[1] In this wise had the weapons of Austria and Turkey broken in their hands.

Although the final solution of the question was thus shelved by the Congress, the way was clearly opened for an entire change of basis, and presumably the ultimate reorganization of the Principalities would be founded on their union. The plan of a plebiscite having been adopted by the Congress, the more detailed features of the report were accepted two days later with only slight amendment.[2] The Principalities were to preserve their existing autonomy, subject to the suzerainty of the Porte; an international commission should make an inquiry into conditions and sentiments in the Principalities and report upon the same to the Powers, who, in congress assembled, should undertake the final reorganization of the provinces; finally, while a national force should ordinarily watch over the defence of these lands, armed intervention on the part of the suzerain might be undertaken, if necessary, to restore internal peace, but only upon preliminary agreement between the contracting Powers and the Porte. Such was the Congress's solution of the question of the Principalities, later embodied in the definitive Treaty of Paris.[3]

It can easily be seen that the reorganization of the Principalities was designed to be a matter for patient study, and that much development would be possible, apart from the general requirement of native autonomy under Turkish suzerainty. The restrictions imposed upon the Porte in the event of turbulence in the Principalities were no doubt intended to safeguard their privileges against encroachments by the suzerain Power. But they had also a deeper significance. It will be noticed that the Powers not only sponsored a new order for the Principalities but assumed a certain joint responsibility for keeping order. Thus, in spite of Clarendon's prejudices, Europe transferred to itself a sort of protectorate over the Danubian Principalities. Whether the British minister had become convinced by this time that there was safety in numbers, we cannot say, but there is no evidence on record that he had spoken for an unrestricted surveillance by the Porte.[4] To a shrewd Wallachian the arrangement merely seemed to denote a replacing of one protector by many, and he lamented that his country was

---

[1] Protocol 8, Mar. 12.

[2] Protocol 9, Mar. 14. The Bourqueney committee had proposed that an international commission, after learning the wishes of the people, should revise the existing statutes. The Congress decided, however, to refer the task to another international conference.

[3] Articles xxii–xxv.

[4] Clarendon's letter of Mar. 29 to Palmerston (no. 91, F.O. 27/1169) alludes only briefly to the discussion of the intervention clause.

not left simply to a suzerainty, 'more nominal than real'.[1] But there is hardly reason to doubt that the Concert of Europe, in thus becoming guarantors of the *status quo*, were consciously trying to buttress the autonomy of the Principalities against possible invasion by the suzerain. It is also to be noticed that precautions against injustice in the elections of the divans were intended by the decision—instigated by Clarendon at the session of March 25— that the firman of convocation should be 'concerted with the representatives of the contracting Powers at Constantinople'.[2] But, on the very day that peace was signed, Buol telegraphed to Prokesch to 'lay emphasis on the necessity of the provisional continuance of the present hospodars in office and of the Austro-Turkish army of occupation until the definitive arrangement',[3] and it is evident that Austria was at once planning how the plebiscite, which circumstances had forced her to accept, could be nullified in the end.

While this testimony of bad faith was, of course, unknown in Paris, the settlement did undoubtedly leave one loophole for intrigue, which convicts the Congress of a strange want of foresight. At the session of April 8 (which had adopted with slight modifications the instructions which a committee had drafted for the international commission of inquiry) the point was raised by Clarendon that the object of the plebiscite could not be achieved if the hospodars continued to possess their present degree of power, and he called attention to the fact that their terms of office were very soon to expire. Buol and Ali made some rather vague objections, but Clarendon, perhaps mindful of Stratford's distrust of Stirbey, was unmoved in his contention; and it was then recalled by several of the plenipotentiaries that in the event of a suspension of the hospodariate, provision was made by the *Règlement organique* for a caimacamie or provisional government. After some discussion it was finally decided at Austria's instance that 'it should be left to the Sublime Porte, if it deemed it desirable, to take measures necessary and proper to carry out the Congress' intentions, combining the free expression of the wishes of the divans *ad hoc* with the maintenance of order and respect for law'.[4] Now, to place so much responsibility on a Power who could not view the plebiscite

---

[1] Boeresco, *Mémoire relative à la question politique et économique de la Moldo-Valachie.* (This interesting pamphlet is not included in Bengesco).

[2] Protocol 14, Mar. 25. In the same session the general instructions to the commission of inquiry were submitted by the Bourqueney committee and adopted.

[3] Buol to Prokesch, Mar. 30, Staatsarchiv, XII/200. Prokesch duly carried out these orders and Fuad Pasha, the Turkish minister of foreign affairs, promised to do nothing to hasten the departure of the armies of occupation, as well as not to replace the hospodars: Prokesch to Buol, Apr. 10, *ibid.*, XII/11.

[4] Protocol 22, Apr. 8.

disinterestedly and whose political morality was justifiably suspect was to jeopardize at one stroke the purpose which the Congress had in view. How far could the 'free expression of the wishes of the divans *ad hoc*' be really combined with the 'maintenance of order and respect for law'? Could not the Porte maintain that a vote for union and a foreign prince must be averted in the interest of law and order? Would not the Porte most certainly see an opening for installing in the Principalities a system of government (in accordance with, or contrary to, the *Règlement*, as it saw fit) which would seek to render the plebiscite illusory? It will be seen that the device of leaving matters thus vaguely to the discretion of the Porte had consequences diametrically opposite to the collective purposes of the Congress. But it might be that one could hardly expect better from a body which had solemnly admitted Turkey to membership in the Concert of Europe itself.

It has been noticed that the decision regarding the temporary government of the Principalities was taken on April 8—more than a week after the definitive treaty was concluded and signed. At the session of March 28—two days before the signature of the treaty—Walewski had pointed out that the Congress had not, with the conclusion of the treaty, finished all its labours, as there were still some matters of detail to be arranged, such as the measures to be taken for the evacuation of Ottoman lands and waters by the Allied forces.[1] The Congress therefore decided to continue in session, and did not actually come to a close until April 16.

The problem of fixing a *terme* for the Allied occupation was not so simple a task as might at first be supposed; for, until the Russians evacuated that part of Bessarabia which had been ceded to Moldavia—and their withdrawal would presumably await a survey of the new frontier by an international commission—it might not be thought expedient for the British fleet to withdraw from the Bosporus or for the Turkish forces to retire from the fortresses in Wallachia which they still held. There was, above all, the Austrian army of occupation, which might serve as a security for the enemy's good faith. To Austria herself, naturally enough, the very thought of evacuation was most distressing, especially as she had long been projecting a system of railways in the Principalities, and her efforts to interest European capitalists, like the Rothschilds, depended unquestionably upon the strength of her political influence there.[2] Yet obviously no arrangement could be made for holding a plebiscite in a country which bristled with foreign

[1] Protocol 17, Mar. 28.
[2] Austria's railway plans (we have mentioned the inception of them, page 27, note 3) were proceeding very hopefully until her compulsion to accept a definite scheme for the withdrawal of her troops speedily brought them to a standstill: Feldakten, 1856, Kriegsarchiv.

bayonets. Moreover, the conduct of the Austrian soldiery had been notoriously oppressive—a fact which even Buol did not deny, though he exculpated himself from blame in the matter, and privately criticized the conduct of the Austrian commander. When the question had been first broached in the session of March 27, Walewski stated that six months might be necessary for the complete withdrawal of the Allied troops, instead of the forty days stipulated by agreement with Turkey, but he desired that the Austrians should withdraw immediately, lest their presence be construed as a means of exercising restraint on the elections to the divans. Buol, according to his own account, resented the insinuation, and declared that it was a matter solely between Austria and the Porte.[1] Then Clarendon, who, according to Cavour, was 'laughing in his sleeve',[2] sustained Walewski's position, and the French minister's acid comments so riled Buol that, in the words of his Austrian colleague, he 'grew quite red, and blew up like a rocket'.[3] One may well imagine how he felt at the idea that Austria was to lose her chief means of making her diplomacy effective; and to find the truth suspected was ground for exasperation. After six hours of discussion it was decided, and incorporated in article xxxi of the treaty, that the Allied Powers and Austria should withdraw their forces 'as soon as possible after the exchange of ratifications', while 'the delays and means of execution should be left to be settled by each Power through a convention with the Porte'.[4] The term, 'as soon as possible', was, of course, still to be interpreted, and the vagueness of the arrangement was designed merely to defer further pressure upon Austria until after the treaty of peace had been disposed of.

For the moment, indeed, Buol felt that he had much cause for feeling relief, for he had feared that the signing of the treaty would be made conditional on immediate evacuation—'and then our situation would have been very delicate. Without doubt', he added to Francis Joseph, 'it will be brought up again, but after the conclusion of peace our position will be freer'. It is clear enough from his own confession that Buol intended, if possible, that the Austrian army should remain 'until the definitive organization of the Principalities'.[5] He accordingly instructed Prokesch to represent to the Turks the great value which Austria ascribed to the Austro-Turkish occupation 'until decision is definitely taken on the points which are still to be settled'. 'The two Powers (he continued) will possess thereby the surest means of neutralizing opposing influences, which may operate on the part of other

---

[1] Buol and Hübner to Francis Joseph, no. 20, Apr. 6, Staatsarchiv, XII/200.
[2] Cavour to D'Azeglio, Mar. 28, *Actes et docs.*, vol. iv, no. 1401.
[3] Hübner, *op. cit.*, vol. i, p. 409.   [4] Protocol 17, Mar. 28.
[5] Buol to Francis Joseph, Mar. 29, Staatsarchiv, XII/200.

governments, much less interested than Austria and Turkey in the decisions that will be made regarding the political and administrative situation in the Danubian Principalities.'[1] As Buol had failed in his effort to keep Stirbey in power, he was now, apparently, thrown upon the defence of his last trench. It is also to be noticed that Austria, when checkmated by the Powers, will, as usual, try a manœuvre from the rear.

Yet the Austrian minister must have realized that, with Clarendon aiding Walewski on the point of a speedy evacuation, it was futile to suppose that the matter would be left simply to Austria's own devices. Whether or not he looked upon his retreat as covered by an overture from Napoleon, who sent Bourqueney to promise that out of regard for his friendship for Francis Joseph he would take account of Austrian interests,[2] Buol had quite altered his position when the question came up again at the session of April 4, and he admitted that the Austrian evacuation could be completed sooner than the withdrawal of the Anglo-French forces from the Crimea.[3] And though he had to listen to a warning from Clarendon, similar to that of Walewski at the former session, he seemed to rest satisfied with presenting a lengthy defence of Austria's attitude. In the end it was agreed that all the armies of occupation should commence their retreat immediately after the exchange of ratifications, six months being allowed the Western Powers for their withdrawal.[4] According to Buol's understanding the complete evacuation of the Principalities should be conditional on the retirement of the Russian forces; the last Austrian withdrawals should be simultaneous with those of the Turks; and the commission of inquiry should not meet until the last Austrian soldier had left the country.[5] For some reason these last stipulations were not incorporated in the protocol, and, as the question of the proper end of the Austrian occupation was frequently raised afterwards, it is unfortunate that these arrangements were not set down in formal fashion. Buol himself cherished the notion (so he wrote to Francis Joseph) that a single Austrian battalion might be allowed to remain until the assembling of the divans, though not—he argued shrewdly —as if Vienna seemed to lay stress on the occupation or employed it for political objects. For the moment, at least, Buol professed to to believe that the Austrian commanders had sadly bungled their opportunities—'they should never have allowed so impractical a question as union and a foreign prince to become current'—and that, if the civil agents were to accomplish anything, they would

---

[1] Buol to Prokesch, Mar. 30, *ibid.*, XII/58.
[2] Buol to Francis Joseph, no. 2, Apr. 6, Staatsarchiv, XII/200.
[3] Protocol 21, Apr. 4. This, however, Walewski and Clarendon did not insist on.
[4] Buol argued later that Austria had the same privilege as these (specified) belligerents.   [5] Buol and Hübner to Francis Joseph, Apr. 6, Staatsarchiv, XII/200.

have better success without depending upon a military occupation.[1] Apparently Buol had learned a lesson. The chief reliance would now be placed on more subtle methods of exercising influence.

The sessions of the Congress were now happily drawing to a close, and nothing remained to trouble the serenity of the atmosphere except the momentary reflection that perhaps, after all, the peace of its making (based, as it was, upon serious injury to Russia) was not as solid as it might be. It was Clarendon who proposed that the Congress should pass a resolution to the effect that in event of any disagreement between the Porte and any one of the other signatory Powers, recourse should be sought in mediation before any resort to force, and, when Buol was assured that this would in no way 'limit the independence' of his government, the Congress unanimously passed this pious measure.[2] The following day (April 15) Great Britain, France, and Austria signed a treaty *extra conventum*, guaranteeing the independence and integrity of the Ottoman Empire, which they agreed, if need be, to defend by force.[3] The idea of such a treaty had emanated from Buol, who sought thus to end that isolation of Austria, which he had scented at the Congress, and perhaps also to revenge himself upon Russia.[4] On April 16 the Congress closed its long and arduous task with felicitations to Walewski 'for the manner in which he had conducted its work' and with the French minister's appropriate reply.[5] Whatever its faults, the Congress of Paris had certainly taken its labours seriously, and the deliberations themselves had revealed little of the rancour that one might reasonably have expected between victors and vanquished. Indeed, one might almost have supposed at times that Austria was the common enemy—but that, of course, is another story.

Already, on March 30, 1856, the Treaty of Paris had been concluded—signed by a quill plucked from an imperial eagle in the Jardin des Plantes; while cannon from the Bastille and the Invalides saluted the task achieved.[6] That night the city of Paris was brilliantly illuminated;[7] and, if Bucharest and Jassy did not similarly rejoice, it was perhaps because the Roumanian people were still far from believing that their prayers had been granted. The following day a great banquet was provided by Walewski for the entire diplomatic corps;[8] and thus France concluded her gracious hospitality. After all, whatever the shortcomings of the Congress of Paris, its advent had marked the zenith of the Second Empire. No clouds were yet to be scanned on the horizon, and, though there

[1] Buol to Francis Joseph, Apr. 6, no. 2.   [2] Protocol 23, Apr. 14.
[3] *Actes et docs.*, vol. ii, no. 492.   [4] Senior, *op. cit.*, vol. ii, p. 72.
[5] Protocol, no. 24.   [6] Hübner, *op. cit.*, vol. i, p. 411.
[7] Thouvenel, *Pages de l'histoire du Second Empire*, pp. 260–1.
[8] Hübner, *op. cit.*, vol. i, p. 412.

were marks of blood on the claws of the eagle, there was nothing yet to sully the grandeur of its plumage. The moment was at least one of triumph for Napoleon. Arbiter of Europe, in so far as he brought the war to a close, he had engraved upon an international treaty the principle of nationality. A people in Eastern Europe were to be permitted to vote themselves a single nation.

Thus the Congress of Paris confirmed the international character of the Rouman question. Divorced from the tutelage of a Power, whose role had been seldom disinterested, the Danubian Principalities were taken under the protecting wing of the Concert of Europe. It was a relation not dissimilar in principle to the mandatory experiment of another congress of Paris; and time was to show whether the scheme would work for good or ill. That a diplomatic controversy should arise over the operation of the programme, thus happily devised, was certainly not evident in what must be considered the most progressive feature of the treaty of 1856.

CHAPTER II

DISCORD AMONG THE PROTECTING POWERS

THE Treaty of Paris had marked the first constructive step in the long struggle for the union of the Danubian Principalities under a ruler of their choice. At least on the initial question of union the people themselves were to be consulted (seeing that they were to express themselves on the problem of their organization); and, to the champions of that principle, convinced as they were of the sentiments of the Moldo-Wallachians, the cause for which they fought might have seemed to be almost won. But the course of French diplomacy, as one may trace it in the dispatches of Walewski for the succeeding months, must persuade us that the Emperor was by no means certain that this section of the treaty would stand firm amid the quicksands of diplomatic vacillation and Ottoman intrigue. Would Austria recall the troops which had occupied the Principalities since June 1854? Would the Porte perform with fidelity the role which had been assigned to her by the Congress? Above all, would Great Britain stand with France in resisting Austro-Turkish intrigues against the established programme? It was not improbable that Turkey, thwarted at Paris, might subject the Principalities to direct pressure—a scheme for which Austrian aid could readily be enlisted.

We have noted the desire of Austria to prolong her occupation of the Principalities, and how it had been frustrated at Paris. Legally the Austrians were under the necessity of withdrawing 'as soon as possible'; logically they should at least commence to withdraw at once. On April 17 an imperial edict authorized the progressive retirement of the army,[1] and by May the numbers had been considerably reduced. Stories, emanating from Austrian sources, that the country would lapse into grave disorder if this army were to retire were discountenanced by both the French and British consuls at Bucharest,[2] and eventually belied by the facts themselves. Whatever acts of violence had taken place had been committed by the Austrians themselves, and their record had been so much worse than that of either Turks or Russians that, according to a newspaper report, the population had begun to regret the cessation of Russian protection.[3] But the country was never more tranquil, and the Austrian commander himself was reported as having no misgivings over the effects of his government's decision.[4]

[1] Kriegsarchiv, no. 1199 CK.
[2] Colquhoun to Stratford, no. 29, Apr. 21, and no. 37, May 25, F.O. 195/529; Béclard to Walewski, Apr. 29, *Actes et docs.*, vol. v, no. 1923.
[3] *The Times*, June 13, Paris correspondent; cf. Sayn-Wittgenstein, *op. cit.*, vol. i, p. 374.　　　　　　　　　　[4] Béclard to Walewski, Apr. 29.

Yet the attitude of Austria was by no means reassuring. France and Great Britain were anxious for a speedy evacuation in order that the commission of inquiry might begin to function and the elections be held as soon as possible.[1] Buol, on the other hand, continued to resent the implications against his government, and, while he maintained that he would stand by the letter of his agreement, he would not advance the time of a complete evacuation 'in order to satisfy exaggerated and ill-founded susceptibilities'. In so far as the Count was moved by pique, one might well discount his statements, but, when he intimated that Austria would 'never order immediate evacuation at the moment when the presence of the European commission and the meeting of the divans *ad hoc* would of necessity greatly rouse the Rouman population'—because otherwise Austria would 'have to re-enter the Principalities' and 'become the laughing stock of Europe'[2]—such reasoning seemed to screen another motive. Did not this 'rousing of the Rouman population' simply mean that Buol feared a landslide for union, which perhaps a few battalions might avert? Prokesch wondered if the evacuation could not be made a subject of bargain—that is, conditional on the exclusion of union and other principles, for which Austria had a distaste, from the plan of reorganization;[3] but Buol, as far as we know, made no reply to the suggestion. Nevertheless he had written to the internuncio that,

'should the Porte itself feel that, during the process of the organization of the Principalities, their own resources were singly and alone insufficient for maintaining public order, it might be represented to them that a reduced number of Austrian and Turkish troops should remain to achieve this single end. In that case, however, your Excellency should avoid the impression that any special Austrian interest is involved—which could give occasion to mistaken assumptions.'[4]

Evidently Austria must be circumspect. Thus—doubtless as a testimony of good faith—Buol pointed out on May 16 that half the Austrian forces had already been recalled;[5] but he insisted anew that the obligation to evacuate the Principalities applied equally

[1] Clarendon to Seymour, no. 171, May 13, F.O. 7/474; Hübner to Buol, no. 36 c, May 7, Staatsarchiv, IX/51; Walewski to Serre, no. 25, May 7, *Aff. étr.*, *Autriche*, vol. 463.

[2] Serre to Walewski, no. 42, Apr. 19, *ibid*.

[3] Prokesch to Buol, May 9, private, Staatsarchiv, XII/60.

[4] Buol to Prokesch, Apr. 28, no. 2, *ibid*., XII/58. Prokesch replied that Fuad agreed, for his part, the occupation should continue till the complete organization of the Principalities, but explained that no decision could be taken until Ali had returned: Prokesch to Buol, no. 38 A–C, May 9, *ibid*.

[5] Buol to Hübner, May 12, no. 1, *ibid*., IX/53. This was communicated to Cowley: Cowley to Clarendon, no. 462, May 16, F.O. 27/1127. But the statement was really false. Investigation in the Kriegsarchiv shows a reduction from 38,632 at the beginning of the evacuation to approximately 32,000 in the middle of May.

to Turkey and Russia, and to Sir George Seymour, British ambassador to Vienna, he expressed the opinion (though not very forcefully) that the presence of the Austrian army would ensure calm in the country, whereas its withdrawal would 'deliver it up to very probable chances of revolutionary outbursts'.[1] There seems little doubt but that Buol was relinquishing with great reluctance the instrument on which Austria had counted so heavily.

At all events, the continued presence of the Russians in Bessarabia remained a point to which the crafty diplomat could shift as a more plausible excuse than speculating about the temper of the people in the Principalities. In vain Clarendon continued his nagging; Buol would do no more than promise that the Austrians would retire simultaneously with the Russians (he had formerly demanded that the Russians should go first), while to the French he hinted that delays in transportation might inevitably hinder the completion of evacuation.[2] Since, during the summer, both French and British residents suffered outrages at the hands of the Austrian soldiers,[3] the irritation of the Western Powers is not hard to comprehend. It is possible that Buol was simply trying in his backhanded way to wear out the patience of his opponents, till in the end he could wring some concession from them. The case of the Russians was, in fact, destined to prove an apple of discord for the Allies. But for the present, at least, France and Great Britain were of one mind on the question of the Austrian evacuation.

Such accord was not so evident at Constantinople. Proud of his long ascendancy over the Porte, whose favour he had held partly through the knowledge that he was the strongest defender of the *status quo* and partly by his browbeating methods, the veteran diplomat, Lord Stratford de Redcliffe, greatly resented the growing influence of a new figure at the Turkish court.[4] Edouard Thouvenel, the French ambassador, who had been accredited to this post in May 1855 was a man of more than ordinary ability. Without possessing that quality of judgement that would enable him to choose infallibly between various courses of action, he had, nevertheless, just the qualities—patience, force, finesse—which an ambassador most needed who had to deal with a timid and shifty court. Stratford noted that he was quick to grasp an opportunity, and that he never allowed his face, and seldom his language,

---

[1] Seymour to Clarendon, no. 340, May 21, F.O. 7/485. He had at first required guarantees that order could be maintained: Serre to Walewski, no. 47, May 10, *Aff. étr., Autriche*, vol. 463.

[2] *Ibid.*; Seymour to Clarendon, no. 369, May 28, F.O. 7/486.

[3] Colquhoun to Stratford, no. 32, May 19, F.O. 195/529, and to Clarendon, no. 36, June 5, F.O. 78/1199.

[4] The 'intolerable arrogance' of Stratford was the subject of an editorial in *The Times*, Sept. 4. *The Times* had previously praised Thouvenel (Aug. 8) as a man of 'great ability'.

to betray him.[1] As a satellite, his services might have been valuable to Stratford—he too knew the East, and had long ago written an account of a journey to Wallachia—but would a man of his force of character and patriotism be willing always to follow the lead of this aged oracle, who had made and unmade ministers and twisted the Turks to suit his whims? While the British ambassador was conscious that the war had left him with greatly diminished prestige (for such is often the penalty of exaggerated prominence), he had come to feel that Thouvenel was aiming at a French ascendancy in that quarter in which he had once reigned supreme.[2] It is doubtful if he was justified in harbouring that much suspicion; yet in one who had almost reigned as an uncrowned king, himself, one can understand the feeling. Naturally enough the relations of the two men, while seldom stormy, were rarely ever cordial; and the temper of the Englishman, now sullen, now querulous, and sometimes even explosive, necessarily made co-operation difficult. There was nothing subtle about Stratford, but he had a way of advising the Turks secretly against the policy which he was supposed openly to favour, and, if these intrigues were sometimes too clumsily executed to be always really effective, they, nevertheless, kept Thouvenel, who knew the extent of his rival's hold upon the Sultan, in a constant state of nervousness. The only other representative of a foreign Power who possessed much weight at Constantinople was Baron Prokesch, the Austrian internuncio, who had once written a valuable study of conditions in the Ottoman Empire. Though it is hard to accept the degree of baseness which Palmerston once ascribed to him,[3] he would hardly have been an Austrian diplomat of that period if he had not sometimes been unscrupulous. He had not, however, a very persuasive personality, and was apt to lose his temper if he failed to attain his end. In general, his chief method was to try to enlist the support of the British embassy to counterweigh the influence of France; and his long period of service seemed to denote that his government well appreciated his value. The test of success for all these diplomats was the degree of pressure which they might exert on the leading Turkish ministers, who at this period were Ali Pasha, the grand vizier, and Fuad Pasha, the minister of foreign affairs. Both political pupils of that would-be reformer, Reshid Pasha, they had reached an importance which enabled them twice to profit by his disgrace, though they felt it necessary to lean a little on the support of the French embassy, since Reshid was the darling of the British. Ali was honest and intelligent, but

[1] Stratford to Clarendon, Apr. 24, Stratford Papers, F.O. 352/44.
[2] Stratford to Clarendon, no. 119, Feb. 2, F.O. 78/1172.
[3] See *The Later Correspondence of Sir John Russell*, vol. ii, p. 198.

seemed, in general, to lack energy and decision.[1] Too often for
his own or Turkey's good he allowed himself to be pushed in one
direction, only to reverse himself with equal suddenness, though
at times, it must be admitted, he showed conspicuously the national
habits of obstinacy and procrastination. Unlike his former patron,
he was a man of humble extraction, his father having been a guard
at one of the city gates. He and his colleague, Fuad, were faithful
friends, forced by numerous vicissitudes to shape their interests
in common, and often in the course of the next decade exchanging
places in the ministry.[2] Fuad had a much keener mind than Ali,
but was said to be thoroughly unreliable. Charming and ingratiating
in his manner, he was emphatically, as a British diplomat called
him, 'a man of expedients', not capable of any really constructive
ideas, and rather childish in his fondness for display.[3] The two
men were, after all, fairly common Turkish types, except that Ali
was less venal than the conventional grand vizier. Had the Sultans
of the period been men of any force, Turkey would probably have
been less the battle-ground of the diplomats. But, as it was, the
ministers were never sure of their tenure, compelled always to
fight intrigues in their sovereign's *entourage*, and much too ready
to seek the support of the foreign embassies to keep themselves in
power. It was against such a background that Thouvenel and
Stratford commenced their struggle for the slippery favour of the
Sublime Porte.

The point of issue at present between the two ambassadors was
the all-important question of the union of the Principalities.
Thouvenel had first believed that this issue—which had been
fathered by his predecessor, Benedetti—was ill-advised, as liable,
by alienating the Turks, to compromise French influence in the
Orient.[4] But when his emperor had definitely espoused the
principle[5] the French ambassador had thrown himself into the
cause with all the enthusiasm and resolution of which his character
was capable—and that meant much. Stratford, on the other hand,
whatever his earlier views, had seemingly acquired a stronger
aversion to union in proportion as his rival had come to favour
it, and it may be true, as Thouvenel surmised, that he felt that
his credit with the Porte had been lowered by the failure of the
Congress to adopt the idea of separation, as suggested by the

[1] This was Bulwer's summary of his character: Bulwer to Russell, no. 87,
Feb. 2, 1859, F.O. 78/1428.
[2] Their fortunes form an interesting study in Challemel-Lacour, 'Les
Hommes d état de la Turquie', *Revue des deux mondes*, 2nd per., vol. 73, pp.
886 ff.
[3] Bulwer to Russell, Feb. 2, 1859, and no. 369, Aug. 4, 1863, F.O. 78/737; cf.
Stratford to Clarendon, no. 1303, Nov. 3, 1856, F.O. 78/1191.
[4] Thouvenel, *Trois Années de la question d'Orient*, pp. 4, 11, 38. Even Walewski
had privately shared his doubts: *ibid.*, p. 44.   [5] See *ibid.*, p. 63.

Protocol of Constantinople.[1] This divergence had already manifested itself during the sessions of the Congress of Paris. 'We
think it very desirable', Clarendon had telegraphed Stratford on
March 8, 'that the union of the Principalities should be discussed, as
opinion is in favour of that arrangement; but Ali has no instructions
to consent to its being discussed. He writes to have that permission. Ask the Porte to give him full power in the matter.'[2]
Thouvenel had, of course, similar instructions, but when it came
to a matter of co-operation, Stratford obscured his government's
telegram, would do no more than send a dragoman to interview
Fuad, and told a member of the French embassy that the Turks
would never consent to union.[3] The fact that Ali had been able
to accept the compromise at Paris may reasonably be attributed to
Thouvenel's persistent efforts.

Once the resolution had been taken by the Congress to consult the
wishes of the Principalities, Thouvenel felt that his chief business
was to see that nothing interfered with the fulfilment of that plan.[4]

'We wish union,' wrote Walewski on April 5, 'and England, who was
at first uncertain, wishes it too. . . . His Majesty wants you to put forth
all your efforts to reach that result, with or without the Porte's consent.
The Emperor would renounce his idea in this regard only if the divans
should pronounce in a contrary sense. For your guidance, I will tell
you that union has an especial odour of sanctity at Windsor. The first
step to take will be relative to the firman which will convoke the divans.
It is desirable that this firman should be conceived in a manner to extend,
as far as possible, the composition of these divans. Austria will oppose
us all she can, but we have Russia on our side. It is essential to show
the Turkish ministry that if in this circumstance it should range itself
on the side of Austria against England, Russia, and France, its existence
would be singularly compromised.'[5]

Such sentiments were, of course, written in the first outburst of
optimism in which the French government indulged itself after
the moderate triumph of its policy at the Congress. Thouvenel
was under no such illusions. Stratford, he told Walewski, had no
instructions to act in the sense of union; he had failed entirely to
co-operate; and all his own logic had been exhausted on the Turks

---

[1] Thouvenel to Walewski, May 8, *Actes et docs.*, vol. iii, no. 526, and Sept. 29,
ibid., no. 701.

[2] Clarendon to Stratford, Mar. 8, telg., F.O. 78/1160. The telegram was
inaccurately deciphered to read: 'We think it very desirable that the union of the
Principalities should be discussed, as *we* are in favour of that arrangement.' It
may have been for that reason that Stratford read the dispatch so fast to Thouvenel as to fail to convey its tenor, and allowed the impression that union was not
even mentioned. Later Stratford was willing to admit that his instructions were
in accord with Thouvenel's: Thouvenel to Walewski, Mar. 13, and Segur to
Thouvenel, Mar. 13, *Actes et docs.*, vol. ii, pp. 497 and 498.

[3] *Ibid.*

[4] This was, in fact, the command which he had received in Walewski's letter
of Apr. 12: *ibid.*, vol. iii, no. 520.   [5] Thouvenel, *op. cit.*, pp. 7–8.

without influencing them a particle.[1] He recognized that the chief immediate problem was to try to overcome the Porte's prejudices against union—no easy matter, for Fuad had told him frankly that if the ministers acquiesced in Napoleon's wishes, the Sultan would no doubt replace them by their predecessors, Reshid Pasha and his friends, and that was presumably what the British wanted. No doubt the ministers were in a difficult position, and the indifference with which Stratford habitually treated the question of union— supporting Thouvenel in such a manner that he plainly desired a rebuff[2]—was not lost on a government which had ever profited by the dissensions of the Great Powers. Clearly, unless Stratford were compelled to alter his demeanour, Thouvenel's efforts would remain in an *impasse*. Impressed by the ambassador's difficulties, Walewski took occasion to remind Clarendon of his recent advocacy of union, but the result was by no means reassuring. In the face of the determined opposition to be encountered at Constantinople, Clarendon made it clear that he proposed to leave the question solely to the decision of the divans.[3]

At first thought it might appear that a policy of neutrality, pending the calling of the divans, was no more than wise and just. But there were many ways in which the Porte, if relieved of all coercion, could scheme to frustrate the decisions of the Congress. When the matter at length came up of providing for a caimacamie in the Principalities, Turkey resolved to appoint a single caimacam in each province instead of a body of three, as the *Règlement organique* had explicitly prescribed. Obviously the Porte could more easily manipulate a single individual. But machinations of of this sort bode ill for the execution of the coming plebiscite. In the meantime Ali, who had stopped at Vienna on his way back from Paris, had been subjected to a pressure that was probably not unwelcome. Not only did Buol voice his opposition to union, but Francis Joseph showed his fear that such a plan would threaten the security of certain of his provinces. When Ali arrived in Constantinople, July 28, he made no concealment of the fact that he was opposed to union, and that, whatever the decision of the divans, he reserved for the Sultan the right to repudiate it.[4]

The policy of Austria was no doubt mainly concentrated in an endeavour to persuade the Porte to keep the whole question out of the divans. Though Buol did not agree with the Porte's conviction (reported by Prokesch)[5] that these assemblies were likely to declare

---

[1] Thouvenel to Walewski, Apr. 10 and 15, *Actes et docs.*, vol. iii, nos. 519 and 521.   [2] Thouvenel, *op. cit.*, p. 10.
[3] Cowley to Clarendon, no. 548, May 24, F.O. 28/1127; Walewski to Thouvenel, May 24 and June 7, *Actes et docs.*, vol. iii, nos. 535 and 542.
[4] Thouvenel to Walewski, July 6, *ibid.*, vol. v, no. 584.
[5] Prokesch to Buol, no. 49 c, July 2, Staatsarchiv, xii/57.

unanimously in its favour, he told the internuncio that it was highly desirable that the Porte should 'pronounce openly and categorically' before either the commission or the divans should begin their work.[1] 'The Porte has the full right', he declared in a later letter, 'to tell the divans that any deliberation on the question of union during their sessions is simply not within their competence'; the existing organization may be modified, if desirable, in the direction of uniformity, but that is all.[2] Such arguments needed little repetition to convince the Turks; and Ali, bristling with unwonted courage, declared, after an interview with Prokesch, that as the Treaty of Paris had made no mention of a project of union, one could not allow the divans to discuss a question that was reserved to the exclusive competence of a congress.[3] About ten days later, on July 31, Fuad issued a circular to the Turkish representatives at the courts of the Protecting Powers, endeavouring to prove the fallacy of the argument that union would produce an effective buffer state or that it would be to the best interests of the Principalities themselves, and declaring that the Porte understood by the Treaty of Paris that the divans were to consider solely the improvement of their existing institutions. While unwilling to 'give a public rejection to this question' in the firman, now being prepared, Fuad appealed to the 'just and loyal spirit of his allies'.[4] One hardly needs to comment on this specious interpretation of the treaty.

The Turkish circular could hardly be called aggressive—a fact which perhaps suggests the desire not to give too great offence to France, whose ambassador was always hounding the Porte to look more favourably upon union. In fact Ali himself was probably trying to repel the charge that he had been a little too lenient on the question.[5] But Walewski, who perceived the enemy in the bush, was incensed at Austria for propagating such a doctrine, and was doubtless much gratified to learn that Clarendon at least 'partook entirely of the views of the French government on the right of the divans'.[6] Undoubtedly the ability with which the Austro-Turkish combination could pervert the meaning of the plebiscite must depend upon the attitude of the other Powers who had fathered it. Prussia, it is true, had rallied to the support of France [7] (no doubt, the result of diplomatic support, lately granted

[1] Buol to Prokesch, July 6, Staatsarchiv, xii/58.
[2] Buol to Prokesch, July 12, *ibid.* Cf. 'We do not recognize to the divans the right to occupy themselves with questions which totally change the political face of the country': Buol to Prokesch, June 28, no. 1, *ibid.*
[3] Thouvenel to Walewski, July 21, *Actes et docs.*, vol. iii, no. 618.
[4] *Ibid.*, no. 632. Cf. Fuad to Callimachi, July 31, Staatsarchiv, xii/58.
[5] See above, page 44, note 3.
[6] Cowley to Clarendon, no. 904, Aug. 8, F.O. 27/1131.
[7] Thouvenel to Walewski, June 30, *Actes et docs.*, vol. iii, no. 575.

by Napoleon),[1] but Russia, according to report, was disposed to leave the question to the arbitrament of Turkey, and, whereas Clarendon, according to Ali, was in favour of union, and counselled the Porte not to oppose it, he gave the vizier no hint that Great Britain would do anything to overcome such opposition.[2] Prokesch, who was perhaps a little premature in regarding Stratford as the barometer of his government's views, believed that the ambassador's reserve showed that Clarendon had changed his mind upon the issue.[3] The point is of capital importance; for, if France and Great Britain were still of one mind on the question which was to come before the divans, the two Powers opposed to union would be less likely to pursue obstructive tactics; but, if Great Britain were to waver on the question, or merely leave the matter to be determined by the plebiscite, then Austria and Turkey would find that they could safely pursue their machinations with an even chance of winning their point against an isolated France. Exactly what, then, was Clarendon's position?

The evidence seems to show that Clarendon had long been wavering on the question. Hübner would have us believe (and he may have got it from Cowley) that Palmerston had 'corrected his ideas' on his return from the Congress of Paris;[4] but there is no available proof that this is so. As early as May 27, however, the French ambassador, Count Persigny, reported that Clarendon did not seem so disposed as formerly to favour union, though, if that plan were realized, he seemed to prefer, curiously enough, a foreign to a native prince. Persigny's theory was that distrust of Russia, who seemed to favour union, was the clue to Clarendon's misgivings.[5] At the time Austria was pressing Turkey to declare the question beyond the competence of the divans, her ambassador at London was reporting that Clarendon had no predilection for union, and that Great Britain was reserving her opinion till the preparation of the Commission's report.[6] It was not, however, until August, when the Turkish ambassador at London deliberately sounded Clarendon on the question of the divans' jurisdiction, that we have any direct record of the British statesman's views. To Cowley he wrote on August 22, that, while he did not agree that the question of union was beyond the competence of the divans (such a view, he had told the Austrian ambassador, had not been

---

[1] Over the question of Neufchâtel in dispute between Prussia and Switzerland.

[2] Thouvenel to Walewski, July 6. Since there is no letter to Stratford on the subject, it is probable that Ali was reporting sentiments conveyed to him by Musurus, the Turkish ambassador at London.

[3] Prokesch to Buol, no. 51 A–E, July 9, Staatsarchiv, XII/57.

[4] Hübner to Buol, no. 12 A–F, Feb. 8, 1857, *ibid.*, IX/54. See page 42, note 3.

[5] Persigny to Walewski, no. 154, May 27, 1856, *Aff. étr., Angleterre*, vol. 705.

[6] Apponyi to Buol, no. 10 B, July 8, Staatsarchiv, VIII/45.

held at the Congress),[1] yet he permitted himself to say that 'although the plan of union appeared at first sight plausible, and likely to be attended with some advantages, a more full and deliberate examination and consideration of the matter has led them [the British ministers] to the conclusion that the injurious consequences which would follow from it would greatly counter-balance any advantages which it could produce, and that it seems, therefore, highly desirable for the general interest that the separate condition of the Principalities should be maintained'.[2] There was no doubt now on what side Clarendon stood. While it was not yet proved that he would not leave the question to the free expression of the divans (in fact, he assured France of his loyalty to the plebiscite),[3] the sentiments of this letter were completely at variance with the position which he had taken at the Congress, and, when a copy of the letter was forwarded to Stratford, the latter did not deny (to Thouvenel) that his government's attitude had under-gone a change.[4]

It now remains to be asked: why had Clarendon reversed him-self? There is no letter of his in evidence that would enable us precisely to understand why he had previously declared for union or had subsequently changed his mind. The Austrian ambassador would have us believe that, just as public sympathy for the Rou-mans had dictated the British attitude in the first place, so a decline of public interest in the question had led the government to believe that it was no longer bound to press the issue.[5] Doubtless this was true in so far as few in England cared about the fate of the Moldo-Wallachians. But, apart from this negative factor, we know that Palmerston had come to believe that union was a danger;[6] and it

---

[1] Apponyi to Buol, no. 14 B, Aug. 18, *ibid.* Clarendon had lately pronounced the same opinion to Persigny: Persigny to Walewski, no. 172, Aug. 12, *Aff. étr.*, *Angleterre*, vol. 705.

[2] Clarendon to Cowley, no. 862, Aug. 22, F.O. 27/1115. About the same time, Count Malaret, the French chargé d'affaires at London, wrote Walewski that Clarendon's view 'each day is further removed from France', and he concluded by saying that it was 'almost incontestable that the British government is almost gained to the cause of those who combat the union of the Principalities': Malaret Walewski, no. 177, Aug. 20, *Aff. étr.*, *Angleterre*, vol. 705.

[3] Malaret to Walewski, no. 172, Aug. 12, *ibid.*

[4] Thouvenel to Walewski, Sept. 11, *Actes et docs.*, vol. iv, no. 673.

[5] Apponyi to Buol, no. 22 C, Sept. 18, Staatsarchiv, VIII/45.

[6] Writing of the Principalities in a private letter to Clarendon, July 8, Palmers-ton remarked that 'union could not essentially contribute to their internal pros-perity, while it would be a step toward the creation of another Greece on the north of Turkey and in immediate contact with Russia. The united provinces would be a field for Russian intrigue and not a barrier against Russia.' Much the same position was taken in a memorandum, dated Aug. 8, emphasizing also the fact that one of the chief objects of the Crimean War had been to preserve the Principalities to Turkey, while independence, on the other hand, would lead to the insoluble question of who should be the ruler. A week later (and a week before Clarendon's letter to Cowley), after racking his brains over a possible federal scheme of union, he wrote to Clarendon: 'My inclination about the

was possibly on this account that Clarendon had revealed that lurking fear of Russia. On a later occasion he told the French chargé d'affaires that he feared that the Principalities, if united, would become strong enough to free themselves from Turkey, and that that would mean, sooner or later, that they would become a prey to Russia.[1] While it is true that such an opinion might equally well have been held at the time of the Congress, it was not till some months later that complications with Russia had awakened the old distrust, and—what was perhaps more serious—the dubious conduct of France was giving at least the impression that Napoleon felt himself now free to regard the Crimean alliance as dissolved.

History has shown that it is rare when two Powers, who have become allies in order to meet a common menace, remain friendly when the occasion for that alliance has been removed. This is even more true in the case of nations which nurse the recollections of old enmities. It is usually about the time or the terms of peace that misunderstandings begin, for it is on such matters that the divergent interests of the two come to the fore. Palmerston had criticized Napoleon for wanting to end the war, and could see none but the meanest motives for his attitude.[2] When it became increasingly clear that public opinion in France was vehemently demanding peace, Napoleon's tendency to temper the punishment of Russia was simply regarded as political manoeuvring. There is some reason for feeling that the Emperor was merely basking in that imperial role which he viewed as an inheritance; 'The Empire is peace' (that was the one modification of the Napoleonic pattern); and he hoped by friendly relations with all the Great Powers to bring them to acknowledge the hegemony of France.[3] Even when he paid homage to the nationalist principle, as when he espoused the cause of the Roumans, one gets the notion that he liked to think of himself as the benefactor of humanity. Why not expect even the Great Powers to look to Paris for the gratification of their favours? What conception could be more Napoleonic? Already Sardinia, under the far-seeing leadership of Cavour, was looking for his aid to shape the destiny of Italy; only recently his timely assistance to Prussia had enabled her to triumph in a controversy

Principalities would be to leave them as to their political relations as nearly as possible in the same condition in which they have been, as it is said, for ten centuries.' (I am indebted to Professor Bell for these quotations.) It was certainly to be regretted that the British government had not faced the question squarely at the time of the Congress.

[1] Malaret to Walewski, no. 172.

[2] Simpson, *op. cit.*, p. 336.

[3] Apropos of the question of the Principalities, Stratford told Prokesch that he believed that Napoleon's motives were 'the inclination and calculation to regain for his country the importance of the First Empire, and to show himself the leading will on the Continent': Prokesch to Buol, Apr. 8, 1856, private, Staatsarchiv, XII/60. See East, *op. cit.*, pp. 64–5.

with Switzerland; and now, when the task of fixing the Russo-Turkish boundary had led to some dispute—the question of whether a town or island should belong to Russia or Turkey—Napoleon essayed to play the umpire, and pronounce a verdict in favour of the Power with whom he had lately been at war. It was a ticklish business—this making new friends at the expense of former ones, more in keeping with the Emperor's magnanimity, one might say, than an evidence of statecraft; but Napoleon always seemed to prefer tortuous methods, and it was not for his contemporaries to appreciate his vision. That he showed sagacity in seeking to make a friend of Russia might also be contended, but there is some reason to think that immediate self-interest should have prompted him to side with Turkey and Great Britain on the questions now at issue. It will be recalled that it was the dispute over the new boundary between Russia and Turkey that prevented the Russian troops from withdrawing from the ceded territory—which delay postponed the Austrian evacuation of the Principalities, and which, in turn, put off the inauguration of the plebiscite. It may be well, therefore, to inquire into this, the principle cause of the estrangement between the former allies.

One of the objects of the Treaty of Paris was to exclude Russia from the Danube. To this end, the Congress, in drafting article xx, had traced a new boundary between Russia and Moldavia, ceding a portion of Bessarabia to the latter, and shutting Russia from all access to the river. For some reason, a little island, known as Serpent's Island, just outside the delta was overlooked; it was of no value except as a location for a lighthouse, but in Russia's possession it would violate the express purpose of the Congress. More unfortunate than this, the maps, which the plenipotentiaries had used—supplied to them, it appears, by the French war office [1]—were found to be inaccurate, and, when a commission of delimitation undertook, under the auspices of the Congress, the survey which was designed to fix the exact frontier, they found that the town of Bolgrad, which had been expressly reserved to Russia, was situated on Lake Yalpuk, through which flowed one of the branches of the Danube delta. One might suppose that Russia would be willing to renounce this point when the error was discovered, but technically her position was unassailable. If the victors made a mistake in stipulating her sacrifices, that was their loss and not hers; besides, she had expressly asked to retain Bolgrad, as the *chef-lieu* of a large Bulgarian community, whose loyalty she desired to preserve, and Napoleon had promised Orloff his support for this request,[2] and he had kept his word. When

---

[1] Walewski to Malaret, no. 87, Aug. 25, *Aff. étr.*, *Angleterre*, vol. 705.
[2] Hübner to Buol, no. 88 D, Oct. 22, Staatsarchiv, IX/50.

later the question arose whether the place, designated as on the Russian side of the line, was this 'Bolgrad', or another town by the same name, farther north, Napoleon declared, 'I understand Bolgrad as the centre of the Bulgarian colony; it is that one, accordingly, which I judge should belong to Russia'.[1] But, apart from any interest involved in these two questions, it was a question whether the spirit or the letter of the Treaty of Paris should prevail.

The matter became acute during August when the commission found itself compelled to refer it to the Powers. While the question of Serpent's Island, though magnified by Turkey, was deemed of relatively slight importance, the disposition of Bolgrad became an issue on which the Concert of Europe was in danger of falling to pieces. Palmerston, who had been the most implacable of Russia's enemies, insisted that Russia should yield the point in question, and privately questioned her good faith during the sessions of the Congress. No doubt, the fact that Russia had demolished the fortifications of Kars before restoring it to Turkey, as stipulated by the treaty, was a contributive cause of British irritation;[2] what was still more likely is that the cabinet was angered by the knowledge that Russia had the sympathy of France, of whose considerate attitude Gortchakoff expressed the warmest appreciation to the British ambassador, taking every occasion to 'draw an invidious distinction between the policy of England and France towards Russia and to throw upon the former whatever is disagreeable to Russia in the conditions of the late treaty'.[3] The British, of course, made much of the fact that Bolgrad would never have been left to Russia if its actual location had been known, and held that Russia, when she had asked for it, should have furnished accurate information as to its site.[4] To yield it to her would make her still a riverain Power and 'give her a point of great strategical importance, by which she will be able to impede the free navigation of the Danube and to intercept the communication of Moldavia with the ceded territory'.[5] To any such suggestion that Russia might keep an armed flotilla there to threaten the river trade Walewski objected that 'Lake Yalpuk was so shallow that even fisher-boats could hardly use it';[6] but certainly such a view was not conclusive. Then the commission itself made an effort to adjust the difficulty by proposing that the shore of the lake which fronted Bolgrad should not belong to the town, though the inhabitants might be free to use the

---

[1] Charles-Roux, *op. cit.*, p. 132.   [2] Ashley, *Life of Palmerston*, vol. ii, p. 112.

[3] Wodehouse to Clarendon, no. 63, July 24, F.O. 65/471.

[4] Clarendon to Wodehouse, no. 274, Aug. 26, F.O. 65/467. The British government tried to make out that the Bolgrad, which by the treaty was left to Russia, was an unimportant village by that name, usually known as Tabak, and situated further north.

[5] Clarendon to Wodehouse, no. 340, Sept. 17, F.O. 65/468.

[6] Ottenfels to Buol, no. 79 A–L, Sept. 10, Staatsarchiv, IX/52.

lake, from which they drew their water and the fish which constituted their food;[1] but Palmerston refused to accept this plan,
urged though it was by Walewski;[2] and Gortchakoff, whose temper
was exceedingly mercurial, did not help matters by lecturing the
British ambassador on his country's isolation.[3] It seemed likely
that the Turks would have been willing to trade Bolgrad for
Serpent's Island, but neither this nor any other compromise was
acceptable to London. Russia had meanwhile suggested the
obvious plan of reconvoking the Congress of Paris, that the plenipotentiaries themselves might interpret the meaning of their
handiwork.[4] But Great Britain would not accept this proposal
either. It was not for Russia to vote on the terms of peace, which
her victorious enemies had dictated,[5] and the question was not, in
British opinion, an arguable one at all. There are times when an
Englishman will not allow himself to be budged. Meanwhile the
rift between Great Britain on the one hand, and France and Russia
on the other, was steadily growing wider. Gortchakoff, on learning
of the British rejection of a conference, was reported to be 'much
out of humour'.[6]

While the deadlock over Bolgrad was more serious from the
standpoint of the peace of Europe, and a more palpable impediment to the welfare of the Principalities, another dispute had arisen
over an interpretation of the Treaty of Paris, which more directly
concerned the interests of the Powers, and furnished the British
with a more rational grievance against France. Long before the
middle of the century foreign capital had looked upon the Principalities as a promising field of investment, and Austria, more
particularly interested because of her proximity, had not only
established important interests in these provinces, but coveted the
right to control the navigation of the Danube.[7] The Treaty of
Paris frustrated this last scheme, for by article xv the principle of
freedom of navigation, invoked for international rivers by the
Congress of Vienna, was definitely extended to 'the Danube and
its mouths'. Nothing was said, however, of the affluents of the
river, although it might be argued from the standpoint of the
general interest that this equitable reform should be considered as
applying to the whole river system. At all events, some months
after the conclusion of the treaty, the hospodar of Moldavia,
Gregory Ghika, had granted to a French company (headed by a

[1] *Annuaire des deux mondes*, 1857, p. 4.
[2] Persigny to Walewski, no. 186, Sept. 23, *Aff. étr., Angleterre*, vol. 706.
[3] Wodehouse to Clarendon, no. 166, Sept. 25, F.O. 65/472.
[4] Such a proposal was actually made by France, and accepted by Gortchakoff
with an air of resignation: Charles-Roux, *op. cit.*, p. 143.
[5] Clarendon to Wodehouse, no. 48, Oct. 14, F.O. 65/469.
[6] Wodehouse to Clarendon, no. 207, Oct. 16, F.O. 65/472.
[7] Xénopol, *op. cit.*, vol. ii, p. 550.

certain Captain Magnan) the monopoly of steam navigation on the rivers Sereth and Pruth, two tributaries of the Danube, which flowed through Moldavia. Bitterly resenting their lost opportunity the Austrians determined to break the concession if they could do so. Accordingly, aware of the advantage of having Stratford join his efforts to those of Prokesch in cajoling the Porte, Buol prepared a memorandum for Clarendon's perusal, alleging that the grant contravened an ancient agreement between Austria and the Porte, whereby freedom of navigation on Turkish rivers had been guaranteed to Austrian subjects,[1] and insisting further that no such concession could be legal without the sanction of the suzerain Power.[2] Clarendon not only concurred with the Austrian view, but contended—with doubtful justification—that the freedom of the Danube, stipulated by the Treaty of Paris, was meant to include its branches.[3] Thouvenel, on the other hand, took the ground that any interpretation of the Treaty of Paris was a matter for the signatory Powers to decide and not for the Porte alone, while the annulment of a hospodarial act of an internal character was an infringement of the autonomy of Moldavia.[4] Besieged by Prokesch and Stratford, yet unwilling to disoblige the powerful French, the Porte had at first desired merely to suspend the grant and leave decision to the commission of navigation which had been set up by the treaty;[5] but the combined pressure of two of the ambassadors proved irresistible, and the Porte finally took the step (though with reluctance) of cancelling the grant.[6] The position of the French had been somewhat analogous to that of the Russians on the frontier question—within the letter of the law, perhaps, but violating its spirit. At any rate, the outcome of the affair was plainly in the general interest.

From the point of view of Anglo-French relations, the controversy over the Magnan grant was a grievous tax upon that spirit of co-operation which was so essential to the faithful execution of the Treaty of Paris. But there is little doubt that the boundary quarrel was a far greater cause of British petulance, and Persigny told

[1] Sened of Feb. 24, 1784: Noradounghian, *op. cit.*, vol. i, p. 379. It might be alleged that a subsequent war between Austria and Turkey had annulled this agreement.

[2] Clarendon to Cowley, no. 725, July 26, enc., F.O. 7/1113; cf. Prokesch to Fuad, July 20, *Actes et docs.*, vol. iv, no. 615, and Prokesch to Stratford, Aug. 30, annex to Prokesch to Buol, no. 64 C, Aug. 22, Staatsarchiv, XII/57.

[3] Clarendon to Cowley, no. 881, Aug. 25, F.O. 27/1115. With more reason Clarendon pointed out to Walewski that the granting of such privileges might result in injury to French interests as well as those of other nations: Clarendon to Cowley, no. 936, Sept. 4, F.O. 27/1115.

[4] Thouvenel to Prokesch, Aug. 8 and to Outrey, Aug. 8, *Actes et docs.*, vol. iv, nos. 640 and 641.

[5] Prokesch to Buol, no. 61 A–F, Aug. 13, Staatsarchiv, XII/57.

[6] Fuad to Balsche, Aug. 6, annex to Prokesch to Buol, no. 59 C, Aug. 15, *ibid.*

Walewski that he believed that if France 'would take into consideration the parliamentary difficulties of the English cabinet on this question, Lord Palmerston would feel more disposed to act with her on the question of union'.[1] There was, however, another —perhaps more serious—cause of British irritation which arose from the multiplicity of complaints that French agents in the Principalities were supporting, if not actually prompting, the public agitation for union. Was there some latent fear, as Bratiano, then sojourning in London, seemed to think, that 'union will operate to the profit of a Bonaparte'?[2] One can readily understand the lurking suspicion with which the British viewed this 'empire of peace'. Was France to solve this problem by single-handed effort?

Uncertain of his ally, and forced to regard Austria and Turkey as covertly determined to vitiate the plebiscite, Napoleon was no doubt relying chiefly on the native appeal; and, if Constantinople were a more fertile field for British or Austrian intrigue, the French had decidedly the advantage in the Principalities. Most accounts seem to agree that all articulate opinion in Wallachia was strongly in favour of union, and even in Moldavia, where some of the greater *boyards* were pleading the danger of the smaller province being sacrificed to the greater,[3] public sentiment was steadily flowing stronger in that direction. True, it may be, that the idea had not yet penetrated the masses[4]—for the bulk of the population had no political consciousness—but even the inert peasantry might be goaded to revolution if the Austrian occupation were to last much longer. Meanwhile the news of the work at Paris had been hailed with pretty general satisfaction.[5] Though there were no noisy manifestations, people seemed conscious that a national transformation had been initiated. At Jassy one even began to discuss the needed reforms, while Bucharest, which was somewhat more conservative, was often the scene of wrangles between the various factions, which saw in the present upheaval a chance to dicker for political spoil.[6] Politics were never very clean in the Principalities—such was the baleful heritage of the Phanariot days—and every one knew that the terms of the two hospodars were to end on June 16. Gregory Ghika, whose hopes centred on the ultimate selection of a foreign prince, was little concerned about the matter of whether his incumbency would be continued,[7]

---

[1] Persigny to Walewski, no. 186, Sept. 23, *Aff. étr., Angleterre*, vol. 706.
[2] Bratiano to Walewski, Dec. 6, *Aff. étr., Mém. et docs., Turquie*, vol. 18.
[3] Place to Walewski, June 24, *Actes et docs.*, vol. iii, no. 566.
[4] Gödel-Lannoy to Buol, no. 29, June 19, Staatsarchiv, xxxviii/106; *The Times*, Mar. 25, Constantinople correspondent.
[5] Béclard to Walewski, Apr. 18, *Actes et docs.*, vol. v, no. 1922.
[6] Béclard to Walewski, Apr. 29, *ibid.*, no. 1923.
[7] Xénopol, *op. cit.*, vol. ii, p. 555. He was said to have wanted to retire from office: Colquhoun to Stratford, no. 10, Feb. 27, F.O. 195/529.

but Stirbey seems to have cherished the idea that union under a native prince would prove the eventual solution, and that hence, if he could manage to get himself chosen as hospodar of Wallachia, the time might come when he would rule over a united Roumania. Unfortunately for Stirbey, it was hardly practicable both to appeal to the native longings for union and to cope with the timid pre-judices of the Porte; while the necessity of standing well with foreign Powers had left the impression that he was nothing but an Austrian tool, who France, for some reason, seemed to favour. When Stirbey essayed to visit Constantinople to try his personal blandishments upon the Porte, he was accused by one of his enemies of putting up 25,000 ducats to purchase re-election.[1] Clarendon instructed Stratford to take pains to spoil his mission;[2] and it is not improbable that Great Britain's friendship was more important to Turkey at this juncture than the long-hallowed custom of selling her favours; and, besides, Ali said frankly that he 'had positive information' that the hospodar 'had done everything in Paris to bring about union . . . and considered that his retention in office was dangerous'.[3]   And so Stirbey's plan miscarried. But Ghika was the worse offender—of whom Prokesch wrote, 'Each day brings us new proofs of his disastrous activities, and whose 'discourse' was most 'seditious'. Hence the Porte doubtless felt that only by a complete change of personnel in the government of the Principalities could the agitation, which, as Prokesch wrote, 'weighed on it like a nightmare',[4] be successfully allayed. When Ali returned from Paris, he decided, with the connivance of Austria, to request the immediate resignation of the hospodars (not waiting for their term of office to lapse, as prescribed by the *Règlement*), and thus to establish a caimacamie as soon as possible.[5] Hence once again the aspirants for office pricked up their ears.

The choice of the two caimacams was a matter which might very well affect the nationalist cause. If weak or venal men were chosen the suzerain Power might, by coercion or corruption, succeed in stifling the movement for union before it had got well under way. Doubtless, material of the right sort was exceptionally hard to find; but it seems evident that neither Austria nor Great Britain wanted any one who had been active in the cause of union, and Thouvenel either underrated the importance of the matter, or felt that Stratford's influence was too paramount to be shaken. Hence for Moldavia Theodore Balsche, a protégé of Austria and head of the

[1] Cretzulesco to Stratford, June 9, enclosed in Colquhoun's letter to Stratford, June 17, Stratford Papers, F.O. 354/60.
[2] Clarendon to Stratford, no. 723, June 27, F.O. 78/1163.
[3] Buol to Prokesch, Apr. 13, Staatsarchiv, XII/58.
[4] Prokesch to Buol, no. 49 c, July 2, *ibid.*, XII/57.
[5] Buol to Prokesch, July 5, no. 1, *ibid.*, XII/58.

separatist faction, received the appointment[1] by the usual venal methods of Ottoman politics, while for caimacam of Wallachia Stratford got the appointment of a candidate, whom Colquhoun had recommended,[2] Alexander Ghika, a member of a large and influential family, and at one time hospodar. Since Prokesch had been strenuously opposed to this selection,[3] it is evident that British and Austrian counsels were not always in unison. When the Porte hesitated at first, Stratford told his dragoman that he hoped that the ministers would realize that it was the representative of Great Britain who was speaking.[4]

If one could judge from symptoms, one might deduce that it was a struggle between the unionists at Bucharest and Jassy, backed by France, and the suzerain Power at Constantinople, supported by Austria and (less directly) by Great Britain, all three of whom had the means of spreading a net over the Principalities. The chief advantage of the cause of 'revolution' was that the ground had already been carefully prepared for its success. Gregory Ghika, whatever may have been his motives, had done much to rouse enthusiasm for union in Moldavia, and his efforts to further the cause at Paris (he had even obtained an audience with Napoleon) were publicly acknowledged at a meeting of the divan.[5] Under the advice of the French consul, Ghika not only had chosen as prefects in all the districts men who could be counted on to agitate for union,[6] but had himself made a tour of the country for that purpose;[7] and already, in May, a unionist club (or 'central committee', as it was called), had been organized at Jassy. Faithful to the views of their leader, the club had placed itself on record as favouring a foreign prince, and, since the necessity of an honest plebiscite was thoroughly appreciated, a committee had diverted itself by drafting an electoral project.[8] Some of the leaders of the club, including Vasili Alexandri and Michael Cogalnitchano, were among the foremost men of the province. Since the press had been freed under the Ghika régime (not the least of Gregory's services), a multitude of addresses had appeared in print, signed by hundreds of partisans of union, both lay and clerical. Yet it must not be supposed that the Roumans were a heroic people, or that they were adept in the art of political agitation. While it is true that nationalism had awakened to new life, it was France whose indirect encouragement gave the

---

[1] The choice was approved by Stratford: Stratford to Clarendon, no. 800, June 26, F.O. 78/1182.

[2] Colquhoun to Stratford, June 30, Stratford Papers, F.O. 352/60.

[3] Prokesch to Buol, no. 49 B, July 2, Staatsarchiv, XII/57.

[4] Stratford to Clarendon, no. 862, July 7, F.O. 78/1183, enc.

[5] *Actes et docs.*, vol. iii, no. 532.

[6] Place to Walewski, June 23, *ibid.*, no. 564.

[7] Place to Walewski, July 4, *ibid.*, no. 581.   [8] *Ibid.*, no. 541.

movement confidence, and it was French intellects which aided in its organization.

From the outset Walewski had made it clear to the French consuls, Béclard at Bucharest and Place at Jassy, that Napoleon favoured union.

'If the Moldo-Wallachian population, as we suppose', he wrote Béclard in May, 'are determined that union shall be accomplished, it is important that they pronounce themselves *hautement*. They should well know that the expression of their wishes, if it is formal, will find support without reserve from the government of His Imperial Majesty.'[1]

It may be inferred that Place, who had lately returned to his post from Paris,[2] had been similarly enlightened. It will be observed that the French minister had not actually encouraged his subordinates to proselyte or even to encourage agitation, but he had definitely thrown responsibility upon the people of the Principalities; and any quick-witted agent could hardly have failed to see the opportunity thus afforded of promoting his government's aim. Béclard seems at first to have let matters take their course, but in Moldavia Victor Place became the active patron and adviser of the partisans of union. A man of great energy and perspicacity, and endowed with a natural bent for politics, Place had soon proved himself invaluable to the nationalist cause. Besides persuading Ghika to employ the prefects as mediums of propaganda, he had given counsel as to the material to be provided for the purpose, even engaging a Moldavian poet to compose an ode in praise of union to be sung to one of the popular airs. But he assured Walewski that he had 'effaced, as far as possible, the traces of my intervention'.[3] Sometimes, indeed, the champions of union became more ardent than he approved, and he had been quite unable to prevent the unionist club from declaring itself in favour of a foreign prince;[4] but the activities of Place were too well known not to cause disquiet at Vienna, and Walewski had felt it necessary twice to warn him against too vigorous a campaign.[5]

A greater difficulty than guiding the unionist propaganda had been that of forestalling or combatting opposition. The influence of the clergy was considerable, and their attitude was decidedly wary, until Place made a special point of allaying their fears—an achievement only possible, however, by reason of the sympathetic attitude of Russia, who had still, when she cared to exert it, a powerful influence over the Church.[6] Of more consequence was

[1] Walewski to Béclard, May 7, *Actes et docs.*, vol. v, no. 1924.
[2] Place to Walewski, June 8, *ibid.*, vol. ii, no. 544.
[3] Place to Walewski, June 23, *ibid.*, no. 564.
[4] Place to Walewski, June 13, *ibid.*, vol. iii, no. 550.
[5] Walewski to Place, July 26, and Sept. 13, *ibid.*, nos. 627 and 677.
[6] Place to Walewski, June 22, *ibid.*, no. 562; Gödel to Buol, no. 33, June 27, Staatsarchiv, xxxviii/106.

the organization of a party, committed to the maintenance of separation, whose first manœuvre was that of trying to discredit the hospodar.[1] Yet Place's struggles did not really commence until Gregory Ghika had retired, and the new caimacam, Balsche, had become installed in his place.

Theodore Balsche had owed his appointment partly to Austria, whose subservient tool he was, partly to the fact that he had headed a petition in favour of separation,[2] and partly, it was said, to the payment of 25,000 ducats to a Turkish banking house, who had acted as broker for the Turks in this transaction.[3] The circumstances of his election, as far as they were known, were quite sufficient to create some apprehension. 'One goes so far as to speak of violent reaction,' wrote Place, 'of destitutions, of individual prosecutions.'[4] Undoubtedly Balsche was wary in the beginning. Efforts made by Austria to get him to cancel the Magnan grant and a concession of a bank to a Prussian interest, as well as to revoke the freedom of the press, met with indifference—or timidity.[5] But both Austria and Turkey knew their man, and it only remained to give him assurances that would strengthen his backbone. As Balsche had the ambition to become hospodar,[6] he was quite ready to become the exponent of Austro-Turkish policy, whether that meant constituting himself the vehicle of Turkish authority in Moldavia, or using his position to undermine the cause of union. When he took the above steps, dictated from Constantinople— the suppression of certain competitors of Austria and the establishment of a censorship[7]—one could see how little he cared that Turkey was invading the autonomy of his land.

The policy of Vienna was to incite the new caimacam to crush the movement for union which had begun so favourably under his predecessor, and to bring out a definite sentiment in favour of the *status quo*. While Gödel-Lannoy, the Austrian consul, was slated for Place's role of major domo, the nucleus of a party of 'separation' was found in the greater *boyards*, who, naturally conservative, were much dismayed at 'Young Roumania's' activity for union as a starting-point for further projects of reform.[8] Adept at planning a campaign of this sort, Gödel left 'no opportunity to strengthen the new caimacam's resolution': Ghika's

---

[1] Place to Walewski, June 24, *Actes et docs.*, vol. iii, no. 566. The effort was made to get up an inquiry into the acts of Ghika's administration.

[2] Prokesch to Buol, no. 49 A–E.

[3] Place to Walewski, July 10, *Actes et docs.*, vol. iii, no. 591.

[4] Place to Walewski, July 19, *ibid.*, no. 612.

[5] Prokesch to Fuad, Aug. 9.

[6] Place to Walewski, July 24, *ibid.*, vol. iii, no. 624.

[7] These measures were not taken until September: *ibid.*, no. 689.

[8] Gödel to Buol, no. 33, June 27, Staatsarchiv, XXXVIII/106.

prefects were to be removed, and in fact 'all politically unqualified officials'. The lesser *boyards* were flattered by the inclusion of one of their number in the caimacam's new ministry, and plans were even made for winning the peasants to the cause through propaganda in the village schools.[1] Not deceived by Balsche's efforts to delude him,[2] Place was speedily made aware that a challenge had come from the other camp that could not be ignored. All he could do was to give assurances that those who stood for union would be 'vigorously sustained', but 'I cannot disguise the fact', he wrote Walewski, 'that great discouragement has seized a certain number of the partisans of union'.[3] There was undoubtedly ground for anxiety. Profuse in testifying his gratitude to Austria,[4] Balsche sought her consul's advice on all matters,[5] and, while he boasted of his neutrality by refusing to allow demonstrations on either side, he chose his ministry from separatists, and as Gödel expressed it, 'worked only secretly against union'. The petitions, which now appeared in defence of separation, were among the first-fruits of the new government's zeal;[6] and with high hopes the Austrian consul was declaring that 'our interests, which under the previous régime encountered only opposition and enmity, face now a bright future, and I will leave no stone unturned to utilize the situation for the best'.[7]

Apparently the enemies of union regarded Moldavia as the more promising of the provinces in which to organize resistance; for no such efforts were expended on Wallachia. Alexander Ghika, though a man of 'no mind' and 'easy to influence',[8] had at least the credit of having once refused to become the tool of Russia, though it had cost him his position.[9] As he was now old, and showed but little force, he was at least negatively acceptable to all parties, and though he gave no quarter to the friends of Stirbey he was not disposed to jeopardize his chance of some day becoming hospodar. Towards the question of union, therefore, Ghika showed benevolent neutrality. While not working for the cause, he did nothing to combat it. If he seemed more disposed to listen to Colquhoun than to Béclard, he was far from being disturbed by the hearty welcome

[1] Gödel to Buol, no. 73, Dec. 31, Staatsarchiv, xxxviii/106.
[2] Balsche had told Place that he favoured union under a foreign prince, but the consul, taking note of his associates, did not believe him: Thouvenel, *op. cit.*, pp. 20–1.
[3] Place to Walewski, July 24, *Actes et docs.*, vol. iii, no. 624.
[4] Gödel to Buol, no. 38, July 12, Staatsarchiv, xxxviii/106.
[5] Gödel to Buol, no. 39, July 16 and no. 40, July 20, *ibid.*
[6] Gödel to Buol, no. 58, Sept. 15, *ibid.*
[7] Gödel to Buol, no. 42, July 20, *ibid.*
[8] Alison to Stratford, July 11, F.O. 78/1184; cf. Prokesch to Buol, no. 49 A–E; also Béclard's comment, 'un viellard, usé, aigri, presque tombé en enfance' in Damé, *op. cit.*, p. 98, cited in East, *op. cit.*, p. 82.
[9] Bulwer to Clarendon, no. 378, Jan. 2, 1858, F.O. 78/1374.

with which Talleyrand, the French commissioner, was greeted in Bucharest in the course of his journey to Constantinople.[1] Whether or not Béclard profited by the caimacam's weakness to encourage the 'National Party', or whether Colquhoun felt that Ghika was slipping from his grasp, the British consul complained that his colleague was actively encouraging the unionist propaganda,[2] and Clarendon, who had to rely chiefly on Colquhoun for information, felt it necessary to remind Walewski that the Powers had agreed not to pre-judge the question of union.[3] It is to be noted that Béclard had made counter-accusations against Colquhoun,[4] and from what we know of the British consul it is hard to believe that he remained neutral. But, at all events, after some discussion between Paris and London, Clarendon and Walewski both agreed to warn their agents to moderate their zeal.[5]

But the feud between the former allies on the question of union was now fairly apparent. Napoleon knew that he could not count on Great Britain to help him circumvent its enemies. And Clarendon, though not disparaging the right of the divans to express themselves, went so far as to write Colquhoun, September 9, that the British government disapproved of union either under a native or under a foreign prince, and would oppose that eventuality 'by all means that they can legitimately employ'.[6] Such 'means', as we have seen, were being employed rather at Constantinople than at Bucharest or Jassy, but it is not to be wondered that Thouvenel found his position painfully isolated, and that he had privately expressed his fear that France would end up as she had done in 1840 over the Egyptian question.[7] An assurance from Walewski (to be communicated to the Porte) that 'union' did not necessarily mean 'a foreign prince'[8] might be looked upon somewhat in the light of a confession of weakness. Neither Walewski[9] nor Thouvenel approved of the Emperor's policy, though Thouvenel, in spite of evidence of discouragement,[10] never faltered in his duty. And, undoubtedly, the ambassador would need all of his stock of skill and resolution to see that the plebiscite was properly protected.

[1] Talleyrand to Walewski, July 19, 1856, *Actes et docs.*, vol. iii, no. 614.

[2] Colquhoun to Stratford, Aug. 26, sent to Clarendon with Stratford's no. 1061, F.O. 78/1186.

[3] Clarendon to Cowley, no. 960, Sept. 9, F.O. 27/1116.

[4] Thouvenel, *op. cit.*, p. 34. Colquhoun admitted that he warned people against union: Colquhoun to Clarendon, no. 95, Oct. 24, F.O. 78/1200.

[5] F.O. to Colquhoun, no. 30, Sept. 24, F.O. 78/1200.

[6] F.O. to Colquhoun, no. 26, Sept. 9, *ibid.*

[7] Thouvenel, *op. cit.*, p. 39. It will be recalled that France's support of Mehemet Ali had left her isolated, and that the final settlement was made in 1840 without consulting her.

[8] Walewski to Thouvenel, Aug. 9, *Actes et docs.*, vol. iii, no. 642. The Austrian chargé d'affaires at Paris also communicated the same view: Ottenfels to Buol, no. 76 C, Sept. 10, Staatsarchiv, IX/52.

[9] Thouvenel, *op. cit.*, p. 42.   [10] *Ibid.*, pp. 38–9, 44–5.

The task of drafting the Sultan's firman for convoking the divans *ad hoc* was begun early in September. Clearly, the degree of accuracy with which the electoral arrangements would serve to evoke the sentiments of the Principalities would be a fair test of the sincerity with which the Powers viewed the treaty of their creation. The inception of the work had been long delayed, partly because of the uncertain length of the Austrian occupation (it may have been the boundary *impasse* which delayed the instructions to Stratford,[1] who as dean of the ambassadors, was the one to call the conferences), partly because the Porte, by utilizing the differences between the Powers, had hoped to exclude the question of union from the divans, and partly, no doubt, because no one hurried at Constantinople. The composition of the document had been confided by the Congress to the Porte in collaboration with the ambassadors, and the initial draft was to be prepared by the Porte itself. Seeing that the question of union could evidently not be debarred from the firman itself, and that the electoral arrangements, however devised, could not absolutely ensure its defeat, the Sultan's ministers had at first hoped to couple the firman with a note, prescribing exactly what the divans might do,[2] intending thus by implication to exclude the hated question. The idea had apparently emanated from Austria,[3] and Stratford was also alleged to favour it,[4] but Gortchakoff showed unqualified disapproval,[5] and, when a similar attitude was displayed by Sardinia and Prussia, the French ambassador was able to get Ali's assurance that the idea would be abandoned.[6] Then a week later it seems to have been revived, and Thouvenel made it clear to Fuad that he would not discuss any project of the firman if it were to be accompanied by a note setting any limitations on the rights of the divans. Without instructions from Clarendon on the subject, Stratford did not venture to thwart his rival;[7] and so Thouvenel had scored in the end—a result due, according to Stratford, to 'apprehension of giving offence to the French embassy and putting M. Thouvenel in the position to execute his threat of refusing to accept the note, or even, perhaps, the draft of the firman'.[8]

[1] Prokesch to Buol, no. 71 B, Sept. 17, Staatsarchiv, XII/57.

[2] As far back as July (before the issuance of the circular of July 31) the Porte had thought to reserve the right by specifying the bases of the divans' deliberations: Prokesch to Buol, no. 49 C.

[3] Koller to Buol, no. 1, Sept. 2, *ibid.*, XII/58. Buol told Prokesch in a private letter, Sept. 13 (*ibid.*) that 'the imperial government would not fail in its support of the firm attitude which the Porte should take regarding the grave question'.

[4] Thouvenel to Walewski, Sept. 15, *Actes et docs.*, no. 678.

[5] Thouvenel to Walewski, Sept. 18, *ibid.*, no. 685.

[6] Thouvenel to Walewski, Sept. 22, *ibid.*, vol. iii, no. 690.

[7] Thouvenel to Walewski, Sept. 29, *ibid.*, no. 701.

[8] Stratford to Clarendon, no. 1254, Oct. 17, F.O. 78/1190.

Thus the Porte would have to bethink itself of some new method of obstruction.

Meanwhile, after some pressure from both Stratford and Thouvenel, the first draft of the firman was duly presented to the embassies, and, except for some of its language, which seemed to assume the separation of the Principalities, Thouvenel not only expressed himself as satisfied in general with its tenor, but considered it superior to plans which had emanated from the Principalities themselves.[1] Walewski, replying to the ambassador's observations, and calling to mind the suspicious changes which the caimacams had made in the personnel of their administrations, impressed it upon him that 'nothing... must interfere with the free expression of the wishes of the Moldo-Wallachian populations'.[2] The machinations of Balsche and the suppression of the freedom of the press in Moldavia were certainly a foretaste of what might happen, and there was no apparent surprise when Fuad issued a circular, October 14, declaring that the Porte reserved its decision respecting union even if the divans voted in favour of it.[3] Such a threat, however, was of no immediate import, and the first meeting of the diplomats on the project of the firman revealed so little difference of opinion that Thouvenel thought he saw 'le désir sincère d'une entente'. It only remained to end the crisis which was holding up the execution of the treaty, and in that regard 'the knot of the question', he told Walewski, was to be found not in Constantinople but in London.[4]

While the struggle over union might already be considered as compromising the outlook for Rouman nationalism, the delay in launching the plebiscite had, undoubtedly, been the occasion for a good deal of this dissension, and for this delay the controversy of the Powers over the Bessarabian frontier was mainly responsible. It will be appreciated how seriously this question had split the Concert of Europe when one finds that Palmerston was now using his influence to strengthen Austria's reluctance to evacuate the Principalities:[5] and Great Britain was so determined not to yield Bolgrad to Russia that she would not hear of a conference lest she and her two partners, Austria and Turkey, be left in a minority. In vain Napoleon said that he would make no effort to convert the other Powers.[6] Even Austria, while consenting to a conference, would not agree to be bound by its decisions, and Turkey withheld

[1] Thouvenel to Walewski, Oct. 6, *Actes et docs.*, vol. iii, no. 706.
[2] Walewski to Thouvenel, Oct. 18, *ibid.*, no. 718.
[3] The circular was addressed to the Turkish representatives at the courts of the signatory Powers: *ibid.*, no. 714. Thouvenel's observations are to be found in no. 734.
[4] Thouvenel to Walewski, Oct. 30, *ibid.*, no. 730.
[5] Note by Palmerston on Seymour to Clarendon, no. 761, Sept. 30, F.O. 7/491.
[6] Walewski to Persigny, Nov. 8, no. 128, *Aff. étr.*, *Angleterre*, vol. 706.

her consent for fear the Powers might effect a compromise that
would sacrifice the little island, which in her opinion conveyed the
control of the Danube delta.[1] Genuinely anxious to find a way out
of the *impasse*, Walewski proposed that the question of Bolgrad be
referred to the arbitration of some disinterested Power, but again
the British government refused to stir from its position, Clarendon
declaring that there was no doubt whatever what was intended by
the treaty, and any question of changing it was simply one of policy
which could not properly be determined by a third party.[2] It was
more logical, he told Persigny, that the allies, who had brought
Russia to terms in 1855, should present her with a new ultimatum
than that Russia herself should cast a vote on the measure of her
punishment; and Palmerston went so far as to aver that Russia was
merely trying to give Europe a spectacle of the differences existing
between her former enemies.[3] Palmerston's own motives, however,
did not pass unchallenged. Persigny expressed the opinion that,
as the British public had greatly magnified the issue, the ministry
was afraid, if it yielded, of being charged with being 'the dupe of a
skilful intrigue'.[4] 'It is the vanity of Lord Palmerston', exclaimed
Walewski in a private letter to Thouvenel,[5] while to Hübner he
declared that the British statesman was always ready to sacrifice the
peace of Europe for the sake of his political interests at home.[6] And
thus the controversy seemed no nearer a solution. Curiously
enough the Porte itself was beginning to resent the somewhat
oppressive solicitude of its friends, and, now that the problem of
carrying out the plebiscite had at last been taken up, Austria was
reminded that the time of evacuation, as stipulated by the treaty,
would elapse in three weeks.[7] Clarendon at once called the Turkish
ministers to order, requesting Stratford to tell the Porte not to
insist on Austria's withdrawal;[8] and that was, of course, sufficient
to end the matter. No doubt it is true that France had lost ground
to her rivals by reason of the support she had given to Russia on the
frontier controversy.[9] It made all the more difficult her champion-
ship of union. Writing to a friend, Thouvenel lamented the reduction of French influence, which for three years had reigned
supreme—and which misfortune he attributed mainly to the

---

[1] Prokesch to Buol, no. 90 C, Nov. 19, Staatsarchiv, XII/57.
[2] Clarendon to Cowley, no. 1276, Oct. 20, F.O. 27/1118.
[3] Persigny to Walewski, no. 190, Oct. 7, *Aff. étr., Angleterre*, vol. 706.
[4] Persigny to Walewski, no. 186, Sept. 23, *ibid.*
[5] Thouvenel, *op. cit.*, p. 42.
[6] Hübner to Buol, no. 85 B, Oct. 18, Staatsarchiv, IX/50.
[7] Fuad to Callimachi, Oct. 10, *Actes et docs.*, vol. iii, no. 709. The Porte was
referring specifically to the obligations of other Powers, but felt that Austria
should follow their example.
[8] Clarendon to Stratford, no. 1201, Oct. 23, F.O. 78/1167.
[9] Thouvenel to Walewski, Sept. 11, *Actes et docs.*, vol. iii, no. 673.

affair of the Principalities.[1] Then a sudden change of viziers at the beginning of November made him realize once again the subterranean influence which gave Stratford his advantage.

The sudden removal of Ali and the reinstatement of Reshid Pasha to the vizirate may well have been due to several causes. It was said that Ali had tried to curb his sovereign's extravagance, whereas Reshid was known from past experience to be more lenient with such delinquencies.[2] But prima facie evidence certainly points to the hand of Stratford;[3] and Prokesch, who was much annoyed because his colleague had not consulted him in the matter, ascribed the success of Stratford's manœuvre partly to the fact that Ali had been able to secure a loan in London (the inference being that an anglophil would have better luck), and partly to the recent conferment of the Order of the Garter upon the Sultan.[4] It can safely be assumed that fear of Reshid's influence had had much to do with Ali's former leanings towards France, and it may account for his recent subservience to Austria, whose policy was fundamentally more pleasing to Turkish hearts. The internuncio, who was, of course, much too jealous of Stratford's influence to respond cordially to his British colleague's efforts to calm him down,[5] realized no doubt that he would now have to yield up all claim to leadership (as far as the embassies were concerned) in the struggle against union. As to the general effect of this convulsion upon Turkish policy, little change might be expected, except in so far as Ali had been more tractable and, at the same time, less timid under pressure than his successor. Reshid was an indolent and dissolute man,[6] of much smaller mentality than the man he had replaced, and had the reputation of being exceptionally venal [7]— even in an environment where venality is a commonplace. As the tool of Stratford he would not feel called upon to seek support in other quarters, and could safely mask his ignorance of statecraft under a demeanour of placid obstinacy, which nothing but fear of some stronger will would move.

---

[1] Thouvenel, *op. cit.*, p. 44.

[2] Prokesch to Buol, no. 86 D, Nov. 5, Staatsarchiv, XII/57. It is not improbably true that Reshid had been intriguing for some time to regain his former post.

[3] Stratford does not wholly admit his instrumentality in any of his letters, but he calls it 'an act not only of justice but of necessity', and he acknowledged that he had expressed his views to those who were in the Sultan's confidence; so that when the latter broached the subject (following Stratford's lead), the British ambassador was able to propose his candidate (Stratford to Clarendon, no. 1303, Nov. 3, F.O. 78/1191). He seems to have denied to Prokesch that he had any hand in the matter, but the latter did not believe him (Prokesch to Buol, no. 88 D, Nov. 12 and no. 92 B, Nov. 26, Staatsarchiv, XII/57). Thouvenel plainly attributed the affair to Stratford (Thouvenel, *op. cit.*, pp. 50–2).

[4] Prokesch to Buol, no. 86 D; also no. 86 C of same date, Staatsarchiv, XII/57.

[5] Prokesch to Buol, no. 88 D. Prokesch would not agree to support the new vizier, though he promised not to intrigue against him.

[6] Thouvenel, *op. cit.*, pp. 222–4.   [7] Prokesch to Rechberg, no. 86 D.

It was not long before the new vizier was conscious of his difficulties. The frontier question was still unsettled, and he soon found himself in a vice between France and Russia on the one hand and Great Britain and Austria on the other.[1] An attempt on the part of the Sultan to prevent Ali from harbouring feelings of revenge foundered on Ali's refusal to accept office under his rival— a decision which, according to Stratford, had 'every appearance of being solicited through a private channel'.[2] Both he and Fuad (who had insisted upon retiring with Ali) were suspected of designs to wreck the new régime.[3] Meanwhile the ministerial upheaval had, of course, suspended all work upon the firman. But one event in November gave promise of removing the chief obstacle to the execution of this measure, and thus paved the way for the resumption of the task of drawing it up. Rather impressed by a suggestion of the French member of the boundary commission to the effect that Russia might be satisfied by a slight territorial compensation for surrendering Bolgrad,[4] and, being assured finally that she would accept a French proposal to that end,[5] the British government at length consented to the reassembling of the Congress of Paris.[6] To this extent, at least, French diplomacy had achieved a triumph, and the question of the Principalities need no longer be postponed. On learning of the decision Thouvenel rejoiced that it seemed to imply a re-establishment of the accord between the former allies.[7]

Deliberation on the firman could now proceed with somewhat more promise of reaching results; and the work was completed in three more meetings. As an act of precaution against too popular a representation of the populations, electoral colleges were constituted from the various classes of society: the clergy, the landed *boyards*, the non-noble landowners (possessed of a certain minimum of land), the peasants, and the urban population. To the extent that each of these bodies should meet after the fashion of committees and form their opinions separately before presenting them to the united assembly, the plan further diverged from the

---

[1] Prokesch to Buol, no. 88, A–D, Nov. 12, Staatsarchiv, XII/57.

[2] Stratford to Clarendon, no. 1386, Nov. 24, F.O. 78/1192. Prokesch was anxious that an effort should be made to persuade him to take office, but Stratford became very angry at the suggestion: Prokesch to Buol, no. 92 B.

[3] Stratford to Clarendon, no. 1358, Nov. 17, F.O. 78/1192; Prokesch to Buol, no. 90 C, Nov. 19, Staatsarchiv, XII/57. Reshid remarked peevishly that they wanted to throw on him the responsibility of the results of their own lack of courage at the Congress of Paris.

[4] Persigny to Walewski, no. 200, Oct. 22, *Aff. étr., Angleterre*, vol. 706. It must be admitted, however, that Walewski himself had at first looked rather askance at the idea.   [5] Charles-Roux, *op. cit.*, pp. 160–1.

[6] Persigny to Walewski, no. 203, Nov. 13, *Aff. étr., Angleterre*. The decision naturally displeased Stratford: Prokesch to Buol, no. 82 A–D, Staatsarchiv, XII/57.

[7] Thouvenel to Walewski, Dec. 1, *Actes et docs.*, vol. iii, no. 755.

Règlement, and one is reminded somewhat of the historic feudal assemblies.[1] The origin of the idea may be found in article xxiv of the Treaty of Paris, which had declared that the divans should be 'composed in such manner as to represent most closely the interest of all classes of society',[2] and the arrangement noticeably appears in the original project of the Porte; likewise that of requiring the reports of each college to be submitted, as well as the results of the deliberations of the assembly as a whole, to the international commission.[3] As each divan was to have 'for its sole mission the statement of wishes', it may be inferred that no work of legislation was entrusted to it. It was not to be, in any sense, a constituent assembly. Most of the present discussion was concerned with the fixing of the various categories and the problem of eligibility. It was no easy task, for conditions in the Principalities were not very accurately known; but Thouvenel seemed better informed than any of his colleagues (even Stratford paid a tribute to his rival's knowledge of the subject),[4] and it was his influence which seems to have been paramount in determining the arrangements. It was at his suggestion that the clergy were narrowed so as to reduce the influence of the priests, whose ignorance would preclude their independence, and to exclude the agents of foreign religious communities holding land in either of the provinces; and it is easy to guess that the French ambassador was guarding against the danger of Russian intrigue. In respect to the peasants, Thouvenel successfully restricted the number of eligibles, here again believing that ignorance might lend opportunity to venality. Of special interest, however, was the French ambassador's fight on *boyarisme*. 'One is not a *boyard* of any rank whatever,' he wrote, 'save by a function, obtained by the favour, the caprice, and even the venality of the hospodars.'[5] In opposition to Stratford's view that title should determine eligibility, Thouvenel felt that only the larger property-owners in that class should constitute a separate category, while the poorer scions of the aristocracy should find their places in one of the other groups. The other ambassadors, Stratford excepted, readily agreed to this attack upon the integrity of the *boyard* class, and the British ambassador finally bowed to the will of the majority. Thouvenel's object, as he wrote Walewski, was to 'paralyse the influence of the great *boyards*, almost all

---

[1] This was one of the targets of attack in a brochure by John Bratiano (*Mémoire sur la situation de la Moldo-Valachie*), one of the Wallachian exiles in Paris. 'Why', he asked, 'should this feudal régime which we have never undergone and for which we have always had an unsurmountable repugnance be imposed upon us when all Europe has definitely abandoned it?'

[2] Holland, *The European Concert in the Eastern Question*, pp. 251–2.

[3] *Actes et docs.*, vol. iii, no. 706, annex and no. 720.

[4] Stratford to Clarendon, no. 1483, Dec. 24, F.O. 78/1194.

[5] Thouvenel to Walewski, Oct. 30, *Actes et docs.*, vol. iii, no. 730.

partisans of the maintenance of separation'.[1] Yet Thouvenel's services must not be overestimated. A shrewd Wallachian, who subjected the firman to a rigorous examination,[2] complained that the *boyards* were allowed twice as many deputies as were awarded to the other colleges, and their very compactness would enable them to attract a following and thus to play a great role in the assemblage. It was stipulated that the electoral lists should be posted thirty days before the elections should begin, as a means of allowing complaints to be considered; and in order to prevent confusion the elections for each college should be held in succession. 'All intervention of authority in the electoral operations that are not for the sole object of maintaining order shall be improper and directly contrary to the intentions of the Sublime Porte.'[3] The firman was finally adopted January 13, 1857.

Such was the effort to compose assemblies that would fitly express the voice of the Principalities. Great Britain had stood with France in concerting a plan, which, while it might be defective in practical details, was in general accord with the resolutions of the Congress of Paris. If the programme met with disaster at any stage in its road to fulfilment, such would come of irregularities not readily foreseen in the Sultan's firman.

[1] Thouvenel to Walewski, Jan. 1, 1857, *Actes et doc.*, vol. iii, no. 779.

[2] Boeresco, *Le Firman turc pour la convocation des divans ad hoc dans les principautés du Danube.* The writer's criticisms were distinctly from a liberal standpoint. He objected, for example, to the fixing of 30 as the age of eligibility for voters and deputies, as this would exclude the younger element, who, he affirmed, were the more enlightened and free of local prejudice. He also disapproved of lumping the liberal professions with the artisans, as they would be left in a minority.

[3] For an English translation of the firman see Wambaugh, *op. cit.* pp. 749 ff.

CHAPTER III

THE REACTION AGAINST THE TREATY

THE convocation of popular assemblies to reflect the sentiments of the Principalities on the nature of their reorganization was a direct appeal to Rouman nationalism that could hardly fail to affect the final result. Yet, if the plebiscite were calculated to elicit the wishes of the population, it was not necessary to suppose that a people with so backward a political training would necessarily know what system of government was most applicable to their needs. It was for this reason, doubtless, that an international commission had been provided by the Treaty of Paris to repair to the Principalities and study the problem at first hand, besides being a convenient medium for transmitting and interpreting the opinions of the forthcoming divans. Nothing was said, however, of its being a vigilance committee to supervise the proper execution of the firman, and the nearest approach to the act of conferring such administrative functions was to be found in the last paragraph of the instructions, passed by the Congress:

'In general, the commission, in the course of its operations, shall not lose sight of its true character. It is charged with an impartial inquiry, and, in its dealings with officials and with private individuals, it will respond exactly to the spirit of its institution only by taking measures against all acts of authority or of interference which may be found in contradiction with the object of its mission.'[1]

Such phraseology would seem to imply that the commission had a right to insist on due co-operation from the governments of the Principalities for their task of making inquiries, but whether a deliberate design on the part of the caimacams to pack the divans would be contrary to the 'spirit of its institution' would clearly be a matter for interpretation. In view of coming events it is unfortunate that the Congress did not clothe the commission with greater authority.

The commission was appointed during the summer of 1856, and, after some debate in which Austrian prejudices were overcome, was made to include members from Sardinia and Prussia. Since neither could the elections take place nor the commission begin its sessions until the end of the Austrian occupation was at least in prospect, there was nothing for this body to do but to repair to Constantinople to await the drafting of the firman. Meanwhile, as an act of courtesy to the suzerain Power, and because the Porte ardently desired it, Safvet Effendi, the Turkish commissioner, who was described by Stratford as 'a man of more than average

[1] Wambaugh, *op. cit.*, pp. 746 ff.

talent',[1] was by general agreement appointed its first president, though
the honour was intended to rotate every month after the sittings
should commence. All the commissioners having arrived at Constantinople, while the firman was in process of preparation, it was
decided that the document, when finished, should be read to the
assembled commission in the presence of the ambassadors, and
answers could thus be given to any questions about its meaning.
The suggestion had been made by the British commissioner and
adopted by Clarendon despite Stratford's disapproval.[2] Clarendon
even went so far as to state that the commission should be allowed
to discuss any points in the firman, 'the insertion or omission of
which should in their judgement tend to create difficulty in the
future settlement'.[3] Such a ruling, if generally adhered to, would
have signified that the Powers did regard the commission as having
some connexion with the firman. But most of the commissioners,
perhaps because they enjoyed the confidence of the ambassadors
with whom they were respectively associated, were indisposed to
raise the question of the extent of their authority.

Sir Henry Bulwer, the British commissioner, was the unique
exception. From the moment he reached Constantinople he
expected the fullest information from Stratford as to the instructions which Clarendon had sent him (a favour which he himself
was ready to reciprocate), and the transmission of all documents
which related to the Principalities. Fundamentally such an
attitude was not unreasonable, especially in view of Clarendon's
own decision; but it would have behoved the new arrival to seek
his end by personal interviews, instead of writing wordy and
meticulous complaints; and, to tell the truth, an inability to view
a question broadly was always to be his handicap as a diplomat—
hardly atoned for by his diligence, resourcefulness, and vigour.
In any case, Sir Henry showed from the outset that he did not
propose to play a passive role at any stage in the proceedings, and
to Clarendon he was constantly harping on the delay in drawing
up the firman [4]—a criticism which might, partly at least, reflect on
all the ambassadors. The effect of all this upon Stratford, who was
accustomed to no competitor in managing his country's business,
can well be imagined. He persistently refused to honour Bulwer
with his confidence, offended him deeply by a whispered conversation with one of the Turkish ministers in his presence, and
betrayed his jealousy by complaining of visits which Bulwer had
paid to or received from Thouvenel, Fuad, and others, implying

[1] Stratford to Clarendon, no. 1386, Nov. 24, 1856, F.O. 78/1192.
[2] Stratford to Clarendon, no. 1408, Nov. 28, F.O. 78/1192.
[3] Clarendon to Stratford, no. 1485, Dec. 12, F.O. 78/1169.
[4] Bulwer to Clarendon, no. 18, Dec. 1, and nos. 20 and 21, Dec. 15, F.O.
78/1195.

that the commissioner was guilty of some intrigue. No doubt Bulwer, who probably owed his appointment to Palmerston's friendship, was a man of too much prominence and experience to be a wise selection for so subordinate a role as he was called upon to play; no doubt he was something of a busybody, too, and over-sensitive on a point of dignity; but the studied way in which Stratford tried to ignore him, making no concealment of his rooted distrust, went far to preclude any possibility of cordial co-operation between the two—an attitude destined to react painfully on the course of British policy in the East. According to Thouvenel Stratford had hoped that Alison would be appointed commissioner; for in that case there would have been no question who was superior in all transactions.[1] As it was, he resented the intrusive-ness of a man so prominent in the foreign service, and he carried his suspicions to such a point that he actually believed that Bulwer was intriguing to supplant him at the embassy.[2] There was some-thing utterly childish in their intermittent quarrels, punctuated as they were by an acrimonious correspondence, and the most charitable thing to say on behalf of both is that Stratford was a frequent sufferer from gout, while Bulwer's liver was periodically deranged. How much the course of history is really affected by pathological conditions is something the historian might well take time to consider.

At the time of the joint meeting of the two diplomatic bodies the ill-humour of Bulwer had reached the boiling-point. According to Talleyrand, the French commissioner, he had expected to be con-sulted in regard to the firman, and was now seeking the first chance of venting his feelings.[3] Hardly had the reading of the firman commenced than he interrupted to know if he were supposed to make observations on each paragraph or upon the document as a whole after it was read; he would apologize for his indiscretion, he added, but he was not well informed on the matters which had taken place. This was, of course, a hit at Stratford, besides reveal-ing the lack of unity in British councils. The other ambassadors present sought to make peace between the two (for Stratford had quickly lost his temper), and, when driven to settle the point of whether the commissioners had a right to discuss the firman, they supported Stratford's contention that the role of the commissioner was solely that of gathering information. Nevertheless, Bulwer insisted upon criticizing the firman, which he declared to be unworkable, and the altercation became so bitter that Stratford had to be silenced, while Bulwer was left to argue to an unsym-

[1] Thouvenel to Walewski, May 22, *Actes et docs.*, vol. iii, no. 533. Thouvenel remarked that Stratford would then have acted with a high hand.
[2] Stratford to Clarendon, Jan. 19, 1857, Stratford Papers, F.O. 352/46.
[3] Talleyrand to Walewski, Jan. 8, *Actes et docs.*, vol. iii, no. 784.

pathetic audience.[1] 'The nature of the relations existing between
the ambassador and the commissioner of His Britannic Majesty
is well known to every one,' wrote Thouvenel, 'and we have more
pain than surprise at seeing it manifested.'[2] The worst aspect of
the quarrel was that it got into the newspapers, and, after this
accident had widened the breach, a long controversy ensued over
whether Bulwer had or had not misrepresented to the Porte his
government's attitude towards union.[3] When the wearisome
quarrel was at length brought before the judgement of the Foreign
Office, Clarendon reminded Bulwer that his functions were not
directive but confined to gathering evidence, and that the consular
agents (this was in answer to a query of Bulwer's)[4] would remain
responsible to Stratford.[5] To Bulwer, who had told his chief that
the commissioners, in general, were in favour of 'supplying
deficiencies [in the firman] by adequate powers, conferred upon
the commission',[6] one may judge how distasteful such a judgement
must have been. As a result of his discomfiture, he was to pursue
a rather pedantic adherence to the letter of his instructions, while
continually complaining of them; and in the meantime he convinced himself that Stratford would meddle with the affairs of the
commission, and try secretly to circumvent it.[7] One may readily
judge that, after so much misunderstanding, the two diplomats
would never be likely to become reconciled.

Meanwhile a much more important matter than dissidence in
diplomatic circles was the execution of the firman, which had
received its full form on January 13, and the Sultan's sanction
some days later. How soon it would be expedited must hinge upon
the outcome of the conference at Paris, which was striving to reach
decision on the long-pending dispute over the Bessarabian frontier.
The result was a compromise, which was said to have given general
satisfaction. Bolgrad and Serpent's Island were both given to

[1] Talleyrand to Walewski, Jan. 14, *Actes et docs*, vol. iii, no. 794. Bulwer also
wrote an account of the episode to Clarendon.
[2] Thouvenel to Walewski, Jan. 15, *ibid.*, no. 795.
[3] According to information, derived by Stratford from one of his dragomans,
Bulwer had told the grand vizier that he thought Turkey should not interfere
in the free expression of the people respecting union, and when Reshid said that
he had every reason to believe that Great Britain and Austria were in accord
against union, Bulwer 'replied that they were not quite clear about it': Revalsky
to Stratford, March 12, Stratford Papers, F.O. 352/45. Stratford at once took
Bulwer to task (Mar. 13, *ibid.*, 352/48), and complained to Clarendon against
what he deemed an encroachment upon his own prerogatives and a misrepresenta-
tion of British policy (no. 235, Mar. 14, F.O. 78/1258). Bulwer explained to
Clarendon that Reshid had seemed to want him to attack union, and that he
considered that his conduct should be impartial (no. 16, Mar. 26, F.O. 78/1279).
Obviously Stratford did not share the commissioner's point of view.
[4] Bulwer to Clarendon, no. 16.
[5] Clarendon to Bulwer, no. 28, Apr. 14, F.O. 78/1279.
[6] Bulwer to Clarendon, no. 3, Jan. 26, *ibid.*
[7] Bulwer to Clarendon, no number, Apr. 18, *ibid.*

Turkey in return for a rectification of the frontier, which would yield certain points to Russia, formerly withheld; the boundary commission should have three months to fix the new line; and, what is chiefly important, the date which should mark the termination of the Austrian occupation was fixed at March 30.[1] 'This event [according to Place] caused great rejoicings in the Principalities', since they were now soon to be relieved of a foreign occupation, and the arrival of the international commission could be expected before long.[2] Meanwhile the Porte was preparing its communications to the caimacams, and the commissioners dispersed to different places to await the withdrawal of the Austrians.

The way had hardly been opened for the elections of the divans when an explosion took place over a trivial matter, which showed up once again the issue that was dividing Europe. While the firman had been received with satisfaction in the Principalities, a rumour became current—fostered, it was said, by Austrian agents —that France had abandoned her support of union. Determined not to be placed in a false light, Napoleon had a notice put in the *Moniteur* to the effect that, while France was always desirous of reconciling the interests of the Ottoman Empire with those of the Principalities, she had believed, and still believed, that the union of the Principalities was the most desirable change to be made in their position, and she did not despair of seeing this view prevail in the councils of the Powers.[3] This pronouncement, coming as it did when the electoral canvass was soon to commence, roused intense indignation in British circles. Answering a question in the House of Commons Clarendon declared that there had been an understanding between the Powers that 'until the divans had met, until the people of the Principalities had been consulted, until the report of the commission had been received, and the Congress had met to consider it, no one of those Powers would do anything to influence opinion in the Principalities or elsewhere upon that particular question'.[4] Parallel with this public statement, Cowley undertook to expostulate with Walewski, though the result was far from affording satisfaction. The French minister not only justified his government's pronouncement but reminded Cowley that Clarendon's own support of union was registered in a protocol.[5] No doubt, regardless of whether or not Clarendon was correct in his understanding of a common 'self-denying ordinance', there was some point in the British contention that the French were

[1] Martens, *op. cit.*, vol. xv, pp. 793 ff. or *Brit. and For. State Papers*, vol. xlvii, pp. 92 ff.
[2] Place to Walewski, Jan. 25, *Actes et docs.*, vol. iii, no. 809.
[3] *Moniteur*, Feb. 4.
[4] Hansard, *Parliamentary Debates*, 3rd ser., vol. cxliv, pp. 332-4.
[5] Cowley to Clarendon, no. 230, Feb. 10, F.O. 27/1189.

guilty of 'interference in the free expression of opinion in the Principalities',[1] but it is difficult to see how foreign Powers could be expected to remain dormant during an electoral campaign in which opposing parties would seek to instruct a backward people, and upon the issue of which the government of Vienna had always laid a suspicious emphasis. Apart from whether Great Britain's encouragement of Austria[2] was itself morally defensible, the methods of the French were at least more lenient and more legal than those which Austria was employing, and we find no British objection to the latter. 'The Principalities will get us into trouble yet', declared Cowley ruefully. 'I always foretold it during the conferences.'[3] Indeed, Cowley came to the conviction that, if union were to mean the forerunner of independence, Napoleon would feel none of Great Britain's anxiety that the integrity of the Ottoman Empire should be maintained at any cost. 'Such being the case,' he told Clarendon, 'it is difficult to argue with His Majesty, for on this question, at least, his philanthropy far exceeds his respect for treaties.'[4] One hardly needs this evidence to see where the shoe was pinching. Great Britain was sincerely afraid that union, after all, would be a danger to the Ottoman Empire.

The more one thinks of it, the more one realizes that Clarendon was largely paying for the tactical blunder which he had made a year ago. How could he reasonably object to the French repeating their adherence to a principle which he himself had espoused? The only solution of such a dilemma—since he could not well retract his opinions publicly—was to show his real views to Austria[5] (a duplicity that must have been distasteful to his Lordship) and to let the whole initiative in British opposition to union pass to the British agents on the spot. Prokesch, who worried over the 'neutral position of Stratford', and confessed his helplessness to move the Turks without that diplomat's assistance,[6] failed to realize that British policy was simply turned adrift until some crisis should arise that might encourage Stratford to assert himself and show his government's colours. In the meantime there was no doubt that British agents had grasped their government's point

---

[1] Cowley to Clarendon, no. 203, Feb. 6, F.O. 27/1189.

[2] The Austrian ambassador reported that Clarendon was decidedly opposed to union, though until the commission's report was submitted, he would not pronounce officially: Apponyi to Buol, no. 22 B, Mar. 28, Staatsarchiv, VIII/47.

[3] Cowley to Stratford, Feb. 7, Stratford Papers, F.O. 352/48.

[4] Cowley to Clarendon, no. 759, May 12, printed in East, *op. cit.*, appx. iii, b.

[5] See above, page 60.

[6] Prokesch to Buol, no. 7 C, Feb. 13, Staatsarchiv, XII/59. Clarendon seems to have explained to Apponyi (Austrian ambassador to London) that British politicians had not yet examined the question at bottom, and that, therefore, the British government could not count on the entire support of public opinion: Apponyi to Buol, no. 12 A–B, Feb. 18, *ibid.*, VIII/47. In April, as we have noticed, he expressed himself more unreservedly.

of view; for even Bulwer, who had thought at first that the dangers attending union had been somewhat exaggerated,[1] prepared a *mémoire* (at Clarendon's request), in which he expressed the opinion that, while union under a foreign prince would create an effective barrier against foreign intervention, such an innovation would be much too like a betrayal of Turkey to be desirable at the present time, and, in short, the disadvantages of union would over-balance the advantages.[2] Sir Henry might have been confronted with a statement of his own, made some time previously, that 'it is now to be feared that the commissioners of the different Powers, instead of visiting the Principalities for the purpose of furnishing their governments with opinions, will visit them for the purpose of maintaining those opinions which their governments have already declared'.[3] Later on Stratford himself prepared a *mémoire*, in which he thought of 'uniformity of institutions' as a substitute for union[4]—a compromise which scarcely helped his government's consistency. In contrast to all these tardy misgivings the attitude of France was thus far unequivocal. In a speech to the legislature on February 16 Napoleon reiterated his faith in union as the arrangement which the Principalities required for their welfare, and declared that his communications with those who thought differently only strengthened his conviction.[5] It is clear that France was not going to help the British government out of the mire of its own making.

But, anxious as the British might be to preserve the Sultan's authority unimpaired, the attitude of Austria was more directly self-interested, and at present more unscrupulous. We have already noticed that her steady policy had been to circumvent the Treaty of Paris by making the fullest use of the authority of the suzerain Power through playing upon the weakness of its ministers. When Clarendon had definitely changed his mind regarding union her commissioner had quietly informed the Porte that there 'was no reason to doubt that the British government is decidedly opposed to union. The Porte has, then, [he continued] only to follow the line which has been traced for it up to this time and use the means of influence which it disposes in the Principalities.'[6] So far, indeed, the Porte's interference in Moldavia had borne considerable fruit, and now that Austrian intrigues had not availed to keep the question of union out of the divans, such action by the suzerain Power was the only way by which the treaty could be flouted. If, more-

---

[1] Bulwer to Clarendon, no. 6, Feb. 9, F.O. 78/1279.
[2] Bulwer to Clarendon, no. 35, Apr. 15, *ibid.*
[3] Bulwer to Clarendon, no number, Aug. 17, 1856, F.O. 78/1195.
[4] Stratford to Clarendon, no. 268, Mar. 23, 1857, enc., F.O. 78/1258.
[5] *Annual Register*, 1857, pp. 226–9.
[6] Koller to Buol, no. 1, Sept. 2, 1856, Staatsarchiv, XII/58.

over, the 'means of influence' were also Turkish garrisons, the outlook would still be brighter. Thus, regardless of the decision at Paris for the definite evacuation of the Principalities, Buol had instructed Prokesch, immediately after the Conference, to tell the Porte that Austria did not object to the continuance of a Turkish occupation, since the Conference had dealt only with foreign troops.[1] Apparently, for the moment, the Porte hesitated; and Prokesch complained that some of the ministers would even prefer union to the danger of incurring the enmity of France and Russia.[2] It was not always, of course, that Austria was able to keep the Porte in harness, so strong were the counter-influences that beset the Sultan's ministers. But, apart from the internuncio's rather awkward manœuvres, the chief immediate reliance was the Austrian consul at Jassy; for if, with the tacit collusion of the Porte, Moldavia could be wrested from the unionists, the coming action of the divans would, of course, amount to nothing.

As far as the authority of the caimacam could be utilized to break the unionist strength, there was little cause for Austria to complain. Picking a ministry of hungry placemen, whom Gödel had nominated (the 'Gödel ministry', it was called),[3] and replacing officials right and left by men whose subservience was assumed, the caimacam of Moldavia set out on a deliberate effort to paralyse the 'National Party'. Many of the progressive element soon found themselves the victims of judicial prosecution, while their opinions (and even foreign brochures favouring union) were excluded from circulation by the rigours of the censorship.[4] Simultaneously no pains were spared to win over the metropolitan, whose influence was paramount with most of the Orthodox clergy. Thanks largely to Place's efforts, the powerful ecclesiastic held firm even against the danger of removal;[5] but the position of the French consul was, of course, rendered difficult by the fear that any resistance to the proscription of his friends would simply serve the Porte as a pretext for claiming the right to intervene to preserve order.[6] Yet, notwithstanding such strenuous efforts to turn the tide, it cannot be said that Austria was very confident of the issue; for it was admitted that as yet no man of weight had espoused the cause of separation, and the opponents of union seemed somehow to hesitate to fight openly for their cause. Apparently it would take time to 'convert the population to the advantages of separation', as

---

[1] Buol to Prokesch, Jan. 17 and 21, 1857, Staatsarchiv, xii/61.

[2] Prokesch to Buol, no. 7 c, Feb. 13, *ibid.* xii/59.

[3] Place to Walewski, Mar. 2, *Actes et docs.*, vol. iii, no. 859. Place wrote that Gödel even resided at the palace, and that the commander of the Austrian troops had moved from Bucharest to Jassy after Balsche's installation.

[4] Place to Walewski, Feb. 23 and 24, *ibid.*, nos. 846 and 848.

[5] Place to Walewski, Feb. 23, *ibid.*, no. 847.

[6] Xénopol, *Histoire des Roumains*, vol. ii, pp. 559–60.

Prokesch put it;[1] and in the meantime such manœuvres threatened foreign complications. A systematic effort to stifle public opinion was naturally disquieting to France, and, after repeated appeals from Thouvenel (who had even raised the question of demanding Balsche's removal), Walewski bade the ambassador impress it upon Turkey that she would be held responsible for any attempt to 'alter the sincerity of the elections'.[2] Had British diplomacy supported France in protecting the common decisions of the Powers, no such distortion of justice would have been probable; but Stratford's dispatches were silent on these scandals[3] (Thouvenel lamented his indifference),[4] and the British consul at Jassy was little more than a cipher.[5] No doubt the blame for British inertia at this juncture may be chiefly laid at Stratford's door. Apart from his prejudices against union, he was too solicitous of retaining his independent initiative with the Porte to care to play the second fiddle in any symphony of which Thouvenel was director. 'It would be a real humiliation', he declared (apropos of the question of union) 'to follow in the wake of a Power who loses no opportunity of influence or ascendancy at our expense'.[6] Once more the rivalry of France and Great Britain was blocking the path to the execution of the collective will of the Powers.

Happily for Rouman nationalism death intervened to arrest the destruction of its prospects; for Balsche thus terminated his caimacamie somewhat abruptly on March 1. Even during the the late caimacam's brief illness the aspirants for the succession had swarmed about the capital, like worms devouring carrion.[7] Foremost among the candidates was a man whom Balsche was said to have designated a few days before his death,[8] and who was then serving as his minister of finance. The son of a former hospodar, a wealthy *boyard* of Bulgarian extraction, Prince Nicolas Vogorides was as eager to make money as he was prodigal in expending it, and public office to him was merely a source of private gain.[9] Determined to get the caimacamie, if any means could win it, he not only made a bid for Place's support (promising,

[1] Prokesch to Buol, no. 7 C.
[2] Walewski to Thouvenel, Feb. 28, *Actes et docs.*, vol. iii, no. 852.
[3] He merely remarked that Thouvenel had pressed for Balsche's dismissal on the ground of his 'known or supposed opposition to union': Stratford to Clarendon, no. 183, Feb. 28, F.O. 78/1257. Stratford seems to have learned of some of Balsche's offences from one of his dragomen: Revalsky to Stratford, Feb. 28, Stratford Papers, F.O. 352/45. On the other hand, Colquhoun had expressed his belief—on what ground we do not know—that Balsche was 'a strictly honest man': Colquhoun to Stratford, telg., Mar. 2, F.O. 195/529.
[4] Thouvenel to Walewski, Mar. 9, *Actes et docs.*, vol. iv, no. 883.
[5] There seems to have been no effort to procure information from Gardner.
[6] Stratford to Clarendon, Mar. 25, Stratford Papers, F.O. 352/46.
[7] Place to Walewski, Mar. 4, *Actes et docs.*, vol. iv, no. 873.
[8] Colquhoun to Stratford, Mar. 5, telg., F.O. 195/529.
[9] Soutzo, *Mémoires*, p. 344.

if chosen, not to interfere in any way with the free expression of Moldavia's desires),[1] but he pleaded his cause at Constantinople by the only means which promised any likelihood of success. Whether or not the Porte would have nominated him in spite of foreign dissuasion cannot be said. As a matter of fact the embassies consulted made no objection, and, though Stratford had thrown his support to a candidate of Prokesch's,[2] a list of names, presented by Thouvenel, had actually included Vogorides, highly recommended, it appears, by Place, whom Thouvenel had consulted.[3] Thus it was the irony of politics that neither Stratford nor Prokesch was particularly gratified, while Thouvenel had contributed indirectly to the selection. After the appointment had been duly made, Place telegraphed Walewski that Vogorides had 'declared that he would support union with prudence, if it should prove certain that this arrangement would triumph at the Congress after being voted by the divans'.[4] The statement reveals an attitude of caution, for Vogorides had, as Place expressed it, a 'blue fear of the Porte',[5] and the French consul strongly suspected that he had received secret instructions,[6] though only time would tell. Apparently the unionists felt anything but easy; yet any one seemed preferable to Balsche, and for the moment Vogorides posed as 'neutral'.[7]

In Wallachia, though political factions never ceased to wrangle, there was no government which became the starting-point for repression, and no party of any sort which avowed itself for separation. Here, as in Moldavia, the activities of the unionists had long centred in the clubs, which were fused into a central organization at the capital; and all citizens, regardless of their personal affiliations, belonged to the so-called 'National Party', which spread the doctrine of union, and looked to France for patronage. As a deputation of the central club declared in its

[1] Vogorides to Place, Mar. 2, *Actes et docs.*, vol. iv, no. 871. Place wrote Thouvenel that Vogorides had declared himself at heart a unionist, though he would be obliged to observe discretion: Thouvenel, *op. cit.*, p. 85.

[2] Stratford to Clarendon, no. 211, Mar. 6, F.O. 78/1257. Prokesch had proposed to Stratford that they should unite on a candidate (Prokesch to Stratford, Mar. 1, Stratford Papers, F.O. 352/48), but Thouvenel's influence was sufficient to prevent his being chosen: Thouvenel to Place, Mar. 11, *Actes et docs.*, vol. iv, no. 887.

[3] Thouvenel to Walewski, Mar. 9, *ibid.*, no. 883.

[4] Place to Walewski, Mar. 14, telg., *ibid.*, no. 897.

[5] Thouvenel, *op. cit.*, p. 88.

[6] Place to Walewski, Mar. 19, *Actes et docs.*, vol. iv, no. 917. Place had a conversation with the kapou kiaya, Photiades, who had arrived with the firman of investiture, and was given to understand that the Porte wanted no change of policy: Thouvenel, *op. cit.*, pp. 87–8. This naturally accorded with Austria's desire: Buol to Prokesch, Mar. 7, Staatsarchiv, xii/61.

[7] Place to Walewski, Mar. 19; cf. Gödel to Buol, no. 21, Mar. 19, Staatsarchiv, xxxviii/108. One critic denounced Vogorides as a 'planariot bey': *Actes et docs.*, vol. iv, no. 878.

address of welcome to Talleyrand, 'Thanks to the constant support
of the government of His Majesty, the Emperor Napoleon, and of
public opinion in France, the desire for union has lost none of its
intensity during the days of trial that we have just passed through.
This desire is to-day unanimous.'[1] These patriots were tactful
enough not to admit that they were also for a foreign prince, but
Talleyrand came to doubt if the Wallachians would vote for union,
unless this further boon were coupled with it. Doubtless the feud
between Ghika and Stirbey (all of whose henchmen had been
turned out of office) made many of them feel that only a foreign
prince could unify the nation; certainly that enmity seemed
sufficient to prevent either one from becoming hospodar.[2] But,
while Stirbey was unwilling to do more than shout for union, the
caimacam, whose government was notoriously unpopular, seems
to have striven to outbid him in the quest of public favour; for
the club which avowed itself openly for a foreign prince was
directed by his nephew, the prefect of police.[3] To be sure, the
very weakness of the caimacam was an asset to the nationalist
cause. When the clubs showed signs of letting their ardour pass
the bounds of discretion, Ghika probably expected that the commission, when it should meet, would assume the task of applying
muzzles, and thus would he himself be dispensed from the
responsibility.[4] Colquhoun was frankly disgusted with the man
he had once so highly praised,[5] and Stratford complained to
Reshid against such evident disobedience of the Porte's injunction
to be studiously impartial.[6] Characteristically enough Ghika
excused himself on the ground that his hand was being forced
by Stirbey and his party, but Talleyrand was perhaps not far from
wrong in his suspicion that, in allowing the demand for a foreign
prince to gather strength, he was hopeful of seeing the cause of
union come to grief.[7] In any event, Ghika was not a man to borrow
trouble, and the personnel of his administration was so unpopular
that only by pursuing a policy of drift could he hope to avoid
disaster. Had Austria and Turkey seriously expected him to play
the role of a Theodore Balsche, it is not impossible that the old
man would have been worried into the grave.

[1] *Ibid.*, no. 916.
[2] Talleyrand to Walewski, Apr. 1, *ibid.*, no. 971; Bulwer to Clarendon, no. 14,
Mar. 25, F.O. 78/1279.
[3] Thouvenel, *op. cit.*, p. 93.   [4] Talleyrand to Walewski, Apr. 1.
[5] Colquhoun to Stratford, no. 12, Feb. 27, F.O. 195/529. As his self-appointed
mentor, he had urged Ghika to appoint prefects on whom he could rely ('Câteva
Farâme din Correspondenta lui Alexandru vodă Ghica' in *Analele Academiei
Romane*, seria ii, vol. xxix, pp. 259–60), but his point of view in such matters
was quite different from the caimacam's.
[6] Stratford to Colquhoun, Mar. 11, Stratford Papers, F.O. 352/46. Such was
not exactly the tenor of the Porte's instructions which accompanied the firman:
Actes et docs., vol. iv, no. 886.   [7] Talleyrand to Walewski, Apr. 1.

The firman having been promulgated, a copy was dispatched to each of the caimacams; and, as the departure of the remaining Austrians was only a mere matter of days, the members of the international commission began to gather at Bucharest where its sessions were to be held. Naturally the Wallachians vibrated to the occasion. A memorial from the clubs was delivered to all the commissioners,[1] and some of them—even the Austrian commissioner, Liehmann[2]—received also separate addresses, all evoking sympathy for the cause of union. The address to Talleyrand, who was accorded the most conspicuous welcome, was eloquent (as we have noticed) in its expressions of gratitude to France; while Benzi, the Italian, was reminded of the bonds of sympathy which united two peoples, inspired by common ideals.[3] Apart from Bulwer, who had gone for a few days' sojourn in the country, the least conspicuous was the Russian commissioner, Basily, who took no pains to win the approval of the Wallachians[4]—an attitude fairly typical of the Russians at this time. The avowed opponents of the Wallachian patriots were Liehmann and the Turkish commissioner, Safvet Effendi; and the latter, under pressure from the former, promised to complain to Ghika of the activities of the clubs, and also to invoke the intervention of his government.[5] By no means loath to take some action, the Porte bade Safvet concert with Ghika and the commission some means of suppressing the clubs.[6] But, as investigation proved that public meetings were not illegal, the commission, to whom Safvet had submitted a coercive measure, merely decided to ask the caimacam to advise that such meetings be suspended until the electoral lists were published.[7] This moderate step seemed to produce the desired results.

It is to be noticed that it was Austria, as usual, who was spurring Turkey to a counter-move against the unionists. Since, from the point of view of Vienna, the struggle was less important—because less hopeful—than that which was being waged in the sister province, Austria's action against Wallachia was somewhat less insidious. But we must recall that in view of her compulsion to evacuate the Principalities, she clung still to the hope that some military measures might yet be employed to hold the unionists in check. Buol had thought at one time of proposing at the Conference at

---

[1] Liehmann to Buol, no. 3, Mar. 30, Staatsarchiv, XII/203.
[2] *Actes et docs.*, vol. iv, no. 913.   [3] *Ibid.*, no. 907.
[4] Thouvenel, *op. cit.*, p. 93.   [5] Liehmann to Buol, no. 3.
[6] Edhem to Safvet, Apr. 6, telg., Staatsarchiv, XII/203. It was Thouvenel who insisted that the commission be consulted, much to Prokesch's regret: Prokesch to Stratford, Apr. 9, Stratford Papers, F.O. 352/48. One can easily gather that Thouvenel did not intend that the Porte should intimidate the caimacam by leaving it entirely to him.
[7] Protocol, Apr. 13, *Actes et docs.*, vol. iv, no. 1037; Bulwer to Stratford, Apr. 14, F.O. 195/558.

Paris that the Turkish troops be authorized to stay in the Principalities until the definite reorganization, but, as France was likely
to dissent from such a proposal, the question was not raised.[1]
Then Buol, as we have seen, made the direct proposal to Turkey,
promising also to take up the question with other courts.[2] Without
coming to a decision the Porte simply took no immediate steps to
withdraw its forces, and Stratford urged Clarendon that, since
the national militia was insufficient to keep order, it might be well
for the Powers to concert with Turkey some plan of intervention,
should such a step prove necessary.[3] Buol remarked to Seymour
that at least a few Turkish troops could be 'left unnoticed in other
places, as well as in the Danubian Principalities'.[4] Harassed
continually by tales of agitation in Wallachia, and pressed re-
morselessly by Prokesch,[5] the Porte finally issued a circular (April 3)
to its representatives at the courts of London, Paris, and Vienna,[6]
declaring, in virtue of article xvii of the Treaty of Paris that it was
now urgent to concert measures of defence, 'in case the public
tranquillity should be troubled in Wallachia or Moldavia during
the exceptional phase which they are to traverse'.[7] Though
Prokesch expressed regret that the Porte had made a *request*,
instead of invoking the treaty as a *right*,[8] Buol was highly delighted
with the success of a manœuvre [9] which he had himself suggested
some time previously.[10] Now, he felt, was the time to put a ban
on the clubs ('we think', he said, 'that the most urgent measures
should be taken to put down political clubs in Bucharest'),[11] and
either the Porte should be authorized to intervene with arms, or,
at least, some step be taken with a view to that contingency.[12]
Unfortunately for Buol's zealous scheming, the circular met with
a chilly response from both the Western Powers. Walewski
expressed surprise, and quite refused to admit the least indications
of any danger; [13] while Clarendon warned the Porte that electoral

[1] Hübner to Buol, no. 4 D, Staatsarchiv, IX/54.
[2] Buol to Prokesch, Jan. 21, *ibid.*, XII/61.
[3] Stratford to Clarendon, no. 150, Feb. 16, F.O. 78/1256.
[4] Seymour to Clarendon, no. 222, Mar. 4, F.O.7/513. According to Apponyi (Mar. 28, Staatsarchiv, XVIII/47), Clarendon raised no personal objection, though he felt that it was legally inadmissible, and suggested that the Turks might perhaps take a position on the frontier. Perhaps his indifference was an encouragement to Buol.
[5] Prokesch's fiery temper must sometimes have got the better of him, for once we find Reshid complaining of his 'insulting and disparaging language': Revalsky to Stratford, Feb. 18, Stratford Papers, F.O. 352/45.
[6] It is curious that the Porte, though basing its action on the Treaty of Paris, addressed only the Powers who had signed the defensive alliance of April 1856. Through inadvertence, however, a copy was sent to Berlin, and the Russian minister was consequently offended by what was apparently a snub to his court: Prokesch to Buol, no. 23 A–D, Apr. 22, Staatsarchiv, XII/59.
[7] Prokesch to Buol, no. 21 B, Apr. 15, annex, *ibid.*   [8] Prokesch to Buol, no. 21 B.
[9] Buol to Prokesch, Apr. 18, *ibid.*, XII/61. [10] Buol to Prokesch, Mar. 21, no. 3, *ibid.*
[11] Buol to Prokesch, Apr. 18.   [12] Buol to Prokesch, Apr. 25, Staatsarchiv, XII/61.
[13] Walewski to Thouvenel, May 1, *Actes et docs.*, vol. iv, no. 1121.

agitation was not the kind of disorder that would warrant intervention—for which, of course (he added), the assent of the Powers was necessary.[1] Foiled of its hopes of keeping its garrisons in Wallachia, or of using them for purposes of coercion, the Porte fell back on Stratford's ready suggestion that the Turkish troops should withdraw to strong positions across the river.[2] For Austro-Turkish policy, it was a rather feeble retreat; for Turks, as well as Austrians, had now ceased to do police duty, and Wallachia was free of every foreign soldier. Meanwhile any idea of a collective menace of intervention by the Powers had happily died stillborn.

While the Austrians and the Turks were fretting over the clubs the chief immediate difficulty was the execution of the firman. Although its authors had made an admirable use of the little knowledge they had of Moldo-Wallachian society, the various arrangements for determining electors and their different classifications were not, perhaps, as comprehensive as they might have been. Since some of the restrictions and exceptions in the process of constituting the colleges had elicited much criticism, Ghika felt, or pretended to feel, that on certain specifications he was in need of further light. Should all priests be given electoral rights, or only those who formed the highest grade in the Orthodox hierarchy? How were the various categories of proprietors to be determined in a country where no reliable statistics were to be had? Was the holder of mortgaged property entitled to vote? Should the requirement that lawyers must possess diplomas in order to be eligible be literally enforced in the face of the fact that only five or six persons held them. And so on.[3] It is not improbable that the caimacam sometimes allowed his personal opinion to creep into the statement of his difficulties, and he was accused by the Austrian commissioner of striving to narrow the group of greater *boyards*, from whom he was known to be estranged;[4] but it would take an intimate knowledge of Wallachian civil law and traditions to penetrate the various complications which he unearthed.

The caimacam submitted his 'doubts' to the commission, which decided that they lacked the authority to pass judgement on them, and that hence they must be referred to Constantinople.[5] Bulwer, who looked with disfavour on the ambassadors and all their acts, lamented that the commission had not been taken into their confidence,[6] but the return of the unwieldy document to its authors may well have afforded Sir Henry a certain vindictive pleasure.

[1] Clarendon to Cowley, no. 664, May 1, F.O. 27/1177.
[2] Stratford to Clarendon, no. 334, Apr. 13, F.O. 78/1260. See above, p. 93, note 4.
[3] Bulwer to Clarendon, no. 35, Apr. 27, enc., F.O. 78/1279.
[4] Liehmann to Buol, no. 29, June 24, Staatsarchiv, XII/203.
[5] Liehmann to Buol, no. 8, Apr. 16, *ibid.*
[6] Bulwer to Clarendon, no. 11, Mar. 9, F.O. 78/1279.

Thouvenel, for his part, expressed the belief that the commission was quite competent to deal with matters of detail, and greatly regretted the delay which would necessarily ensue in submitting the question to the Porte and the ambassadors.[1] Such misgivings were justified, for any dispatch of business by the Porte was ever a slow affair; and meanwhile, as far as Wallachia was concerned, preparations for the elections were necessarily suspended. The full effect of this postponement could hardly have been perceived by even this keen-witted diplomat.

While the suspension of the firman necessarily interrupted the work of the commission, it was not long before its attention was summarily aroused by the news of what was happening in Moldavia. After some weeks of hesitation, Vogorides made it evident that he was quite prepared to follow in the footsteps of his predecessor. A man of small education and very limited intelligence, he had owed his prominence partly to his adoption by a wealthy and distinguished *boyard*, and partly to his marriage with the richest heiress in Moldavia. We have already alluded to his moral limitations. Supple rather than strong, and solicitous only of his own interests, 'Nicholas Vogorides might be compared', wrote one of his compatriots, 'to one of those young pashas, emerging from the swaddling clothes of the harem.'[2] Since, in fact, his father was a prominent Turkish dignitary, his brother a secretary to the embassy in London, and a Greek brother-in-law, Photiades, the Moldavian kapou kiaya at Constantinople, one may readily agree that 'the Phanariot régime seemed to have returned'.[3] Certainly the opportunity for Turkish intrigue in the Principalities could hardly have been better; and from the outset of his administration the Porte regarded Vogorides as the instrument by which the Moldavian divan should be packed to the detriment of union. True, the firman of installation had instructed the new caimacam to 'act with entire justice and equity';[4] but the attitude of the Turks can seldom be read in a public document, and Photiades, who had come to Jassy with the firman, was so indiscreet as to tell Place that 'the Porte would not have union at any price, and that the man she had named as caimacam would fail in his duty if he did not work to prevent it'.[5] No wonder Place suspected that instructions of this character had been secretly imparted;[6] and, as time went on, it became evident that Photiades himself was the private channel through which the Porte encouraged the caimacam, whom Austria was busily coaching. 'Follow her blindly,' was the substance of a letter from the brother in London, 'for, if union is

---

[1] Thouvenel to Walewski, Apr. 13, *Actes et docs.*, iv, no. 1040.
[2] Soutzo, *op. cit.*, p. 344.   [3] Xénopol, *op. cit.*, vol. ii, p. 562.
[4] *Actes et docs.*, vol. iv, no. 915.   [5] Thouvenel, *op. cit.*, p. 87.   [6] Page 90.

voted, Austria will hold you to account.'[1] 'Take 12,000 ducats from the Moldavian treasury' was the meaning of some advice which Vogorides, *père*, imparted from Constantinople. 'The English ambassador is beginning to have a good opinion of you', the father assured his son;[2] while a personal letter from the internuncio promised support from another quarter.[3] Also from London came the assurance that Palmerston was 'tout-à-fait contraire à l'union', and the caimacam must prove worthy of his support.[4] With so much appeal to fear and cupidity, and so strong an indication of backing from the Porte and its two allies, it is hardly to be wondered that a man like Vogorides should have succumbed. When some time later all these letters fell into the hands of the French consulate[5] the whole sordid story came to light.

With so excellent a machinery of intrigue in operation the position of the Austrian consul was more impregnable than ever. Place, on the other hand, had very soon discovered what the professions of his chosen candidate had been worth. When he urged a change of ministers (in order to get rid of Balsche's questionable staff), he was told that the Porte wanted as few changes as possible. Place then became exasperated, and according to Gödel's story assumed a threatening tone. He warned Photiades of the intense feeling of the unionists, and hinted that he, their leader, would no longer hold them in check.[6] But a veiled threat of revolution proved altogether futile. 'M. Photiades', wrote Place, 'did not leave me unaware that he brought M. Vogorides the formal order to keep the ministry of M. Balsche, and to employ the same means to fight union.' A programme was thus arranged ere Photiades departed. One of the former ministers, Costin Catargi (whom Austria had wanted for the caimacamie), was transferred to the ministry of the interior on the understanding that he would take the full responsibility of seeing that the coming elections were unfavourable to union.[7]

We have already noticed that the unionists in Moldavia had looked with some disquiet upon the choice of the new caimacam.[8] How long would he observe this 'benevolent neutrality'? Taking advantage of the brief interval before the new caimacam had inaugurated his policy, the 'Unionist Electoral Committee', as

[1] *Actes et docs.*, no. 1047. [2] *Ibid.*, no. 1090.
[3] *Ibid.*, no. 1056. [4] *Ibid.*, no. 1042.
[5] According to the story which Stratford heard, Vogorides's sister, who had access to the caimacam's room, was persuaded by Place (possibly with liberal offers of unionist money) to purloin such papers, if they were to be found. As the caimacam was very careless, the papers were easily discovered and secured: Stratford to Clarendon, no. 888, Oct. 14, F.O. 78/1272.
[6] Gödel to Buol, no. 21, Mar. 19, Staatsarchiv, xxxviii/108.
[7] Place to Walewski, Mar. 25, *Actes et docs.*, vol. iv, no. 943. [8] Page 90.

the central club was called, had formulated its platform, which included union under a foreign prince, respect for autonomous rights, the abolition of extraterritoriality (all of this under the collective guarantee of the Powers!), and only vaguely hinted at a connexion with the Porte.[1] If the gauntlet was thus thrown down, the government eagerly picked it up. Denied the liberty of the press, the party of union had hoped to sustain their movement by means of public meetings; but no indulgence whatever was to be expected from Catargi, and it was announced that all such clubs were to be suspended. Satisfied that he had found the man who could not flinch at anything, Vogorides practically turned over the whole administration to his subordinate. And Catargi responded in every way to expectations. He exacted pledges from all officials to fight union, employed the prefects to enforce his measures, and already began making up lists of eligible electors in accordance with their attitude towards union.[2] Some unionist agitators were even thrown into prison, and, when Place demanded to know the reason, Vogorides sheltered himself behind the excuse that these were acts of internal administration—an inference that all this was none of Place's business.[3] The appeal to Moldavian autonomy was not the less amusing because, in all probability, the response had been drawn up with the aid of the Austrian consul. Helpless to combat such measures, the unionists drew up an appeal to the commission, demanding that freedom of press and association be restored, and 'that all direct or indirect action of the government on the elections and on the voting of the divans be prevented'. 'We no longer have any hope [so ran the petition] save in the intervention of the high international commission, which, alone, can still at the last moment save us from the danger with which we see ourselves threatened.'[4]

Thus the commission, which had not yet disposed of difficulties in Wallachia, was called upon to deal with a more serious question. At a meeting, which had been called for a minor purpose, Talleyrand, Benzi, and Richthofen (the Prussian commissioner) called attention to the deplorable conditions in Moldavia, and, backed by documentary evidence, requested Safvet to enforce in Moldavia, as in Wallachia, the impartial execution of the firman. The Turkish commissioner (and Bulwer as well) pleaded ignorance of these stories, while Liehmann wisely met the charges in silence. When, however, a deputation arrived next day with the unionist petition, Safvet declared that the intelligence 'pierced his heart', and that, in spite of ill health, he would betake himself to Jassy.[5] Probably because

[1] *Actes et docs.*, vol. iv, no. 923.
[2] Place to Walewski, Mar. 31, *ibid.*, no. 965; cf. Gödel to Buol, no. 27, Apr. 5, Staatsarchiv, xxxviii/108. [3] See *Actes et docs.*, vol. iv, nos. 983, 990, and 991.
[4] *Ibid.*, no. 962. [5] Talleyrand to Walewski, Apr. 14, *ibid.*, no. 1043.

they did not wholly trust him most of the commissioners followed
his example, though Bulwer, who seemed to glory in a policy of
detachment, preferred to stay behind, while an inexperienced agent
served him with roseate reports on the character of the new
caimacam.[1] The visit of the commissioners soon convinced those
who wished to be convinced that the reports were not exaggerated.
Talleyrand had a taste of the government's attitude when he
found that all telegrams announcing his arrival were intercepted—
a step which, nevertheless, did not prevent his being received at
different places with shouts of 'Vive l'Empereur! Vive la France!
Vive l'Union!'[2] No doubt the unionists had readily seen the value
of such ovations, and, if we are to believe the jealous pen of
Liehmann, the French commissioner made a point of meeting
as many people as possible in the towns *en route* to the capital,
went out of his way to flatter the army and stir up the clergy, and
allowed his house in Jassy to become the rendezvous of all partisans
of union.[3] Yet one need not really question the spontaneity of his
welcome; and, according to Place, Benzi likewise received a cordial
reception, while that accorded to Safvet and Liehmann was
correspondingly cold[4]—though the latter had, at least, the satisfaction of tendering his encouragement to the caimacam. No
doubt both sides doffed restraint for the moment. Place considered it unfortunate that the unionist colours, 'which were not yet
legally those of the state', were so conspicuously displayed;[5] but
such an act, if rather imprudent, was at least perfectly natural
to a people whose demonstrations were more childlike than
belligerent. More impressive to Talleyrand was the steadfast
attitude which he found among large numbers of the clergy;[6]
and it was this fact, doubtless, which induced Vogorides to accuse
the metropolitan of conniving at an alleged demonstration on the
part of his flock—a charge which that prelate indignantly denied.[7]
Even Liehmann acknowledged that for the first time the clergy
had come out openly for union—a fact which he attributed to
Russian influence.[8]

The visit of the commission was not wholly barren of results;
for even Safvet was persuaded that Catargi must be sacrificed.
There was never any scruple among the Turks against picking
out a scapegoat, and Safvet, who was by nature more subtle in his

[1] Bulwer to Clarendon, no. 59, May 23, F.O. 78/1280.
[2] Thouvenel, *op. cit.*, p. 96.
[3] Liehmann to Buol, no. 13, Apr. 30, Staatsarchiv, XII/203.
[4] Liehmann wrote, however, that he received a hearty demonstration from the
separatists: Liehmann to Buol, no. 10, Apr. 22, Staatsarchiv, XII/203.
[5] Place to Walewski, Apr. 22, *Actes et docs.*, vol. iv, no. 1076.
[6] Talleyrand to Walewski, Apr. 23, *ibid.*, no. 1084.
[7] *Ibid.*, nos. 1085 and 1095.
[8] Liehmann to Buol, no. 11, Apr. 27, Staatsarchiv, XII/203.

methods, was perhaps satisfied that a quieter, though no less dangerous man, was chosen in his place.[1] There was in fact no change in policy. Gödel saw to it that the electoral lists, soon to be drawn up by the new minister of the interior, should be submitted to his inspection, 'and I will personally see to it', he wrote to Buol, 'that every name is removed that is not fully justified according to the firman'.[2] Since he had earlier stated that 'the elections should be conducted in an anti-unionist sense',[3] we need have no doubt whatever as to his meaning.

Considering the partisan activities of the French and Austrian consuls and the suspected collusion of Vogorides and the Porte, the position of the commission, especially now that it was divided against itself, was, to say the least, unenviable. Bulwer, who felt that his cautious, neutral attitude would give him a strategic advantage which he feared to lose if he should back the enemies of union,[4] had refused, on the other hand, to give any opinion on the case of Catargi,[5] and evidently shrank from accepting the charges against Vogorides, which he told Stratford he had no chance to investigate.[6] But the time was rapidly approaching when such an ostrich-like attitude would be very hard to maintain. Thouvenel, who knew only too well the source of the difficulties, wrote to Walewski that what was needed was constant pressure upon the Porte, and for that purpose an understanding must be reached between the French and British governments.[7] On the question of concerting a plan of military interference the two governments were, as we have noticed, in perfect accord; but French complaints to Cowley that Vogorides was falsifying the plebiscite left Clarendon indifferent; his conduct was natural, he contended, and due to the attempts which had been made to carry union.[8] It was doubtless unfortunate for the Emperor's policy that his ambassador to London, Count Persigny, was known to be out of sympathy with his sovereign's views.[9] Persigny argued at length to Walewski that the advocacy of union not only compromised the future of the Ottoman Empire but (what was more serious in his eyes) was

---

[1] Talleyrand wrote that he himself had forced Catargi's retirement by threatening to leave Jassy at once: Talleyrand to Walewski, *Actes et docs.*, vol. iv, no. 1134.
[2] Gödel to Buol, no. 44, May 20, Staatsarchiv, xxxviii/108.
[3] Gödel to Buol, no. 24, Mar. 26, *ibid.*
[4] Bulwer to Clarendon, no. 28, Apr. 11, F.O. 78/1279.
[5] Bulwer to Clarendon, no. 45, May 7, F.O. 78/1280.
[6] Bulwer to Stratford, no. 9, Apr. 10, F.O. 195/558.
[7] Thouvenel to Walewski, May 11, *Actes et docs.*, vol. iv, no. 1158.
[8] Cowley to Clarendon, no. 636, Apr. 23 and Clarendon's note thereon, F.O. 27/1195.
[9] Ollivier, *L'Empire libérale*, vol. iii, p. 411. Apparently his recall had been once thought of, but Napoleon had decided not to risk the impression it would create in England: Thouvenel, *Trois années*, p. 64.

a danger to the Anglo-French alliance.[1] It is hardly to be supposed that the British ministers were unaware of Persigny's views, and nothing, certainly, deterred them from telling Austria and Turkey that Great Britain was herself opposed to union.[2] In the face of the rising storm, the French government bade its agents urge the unionists to drop the idea of a foreign prince,[3] and, while an assurance to that effect was given to Vienna,[4] Walewski suggested to Hübner that he might even go further, if only Austria would acknowledge the principle of union. Under these circumstances it was no great wonder that Napoleon was suspected of simply fleeing to escape a diplomatic defeat.[5] But such overtures were hardly more than a gesture—probably with a view of moderating Austria's zeal—and, though Buol took them seriously,[6] there is no evidence to show that he relaxed his policy in the least. When later, Bourqueney, inspired by Austria, suggested some looser definition of union than his government had contemplated,[7] one may feel that Walewski's manœuvres had had a rather sorry result.

Unhappily the hitch in executing the firman allowed the situation to become aggravated. After considerable delay (which even Bulwer considered grave) the Turkish ministers and the embassies agreed—after much hesitation on Stratford's part—that the doubt-

---

[1] Persigny to Walewski, no. 13, Feb. 18 and no. 29, Apr. 13, *Aff. étr., Angleterre*, vol. 707.

[2] Clarendon to Stratford, no. 315, Apr. 14, F.O. 78/1246, &c. Clarendon affirmed that he considered union 'would be a first step towards the independence of the Principalities and, consequently, towards a dismemberment of the Ottoman Empire'.

[3] Walewski to Talleyrand, Apr. 18 and to Thouvenel, Apr. 25, *Actes et docs.*, vol. iv, nos. 1059 and 1091.

[4] Walewski to Bourqueney, no. 59, May 27, *Aff. étr., Autriche*, vol. 467. Bourqueney had hinted the advisability of giving up the idea of a foreign prince on the ground that France, who was now confronting Palmerston again, might find herself isolated in Europe, as had been the case in 1840 (Bourqueney to Walewski, no. 76, Apr. 29, *ibid.*). One might feel, indeed, that a sudden panic was afflicting the French diplomats.

[5] Hübner quoted Cowley as believing that the Emperor, fearing another 'Bolgrad', was now ready to be content with only 'the word, union', and would on that ground agree to 'any sort of transaction': Hübner to Buol, no. 42 B, May 13, Staatsarchiv, IX/54.

[6] Seymour to Clarendon, no. 512, May 12, F.O. 7/516 and no. 533, May 19, F.O. 7/517. Mr. East (*op. cit.*, pp. 77–8) seems to think that France was genuinely wavering on the question of union; and it is, of course, true that Napoleon later seemed to care more for an ostensible victory on this question than one that was really solid. But I doubt if one should go further than charge Walewski with momentary timidity. The idea of a foreign prince had always been kept in the background, and an examination of the 'overture' will show that Walewski did not yield anything definite on the question of union. When Buol suggested a plan (as we shall notice later) of a non-political union, Walewski would have none of it—possibly because the Emperor had seen the mistake of all such floundering. My own feeling is that Walewski's conciliatory efforts were nothing but a rather stupid ruse, prompted largely by the fear that a controversy (on the merits of which he had some doubts) was beyond his capacity. See below, p. 110.

[7] Bourqueney to Walewski, no. 91, May 31, *Aff. étr., Autriche*, vol. 467.

ful points in the firman should be referred back to the commission
to interpret. At last the commission—whenever it should receive
the formal notice—would have something definite to do.[1] But the
question then arose: should the caimacam of Moldavia be asked
to wait until the commission had settled this complication, in
order that the firman should be applied in the same manner
in each principality? Bulwer had considered that such would be
the logical procedure,[2] and the commissioners, favourable to
union, were eager to grasp the occasion for putting a rein on
Vogorides. As at any moment the vicious staff at Jassy might
begin the choice of electors, there was no time to be lost. Accordingly, since Bulwer refused their request to come to Moldavia
and join a concerted movement (on the ground that the commission
had no authority to interfere),[3] Talleyrand, Benzi, and Richthofen
took the step themselves of urging it upon the caimacam to wait
until an answer had been received to Ghika's questions. Vogorides
simply replied that the difficulties suggested by Ghika did not
exist in Moldavia. The three commissioners then tried to get
Safvet to order the caimacam to halt proceedings, but again met
with a rebuff.[4] Quick to take advantage of a victory which might
not be decisive, the sedulous Gödel urged the caimacam to act
that very evening; 'stand by your authority,' he wrote, 'and lose
not a moment'.[5] Vogorides no longer hesitated. Instructions were
sent to the prefects to draw up lists of eligible electors and were
simultaneously published in the official journal,[6] while Liehmann
at once telegraphed to Prokesch, urging him to prevent these
orders from being suspended, else the caimacam would be 'sacrificed'.[7] Almost immediately Prokesch telegraphed in reply that
the Porte considered that the Wallachian 'doubts' were not
applicable to Moldavia[8]—a decision which, of course, may be
ascribed to Prokesch and Stratford. The internuncio wrote to his
chief that Talleyrand and company had clearly acted beyond their
competence; 'there is no word in the instructions [to the com-
mission] to meddle with the electoral preparations'.[9]

[1] Thouvenel to Walewski, Apr. 27, *Actes et docs.*, vol. iv, no. 1103.
[2] Bulwer to Stratford, no. 17, May 21, F.O. 78/1280.
[3] Bulwer to Clarendon, no. 56, May 22, encs., *ibid.*
[4] Safvet replied that the only points raised by Ghika which might be applicable
to Moldavia had been settled by the Porte in response to an inquiry from Vogorides (Safvet to Talleyrand, May 4, Staatsarchiv, XII/203). It is quite true that
Vogorides had questioned the Porte, and that the answer had seemingly left the
matter to his own interpretation (Stratford to Clarendon, no. 310, Apr. 6, encs.,
F.O. 78/1260), but the Porte had no authority, by itself, to interpret the meaning
of the firman, since it was the work of collaboration, and responsibility was
collective.　　　　[5] Gödel to Vogorides, May 4, *Actes et docs.*, vol. iv, no. 1128.
[6] Liehmann to Buol, no. 15, May 5, Staatsarchiv, XII/203.
[7] Liehmann to Prokesch, May 6, telg., *ibid.*, XII/59.
[8] Prokesch to Gödel, May 8, *ibid.*
[9] Prokesch to Buol, no. 28 A–B, May 13, *ibid.*

On the basis of their prerogatives it is more than doubtful if the intervention of the three commissioners had been legally justifiable, for the commission itself had no authority to supervise the execution of the firman, and, even if it had had such authority, the performance of these three was the action of a minority of that body. But it may fairly be presumed that Talleyrand and his friends had seen enough to realize that, if the lists were made up now, they would certainly be composed in such a way as to prevent the real sentiments of Moldavia from being expressed; and the fact that Vogorides was just about to take the decisive step was no doubt the reason for not referring the question to Constantinople, where authority really resided.[1] One can only be impressed with the shortsightedness of the Congress of Paris, which had condemned the commission to be passive spectators of abuses it could not prevent. The execution of the firman was, indeed, no longer an affair of international concern, attesting to the good faith of the Powers who had sponsored it. On the contrary, the Protecting Powers were hopelessly divided, and the result of the elections had become solely a national interest, in which each Power was playing its own hand, regardless of all collective responsibility. Stratford himself had foreseen the rift, and as far back as March had suggested to Prokesch that an understanding should be reached between his government, Austria, and the Porte, on the ground that union was likely to be voted by the divans and that the others Powers could be expected to support such a decision.[2] One is impressed with the fact that it was these agents of the Powers who were chiefly responsible for the widening of the rift. 'It is certain', wrote Prokesch to Buol, 'that, in states like the Principalities, and in face of adversaries without scruples,[3] any means should appear good to us, and they will be so, if they are employed promptly and liberally. We should, then, fear no sacrifice in order to assure ourselves on that score.'[4]

It was perfectly obvious that Austria and Turkey wanted the issue to be decided in Moldavia while proceedings in Wallachia were still held in abeyance. If the electoral lists were now prepared (under the zealous care of Gödel, we must remember), the whole business could be quickly expedited; any influences from Wallachia would be slight, since the clubs had been suspended; and the result would be a divan that would not approve of union. Once

---

[1] Apart from direct pressure upon Vogorides, Talleyrand did send a special messenger to Thouvenel to lay the situation before him and see what could be done: Talleyrand to Walewski, May 4, *Actes et docs.*, vol. iv, no. 1134.

[2] Prokesch to Buol, March 25, private, Staatsarchiv, XII/60.

[3] Prokesch held the view that Ghika's 'doubts' had been simply a unionist intrigue: Prokesch to Buol, no. 28 A–B, May 13, Staatsarchiv, XII/59.

[4] Prokesch to Buol, no. 21 A–E, Apr. 15, *ibid.*

the Moldavian divan had spoken, it would make no difference whatever what transpired in Wallachia. These Powers wanted, in short, to hurry up proceedings. It was correspondingly important to the Powers, who wished the Principalities to develop an overwhelming desire for union, and to be free to express that desire, that all official manipulation should be stopped without delay. Whether the commission's view of the firman would seriously affect the choice of electors in Moldavia may be doubted; but at least an enforced delay would call attention to the duty of administering the firman fairly, and also enable the preparations in the two provinces to march together. Since the commissioner of France had failed in his manœuvre, responsibility must now be shouldered by her embassy. Fully informed by Talleyrand of the present state of affairs,[1] and having obtained the concurrence of the Russian and Prussian ministers, Thouvenel, accordingly, demanded of Reshid on May 12 that Vogorides be requested to suspend his preparations till the answer of the commission to Ghika's points had been announced, and that Safvet, who with Liehmann, was still lingering in Moldavia, and whose absence from Bucharest was naturally holding up the commission's decision, be requested to return without delay. The grand vizier, after vainly pleading Vogorides's excuses, asked time for reflection— a ruse which usually meant a refusal, if properly supported. Two days later Reshid sent word to the French ambassador that he must consult Prokesch and Stratford on the matter;[2] and, while he was conjuring in his mind the notion of demanding the degradation of Vogorides and his ministers,[3] Thouvenel learned that both Prokesch and Stratford were opposed to the extension of the commission's rulings to Moldavia, and that the Turkish council had acquiesced in this view.[4] The only satisfaction accorded to Thouvenel was that Safvet, who was awaited impatiently at Bucharest,[5] should be ordered to return.[6]

But Thouvenel was not yet prepared to acknowledge defeat on the main issue. On May 20 he besieged Reshid again, and insisted either that a conference be held of the Turkish ministers and the ambassadors or that the question of Vogorides's course be referred to the commission. Although both Prokesch and Stratford were

---

[1] On information from Talleyrand, Thouvenel had just warned the Porte against agreeing to the destitution of the metropolitan, demanded by Vogorides: *Actes et docs.*, vol. iv, no. 1156.

[2] Thouvenel to Walewski, May 14, *Actes et docs.*, vol. iv, no. 1169.

[3] Thouvenel to Walewski, May 18, *ibid.*, no. 1179.

[4] Outrey to Thouvenel, May 19, *ibid.*, no. 1183; cf. Prokesch to Buol, no. 31 A–B, Staatsarchiv, XII/59.

[5] Talleyrand to Walewski, May 15, *ibid.*, no. 1171.

[6] Outrey to Talleyrand, May 19, *ibid.*, no. 1183.

averse from holding a meeting[1] (Stratford arguing oddly that the
Sultan had complete authority over the execution of the firman),
they gave way at length;[2] and a conference (which Stratford
expected to be 'tempestuous') took place on May 30. According
to the accounts we have from the pens of the French and British
ambassadors, Stratford and Prokesch again opposed the idea of
intervention on the part of the commission in the work of Vogorides, while Thouvenel, supported by the three other ministers,
insisted that the firman should operate identically in both principalities.[3] After much 'tempestuous' discussion it was decided
that a dispatch should be sent to Safvet instructing him to the
effect that the commission's solution of the pending questions in
dispute should be communicated to Vogorides 'to the end that they
should be applied as exactly as possible save for exceptional cases
that might be peculiar to Moldavia'.[4] While at first sight the
result might seem a triumph for the unionists there was, of course,
nothing in the decision to prevent Vogorides himself from being
the judge of what was applicable to Moldavia. The mistake was
made of not specifically allowing the commission to review his
interpretations. Nevertheless, the suspension of preparations in
Moldavia was clearly a point gained; and the Conference had
obviously gone much further than implied by Stratford's statement
to Clarendon that the 'Ottoman commissioner should be directed . . .
to convey to Prince Vogorides the terms in which it is hoped the
doubts, entertained at Bucharest, are by this time solved'.[5] Of
course, the enclosure of the actual order to Safvet enabled Clarendon to see the case precisely as it stood—and Clarendon himself
seems to have approved the Conference's decision[6]—but one
wonders a little that Stratford had not represented the matter in
its true and proper light.

[1] Thouvenel to Walewski, May 21, *Actes et docs.*, vol. iv, no. 1193; Prokesch
to Buol, no. 30 A–B, May 20, Staatsarchiv, XII/59. Thouvenel wrote that Reshid
had at first yielded to their veto.

[2] Stratford to Clarendon, no. 447, May 22, F.O. 78/1262. According to
Thouvenel, Stratford and Prokesch had even questioned the validity of the
agreement to refer Ghika's queries to the Commission: Thouvenel to Walewski,
May 25, *Actes et docs.*, vol. iv, no. 1204. Stratford makes no mention of this in
his letters.

[3] Stratford to Clarendon, no. 473, May 30, F.O. 78/1263; Thouvenel to
Walewski, June 1, *Actes et docs.*, vol. iv, no. 1238.

[4] Thouvenel to Walewski, June 1, *ibid.*, no. 1238; The Porte to Safvet, May 31,
ibid., no. 1232.

[5] Stratford to Clarendon, no. 473.

[6] Writing later of the proposed contention on the part of a majority in the
commission that a divan, elected under Vogorides's influence, should be regarded as illegal, Clarendon stated to Apponyi that he 'thought the best way of
defeating it would be to place the Principalities as far as possible on the same
footing with regard to the electoral lists': Clarendon to Seymour, no. 438,
June 30, F.O. 7/505; cf. Apponyi to Buol, no. 45 A–C, June 30, Staatsarchiv,
VIII/47.

But it is not improbable that Stratford, determined as he was to contest every inch of the ground with the friends of union, was anxious to discourage his government from interference. He had sent no telegram to the Foreign Office on the subject, and had made no proposal to enlarge the competence of the commission. More than that, he had really taken no pains to acquaint himself with occurrences in Moldavia. To Thouvenel he admitted that he knew nothing of the scandals which the French ambassador had aired before the meeting of May 30;[1] and Thouvenel considered that such ignorance was 'extraordinary'.[2] The fact of the matter is, Stratford did not care whether Vogorides was manipulating the elections. As far back as March, in submitting his own plan for the reorganization of the Principalities, he had declared that, while the unionists seemed to have the advantage, 'the Porte, even at the eleventh hour, if ably seconded by the local authorities, may exercise a preponderating influence'.[3] Thus it is not improbable that Stratford, knowing full well what this 'seconding' by 'local authorities' would mean, preferred that matters should take their course. The only fear, of course, was that Thouvenel would eventually get his government to take some means of scaring the Turks into good behaviour. 'His fear of France', wrote Stratford of the grand vizier, 'is quite puerile. It is only by acting like a bully that I can at all keep him up to the mark.'[4]

What should really be the 'mark' was, of course, the debatable question. Stratford's opinion (in which Bulwer seemed to concur)[5] that Vogorides was not bound to respect difficulties which Ghika alone had raised[6] was plausible enough, as far as it went, but, now that the commission had been given the right to settle the difficulties in Wallachia, the French view that it should supervise the general application of the firman[7] possessed a certain amount of logic. Broader, however, than these rather technical points was the moral necessity of seeing fair elections in the Principalities, and here one finds the fundamental question which divided Austria, Turkey, and Great Britain, on the one hand, and France, Sardinia, Russia, and Prussia, on the other, into two opposing camps. The former Powers, not wanting union, were unwilling to risk the

[1] Stratford to Clarendon, no. 473. 'I have no advice from any official correspondent of mine', wrote Stratford, 'to warrant a suspicion of his [Vogorides's] acting with unfairness in preparing the electoral lists.'
[2] Thouvenel to Walewski, June 8, *Actes et docs.*, vol. iv, no. 1258.
[3] Stratford to Clarendon, no. 268, enc.
[4] Stratford to Clarendon, May 25, Stratford Papers, F.O. 352/48. We may compare this remark with Prokesch's: that the Porte 'has always the air of imploring from the friend who counsels it a charitable regard for its feebleness': Prokesch to Buol, no. 24B, Apr. 24, Staatsarchiv, XII/59.
[5] Bulwer to Stratford, no. 24, May 26, F.O. 78/1280.
[6] Stratford to Thouvenel, May 17, Stratford Papers, F.O. 352/46.
[7] Walewski to Talleyrand, May 27, *Actes et docs.*, vol. iv, no. 1214.

moral evidence of an honest plebiscite, while France and her allies, committed to the cause of union, and holding firmly to that right of free election, which had been accorded by the Treaty of Paris, were ready to pounce on every evidence of Turkish duplicity, and to hold the Porte strictly responsible for the conduct of its tool. And there was clearly ground for intervention. Apart from all the evidence which the French diplomats accumulated even Bulwer admitted: 'There is too evident a desire to obtain a majority by any means.'[1] The warning should have been heeded. As a matter of fact, if this statement, sent to Clarendon, had been telegraphed to Stratford[2] it might have reached him before the meeting of May 30, when his ignorance was so amazing. But regardless of what might have been its possible effect (and one must feel a trifle dubious about that) it is evident that the entire want of sympathy between ambassador and commissioner may partly explain why the British government, which leaned chiefly on Stratford's counsels, was not more adequately informed of conditions in Moldavia. Yet that ignorance was undoubtedly gratuitous. The government at London could have taken pains to learn the truth if it cared to; that it did not do so can reasonably be ascribed to its enmity towards union, its willingness to see that movement quashed 'by any means'. 'No one doubts any longer', wrote Talleyrand, 'that England is to-day systematically hostile to the programme of the unionists.'[3]

Much more serious, however, than the more or less negative opposition of Great Britain to the execution of the treaty was the policy of intrigue and obstruction which Turkey, with the connivance of Vienna, was pursuing. The Porte's message to its commissioner, acquainting him with the decision to confer authority upon the commission to answer Ghika's questions, was dated May 1; yet the only intimation of this decision had been received by the other members through the ordinary diplomatic channels, and, manifestly, the commission could not act without formal authorization. Moreover, it was not till after the meeting of May 30 that Safvet had—by order from Constantinople—rejoined his colleagues in Bucharest. When the sessions of the commission were resumed on June 2, the Turkish commissioner produced a copy of his instructions of May 31:

'As the Sublime Porte hopes that at the present time the doubts raised in Wallachia have been settled by a confidential understanding between

---

[1] Bulwer to Clarendon, May 27, telg., F.O. 78/1280.
[2] Bulwer himself was never at his ease in writing to Stratford, and that is perhaps why he reserved for Clarendon his suspicions regarding proceedings in Moldavia. He also stuck to his contention that, even if there were abuses, the commission had no authority to correct them. See below, p. 119, note 2.
[3] Talleyrand to Walewski, June 12, *Actes et docs.*, vol. iv, no. 1282.

the caimacam and the commission, you are invited to bring the terms of this solution to the knowledge of the caimacam of Moldavia in order that the firman may be applied with as much exactness as possible, save for the exceptional cases which are peculiar to Moldavia.'

At once the commissioners ejaculated, 'How is it to be supposed that we have settled the difficulties of the firman in this province, when we have never yet heard that we had the power of doing so?' Basily, in particular, demanded to know what this earlier instruction might be, the existence of which was now clearly proved. Only then did Safvet bring out of his portfolio the communication of May 1:

'As the European Commission is in agreement on the subject of the explanation, requested as to certain points of the firman of convocation of the divans *ad hoc*, the Sublime Porte, in concert with the representatives of the contracting Powers, refers the matter to the Commission.'

Obviously the Turkish commissioner had some explanations to make. When asked why he had withheld the paper so long, he answered that he had shown it to Liehmann, who declared that it was not valid, as Prokesch had told him that it could not have been framed 'in concert', since he himself had not been informed of it.[1] In so far as no meeting had been called on the question, the allegation was, perhaps, technically correct; but since—if we are to believe Thouvenel—all the ambassadors had considered the matter, and had agreed upon the course of action to be taken,[2] one must come to the conclusion that Austria and Turkey were deliberately using this pretext for holding up the execution of the firman in Wallachia. As the keen-witted Talleyrand remarked to Bulwer, 'Everything has been done here to hold back the elections until those in Moldavia could be hurried on'.[3] A secret dispatch of Photiades on May 6, bidding Vogorides 'hasten as much as possible' the holding of the elections in Moldavia,[4] is probably all the evidence one needs to confirm this charge.

The Austro-Turkish programme thus becomes clear. Without waiting for the commission's rulings on the firman Vogorides was expected to proceed with his preparations, while those in Wallachia remained suspended. By dint of force and fraud the divan in Moldavia should be so constituted as to vote decisively against union. In such a case the results in Wallachia (which, if reached simultaneously, and if favourable to union, might have influenced the outcome in Moldavia) would obviously be nugatory. It now remains to be seen whether this programme would succeed.

---

[1] Bulwer to Clarendon, no. 83, June 18, F.O. 78/1280.
[2] Talleyrand to Walewski, Apr. 20, no. 1062 and Apr. 27, no. 1103, *Actes et docs.*, vol. iv.   [3] Bulwer to Clarendon, no. 83.
[4] *Actes et docs.*, vol. iv, no. 1138.

CHAPTER IV

THE CRISIS OF 1857

THE delay of more than a year in the holding of the plebiscite had produced so many oscillations, tergiversations, and cabals that it might seem to require more than an ordinary show of firmness to win the battle for Rouman nationalism. How much influence Napoleon III may have had on the course of French policy during these tangled months is not revealed in any evidence we have at hand. It is not easy to conceive that he was righteously indignant at a threatened miscarriage of justice or at the perversion of a treaty; but, having—with laudable intentions—committed French policy to a certain course of action, he probably held the view that a diplomatic defeat would mean a lowering of prestige for himself and for France.[1] Yet the 'explosion' in the *Moniteur*[2] and a penned note on one of Thouvenel's letters are the only traces of his personal intervention.[3] Though he meditated a visit to Queen Victoria,[4] he seems to have made no personal move to reach an understanding, albeit British policy was decisive at this juncture. Yet, withal, a man of such manifold interests may well have preferred to rely mainly on the discretion of his foreign minister, content that his views should be thoroughly understood, and that his general object should be steadily pursued. Walewski, for his part, had unfortunately none of the resourcefulness of a Cavour or the businesslike effrontery of a Palmerston. Had he been gifted with ordinary penetration, he would have realized that the Austro-Turkish manœuvres, unless decisively arrested, were certain to bring disaster to the cause of union, and that Great Britain's pose of neutrality was amounting to a benevolent neutrality towards the criminals. When Clarendon protested that the three commissioners, who sought to interfere with Vogorides, were exceeding their authority,[5] it was not enough for Walewski to justify their action; surely that was his opportunity for suggesting

[1] 'He is convinced', wrote Cowley, 'that the governments, which preceded him, fell because they neglected to uphold the dignity of France, and he is resolved to recover for her that position in the councils of Europe, which had been lost through the feebleness of others': Cowley to Clarendon, no. 753, May 11, 1857, printed in East, *op. cit.*, appx. iii, a.   [2] Page 85.
[3] This note read: 'Insist strongly on obtaining the aid of Reshid Pasha for union. Spare nothing to obtain this result': *Actes et docs.*, vol. iv, no. 977.
[4] The idea seems to have been prompted by Persigny, who had long been troubled over the state of Anglo-French relations, and Napoleon evidently seriously considered the plan (Martin, *op. cit.*, vol. iv, pp. 53–4), but, when its execution was postponed to suit British convenience, the Emperor made no further overtures for some time.
[5] Clarendon to Cowley, no. 775, May 19, F.O. 27/3178; Cowley to Clarendon, no. 826, May 27, F.O. 27/1197.

that the firman should be scrupulously observed, and that the commission's instructions could be amended in such a manner as to enforce its honourable execution. The whole difficulty lay in the fact that the way in which the authority of the commission had been defined left it singularly impotent to check abuses; and Bulwer, chafing as he did under the restrictions thus imposed, was nevertheless so anxious to preserve his 'balance of power' that he preferred to shelter himself behind a screen of academic rectitude instead of joining those members of the commission who chose to subserve the letter of their instructions to the spirit. It is obvious that, as formerly at the Congress of Paris, Great Britain was peculiarly able to tilt the scales in either direction. The fact that she was now conniving at the distortion of the plebiscite should have spurred Walewski to demand a *modus vivendi*. Thouvenel had insisted all along that what was needed was a workable understanding between the French and British governments.

Instead of seeking to come to terms with Clarendon, Walewski hàd made (as we have noticed)[1] some foolish advances to Buol. Such efforts at conciliation could only be misunderstood, and would probably be interpreted as an indication of weakness. In the mistaken belief that France was wavering on the principle of union, and that even Thouvenel despaired of its attainment,[2] Buol outlined a plan of his own, which should constitute the basis of the organization of the Principalities. Needless to say, the underlying principle of the scheme was separation (for Buol chose to assume that the unionists would lose their fight in Moldavia at least), but the Austrian was willing to make concessions to national feeling in the shape of 'assimilation in respect to administration and legislation' (whatever that might mean), 'a common defensive system, organized in conjunction with the Porte', and 'a customs union'.[3] The plan agreed in principle with Stratford's earlier scheme of 'uniformity without union'; and Clarendon signified his approval (as he had done in the case of Stratford's),[4] expressing the hope that these proposals would prove acceptable to France,[5] who, he believed, would now be willing to 'put a little water into her wine'.[6] The plan was duly submitted through Hübner to the French government, but Walewski carefully refrained from expressing an opinion.[7] Indeed, this cautious diplomat was already drawing back

[1] Page 100.
[2] Seymour to Clarendon, no. 533, May 25, F.O. 7/517. This information had come to Seymour rather than to Buol, but there is little doubt that Buol also received it. [3] Clarendon to Seymour, no. 577, June 9, F.O. 7/504.
[4] Clarendon to Stratford, no. 512, June 12, F.O. 78/1247.
[5] Clarendon to Seymour, no. 432, June 23, F.O. 7/504.
[6] Apponyi to Buol, no. 38 B, June 4, Staatsarchiv, VIII/47.
[7] Hübner to Buol, no. 48 B, June 5, *ibid.*, IX/54. According to his own account Walewski found Buol's scheme very indefinite.

from a flirtation, which, as he told Bourqueney, 'seemed to imply
the sacrifice of the principle of union'.[1] Elimination of a foreign
prince[2] did not mean, therefore, that Walewski was converted to
the idea of 'assimilation'. It is true that this 'diluted' form of
union, which was calculated, as Stratford put it, to 'save Europe
from a scratched face',[3] might prove in time the basis of a temporary
compromise; but not until the struggle had been carried to a
climax was France disposed to bend in her fidelity to union. Not
improbably the Emperor himself had stiffened the backs of his
faithful servants.

Meanwhile the tide of battle flowed still in the same direction in
Moldavia. It had been expected that the caimacam would wait for
the commission's decision on the disputed points in Wallachia, and
eventually draw up new instructions for the preparation of the
electoral lists, with due regard for the commission's rulings. In
evident consternation, the Austrian commissioner groaned that
'by this turn of affairs . . . his authority is broken, [and] the conservative party reduced to a critical condition'.[4] As a matter of
fact, nothing of the sort occurred. Vogorides had received no
formal communication beyond the fact that when he should
proceed to the execution of the firman, it was to be 'loyally
applied, according to its true spirit'.[5] One can hardly blame the
caimacam for not reading between the lines—or perhaps one
should say that he read exactly what the Porte intended him to
read.[6] Accordingly, while the ambassadors doubtless supposed
that the decision of May 30 had been executed, and the commission continued to wrangle over the extent of their 'moral authority',
Vogorides went merrily on with his task of padding and pruning
his lists to the end that the coming divan should reflect the views
desired by his superiors. Gödel wrote with evident glee of the
exclusion of some of the most zealous of the unionist leaders—
only regretting that some, like Cogalnitchano, seemed beyond
their legal reach—and declared that short shrift would be made

---

[1] Walewski to Bourqueney, no. 60, June 2, *Aff. étr., Autriche*, vol. 468.
[2] Walewski even went so far as to say that Austria had misunderstood his
attitude towards a foreign prince. While he was prepared to see only the question
of union considered by the Moldo-Wallachians themselves, 'it is the duty', he
said, 'of the governments to examine in what measure it may be convenient to
confide the administration of the Principalities to a foreign prince': *ibid.*
[3] Stratford to Bulwer, June 13, Stratford Papers, F.O. 352/48.
[4] Liehmann to Buol, no. 24, June 7, Staatsarchiv, XII/203.
[5] The Porte to Vogorides, May 31, *Actes et docs.*, vol. iv, no. 1231.
[6] As a matter of fact, Vogorides knew the nature of the decision of May 30 for
the commission had decided to send him a copy of the communication which the
Porte had addressed to it on May 31, and though some of its members had
objected to sending him a request to delay the elections, Safvet himself took the
liberty of making it known to Vogorides that the commission expected his lists
to be revised: Bulwer to Clarendon, no. 115, July 16, F.O. 78/1281.

of the rank and file, unless a sudden reaction should set in.[1] Once again we are impressed with the duplicity of the Porte, now covertly leaving the question to the 'discretion' of the caimacam. No injunction had been sent him to await the commission's findings; no command that he was to apply them 'save for exceptional cases that might be peculiar to Moldavia'.[2] Stratford—who may or may not have been privy to this intrigue—held the view that, even if the French did find evidence of irregularities, that was no reason for holding up the execution of the firman, as the commission's solution of the doubtful points was not mandatory for Moldavia.[3] Such, of course, was stultifying the purpose of the recent decision. Thus neither from Constantinople nor from Bucharest was any hindrance offered to the caimacam's machinations, and on June 11 he announced that the electoral lists had been completed.[4] By an amusing irony, on the following day, Safvet sent word to Vogorides that he 'would not fail to acquaint' him with the decision of the commission.[5] It is true that, in accordance with the firman, it would be necessary to wait thirty days before holding the elections, in order to give time for electoral claims to be considered. But now that the lists were prepared the first stage in the struggle was over.

The manipulations of the firman by Vogorides were probably but little exaggerated by his numerous enemies. The electoral lists, prepared in the first instance by 'instructed' prefects, had been subjected to a final examination at Jassy under the supervision of the Austrian consul. Every advantage had been taken of the absence of statistics and adequate land-registers and the various complications involved in property-holding to exclude thousands of eligible voters for the simple reason that they were known to be unionists. Not only was the existence of a small mortgage cited as reason for disqualifying certain property-holders (this was one of the points to be considered by the commission in relation to Wallachia), but members of the clergy and of the liberal professions were excluded on even flimsier grounds.

'The lists', wrote an eminent Roumanian author, '. . . constituted a veritable insult to the prescriptions of the Treaty of Paris, which ruled that the divans *ad hoc* should be the most faithful expression of the opinion of all classes of society. Of 2,000 great proprietors in Moldavia, they contained the names of only 350; of the 20,000 and more small proprietors, they had inscribed only 2,264. Among the electors of the

---

[1] Gödel to Buol, no. 48, June 12, Staatsarchiv, xxxviii/108.
[2] See page 104.
[3] Stratford to Clarendon, no. 564, June 26, F.O. 78/1265.
[4] Vogorides to the Porte, June 11, F.O. 195/561. This may, perhaps, be misdated, as Place on June 15 writes of the lists as 'just published': Place to Walewski, June 15, *Actes et docs.*, vol. iv, no. 1292.
[5] Safvet to Vogorides, June 12, *ibid.*, no. 1281.

cities one had found to register in the whole state of Moldavia only 11 persons who exercised the liberal professions. In all the lists were comprised [but] 4,658 electors of the upper classes instead of 40,000, which they should have contained. One made, it is true, a great parade of the 167,922 peasants inscribed; but these latter, seeing the manner in which they had to choose their delegates, signified absolutely nothing.'[1]

It was evident enough that, if these results were allowed to stand, the elections would result in a divan opposed to union. Many and great were the lamentations which arose from the outraged patriots. Petitions poured in to the central unionist club at Jassy from the various provincial clubs or from divers individuals testifying to the arbitrary conduct of prefects and police and to the wholesale exclusion of unionists from the lists. Even Pano, Mavrogheni, and other well-known leaders of the party were disqualified; and some cases were brought to the direct notice of the consuls, the metropolitan appealing naturally to Popoff, the Russian consul,[2] while others sought the sympathetic ear of Victor Place.[3] In some cases it was stated that the officials themselves shrank from performing the task assigned to them, and something of a stir was caused by the resignation of a certain Colonel Couza, prefect of Galatz,[4] who wrote his explanation to Vogorides, and requested Place to lay it before the European commission. Couza complained specifically of the stuffing of the electoral lists, of the dismissal of officials without adequate reason in order to be replaced by men 'incapable and dangerous', and of 'the system of terrorism, adopted generally', in his district.[5] The one source of relief in sight was presumed to be the commission. A petition, sent to that body, and bearing, it was said, thousands of signatures, declared in part that

'ever since the establishment of the caimacams they [the undersigned] had not ceased to protest against the illegality of their institution, against the powers that are ascribed to them, and also against the pressure, dictation, and partiality of which the provisional governments in Moldavia have been guilty. Our complaints of February 19, March 30, and May 4, 1857, addressed to the representatives of the Great Powers testify to it. . . . Not only the *exposé* of our legitimate complaints, supported by the most authentic, the most irrefutable proofs, have procured for us no change in the system of pressure and dictation which crushes us, but this system is still aggravated *sans relâche*, and to-day has come to a climax. The electoral lists, which the government has just published, are the evident proof and the crown of that work of repression and fraud, which has attained the proportions of a scandal.'

---

[1] Xénopol, *op. cit.*, vol. ii, p. 569. According to Place (from whose analysis these figures were taken) the peasants had been subjected to intimidation by the sub-prefects: *ibid.*, no. 1319.

[2] *Ibid.*, vol. v, no. 1415.

[3] *Constitutionel* (Paris), July 13.

[4] *Actes et docs.*, vol. v, no. 1436.

[5] *Ibid.*, nos. 1434 and 1435.

The address provided full particulars regarding the falsification of the lists, and made a point of the fact that, despite these provocations, 'the tranquillity and public order have not been disturbed a single instant'.[1] 'We hope for justice', declared another petition (sent to the central club);[2] while the poet Rossetti, addressing the commission, affirmed that 'ever since the inauguration of the present régime, we have never ceased in our complaints to call the attention of *Messieurs*, the commissioners of the Powers, that the caimacamie pursued only one end: that of annulling the benevolent dispositions of the Treaty of Paris'.[3] Of special importance was a protest from the metropolitan,[4] not only because his position added weight to his contentions, but because his appeal was bound to rouse the Russian commissioner to some action.

The commission was certainly not left unaware of electoral abuses, as petitions and complaints from the disqualified poured in; but conflicting interests, as ever, prevented its assuming a united front, and, while the members who favoured union were loud in their invectives against the caimacam, his apologists were equally ready to defend him. Bulwer essayed to play the role of umpire between the factions, but the narrowness of his instructions (and perhaps also a sense of his government's inveterate prejudices) completely blunted his power of initiative, while it inspired his pen to the point of weariness. Some action, at least, must be taken in regard to the petitions, which threatened more than once to disrupt the commission. After an unsuccessful effort on the part of the Austrian and Turkish members to prevent their reception or consideration, the commission voted to accept them as 'information', but 'must protect itself against all acts of authority or interference which are in formal contradiction with the object of its mission and of its consultative character'.[5] The compromise was due to Bulwer, who was fixed in his idea that its functions were strictly limited.[6] A pitched battle between Basily and Liehmann over the former's motion to censure the caimacam brought almost as little result; for, though Talleyrand, Richthofen, and Benzi had sustained the Russian commissioner, Bulwer held that such a measure was beyond the competence of the commission, and Liehmann succeeded in the end (after a 'long and hard battle', as he expressed it) in getting it recorded that any expression of opinion was solely the affair of each individual commissioner.[7] It

---

[1] *Ibid.*, vol. iv, no. 1320.   [2] *Ibid.*, no. 1303.   [3] *Ibid.*, no. 1317.

[4] *Ibid.*, no. 1301. It was only after three efforts, however, that Basily obtained a reading of this petition.

[5] Protocol 5, June 8, Wambaugh, *op. cit.*, pp. 775 ff.

[6] Bulwer to Clarendon, no. 76, June 12, F.O. 71/1280. Clarendon sustained this action: Clarendon to Bulwer, no. 80, June 30, F.O. 78/1277.

[7] Liehmann to Buol, no. 26, June 11, Staatsarchiv, XII/203; Talleyrand to Walewski, June 12, *Actes et docs.*, vol. iv, no. 1280.

only needed the insistence of Liehmann, Safvet, and Bulwer, that the commission could take no action without a unanimous vote, to paralyse effectively its powers of intervention. 'What will the populations of the two principalities think', wrote Talleyrand in despair, 'when they see us as passive spectators of abuses all around us?'[1]

Nevertheless, even Safvet had told the commission that he would try to get the firman applied identically in both principalities,[2] and when the commission's rulings were finally announced on June 17,[3] and it was known that Vogorides had acted without any regard for them,[4] the temper of most of the commission was, at least, sorely strained.[5] Uncovering a little of the truth, Bulwer bade Stratford 'take a little discount of views you get from Prokesch, for the Austrian consul at Jassy overacts his part', and then he acknowledged that, while Vogorides 'will end by getting a divan together, favourable to his and our own views', 'to do this, government influence will have been too much and too evidently exerted, and the spirit and even the letter of the firman too far departed from'.[6] In reply, Stratford wrote that, if the caimacam had 'erred', it would be 'difficult to shield him from the consequences of his folly', but 'to sacrifice him unfairly or even prematurely would be playing the game of those whose object we cannot approve'.[7]   The time had come, indeed, when the British diplomats, whatever their reluctance, were forced to believe that frauds had been practised in Moldavia. Clarendon, to whom Bulwer had expressed his fears without reserve,[8] was ready to accept the results in spite of 'irregularities',[9] and Thouvenel hazarded the opinion that 'neither at Constantinople nor at Vienna was the centre of resistance, which we have to overcome, but at London'.[10] But such a view was only correct in so far as Clarendon was simply following Stratford's lead, and thus allowing British policy to reach its logical climax. Still, as Paris did not choose to quarrel with London, the only apparent recourse was to charge the enemy's lines where they were weakest.

[1] Talleyrand to Walewski, no. 1280.
[2] Bulwer to Clarendon, no. 79, June 18, F.O. 78/1280.
[3] Bulwer to Clarendon, no. 80, June 18, *ibid*.
[4] The Prussian commissioner established this fact at the session of June 17: Protocol 6, June 13, 15, and 17, Wambaugh, *op. cit.*, p. 780.
[5] Writing to Stratford on July 7, Bulwer declared: 'Vogorides made an immense blunder in not waiting to see our solutions before publishing his own lists. . . . At the same time I am for sustaining Vogorides now whenever we can do so with anything like justice: Stratford Papers, F.O. 352/48.
[6] Bulwer to Stratford, June 23, *ibid*.
[7] Stratford to Bulwer, June 27, *ibid*.
[8] Bulwer to Clarendon, July 6, telg., F.O. 78/1281. Bulwer believed that some of the commissioners would not recognize the divan, when constituted, and feared that they would have 'some very plausible ground' for their action.
[9] Clarendon to Bulwer, no. 92, July 9, F.O. 78/1277.
[10] Thouvenel to Walewski, June 15, *Actes et docs.*, vol. iv, no. 1293,

There was no escaping the fact that the Porte must become the centre of the struggle. Thouvenel had followed this view, when he intervened in May to procure the extension of the commission's authority to deal with electoral questions in Moldavia; and, though the result had been only partially successful, it was becoming clearer every day that the only check on Vogorides must be sought at Constantinople. Accordingly, in June—just before learning that the Moldavian lists were being published—the French ambassador warned Reshid that the Porte would be held responsible for the conduct of the caimacam. 'I would have been franker', wrote Thouvenel afterwards, 'if I had then possessed the information which M. Place sent me by a telegram of yesterday.' Yet the vizier must have been frightened, for he decided for the moment to demand an explanation of Vogorides, though Stratford and Prokesch spared no effort to dissuade him.[1] Clearly the diplomatic battle was growing keener now that Thouvenel was again crossing swords with his rival. Was it exactly a coincidence that Stratford had given a dinner party on the anniversary of Waterloo? 'Briefly', wrote Thouvenel, 'I repeat my *Carthago delenda*. Strike hard!'[2] No wonder the French ambassador was reported to have given up an intended leave of absence from his post;[3] and it was doubtless the gravity of the situation which had lately induced Cowley to cross the Channel to consult with Clarendon. On his return to Paris, Cowley warned Walewski that 'the demand, made by M. de Thouvenel for the dismissal of the caimacam of Moldavia was an attack on the independent authority of the Sultan, which Her Majesty's government could not countenance'.[4] There is no evidence in Thouvenel's letters that he had done more than threaten to make such a demand,[5] but there is no doubt that the fear lest Reshid, overborne by French pressure, would call the guilty caimacam to account was the chief preoccupation of the British. For, much as Clarendon might admonish firmness,[6] there was too much reason for believing that the Porte, if driven into a corner, would sacrifice its instrument to save itself.[7]

---

[1] *Ibid.*

[2] Thouvenel, *op. cit.*, pp. 125–6.   [3] *The Times*, June 5, Paris correspondent.

[4] Cowley to Clarendon, no. 882, June 18, F.O. 27/1199.

[5] This was back in May, at the time of the struggle which led to the decision of May 30. Thouvenel had said on one occasion to the vizier: 'I have all the powers to demand the destitution of Prince Vogorides, but I abstain from doing so': *Actes et docs.*, vol. iv, no. 1216. Mr. East (*op. cit.*, p. 110) is very misleading on this point when he writes: 'In June Thouvenel launched a powerful offensive against the Porte, which began with the demand for the dismissal of Vogorides.' The telegram of Stratford, which he cites (June 5, F.O. 78/1564) states, 'The French ambassador has written home for permission to require directly from the Sultan that the caimacam of Moldavia be dismissed.'

[6] Clarendon to Stratford, June 13, telg., F.O. 78/1247.

[7] 'There are people without crowns on their heads', wrote Stratford in a

In the meantime Vogorides had done his worst, and something must be done to save the divan in Moldavia. Thus, encouraged by the vigorous stand of Talleyrand and his associates on the commission,[1] and fortified by instructions from Walewski, who emphasized the Porte's responsiblity,[2] Thouvenel got his Sardinian, Prussian, and Russian colleagues to join him, June 25, in an 'identic' note of protest to the Porte:

'The representatives of France, Prussia, Russia, and Sardinia cannot forbear expressing to the Sublime Porte the surprise with which they learn of the manner in which one continues in Moldavia to proceed to the execution of the firman; it is always the same system of open intimidation, of violent pressure. That is why it is not in keeping with the dignity of the commission, itself an emanation of the Congress of Paris, to put itself in touch with a divan, which will not be composed in a manner to be able to pass for the true expression of the wishes and needs of the State, and which will respond so badly to the intentions of the Congress of Paris in this regard.

'The Sublime Porte disavows, it is true, all collusion in this regard with its agents in Moldavia; but this declaration does not suffice to exonerate it of responsibility, which will truly weigh upon it in this circumstance, unless it shall have disavowed formally these same agents and shall have obliged them to modify their conduct.'[3]

The protest was mild enough in tenor, but the concerted action of four ambassadors could not fail to make an impression. In an interview with Reshid some days later Thouvenel alluded to some of the letters (already shown the vizier) which Photiades had written to the caimacam. Greatly taken aback, the vizier heaped abuse upon his agent, but swore to Allah that he himself was innocent. Thouvenel reminded him that Photiades was the official intermediary between the Porte and the caimacam, and that both offenders were appointments of the Porte itself. 'The embarrassment of Reshid Pasha', wrote Thouvenel afterwards, 'was extreme'. For the moment the French ambassador believed it unnecessary to make specific demands, but he pointed out that if he (Thouvenel) did not require the caimacam's removal, his colleagues had no right to insist on his retention: 'You are free, and, being free, are responsible.' In concluding his account to Walewski, Thouvenel hinted once more that his government should deal directly with Great Britain. 'The real protector of Prince Vogorides is Lord Stratford.'[4]

The joint intervention had the effect of placing responsibility where it belonged, but, if any tangible results were looked for, it

private letter to Bulwer (June 27), 'who incline from constitutional timidity to have a scapegoat always at hand': Stratford Papers, F.O. 352/48.

[1] Thouvenel to Walewski, July 1, *Actes et docs.*, vol. v, no. 1419.
[2] Walewski to Thouvenel, June 13, *ibid.*, vol. iv, no. 1287.
[3] *Ibid.*, no. 1348.   [4] Thouvenel to Walewski, July 1.

must soon have been evident that the four assailants had not captured a single trench. It is true that Reshid had thought at first of
sending a special deputy to investigate the charges against the
caimacam, but this resolution raised such a storm of protests from
Stratford and Prokesch (whose temper, Stratford tells us, had
occasionally to be 'iced')[1] that the vizier finally dropped it.[2] It is
interesting, however, to notice in this connexion that Stratford
himself felt moved to conduct a personal investigation, and on
July 7 sent Alison to Jassy.[3] This emissary was to 'obtain complete
information respecting the manner in which Prince Conaki
Vogorides has carried into effect the firman of convocation';[4] and
there is evidence to show that Stratford really wanted to know the
truth. Alison, after questioning Vogorides (who trembled for fear
the Porte intended to sacrifice him),[5] and after making further
inquiries, gave his chief a guarded answer: 'The electoral lists
cannot be regarded as altogether free from stain or reproach, but
they have been conducted with general regularity and propriety.'[6]
Much later—after the value of his evidence was past—Alison
confessed that he really could not get the truth about the framing of
the lists, or whether the charges against the caimacam were justified
or not.[7] As his first reports were decidedly less dubious, it is doubtful if Stratford felt appreciably disturbed.

Meanwhile matters were clearly hastening to a crisis. Despite
the action of commissioners and representatives, the elections,
based on the unrevised lists, were to begin on July 12; and some
of the peasants, contrary to the time allowed by the firman for
inspecting the arrangements, were already choosing their delegates
—subject to the government's interference.[8] The further conduct of the caimacam added fuel to the fire. The special commission,
designed to receive electoral claims, was so packed as to make it
hopeless to look for any reparation for the unionists.[9] 'My impression', wrote the distracted Bulwer, 'is that if the Russian,
French, Sardinian, and Prussian cabinets carry out the positive
threats of their commissioners not to recognize the Moldavian

---

[1] Stratford to Clarendon, July 1, Stratford Papers, F.O. 352/48.
[2] Thouvenel to Walewski, July 8, *Actes et docs.*, vol. v, no. 1451.
[3] Stratford explained that Alison was sent 'in the hope of terminating the
uncertainty and consequent embarrassment arising out of the view which is
taken by the French consul at Jassy and other zealous unionists of the late proceedings of Prince Vogorides': Stratford to Clarendon, no. 604, July 8, F.O.
78/1266. This mission gave great offence to Bulwer, who had not been informed
of it: Bulwer to Clarendon, no. 102, July 9, F.O. 78/1281.
[4] Stratford to Alison, no. 1, July 7, *ibid.*
[5] Alison to Stratford, no. 11, July 14, F.O. 195/561.
[6] Alison to Stratford, no. 8, July 14, F.O. 78/1268.
[7] Alison to Stratford, no. 70, Aug. 7, F.O. 78/1269.
[8] *Actes et docs.*, vol. iv, no. 1325, and vol. v, no. 1448.
[9] Place to Walewski, July 5, *ibid.*, no. 1431.

divan, they will have a strong case for the public, while the Porte will stand in an awkward position.'[1] Already Talleyrand and his allies were urging their governments to allow them to protest against the violation of article xxiv of the Treaty of Paris, and to refuse to have any relations with the coming divan.[2] And Thouvenel put his case on the firmest ground when he wrote, 'Once again, it is not a question of the union of the Principalities, but of the *loyal* execution of the Treaty of Paris.'[3]

It must be admitted that even Walewski was beginning to be stirred by these events. He had already taken the view that, inasmuch as the perversion of the plebiscite would have the effect of misleading the ultimate conference of the Powers, the commission should be considered 'a delegation of the Congress', empowered to ascertain and transmit (as the treaty had said) the free desires of the Principalities, and thus 'to denounce and combat any irregularities which are presented before it'. He unhesitatingly blamed Stratford for the conduct of the caimacam, and supplied Persigny with the evidence which Thouvenel had forwarded.[4] When Clarendon expressed his disbelief that Stratford had the influence over Turkey which had been ascribed to him, French logic answered, 'If it is true that Lord Stratford has not intervened in this affair, and that the Turkish government has acted alone, then there is no longer any difficulty between us; the question is entirely between France and Turkey, and, as we have been tricked, it is very just that we should demand and obtain reparation.'[5] That desired reparation, as Persigny understood, was the dismissal of Vogorides;[6] though this end was probably proposed as a means of forcing Clarendon's hand, and thereby bringing Stratford to reason. Clarendon, much embarrassed by the turn the argument was taking, found shelter in the excuse that more information was necessary, and then deplored the fact that for such petty interests 'in a little barbarous province at the end of Europe—the question of whether some persons should or should not vote—the policy of Europe should be upset'.[7] It was evident that the problem was quite too much for Clarendon.

Thus the struggle was being waged in three arenas. Among the cabinets Walewski was at last taking the offensive, while at Bucharest, as well as at Constantinople, the atmosphere was becoming more and more tense. The meetings of the commission were 'long and stormy',[8] according to Bulwer, and even its arid protocols bear

[1] Bulwer to Stratford, no. 96, July 8, F.O. 78/1281.
[2] Talleyrand to Walewski, July 8, *Actes et docs.*, vol. v, no. 1443.
[3] Thouvenel, *op. cit.*, p. 121.
[4] Walewski to Persigny, no. 65, June 20, *Aff. étr., Angleterre*, vol. 708.
[5] Persigny to Walewski, no. 65, July 24, *ibid.*
[6] Persigny to Walewski, no. 64, July 21, *ibid.*
[7] Persigny to Walewski, no. 63, July 20, and no. 65.
[8] Bulwer to Stratford, no. 96, July 8, F.O. 78/1281.

evidence of the fact. At the session of July 2 Basily proposed a vote of censure upon the caimacam for having ignored the commission's rulings, as well as for gross 'injustice and corruption in the administration of the firman'.[1] Naturally Bulwer's pedantic soul would not submit to so decisive a commitment on the part of the commission, but, while adhering to his point, he proposed at a later session that the incriminating documents, which the commission had received, should be referred without comment to the Porte and the ambassadors. This was much too mild for Talleyrand, who, availing himself of instructions from Walewski, protested formally against the elections, which he declared to be 'null and void'. The four commissioners favourable to union then declared that they would refuse to recognize a divan elected on the present basis.[2] Such action meant, of course, that the commission would no longer act as a body. The time had come, as Basily told the Austrian consul afterwards, for each Power to act separately, and, when it was suggested that discord in the commission was preventing an understanding among the cabinets, the Russian commissioner answered rather gloomily that 'if there is no understanding, there will be cannon shots'.[3] As by this time the results of the elections had produced a veritable explosion, and as the commission had reached a point where even a semblance of unity was impossible, its sessions were suspended by common consent to await the issue of the struggle, now pending, in Constantinople.[4]

The question of an honest plebiscite had obviously proved to be beyond the capacity of the commission, and hence the issue must be fought out among the embassies, with the possibility that the cabinets themselves might be forced to take a hand in the affray. Moved by a warning from Place, that if the electoral lists were not rectified an insurrection might be feared,[5] Thouvenel had again invoked the aid of the ambassadors who stood with him, and the four diplomats instructed their respective dragomen, July 7, to ask the Porte for categorical answers to the questions: (1) whether the commission's rulings in Wallachia were mandatory on Moldavia, except for cases peculiar to the former province; (2) whether the thirty days, stipulated by the firman for inspection of the electoral lists, should not be held to begin *after* the electoral lists had been rectified; and

[1] Bulwer to Stratford, no. 111, July 15, *ibid.*; cf. Protocol 9, *Actes et docs.*, vol. vi, part 2, pp. 430 ff.
[2] Protocol 13, July 29, Wambaugh, *op. cit.*, pp. 788 ff. Talleyrand gives an amusing sidelight on Bulwer at this meeting. He reports him as saying, 'My position is very difficult. I am obliged to send copies to Lord Stratford of all my dispatches; I cannot, therefore, blame openly what he approves of': Talleyrand to Walewski, July 30, *Actes et docs.*, vol. v, no. 1627.
[3] Eder to Buol, no. 57 C, July 29, Staatsarchiv, XXXVIII/109.
[4] Talleyrand to Walewski, July 30.
[5] Place to Thouvenel, July 4, telg., *Actes et docs.*, vol. v, no. 1429.

(3) whether the caimacam should not be invited to suspend all electoral preparations until he had given consideration to the aforesaid rulings.[1] Reshid's reply was to propose a conference of the diplomats, presumably in order that the caimacam's duty under the firman might be thoroughly threshed out. It is not impossible that a conference might have terminated the wrangle, and certainly it would have avoided the subsequent confusion; but the exponents of decisive action would have none of the proposal which they denounced as ridiculous and flatly rejected. 'We don't understand', said Thouvenel, 'the use of holding a conference to discuss what has already been resolved upon twice.'[2] The French ambassador did not feel that the decision of May 30 needed further clarification; the action of the four had been designed merely to force its confirmation by the Porte.

As a matter of fact, Thouvenel, far from wanting a conference, was relying on other weapons. A hint from the French foreign office that he might force the hand of the vizier by direct appeal to the Sultan[3] was not without effect. Moreover, he knew that Ali and Fuad were ready to knife Reshid in the back.[4] These facts may well explain a decision of the Turkish council to postpone the elections fifteen days and to send an instruction to Vogorides to revise his lists in conformity with the commission's interpretations. On learning that the Sultan himself had sanctioned this decision,[5] Prokesch and Stratford saw themselves hoodwinked, and their anger knew no bounds.[6] After a brief consultation they drew up an 'identic 'protest to the Porte, declaring that it had no right to

[1] *Actes de docs.*, no. 1444.

[2] Thouvenel to Walewski, July 8, *ibid.*, no. 1451. 'It is for you alone', Thouvenel told Reshid, 'to convince M. the ambassador of England and M. the internuncio of Austria, or to decide, notwithstanding their opposition, what you have to do in order to shield yourself against a responsibility which they do not share with you. The Congress, I repeat, has left solely to the Porte the task of combining the maintenance of legal order in the Principalities with the free expression of the wishes of the populations. The system, followed by Prince Vogorides under your patronage represses the wishes of the Moldavians and compromises the security of the state.' The argument was somewhat captious, for it overlooked the fact that the firman had been concerted between the Porte and the Powers; but it was reasonable to expect the Porte to enforce the execution of the decision of May 30—which was clearly the object of the questionnaire of the four ambassadors. Such enforcement hardly required a conference.

[3] Thouvenel, *op. cit.*, pp. 124–7.

[4] Thouvenel to Walewski, June 15. Stratford suspected collusion between Thouvenel and 'the party averse to Reshid Pasha in the cabinet': Stratford to Clarendon, no. 621, July 15, F.O. 78/1266.

[5] Letters of Prokesch attest to a visit of the French dragoman to the Sultan, and also one from Thouvenel himself.

[6] Thouvenel to Walewski, July 15, *Actes et docs.*, vol. v, no. 1479; Prokesch to Buol, no. 43 C, July 10, Staatsarchiv, XII/60; Stratford to Clarendon, no. 621. According to Prokesch, he and Stratford reproached Reshid for not having submitted to them the communication of the four ambassadors before it was brought before the Turkish council.

make such a decision apart from the other signatory Powers, and insisting that a conference be held.[1] In a separate communication to the Porte Stratford held that the accusations against the caimacam had not been proved, and that, until denial could be made, no action should be taken to impede the local authorities.[2]

Pushed this way and that, the grand vizier was ready to bow to any momentary coercion. After getting ready to act in accordance with the council's decision, he succumbed to pressure from Stratford and Prokesch, who would agree to only eight days' delay,[3] and, accordingly, telegraphed to Vogorides to defer the elections eight days and to send immediately an explanation of his reasons for rejecting the commission's interpretations.[4] We need not pause to consider Vogorides's answer, which simply contended that he had applied all the provisions that were applicable to Moldavia.[5] Though no conference was held, the result had been a triumph for the obstructionists, since the caimacam was now under no compulsion to change his lists, and the small respite allowed—the elections would begin on July 19—would not avail the unionists. Yet the Porte was so irresolute that Thouvenel was not told of the second decision, and Reshid informed the dragoman of the French embassy that the commission's rulings were obligatory in Moldavia.[6] In the maze of letters, telegrams, and interviews, with dragomans going to and fro, and the Turkish ministers forming a decision one moment, only to alter it the next—one can well understand that a serious tangle would result.

Unfortunately, Clarendon and Waleweski, to whom these disputes had been referred, were themselves confused by so much oscillation. On July 9 Thouvenel had telegraphed Walewski:

'The Porte has decided, on a new *démarche* of the embassies of France, Russia, Prussia, and Sardinia, and notwithstanding the opposition of those of England and Austria, to order the Moldavian government to recast the lists, conformable to the interpretation of the commission, and to delay for 15 days the elections, set for July 12.'[7]

[1] *Actes et docs.*, vol. v, no. 1459.
[2] *Ibid.*, no. 1458.
[3] This much concession Reshid required for the purpose of getting together the desired conference, though he had to inform Stratford later that the proposal of a conference was rejected by the four ambassadors: Stratford to Clarendon, July 11, telg., and no. 621. (According to no. 621, Reshid had demanded a week, but, for some reason, eight days was finally resolved upon).
[4] Stratford to Clarendon, July 11, telg., F.O. 78/1260.
[5] Stratford to Clarendon, no. 620, July 15, enc.
[6] *Actes et docs.*, vol. v, no. 1499. Reshid seems to have lost his head completely. On July 13 word was sent to Safvet that the elections were to be adjourned 'to the end of July' (*ibid.*, no. 1473)—a step which Prokesch deplored as 'granting a new success to the adversaries of the Porte': Prokesch to Stratford, July 16, Stratford Papers, F.O. 352/48.
[7] *Actes et docs.*, vol. v, no. 1454.

Walewski telegraphed in reply:

'We consider it a sufficient satisfaction, if loyal effect is given to the orders, transmitted by the Porte to Jassy.' [1]

But in the meantime Stratford had telegraphed to Clarendon, July 11:

' . . . The Porte has ordered Prince Vogorides to defer the elections for eight days, and to send up immediately a full explanation of his reasons for rejecting the Wallachian decisions as inapplicable to Moldavia.'[2]

To this, Clarendon (learning from Cowley no specific time of adjournment)[3] telegraphed the answer, July 14:

'The French Government have sent orders to their agents at Constantinople and Bucharest to accept the delay in the Moldavian elections as a complete satisfaction and not to continue the struggle respecting the elections any further.'[4]

The question then was, how much delay did Walewski signify as satisfactory?[5] Thouvenel, mindful of his own dispatch, knew, of course, that fifteen days were meant; while Stratford, who had telegraphed the later resolution of the Porte (the one, which had been actually carried into effect), contended that eight was what the French minister must have intended. Harassed by both ambassadors, Reshid proposed, July 18, that the elections, which were now to begin on the following day, should be postponed for five days in order that Paris and London might be reached by telegraph, and the question of the length of the adjournment be thus settled by agreement between the French and British cabinets.[6] Such a measure would seem reasonable, for both ambassadors had been under an honest misapprehension (Thouvenel not knowing of the second decision, and Stratford supposing naturally that this was the basis of action), and the respite of another week (assuming that the 'fifteen days' would prove acceptable to Clarendon), while it would

[1] *Aff. étr., Turquie*, vol. 331. (Curiously enough, this important telegram is not found in the Sturdza collection).
[2] F.O. 78/1260.
[3] Cowley's telegram of July 14, though referred to by Clarendon as having been sent to Stratford (no. 1117 to Cowley) is not to be found in the British archives. Cowley, however, later admitted his negligence: Cowley to Clarendon, no. 1120, Aug. 4, F.O. 27/1201.
[4] F.O. 78/1266.
[5] Walewski's want of precision was a strange piece of carelessness. He had been more explicit to Talleyrand, to whom he had telegraphed on July 12 (*Actes et docs.*, vol. v, no. 1464) that: 'the Ottoman Porte having ordered the caimacam of Moldavia to recast the lists in conformity with the interpretation of the commission and to delay the elections fifteen days, there is no need to give effect to the plan of protest [see p. 118]. The decision of the Ottoman Porte being, moreover, a striking testimony of deference towards the Four Powers, one may consider it as satisfactory, and it is desirable that the elections take place on the 27th.'
[6] *Ibid.*, no. 1510.

have satisfied the French, would hardly have insured them a victory
at Constantinople. It is not certain that the Porte could have been
persuaded to force a revision of the lists, or that Clarendon would
have yielded to that extent; at most, it would have simply given
Thouvenel a chance to renew the battle. Unhappily, Stratford's
stubbornness had been intensified by opposition, and he was not
willing to give either the French or the Moldavians the benefit of
any doubt. Accordingly, he and Prokesch, on their own responsibility, rejected the Porte's proposal.[1] 'If Thouvenel be not curbed',
wrote Stratford to Clarendon, 'he will ride roughshod over the
whole of us.'[2] It was Stratford, however, who was at present
guilty of the rough-riding. When Reshid remonstrated with him
for refusing to accept the proposed delay,[3] both he and Prokesch
were said to have flown into a rage, and accused the grand vizier of
subservience to the French.[4] It was clear enough that Stratford
was doing his utmost to guard the bogus plebiscite from any
interference.

For the moment, indeed, the British ambassador had his way.
When Clarendon telegraphed, July 20, that he had 'no objection to
the delay of fifteen days in the Moldavian elections, to which we
understand the Porte agrees',[5] Stratford replied that the dispatch
had come too late, as the elections had already begun.[6] The
British government had been dragged into a perilous commitment
by the mistake it had made of leaving the initiative to its most
domineering and dangerous ambassador. Writing with pardonable
exaggeration, Cavour compared the attitude of the British on the
question of the Principalities with that of the Austrians in Italy.[7]

But, while Great Britain had her scene with France to face,
Clarendon had no intention of allowing Stratford's action to go
unchastened. On August 4, after accumulating all the facts on the
pending controversy, Clarendon wrote to Stratford as follows:

'. . . It appears from your despatch no. 641 and its enclosure that the
Porte would very willingly have deferred for five days longer the
Moldavian elections, but had yielded to the representations in a contrary
sense, addressed to it by Your Excellency and the Austrian internuncio;
and it is my duty to state to your Excellency that Her Majesty's govern-

---

[1] Stratford to Clarendon, no. 641, July 22, F.O. 78/1267.
[2] Stratford to Clarendon, July 22, Stratford Papers, F.O. 352/48.
[3] Prokesch wrote that Reshid defended his proposal with 'remarkable tenacity'
(Prokesch to Buol, no. 46 B, July 22, Staatsarchiv, XII/60), and, according to
Stratford, he even threatened to resign unless the plan was accepted: Stratford
to Clarendon, no. 643, F.O. 78/1267. No doubt Reshid had a wholesome fear
of what might happen to him when Thouvenel learned of his duplicity, and a
timely concession might avert that catastrophe.
[4] Outrey to Thouvenel, July 20, *Actes et docs.*, vol. v, no. 1552.
[5] F.O. 78/1248.
[6] Stratford to Clarendon, July 25, telg., F.O. 78/1267.
[7] Cavour to D'Azeglio, July 27, Bianchi, *op. cit.*, p. 253.

ment must regret that the proposal of the Porte in this respect was not accepted.

'The great desideratum was that the English and French governments would come to an understanding with each other, and Her Majesty's government think that the proposition of the Porte to give a delay of five days in order to communicate with London and with Paris was a reasonable one, with reference to two telegrams which the English and French ambassadors construed differently. If this had been agreed to, all the complications which have since arisen would have been avoided.

'The telegram, which I addressed to Your Excellency on the 14th ultimo, simply announced that the French government were satisfied with the delay accorded, and it was a matter of indifference whether the delay was of eight or of fifteen days, provided that the painful differences respecting the Moldavian elections were put an end to.'[1]

Stratford, in reply to this reprimand, expressed 'deep concern', but insisted that his course of action had been warranted.

'I was given to understand', he declared, 'that a fresh postponement would so discourage the parties who most sympathized with the government that the turbulent and intriguing partisans of union would hardly fail to obtain a decided ascendancy in the elections. Such a result would have been the more regrettable, as it must have placed the caimacam in a very humiliating position, and confirmed the prospect of that European embarrassment, which would infallibly occur, if the question of uniting the two Principalities under a single hospodar were to go before the Congress of Paris with a majority of both divans in its favor.'[2]

There is no clearer evidence that Stratford had made up his mind that, whatever the means, the elections must produce a divan which would oppose the idea of union. It was union which he had declared to be the real stake in the diplomatic battle,[3] and that movement must be stifled at any cost. It may be of interest to add, however, that Clarendon did not accept the ambassador's excuses, reaffirming his opinion that his

'telegram of July 14 may not have stated the precise number of days for which delay was to be granted, but it clearly indicated that the English and French governments were in communication, and that the delay, understood between them, would have put an end satisfactorily to the differences which then existed'.[4]

---

[1] Clarendon to Stratford, no. 695, Aug. 4, F.O. 78/1249. I agree with Mr. East (*op. cit.*, pp. 125–6) that 'it does not seem obvious that Stratford should have known that an Anglo-French understanding was "the great desideratum",' but it seems to me that the rest of his apology is unconvincing. Surely the misunderstanding over the telegrams and advices received from Jassy were no excuse for rejecting the Porte's proposal to wait long enough for that misunderstanding to be cleared up. With all his indifference to the question of an honest plebiscite, Clarendon hardly erred in calling the Porte's proposal 'a reasonable one'.

[2] Stratford to Clarendon, no. 727, Aug. 18, F.O. 78/1269.

[3] Stratford to Clarendon, no. 621, July 15, F.O. 78/1266.

[4] Clarendon to Stratford, no. 810, Sept. 9, F.O. 78/1250.

Bulwer, while distributing blame liberally among the diplomats whose slights he had not forgotten, declared that it was not for a representative of Great Britain to hurry on the elections 'at a moment when their legality is questionable, and when some mistake appears to have existed between the governments of France and England as to some arrangement that both governments would receive as satisfactory.[1]

But in all his manœuvres there was one result on which the British ambassador had not calculated. That the elections (which began on July 19 and lasted three days) would end in bringing about a divan opposed to union, he did not doubt; but the detail that he had not foreseen was the abstention from the polls of practically all the electors who believed in union. Of the 193 priests registered (out of a total of 3,263) only 17 voted; of the 465 electors among the 3,000 great proprietors, but 207 cast their votes.[2] Even to the end, the officials of the government interfered to influence the results, and a case was cited where a self-appointed committee took possession of the ballots at one of the polling places of Jassy and wrote on them the name of the anti-union candidate.[3] But the absence of the great majority of citizens from the elections was a ridiculous commentary on the means devised for securing the opinions of the province. As a medium for registering the wishes of Moldavia the plebiscite was a farce.

Such occurrences only hardened the resolution of the Powers who favoured union. France, for her part, did not propose to lose the fight to an unscrupulous ambassador, a timid court, and a corrupt subaltern. The report (though probably untrue) that Stratford's deputy, Alison, was 'presiding over the electoral operations'[4] and 'haughtily declaring that the present elections will be maintained, because Lord Redcliffe will not permit them to be annulled',[5] was certainly adding bitterness to a cup already full. Once more—and this time, once for all—the Porte must be compelled to give adequate redress. Reshid undoubtedly was a weak creature, and Stratford's report that he was stronger and that intrigues against him in the cabinet had been checked[6] must be set beside the French story that the vizier had lately talked of resigning and hoped that France, seeing that he was not free to act, would insist that the elections be annulled.[7] Already Napoleon had decided that this should be the point of attack. After considering the feasibility of demanding the destitution of Vogorides

[1] Bulwer to Clarendon, no. 128, July 23, F.O. 78/1281.
[2] Place to Walewski, July 24, telg., *Actes et docs.*, vol. v, no. 1573.
[3] Wambaugh, *op. cit.*, p. 112.   [4] Thouvenel, *op. cit.*, p. 135.
[5] Place to Walewski, July 25, *Actes et docs.*, vol. v, no. 1578.
[6] Stratford to Clarendon, no. 664, July 30, F.O. 78/1268.
[7] Outrey to Thouvenel, July 20, *Actes et docs.*, vol. v, no. 1552.

(possibly this was relinquished because of Clarendon's dis-approval),[1] Walewski consulted the cabinets of Russia, Prussia, and Sardinia on the plan of demanding the annulment of the elections,[2] and, as soon as favourable answers were received, the Emperor got Walewski to instruct Thouvenel that he was to demand the annulment of the elections, and that, in event of a refusal to comply, he should sever diplomatic relations.[3] Acting in the spirit of the Emperor's orders, Walewski telegraphed the ambassador, bidding him concert this demand with his three followers, and if necessary, threaten the Porte with a breach of diplomatic relations.[4] Accordingly, the ambassadors of the four Powers presented their ultimata—the French and Sardinian on the 28th, the Russian on the 29th, and the Prussian on the 30th.[5]

At last came the crisis of the hard-fought battle. Even Persigny, who feared that they were 'setting ablaze the edifice of the Anglo-French alliance', was recognizing, according to report, that 'our allies [meaning the Crimean allies] are going beyond all bounds',[6] and Thouvenel declared that, while the Turkish council was de-bating the nature of its response, it was certain that, if the response was unsatisfactory, he would leave Constantinople.[7]

Yet the Porte had weathered so many storms that, once more, it hoped to avoid a crash by temporizing. Perhaps the Turks were shrewd enough to see that, after all, the struggle was primarily between two factions among the Powers, and that, should the quarrel lead to war, any action which the Sublime Porte had taken would pale into insignificance. After due deliberation Turkey declared that she could not, merely as a co-signatory of the Treaty of Paris, annul the elections on her own responsibility, but that she was willing to suspend the convocation of the divans until the Powers, reassembled, should decide on the whole question.[8] The answer was clever, for, at first sight, it might seem technically unassailable. Yet when we recall that the execution of the firman had been confided to appointed instruments of the suzerain Power, and that one of these instruments had proved derelict in duty, it is not surprising that Thouvenel should denounce the proposal as '*dérisoire*'.[9] Thus, the answer quite failed to move the four redoubtable ambassadors, and Thouvenel merely decided that the vizier had been intimidated.[10] He himself was straining every nerve to snatch a victory for his government. He had even ob-

---

[1] Clarendon to Stratford, July 28, telg., F.O. 78/1248.
[2] Walewski to Thouvenel, July 23, *Actes et docs.*, vol. v, no. 1571.
[3] Napoleon to Walewski, July 26, telg., *ibid.*, no. 1584.
[4] Walewski to Thouvenel, July 27, telg., *ibid.*, no. 1591.
[5] *Ibid.*, nos. 1600, 1601, 1618, and 1631.   [6] Thouvenel, *op. cit.*, p. 134.
[7] *Ibid.*, p. 136.   [8] *Actes et docs.*, vol. v, no. 1633.
[9] Thouvenel to Walewski, July 30, telg., *ibid.*, no. 1634.
[10] Thouvenel to Walewski, Aug.6, *ibid.*, no. 1662.

tained a personal interview with the Sultan, and contrived by implication to throw upon Reshid all the blame for the present crisis.[1] On the 30th he telegraphed Walewski, asking to be authorized not only to threaten but to sever his relations with the Porte.[2] When Walewski promptly telegraphed assent,[3] the French ambassador had his armoury complete.

For several days longer the battle of wills and wits went on. Clarendon would not hear of an annulment of the elections,[4] warmly approved the Porte's action,[5] and reverted to Stratford's proposal of a conference of the ambassadors.[6] Such a proposal was far too late,[7] and even Stratford had ceased to urge it. Truly enough, the French ambassador showed no signs of leaving his post,[8] but Stratford told Clarendon that his rival's 'main object is to upset the ministry',[9] and doubtless the intrigue at the palace was not without effect. At all events, on July 31 Reshid Pasha relinquished office, and Stratford supposed that his object was to 'scramble out of responsibility'.[10] The new vizier, Mustapha Pasha, was reputed to be a friend of France, while the re-entrance of both Ali and Fuad into the ministry might seem to denote an omen of conciliation. But, although Reshid's sacrifice was a move to propitiate France, it was to be seen whether the change was one of policy as well as persons. Quick to follow up his victory, Thouvenel assured the two ministers that they were mistaken if they supposed that the change of ministry would have any effect upon his demand, and he showed them the dispatch which authorized him, if necessary, to request his passports.[11] Thus, according to the French design, the fall of Reshid was but a means, not an end. Walewski, when asked by Clarendon whether France

[1] Thouvenel to Walewski, July 22, *ibid.*, no. 1567. Thouvenel followed this interview by a week later by addressing a letter to the Sultan—a step which he justified on the ground that he had exhausted all his resources with the ministry. He repeated the Emperor's 'peremptory' demand for the annulment of the elections, and alluded casually to the sacrifices which France had made on behalf of Turkey and of her sovereign: *ibid.*, no. 1612.

[2] Thouvenel to Walewski, July 29, *ibid.*, no. 1615. In a telegram on the following day Thouvenel asked to be allowed to break relations, but to adjourn his departure eight days. 'On ne me laissera pas partir,' he added: *ibid.*, no. 1636.

[3] Walewski to Thouvenel, July 30, *ibid.*, no. 1635.

[4] Clarendon to Cowley, no. 1118, Aug. 3, F.O. 27/1181.

[5] Clarendon to Stratford, July 31, telg., F.O. 78/1249.

[6] Clarendon to Cowley, no. 1097, July 31, F.O. 27/1180; cf. Persigny to Walewski, no. 68, July 31, *Aff. étr., Angleterre*, vol. 708.

[7] In rejecting this proposal Walewski told Clarendon that France, having made a peremptory demand of the Porte, could not recede from that position: Cowley to Clarendon, no. 1099, Aug. 2, F.O. 27/1201. To Persigny he explained that the request for revision of the electoral lists—which, under Vogorides's direction, would furnish no guarantee of fairness—was France's 'utmost act of conciliation': Walewski to Persigny, no. 85, Aug. 2, *Aff. étr., Angleterre*, vol. 708.

[8] See above, n. 2.

[9] 'Stratford to Clarendon, July 30, Stratford Papers, F.O. 352/48.

[10] Stratford to Clarendon, July 31, *ibid.* [11] Thouvenel to Walewski, Aug. 6.

would be satisfied with Reshid's downfall, answered, no—it would 'expose' her to the 'reproach of following in Turkey a personal policy'.[1] Everything, of course, depended on the action of the new ministry, of which Ali was undoubtedly the leading spirit; and whether Stratford and Prokesch had an influence on its attitude is not evident in any of the dispatches. But from Thouvenel's report it would seem that Clarendon's recent proposal of a conference (which he had coupled with the suggestion that, if this proved unavailing, the whole affair should be submitted to the governments),[2] encouraged the Turks to try one last resource to escape surrender.[3] To the four ambassadors the Porte proposed that the two caimacams should be summoned to Constantinople for examination, and that the result should then be submitted to a conference of the ambassadors.[4] Such a proposal had less merit than the one which Reshid had made—which Thouvenel had labelled '*dérisoire*'[5]—and, of course, it was foredoomed. Satisfied now that their threats would not extort the price demanded, the four ambassadors declared a breach of diplomatic relations with the Porte.[6] Though Thouvenel still remained at his post the flag of the French embassy was not raised on August 5.[7]

The controversy had now reached the point where the Anglo-French alliance seemed to be shattered, and Europe brought to the brink of war over the question of whether the Treaty of Paris should be honestly carried out. 'If a question like this', exclaimed Clarendon (meaning the accuracy of the electoral lists) 'should enkindle a war in the world, never could History believe in so slight a cause for events so great!'[8] But surely the issue was much more fundamental than whether certain prescriptions for voting were accurately applied, or whether, indeed, the French had gone so far that they could not recede without a national humiliation. Unless the Treaty of Paris were meaningless the Moldo-Wallachians were entitled to express their views on the question of their political reorganization. None of the European Powers had enough at stake to want a war over the question, but it behoved the Concert of Europe either to appreciate the gravity of their own contribution to the public law of Europe, or else to re-examine

---

[1] Clarendon to Cowley, no. 1118; Cowley to Clarendon, no. 1120, Aug. 4, F.O. 27/1201; Walewski to Persigny, no. 84, Aug. 3, *Aff. étr.*, *Angleterre*, vol. 708.

[2] This was communicated in a telegram of July 31 to Stratford.

[3] We learn from Prokesch, however, that he and Stratford had been consulted by Ali, and that the rejection of the Turkish overture 'changes nothing in the situation': Prokesch to Buol, Aug. 4, telg., Staatsarchiv, XII/60.

[4] Thouvenel to Walewski, Aug. 6, *Actes et docs.*, vol. v, no. 1662.

[5] Page 126. [6] *Ibid.*, no. 1657.

[7] Stratford to Clarendon, Aug. 5, telg., F.O. 78/1268.

[8] Persigny to Walewski, no. 63, July 20, *Aff. étr.*, *Angleterre*, vol. 708.

their acts and seek some workable compromise. Since the moral aspects of the question had been quite lost sight of in the heat of battle, it was apparent that only by reciprocal concessions could the deadlock be relieved. After all, it is only, as a rule, by slow and painful plodding that a step is taken in the onward march of civilization.

CHAPTER V

COMPROMISE: THE PACT OF OSBORNE

THE Roumanian question received more general attention in the summer of 1857 than at any time before or since.[1] It was not because the fate of a nationality depended on the complexion of the Moldavian divan, for the Moldo-Wallachians were not looked upon as having any of the charm with which the romantic spirit of the nineteenth century had clothed the revolting Greeks, and, west of Vienna, Europe was not greatly interested in the Danubian Principalities. It was, rather, because the question presented, as somewhat remote questions often did, a test of strength between opposing parties among the Powers. The Concert of Europe could not, apparently, undertake the settlement of an international problem without letting their interests or their 'honour' push them to such a degree that a small difference came to assume gigantic proportions. During the brief interval between the Congress of Paris and the Italian War of Liberation the devil must needs find somewhere the means with which to shatter the frail idealism of collective Europe. The Roumanian question brought one more rift in a body, whose unity, even at Paris, had been manifestly superficial, and whose corporate energy would soon be found quite too weak to withstand a Bismarck. Unhappily, the nations of the world are seldom internationalist save when contemplating a problem from a distance.

More particularly it was a tilt between France and Great Britain. While the basic question would more naturally have involved Paris and Vienna, the intransigence of Stratford (of whom Clarendon once said that 'having for a number of years occupied the Eastern dunghill without competitors, he could not find an inch of room upon it for the French ambassador')[1] had seemingly forced his government to take the lead in the opposition to union. Was the present crisis to prove the last painful gasp of the Anglo-French accord, and the episode at Constantinople to presage a new alignment among the Powers? Certainly the moment was heavy with possibilities. 'We are ready for any eventualities, however painful they may be', wrote Palmerson to Persigny,[2] and it was some such letter as this that so exasperated the Emperor that he declined to read any more of the British minister's communications.[3] Facing each other in what had come to be a personal struggle, the two governments seemed to be racked

---

[1] Maxwell, *Life and Letters of George William Frederick, Fourth Earl of Clarendon*, vol. ii, p. 159.

[2] Palmerston to Persigny, no number, Aug. 3, *Aff. étr., Angleterre*, vol. 708.

[3] Martin, *op. cit.*, vol. iv, p. 105.

by a conflict of wills. The redoutable Palmerston was not wont to accept defeat in a diplomatic battle, while, to Napoleon, the granting of his demand at Constantinople had come to be a 'point of honour' [1]—a position which inherently precluded all concession. The French press—not merely the government organs [2] but the slightly more independent papers, like the *Siècle* [3] and the *Patrie* [4]— were inflexible in their support of the Emperor and his ambassador. With somewhat less assurance the British press rallied to Palmerston and Clarendon, though the *Saturday Review* scolded the Premier soundly for 'the contemptible position into which the country has been placed', [5] and Disraeli's organ launched an angry invective against a policy which had endangered the *entente cordiale*, violated a sacred treaty, and involved the country in complications which 'threaten to plunge us into difficulties of prodigious extent'. [6] No comment, perhaps, is necessary on the conduct of the British opposition in a crisis which is not likely to lead to war. But the basis for all this public criticism is quite clear. The Liberal ministry had pursued a policy in the Near East which had neither the merit of consistency nor the accident of success. And out of such an *impasse* even the dexterous Palmerston could hardly hope to extricate himself with credit. Fortunately, however, for the ministry—and perhaps this was another case of Palmerston's luck —the Great Mutiny had much more interest for the British public than the question of whether the union of the Principalities was likely to endanger the Ottoman Empire. It was under cover of this distraction that Palmerston and Clarendon could plan the nature of their retreat.

But, while the British ministers were doubtless aware of the untenable position into which their own ineptitude and Stratford's folly had led them, it was clear that Napoleon was statesman enough to see the unwisdom of pressing his advantage. Already much unnecessary heat had been generated over whether France should, or should not, have consented to a conference at Constantinople; whether Thouvenel was a 'second Menschikoff', as Clarendon had depicted him, [7] or whether the uncompromising Stratford was the arch-villain of the drama; and poor Persigny, who had to bear the brunt of Palmerston's wrath, complained on one occasion to Walewski that he was not adequately informed of the course of events. [8] Such, of course, were repercussions of a

---

[1] Cowley to Clarendon, no. 1120, Aug. 4, F.O. 27/1201; Thouvenel, *op. cit.*, p. 150. See Clarendon's interesting observations in Martin, *op. cit.*, vol. iv, pp. 106-7.
[2] e.g. *Constitutionel*, Aug. 10, roundly accused Palmerston of duplicity.
[3] *Siècle*, Aug. 9.   [4] *Patrie*, Aug. 8.   [5] *Sat. Rev.*, Aug. 15.
[6] *Press*, Aug. 8.   [7] Clarendon to Cowley, no. 1103, Aug. 1, F.O. 27/1181.
[8] Persigny to Walewski, no. 69, Aug. 2, *Aff. étr., Angleterre*, vol. 708.

quarrel which had for a time got beyond the reach of the home governments. But, now that the latter were forced to assume the burden of cutting a way through the tangle, it might seem possible for France and England to view the question soberly, and try to seek an adjustment on a fairly restricted basis. It was suited to the magnanimous disposition of the Emperor that he should make the first overture. It was also characteristic of his judgement that he should regard his accord with England as worth an effort to preserve. We have noticed that, as far back as April, he had meditated a visit to Victoria, who had now begun her summer's sojourn at Osborne on the Isle of Wight. What could be more desirable than to carry out this plan, and try to find, if possible, the basis for a compromise?

The Emperor's yacht, bearing himself and the Empress, reached Osborne on August 6; on the 10th it sailed away again, bearing them home. Writing of the visit afterwards, Victoria said, 'Politically it was, as Lord Clarendon said, a "godsend", for the unhappy difficulties in the Principalities have been *aplanis* and satisfactorily settled.'[1] The visit made, in fact, a very favourable impression. Albert talked politics with his imperial guest, and, though they were not agreed on every point, especially in regard to Russia, whom the Prince accused of using France to secure the independence of the Principalities to further her own ends, there was no trace of any ill-humour in these discussions as Albert recounts them.[2] But neither the Queen nor the Prince Consort was instrumental in reaching the settlement of the pending crisis. Both Palmerston and Clarendon had come to Osborne for that purpose, while Napoleon had with him Persigny and Walewski. On these five rested the responsibility of the denouement.

On the conferences which led to an agreement we have very little evidence. An important meeting took place between Palmerston and the Emperor during the evening of August 7, and, though it lasted, according to report, until after two in the morning, there was no apparent prospect of an understanding. On the following day a conference, probably of all the diplomats, was held, and an agreement seems then to have been reached.[3] From Walewski we learn that the British ministers were duly enlightened on the frauds which had been perpetrated in Moldavia, and, though they hoped at first that Napoleon would not insist on the annulment of the elections, they finally, albeit reluctantly, gave way. He also tells us (if Hübner is to be trusted) that he tried to get assent to a personal union of the Principalities, that is, the institution of a

[1] Martin, *op. cit.*, vol. iv, p. 95.
[2] *Ibid.*, pp. 102–3.
[3] Vitzthum von Eckstädt, *St. Petersburg and London in the Years 1852–64*, vol. i, p. 225.

common hospodar, but that the proposal was rejected.[1] According to Clarendon, as reported by Apponyi, Napoleon manifested great exasperation against the Turks, whom he would fain have seen driven out of Europe, whereupon the British ministers took pains to impress upon him the necessity of having Turkey for the equilibrium of Europe.[2] Such are a few inklings we have of the discussions, which must at times have brought out a good deal of disagreement. But on August 9—if not before—the bargain was struck.

The agreement reached at Osborne on August 9 was not embodied in any signed document, though, at Albert's suggestion,[3] the British understanding of that decision was set forth in a memorandum and presented to Walewski, who assented to its accuracy while declining to affix his signature to the paper. According to that statement it was agreed that the Porte should be requested by Great Britain (the concurrence of Austria being also solicited) to annul the electoral lists in Moldavia and order a revision of the same in conformity with the decision of May 30. At the same time it was agreed that an internal organization should be devised for the Principalities, which, while insuring Turkish suzerainty and the maintenance of the ancient privileges of the Principalities, should entail for them 'similar organic institutions', and that 'while retaining their separate governments, they should have a common system in respect to all things civil and military'. It appears that an earlier draft of the memorandum had stated more exactly what was meant by the last expression,[4] but appar-

[1] Cowley to Clarendon, no. 1144, Aug. 15, F.O. 27/1202; Hübner to Buol, no. 62, Aug. 13, Staatsarchiv, IX/55. According to Hübner, Walewski told him 'the English ministers asked us to renounce political union, dissolve the commission at Bucharest, not to convoke the divans, and to refer this whole affair to the Congress. We had to decline this proposal.' Hübner gives some further details in his letter of August 22 (no. 57 A–C), but they add nothing to our knowledge. Walewski wrote the French minister at Turin (Aug. 13) that 'les explications que nous avons échangeés en édifiant Lord Palmerston et Lord Clarendon sur plusieurs points dont ils n'avaient qu'une connaissance imparfaite, ont conduit les deux ministres à reconnaître que la sincérité des élections qui ont eu lieu en Moldavie pouvait être contestée': *Aff. étr., Sardaigne*, vol. 342, no. 29.

[2] Apponyi to Buol, no. 55 A–E, Aug. 12, Staatsarchiv, VIII/48.

[3] Martin, *op. cit.*, vol. iv, p. 113.

[4] Mr. East has printed not only the memorandum of Aug. 9 but the suppressed passage (to be found in an enclosure of Cowley's to Malmesbury, June 4, 1858), which reads as follows: 'Such arrangements would include a coinage which should pass current in both provinces, a tariff that should be the same in both, a customs union, and the absence of any customs duties payable on goods passing from one province to the other, a provision that decrees of courts of justice in one province should have force against persons who might have withdrawn from that province to the other, and a common system of military arrangements for the defence of the two provinces.

'All these arrangements, when completed, to be placed under the collective guarantee of the Six Powers': *Eng. Hist. Rev.*, vol. xliii, p. 412.

ently the French were unwilling to go that far;[1] for the passage which was substituted at Persigny's suggestion merely stated that

'in regard to the details of the arrangements, which should be established according to this principle, the two governments of England and France should come to an understanding on this subject before the meeting at Paris of the conference which should have to pronouce definitely, [and that] until then it is understood that the present arrangement should remain quite secret between the two governments'.[2]

Clarendon gave substantially the same account of the transaction to Stratford and Apponyi. Regarding the element of secrecy he told Stratford that

'in deference to the request of the Emperor of the French, and with a view the better to arrive at the results which Her Majesty's government wish to attain, it is agreed between the two governments that the arrangement, mentioned in this dispatch, should be regarded as strictly confidential, and it is of the utmost importance that secrecy on this subject should be maintained. This prospective agreement, if made known, might be considered as forestalling the decision of the Congress, and His Imperial Majesty, who does not feel entitled to answer for the three Powers, who have hitherto adopted his views respecting union, naturally desires, himself, to explain to them the grounds upon which that policy has undergone an important modification.'[3]

To Apponyi Clarendon stated that the Emperor had demanded 'the most absolute secrecy for the grave concessions he had made', and that, while it was agreed that it was necessary to confide in Austria, Napoleon said that he would not ask for this privilege for his own allies, but 'asked only time and opportunity to prepare them for the change in their views and intentions, as though (added Clarendon) it was a question of satellites, submitted blindly to his will'.[4] Such, according to the British version, was the general nature of the Pact of Osborne. The essence of the bargain was the convocation of a new divan on the basis of revised electoral lists, in return for which Napoleon should relinquish his support of union, it being understood that the agreement should remain secret for the present.

Naturally one wishes to know the French version of the agreement, particularly as the nature of France's concession became a

[1] Napoleon was reported to have stated he 'had gone too far to abandon at a single stroke the principles which he had openly professed up to the present': Apponyi to Buol, no. 55 A–E, Aug. 12, Staatsarchiv, VIII/48.

[2] Memorandum, Aug. 9, F.O. 93/67x, no. 19. The whole memorandum is printed as an appendix to Mr. East's article, 'The Osborne Conference and Memorandum of August, 1857' in *Eng. Hist. Rev.*, vol. xliii, pp. 411–12. Extracts from the memorandum and also from Walewski's somewhat different version are printed in Riker, 'The Pact of Osborne', *Amer. Hist. Rev.*, vol. xxxiv, pp. 237 ff.

[3] Clarendon to Stratford, no. 740, Aug. 13, F.O. 78/1249.

[4] Apponyi to Buol, no. 55 A–E.

subject of later controversy. Writing to Bourqueney on August 9, Walewski affirmed that the two governments

'will come to an understanding on the conduct to hold at the Congress of Paris respecting the definite organization. The ground of these transactions will be that of a broad administrative union, which, in our eyes at least, can be the prelude of a complete union. Nothing definite or precise has been determined, but we told the English government, after it manifested a willingness to act *dans notre sens* at Constantinople, that . . . if complete union and a foreign prince (the plan we deem the best) should encounter too great difficulties, we would be ready to modify our views in order to avoid a disagreement with our allies.' [1]

The pith of the French concession, as here declared, was abandonment of complete union for a 'broad administrative union', whatever that might mean. Later Walewski was reported as telling Cowley that 'although union under a foreign prince was given up', he 'distinctly declared to Her Majesty's ministers who were at Osborne that he must continue to insist on the principle of legislative union, that is, on some sort of common parliament between the two provinces, and that his declaration was not objected to'.[2] On returning to Paris, Walewski sent to Persigny his letter to Bourqueney to be forwarded to Vienna, telling him in a covering letter that, while 'the entente at Osborne rested on no precise agreement outside of the resolution taken by the British government', it was desirable that 'a trace of it should remain in the archives of the embassy'.[3] Finally, he told Hübner that 'we made no arrangement, no transaction, and could make none', because it was necessary to await the action of the divans, the report of the commission, and the concurrence of France's allies.[4] 'No agreement whatever has been entered into with the British government, but we are ready to examine the proposition made by them.'[5] Thus we have at least three different versions from the same individual: a broad, administrative union was agreed upon, legislative union was tacitly accepted, no agreement at all was made regarding reorganization—only a tentative or qualified arrangement, or perhaps one that might simply be taken under advisement. And, apart from all these contradictions, we have fairly conclusive evidence that Walewski assented to the accuracy of the British

[1] Walewski to Bourqueney, no number, Aug. 9, *Aff. étr.*, *Autriche*, vol. 468. This letter bears the note : 'Cette lettre a été communiquée avant d'être expediée à Lord Palmerston et à Lord Clarendon, qui en ont approuvé tous les termes comme reproduisants fidèlement l'accord qui s'est établi à Osborne entre eux d'une part et M. le Comte de Walewski de l'autre.'

[2] Cowley to Malmesbury, no. 593, June 4, 1858, F.O. 27/1251.

[3] Walewski to Persigny, no. 87, Aug. 17, 1857, *Aff. étr.*, *Angleterre*, vol. 708.

[4] Hübner to Buol, no. 62, Aug. 13, Staatsarchiv, IX/55.

[5] Cowley to Clarendon, no. 1144. Cowley was quoting Hübner's rendering of a statement of Walewski's.

memorandum, though refusing to honour it with his signature.[1]
It is certainly regrettable that some written record of the transaction, acceptable to both sides, was not signed and docketed for
future reference. But how are we to account for Walewski's strange
behaviour? Why was he unwilling to sign the aforementioned
memorandum? How shall we reconcile these numerous conflicting
stories of what the French conceded? When was Walewski telling
the truth, and when was he prevaricating?

On the whole it seems fair to deduce that a 'broad administrative union', which the British defined in equally general terms, was
intended to mean—if anything at all—a tariff union and common
judicial and military organizations. Hübner understood from
Walewski himself that this was what was meant,[2] and a memorandum of the French foreign office also sustains this view.[3] If
Walewski treated the matter vaguely, it was partly because the
French government wanted at first to give the impression that its
victory had been decisive—a feeling which prompted Walewski's
contention that the annulment of the elections was anterior to, and
not conditional upon, any concessions which France had made.[4]
Partly, too, it was because Napoleon did not care to admit to his
allies how completely he had reversed himself behind their backs.
This 'broad administrative union' was, in truth, originally Buol's
scheme,[5] and might serve as a common denominator for the
moment. The idea of 'legislative union' was a later interpretation,
and fabricated for special ends in view, as will later appear. The
statement that 'no agreement whatever had been entered into'
(probably Walewski used the word, 'precise')[6] was, no doubt, a
safeguard against the possibility of the secret being divulged.
Diplomats cannot afford to trust each other too much in a delicate
affair involving the relations of their country with several Powers;
and it was possibly for that reason that Walewski had declined to
affix his signature to any record of the pact. If the secret were
revealed before the Powers who had supported the *démarche* at
Constantinople were prepared for this denouement, or before
Thouvenel had taken full advantage of the Austro-British concession, Walewski could deny the whole story of his government's
surrender. Clarendon told Stratford that, whereas the actual
divulgence of the secret might have absolved the Emperor from

---

[1] Besides Albert's statement to this effect (Martin, *op. cit.*, vol. iv, p. 114), we have
in evidence a letter of Clarendon to the Queen, dated Aug. 10, 1857, to be found in
the Royal archives at Windsor. The two are verbally almost identical. Hübner
must certainly have been at fault when he wrote that Walewski showed him a
copy which he had signed. The original memorandum certainly bears no
signature.   [2] *Ibid.*, p. 43.   [3] *Actes et docs.*, vol. v, no. 1740.
[4] See Albert's statement in Martin, *op. cit.*, vol. iv, p. 114; Walewski to Thouvenel, Aug. 21, and Sept. 3, *Actes et docs.*, vol. v, nos. 1727 and 1750.
[5] Page 109.   [6] See the phraseology in Walewski's letter to Bourqueney (p. 135).

his observance of the pact, Walewski had decided, instead, to deny that any such engagement had been taken.[1] Probably, on the whole, Walewski made the choice that a diplomat, so situated, could best have made. To renounce the pact would have run the risk of compromising the reconciliation with Great Britain, which had been the Emperor's chief immediate desire; while denial of the pact would not really deceive the British, and might enable him to gain time to smother the flames of indignation from various capitals of Europe. Only in his relations with Thouvenel was Walewski's floundering inexcusable. Surely there was no point in withholding from that trusted ambassador the admission of the price which France had paid for the annulment of the elections.

The situation of Thouvenel had at first rather unexpectedly brightened. Ali, who was now once more the Sultan's minister of foreign affairs, had agreed, without apparently waiting to hear from London or Vienna, that the elections should be annulled, and the only point under debate was whether all parties should agree to be bound by the future decision of the Conference of Paris.[2] Then to the Turkish ministers, as well as to Prokesch and Stratford, came the news of the Pact of Osborne, though Thouvenel learned by telegraph only the concession which London had made,[3] and a letter, containing the whole truth, did not reach him until several days later.[4] Meanwhile, in spite of all the precautions taken,[5] some one in Turkish circles had let out the secret—no doubt the temptation to refute the charge of an abject surrender was very hard to resist—and Reshid's party made the story common property.[6] 'The rumour of the abandonment of union', wrote Thouvenel in consternation, 'fills the city.' All that Thouvenel could do was to say that the Turkish ambassador at London must have misunderstood Clarendon; but he spent a very unhappy hour when the Russian minister quizzed him about the rumour ('the confidence which sustained and fortified our

[1] Clarendon to Stratford, Aug. 25, telg., F.O. 78/1249. Clarendon added (partly with a view of scolding Stratford) that Walewski had been 'led to adopt this course with reference [*sic*] to the humiliating position in which the French ambassador has been placed in consequence of our instruction not having been at once acted upon'.

[2] Thouvenel to Walewski, Aug. 11, *Actes et docs.*, vol. v, no. 1683.

[3] The dispatch informed Thouvenel that 'this conference had led to a general exchange of ideas respecting union, but nothing precise had been agreed upon'. The reason given was that before a plan of organization could be decided upon, it was necessary for the commission to end its work and France reach an agreement with Russia, Prussia, and Sardinia: *Actes et docs.*, vol. v, no. 1671.

[4] Walewski to Thouvenel, no. 52, Aug. 14, *Aff. étr., Turquie*, vol. 332. The information was conveyed by the enclosure of Walewski's letter to Persigny.

[5] Clarendon to Stratford, Aug. 10, telg., F.O. 78/1249; Musurus to Ali, Aug. 10, telg., *Actes et docs.*, vol. v, no. 1689.

[6] Thouvenel to Walewski, Aug. 17, telg., *ibid.*, no. 1702.

action . . . ', he complained to Walewski, 'has been evidently attacked, and I suffered in not being able to re-establish it'), and he could only meet Boutenieff with the weapon of his own honest ignorance of his government's duplicity. Meanwhile Stratford went about with the air of 'knowing something that he could tell if he wanted to',[1] and actually both he and Prokesch were so furious that the position which they had taken had been reversed that they made no haste to execute the instructions, which both had received, to urge the Porte to annul the elections.

The effrontery of Stratford, in again trying to obstruct the paths of peace, must convince us that that diplomat was incorrigible.[2] Clarendon had telegraphed on August 10 the substance of the Pact of Osborne.[3] Two days later Stratford replied that, as he was not instructed to act at once, he supposed that Austria's concurrence was still awaited, and then gave vent to his disapproval of the concessions which his government had made.[4] Clarendon accordingly replied that all the disadvantages of the Porte's yielding were considered to be outweighed by the advantages, and 'we rely (he said) upon your zeal and ability for persuading it to do so'.[5] Yet Stratford implied that he did not consider this statement 'positive instructions'[6] (this, notwithstanding the fact that Prokesch had received precise orders from Vienna),[7] and, when Thouvenel informed his government that no action had been taken,[8] Walewski telegraphed him in reply, August 18, that if annulment were not granted in three days he might be required to leave his post forthwith, though he was to telegraph first.[9] Only on receiving a sharp demur from his chief[10] did Stratford finally bestir himself; and Clarendon not only expressed himself forcibly to Apponyi (including Prokesch also in his strictures),[11] but was almost ready to admit to Persigny that perhaps Stratford had revealed the secret portion of the pact—a circumstance which, he acknowledged, would release France from the agreement.[12] Fortunately France was as anxious as Great Britain to avoid a fresh quarrel, and, when

---

[1] Thouvenel to Walewski, Aug. 18, *Actes et docs.*, vol. v, no. 1708. Stratford was under the misapprehension that Thouvenel was deliberately withholding the truth: Stratford to Clarendon, no. 738, Aug. 19, F.O. 78/1269.

[2] *The Times* expended some sarcasm at his expense in an editorial on Sept. 8 (quoted in *Amer. Hist. Rev.*, vol. xxxiv, p. 247).

[3] Clarendon to Stratford, Aug. 10, telg., F.O. 78/1249.

[4] Stratford to Clarendon, Aug. 12, telg., F.O. 78/1269.

[5] Clarendon to Stratford, Aug. 13, telg., F.O. 78/1249.

[6] Stratford to Clarendon, no. 756, Aug. 26, F.O. 78/1269.

[7] Buol to Prokesch, Aug. 15, Staatsarchiv, xii/61.

[8] Thouvenel to Walewski, Aug. 17, telg., *Actes et docs.*, vol. v, no. 1702.

[9] Walewski to Thouvenel, Aug. 18, telg., *ibid.*, no. 1710.

[10] Clarendon to Stratford, Aug. 20, telg., F.O. 78/1269. Mr. East (*op. cit.*, pp. 140–4) gives a vivid account of Clarendon's tilt with Stratford on this occasion.   [11] Apponyi to Buol, no. 59 A, Sept. 8, Staatsarchiv, viii/48.

[12] Persigny to Walewski, no. 72, Aug. 21, *Aff. étr., Angleterre*, vol. 708.

Ali announced, August 23, that the elections were annulled,[1] the four ambassadors resumed diplomatic relations with the Porte.

Thus calm was restored at Constantinople, and the two great western Powers were at last in happy accord. As so often, however, when governments have wandered from the straight road, and have to find it again by groping, the Pact of Osborne was not wholly creditable to either party. The agreement to face the Conference of Paris with a general scheme, already formed, regardless of the prospective action of the divans and of the European commission, was scarcely to be reconciled with Clarendon's earlier principles against 'prejudging the question'.[2] Equally questionable was Napoleon's readiness to make a bargain *à deux* without taking into his confidence the three Powers who had stood by him so loyally. Clarendon had been not a little astonished, as we have noticed, that Napoleon should treat them as 'satellites, submitted blindly to his will'.[3] Smooth words, however, seem a sufficient balm sometimes to cover insult when both parties wish to see none.[4] To St. Petersburg and Turin Walewski wrote that France had not decided on bases of organization for the Principalities, as she had told the British government that she could not act without her allies, though she was ready, of course, to enter upon 'reciprocal concessions'.[5] Gortchakoff seemed a little puzzled at what was meant by 'reciprocal concessions',[6] but he was obliging enough not to ask embarrassing questions, and Cavour, who had no wish but to gratify the Emperor's wishes, seems to have ignored the hoax entirely. Only Prussia was slightly sullen at first, having been goaded, it seems, by Austrian gibes that France had wantonly let her down. But on reflection she proved no less willing than the other courts to defer to the great monarch, whose tactful references to his 'allies' could not fail to denote goodwill, and in the end the French ambassador was able to report that Prussia also had pronounced her 'satisfaction'.[7] It is probably an evidence of the striking prestige that Napoleon enjoyed in 1857 that, in spite of the awkward diplomacy of his minister, France stood forth as the sponsor, for the moment, of a common programme, the pivot of international politics, and in a sense the arbiter of Europe.[8]

---

[1] *Actes et docs.*, vol. v, no. 1720.   [2] Page 85..   [3] Page 134.

[4] Benedetti, who was then director of political affairs in the department of foreign affairs at Paris, also remarked upon the 'docilité' of the three Powers, but concluded that they had been satisfied to see the other side fail of their point, and were anxious not to aggravate the crisis: Thouvenel, *op. cit.*, p. 163.

[5] Walewski to Baudin, no. 60, Aug. 19, *Aff. étr.*, *Russie*, vol. 214; and to Grammont, no. 29, Aug. 13, *ibid.*, *Sardaigne*, vol. 342. Similar to Prussia in telegram to Belcastel, Aug. 13.

[6] Baudin to Walewski, no. 38, Aug. 27, *ibid.*, *Russie*, vol. 215.

[7] Belcastel to Walewski, no. 6, Aug. 14, *ibid.*, *Prusse*, vol. 330.

[8] This was still more apparent when Napoleon met the Tsar at Stuttgart in September (to be noticed later).

The international crisis being ended, one may naturally inquire: What was the cost of the resultant compromise? Stratford declared that the Turks were the real gainers,[1] but he omitted to give the basis of his reasoning. Clarendon told Apponyi that his government thought it wise to 'sacrifice the form to obtain the fundamentals',[2] and, this sentiment being also expressed by Musurus, the Turkish ambassador to London, in a telegram to his chief, and subsequently reported to Paris, Walewski was highly indignant at that view of the situation, and once more insisted that Great Britain's yielding on the question of annulment was wholly independent of any concessions which France had made.[3] Such casuistry might prove how really superficial was the Emperor's arbitral eminence. And yet one cannot but feel that his government had some ground for satisfaction at even the appearance of victory. In answer to questions in Parliament both Palmerston and Clarendon mentioned only the concession which the British government had made, and, in alluding to the elections, not only did Clarendon admit '*prima facie* proof of irregularity',[4] but Palmerston went so far as to charge the Turkish officials with negligence for having so long suppressed the decision of the ambassadors on the injunctions Vogorides was to follow.[5] Speaking later in debate, Lord John Russell said that if the divans 'should express a strong wish that the Principalities should be united', he did not think it 'would be right or practicable for the Powers to do otherwise than advise the Porte to concur in that opinion', much as he would regret to see Turkey 'between the kingdom of Greece on the one hand and the kingdom of Moldo-Wallachia on the other'.[6] It is just in such a remark that one can gauge the chief outcome of the crisis and its solution. Whether or not France would be faithful to her side of the bargain—and Walewski wrote Talleyrand that 'we aim at the same end, though we have always intended to lend ourselves to concessions, which, while adjourning solution, will render it more certain'[7]—the fact remains that it would be difficult for the Powers to flout permanently the expressed wishes of the Principalities. In obtaining the election of a new divan, Napoleon gave the Moldo-Wallachians their opportunity. It was the future, then, to reveal which Power had won the 'form', and which the 'fundamentals'. In the meantime moral factors paid obeisance to diplomacy, and the compromise at Osborne put nationalism in storage.

[1] Stratford to Clarendon, Aug. 26, Stratford Papers, F.O. 352/48.
[2] Apponyi to Buol, no. 55 A–E.
[3] Walewski to Persigny, no. 92, Aug. 31, *Aff. étr., Angleterre*, vol. 708.
[4] Hansard, *op. cit.*, vol. 147, pp. 1388–90.   [5] *Ibid.*, pp. 1526–7.
[6] *Ibid.*, pp. 1688–9.
[7] Walewski to Talleyrand, Aug. 17, *Actes et docs.*, vol. v, no. 1704.

CHAPTER VI

THE LIQUIDATION OF THE COMPROMISE: THE CONVENTION OF AUGUST 19, 1858

IT is undoubtedly true that the Pact of Osborne shelved rather than solved the problem of the Principalities. The basis which had been agreed upon for the reorganization of these lands might have the effect of bolstering up the *status quo* in the Ottoman Empire for a year or two, but neither Napoleon nor the Moldo-Wallachians themselves would accept as final so incomplete a system of union as must proceed from the understanding of August 9. One has simply to reflect that a revolution, whether peaceful or otherwise, seldom makes a solid advance save by dint of slow and painful adjustments. It was obvious that peace must reign once more within the ranks of the Protecting Powers before reason and logic could be applied to this complicated problem; and the foreign office at Paris had shown creditable insight when it reflected (in a cabinet memorandum) that if the coming Conference of Paris were to find itself divided into irreconcilable groups, its sessions would terminate without arriving at any decision whatever.[1] For the present, whatever the sacrifice, the Concert of Europe must be preserved.

It is more difficult to justify the encouragement of the public belief that the crisis had ended in the complete triumph of the unionists. Faithful to the equivocal language of his court, Thouvenel was still protesting, as late as September, that France had not renounced the idea of union,[2] though, in alluding to the 'enigma of Osborne', as he called it in a private letter, he expressed the conviction that his government did not have any policy at all. It was a comfort, however, to feel, as he recalled his earlier misgivings, that 'the only reasonable union implied the choice of the prince by the Porte and the establishment of a Turkish fortress at Ismail; and I know not what we should gain', he added, 'by upholding the illusions of the Roumans'.[3] No such pessimism, however, reigned at Bucharest and Jassy. Place and Béclard rejoiced at France's 'great success', as the latter put it,[4] and neither seems to have harboured any suspicion of a skeleton in the closet. As for Talleyrand, there is no evidence that he had received any inkling of the truth, but the award of the dignity of commander of the Legion of Honour[5] was at least a cause of personal gratification, and, in the

---

[1] *Ibid.*, no. 1740.
[2] Thouvenel to Outrey, Sept. 6, 1857, enclosed in Stratford's no. 845, F.O. 78/1271.
[3] Thouvenel, *Trois Années*, pp. 179–80.
[4] *Ibid.*, p. 157.   [5] *Ibid.*, p. 158.

meantime, to Bulwer's amazement, he still supported union.[1] Public opinion in the Principalities was naturally full of gratitude to France, who had given them the chance of registering their wishes.[2] One may picture the French ambassador's ironical smile when Place wrote him, 'You are regarded as the protector, the saviour of Moldavia.'[3] But, in truth, the Moldo-Wallachians were too much the victims of joyful astonishment to cherish any suspicions for the present. The annulment of the elections and the privilege, recently accorded, of welcoming back the exiles of 1848,[4] were quite enough to make them all believe that the future was in their hands.[5] On the surface, at least, every one seemed to be hugging an illusion.

Among the Powers, despite occasional grumbles from Vienna, a state of unusual harmony seemed to prevail. Following a plan which had been made in the late spring,[6] Napoleon met the Tsar at Stuttgart on September 25, and had then the chance of removing any misunderstanding which might have arisen regarding Osborne. While the continental press played up the meeting as a significant stroke of diplomacy, and one historian has imagined that Russia had agreed not to oppose French policy in Italy in return for a French promise not to abandon the Principalities,[7] there is no archival evidence to support such a theory. It is probably true that Gortchakoff had really wanted some binding treaty, but that Walewski (and that meant, of course, Napoleon) was unwilling to go that far; and, apparently, the most that was entered into was a verbal agreement that the two governments would not be found on opposite sides in European affairs and that in the Eastern Question they should march in perfect accord.[8] When questioned afterwards

[1] Bulwer to Clarendon, no. 249, Oct. 12, F.O. 78/1283. According to Bulwer, Talleyrand said that he knew 'nothing positive as to any arrangement at Osborne', and that his instructions were simply to be 'conciliatory'.

[2] Béclard to Walewski, Aug. 6, *Actes et docs.*, vol. ix, no. 2592.

[3] Thouvenel, *op. cit.*, pp. 154–5.

[4] Stratford had contended ever since the close of the Crimean War for this permission to be accorded, but the Porte had been afraid that these men of 1848 would engage too actively in agitation while the question of union was still pending. By special dispensation two of the Golesco brothers were allowed to return during the spring of 1857, and Nicholas justified expectations by becoming vice-president of the leading club at Bucharest. Nevertheless, in spite of Austrian opposition, the Porte finally yielded to Stratford's creditable efforts; and in July these zealous patriots made their triumphal entry into Bucharest: Eder to Buol, no. 55 A, July 17, Staatsarchiv, XXXVIII/109. There were about twenty of them in all.

[5] According to the Austrian consul at Bucharest, 'No credence is given here to the news, printed in different newspapers, that the Emperor Louis Napoleon had made the concession at Osborne not to go on with the union of both Principalities. . . . The view is held that France will support with all energy the development of union': Eder to Buol, no. 66, Sept. 3, Staatsarchiv, XXXVIII/109.

[6] Charles-Roux, *op. cit.*, p. 213.

[7] Débidour, *Histoire diplomatique de l'Europe*, vol. ii, p. 172.

[8] Charles-Roux, *op. cit.*, pp. 219–20.

by Cowley, Walewski refused to admit that there had been any understanding, and asserted that Gortchakoff was plainly opposed to the union of the Principalities, and that he, for his part, had given no encouragement to the project.[1] Cowley, in recalling the insolence with which Russia had greeted the *Coup d'État*, told Walewski that he considered the meeting 'to be perhaps the greatest external triumph which the Emperor had yet attained'.[2] If the affair had any significance, it may be said to have enhanced the prestige of Napoleon—now more than ever the arbiter of Europe—and to have paved the way for a co-operation of the two governments on Eastern affairs. Perhaps also it was designed as a warning to certain Powers that neither France nor Russia were willing to play second fiddle in the European concert. The government of Vienna, which had most reason to feel alarm, was not content until the Tsar should show an equal deference to Francis Joseph, and a meeting took place between the two sovereigns at Weimar two weeks after the Stuttgart interview. Buol, though he was said to have desired to anger Napoleon by arranging this countermove,[3] told Bourqueney that the two meetings had the effect of achieving the general reconciliation',[4] and both he and the Tsar denied that the meeting had any 'political significance'.[5] The British government had perhaps the most reason to be disturbed by these cryptic exchanges of courtesies, but there is no evidence that Clarendon was alarmed or even suspicious. Cowley, for his part, was quite convinced that France had really abandoned union,[6] and was also gratified when Walewski further announced that the downfall of Reshid had been Thouvenel's own manœuvre, and that he (Walewski) had disapproved of it.[7] Whatever her secret intentions, France did not propose to allow any slight misunderstandings to rob her of the fruits of Osborne. 'We desire,' Walewski had written Talleyrand, 'as far as we can, to pass a sponge over the past.'[8] It is obvious that France had more occasion to watch the present.

It will be recalled that by the Pact of Osborne fifteen days were to be allowed for the revision of the electoral lists in Moldavia in

[1] Cowley to Clarendon, no. 1419, Oct. 13, F.O. 27/1204, reprinted in East, *op. cit.*, appx. ii.
[2] Cowley to Clarendon, no. 1379, Oct. 4, *ibid.*
[3] Hübner, *Deux Années*, vol. ii, p. 49.
[4] Thouvenel, *Trois Années*, p. 178. Lord Loftus, who was soon to succeed Seymour as British ambassador to Vienna felt, on the other hand (*Diplomatic Reminiscences*, vol. i, p. 345), that relations between Austria and Russia were not improved by the meeting, as Gortchakoff had been particularly anxious to get Buol dismissed, and had failed in his object.
[5] Seymour to Clarendon, Sept. 23, telg., F.O. 7/522.
[6] Cowley to Clarendon, no. 1419.
[7] Cowley to Clarendon, no. 1382, Oct. 4, F.O. 27/1204.
[8] Walewski to Talleyrand, Aug. 10, telg., *Actes et docs.*, vol. v, no. 1678.

accordance with the commission's rulings. That the real wishes of Moldavia would be expressed there could now be little doubt, seeing that Vienna and Constantinople had been forced to admit their defeat, and even the erring caimacam must now trim his sails with the winds. One might not readily understand how Vogorides could so speedily and completely reverse himself, but oriental politicians are not squeamish about their record as long as they believe themselves to be promoting their own interests, and the caimacam had no other thought than to justify his conduct, past, present, and future to the Porte.[1] If he had got himself into trouble for using his position to frustrate union, he was now prepared to throw himself as heartily into the opposite camp, if only he could satisfy his sovereign and save his political skin. On this ground we can explain the removal of some of his ministers, whom he frankly declared to be venal and subservient to Austria[2]—an enlightening commentary on his previous management of the elections. On the other hand, though Place's statement that Vogorides was 'strictly impartial'[3] is probably an exaggeration, and though Bulwer noted that most of the peasants and small proprietors were suspiciously changing sides,[4] there was no need of corrupting Moldavia to enlist her vote for union. Besides the presence of those voters who had boycotted the previous election, a considerable number of new names had been added to the electoral lists.[5] For these reasons the new elections, which began on September 20, brought out a much greater vote than the first plebiscite (all the clergy seem to have turned out),[6] and enthusiasm was general.[7] When the votes were counted, it was found that, of the eighty-seven deputies chosen, sixty-six were known to be unionists, six were separatists, and fifteen peasants were classed as doubtful but probably favouring union.[8] It was not, of course, foreseen that all but two deputies would eventually vote for union, but it was clear that the nationalist cause had won an overwhelming triumph.

The result was, of course, a blow to Austria and Turkey, though they could hardly have been astonished. Clarendon, as a matter of fact, seemed the most immediately perturbed, as he feared that British opinion might sympathize with the Moldavians, and hence began to wonder if union under a native prince was the best result

---

[1] Vogorides to Ali, Sept. 9, F.O. 78/1271.
[2] Bulwer to Clarendon, no. 209, Sept. 12, F.O. 78/1283.
[3] Place to Walewski, Sept. 18, *Actes et docs.*, vol. v, no. 1768. Some abuses were reported (Bulwer to Clarendon, no. 64, Oct. 13, F.O. 78/1283), and doubtless an absolutely fair election in an oriental country was hardly to be expected.
[4] Bulwer to Clarendon, no. 232, Sept. 25, F.O. 1283.
[5] Gardner to Stratford, Sept. 10, F.O. 78/1271.
[6] Place to Walewski, Sept. 10, *Actes et docs.*, vol. v, no. 1758.
[7] Talleyrand to Walewski, Sept. 11, telg., *ibid.*
[8] Place to Walewski, Sept. 18.

that could be hoped for.[1] But his friends were less disposed to accept the outlook. Under persistent pressure from Austria[2] (who had urged the step as far back as July) the Porte sought consolation in issuing a circular, September 22, declaring that the question of union tended to attack its legitimate rights, and reiterating the sentiment, contained in the circular of a year ago,[3] that it reserved its final decision regarding union.[4] While this move was endorsed by Buol,[5] and denounced by Clarendon[6] and Walewski,[7] there is no reason to take it too seriously. Ali assured Thouvenel that, while feeling that it was its duty to clarify the issue, the Porte had no intention of proposing the exclusion of the question of union from the deliberations at Paris;[8] and his colleague Fuad seemed actually to favour the acceptance of the principle, if only the Porte were permitted to name the hospodar and to establish a garrison at Ismail.[9] It is not improbable, apart from the persuasiveness of Prokesch, that the suzerain Power had merely wished to remind the world of its right to be considered, and especially to recall to the Powers their own repudiation of the Rouman conception of union.

The resounding victory of the unionists in Moldavia was hardly needed to inspire the electors in Wallachia, where the general result had long been conceded to the National Party. Indeed, it might be supposed that the course of politics in Wallachia would furnish little interest or excitement. But public opinion there had long enjoyed a degree of freedom that had not been permissible in the sister province, and the occasion of Napoleon's name-day, August 15, was seized upon to stage a more than usual demonstration. There was a torch-light procession, accompanied by the band of the provincial militia, and the celebration wound up with an address to Talleyrand. Whether or not there were shouts of 'Vive l'union!' is not quite clear, but much was made of the story that a handkerchief had been waved in defiance under the window of the Turkish commissioner, who was, himself, unaware of it.[10] When

---

[1] Malaret to Walewski, no. 79, Oct. 9, *Aff. étr., Angleterre*, vol. 708.

[2] Buol to Prokesch, Aug. 26, telg., and Aug. 27, Staatsarchiv, XII/61; Prokesch to Buol, no. 60 A–D, Sept. 9, and 61 A–D, Sept. 11, *ibid.*, XII/60. Ali had shown some hesitation at first for fear lest France would think that his government was trying to influence public opinion. [3] Page 75.

[4] *Actes et docs.*, vol. v, no. 1780.

[5] Buol to Prokesch, Sept. 26, Staatsarchiv, XII/61.

[6] Malaret to Walewski, no. 81, Oct. 22, *Aff. étr., Angleterre*, vol. 708.

[7] Walewski to Thouvenel, Oct. 16, *Actes et docs.*, vol. v, no. 1820.

[8] Thouvenel to Walewski, Oct. 7, *ibid.*, no. 1804. Cf. Prokesch to Buol, no. 66 A–C, Sept. 30, Staatsarchiv, XII/60. Ali complained, however, to Prokesch of the hardship which the Treaty of Paris imposed upon the Porte in requiring the concurrence of the Powers in settling the question.

[9] Thouvenel to Walewski, Sept. 22, *ibid.*, no. 1778. Such a view was an odd reproduction, in part, of Thouvenel's own reflections (*supra*, page 141).

[10] Béclard to Walewski, Aug. 23, *ibid.*, vol. ix, no. 2594; Bulwer to Stratford, no. 50, Aug. 18, F.O. 195/559.

Liehmann and Bulwer called on Ghika to account for allowing officials to participate and the band to contribute its share in the demonstration, the caimacam defended himself on the ground that he could not be responsible for the conduct of all government employees, that there was no law to prevent the band from being hired for this occasion, and he denied that it was a unionist demonstration. The two objectors having put their protests in writing, Ghika believed that they were aiming to bring about his fall;[1] nevertheless, he refused to punish the offenders,[2] being probably more afraid to defy the force of public sentiment than to incur the hostility of foreign agents.

Talleyrand himself seems, in general, to have escaped criticism in connexion with this affair, which one may believe was entirely spontaneous. But a few weeks later Prokesch heard that the French commissioner was taking part in the electoral agitation and that the clubs were once more active. Stratford passed on the information to Clarendon and Bulwer, and the former sent it to Cowley to be digested by Walewski.[3] Bulwer, for his part, felt that Stratford was magnifying trifles;[4] he did not feel that the attitude of the clubs mattered much; and he doubted the truth of the accusations against Talleyrand.[5] As a matter of fact, the Ghika and Stirbey-Bibesco factions were much more intent on knifing each other than on agitating for a cause that was already won.

The elections in Wallachia were as orderly as those in Moldavia.[6] Stirbey's party won in the country and the Ghika interest carried the capital, but no one opposed the national programme,[7] though some effort had been made to impose upon candidates a *mandat impératif*, pledging them to vote for it, if elected.[8] It really did not need the news of the elections in Moldavia to create unionist deputies in Wallachia, and the suppression of a paper which published the outcome across the border under the caption 'Vive l'Union' was probably a harmless bit of posing on the part of the caimacamie.[9] Bulwer had forecast the result of the elections when he had previously written to Clarendon, 'The truth we must acknowledge to ourselves is that almost every man in this principality is, or says he is, for uniting the two Principalities under a foreign prince.'[10]

[1] Béclard to Walewski, Aug. 23; Bulwer to Stratford, no. 11, Aug. 20, F.O. 195/529.
[2] Béclard to Walewski, Aug. 26, *Actes et docs.*, vol. ix, no. 2595.
[3] Stratford to Clarendon, no. 785, Sept. 2, F.O. 78/1270; Clarendon to Cowley, no. 1297, Sept. 8, F.O. 27/1182.
[4] Bulwer to Clarendon, no. 202, Sept. 4, F.O. 78/1283.
[5] Bulwer to Stratford, Sept. 3, Sept. 15, and Sept. 21, F.O. 195/529.
[6] Talleyrand to Walewski, Oct. 3, *Actes et docs.*, vol. v, no. 1798.
[7] This consisted of the 'four points' which were later brought up in the divans.
[8] Dalyell to Bulwer, Oct. 16, F.O. 78/1283.
[9] Bulwer to Stratford, no. 57, Sept. 15, F.O. 195/559.
[10] Bulwer to Clarendon, Sept. 4, F.O. 78/1283, cited in East, *op. cit.*, p. 144.

Apparently Bulwer did not feel that the ambition of the factional leaders would be able to stand proof against the current.

There was in fact no longer any doubt among the Powers that the divans would vote for union, and the only thing that worried any of the cabinets was the possibility that the idea of a foreign prince would be coupled with it. At first it seemed—if we may believe the Austrian ambassador [1]—that Clarendon was opposed to a notion (emanating from Talleyrand) that the divans must be told that they were not to broach this thorny subject, fearing that such injunctions would look like unwarrantable interference. But a week later he turned completely around, and proposed that the French and British governments should unite in telling them that the question of a foreign prince was 'beyond the competency of the divans'.[2] Walewski, while admitting that this desirable innovation was at present impracticable, seemed unwilling to do more than consent to a joint protest if the divans should actually take this action.[3] At the same time an Austrian view that a declaration of the divans in favour of a foreign prince and representative government was likely to produce dissension in the commission led him to agree with the Vienna government that the commission should merely report the wishes of the divans and not discuss these thorny points in the preparation of its report.[4] Since Russia also adhered to this opinion, it seems to have been adopted, much to the disgust of Bulwer,[5] who was averse from losing any opportunity of expressing a personal judgement. Even the Porte, after some hesitation, decided that its commissioner should make no protest in the event of the dreaded declaration being passed.

The Moldavian divan opened on October 4 amid general enthusiasm.[6] After the first few sessions had been spent in matters of organization, the divan proceeded to proclaim the principles of religious and civil equality,[7] and finally on October 19 a motion was read containing the four points: automomy, union, a foreign prince, and representative government, with the addition of a fifth point, the neutrality of the Principalities. 'In Moldavia and Wallachia', declared the resolution in part, 'we are a single people, homogeneous and identical . . . the advantages and salutary consequences resulting from the union of these two peoples cannot be called in question.' Michael Cogalnitchano supported the national programme in an impassioned speech, and it was creditable to the

---

[1] Apponyi to Buol, no. 63 B, Oct. 3, Staatsarchiv, VIII/48.
[2] Clarendon to Cowley, no. 1435, Oct. 8, F.O. 27/1182.
[3] Cowley to Clarendon, no. 1418, Oct. 13, F.O. 27/1204.
[4] Walewski to Thouvenel, Oct. 9, *Actes et docs.*, vol. v, no. 1808.
[5] Bulwer to Clarendon, no. 247, Oct. 11, F.O. 78/1283.
[6] Place to Walewski, Oct. 5, *Actes et docs.*, vol. v, no. 1801.
[7] Place to Walewski, Oct. 11, *ibid.*, no. 1812.

temper of the house that an address by one of the few opponents of union was listened to without any interruption. According to the firman the divan should have broken up into its various categories or class divisions for the submission of all questions before taking any collective parliamentary action, but there was so little difference of opinion on these fundamental points that the assembly took the shortest cut to its goal. When the five points were put to vote, only two dissenting voices were counted out of a total of eighty-three. Announcement of the result was greeted with prolonged shouts of 'Vive l'union!'[1] The principality, whose sentiments had so long been a bone of contention, had spoken with no uncertain voice.

It apparently mattered little that Stratford and Bulwer were annoyed at the irregularity of the divan's proceedings.[2] Since, moreover, the commission had condemned itself to inertia, the divan took whatever action it saw fit, dividing now into its component elements, which prepared elaborate projects of reform for the consideration of the assembly as a whole. When the question of a foreign prince came up for further discussion, the divan registered its disapproval of the choice of a ruler from any neighbouring Power, and Victor Place imagined that a Frenchman might be generally acceptable.[3] In the designation of the new state as 'Roumania' there was, of course, no disagreement.[4] It was not, however, the application of the principle of union that proved an obstacle to harmony in the divan. When that body came to deliberate on the details of reconstruction, the agrarian question showed at once the sharp cleavage between *boyards* and peasantry.[5] As the divan became more and more the scene of futile wrangling it soon became evident that its usefulness was at an end.

In Wallachia, though there was a similar disregard of the firman, no such muddle disfigured the deliberations of the divan, which began its sessions on October 11. After the usual preliminary formalities had been completed, the divan deliberately followed the lead of the sister assembly in Moldavia and on October 21, with shouts of 'Long live Roumania! Long live the Protecting Powers!', unanimously passed 'the four points': autonomy, union, a foreign prince, and representative government.[6] It then sent a memorial to the commission, setting forth in rather grandiloquent phrases the moral argument of Rouman nationalism for union,

---

[1] Procès-verbal no. 7, *Actes et docs.*, vol. vi, part 1, pp. 549 ff.
[2] Bulwer to Stratford, Oct. 27, Stratford Papers, F.O. 352/48; Stratford to Clarendon, no. 931, Oct. 28, F.O. 78/1272.
[3] Place to Walewski, Oct. 21, *Actes et docs.*, vol. v, no. 1825.
[4] Stratford to Clarendon, Oct. 22, telg., F.O. 78/1272.
[5] Place to Walewski, Dec. 16, *Actes et docs.*, vol. v, no. 1869. The agrarian question was also aired to a certain extent in the Wallachian divan: *ibid.*, vol. vi, part i, pp. 383–5.
[6] Procès-verbal no. 6, *ibid.*, pp. 202 ff.

and justifying the demand for a foreign prince on the ground that
such a departure would promise stability and prestige to the new
nation, end internal rivalries, and ensure it a place in the family of
nations; until it were known, however, whether the fundamental
points, recommended in the vote of the divans, were acceptable to
the Powers, it was useless to proceed to the further work of
reorganization.[1] Such a view was logical, and, since the divan was
quite adamant on the subject, an effort of the commission to induce
it to continue its labours proved altogether futile.[2] The assembly
was apparently swayed by the 'men of '48', a great number of
whom had composed the commission which had drawn up the
document proposing 'the four points'; and the Russian consul
deplored the confusion of classes, which he compared to conditions
in the estates-general of 1789 in France.[3] The implication was
hardly apt, however, as the divan was very far from revolutionary,
and never claimed to enforce its will without regard to the Protecting Powers.

While the thus far tranquil temper of the Wallachian assembly
was cause for reflection, the radical principles, proposed by both
assemblies, could not fail to harass the uneasy sensibilities of the
cabinets. Clarendon, always anxious about the stability of the
Pact of Osborne, tried to persuade Walewski that the Powers
should at once convene and impose their veto on the resolutions
for union and a foreign prince.[4] But Walewski was not quite so
stupid as to fall into such a trap. If his government had bartered
in advance the aspirations of its protégés, it was not going to show
them gratuitous offence. The vote of the divans, he told Cowley,
meant no more than the indications of a desire, and they themselves knew well enough that they would not be allowed a
foreign prince. Moreover, it would be ungracious to tell them
what could not be granted without at the same time informing
them what they could obtain. He did not agree with Cowley that
an insurrection was more likely to break out if the matter were
left to the Conference to settle than if a veto were imposed now;
and he declared that the thing to do was to press the divans to
complete their work and to get the commission's report as soon
as possible in order that the divans might be dissolved and the

[1] *Ibid.*, pp. 268 ff. Bibesco had made a strong speech on Oct. 19, demanding
a thorough-going reform of the governmental system—in other words, the revision of the *Règlement*, which had been the prescribed duty of the divan—but
he, as well as Stirbey, had been excluded from the commission which formulated
the divan's wishes: Talleyrand to Walewski, Oct. 25, *ibid.*, vol. v, no. 1828. It
was another evidence that the 'Forty-eighters' controlled the assembly.
[2] *Ibid.*, no. 1853.
[3] Basily to Boutenieff, Oct. 12, *Aff. étr., Russie*, vol. 215.
[4] Clarendon to Cowley, Oct. 26, telg., F.O. 27/1187; Walewski to Malaret,
no. 105, Oct. 31, *Aff. étr., Angleterre*, vol. 708.

Conference open its sessions.[1] As Walewski had lately alluded to
the Pact of Osborne and had expressed the view, according to
Cowley, that the divan should be constantly told that these wishes
were not practicable, it is perhaps not astonishing that Clarendon
had put him to the test; but Cowley believed that France was still
prepared to stand by the Pact, and it was better to let well enough
alone.[2] Clarendon, accordingly, sent word to Buol that it would
be well not to send any instructions of which France was likely to
disapprove, as the all-important thing was for the Powers to stand
together.[3] It is noticeable that Austria at no point played a decisive
role during these incidents, though she had threatened to make
trouble if the divans voted for union,[4] and she had, after her usual
fashion, encouraged the Porte to make difficulties.[5]

The Porte was not averse from letting its position be known,
though it seemed to realize that its recent action had been somewhat too peremptory. On October 28 a new circular appeared,
which was simply critical of the conduct of the divans. It deplored
the radical pronouncements of these bodies as well as the omission
of the word 'suzerainty' in the debates—a fact which seemed to
show clearly what the Principalities 'wished to attain'. Then, with
a bit of characteristic subtlety, the Porte expressed some distrust
of the divans' avowed respect for the capitulations, and alluded to
the 'sovereignty' which it had long exercised over these countries
(a designation which incurred sharp criticism from Russia);[6] but
one could not, of course, expect a different result from assemblies
composed of the men of '48! Yet, 'trusting in . . . the sincerity of
its ancient allies', the Porte 'would await with assurance the
reassembling of the Conference of Paris to discuss and combat
the so-called national demands of the assemblies in question'.[7]

It is not improbable that the Porte felt that its dignity required
this much venting of its feelings. It may also be true that a new
vizier felt called upon to show his colours. Just six days before,
the Sultan had reinstated Reshid, much to the disgust of Thouvenel,
and greatly to the satisfaction of the wily Turk, who had been
trying to get back into power ever since his fall. 'I am little
inclined to exclusive preferences,' wrote Thouvenel, 'but in point
of antipathy Reshid merits in the highest degree the honour of an
exception to our system of impartiality.'[8] One can hardly blame
the Sultan for seeking this balm for the wound to his dignity which

[1] Cowley to Clarendon, no. 1497, Oct. 31, F.O. 27/1205.
[2] Cowley to Clarendon, no. 1467, Oct. 23, F.O. 27/1204.
[3] Clarendon to Seymour, no. 760, Nov. 7, F.O. 7/507.
[4] Clarendon to Seymour, no. 716, Oct. 20, F.O. 7/507.
[5] Prokesch to Buol, no. 69 c, Oct. 16, Staatsarchiv, xii/60.
[6] Gortchakoff to Boutenieff, Nov. 17, *Actes et docs.*, vol. v, no. 1842.
[7] *Ibid.*, no. 1830.   [8] Thouvenel, *Trois années*, pp. 180–1.

Thouvenel had inflicted, but, as Ali and Fuad consented to remain in the ministry,[1] the affair could hardly be regarded as a political upheaval. Moreover, Reshid, for his part, must have had some momentary qualms, for he sent a private emissary to plead his cause in Paris, and this person (a former employee of the French legation) proved so skilful in the arts of ingratiation that Walewski came to believe that the new vizier would 'adhere to union on conditions which we ourselves impose'.[2] The only thing that ruffled the French was the thought that the change of viziers would now be looked upon as a British triumph, and Walewski was highly annoyed when he learned that Stratford had telegraphed his government that the Sultan had 'asserted his independence and vindicated his character'.[3] The Anglo-French rivalry at Constantinople only slumbered at best.

In the meantime the proper mode of dealing with the divans continued to puzzle and harass the European chancelleries. If the Moldavian divan gave offence by trying to do too much, the Wallachian divan was equally annoying in refusing to do anything —except to raise a hubbub! For several weeks, it appears, the latter body had done little but mark time, the 'Forty-eighters' wishing to stay in session in order to protest against the action of the Powers if they failed to grant union, and winning over the peasant deputies by promising agrarian reform. A second request from the commission to proceed to the task of revising the *Règlement* was only met by a second refusal, the divan reserving, as it said, the right to frame a new electoral law as a basis for a constituent assembly.[4] To offset the effect of this action the Left would have passed a new vote of gratitude to the Powers, but the proposal was rejected—probably by the votes of the Right—while Napoleon's name, uttered in the course of the debates, was greeted with wild enthusiasm from the radical benches.[5] Stirbey and Bibesco finally resigned, rather than seem to approve of the divan's futile turbulence, and before the close of the session thirty-eight conservatives refused, or threatened to refuse, to attend any further deliberations.[6] Meanwhile at Jassy almost every conceivable question was being solemnly and somewhat noisily discussed—

---

[1] Stratford to Clarendon, no. 928, Oct. 28, F.O. 78/1272. This seems partly to have been due to Prokesch's persuasion, as he always regarded Reshid as Stratford's man, and had more confidence in Ali: Prokesch to Buol, no. 72 C, Oct. 28, Staatsarchiv, XII/60.

[2] Thouvenel, *op. cit.*, p. 200; cf. *Actes et docs.*, vol. v, no. 1852.

[3] Stratford to Clarendon, Oct. 22, telg., F.O. 78/1272; Thouvenel, *op. cit.*, p. 198.

[4] Bulwer to Clarendon, no. 363, Dec. 26, F.O. 78/1285; Talleyrand to Walewski, Dec. 19, *Actes et docs.*, vol. v, no. 1872.

[5] Talleyrand to Walewski, Dec. 31, *ibid.*, no. 1874.

[6] Bulwer to Clarendon, Dec. 25, telg., F.O. 78/1285.

from a system of gratuitous and compulsory education to the demand for the suppression of consular jurisdiction;[1] and even Victor Place was aghast when a motion was introduced to impeach the existing ministry.[2] It is no wonder that the patience of the tutelary Powers was somewhat strained by all this parliamentary comedy; and, though Talleyrand declined a British suggestion to join with Bulwer in pronouncing against these 'revolutionary tendencies',[3] it was felt on all sides that the time for drawing the curtain had arrived. Interestingly enough, while the Powers were still debating whether to ask the opinion of the commission or to leave it to the Porte to decide the moment of terminating the discussions, the Wallachian divan on its own initiative adjourned till February 1. Although the Moldavian divan was still in session, it was only waiting to learn if the commission had questions to put to it, and the commission decided unanimously that it would forgo this privilege.[4] Hence, at the request of the Powers, the Porte issued a firman dissolving both divans.[5] So decisive a procedure had the effect of quashing the plans of the Wallachian divan, which had constituted itself the 'guardian of the national programme',[6] and evidently was arming for a renewal of the struggle; but, under these circumstances, dissolution, rather than prorogation, was no doubt the wiser course. Yet the wisdom of the cabinets in having let the Principalities enjoy their brief triumph without hindrance can hardly be questioned after the experiences of the summer. Even Stratford contented himself with the thought that 'the unionists could be safely left to work out their own failure'.[7]

Much less impressive, on the whole, than the role of the divans was that of the European commission. The factional divisions and general helplessness of that body had been amply demonstrated during the crisis of the summer; and, but for the Pact of Osborne, it would probably have ceased to function altogether. Some time after the crisis was past (there were no meetings for nearly a month),[8] it had returned to its original task of observing

[1] Place to Walewski, Nov. 19, Dec. 3, and Dec. 16, *Actes et docs.*, vol. v, nos. 1843, 1863, and 1869.

[2] Place to Walewski, Dec. 16, *ibid.*, no. 1869.

[3] Talleyrand to Walewski, Dec. 26, *ibid.*, no. 1881; cf. Bulwer to Clarendon, no. 365, Dec. 26, F.O. 78/1285.

[4] Bulwer to Clarendon, Jan. 20, 1858, telg., F.O. 78/1374.

[5] *Actes et docs.*, vol. v, no. 1882. Opinion in the Moldavian divan was much offended by the expression in the firman 'an integral part of my empire', which was regarded as placing the Principalities in a status below that which the Treaty of Paris had determined for them: Place to Walewski, Jan. 26, *ibid.*, vol. ix, no. 2603.

[6] Bulwer to Clarendon, Dec. 25, 1857, telg., F.O. 78/1285.

[7] Stratford to Bulwer, Nov. 25, telg., F.O. 78/1274.

[8] The protocols will be found in *Actes et docs.*, vol. vi, part 2.

the course of public opinion in the Principalities, and, though its sessions were virtually suspended, at Bulwer's instance,[1] during the elections, it met frequently during the sessions of the divans, and wasted countless hours worrying over the behaviour of those bodies. Faithful to its habits of ineffectiveness, however, it studiously refrained from interfering with their proceedings, and declined to give advice to the ambassadors. When at length the serious work of the assemblies came to a close, the commission got to work in earnest on its report, assigning to various of its members the task of drawing up a précis of separate aspects of the existing administration, like the judicial, the financial, the ecclesiastical, and so on. As the commission had also the special duty of taking cognizance of the wishes of the inhabitants, a lengthy memorial was drawn up as a sort of commentary on the formally expressed wishes of the divans, and this document formed the preamble of the report. One might judge that the attitude of the divans might easily give occasion for new controversies in the commission, but, either because its members were tired of their former wrangling, or because the cabinets were in a hurry to get its work expedited, the commission had early decided to confine its report to expressions of opinion on which there was little or no divergence, leaving individual differences to the separate judgement of its members, who might enlighten their respective governments as they saw fit.[2] In consequence the exposition of the divans' *vœux*[3] was, on the whole, a rather colourless document, the commission deliberately forbearing to discuss thorny questions, like a representative legislature, the separation of powers, and ministerial responsibility, for which the Moldavian divan had contended, and limiting itself to a dry record of facts and fancies, leaving it to the Conference of Paris to draw its own conclusions. After a brief survey of the régime of the *Règlement organique*,[4] the main body of the report took up in succession 'administration', 'judicial organization', 'ecclesiastical affairs', 'commerce', 'public works', public instruction', 'military organization', and 'financial

[1] Bulwer to Clarendon, Aug. 28, telg., F.O. 78/1282. Walewski supported Bulwer's and Talleyrand's opinion on this point in spite of Gortchakoff's desire that the meetings should be resumed without delay: Walewski to Baudin, no. 66, Sept. 3, *Aff. étr., Russie*, vol. 215. There was one brief meeting, however, after the Moldavian elections and before the Wallachian for the purpose of sending Basily and Bulwer to get in touch with the Moldavian divan. Talleyrand wrote that these two were selected because they were the only members of the commission who had not visited Moldavia: *Actes et docs.*, vol. v, no. 1767.

[2] This had been Bulwer's view (Bulwer to Clarendon, no. 381, Jan. 2, 1858, F.O. 78/1374), and the protocols show that the rest of the commissioners tacitly adhered to it.

[3] *Actes et docs.*, vol. vi, part 2, pp. 559 ff.

[4] The commission had dealt gently with this point owing to the susceptibilities of the Russian commissioner: Bulwer to Malmesbury, no. 443, Mar. 28, 1858, F.O. 78/1375.

system'.[1] The report was finally completed at the end of March, and Talleyrand noted with much amusement that it was dated April 1 according to the Greek calendar and the 13th according to the Roman, so that one might regard the work as an act of folly or as a portent of disaster.[2] No doubt it could add much to the enlightenment of diplomats, who, with one or two exceptions, knew little of the character of these distant lands, but whether the Powers would bear out their promise of approaching this problem in a scientific spirit could reasonably be doubted in view of the shabby bargain made at Osborne. Thus far, indeed, the clash of national interests had influenced the fate of the Principalities far more than either their wishes or their needs.

Between the time of the dissolution of the divans and the opening of the Conference of Paris the question of the Principalities slipped somewhat into the background, much more attention being given to a palace revolution in Servia, and, in particular, to an attack by Montenegrins upon some Turkish border villages. It would be impracticable for us to consider at length the latest chapter of this perennial feud which intermittently racked the Balkans. Turkish reprisals on this occasion were, as usual, unsuccessful; but Russia did not choose to risk the possibility of a war of conquest, and she persuaded France to join her in a naval demonstration off the Montenegrin coasts. The Turks took the hint, and the boundary dispute was referred to an international commission[3]—a measure, which, of course, was only a palliative.[4] Yet the episode was not without its importance if Napoleon, by playing Russia's game, expected to find an ally at the Conference. Since Gortchakoff had shrewdly maintained a scrupulous reserve regarding his government's attitude toward union[5] (contending that its only insistence was the maintenance of the Treaty of Paris[6] and that no one would know Russia's decision until the Conference should meet),[7] it was deducible that Russia was waiting simply to consult her own

[1] *Actes et docs.*, vol. vi, part 2, pp. 599 ff.

[2] Thouvenel, *Trois années*, p. 233.

[3] Alison, the British chargé d'affaires, lamented that Bulwer (designated as Stratford's successor) was not on hand to 'remedy all this': Alison to Hammond, June 13, 1858, F.O. 78/136.

[4] Monicault, *Le Traité de Paris et ses suites*, pp. 189–92.

[5] The Austrian ambassador was continually trying to extract information, but with scant results. In November Gortchakoff mischievously admitted that he was not averse from the principle of a foreign prince, but he acknowledged that he doubted if any one could be found to fill that role: Szechenyi to Buol, no. 54 A, Nov. 21, 1857, Staatsarchiv, x/40.

[6] Szechenyi to Buol, no. 41 A, Aug. 28, *ibid.*; Wodehouse to Clarendon, no. 386, Aug. 27, F.O. 65/497. Gortchakoff had persistently declared for a free expression of opinion on the part of the divans.

[7] Szechenyi to Buol, no. 35 A, Aug. 7, and no. 41 A, Staatsarchiv, x/40. 'Outside of the Emperor, my august master, and myself,' he had said, 'there is not a man who knows.' Cf. Wodehouse to Clarendon, no. 470, Oct. 23, F.O. 65/498.

advantage. Whether that advantage lay in strengthening the Stuttgart Pact was only for the future to disclose. Meanwhile some changes on the immediate political stage were taking place. Stratford, who felt at last that things were sufficiently quiet to enable him to take a long-promised furlough, departed late in December from Constantinople. As a matter of fact, Clarendon was only too glad to authorize his leave, as a concession to pressure from Paris,[1] and Stratford himself could hardly have imagined that his role as ambassador was closed. On January 7 Reshid died rather suddenly after a brief illness but a long career of dissipation, and once more his rival Ali was elevated to his place—not improbably at the instigation of the French embassy.[2] Meanwhile, before the close of the year, had come the downfall of the Palmerston ministry in England, and soon afterwards—what was of great interest to Near Eastern circles—the resignation of Lord Stratford de Redcliffe, which, to his great regret,[3] the Tory government accepted. True, it was not his final bow; for he journeyed back on an unofficial mission during the spring of 1858, and even the proximity of this blusterer caused his successor some uneasiness.[4] But, whatever the marks of his long sojourn at the Sultan's court, the formidable diplomat had really closed his long career, and we know that France, at least, was far from feeling any displeasure. The succession of Sir Henry Bulwer to his place would mean the appearance of another strong character, but with probably somewhat different methods and a more tractable disposition.

The new year had opened with exceptionally cold weather at Constantinople, and for some weeks official business was practically suspended.[5] As the winter wore on, the diplomats began to think of the coming conference at Paris. The return of Ali to power was a bit of luck for France, as Reshid's recent cringing could hardly be thought sincere,[6] and Ali and Fuad, while certainly not favourable to the idea of union, were much more likely to yield something to persuasion. They both talked of preparing a plan to submit to the Conference as soon as they should come to know the opinions of France;[7] and Walewski, who noted with pleasure that they had suggested the designation 'United Provinces' or 'United Principalities' for the countries under discussion, accordingly sent to

[1] Persigny to Walewski, no. 91, Dec. 1, *Aff. étr., Angleterre*, vol. 708. Clarendon expressed the hope that France would reciprocate by treating Thouvenel in the same manner. [2] See Thouvenel, *Trois années*, p. 226.

[3] Lane-Poole, *Life of Stratford de Redcliffe*, vol. ii, p. 448.

[4] Thouvenel, *Trois années*, pp. 309–10. 'Bulwer took to his bed to be cured of his emotions', wrote Thouvenel.

[5] Prokesch to Buol, no. 7 A–B, Feb. 3, Staatsarchiv, XII/62.

[6] Thouvenel, *op. cit.*, p. 219; cf. Thouvenel to Walewski, Dec. 29, 1857, *Actes et docs.*, vol. v, no. 1883.

[7] Thouvenel to Walewski, Feb. 3, 1858, *ibid.*, vol. vii, no. 2009.

Thouvenel some ideas of his own which he felt would accord with Turkish views, and were, of course, subject to the eventual approval of Russia and Great Britain.[1] As a matter of fact, Thouvenel had already discussed with Ali a scheme which he had himself drafted during the previous November, and, after some amendment,[2] Ali had said that 'except for some modifications which reflection could suggest to him, it was, in his opinion, an honourable transaction for every one'. While not departing from the system of two hospodars, the essence of the scheme was a kind of legislative union, which, apart from the new denomination of the Principalities, was the most striking innovation recommended;[3] and it is reasonable to surmise that this idea, which had emanated from both Thouvenel and Walewski, was the issue on which the Emperor had resolved to make his fight. Ali spoke again of having a plan drawn up on behalf of the Porte,[4] but, fearing to incur the odium of Austria, he eventually accepted the bases of Thouvenel's memorial as a 'preliminary entente', only stipulating that they should not be attributed to the Porte's initiative, and that France should seek the opinion of other Powers, notably Great Britain.[5] Manifestly, the docility of the Turks did not necessarily mean that the Emperor would have his way. He had still to reckon with the cabinet at London.

It is easy to conjecture that the British Tories would not be likely to be more friendly to the Moldo-Wallachians than had been the Palmerston ministry. But it is interesting to notice that British opinion was beginning to be more interested in the merits of nationalism on the Danube—a fact which was doubtless due to the impression created by the crisis of the previous summer. On May 4 Gladstone moved an address in the House of Commons, expressing his 'earnest hope' that 'in the further prosecution of the important subject just weight may be given to those wishes of the people of Wallachia and Moldavia which through their representatives elected in conformity with the said treaty [the

---

[1] Walewski to Thouvenel, Mar. 5, *Actes et docs.* vol. v, no. 2018. A draft of Walewski's plan does not seem to be extant, but one may gather something of its nature from an analysis made by Thouvenel (*ibid.*, no. 2021). It evidently provided for two hospodars, a common legislative assembly, and a senate.

[2] This plan, which would call the new state 'The United Provinces of Moldavia and Wallachia' provided, among other things, for a single hospodar at Bucharest (represented, however, by a caimacam at Jassy), chosen for life by the Porte from a list of three nominees, designated by some form of election to be determined; for an 'ordinary general assembly' common to both principalities; and for a council of state, appointed by the hospodar in equal number from both principalities, and entrusted with projects of law to be submitted to the assembly.

[3] Thouvenel's amended scheme dropped the idea of a single hospodar, and proposed that the common assembly should sit alternately at Bucharest and Jassy; but, otherwise, the original plan was not appreciably modified.

[4] Thouvenel to Walewski, Mar. 16, *Actes et docs.*, vol. vii, no. 2020.

[5] Thouvenel to Walewski, Mar. 30, *ibid.*, no. 2028.

Treaty of Paris] they had recently expressed'. In a long and very able speech Gladstone reviewed the course of European policy towards the Principalities and the encouragement which the Powers had given them to believe that their wishes would be respected. He argued that no supposed considerations of danger from Russia should militate against the desire for a foreign prince—a desire evidently intended to put an end to inner dissension—and he scoffed at the notion that union under a foreign prince would be injurious to Turkey.

'I beseech this house', he said, 'to consider well before it determines that the fate of these two countries is to be governed by considerations other than the welfare of the people. It will be a dangerous and slippery course on which to embark when we refuse that which is suited to four and five millions of men and when we say that God Almighty put them into the world not to pursue their own happiness and welfare by such lawful and reasonable means as are in their power but to be made the victims of those whose public and private interests are subserved by other views extraneous to their interests but which an overwhelming force has determined to carry into effect.'

This declaration, couched in the familiar Gladstonian style, did immortal credit to the most liberal of British statesmen, and received a generous acknowledgement from the people he had thus befriended.[1] But neither the Tories nor the supporters of the old Whig tradition showed much sympathy for the views of this astounding liberal. Palmerston replied that the Principalities demanded union under a foreign prince because Wallachia would not submit to be ruled by a Moldavian or Moldavia by a Wallachian, but that a foreign prince would undoubtedly mean a Russian prince, and that then the Principalities would become an appanage of Russia. He reminded the house that Great Britain had undertaken a war in defence of the integrity of the Ottoman Empire, and pointed how incongruous it would be now to 'take a step which the Turkish government considers, as I think every reasonable man will pronounce, to be the first step towards the dismemberment of that empire'. Lord John Russell found a middle position between that of his former chief and the new spokesman of nationality, and pronounced himself in favour of union without the corollary of a foreign prince. Naturally the Tories, led by Disraeli, rallied in opposition to the motion, and it was defeated by a vote of 292 to 114.[2] The most liberal of all nations was not invariably the friend of the small nationalities.

Meanwhile the Porte had been pressing for some time for the opening of the Conference,[3] and, as the commission's report had

---

[1] See *Actes et docs.*, vol. vii, pp. 206–9.
[2] Hansard, *Parliamentary Debates*, 3rd ser., vol. cl., pp. 44–106.
[3] Thouvenel to Walewski, Mar. 3, *Actes et docs.*, vol. vii, no. 2017; Alison to Malmesbury, no. 197, Mar. 1, F.O. 78/1356.

been handed in on April 15, the French government issued the formal invitation. At a legislative session on January 8 Napoleon had stated in his address that France had supported the wishes of the Principalities, but that the coming conference would meet in a conciliatory attitude. 'The relations of France with foreign Powers', he declared, 'has never been better', and he alluded pointedly to the meetings at Osborne and Stuttgart to show the harmony which reigned.[1] Such a view was doubtless encouraging, but who could tell how long that paradise would last? In anticipation of the task of concerting a programme for the Conference, Cowley sounded Walewski on the attitude of France towards the question of the Principalities, and the Emperor's minister told him frankly that he proposed to put his country on record as favouring union and a foreign prince.[2] This was not, of course, intended to mean that France would press the issue, but it did open the way to a discussion of just what the Pact of Osborne signified. As Lord Malmesbury, the new foreign secretary in the Derby cabinet, could only learn from others the nature of that agreement, it was probably on that ground that Napoleon cherished the hope of securing at least the boon of legislative union.[3] But others besides France were sharpening their swords for the coming struggle. When Fuad stopped at Vienna on his way to attend the Conference, he was greeted with an unusually warm reception. In an audience with the Austrian Emperor he was told that Turkey should take the initiative in the coming deliberations, and that Austria would support her.[4]

The Conference of Paris opened its sessions on May 22, 1858.[5] Each Power was represented by one plenipotentiary: Austria, Prussia, Russia, Sardinia, and Great Britain by their resident ambassadors at Paris (Baron Hübner, Baron Hatzfeldt, Count Kisseleff, Count Villamarina, and Lord Cowley respectively), while Fuad Pasha, as we have already noticed, had come from Constantinople to represent Turkey. Count Walewski resumed his role of presiding over the deliberations and determining the order of business.[6] At the opening session it was decided that absolute secrecy should be preserved regarding the deliberations, and that

[1] *Annual Register*, 1858, p. 220.

[2] Cowley to Malmesbury, no. 506, May 21, F.O. 27/1250.

[3] Walewski took care to impress upon Malmesbury the indefiniteness of the Pact of Osborne: Walewski to Malakoff, no. 71, May 21, *Aff. étr., Angleterre*, vol. 710.

[4] Malmesbury to Loftus, no. 655, May 11, F.O. 7/543 (cited in East, *op. cit.*, p. 151).

[5] The protocols of the Conference may be found in Martens, *op. cit.*, vol. 16, part 2, pp. 14 ff., in Hertslet, *op. cit.*, vol. xlviii, pp. 81–132, in *Actes et docs.*, vol. vii, pp. 266 ff. or in *Archives diplomatiques*, 1866, vol. ii, pp. 113 ff.

[6] Some incidental attention was given to a report of a commission on the Danube navigation, but the matter was not taken up till near the close of the Conference.

each plenipotentiary should request his government to respect this rule.[1] Sometimes, of course, the press got an inkling of what was going on; sometimes it used its imagination; but, in general, it may be said that the Conference attracted little attention from the public.

After the pledge of secrecy was taken, Walewski read the clauses of the Treaty of Paris which provided for the present conference, and laid the report of the international commission before the plenipotentiaries. The Conference decided to give it immediate consideration, and it was duly read. We are not told how many of its auditors went to sleep during the performance, but the Conference adopted Walewski's proposal to register its satisfaction in the protocol.

Walewski was now ready to fire the first gun of the Conference. The solution of all other questions, he said, depended on the attitude of the Conference towards the question of union; and France, for her part, still believed in union and a foreign prince. It would add to, rather than detract from, the stability of the Ottoman Empire, and would conform both to the interests and to the wishes of the Principalities. He admitted, however, under pressure from Cowley, that the Porte had a special interest in the matter, and that its opinion deserved to be heard first of all. Fuad then spoke for Turkey, and affirmed her adherence to the existing separation of the provinces—a position in which he was sustained by Hübner for Austria. Kisseleff then rallied to Walewski's opinion —with even more vehemence than the Frenchman had displayed, so Cowley reported in a dispatch to his government. No settlement, declared Kisseleff, could be final that was not based on union and a foreign prince.[2] Now that this vexing question had been forced upon the Conference, Cowley had, of course, to explain his own government's change of heart: the granting of union had been found on examination to promise too many difficulties and inconveniences, but it would perhaps be possible, while maintaining separation, to bring about an 'assimilation of the administrative institutions' of the two provinces. The British diplomat could not, of course, refer specifically to the Pact of Osborne, which had no validity for the Conference as a whole (Walewski's advantage had been only too obvious), but the position which Great Britain had taken at Osborne was now clearly set forth as the basis of her

---

[1] Hübner to Buol, no. 54 F, May 23, Staatsarchiv, IX/56.
[2] Objection was made to this statement as reflecting on the work of the Conference, which would perhaps reach a different decision; and, under pressure from Cowley and Hübner, Kisseleff consented to withdraw the expression on the understanding that some remarks of Hübner, which had occasioned it, should also be omitted from the protocol: Hübner to Buol, no. 56, May 21, Staatsarchiv, IX/58; Cowley to Malmesbury, no. 540, May 26, F.O. 27/1250.

policy at the Conference. Hatzfeldt, who spoke next, was somewhat cautious, pointing out the importance of the expressions of the divans, but adding that the existing relations between the Porte and the Principalities deserved examination. Villamarina bespoke Sardinia's predilection for union, but expressed his readiness to comply with the decisions of the Conference, whatever they might be.[1] It is doubtful if any of the plenipotentiaries took the advocacy of union very seriously. Russia was merely playing the diplomatic game, as had already been shown. As for Walewski, he knew that he could not carry such a proposal without Great Britain, and he could not have entertained a doubt as to what her attitude would be. It was sufficient for the moment that he had placed France's position on record, and that, when the protocols should become public, there would be left no doubt in the minds of the Moldo-Wallachians that France still sympathized with their cause. After the diplomats had all expressed themselves, he assured the Conference that no Power wished to impose its opinions on the others, and he hoped that the Conference would be able to work out a plan based on 'mutual and reciprocal concessions'. This was talking the language of the Pact of Osborne.

The purpose of France was evidently to work within the principle of separation for as close an approximation to union as the Conference would permit. Although it was suggested by Hübner that the initiative in making proposals should be taken by the Porte,[2] Walewski had no notion of letting France be deprived of this advantage; and at the second session, May 26, he introduced a plan of organization—not, he assured the Conference with a rather extraordinary timidity, as purporting to be France's own recommendations, but as 'emanating from the negotiations and the ideas of all the plenipotentiaries'. After a brief discussion, which brought out plenty of opposition, the Conference decided to evade the proposal by refusing to take it up until it was divested of its anonymity, and meanwhile the details of the plan could be examined by the plenipotentiaries at their leisure.[3]

The Power which might most fittingly have presented a plan of organization was Great Britain, but no such idea seems to have occurred to the British cabinet, which, like Austria, seemed to prefer that the Porte should assume the initiative. The only plan of British authorship was one which had been voluntarily prepared by the indefatigable Bulwer, who pointed out that, as the commissioner

---

[1] Protocol 1.

[2] Buol blamed the Porte for its 'sträflichen Lässigkeit': Buol to Prokesch, June 1, telg., Staatsarchiv, XII/64.

[3] Cowley to Malmesbury, no. 542, May 26, F.O. 27/1250; Hübner to Buol, no. 56, May 27, Staatsarchiv, IX/58. All this is omitted from the brief protocol of the second session.

who had mediated between contending forces on the commission, he best knew how to reconcile conflicting opinions; and he pressed Cowley to sponsor his proposal. An examination of Bulwer's scheme, however, would convict it of over-elaboration of detail, and Cowley did not see fit to ask his government's permission to introduce it. In his own opinion, no scheme, short of granting union, would satisfy the Principalities, and he did not believe that Great Britain should take the responsibility of backing anything that would prove so unpopular as to be probably unworkable.[1] Such a view is, in truth, an interesting commentary on the attitude which British statesmanship was assuming towards the rehabilitation of a people. If the cabinet at London had nothing more positive in mind than to cavil at the suggestions of others or to amend them in the interest of harmony among the Powers, then one cannot but feel that Napoleon was making a far more creditable showing. The unfortunate feature of the French scheme was that it threw the preponderant weight not on a single hospodar (which was at present out of the question) but on a body which would have little organic connexion with either executive.[2] Yet it was not Napoleon's fault that union had to be pushed in the wrong direction, and he himself doubtless felt that any furtherance of consolidation was a forward step.

Walewski's plan, to begin with, assured to the Principalities the continuance of their privileges and immunities under the collective guarantee of the Powers who had signed the Treaty of Paris; it then suggested as the designation of the new state 'The United Principalities, or Provinces'. The executive power in each province was to be lodged in a hospodar, elected for life; the legislative power to be vested in two assemblies (one for each province) and in a central commission, consisting of eighteen members, nine chosen by each assembly, which should sit at Focshani in Moldavia, close to the frontier line between the two provinces. This body, designed to produce a certain amount of harmony of action, was the cornerstone of the new structure, as conceived by its author. It should make laws which pertained to the common interest, and should decide whether such laws as emanated from the assemblies were compatible with general legislation; it should determine the sources of revenue for the two principalities, and its assent should be necessary for every impost voted by either assembly; it should have the task of codi-

---

[1] Cowley to Malmesbury, no. 542.

[2] Malmesbury would have liked each hospodar empowered to name one member of the central commission (Malmesbury to Cowley, no. 428, May 25, F.O. 27/1236), but this would obviously have been quite insufficient to bring about unity of policy. When it is also to be realized that there were two hospodars to be considered, it is easy to see that all initiative, as far as general policy was concerned, must pass to the commission.

fying the laws, of establishing monetary, postal, telegraphic, and customs union, of reorganizing the two militias in such manner that they preserved in all respects the character of two corps of the same army, and of nominating the commander-in-chief at all times when these should meet as one army, notably for the common defence. Measures of strictly local import, such as the preparation of the annual budget, were left to the cognizance of the assemblies on the initiative of the hospodars. In addition to the unitary devices mentioned above a court of cassation should be instituted to pass upon judgements emanating from all courts in the two provinces, and there should be a common flag for the use of the two militias.[1] Manifestly, this draft-scheme was only a method of approach to the task before the Conference, but its interest lay in the fact that it contained as wide a realization of union as France could possibly hope to see enacted by the Conference.

It can readily be seen that such a project was too radical in some particulars to pass unchallenged. While the conventional scheme of two hospodars remained unaltered, the proposal of a central legislative organ, endowed with so much authority, was hardly more than a veil under which the Principalities were to be granted legislative union. Naturally Turkey was somewhat shocked at the interpretation of the principle she had accepted, Thouvenel failing to convince Ali that the movement towards union would be weakened rather than strengthened by this federal scheme;[2] and Walewski was disappointed when Fuad refused to discuss it until further instructions came. This attitude, according to the French minister, did not respond to the assurances given as to the content of Fuad's instructions, and 'at bottom there is almost complete identity' between his project and the bases which Ali had accepted at Constantinople.[3] But the mystery was somewhat clarified when the Russians supplied evidence—some intercepted instructions to Prokesch from Vienna—that revealed Austria's insistent pressure upon the Porte.[4] Austria, for her part, was very positive in her disapproval. The power given to the central commission would, as Hübner saw it, 'make union a fact—not under a prince, it is true, but under a republican form'.[5] With a strange perversion of logic Buol looked upon the project as union and anarchy combined.

---

[1] Enclosed in Cowley's no. 521, and appended to protocol 3.

[2] Thouvenel to Walewski, no. 45, June 9, *Aff. étr., Turquie*, vol. 336.

[3] Walewski to Thouvenel, no. 41, June 10, *ibid.* Walewski must have had some doubt about Turkey, however, as he told Cowley after the first session of the Conference that he feared that Hübner would persuade Fuad not to assent to what represented the *ne plus ultra* of French concessions: Cowley to Malmesbury, no. 565, May 30, F.O. 27/1251.

[4] Thouvenel to Walewski, no. 46, June 15, *ibid.*, cf. Buol to Prokesch, June 1, telg., &c. Staatsarchiv, XII/64.

[5] Hübner to Buol, no. 56, May 27, *ibid.*, IX/58.

His government was opposed not only to this plan but to the proposed name for the Principalities, and to the idea of a common flag.[1] On these three questions Austria declared herself inflexible; and Hübner, who was instructed to support Fuad in opposition, hinted to Cowley that his government might go so far as to retire from the Conference.[2] Yet Walewski felt, for his part, that he had gone to the limit of concession, and bade Hübner so inform Buol.[3] Already the lines were drawn for battle.

After the plenipotentiaries had ruminated for nearly a week over his project, Walewski, in spite of Cowley's warning not to drive Austria to a premature declaration,[4] presented his plan once more at the session of June 5, and wished it incorporated in the protocol. Hübner at once countered this move by demanding that the Conference, in conformity with article xxiii of the Treaty of Paris, should proceed to revise the existing constitution, the *Règlement organique*. This meant, of course, shifting to a more conservative basis, and would obviously be shelving the mooted innovations to which Austria was opposed. Fuad, having no mind but Hübner's when forced to a decision, supported this view. But Walewski, of course, perceived the Austrian game readily enough, and frankly declared that he must oppose this suggestion, as the *Règlement* had been made for separation and France believed in union. Cowley then cut short the discussion by saying that he could not discuss the project until he had received further instructions; and the meeting seems to have closed with Walewski's warning that 'if no entente could be found on the basis of this project, France would go back to her former idea of union and a foreign prince'.[5]

Such a bluff was doubtless needed in response to so much shilly-shallying. The resort to delaying tactics was not a brilliant stroke of politics[6] when the question had already been so long pending, but the British statesmen were consistently averse from taking a stand on either side. Moreover, Cowley had his suspicions of France's good faith, as Walewski had told him privately that legislative union had been tacitly agreed upon at Osborne, and his own copy of the memorandum of August 9, 1857, did not tally with this view. Would it not be prudent to stand with Austria and resist the smallest concession towards legislative union?[7] Malmesbury's reply was characteristically wary. He agreed that discussion should be

[1] Buol to Hübner, June 3, telg., Staatsarchiv, ix/60.
[2] Hübner to Buol, no. 56, June 1, *ibid.*, ix/57.
[3] *Ibid.*
[4] Cowley to Malmesbury, no. 600, June 5, F.O. 27/1251.
[5] *Ibid.*; Hübner to Buol, no. 59 B, June 6, Staatsarchiv, xii/57; Walewski to Thouvenel, no. 45, June 18, *Aff. étr., Turquie*, vol. 336.
[6] According to Hübner, it was in order to gain time to avoid a breach with Austria: Hübner to Buol, no. 59 c, June 6, Staatsarchiv, ix/60.
[7] Cowley to Malmesbury, no. 593, June 4, F.O. 27/1251.

carried on strictly according to the terms of the Treaty of Paris; he wished Austria to be encouraged to oppose France on all the three points of the controversy; and he not only disapproved of Walewski's project but he relied on Cowley to rid it of its 'mischievous' features. At the same time he preferred that the Porte should take the lead in the opposition, and told Cowley that there was no reason to insist on points on which the Turkish plenipotentiary might be prepared to give way; for, if the Porte were to agree to a 'modified system of union', there was no obligation on the part of Great Britain, however much she wished the principle of separation to be maintained, to out-Turk the Turk in this connexion.[1] Both Austria and Great Britain would have liked to shift to Turkey the burden of opposition; and, while Buol plied Ali through Prokesch, Cowley and Hübner tried to infuse some courage into Fuad, who was strongly suspected of wavering on the question of the central commission.[2] Meanwhile the French, as we have noticed, were beginning to show impatience, and Napoleon seems to have decided to unmask his minister; for Walewski was said to have told Cowley that 'it had been decided at Fontainebleau' that he should present the plan 'not as a French project but in the name of France'.[3] This was no doubt designed to let Walewski down gently, though it contrasted with a former statement of the minister that he did not know whether his government would support the measure he proposed.[4] One wonders if the Count had been rather fearful of the effect of his distortion of the Pact of Osborne. At any rate, Napoleon himself seems to have had no such misgivings. On June 8 Cowley telegraphed his chief that he had it on good authority that the Emperor would break up the Conference if the project were not discussed at the next session.[5]

Perhaps Cowley was right in thinking that Buol had made a mistake in threatening Austria's defection from the Conference[6]—a move which may well have stiffened Napoleon's attitude on the

---

[1] Malmesbury to Cowley, no. 481, June 7, F.O. 27/1251.

[2] Hübner to Buol, no. 59, June 6, A–G, Staatsarchiv, IX/57. Cowley told Hübner that Fuad actually intended to propose the institution to the Conference, and though Hübner promptly extorted from him the most explicit assurances, he admitted to Buol that he 'did not know what passed between him and Walewski outside the Conference'.

[3] Hübner to Buol, no. 59 A–G. He so introduced it at the Conference: Hübner to Buol, no. 59 B.

[4] *Ibid.*; Cowley to Malmesbury, no. 565. It is, of course, possible that Walewski had not really known whether Napoleon would care to make the project official and, consequently, put up a fight for it. In giving it anonymity at first, he had been able to sound the views of the plenipotentiaries. Clarendon hazarded the belief that the plan was 'of Imperial, not Walewskian origin' (Malmesbury, *Memoirs of an ex-Minister*, vol. ii, p. 124), but, if so, then Walewski had probably been prompted by the Emperor to suggest legislative union to the Turks back in March. It is not improbable that it was Napoleon who had decided to gain this measure of union if he could, and that it was Walewski who elaborated the plan.

[5] Cowley to Malmesbury, June 8, telg., F.O. 27/1251.

[6] Cowley to Malmesbury, no. 599, June 5, *ibid.*

question. At all events, there was really no use in dodging the issue any longer, as Cowley himself had begun to perceive—more especially as the Porte was believed to have agreed to the central commission in principle,[1] and that settled Great Britain's objection to its discussion. Hübner wrote that his British colleague told him that, while Great Britain would assent to a central commission, it 'will be reduced to zero', and the Austrian believed that he (Cowley) would demolish it, bit by bit, and thus avoid Austria's withdrawal from the Conference.[2] As Vienna felt sure of Turkish opposition to the common flag,[3] the chief point of attack at present was still the central commission. Buol had followed British lead to the extent of being willing to discuss the Walewski project,[4] but the central commission was 'union in germ', and, if necessary, Austria would simply stand on the Treaty of Paris, and, as Hübner expressed it, 'withdraw from the Conference with the honours of war'. If the proposed institution were to meet with Austria's indulgence, its powers must certainly be whittled down;[5] and the shifty Walewski gave the impression that perhaps, after all, France might be satisfied with a more impotent body, designed merely to 'cover her abandonment of union'.[6]

It was probably some hint of concession on the part of Walewski[7] that led Cowley to believe that he might find a basis of compromise that would make the central commission more palatable to Vienna. He was aware, of course, that it was not Walewski's resolution that must be shaken but Napoleon's; and, as possession of the *bouton de chasse de l'Empéreur*[8] gave him the privilege of attending the imperial hunt at Fontainebleau on June 12, he took that opportunity of approaching the Emperor on the questions under discussion; and an informal conference of some length was the result. Napoleon seemed very much put out at the course which the Conference was taking, especially the way he was being forced to deviate from his original plan of union, and he affirmed that he had only gone so far as to agree to two hospodars and the relinquishment of a foreign prince. He 'now found [to quote Cowley's

---

[1] See page 164, note 2.

[2] Hübner to Buol, no. 59 C, June 6, Staatsarchiv, IX/57.

[3] Hübner to Buol, no. 64 D, June 15, *ibid.*

[4] Buol to Hübner, June 9, telg., *ibid.*, IX/60. Buol fumed about the failure of the British to support him, and deplored that they had not taken the same high tone which had been so successful during the controversy over Bolgrad: Loftus, *op. cit.*, vol. i, p. 346.

[5] Cowley and Hatzfeldt tried to get Hübner to say what Austria would be likely to accept, but without success: Hübner to Buol, no. 60, June 9, Staatsarchiv, IX/57.

[6] Hübner to Buol, no. 59 C.

[7] Hübner got that impression from Cowley's recital of a conversation which he had had with Walewski (*ibid.*), but Cowley's letters to Malmesbury make no mention of it.   [8] Hübner to Buol, no. 64 G, June 15, Staatsarchiv, IX/57.

words] resistance to everything which he proposed, and he had at length been forced to abandon all but the mere shadow of union'. While he reserved his chief strictures for Austria, he was very emphatic in blaming the British government, which he accused of deserting him despite the Pact of Osborne. Cowley rejoined that there must have been some misunderstanding of that agreement, as Great Britain had assented to nothing but a common administration in certain things, and was not bound to go beyond the memorandum of August 9, which, though not signed by Walewski, was no less binding on the honour of France.[1] Manifestly, the question between the two men was whether a central commission, clothed with considerable power, did, or did not, conform to the substance of the Pact. An examination of Walewski's scheme could hardly leave any doubt that France was trying to stretch the Pact quite beyond its original meaning. After a time, Napoleon shifted the discussion to the common flag, which had already aroused bitter opposition from Austria, and declared that, if he yielded somewhat on the other question, he would withdraw from the Conference sooner than yield on this. The fact, however, that he hinted that he might yield at all was encouraging, and put the key to the situation more securely in Walewski's hands. On the following day Cowley had an interview with the minister himself, who now asked him to prepare a counter-project, embodying his objections to the original scheme, and to lay it before the Conference.[2] The British ambassador's role as mediator seemed bright with possibilities.

The conviction had been growing on the part of Walewski that his hopes of making something out of the central commission were vain. On one occasion, when he was forced to meet a storm of objections, he had declared that he meant it to be merely the guardian of the constitution;[3] he was ready now to assure the Conference that it was just intended as a link between the Principalities[4] (he felt, indeed, that that much was due to the Principalities in response to their desires);[5] and so, when he brought his project for the third time before the Conference on June 14, he was clearly willing to consider large modifications of the institution in question. Alone among the plenipotentiaries, Hübner refused to budge an inch.[6] But simultaneously, a message of Walewski through Cowley to the effect that France might yield on the question of the flag

---

[1] Cowley to Malmesbury, no. 669, June 15, F.O. 27/1252.
[2] Cowley to Malmesbury, no. 670, June 15, *ibid.*
[3] Cowley to Malmesbury, no. 600, June 5, F.O. 27/1251.
[4] Hübner to Buol, no. 64 E, June 15, Staatsarchiv, IX/57.
[5] Walewski to Bourqueney, no. 46, May 28, *Aff. étr., Autriche*, vol. 471. This had also been Kisseleff's contention at the second session: Hübner to Buol, no. 56, May 27, Staatsarchiv, IX/57.
[6] Protocol 5; Hübner to Buol, no. 64 E.

if Austria would accept the principle of a central commission elicited from Hübner the statement that his government would not 'absolutely refuse to make an accommodation on a central commission', though on the other two questions Austria would not give way.[1] (We shall note later that he offered on June 23 to yield also on the question of the new denomination.)[2] That much achieved, it was not difficult to work out a scheme sufficiently moderate to obtain her acceptance. At the next session (June 19), while Cowley's plan was rejected as too complicated[3] (though accepted, it was said, by Napoleon),[4] the composition of the body was decided upon with little debate, and an effort of Hübner to withhold from it the right to revise the *Règlement* was eventually defeated.[5] Finally, at the session of July 3, Walewski introduced a revision of his project, shaped to meet the views of his British colleague, and intended, if possible, to bring Vienna to reason. The central commission should be restricted to the right of initiative in matters of legislation in the common interest, should be empowered to pass upon measures of that character, and should have both the making of a new constitution and its custody when adopted. As to the army, the idea of giving the central commission a right of inspection was dropped, but Walewski tried still to save for it the right of nominating the commander-in-chief. 'The central commission, having been deprived of all power, authority, and influence', should, at least, he declared, 'preserve the semblance of authority', but, when Hübner, in the midst of a profound silence, declared that if this were granted all chance of an accommodation with Austria would disappear, the French minister did not pursue the subject further.[6] After all, France had slightly widened the scope of union; and perhaps the reconstructed central commission would be less cumbersome than the one which she had first proposed.

The proposed designation of the new state as 'The United Provinces' was another point on which Austria was resolved not to give way, contending that it would have the effect of encouraging

[1] Hübner to Buol, no number and 64 F, June 15, Staatsarchiv, IX/57.
[2] See below, page 172, note 4.
[3] Cowley's plan provided for a council of state as an upper chamber of each legislature and included also the central commission, though restricted to a supervisory capacity, the operation of which was not made clear (Cowley to Malmesbury, no. 670, June 15, enc., F.O. 27/1252). According to Cowley, the plan received Fuad's assent, and several of the plenipotentiaries had been consulted in its preparation, but, in the end, 'considerable difficulties were raised to its acceptance': Cowley to Malmesbury, no. 700, June 19, *ibid*.
[4] Hübner to Buol, no. 66, A–B, June 20, *ibid*.
[5] Protocol 6; Hübner to Buol, no. 66 B, June 20, *ibid*. On Kisseleff's remarking that a commission of experts had drawn up the *Règlement*, Hübner had suggested the same device for drafting a new constitution, but the Russian pointed out that this would impair the prestige of the central commission.
[6] Hübner to Buol, no. 70 B, July 4, *ibid*.

agitation in her dominions;[1] and the Porte, probably prompted from Vienna, was now opposed to an innovation[2] which it had previously accepted.[3] The resourcefulness of Cowley, however, found a way out of the dilemma. At the session of June 10 he proposed the addition of the words 'of Moldavia and Wallachia', and Fuad then withdrew his opposition.[4] Since Austria had by this time decided to concentrate her strength on other issues, the proposal was passed without dissent.[5] Again we have the illusion of both union and separation.

The position of the two executives was naturally of considerable importance, and one of Austria's reasons for disapproving of a strong central commission was the fact that it would overshadow the hospodars.[6] Malmesbury was very anxious that the institution should be hereditary on the ground that it would thereby discourage intrigues and make for stability,[7] but the Porte was so opposed to the idea (Ali feared that the Principalities might be absorbed by a neighbouring Power through some sort of hold it might obtain over the incumbents)[8] that Great Britain, true to her general attitude of humouring Turkish sentiment, reluctantly dropped the proposal.[9] It was generally agreed that the hospodars should be elected by the assemblies and serve for life, though Walewski had at first favoured a seven-year term—hoping, according to Hübner, that an occasion would be found for bringing about union.[10] On the question of the provisional government to serve until the new hospodars were elected, there was, however, considerable difference of opinion,[11] until finally Walewski carried the proposal that caimacamies, chosen in accordance with the *Règlement organique*, should call the assemblies which would choose the hospodars.[12] Hübner, who had fought a long battle for the

---

[1] Buol to Hübner, June 9, telg., Staatsarchiv, IX/57.
[2] Walewski to Thouvenel, no. 45, June 18, *Aff. étr., Turquie*, vol. 336.
[3] See page 155.
[4] Cowley to Malmesbury, no. 639, June 10, F.O. 27/1251.
[5] Protocol, no. 4. 'Principalities' was substituted in the final form for 'Provinces'.
[6] Bourqueney to Walewski, no. 77, June 2; Walewski to Malmesbury, no. 51, June 7, *Aff. étr., Autriche*, vol. 471.   [7] Cowley to Malmesbury, no. 639.
[8] Thouvenel to Walewski, no. 52, June 30, *Aff. étr., Turquie*, vol. 336; Alison to Malmesbury, no. 366, June 14, F.O. 78/1362, and no. 401, June 18, enc.
[9] Cowley to Malmesbury, no. 826, July 8, F.O. 27/1254. Malmesbury then thought of suggesting that hospodars be designated by their predecessors, since he did not believe that an honest election could be held: Malakoff to Walewski, no. 97, July 8, *Aff. étr., Angleterre*, vol. 711.
[10] Hübner to Buol, no. 76 F, July 19, Staatsarchiv, IX/57.
[11] Kisseleff proposed that provisional hospodars be chosen by the Powers, while Hübner and Fuad spoke for vesting the responsibility solely in the Porte, and Walewski at first suggested that the Conference might make selections from a list submitted by the Sultan's government. None of these original suggestions was carried, however, and, for some reason, the question hung fire for over a month. Discussion is found in Cowley to Malmesbury, no. 637, June 10, F.O. 27/1257.
[12] Hübner to Buol, no. 77, July 22, Staatsarchiv, IX/57.

right of the Porte to nominate temporary hospodars (one remem-
bers Austria's opportunity for intrigue in 1857), reminded Kisseleff
that he had formerly advocated it himself on the ground that an
elected hospodar might be dangerous. Kisseleff replied that
according to his information the Principalities had never been
more tranquil, whereupon Hübner declared that from what he
had learned they had seldom shown so disturbing a character.
This was, of course, a familiar contention, and got nowhere. Once
the hospodars' responsibility to their respective subjects was safe-
guarded, there was little debate on the nature of their prerogatives,
though the question of qualifications for the office brought forth
various suggestions. A proposal of Hübner, supported by Kisseleff,
that a candidate must have been a high official was rejected on the
ground that this class was too corrupt to be deserving of consideration;[1] likewise a proposal of Cowley's to restrict the choice
to the greater *boyards* failed to find favour;[2] and the basis of
eligibility was, in the end, made fairly broad. The Conference
was guilty of a great oversight, however, in not determining more
exactly the relations of the executive and the legislature. The
hospodars were to govern 'with the concurrence of the ministers',[3]
but did that mean that the ministers were responsible to the
hospodar by whom they were appointed, or were they to have
equal weight with him, and thus, perhaps, by implication, to voice
the wishes of the assembly? If they were not, indeed, to rest on
legislative confidence, how were they or the hospodar to work
with the assembly? Merely to allow the hospodar the right
of dissolution was no assurance that he would get an assembly
of different sentiments? Yet, as the stipulation is far from clear
and there was apparently no discussion of the point, one can hardly
infer that the Conference meant to grant ministerial responsibility.
When it is realized that most of the Protecting Powers had not yet
adopted that institution for themselves, and that the Conference
was taking as its model the *Règlement organique*, one may reasonably conclude that no such innovation was intended. Yet therein
lay the germ of future trouble for the Principalities.

On the composition and functions of the assemblies there was
little disagreement; and neither Great Britain nor France seems to
have ventured to propose a broad representative basis.[4] At the

[1] Hübner to Buol, no. 79 A–B, Aug. 4, *ibid.*
[2] Cowley to Malmesbury, no. 923, July 23, F.O. 27/1255. As a matter of fact,
the property qualification adopted would have practically the effect, as Walewski
pointed out, of restricting such candidates to the upper classes: Hübner to Buol,
no. 79 A–B.
[3] Protocol 14, annex 2.
[4] Bulwer's plan would have given some influence to non-propertied classes,
but Cowley thought his scheme too complicated, and, though he himself proposed granting the suffrage to some who did not possess property, he seems to

session of June 19 a property qualification for electors was agreed upon without dissent,[1] and at the session of July 10 a detailed scheme was passed, which continued the practice of indirect election, and fixed the suffrage requirements in such a manner as to place the assemblies under the control of the *boyards*. It was understood, however, that, in the absence of sufficient statistical information, the electoral arrangements should be regarded as tentative—subject, if necessary, to later revision by the assemblies[2] with the sanction of the Porte and the Protecting Powers.[3] Hübner's objection to designating the assemblies as 'representative' was met by the decision to call them 'elective'[4]—which was, after all, perhaps a little nearer the truth.

Meanwhile the third contentious point, the question of the common flag, had already cast its sinister shadow upon the Conference, and threatened, as time went on, to wreck its entire work. 'The knot of the situation', wrote Hübner, 'is always the question of the flag.'[5] To Austria, as the possessor of nearly two million Roumans, the proposal smacked of serious danger to her integrity. Any variant of the expression, 'The United Principalities', was enough cause for alarm without the emotional appeal that would be furnished by a visible standard of the union of the Roumans on the Danube. No effort was spared, in consequence, to stiffen the Porte's resistance to the dreaded innovation,[6] and Hübner told Fuad that, if Turkey should consent to this departure, he would get up and leave the Conference.[7] Since Napoleon, on his side, was simultaneously threatening to quit if the flag were not approved,[8] it is evident that, on this issue at least, the Conference was facing a perilous deadlock.

France's position is not hard to fathom. Walewski, who had set more store on legislative union than on the common flag, had offered, as we have noticed, to compound with Austria on the basis of mutual concessions; but without doubt he had been overruled by the Emperor,[9] who saw no adequate gain in a mutilated central commission. Walewski now explained that the common flag of the Principalities was needed to afford them 'moral security'.[10]

have made no special effort to carry his point: Cowley to Malmesbury, no. 710, June 21, F.O. 27/1250.   [1] Hübner to Buol, no. 66 B, June 20, Staatsarchiv, IX/57.
   [2] While the protocol did not explicitly say this, but merely used the expression 'during the second legislature', it was later understood that the Conference had meant to give the initiative in the matter of revision to the legislative arm of the government, presumably the central commission.
   [3] Protocol 9.   [4] Hübner to Buol, no. 84 A–H, Aug. 15, *ibid.*, IX/58.
   [5] Hübner to Buol, no. 69 B, June 29, *ibid.*, IX/57.
   [6] Hübner to Buol, no. 64 D, June 15, *ibid.*; Buol to Prokesch, June 24, *ibid.*, XII/64.
   [7] Hübner to Buol, no. 64 A–K, June 15, *ibid.*, IX/57.
   [8] Cowley to Malmesbury, no. 669, June 15, F.O. 27/1252.
   [9] Hübner, *op. cit.*, vol. ii, p. 185.
   [10] Walewski to Malakoff, no. 87, June 18, *Aff. étr., Angleterre*, vol. 711.

Actually there is little doubt that it was intended as a device for promoting union; and, once his pride had been involved by taking a resolute stand, Napoleon refused to accept defeat.

The task for the other diplomats to find a way out of the *impasse* was certainly not encouraging. Cowley wrote to Malmesbury that he did not believe that Austria would give in, but that the French contention, being based on *amour propre*, was still more difficult to handle.[1] Apparently Walewski felt that, if the Porte and Great Britain could be brought around to France's position, and Austria thus isolated, the first step would be taken towards the success of the French project. Thus far, indeed, Turkey had refused to yield to pressure; but Cowley told Hübner (in answer to a query) that Great Britain could not refuse to yield, if Turkey did.[2] Walewski was meanwhile besieging the British with every weapon at his command. He told Cowley that, as he had adopted the British view in the matter of the central commission, it was the more necessary that France should win her point on the question of the flag.[3] Through Count Malakoff, French ambassador at London, he went further, complaining of British partiality to Austria, and threatening that if the British continued their opposition to his project, France would revive her demand for union and a foreign prince.[4] Sometimes the Pact of Osborne entered into the discussion both at London and at Paris, Malmesbury contending that Great Britain had faithfully observed that covenant and expected France to do the same, while Walewski argued that the common flag was quite within the scope of that agreement.[5] To the suggestion of Malmesbury that the Turkish crescent might be added to the common flag, Walewski replied that he feared that the Principalities would not consent to such a mark of vassalage. Cowley seems to have been convinced that Walewski himself might have been willing to make concessions, but that the adoption of the French proposal was a '*sine qua non* with the Emperor'.[6] Since Hübner told his British colleague that Austria would sooner leave the Conference than yield (especially after giving way on the other two points of contention),[7] the matter did not seem any nearer of solution. Both sides had, in fact, the feeling of having already been too generous. 'We have made numerous concessions,' Walewski telegraphed the French ambassador to Russia, 'but on this point we shall not yield.'[8] Gortchakoff responded to this

[1] Cowley to Malmesbury, no. 675, June 16, F.O. 27/1252.
[2] Malmesbury to Cowley, no. 548, June 21, F.O. 27/1237.
[3] Cowley to Malmesbury, no. 670, June 15, F.O. 27/1252.
[4] Malmesbury to Cowley, no. 548, June 21, F.O. 27/1237.
[5] *Ibid.*; Cowley to Malmesbury, no. 709, June 21, F.O. 27/1253.
[6] Cowley to Malmesbury, no. 722, June 22, *ibid.*
[7] Cowley to Malmesbury, no. 723, June 22, *ibid.*
[8] Walewski to Montebello, June 16, telg., *Aff. étr., Russie*, vol. 216.

feeler that he believed it might be expedient to yield to *la forme des choses*; yet he was prepared to resume their former position of demanding union and a foreign prince.[1]

It is not improbable that the·threat to throw over the Pact of Osborne and go back to the idea of union in an extreme form may have weighed sufficiently with Great Britain to induce her to bend a little towards France. The fact that the Emperor was displeased with Walewski (as the latter confessed) for having made any concessions at all made Cowley all the·more certain that a rupture of the Conference was inevitable if France were not satisfied, and the British diplomat did not relish the impression which would be forced on the British nation if the Conference were broken up— no doubt a 'condemnation of me and all those engaged in the negotiation'. There was more danger, he argued to Malmesbury, in flouting France and Russia than in now giving in to their demand, and his advice was 'an acquiescence, and, if necessary, a full acquiescence' on the question of the flag.[2] This sudden change of heart was, of course, unknown to the French, but Hübner, when apprized of Cowley's wavering, remonstrated with him strongly, and urged that if only Great Britain would stand firm, France would certainly think twice before executing her threats.[3] But, whether or not he was partially placated by a direct overture from Hübner to Walewski,[4] Napoleon finally consented to a Prussian proposal that the militias when united should use the same standard, consisting of the two flags, side by side;[5] and Malmesbury urged Austria through Loftus (British ambassador to Vienna) to accept this as a compromise.[6] The hope was vain, however. 'A flag of peace', exclaimed Buol to Bourqueney, 'and then a flag of war! . . . No, we cannot put our signature to such a plan. We have given our last word in the way of concession.'[7]

Up to this time the negotiations on the question of the flag had been conducted outside the Conference through the medium of

---

[1] Montebello to Walewski, June 17, *Aff. étr., Russie*, vol. 216.

[2] Cowley to Malmesbury, no. 742, June 25, F.O. 27/1253.

[3] Hübner to·Buol, no. 69 D, June 29, Staatsarchiv, IX/57.

[4] Hübner to Buol, no. 69 C, *ibid.* Hübner had not heretofore deigned to parley with Walewski outside the Conference, but this time he tells us that he sought and received an interview, which took place on the night of June 23, just before Walewski was to see the Emperor. Hübner had then offered to accept a modified central commission and the proposed denomination of the Principalities, though he insisted that Austria would not yield on the question of the flag. Cowley expressed his regret that these concessions had not been made sooner: Cowley to Malmesbury, no. 722.

[5] Cowley to Malmesbury, no. 760, June 28, F.O. 27/1253.

[6] Malmesbury to Loftus, July 6, telg., F.O. 7/536. Malmesbury urged that this would simply indicate a 'temporary alliance' in time of war, and would in no way infringe upon the normal condition of separation: Malmesbury to Loftus, no. 121, July 7, F.O. 7/536.

[7] Bourqueney to Walewski, no. 96, July 6, *Aff. étr., Autriche*, vol. 471.

dispatches, telegrams, and informal conferences. At the seventh session, however, on July 3, Walewski introduced his revised project of reorganization, much of which had to do with the army. After a discussion, in the course of which it was decided that the commander-in-chief should be appointed by the hospodars alternately, Walewski formally proposed the common flag. While the Opposition was marshalling its forces, Hatzfeldt introduced his counter-proposal—two flags on a single pole when the militias met as one army. Hübner said (pursuant to Buol's instructions) that he could admit this amendment only if a Turkish emblem were added to the flag, and Fuad rallied to this position; but most of the plenipotentiaries felt that this would wound too deeply the suscepti-bilities of the Moldo-Wallachians; and thus the session ended without decision.[1] Cowley told Hübner afterwards that he did not believe that Napoleon would yield beyond his acceptance of the Prussian proposal;[2] and, when a violent brochure appeared, discuss-ing the imminence of war with Austria, the fact that it was attributed to the government precipitated an immediate panic on the bourse.[3]

There was, of course, no danger of war; but it was evident that both France and Austria intended to contest every inch of the ground, and it looked as if the Conference was doomed. Napoleon flatly refused to consider the addition of a Turkish symbol to the flag (though Cowley seemed to feel that Walewski regretted his decision),[4] and Buol took the view that a common flag, even in the manner proposed, would encourage the unionists to impose their ideas by a 'military revolution'. In short, he rejected the Prussian proposal. At the same time, adopting a suggestion which is credited to Cowley,[5] Buol offered to accept, as a substitute for a common flag, a pennant of any colour, affixed to each flag-pole.[6] Since, at first, the device was proposed only for the militias when united, neither Walewski nor Cowley was sanguine that the Emperor would acquiesce;[7] and, after a moment's wavering, Napoleon decided to stand firm on the Prussian proposal.[8] Then, at Cowley's suggestion (communicated through Loftus),[9] Francis Joseph was persuaded to resort to a manœuvre that might perhaps assuage his fellow sovereign's *amour propre*: he sent word to

[1] Hübner to Buol, no. 70 B, July 4, Staatsarchiv, IX/57.
[2] Hübner to Buol, no. 70 A–G, July 4, *ibid.*
[3] Hübner to Buol, no. 70 F, July 4, *ibid.* Cf. Hübner, *op. cit.*, vol. ii, p. 192. Walewski took pains to deny to the Conference that his government was respon-sible for this brochure. The title, *L'Empéreur Napoléon et les principautés roumaines*, was reminiscent of other pamphlets on international questions which were almost certainly inspired by the government.
[4] Cowley to Malmesbury, no. 825, July 8, F.O. 27/1254.
[5] Loftus, *op. cit.*, vol. i, p. 364.
[6] Buol to Hübner and Apponyi, July 9, Staatsarchiv, IX/60.
[7] Hübner to Buol, no. 72 A–B, July 9, *ibid.*, IX/57.
[8] Hübner, *op. cit.*, vol. i, pp. 193–4.   [9] Loftus, *op. cit.*, vol. i, p. 363.

Napoleon that he would regard it as a personal favour if the Emperor would relinquish his demand for the common flag.[1] This *coup de théâtre* proved decisive. France gave up the common flag; Austria accepted the permanent pennant;[2] and at the session of July 30, the Conference formally agreed that 'the two militias should preserve their present flags, but that these flags should carry for the future a blue pennant, conforming to the model annexed to the present protocol'.[3] Thus, at last, the work of the Conference was saved from shipwreck.

While the three paramount points of contention between France and Austria were the most difficult that the Conference had to settle, the conduct of Russia was at times a source of anxiety, both to Austria and to Great Britain. If she 'blindly followed France',[4] as Hübner once complained, it was undoubtedly for reasons of her own. It was quite natural, of course, that Russia, in view of the abrogation of her protectorate, should take pains to show a special solicitude over the relations of her recent charges with the suzerain Power; and Kisseleff, it must be remembered, had been the chief author of the *Règlement organique*. The Russian plenipotentiary had introduced a paper on this subject at the second session;[5] but, after some debate, it was decided that the introduction of such questions at that time would interrupt the work of internal reorganization, and so the matter was deferred. Cowley believed he saw a snare in the Russian proposal that the Powers should be authorized to come to an entente with the Porte in any dispute arising between it and the Principalities, suspecting that Russia was looking for an opportunity to meddle; and he also doubted the wisdom of tempting the Principalities to bring their grievances to the Powers rather than to their suzerain.[6] At the meeting of June 14, Kisseleff again brought up his *mémoire* and wished it incorporated in the protocol, but it was not till July 15 that it was, at length, admitted as a basis of discussion. It was then agreed as the *mémoire* proposed, that the annual tribute, due to the Porte, should be augmented in consideration of abolishing the extra-ordinary tribute customarily paid on the investiture of a hospodar. This brought up the question of whether the Porte might refuse investiture—in other words, veto the choice of hospodars by the Principalities. Fuad, supported by Hübner, asserted such a claim on behalf of the Porte, and Cowley seemed also inclined to support

[1] Buol to Hübner, July 9, no. 6, Staatsarchiv, IX/58.
[2] The Porte, under pressure from Malmesbury, also acquiesced: Bulwer to Malmesbury, no. 37, July 14, F.O. 78/1364.
[3] Protocol 13.
[4] Hübner to Buol, no. 59 C. Kisseleff had made a few suggestions regarding the central commission but only on non-essentials.
[5] The date of the copy in the Austrian archives is June 10. It will be found in protocol 10.   [6] Cowley to Malmesbury, no. 801, July 5, F.O. 27/1254.

it, but Kisseleff was so vehement in opposition that the proposal
failed to carry;[1] yet in a later session it developed that the Russian
plenipotentiary was willing that such a power might be exercised
in accord with the Protecting Powers, and, after a somewhat
spirited debate, the Conference decided to beg the question and
leave the right of investiture 'as in the past'.[2] When it came to the
Porte's part in the defence of the Principalities against aggression,
Cowley urged (in accordance with instructions from Malmesbury)[3]
that it be given the right to send such aid, if it were invoked by a
hospodar. This proposal was a fair illustration of the ever-present
anxiety of the British to uphold the power of the Sultan in his
dominions, but the Conference easily swept it aside on the ground
that it contravened the Treaty of Paris, which called for an entente
with the Powers in any occasion for intervention. When Walewski
remarked that native troops should be relied upon in such an
emergency, Cowley had exclaimed, 'But what if they should
revolt!'[4] Even Buol, who approved of the plan of having a hospodar
invite the Porte's intervention, admitted that the concurrence of the
Powers was obligatory.[5] Thwarted in the prospect of seeing Turkey
given a greater scope for interference, Fuad now proposed that the
Porte be allowed to send commissioners into the Principalities to
investigate any alleged disturbances; but here again the opposition of France and Russia was sufficient to block the measure, and
the privilege was made dependent on whether the Principalities
should come to an agreement with the Porte in the matter.[6] Such
was, of course, a delicate way of rendering it impossible.

Most of these questions merely got an airing at the session of
July 15, but it is noticeable that Russia strove, as far as she could,
to weaken the position of the suzerain Power. When the question
arose whether the Porte's international treaties might be applied
to the Principalities, Kisseleff expressed his opinion that the
Principalities should have an independent right to conclude
treaties.[7] Again, it was a feature of Kisseleff's *mémoire* that no
commercial treaty affecting the Principalities should be concerted
without their approval. Such a proposal met, of course, a storm
of resistance from Hübner, who insisted that the Conference had

---

[1] Cowley to Malmesbury, no. 873, July 16, *ibid.*
[2] Hübner to Buol, no. 84 A–H, Aug. 15, Staatsarchiv, IX/58.
[3] Malmesbury to Cowley, no. 576, June 21, F.O. 27/1237.
[4] Cowley to Malmesbury, no. 871, July 16, F.O. 27/1254.
[5] Buol to Hübner, July 29, Staatsarchiv, IX/60. Cowley's argument was that
the Treaty of Paris, as it stood, did not adequately protect the integrity of the
Ottoman Empire, since the Principalities might be appropriated by some foreign
Power before the Powers collectively could enter into an agreement for their
defence.
[6] Hübner to Buol, no. 76 C, July 19, *ibid.*, IX/57.
[7] *Ibid.*; Hübner, of course, objected and the question was adjourned.

no authority to grant new rights either to the Porte or to the Principalities; and Walewski, in his quality of arbiter, remarked that, while he would be glad to see the innovation adopted, he must needs, in view of his judgement of the British and Austrian attitude, advise Kisseleff to drop the proposal. Kisseleff then merely requested that his idea be inserted in the protocol. 'Constantly beaten,' wrote Hübner to Buol, 'Russia wants at least to leave in the protocols the proofs of her desire to arrogate to herself the protection of the Principalities, and to throw on other Powers the responsibility for the failure of her efforts.' In the end the Russian plenipotentiary was deprived of even this modicum of satisfaction.[1] At the same session, July 17, a determined effort was made by Walewski and Kisseleff to defeat a proposal of Fuad that the size of the militias should be fixed with the consent of the Porte, but Cowley succeeded in forcing an adjournment of the issue,[2] and the question was finally decided against the Powers friendly to the Principalities.[3] Hübner records with glee in his diary that the Russians were beaten at every point.[4]

No doubt much of Russia's action at the Conference was due to the conviction that if the Russian-made constitution were to be superseded by one concerted by the Powers, it was clearly the duty of those Powers to make the new régime more progressive than the old. Kisseleff was not averse from making even Walewski feel uncomfortable, when he pointed out that the *Règlements* had had union in view, whereas 'the two principalities were less united now than at the moment when the *Règlements* had been promulgated'. 'It was the funeral oration of union', declared Hübner with satisfaction.[5] But the Austrian seemed to have missed the point of the old diplomat's remark. If the Powers were to take the place of Russia in guarding the interests of the Principalities, the character of that guardianship should justify the change. Internationalism should be effective in its present role, or the experiment was morally bankrupt. Why, then, should not the Powers play an arbitral role in all questions between the suzerain and his vassals? The logic of such a view was evident, but it reckoned unfortunately without the traditional conservatism of British policy towards the Eastern Question. Thus, a feature of Kisseleff's *mémoire*, already noted, which would authorize the Powers to 'regulate by diplomacy or by entente with the Powers every controversy that might arise between it and the Principalities' led the British to fear that they might be drawn into quarrels between the Principalities and their suzerain, and Malmesbury contended

[1] Hübner to Buol, no. 76 D, July 19, Staatsarchiv, IX/57.
[2] Cowley to Malmesbury, no. 886, July 18, F.O. 27/1255.
[3] Protocol 17.
[4] Hübner, *op. cit.*, vol. ii, p. 195.   [5] *Ibid.*, p. 183.

successfully that the reciprocal rights of the Porte and the Principalities might be determined, but not the rights of the Protecting
Powers.[1] Perhaps the most feasible way of making the tutelage of
the Powers mean something would have been to allow such differences to be referred to the representatives at Constantinople, but
British objections were insurmountable. 'Nothing, in my judgement,' wrote Cowley, 'would do more to weaken the authority of
the Porte than to establish at Constantinople a sort of tribunal to
sit in judgement upon its dealings with the Principalities.'[2] There
is little doubt but that in British opinion the dignity of the
Sublime Porte had precedence over the interests of the Principalities.

Not only was Russia the champion of the Principalities against
the Porte, but on one question—that of the rights of extraterritoriality—she espoused their cause against the Powers.
Whether or not Russia herself had been an offender in this regard,[3]
it is fairly evident that too many foreign residents were able to
evade the course of justice by invoking consular aid. Unfortunately,
when Kisseleff moved that the governments of the Principalities
should be invited to prove abuses of the rights of protection, as a
basis for the consideration of some measures of reform, the Conference was so divided on the question (France, Russia, and
Sardinia supporting the proposal, while Austria, Turkey, and
Great Britain dissented) that any action seemed out of the question.
Cowley wrote Malmesbury that it would be 'very derogatory of the
great Powers of Europe to call upon the local governments of the
Principalities to prove delinquencies on the part of the agents of
those Powers', but it is clear that he distrusted the Russian proposal
and doubted its sincerity.[4] Sometimes, however, it takes a step
like this to uncover evidences of guilt. Hübner was sure that the
suggestion of giving the hospodars such a right of complaint was
deliberately aimed at Austria; it was Walewski, he noted, who
obviated a 'blow fatal to the influence of Austria in these states'.[5]
In the end only Sardinia had supported the proposal.[6] Yet it must
be admitted that the rapid growth of nationalism in the Principalities clearly justified a study of this question, as the Powers were
soon to discover from rather painful experience. Apart from the
desire to support France and to pose as the benefactor of the
Principalities, Russia's chief consideration at the Conference was

[1] Malmesbury to Cowley, no. 634, July 8, F.O. 27/1237.
[2] Cowley to Malmesbury, no. 856, July 13, F.O. 27/1254.
[3] Cowley wrote that she was the chief offender (Cowley to Malmesbury, no.
666, June 15, F.O. 27/1252), but he wrote, of course, only from hearsay, and
consular evidence does not seem to support his contention.
[4] Cowley to Malmesbury, no. 1072, Aug. 17, F.O. 27/1257.
[5] Hübner to Buol, no. 85 E, Aug. 20, Staatsarchiv, IX/58.
[6] Hübner to Buol, no. 85 B, Aug. 20, *ibid.*

the welfare of the dedicated convents [1]—another contentious question, which the Conference deliberately shirked.

But the Conference was already wearied by its labours, and must have realized—as one of its members certainly did [2]—that its work had little of the virtue of finality. The new constitution [3] which had been provided was more definite than the *Règlement organique* and, in some respects, a little more progressive; but withal it was a clumsy piece of machinery, chiefly because its makers could not agree on the plans for its construction. Two hospodars in order to insure administrative separation, and the legislative power shared between hospodar and assembly and concentrated for certain purposes in a central body divided equally between the representatives of each land, did not somehow promise much in the way of governmental harmony. The hospodar, elected for life by the assembly, must be the son of a native of one or other of the principalities, and be able to show that he had an income of 3,000 ducats and had held public office for at least ten years; he was to govern with the concurrence of ministers appointed by himself and had the right to sanction or veto all legislation. The ministers need not be members of the assembly, but they might be impeached before the court of cassation at the request of two-thirds of the assembly. The central commission, composed of eight Moldavians and eight Wallachians (half of each contingent being chosen by the hospodar and half by the assembly), should draft and submit to the assemblies projects of legislation of general import, which should include those having as their object the maintenance of customs, postal, and telegraphic union. The assembly, chosen by indirect election on a restricted suffrage for a period of five years (though subject to dissolution by the hospodar), should consider (that is, accept, reject, or amend) measures presented to it by the central commission and was empowered to vote the budget each year—though, in default of such action, the executive power might provide for the public services on the basis of the previous budget. While the existing judicial system remained practically unchanged, a high court of justice and cassation was to be established at Focshani. The size of the two militias was placed at the figure fixed by the *Règlements organiques*, though it might be increased by a third with the preliminary assent of the Porte. They should be separately organized but have a common

---

[1] Action of a sort was taken on this question at the session of July 30: Protocol 13. See chap. xii.

[2] Hübner to Buol, no. 85 G, Aug. 20, Staatsarchiv, ix/58.

[3] The text of the Convention of Aug. 19, 1858 will be found in Martens, *op. cit.*, vol. xvi, part 2, pp. 50 ff., or in *British and Foreign State Papers*, vol. xlviii, pp. 70 ff., or in *Actes et docs.*, vol. vii, pp. 306 ff., or in *Arch. dip.*, 1866, vol. ii, pp. 102 ff.

commander-in-chief who should be named alternately by each hospodar, though only after consultation with the Porte. The decision regarding the flag has been noted. Perhaps the most drastic provision of the Convention was the article which decreed that 'all privileges, exemptions, or monopolies which certain classes still enjoyed shall be abolished'. Individual liberty and equality before the law were now for the first time formally guaranteed.

But if, on the side of inner organization, the lot of the Moldo-Wallachians was given a brighter outlook, the organic relations of the Principalities to the suzerain Power were practically unaltered. The autonomy of the Principalities, provided by the Capitulations, was confirmed under the guarantee of the Protecting Powers. In event of external aggression the Porte should undertake measures of defence in common with the Principalities, such measures having been determined 'by an entente with the Protecting Powers'. Treaties, concluded between the Porte and the Protecting Powers, should be applicable to the Principalities in so far as they did not attack their immunities. In event of the violation of these immunities the hospodars would have recourse to the suzerain Power, and, if satisfaction were not obtained, might appeal to the representatives of the Protecting Powers at Constantinople. The amount of tribute for each principality was fixed, and the right of the Sultan to invest the hospodars was confirmed. By a curious irony —seeing that Russia had sought to weaken the suzerain Power in the interest of the Principalities—the Convention substantially confirmed a condition which Russian treaties had long ago ordained; for, after all, apart from the fact that Turkey was a co-signatory of the Convention, the Conference itself was quite unequal to daring innovations. It was only gradually that Europe gave ground to Rouman nationalism.

Such, then, were the outstanding arrangements provided by the Convention. That the Conference regarded its work as only tentative seems to be proved not only by the temporary character of the electoral arrangements (appended to the constitution) but especially by the fact that the central commission was explicitly empowered to undertake a revision of the *Règlements organiques*—which, by implication, were still in force, where not obviously superseded by the new constitution. Viewing it broadly, the work of the Conference was essentially a compromise between contending principles, as was well illustrated by the designation of the new state—'The United Principalities of Moldavia and Wallachia'. 'A sort of homage rendered to union' was the comment of Walewski, who pointed out the virtues of the Convention, while signifying his regret that the principles which France had stood for had not been fully realized.[1] Indeed, the fundamental defect of the new constitution was that it did not establish union or separation but set up a sort of hybrid régime, for the operation of which the ineffective central commission was relied upon to produce a reasonable harmony. And, strangely enough, the weakness of this coping stone was not readily perceived at this time. But a searching analysis[2] of the Convention was written shortly afterwards by an able Wallachian, who pointed out that the hospodars would inevitably have difficulty with the assemblies (he also considered their duration much too long), and contended that the rights of the suzerain Power greatly hampered the Principalities in suddenly meeting the problem of national defence. On the other hand, he pointed out that for the first time the Capitulations, which registered the national autonomy, were incorporated in the public law of Europe, and that the establishment of equality before the law was a distinct step forward. And even though this compromise but meagrely satisfied the aspirations for union, half a loaf was better than none. 'It is not complete union,' he declared, 'but the principle is proclaimed. It is for us, Roumans, to do the rest; and we owe thanks to Europe, who has shown us that union is possible.'

[1] Circular of Walewski to diplomatic agents, Aug. 20, *Actes et docs.*, vol. vii, no. 2071.

[2] Boeresco, *Examen de la convention relative à l'organisation des principautés danubiennes.*

CHAPTER VII

THE NATIONALIST REJOINDER

O F the general trend of the work at Paris some inklings naturally reached the Principalities,[1] though none of such information was official, and, manifestly, much was still in doubt. But the long period of waiting could not have been anything but hurtful to the best interests of the country. Victor Place gives a gloomy picture of financial conditions in Moldavia:

'The revenue from the taxes levied up to the coming November', he writes, 'has been completely absorbed and expended. . . . The Jews, who up to this time had consented to lend, refuse to make new advances even at the most usurious rates, and thus recourse to loans seems closed. Employees have not been paid for several months, [and] the few, who by dint of importunity have been able to obtain something on credit, receive in reality only ministerial warrants which carry a depreciation of 40 per cent. . . . The numerous creditors of the state loudly demand their money, and are not able to obtain anything. But what is most serious is that the militia not only receives no pay but is on the point of lacking the necessaries of life.'[2]

Yet the patience of the Moldo-Wallachians seemed to stand any test; for we hear of no turbulence as the result of this depression, and the greatest stir was made by men whose economic needs were less poignant than their political ambition. When the report was circulated that the Porte might be empowered, as of old, to nominate the hospodars, the thought 'awakened the most shameful ambitions', as one observer put it, and the number of candidates who would sell their country to obtain the coveted prize was 'incredible'. Naturally there was a scramble to obtain the Porte's favour, and in Moldavia Vogorides and Gregory Sturdza were busily engaged in getting petitions signed and transmitted to Constantinople.[3] How many ducats the different aspirants expended is unfortunately not told us; 'but every *boyard*', as one remarked, 'seemed to feel that he was capable of being prince'.[4]

But the story about the hospodars was only one of the false reports which besieged an expectant public. Relying on a telegram from Paris, Constantin Rosetti, the radical editor of the *Roumanul*, published the statement that the new constitution was to be modelled after the American constitution; and there was, at first,

[1] In spite of the supposed secrecy of the Conference of Paris, some agents of Alexander Ghika had been able to send some knowledge of its transactions, and Ghika gave out some of this information to the public: Béclard to Walewski, Sept. 3, 1858, *Actes et docs.*, vol. ix, no. 2614.
[2] Place to Thouvenel, June 24, annex to Thouvenel's no. 52, *Aff. étr.*, vol. 336.
[3] Place to Walewski, July 7, *Actes et docs.*, vol. vii, no. 2061.
[4] Vaillant to Walewski, Mar. 15, *Aff. étr.*, *Mém. et docs.*, *Turquie*, vol. 55.

much rejoicing on the part of persons who had not the remotest idea of what that really meant. When the mistake was discovered and the real truth about the Convention came to be known, the radical element began to plan a demonstration against the Powers —to take place as soon as the text had been officially received.[1] Though it was only, of course, a ripple on the surface, these men of '48 were, after all, the guardians of what was best in Rouman nationalism, and even their hot-headedness bespoke a certain vitality without which the nationalist cause would surely have been vain.

Yet, in general, the Moldo-Wallachians received the shock to their hopes with characteristic passivity. Perhaps this was partly because they had heard, before the Conference met, that union and a foreign prince were likely to be abandoned, and they had only clung to a vague hope that something good might come out of it all.[2] A French traveller, who had talked with several Wallachians on a Danube steamer, reported that all seemed well pleased with the stipulations of the Convention, as being the best that could be hoped for for the present, and, on the whole, a step forward.[3] And Baron Eder, the Austrian consul at Bucharest, has testified that 'one seems to have forgotten that one had asked for union and a foreign prince'.[4] When the full import of the Convention became known, the British consul at Jassy noted a fair degree of satisfaction—or at least an absence of complaint;[5] though some of the *boyards*, it is true, were indignant at the loss of their special privileges, and the radicals were, of course, disappointed at the narrowness of the suffrage.[6]

The only provision of the Convention which really caused any flurry was the one which provided for a special caimacamie, consisting in each case of three ministers[7] of the last reigning hospodar, to take charge of the elections and to hold office until the new hospodars were chosen. Such an arrangement, calling unexpectedly for the removal of the existing caimacams, produced something like consternation in official circles. In the camp of the Ghikas it was a veritable bombshell. For some time past the crafty old caimacam had been turning men out of office, and filling the posts

---

[1] Eder to Buol, no. 49, Aug. 4, Staatsarchiv, XXXVIII/112. Rosetti's misinformant had been Ubicini, a well-known student and friend of the Principalities: Colquhoun to Malmesbury, no. 4, July 23, F.O. 78/1378.

[2] Place to Walewski, May 15, *Actes et docs.*, vol. vii, no. 2047.

[3] Schickler, *En Orient; souvenirs de voyage*, p. 12.

[4] Eder to Buol, no. 53, Aug. 15, Staatsarchiv, XXXVIII/112.

[5] Ongley to Bulwer, no. 2, Sept. 13, F.O. 78/1379. A circular of the National Party at Jassy took special note of the important role assigned to the central commission, and emphasized the importance of the coming elections to the assembly: *Actes et docs.*, vol. vii, no. 2077.

[6] Place to Walewski, Nov. 6, *Actes et docs.*, vol. vii, no. 2137.

[7] The president of the *divan princier*, the minister of the interior, and the minister of justice.

thus vacated with his own adherents; and his excuse to Colquhoun, who disapproved of his selections, was that he had to reward his partisans, but that he intended to replace them as soon as practicable. Yet, with very few exceptions, these men had been retained, and Colquhoun lamented that the department of the interior had never been in the state that it was now in, the vast majority of the prefects being 'men of no character'.[1] Making allowance for the British consul's tendency to exaggeration, it is undoubtedly true that Ghika had deliberately created a machine designed especially to control the elections and to secure for its creator the Wallachian hospodariate. Such a blow now to his hopes was certainly bad enough, but when it also meant that the new caimacams would be adherents of his arch-enemy, Stirbey, the old man was almost beside himself.[2] Useless as any one might perceive such a course would be, he sent a messenger to the Porte to protest against the resolution of the Conference, declaring that if it were persisted in, he could not vouch for the public tranquillity; while, at Bucharest, in order to fortify himself against the Stirbey interest, he formed a coalition with the radicals (the so-called National Party), receiving the promise of their support unless they should insist upon favouring Nicholas Golesco, in which case he should tender his support to the radical leader.[3] It was uncertain, as a matter of fact, whether Ghika was really eligible for the hospodariate,[4] since he was not the son of a native-born Wallachian, although his family had been residents of that province for generations, and many of its members had been hospodars in the past. It was perhaps for that reason that he bestowed a bribe of a thousand ducats on Balliano, one of the new caimacams;[5] and up to the very moment of his retirement, he distributed 'gratifications' at the public expense.[6] One may judge from this recital wherein lay the source of any possible danger to the public 'tranquillity'.

Foiled in their hopes of remaining in power, the two caimacams hoped at least that the personnel of their administrations would be retained.[7] This might seem to involve an interpretation of the firman of investiture, and Walewski had already bidden Thouvenel warn the Porte against the intrigues which were going on in the Principalities to falsify the meaning of the Convention;[8] but it must be confessed that when the firman appeared,[9] it was no more

[1] Colquhoun to Bulwer, no. 10, Sept. 15, F.O. 78/1378.
[2] Eder to Buol, no. 54 A, Aug. 19, Staatsarchiv, XXXVIII/112.
[3] Béclard to Walewski, Sept. 3, *Actes et docs.*, vol. ix, no. 2614.
[4] Béclard to Walewski, Sept. 22, *ibid.*, no. 2618.
[5] *Ibid.*, no. 2617; Colquhoun to Bulwer, no. 10.
[6] Colquhoun to Malmesbury, no. 15, Oct. 30, F.O. 78/1378.
[7] Thouvenel to Walewski, no. 71, Sept. 8, *Aff. étr., Turquie*, vol. 337.
[8] Walewski to Thouvenel, no. 78, Sept. 24, *ibid.*
[9] See *Actes et docs.*, vol. vii, no. 2105.

definite in this regard than was the Convention itself. On the other hand, there is hardly any denying Thouvenel's logic that if the old caimacams were to retire, their henchmen ought to go with them, else the Convention, which had planned a new régime to handle the elections, would indeed be falsified.[1] On this point it appears that most of the Powers were agreed: the new caimacams should be free to choose their own ministers;[2] and Bulwer, who had taken the contrary view, could only lament that the question had not been referred to the representatives of the Powers at Constantinople.[3] Malmesbury's characteristic comment on this last asseveration was that Great Britain was only too likely to find herself in a minority at Constantinople, and telegrams from the home government were quite expeditious enough to decide such a question.[4] Meanwhile, Ghika, who saw that he had lost, was now asserting that the caimacams should even recover the official functions which they had held under Stirbey.[5]

On this question of whether the new caimacams should resume their old portfolios agreement was less easy. Most of the Powers took the contrary view, but Russia proved so strong a supporter of the privilege, that the caimacams finally decided the matter in their own favour.[6] It was, meanwhile, agreed by the Moldavian caimacams that in case of disagreement on a question a majority vote should prevail [7]—a reasonable decision, on the whole, though one may wonder if matters could have turned out worse under the rule of unanimity. In Wallachia the three caimacams, Mano, Balliano, and Philippesco, were all unionists, but Mano, though a man of ability, was not popular,[8] and did not mind doing the unpopular thing. In Moldavia Catargi was a conservative, and little likely to agree with his unionist colleagues, Pano and Sturdza. But on the proscription of the men of the former administration there was no apparent dissent. All of Vogorides's ministers (some of whom had shown themselves unpleasant) were summarily dismissed;[9] and, though Mano, on the plea of being non-partisan, was rather disposed to caution,[10] it was not long before the caimacams of Wallachia made a clean sweep of the Ghika crowd, even to the humble turnpike keepers—all 'for the purpose [so Bulwer charged them] of advancing the electioneering prospects of their

[1] Instructions to Outrey, Sept. 28, annex to Thouvenel's no. 76, *Aff. étr.*, *Turquie*, vol. 337.
[2] Walewski to Béclard, Oct. 12, *Actes et docs.*, vol. ix, no. 2624.
[3] Bulwer to Malmesbury, no. 306, Oct. 27, F.O. 78/1369.
[4] Note by Malmesbury on Bulwer's no. 306.
[5] Béclard to Walewski, Nov. 4, *Actes et docs.*, vol. ix, no. 2631.
[6] *Ibid.*; Place to Walewski, Nov. 6, *ibid.*, vol. vii, no. 2139.   [7] *Ibid.*
[8] Colquhoun to Malmesbury, no. 27, Nov. 29, F.O. 78/1378.
[9] Place to Walewski, Nov. 6, *Actes et docs.*, vol. vii, no. 2137.
[10] Colquhoun to Malmesbury, no. 17, Oct. 31, F.O. 78/1378.

own party'.[1] Since few had any tears to shed for Ghika, such violence was not likely to disturb the peace in Wallachia, but one cannot but feel that the suppression of public meetings, as well as much petty interference with Ghika's efforts to combine with the radicals,[2] was a fair demonstration of the unfitness of the new board that was to preside over the coming elections in Wallachia.

In Wallachia, notwithstanding some differences between Philippesco (said to be a Russian tool)[3] and the other caimacams, the administration worked with at least a fair degree of harmony; but in Moldavia the situation was far otherwise. According to the French consul (who was certainly not unbiased), Catargi had been especially anxious to resume his old portfolio, since it was the department of the interior, and he could hope, by controlling the choice of prefects, to further his aspirations for the hospodariate. The other two caimacams, divining his purpose, had made a show of impartiality, and preferred that all three should exclude themselves from ministerial office; but in the end they had yielded the point; and all three had united in getting rid of Vogorides's placemen—Sturdza and Pano—because they feared that Vogorides would throw his support to Michael Sturdza, a conservative and a separatist, and Catargi, because he wanted the princely honour himself. The plan at first agreed upon, of letting Pano nominate the judges, and Catargi the prefects, might seem a fair division of the spoil as far as the determination of the electoral lists was concerned, but the fact that the police were subject to Catargi's department and its chief was that minister's nephew gave to one party an advantage which the other would not countenance. Further complications arose when Catargi—possibly at Austria's instigation[4]—refused to sign the decree, prepared by his colleagues, restoring the liberty of the press. But the chief rock on which they split was the choice of some of the new prefects, Sturdza and Pano objecting to the nomination of some of Catargi's own kinsmen, and undertaking, themselves, to make appointments, which Catargi, on the ground that this was an unwarrantable interference with his department, refused flatly to accept. Since fifteen of the twenty days allotted for the preparation of the electoral lists had elapsed, the discord in the caimacamie had begun to take on a serious character. Catargi refused finally to attend any more meetings of the executive body, and his two colleagues then completed the list of appointments, merely invoking the will of the

[1] Bulwer to Malmesbury, no. 382, Nov. 24, F.O. 78/1370.

[2] Béclard to Walewski, Nov. 17, *Actes et docs.*, vol. ix, no. 2635.

[3] Béclard to Walewski, Nov. 4, *ibid.*, no. 2631.

[4] If so, it was private encouragement, as there is no evidence from Gödel-Lannoy's own dispatches that he exerted any pressure.

majority.[1] Matters reached a climax when Catargi appealed to the Porte through its commissioner, Afif Bey, requesting the 'legitimate intervention of the suzerain court'.[2]

The Porte acted with unwonted promptness in the matter. A communication of the Turkish commissioner (presumably dictated by the Porte) rebuked the caimacams for having acted in contravention of the firman, specifying particularly 'the change *en masse* of functionaries and employees', and warned them against gratuitous interpretations of the Convention.[3] Had Turkey stopped there, one might possibly feel that her action had some degree of justification, even though Walewski did denounce her for venturing to interpret the Convention without the concurrence of the Powers.[4] But the suzerain Power, whenever roused from her accustomed lethargy by the truculence of a vassal, seldom failed to essay the congenial role of bully. Two more communications were sent to Jassy, one requesting the Moldavian government not to act on the question of the dedicated monasteries until the Porte had ruled on the matter,[5] while another ordered the caimacamie to revoke the decree granting the liberty of the press.[6] The fractious caimacams, who had boldly challenged the commissioner's right to act as intermediary,[7] now held up his ciphered telegrams,[8] and, according to report, had ordered him out of the country.[9] Seeing that Afif's sole claim on the Moldavian treasury had been his role of communicating the firman—a task already executed—one can hardly denounce the Moldavians for objecting to his presence. Nor can one blame the caimacams for resisting all attacks upon Moldavian autonomy. But, regardless of their reason and their rights (and it was reported that Afif's expense-bill was becoming enormous),[10] it hardly behoves the weaker party in a controversy to close the door to compromise, especially when some of its own acts are seriously open to question. In any event, the Porte's admonition had found Pano and Sturdza as incorrigible as ever, for an order of recall was received by Photiades,[11] the disloyal kapou kiaya, who had figured in the scandals of 1857.[12]

[1] Place to Walewski, Nov. 18, *Actes et docs.*, vol. vii, no. 2182; Churchill to Bulwer, no. 3, Dec. 14, F.O. 78/1379.

[2] Catargi to Ali, Nov. 15, *Actes et docs.*, vol. vii, no. 2164; Lallemand to Walewski, no. 94, Nov. 30, *Aff. étr., Turquie*, vol. 338.

[3] *Actes et docs.*, vol. vii, no. 2185.

[4] Walewski to Lallemand, no. 92, Dec. 2, *Aff. étr., Turquie*, vol. 338. Buol held the contrary view: Buol to Prokesch, Dec. 5, no. 1, Staatsarchiv, XII/64.

[5] *Actes et docs.*, vol. vii, no. 2191.   [6] *Ibid.*, no. 2303.   [7] *Ibid.*, no. 2186.

[8] Lallemand to Walewski, no. 94.

[9] Bulwer to Malmesbury, no. 401, Dec. 2, F.O. 78/1370.

[10] Place to Walewski, Nov. 9, *Actes et docs.*, vol. vii, no. 2140. Even Bulwer declared that he was a man of 'no capacity', and ought to be recalled: Bulwer to Malmesbury, no. 382.

[11] Lallemand to Walewski, no. 93, Nov. 24, *Aff. étr., Turquie*, vol. 338

[12] See p. 95.

The Protecting Powers were of course in touch with all this singular behaviour of their charge, and Bulwer, whose active mind never allowed a malady to grow worse for want of treatment, kept the telegraph wires hot with his suggestions. His idea, as far back as September, was that the Congress itself should act as the interpreter of its own decisions;[1] but Malmesbury had felt that this would only cause unnecessary delay, and that all questions of interpretation should be left to the decision of the Porte, subject only to the advice of the embassies at Constantinople.[2] Then, as we have noticed, Malmesbury changed his mind (preferring to leave such questions to the cabinets)[3] and finally it appears that he decided that an international conference should be called. Walewski, though unconvinced that this was necessary, had communicated with the Powers, only to learn that Austria considered that such a proposal should originate with the Porte.[4] So far, indeed, the suzerain Power had preferred to act alone.

But the Porte now decided to bring the whole affair before the embassies on the plea that the validity of the coming elections was involved.[5] Accordingly, Bulwer, acting as dean of the ambassadors, called a conference, which met at the British embassy on November 27. While it was felt that some caution should be taken lest the two caimacams resign in a huff and throw all the electoral preparations out of gear,[6] the representatives were unanimous in feeling that they should be thoroughly admonished. Bulwer presented the project of a note, which was discussed *seriatim*,[7] and the result was a complete refutation of the position which the two caimacams had assumed. They were warned to show respect for the Sublime Porte, whose commissioner had a right to prolong his stay, and the failure to send on his telegrams had been a derogation of respect. While all nominations should be subject to the approval of the majority, account should be taken of the opinion of the caimacam whose department was concerned, and the degradation of employees in the department of the interior was an abuse that was 'just to redress'. The caimacams had passed the limits prescribed by the firman, and, while they were allowed to decide 'current matters' (whatever that meant) by majority vote, any interpretation of the Convention or of the firman must be

[1] Bulwer to Malmesbury, Sept. 27, telg., F.O. 78/1367.
[2] Malmesbury to Bulwer, Oct. 1, telg., F.O. 78/1368.   [3] See p. 184.
[4] Walewski to Malakoff, no. 152, Nov. 22, *Aff. étr., Angleterre*, vol. 711.
[5] Fuad to Bulwer, Nov. 26, enclosed in Bulwer's no. 401.
[6] Bulwer to Malmesbury, no. 401, Dec. 2, F.O. 78/1370.
[7] Lallemand to Walewski, no. 94, Nov. 30, *Aff. étr., Turquie*, vol. 338. Lallemand, the French chargé d'affaires, felt (in opposition to Prokesch) that none of the official changes in the department of the interior should be annulled except those to which Catargi had objected, but the point was not made clear in the memorandum of the Conference or the note sent to the caimacams.

referred to the Sublime Porte.[1] Such was the substance of the note which was dispatched to the erring caimacams.

It is hard to measure the exact effect of this collective pronouncement. According to the British consul, Sturdza and Pano refused to alter their ways, and were deaf to the remonstrances which Bulwer bade him make.[2] Place, on the other hand, who was universally credited with having egged the caimacams on, insisted at length that they made all possibe efforts to become reconciled to their colleague, but that Catargi still refused to exercise his functions.[3] It is not improbable that Catargi's obstinacy had been strengthened by the note from Constantinople, but it is hard to resist the feeling that the other two regarded the imminence of the elections as insuring them immunity. When several messages of remonstrance[4] failed to achieve the desired results, the Porte contemplated suspending the elections, and so informed the embassies.[5] Such a plan would, of course, be bound to lead to further complications, and Russia warned the Porte that such action would be tantamount to suspending the Convention itself—'a very grave responsibility for the Porte to assume'.[6] No doubt Turkey looked upon the matter very much as a family affair, and a rather impudent message from Pano and Sturdza[7] was a further strain on vizirial patience. But the problem was clearly too much for Turkish ingenuity; and, dissuaded, at length, by France from issuing an order suspending the elections, the Porte decided on the alternative of bringing the whole matter before the Powers.[8]

The idea of having the whole question thrown back upon the Powers was not a pleasant reflection for governments whose plenipotentiaries had supposedly settled the fate of the Principalities at the recent conference at Paris. On the face of it, it

[1] *Actes et docs.*, vol. vii, no. 2178. The document is here wrongly dated Nov. 18. The memorandum (see annex to Lallemand's no. 94) bears the date of Nov. 28, and the note to the caimacamie immediately followed.

[2] Churchill to Bulwer, no. 3, Dec. 14, F.O. 78/1379.

[3] Place to Walewski, Nov. 30, *Actes et docs.*, no. 2214.

[4] *Ibid.*, nos. 2234, 2249, and 2297. Pano and Sturdza, on their side, appealed to the consular body against their colleague and to Walewski against both Catargi and Afif: *ibid.*, nos. 2284 and 2286.

[5] Lallemand to Walewski, no.100, Dec.15, *Aff. étr.,Turquie,*vol.338. Lallemand attributes this to Bulwer (no. 98, Dec. 10, *ibid.*). Since Bulwer had great fear that the elections would lead to union and independence (Bulwer to Malmesbury,Jan. 8, telg., F.O. 78/1427) this may be true.

[6] Lobanoff to Gortchakoff, Dec. 18, *Aff. étr., Russie*, vol. 192.

[7] *Actes et docs.*, vol. vii, no. 2313. They took exception to the omission in the Turkish note of the last paragraph of the memorandum of Nov. 28, which had expressed the wish that the Porte might see fit to instruct its commissioners at Bucharest and Jassy to reach an understanding with the consular corps. It might be noted also that the Turkish note omitted the clause which had to do with the contingency of a vacancy in the caimacamie and the stipulation that Afif was not to interfere in the affairs of Moldavia.

[8] Lallemand to Walewski, no. 101, Dec. 22, *Aff. étr., Turquie*, vol. 338.

might seem that a body so closely in touch with the problem as the representatives at Constantinople might, in concert with the Turkish ministers, be trusted to rule authoritatively on the meaning of the Convention;[1] and such, indeed, seems for the moment to have been Malmesbury's view. But Walewski felt that local conditions would make it difficult for any wise decision to emanate from Constantinople, and that questions touching the Convention might better be settled by the body which had drafted it.[2] Then Russia rejected Malmesbury's proposal to refer the matter to the embassies,[3] and so, what was left but a congress, after all?

Unable to carry his last proposal, and rather pedantic in his insistence upon accuracy in details, Malmesbury now harked back to his earlier request that the Conference of Paris should reconvene to interpret the Convention. He wished that body, he told Cowley, to ratify the decision of November 28, and thus show the Moldavian caimacams that they 'would not be countenanced or upheld in resisting the authority of the Porte'.[4] Walewski, while feeling that a congress was preferable to any other means of settling the difficulties, was plainly not at all enthusiastic over the idea, believing that the gravity of the whole affair had been exaggerated; that the dismissals, however unjustified, could not very well be annulled; and that collective action by the Powers would only aggravate the situation in the Principalities.[5] Yet after some hesitation he promised, in deference to Great Britain, to call a conference if assured that all the signatory Powers desired it.[6] Gortchakoff as usual followed France's lead,[7] though Austria was, of course, uncertain. Then Walewski learned of the Porte's intention to appeal to the Powers, and decided that, after all, a conference could not be avoided.[8] But the really insuperable obstacle was Buol, who felt that Austria would only be a minority in such a body, and that she did not care to repeat the experience of the preceding summer.[9] Malmesbury was much annoyed at the baffling of his plan, but there was, of course, nothing to be done about it. So the upshot of all this discussion was that things were allowed to drift, and the Powers

---

[1] According to Bulwer, he himself and most of his colleagues (not, however, Lallemand) came to believe that the Porte, which had conveyed the substance of the Convention by means of the firman, and was responsible for its execution, should be the one to interpret its provisions: Bulwer to Malmesbury, no. 1448, Dec. 21, F.O. 78/1271.
[2] Walewski to Lallemand, no. 172, Dec. 2, *Aff. étr.*, *Turquie*, vol. 338.
[3] Chateaurenard to Walewski, no. 84, Dec. 12, *ibid.*, *Russie*, vol. 217.
[4] Malmesbury to Cowley, no. 1252, Dec. 9, F.O. 27/1240.
[5] Cowley to Malmesbury, no. 1607, Dec. 22, F.O. 27/1264; cf. Walewski to Chateaurenard, no. 85, Dec. 15, *Aff. étr.*, *Russie*, vol. 217.
[6] Cowley to Malmesbury, no. 1594, Dec. 18, F.O. 27/1264.
[7] Chateaurenard to Walewski, no. 87, Dec. 29, *Aff. étr.*, *Russie*, vol. 217.
[8] Walewski to Chateaurenard, no. 89, Dec. 23, *ibid.*
[9] Malmesbury to Cowley, no. 1252, Dec. 29, F.O. 27/1240.

had the uneasy feeling that the Porte might refuse to recognize the results of the elections.

In both Principalities candidates for the hospodariate had already begun an active canvass. Naturally both of the caimacams had aspirations, but neither of them was sure of his eligibility, since Ghika's father, as we have noticed, happened to be born outside of Wallachia, while Vogorides, whose father was a Bulgarian, had to base his claim on the fact that he had been adopted, as a child, by a native of Moldavia. Since, for some reason, the caimacamie had left untouched the judicial appointments made during the last days of the Ghika administration, it was not impossible that the ex-caimacam controlled the courts which would rule on his case;[1] though more serious handicaps to his success were the rivalry of Golesco and the strength of the Stirbey-Bibesco interest, which had the advantage of including in its influence the caimacamie itself. Ghika's party was supposed to be the 'moderate liberals', while the other two were radicals and conservatives respectively, but none of them was avowedly opposed to union, and, with all but the radicals at least, it was a question more of persons than of principles. In Moldavia the unionists had not yet united on a candidate, and the leading aspirants (both conservatives) were the ex-hospodar Michael Sturdza and his son Gregory, formerly an officer in the Turkish army. While the former's wealth was doubtless of practical value in such a campaign, the latter had made the most strenuous efforts during the absence of his father (who did not return from Paris until shortly before the elections) to control the selection of deputies,[2] and he had also, it appears, the support of the French consul.[3] Clearly the situation was complicated in both Principalities. Viewing the mêlée from a distance, Buol ventured the prophecy that the choice of one of the Principalities would become the choice of the other.[4] Some said it would be Golesco,[5] though no one had the foresight to pick the actual winner. But it is interesting to notice that certain Wallachians hazarded the opinion that, if it were necessary in order to beat Stirbey or Bibesco, Ghika and the radicals would come to the point of agreeing to support the one elected at Jassy, and in that way the union of the Principalities might be partially achieved.[6] Such would scarcely argue the existence of any sentiment to seek the national welfare in place of personal interest.

Meanwhile electoral preparations proceeded, and, as might be

---

[1] Colquhoun to Malmesbury, no. 5, Jan. 12, 1859, F.O. 78/1441.
[2] Soutzo, *op. cit.*, pp. 361–2.
[3] Gödel to Buol, no. 33, Aug. 30, 1858, Staatsarchiv, xxxviii/119.
[4] Banneville to Walewski, no. 161, Nov. 30, *Aff. étr., Autriche*, vol. 474.
[5] Churchill to Bulwer, no. 6, Dec. 31, F.O. 78/1379.
[6] Vaillant to Walewski, Sept. 7, *Aff. étr., Mém. et docs., Turquie*, vol. 55.

expected, complaints arose on every hand. If it be true that in Moldavia residents of the districts were in some cases enrolled among the voters for the towns,[1] then there was some ground for the belief that Pano and Sturdza were overactive in support of the unionist cause. Place had been so active a supporter of the two that Malmesbury bade Cowley protest to Walewski against his conduct.[2] No doubt the French consul had all along been overzealous in his partisanship (Lallemand virtually admits it), and he had lately convinced himself that the Porte was working towards the recall of Pano and Sturdza, and the direct nomination of a hospodar by the Sultan;[3] but Churchill, the British consul, while he blamed Place for his interference, believed that Catargi was being encouraged 'from another quarter'—possibly meaning Austria. At all events, although the caimacams accepted the pronouncement of the ambassadors, the deadlock within their midst was still unbroken, Catargi demanding the appointment of the men whom he had nominated, and his colleagues merely agreeing to revise all nominations—which, of course, meant that they might assert their majority voice, if they should choose.[4] Yet Pano and Sturdza did apparently make overtures to their colleague,[5] while even the British consul admits that Catargi showed no spirit of compromise, merely explaining (to Churchill) that his intransigence meant nothing anyway, as the electoral lists ('based', he declared, 'on erroneous principles') had already been drafted, and there was nothing further for the caimacamie to do.

'With regard to the elections', wrote Churchill to Bulwer, 'I beg to state that everybody acknowledges their imperfections, though little has been done by the party in power to correct those imperfections. . . . Those who protested against the appearing on the lists of persons unqualified to vote for the elections were required to prove their assertion —a thing which scarcely any one was naturally able to do. The party in power have spared themselves no effort to obtain the majority of deputies of their own political opinions, and, in order to succeed more effectually, many instances of abuse of power have been committed; in some cases the police force were employed in their favour. On the other hand, I must add that cases have been brought to my notice of

---

[1] Churchill to Bulwer, no. 6. While Churchill declared, 'The elections are, more than most, irregular', Place affirmed, 'The caimacamie has not deviated a single instant from the most absolute legality; contrary assertions are only calumnies. I am witness of its sincere efforts to make the electoral lists as exact as possible considering the short interval and a system so difficult to apply': Place to Walewski, Dec. 23, telg., *Actes et docs.*, vol. vii, no. 2333.

[2] Malmesbury to Cowley, no. 8, Jan. 3, 1859, F.O. 78/1279.

[3] Place to Walewski, Dec. 23, 1858, telg., and Dec. 28, *Actes et docs.*, vol. vii, nos. 2333 and 2348.

[4] Churchill to Bulwer, no. 6. Churchill telegraphed later that the two caimacams resented the interference of Bulwer, and declined to accept any further representations from him (Churchill): Jan. 3, telg., F.O. 78/1441.

[5] Place to Walewski, Dec. 25, *Actes et docs.*, vol. vii, no. 2341.

large sums of money having been given by the partisans of Michael and
Gregory Sturdza to be elected deputies. The same argument must
naturally have been used by both sides. Your Excellency is too well
acquainted with the immorality of this people to doubt the interest that
money can command in these countries, and, though it is to be regretted
that compulsion has been used on one side to bias the elections, it is
likewise a source of regret that bribery is resorted to, to counteract that
influence. Thus the Prince elected will be, not the choice of the people
to fill the important post of hospodar, but one belonging to the party
who will have spent the most money on the elections.' [1]

Such was, of course, a natural inference as conditions then appeared. But History has so many secrets up her sleeve that mere
mortals should not prophesy.

Whatever the truth about the elections, the determination of the
two caimacams to assert their independence was becoming more
and more evident. Since Catargi's refusal to exercise his functions
appeared final, his colleagues took the step of declaring him deposed, and replaced by one John Cretzulesco. [2] A few days later
they requested the ambassadors to bring about the recall of the
Turkish commissioner on the ground that his continued presence
was an attack upon the autonomy of Moldavia. [3] There is little
reason to doubt that Turkey had kept Afif there as her whip to
secure the desired results in the elections, and the suppression in
the Turkish note of the stipulation in the memorandum of
November 28, that he was not to interfere in Moldavian affairs,
is certainly not without significance. For some reason, Durando,
the Sardinian minister, espoused warmly this demand, and urged
his colleagues to support it; but Bulwer and Prokesch felt that
compliance would be humiliating to the Porte, which, as they
acknowledged, should have taken the initiative in the matter. [4]
Though Afif was not recalled, it does not appear that the remaining
months of his sojourn were marked by any fresh ground of complaint. [5] Meanwhile the Porte, outraged by the treatment which
had been accorded to her various admonitions, had informed the
ambassadors, January 12, that it reserved its right to accept the
elections. [6] This action had apparently been instigated by Buol, [7]

[1] Churchill to Bulwer, no. 6, Dec. 31, F.O. 78/1379.
[2] Bulwer to Malmesbury, no. 60, Jan. 21, 1859, F.O. 78/1427.
[3] Pano and Sturdza to the ambassadors, Dec. 26, 1858, *Actes et docs.*, vol. vii,
no. 2342.
[4] Prokesch to Bulwer, no. 5 B, Jan. 19, 1859, Staatsarchiv, XII/65. Prokesch
told Bulwer that, if the commissioner were expelled, the Austrian consul would
leave Jassy. Lallemand reported that his colleagues felt that Afif should remain
until the elections in order to see that they were properly conducted: Lallemand
to Walewski, no. 96, Dec. 7, *Aff. étr.*, *Turquie*, vol. 338.
[5] *Actes et docs.*, vol. viii, no. 2539.
[6] Prokesch to Buol, no. 3 A–D, Jan. 12, 1859, Staatsarchiv, XII/65.
[7] Buol to Prokesch, Jan. 8, *ibid.*, XII/66.

but met with no sympathy from Great Britain, who felt that a conference ought to have been called when the British had desired it;[1] and a message to Churchill stated that 'Her Majesty's government consider some latitude should be given to a new state of things, and the essential thing is to establish a government in the Principalities.'[2]

In Wallachia the elections were to be held about a fortnight later than in Moldavia; and at the beginning of the new year a controversy over the framing of the electoral lists made one wonder if the Wallachian caimacamie would become shipwrecked like the Moldavian. On the basis of article ix of the electoral law, prescribed by the Convention, the caimacamie had issued an ordinance which had the effect of disqualifying for the assembly two radical journalists, of whom one was Constantin Rosetti, the editor of the *Roumanul*. It is not at all certain that a measure of general application had any ulterior object; but the court which had competence over certain electoral cases, being made up of henchmen of Alexander Ghika, promptly declared the two to be eligible.[3] Accordingly, Mano and Balliano appealed to Philippesco, as minister of justice, to request them to revise their decision. But, whether from respect for the independence of the judiciary or desire to court popularity, Philippesco declined to do this; and even an alleged opinion of Fuad, adverse to the court, failed to move him.[4] Three of the consuls then issued an appeal to the Porte, and Fuad was induced[5] to transmit his opinion directly to the caimacams, which was to the effect that judgements on questions of eligibility to the assembly were reserved to the assembly itself[6]—which was the evident purport of the Convention. Since, in the meantime, further disputes had arisen between Mano and Balliano on the one hand, and Philippesco on the other, the consuls undertook the task of restoring harmony, and were not only able to persuade the caimacams to apply the Porte's decision in the Rosetti case,[7] but succeeded also in settling other causes of irritation.[8] To some extent, however, the conflict between the

[1] Malmesbury to Bulwer, no. 45, Jan. 13, F.O. 78/1422.
[2] F.O. to Colquhoun, Jan. 10, telg., F.O. 78/1441.
[3] The question was whether the qualification of 400 ducats applied to landed property, in which case the two men could not qualify, as their incomes were derived from their profession. Article ix, unlike article iii (regarding qualifications for electors), did not specify. Hence, the court had some ground for its action.
[4] Béclard to Walewski, Jan. 6, *Actes et docs.*, vol. ix, no. 2662; Colquhoun to Bulwer, no. 1, Jan. 3, F.O. 78/1441. Fuad's opinion had been communicated through the Wallachian kapou kiaya on the two caimacams' telegraphic inquiry.
[5] Apparently by Prokesch: Prokesch to Buol, no. 2, Jan. 7, Staatsarchiv, xii/65.
[6] Annexes to Prokesch's no. 2.
[7] *Actes et docs.*, vol. ix, nos. 2670 and 2673.
[8] Colquhoun seems to have taken the lead, judging from his and Béclard's letters.

courts and the caimacamie continued up to the day of the elections. While the caimacams were hardly innocent of partisan activity, Colquhoun placed more blame on the liberal Opposition, accusing them of trying deliberately to embarrass the provisional government, and howling at every attempt to check their irregularities.[1] According to Béclard (who was less sympathetic with the conservatives than his colleague), Ghika and the radicals were hoping that the conduct of the exasperated caimacamie would lead to a suspension of the elections, and that they would then have more time to gather strength for the coming contest.[2] But the hope was vain. The conservatives were in control in Wallachia, and it was Moldavia, 'the Piedmont of Roumania',[3] as one patriot fondly called her, which must point the way to progress.

The elections in Moldavia were held without undue excitement, but the keenest interest was shown in the result; for, if bribery were effective (and such, unhappily, was not impossible in Moldavia), one of the Sturdzas might carry the day. Michael Sturdza had the support of the more substantial *boyards*, while Gregory had the backing of Vogorides, who was finally convinced that his own candidacy was hopeless.[4] But the conservatives could hardly hope to win unless the two factions united, and the implacable hatred of Gregory for his father made fusion quite impossible.[5] To the unionists, or 'National Party', the problem was to keep its numbers intact. It had pursued an active campaign,[6] and had won a great majority of the deputies; and, while several in its membership naturally cherished aspirations for the hospodariate, the settled desire of the party seems to have been to make its principles transcend all personal attachments. In order to avoid being seduced by the blandishments of some *boyard*, and especially in order to prevent the split which had weakened the conservatives, it was agreed to hold a caucus on several successive evenings, and whosoever should be able in the course of repeated ballots to poll a majority of votes should receive the united support of the party.[7] Thus by the faithful fulfilment of their pledges these thirty-two unionists would designate the future hospodar.

It often happens that important events proceed from very small beginnings. There were so many possible selections for the honour that it seemed for a time impossible to make a choice; and, as these eager but baffled patriots looked through the open doorway at a

[1] Colquhoun to Bulwer, no. 14, Jan. 18, F.O. 78/1441.
[2] Béclard to Walewski, Jan. 16, *Actes et docs.*, vol. ix, no. 2675.
[3] B., *L'Autriche, la Turquie, et les Moldo-Valaques*, p. 107.
[4] Ongley to Bulwer, no. 121, Oct. 26, 1858, F.O. 78/1379.
[5] Gödel to Buol, no. 6, Jan. 20, 1859, Staatsarchiv, xxxviii/119.
[6] See their election circulars, printed in vol. vii of *Actes et docs.*
[7] Gödel to Buol, no. 6; Place to Walewski, Jan. 18, *Actes et docs.*, vol. vii, no. 2681; Soutzo, *op. cit.*, p. 363.

skeleton of an elephant (for the meetings were held in the Museum of Natural History), they must at times have felt as hopeless as this mute and silent relic. Finally, at the last caucus but one, when no one as yet had polled a majority, one of the members locked the doors lest the party should succumb to despair and dwindle away, and still another—so it was said—threatened to kill himself if no decision were reached.[1] It was then that the name of Colonel Couza, who may be remembered as the prefect who had defied Vogorides during the campaign against the plebiscite,[2] was entered into the contest, without, as a matter of fact, any attention being paid to his technical qualifications, or any effort on the part of the candidate (he was not among those present) to get himself elected. At the first ballot Couza received only five votes—probably from the friends who had brought him forward as a candidate; but, after the initial amazement which his candidature had produced, he increased his strength with every succeeding ballot, until he finally obtained a majority of nine.[3] One can well understand his shock when his friends imparted the tidings; as his wife has testified, he turned faint, and at first refused to believe it.[4] Yet it was the relative insignificance of the colonel that doubtless attracted many, who believed that they could sway him.[5] Moreover, the fact that he was at the time acting hetman of the army was not without some value (Churchill believed that that partly explained his nomination); for Gregory Sturdza bore a sinister reputation, and the caimacams were on their guard against a plot. Both before and during the opening of the assembly soldiers were freely employed to guard the hall.[6]

On January 17 the assembly met in session to elect a hospodar. It seemed a foregone conclusion that the candidate of the unionists would win the day, for the Austrian consul did not even deign to be present, and the opposition had only the slender hope that the metropolitan, instead of presiding over the assembly, would be found among the absent, with the intention of impugning the election.[7] It was a vain hope; for the primate was not only there, but made a short speech in favour of Couza. After an address of thanks to the Powers for the Convention and a new resolution in favour of union and a foreign prince, a poll was immediately taken for hospodar, and a unanimous vote recorded for Alexander John Couza.[8]

[1] Xénopol, *Domnia lui Cuza-Vodă*, vol. i, p. 35. [2] Page 112.
[3] Gödel to Buol, no. 6; Place to Walewski, Jan. 18.
[4] *Dimineata* (Bucharest), Jan. 25, 1929.
[5] Xénopol, *op. cit.*, vol. i, p. 36.
[6] Churchill to Bulwer, no. 3, Jan. 27, F.O. 78/1443.
[7] Place to Walewski, Jan. 18, *Actes et docs.*, vol. ix, no. 2681.
[8] Procès-verbal, Jan. 17, *ibid.*, vol. viii, no. 2429.

One may wonder what became of the conservatives—especially the well-known enemies of union. Apparently the realization that they had lost caused some of them to absent themselves,[1] while others were not ashamed to seek the rising star.[2] None of them had even ventured to bring forward any candidate. Now, indeed, at last a Moldavian assembly had the consciousness that its will was being translated into fact, and there was nothing to sully the completeness of the victory.[3] 'For the first time in Moldavia', wrote Place, 'an election has been accomplished without the expenditure of a ducat. . . . The election of Colonel Couza is the complete triumph of unionist and liberal ideas against the old system of corruption. . . . It is difficult to form a conception of the enthusiasm.'[4]

The man, so suddenly elevated to the highest honour in his country, belonged to a family of lesser *boyards*, who had for several generations held small administrative posts, and it appears that his father, a man of too slender means to become attached to the *status quo*, had been a participant in the revolution of 1848.[5] Young Couza went to school at Jassy, where he had as classmates, among others, Vasili Alexandri the poet and Michael Cogalnitchano the future statesman. After a brief period of military service, he was sent to Paris to finish his schooling and to take a course in law, but he failed to complete the requirements for a degree. Returning to his native heath in 1840, he subsequently married a Moldavian lady named Elena Rosetti, and for some years held a small judicial post; in the meantime the liberal ideas he had gleaned in the West made him a member of the group known as 'Young Moldavia'. Like his father, he took part in the revolution at Jassy, and, after the failure of that movement, was for a time under arrest. In an effort to make his escape he was captured, but, after convincing his captors that he was willing to disclose the whereabouts of his fellow-conspirators, he led the officer who had charge of him straight to the British consulate, where he thanked his escort with a fine flourish, and left him to realize that he had been duped. After taking refuge at Vienna for a time, he went again to Paris, but returned in 1849 to Moldavia, being appointed prefect of Galatz by Gregory Ghika, who wished to attach himself to the liberals. Under Vogorides he received rapid promotion in the militia, finally attaining the rank of major, but this bribe—if bribe

[1] Churchill to Bulwer, no. 3, Jan. 27, F.O. 78/1443.
[2] Gödel to Buol, no. 6; cf. Place to Walewski, Jan. 18.
[3] The general enthusiasm may be read in the telegrams of congratulation and the articles in the press, as well as other manifestations. See *Actes et docs.*, vol. viii, nos. 2434-41, 2444-50. The election of Couza was plainly regarded as a triumph of the principle of union.
[4] Place to Walewski, Jan. 18, *Actes et docs.*, vol. ix, no. 2681.
[5] Ghibanescu, *Cuzeștii*, p. 159.

it was—failed to turn him against his principles, and in July 1857 he attracted considerable attention, as we have already noticed, by resigning from his prefecture as a protest against the caimacam's manipulations of the elections. Naturally Galatz chose him as her deputy to the divan *ad hoc*, but, though he supported a measure of agrarian reform, he took no part in the debates, believing that he was not an effective speaker. Under the caimacamie which immediately followed the Convention of 1858 he was promoted to a colonelcy besides being made hetman of the Moldavian militia, and he was naturally one of the lesser *boyards* elected to the present assembly.[1] He was now just under thirty-nine years old.

We shall not draw an elaborate portrait of Couza, since his salient characteristics will reveal themselves in his acts. Various incidents in his previous career had shown him to be a man of courage and of more than an average degree of oriental cunning. By nature rather indolent, he was probably much less fond of politics than of the gaming-table, and he was not more moral than most of his compatriots of that day. His biographer credits him with an almost abnormal sense of humour, which he was not judicious in displaying,[2] but he had a winning personality, and was a contrast to most of his fellows in caring nothing for luxury or personal aggrandizement.

In spite of the general enthusiasm that greeted his election[3]—and only a few irreconcilables were sullen over the result[4]—the new hospodar was under no delusion as to the meaning of his victory. To the old *boyards* it was not a pleasing reflection that they had chosen as their prince a man of low estate, little better than a bourgeois;[5] and, if the magnates of his own party deserve some credit for having picked a dark horse to avoid possible disruption, can we not also discern the lingering longing for a foreign prince? Mindful of the vote of the assembly which had tendered him the honour, they looked upon Couza not only as a mandatory of the national will to achieve union but—paradoxically as it may seem— as the pledged instrument to bring about a foreign prince. A strange mission, indeed, had Moldavia imposed upon her chosen leader in the cause of union!

It was no wonder that the new hospodar saw no ground for self-aggrandizement. It might have been better, he thought, if the assembly had taken the step of choosing a foreign prince, and, for his part, he was ready to yield the throne whenever the nation wished it.[6]

---

[1] Xénopol, *Domnia lui Cuza-Vodă*, vol. i, pp. 18–25. [2] *Ibid.*, p. 28.
[3] Place to Walewski, Jan. 17. telg., *Actes et docs.*, vol. ix, no. 2676.
[4] Gödel to Buol, no. 6, Jan. 20. Gödel says there were four inveterate separatists besides Michael Sturdza.
[5] Place to Walewski, Jan. 24, *Actes et docs.*, vol. ix, no. 2688. [6] *Ibid.*

'Couza expressed himself', said the Austrian consul, 'as regarding his position as only provisional; he disdains to envelop himself in a princely cloud, and wears a civic simplicity; persons who know his cynical nature and do not trust the integrity of his conduct are of opinion that under present circumstances it ought not to be hard for him to relinquish a position he did not seek, and which greatly cramps his former manner of life.'[1]

The Austrian consul was not at all favourably impressed with him at first, but the British consul liked his frankness and his modesty, though doubted if he had the dignity that would keep him from intrigue. To Churchill the Prince expressed astonishment at the fortune which had lifted him in a few years from a humble cadet to the highest post in the land.[2] Perhaps beneath all the public rejoicings in his triumph there was a feeling of relief that a less desirable person, such as Gregory Sturdza, had not been chosen; and, so far as one could see, only Gregory Sturdza was unwilling to accept the result. His plot to raise the peasantry and proclaim union seems fatuous enough, but it might have provoked more trouble with Turkey had not Couza been able to prevent it from attaining serious dimensions.[3] So far the hospodar was prudent enough even to win some approbation from the Austrian consul, who wrote that he 'seemed quite resolved to rule according to constitutional forms'.[4]

With the British and Austrian consuls benevolently neutral, and the French consul extravagantly favourable to the newly elected hospodar, one would hardly expect the Protecting Powers to display objection to the results in Moldavia. But the Porte was in no such amiable mood. The gross mishandling of the elections had resulted in what the Turks had feared—a triumph of the unionists. Was it not fitting now to make use of its reservation, and refuse to accept the choice of the Moldavian assembly? Various technicalities, such as the alleged illegalities in the preparation of the electoral lists, the question of whether enough deputies had been present on the day when the hospodar was chosen,[5] and the possibility that Couza did not possess the qualifications[6] prescribed by the Convention, were all convenient grounds for con-

[1] Gödel to Buol, no. 8, Jan. 23, Staatsarchiv, xxxviii/119.
[2] Churchill to Malmesbury, no. 3, Jan. 21, F.O. 78/1443.
[3] *Ibid.*   [4] Gödel to Buol, no. 8.
[5] By article xii of the Convention three-quarters of the assembly were required to be present to choose a hospodar. Since five deputies had not been elected by the time the assembly met, there were only sixty-two instead of sixty-seven deputies who could have voted. Couza polled forty-eight votes (a unanimous vote save for his own abstention), which was more than three-fourths of the former, but less than three-fourths of the latter. See *Actes et docs.*, vol. viii, p. 349 and ix, no. 2694.
[6] It was said that the amount of income required of Couza to be eligible for the hospodariate was partly that of his mother: Gödel to Buol, no. 8, Jan. 23, Staatsarchiv, xxxviii/119.

testing the election. Buol, who had come to the conclusion that something should be done—he did not know quite what—telegraphed Prokesch to inform him as soon as possible what might be the Porte's intentions.[1] To Prokesch's inquiries the grand vizier said that he felt that the Porte was obliged to make use of its reservation, and, since he feared that Couza might be encouraged by the French consul to dispense with the Sultan's sanction, he thought that the best idea would be to call a conference—not at Paris, however, where the Porte had no ambassador at present, but at London, where Musurus could be relied upon to put the matter skilfully; and Ali added that he believed that Great Britain would welcome this proposal. At the back of the vizier's mind lurked the idea that the conservatives might, in the meantime, turn out Couza, and install a provisional government with Michael Sturdza at its head.[2]

British policy would, of course, be shaped with caution, after due consultation of the barometer at Paris. In his first interview with Walewski on the subject Cowley had deliberately displayed doubt as to whether Great Britain would recognize Couza.[3] Walewski, on the other hand, showed equally plainly that he believed that the alleged abuses in Moldavia would not suffice to justify withholding recognition;[4] to Lallemand he wrote that, while regretting the fact that Couza had begun to exercise his prerogatives before receiving investiture, he hoped that the Porte would raise no difficulty about the election, for, even if it were proved that Couza was ineligible, it was the duty of the assembly, and the assembly alone, to disqualify him.[5] It was, of course, manifestly absurd to suppose that the body which had chosen Couza should turn around and condemn its own work, but it was in just such anomalies that the Convention of Paris abounded. Malmesbury, for his part, was still somewhat sullen over the rejection of his plan of a conference in November, and refused to be moved by Bulwer's arguments in favour of the Porte's demand.[6] 'The point of paramount importance', he told Cowley, 'is that the tranquillity of the Principalities should not be disturbed.'[7] Gortchakoff was hardly less indifferent. A conference might, he thought, be held if necessary, but the Porte had no right to refuse investiture

---

[1] Buol to Prokesch, Jan. 13, no. 1, *ibid.*, XII/66.
[2] Prokesch to Buol, no. 5, A–F, Jan. 19, *ibid.*, XII/65.
[3] As Cowley had received no instructions from Malmesbury, he was acting on his own initiative.
[4] Cowley to Malmesbury, no. 145, Jan. 24, F.O. 27/1289.
[5] Walewski to Lallemand, nos. 3 and 6, Jan. 21 and 24, *Aff. étr., Turquie*, vol. 339.
[6] Bulwer to Malmesbury, no. 61, Jan. 21, F.O. 78/1427, and no. 71, F.O. 78/1428.
[7] Malmesbury to Cowley, no. 108, Jan. 25, F.O. 27/1279.

to Couza,[1] and his election had shown that the Moldo-Wallachians had voiced their mind, regardless of all corrupting influences.[2] Meanwhile a deputation was supposed to be on its way to Constantinople to communicate officially the fact of Couza's election, and the Porte's indecision allowed an interval of calm. Was Vienna prepared to disturb it?

It is not improbable that Austria would have welcomed a conference, were she sure in advance that France would admit that the elections should be annulled, but, having already sounded Walewski on that point and found that he declined to be disturbed by the caimacamie's manœuvres,[3] Buol urged Turkey to accommodate with Couza and thereby avoid a conference; at least, before deciding anything, it should await the result at Bucharest.[4] It has already been shown that Austria had no hankering after conferences that left her isolated, and the fact that Lallemand and Bulwer were urging such a course was enough to rouse her suspicions. In the end the Porte decided to wait and see what worse disaster might transpire in Wallachia.[5]

The news of the events in Moldavia had caused some excitement in Wallachia, and the National Party got up a banquet in Couza's honour.[6] The elections, which took place January 20 to 22, passed off peacefully enough, and the result was not unexpected. Bucharest was, of course, strongly radical, and returned Rosetti, Boeresco, and Nicholas Golesco,[7] but elsewhere the party showed little strength, and so far, the 'National Party' adopted the scheme of the corresponding group in Moldavia, and refrained from pledging itself to any one candidate. It was the conservatives who triumphed in the country at large, obtaining nearly two-thirds of the seventy-two seats,[8] though like the corresponding party in Moldavia, they were divided in their allegiance between men of the same blood, Bibesco and his brother Stirbey, both former hospodars.[9] Bibesco, though out of the country, was expected to return at any moment; while Stirbey, generally the victim of ill health, was living in the closest retirement. Alexander Ghika had waited to learn the character of the returns before deciding whether he would submit his qualifi-

[1] Chateaurenard to Walewski, no. 7, Jan. 22, *Aff. étr., Russie*, vol. 218.
[2] Crampton to Malmesbury, no. 30, Jan. 20, F.O. 65/534.
[3] Buol to Hübner, Jan. 13, no. 2, Staatsarchiv, IX/63; Hübner to Buol, no. 10, litt. c, *ibid.*, IX/61.
[4] Buol to Prokesch, Jan. 23, telg., *ibid.*, XII/66. 'You can await the result at Bucharest', said Prokesch to Fuad. 'If it is good, sanction of Couza is without danger. If it is not, the gravity of the danger will loom higher in the eyes of Europe': Annex (Jan. 25) to Prokesch's no. 7 A–B.
[5] Prokesch to Buol, no. 7 A–B, Jan. 26, *ibid.*
[6] Eder to Buol, no. 7, Jan. 20, *ibid.*, XXXVIII/119.
[7] Colquhoun to Bulwer, no. 16, Jan. 24, F.O. 78/1441.
[8] Colquhoun credited them with forty-six, Béclard with forty-three.
[9] *Ibid.*; Bulwer to Malmesbury, no. 10, Jan. 29.

cations to the caimacamie, and the result—Béclard credits him with six deputies—did not seem to warrant his entering the field. Golesco, also in doubt about his status (since he lacked the requisite income) played a waiting game.[1] The combination of Ghika's followers and the radicals might, of course, decide the winner, if the conservatives refused to choose between the brothers, but, at the opening of the assembly it was universally believed that Bibesco, who controlled twenty-four deputies, would be chosen to resume the position from which he had been dethroned in 1848.[2] Still evidence was not wanting that constitutional procedure might prove ineffective; for, two days before the deputies were to gather, the peasants were being impressed by the National Party to crowd round the assembly hall and make a demonstration, and the caimacams found on investigation that there actually was a conspiracy to force the choice of Bratiano or Golesco.[3] Unlike the dangerous element in Moldavia, the minority in Wallachia were able, by exploiting the popular hatred of the *boyarie*, to appeal more directly to the masses.[4]

The assembly opened on February 3, and exhibited on this and the following day scenes of wild disorder. Since some of the outer gates had been carelessly left open (it is probable that the police were in the plot) a great many peasants and people from the faubourgs had swarmed into the city, and it was noticeable that on the first day the galleries were full of noisy spectators. There was little doubt but that the radicals had forged a weapon to use if necessary. When the caimacams left the hall on the morning of the 3rd they were hooted by the mob. But the following day the situation was far more serious, the guard at one of the city gates being disarmed by a mob of peasants, and crowds thronged the streets during the night, harangued by persons who declared that, whatever the *boyards* wanted, the people had a right to choose Golesco or Bratiano. Colquhoun wrote that agitators in the gallery of the assembly hall gave a signal through the window to the crowd outside when clamour was desired, and the president seemingly lacked the courage to keep order. The caimacams had begged the consuls to attend the session in the hope that their presence might have a restraining effect, and some of them were witnesses of this hectic drama;[5] while, three hundred miles away

---

[1] Eder to Buol, no. 7.

[2] Eder to Buol, Feb. 12, no. 14 A, *ibid.*

[3] Colquhoun to Bulwer, no. 20, Feb. 1, F.O. 78/1441.

[4] Béclard wrote that the conservatives were full of confidence, and that the first plan of the radicals was to contest the validity of the elections, and, if that failed, to quit the chamber and appeal to the nation: Béclard to Walewski, Feb. 7, *Actes et docs.*, vol. ix, no. 2700.

[5] Colquhoun to Bulwer, no. 23, Feb. 3, and to Malmesbury, no. 15, Feb. 5, F.O. 78/1441.

in Jassy, Colonel Couza was said to be meditating a march on
Bucharest at the head of his troops for the purpose of restoring
order.[1]

The effect of all this commotion upon the harassed deputies can
well be imagined. While the conservatives sat, cowed, in their
seats, the radicals gave the colour to the proceedings, and showed
their confidence in the outcome. On the first day of the session a
rumpus had taken place over the verification of powers, when
Alexander Ghika and others attacked the caimacamie for their
manner of conducting the elections.[2] Then Demetrius Ghika, a
prominent *boyard*, who had been debarred from standing for the
hospodariate, rose in protest against the election of some of the
deputies, including Alexander himself (his uncle, by the way), who
had failed to obtain an absolute majority.[3] The ex-caimacam
acknowledged his disability, and promised to withdraw, but the
next day he not only reappeared, but took part in the discussions.[4]
Eder, the Austrian consul, charges him with also seeking support
from the mob, aiming, if possible, to make any election impossible,
and thereby to secure the nomination from Constantinople.[5] But
the manœuvres of Ghika were only a characteristic interlude—the
last agonies of a man politically dying. The real drama was a
struggle between the conservatives, relying on the strength of
their numbers in the assembly, and the minority, backed by the
revolutionary elements outside.

Meanwhile, in the lobbies and in private houses the game of
picking a likely winner from the various candidates went on without cessation. Some of the conservatives, in fear that Bibesco
would not unite their forces, were now turning to Philippesco,
who had not at first possessed a single adherent in the assembly,
but had gained some popularity from his show of independence in
the recent broils within the caimacamie. According to Eder, who
is usually well informed, the Prussian and Russian consuls were
active in working for Philippesco, and hoped to win over Stirbey
by promising that his son should be chosen as Philippesco's
successor. But such were only projects. On the evening before
the election one of the conservatives came to Eder and admitted
that his party were terrorized, whereupon the Austrian consul
tried to persuade them either to retire as a body and send a petition
to the Porte, showing that a fair election was impossible, or else to

[1] Béclard to Walewski, no. 160, Mar. 1, *Aff. étr., Turquie, Bucharest*, vol. 19.
Béclard says that Couza told him later that such had been his intention, and we
may suppose that the Prince appreciated the irony of that impulse.
[2] Béclard to Walewski, Feb. 7, *Actes et docs.*, vol. ix, no. 2700.
[3] Colquhoun to Bulwer, no. 23, Feb. 3, F.O. 78/1441.
[4] Colquhoun to Malmesbury, no. 15, Feb. 15, *ibid.*
[5] Eder to Buol, no. 14 A, Feb. 12, Staatsarchiv, XXXVIII/119.

move to another city and hold a rival session. Since the latter device would have meant civil war, one cannot wholly trust the Austrian's motive. But no one seemed then to expect an election on the following day, and many were misled by rumours that Philippesco was gaining recruits.[1] Either because they wished to test their numerical strength, or because fear paralysed their power of decision, the conservative majority still drifted with the stream.

While the conservatives were spending the night in trying to make up their minds, the chiefs of the National Party were gathered at their club in Bucharest to see if they could pick a likely winner and to lay their plans for the morrow. Demetrius Ghika seems to have been able to take the lead at the meeting, and, when he found that his own candidature would not prevail, and that Golesco and Bratiano were too radical to procure a large enough following, he suddenly proposed that the party should throw its strength to Couza [2]—as a means, no doubt, of furthering the cause of union. We have noted that such an idea had entered the heads of certain Wallachians,[3] but this is the first evidence we have since his election that the hospodar of Moldavia had been thought of for Wallachia. While it is also true that the idea of choosing the same hospodar in both Principalities had occurred to some of the adherents of Golesco before the elections had taken place in Moldavia,[4] there is no evidence that his candidature for the Moldavian hospodariate—if we can go so far as to call it a candidature —had played any serious part in the electoral canvass at Jassy, and it is extremely doubtful if the National Party, even if they had been so disposed, could have elected a Wallachian. It would seem that the unexpected triumph of the liberal element at Jassy had now opened the way for a reconsideration of such a manœuvre. Could it be possible that by a strange trick of fate the man who had been elected as a dark horse in one principality would encounter the same fortune in the other?

The query has often been made whether any serious movement had been on foot to elevate the hospodar of Moldavia. Had the Moldavians been intriguing at Bucharest in favour of Couza, and had an understanding been reached between the two 'national' parties? Michael Sturdza, in congratulating his successful opponent, had expressed the wish that he would be chosen in Wallachia as well,[5] and it is further said that a Moldavian deputation, which had as its mission to inform the Porte of the results at

[1] *Ibid.* The most they would do was to agree among themselves that they would give up Stirbey and Bibesco if the radicals would drop Bratiano and Golesco, though whether this proposal was ever made to their rivals, we cannot say.   [2] Eder to Buol, no. 14 A.   [3] Page 190.

[4] Ongley to Bulwer, no. 15, Nov. 9, 1858, F.O. 78/1379.

[5] Xénopol, *Domnia lui Cuza-Vodă*, vol. i, p. 45.

Jassy, and which had stopped *en route* at Bucharest, had taken this occasion to feel out the situation.[1] But this story is explicitly denied by the French consul, who said that none of the radicals had been anxious to yield up their private ambition for the sake of a principle;[2] and the fact that none of the consuls had written of any movement in his favour would seem to show that the idea,[3] if cherished at all, had certainly made no headway. There is also evidence that Couza himself had no such expectation.[4] Finally it is stated that Ghika's proposal at first encountered some opposition, for, though article xiii of the Convention allowed a Moldavian to be eligible to the throne of Wallachia and vice versa, it was feared by some that the election of the same man in both principalities would be regarded by the Powers as an attempt to force their hands. Actually the radicals were probably reluctant to give up what must have seemed a unique opportunity of capturing the government and executing their programme. But, nothing daunted, Ghika eloquently urged his compatriots to put aside all partisan feeling, and, when the caucus ended its session, the party had agreed to unite on Colonel Couza. If necessary, it was fully determined to carry the election by force.[5]

On the following day (February 5) the masses of peasants and small shopkeepers who composed the mob at the disposal of the radicals were distributed to the number of fifteen thousand among the adjoining gardens, where they were fairly invisible to passers-by, but able to mobilize and march to the assembly hall if required. The deputies met at twelve, and Demetrius Ghika then proposed that the chamber should resolve itself into secret session to hear a statement from his party. This suggestion being accepted, Boeresco, a prominent young orator of the Left, begged the assembled deputies to end animosities and to adopt the plan which his party felt would terminate the deadlock—namely that of electing Colonel Couza. 'United as we are to the principle of union, we are attached', he declared, 'to the man who personifies that principle—Alexander Couza, Prince of Moldavia. Let us

---

[1] Bolintineanu, *Viata lui Cuza-Voda*, p. 14.

[2] Béclard to Walewski, no. 159, Feb. 24, *Aff. étr.*, Turquie, Bucharest, vol. 19.

[3] Writing after the event, Eder said that he could state positively that on the day before the election no one had foreseen that the election would take place the following day or that Couza would be chosen, and that, further, no foreign agency had been concerned in bringing it about: Eder to Buol, no. 15, Feb. 15, Staatsarchiv, xxxviii/119.

[4] Couza had announced that, as soon as a 'brother ruler' were chosen in Wallachia, steps would be taken to organize the central commission: Xénopol, *Domnia lui Cuza-Voda*, vol. i, p. 43. Xénopol did not believe that there was any understanding between the two 'national' parties.

[5] Eder to Buol, no. 14 A, Feb. 12, Staatsarchiv, xxxviii/119. Béclard does not tell us that force was contemplated, and, in contrast to Eder and Colquhoun, he rather minimizes this element in the episode.

unite under his name, and our memory will be blessed by our descendants.' He concluded by expressing the hope that the Porte and the Powers would consent to the choice, and recognize it as an act of conciliation. Taken by surprise, the conservatives had almost nothing to say in defence of their interests, only one of them daring to point out that such a choice was a violation of the Convention. These *boyards* were in fact overmastered by their fears, and ready to believe that their lives were in danger if they resisted the popular will. It was Stirbey's own son who moved that each member pledge himself to the support of Couza, and not one deputy present refrained from signing the pact. Thus was Alexander John Couza elected by acclamation hospodar of Wallachia.[1]

Great was the joy in the radical camp. Couza was, after all, a 'forty-eighter', and it might be hoped that he would support the radical programme.[2] Meanwhile it was a great thing to be able to exorcize the spirit of revolution when necessary. Demetrius Ghika was boasting that if the Powers sought to force Stirbey or Bibesco on the country, he would call forth another popular outbreak, calculated to show the national preference.[3] No less joy was exhibited in Moldavia over the triumph of the common cause. Place, who, in spite of having preferred the younger Sturdza,[4] had looked upon Couza's election in Moldavia as a victory for France,[5] was now beside himself with joy at the doubling of the triumph. 'To describe the enthusiasm with which this news was greeted here', he declared, 'would be impossible. For three days the capital has been illuminated, and processions have been held in the city, with torches and shouts of "Vive l'Empereur".'[6] Of course, the Austrian consul nursed his chagrin in silence, but Churchill telegraphed that 'Couza's election to [*sic*] Wallachia has created great enthusiasm here. It is considered a grand step towards union, which will be effected if the strongest measures are not taken to oppose it. In the Moldavian journals it is clearly declared that, should the Porte dare to refuse investiture, the Roumans will reject its authority, and will, one and all, defend their rights to the

---

[1] Eder to Buol, Feb. 12; Béclard to Walewski, Feb. 5, telg., and 12; Colquhoun to Malmesbury, no. 16, Feb. 6, F.O. 78/1441.

[2] According to Eder, the radicals hoped that Couza would leave the government of Wallachia largely in their hands, as if Golesco had been elected, and for that reason were glad to see the Prince compelled to divide his time between two capitals: Eder to Buol, no. 17, Feb. 22, Staatsarchiv, XXXIII/119. This would mean, of course, that they were satisfied (at least, for the present) with personal union. But the Left had not as yet, in truth, taken the measure of Couza's radicalism.   [3] Eder to Buol, no. 14 A.

[4] *Actes et docs.*, vol. ix, no. 2712.

[5] Place to Walewski, Jan. 24. Place dwelt upon Couza's French training, and credited him with the desire to mould his state on the model of France.

[6] Place to Walewski, Feb. 9, *ibid.*, no. 2702.

last'.[1] Thus was Moldavia somewhat ingenuously resolved to stand by the *fait accompli*. Whatever the force of the personal element, it was on the part of both Principalities an overwhelming manifestation in favour of union.

But there is no denying that the position of the new hospodar was one of exceptional difficulty. Whether it is true or not that he hesitated at first to accept the honour tendered him[2] (he had had inklings of the movement in his favour before it culminated in his election), he speedily telegraphed his acceptance 'with pride and gratitude',[3] and was thereafter left to reflect upon his new responsibilities. As a Moldavian, he was not fully acquainted with conditions in Wallachia, and the fact that he had owed his election to a doctrinaire and turbulent minority was hardly a pleasing thought to so inexperienced a statesman. Worse than that, he was soon to learn—if he had not already done so—that the majority of that assembly which had chosen him had done so against their will under a paroxysm of terror; and Eder wrote that they were sorely afraid that the Powers would accept the result, or at least allow the hospodar his choice of the two thrones.[4] The problematical attitude of the Powers was in fact the keenest phase of Couza's problem. He had, of course, no assurance that the Powers would sanction a step that not merely extended arbitrarily the scope of the Convention, but consummated, indeed, the moral union of the Principalities. Furthermore, the impatience of the Moldavians to bring about complete union (legislative and governmental, as well as personal),[5] and even to obtain a foreign prince, was a factor that not only affected his individual future but threatened to involve him still more with the Porte and the Protecting Powers. Whether or not he could hold back the impatience of his countrymen, he saw from the outset that he must count on some external support; and his likeliest ally was France. So, on the day that he was elected at Bucharest, Couza wrote to Walewski, begging him to place before the Emperor a letter which he proposed to address to the Powers, as well as a personal letter to the Emperor himself, written on the same day as the message to Walewski, but sent by special courier.[6] 'The fate of the Roumans is in the keeping of Your Majesty', he wrote Napoleon. ' . . . I have no longer any fear, and am assured that Providence will aid us.'[7]   In the meantime he

[1] Churchill to Bulwer, Feb. 6, telg., F.O. 78/1443.

[2] Gödel is responsible for the story, and says that he was persuaded to accept by the French and Russian consuls (no. 12, Feb. 6). But Place makes no mention of this, and one knows that the Austrian consul was ever ready to put Couza in an unfavourable light.

[3] *Actes et docs.*, vol. viii, no. 2507, annex C.   [4] Eder to Buol, no. 15.

[5] Churchill to Malmesbury, Feb. 7, telg., F.O. 78/1443.

[6] *Actes et docs.*, vol. ix, nos. 2696 and 2697.

[7] *Ibid.*, vol. viii, no. 2500. Since neither this letter nor the two to Walewski of

penned another letter to the French minister, in which he wrote of his election as 'completing the union of the Principalities which the Rouman nation wished to establish'. But, while declaring himself the embodiment of that principle, he did not accept the honour 'without making a supreme appeal to the magnanimity of the Great Powers who have already given us so many proofs of their interest'. 'Permit me to believe', he concluded, 'that, thanks to the powerful intervention of the cabinet at Paris, the fate of the Roumans will be fixed conformable to the wishes they have just expressed.'[1] In view of the Prince's consciousness of the gravity of his position, the speech of Napoleon, February 7, on opening the French legislature, must have been a welcome reassurance. While this speech is more famous as proclaiming France's sympathy with the Italians, the Emperor did not fail to allude to his differences with Austria over the status of the Roumans.

'. . . The reorganization of the Danubian Principalities', he declared, 'could only be effected after numerous difficulties, which have hindered the full satisfaction of their most legitimate desires; and, if I were asked what interest France has in those distant countries which the Danube waters, I should reply that the interest of France is everywhere where there is a just and civilizing cause to promote.'[2]

Nothing was clearer than that France, however much she may have felt forced to accept the compromise of 1858, was still the avowed friend of the Moldo-Wallachians.

While Couza was thus assuming the role of spokesman for his people, there was still the impetuous current of public feeling in Moldavia to be considered; and Couza was fully aware, as we have said, that he was morally bound to admit the principle of an eventual foreign prince. However much he might disagree with his fellow countrymen on the wisdom of immediately proclaiming union, he was willing to make a concession to their favourite *arrière pensée*. In the address to the Powers, which he issued on February 6, he not only emphasized the 'persistence of the Roumans in the wish for union' and appealed for the 'consecration of the great act' which they had achieved in confidence of the 'justice' of the Powers, but then alluded pointedly to the resolution of the Moldavian assembly, requesting union and a foreign prince.

'As for me personally,' he continued, 'I have always worked for the success of this design, and my election has lessened none of my previous convictions. Devoid of all personal ambition, and desiring only the

the same date were, apparently, telegraphed, Couza could hardly have been waiting for a reply before accepting the hospodariate. It shows, rather, that he had made up his mind to accept it on the day he received the announcement from the Wallachian metropolitan, namely on Feb. 5 (*ibid.*, no. 2499).

[1] Annex to Place's no. 4, Feb. 9, *Aff. étr.*, *Turquie*, *Jassy*, vol. 9.
[2] *Annual Register*, *1859*, p. 198.

welfare of my state, as far as it understands and requests it, I must needs declare that I shall always be ready to enter into private life, and will not consider my renunciation a sacrifice, if the Great Powers, taking into consideration the legitimate wishes of a nation which aspires to self-development and sees opened before it the way to a new future, will consecrate by their decision a design which will accomplish all the hopes of the nation.'[1]

This public self-abnegation of Couza (which made a great sensation when it was read before the Moldavian assembly) may have been, from the point of view of practical politics, rather questionable. While conforming to the pledges of his party, and tending to make him popular for the moment, it was consecrating an idea that might loom up, like an evil spirit, across the path of his ambition, as well as opening the door to intrigue of the basest sort. But it must be realized that Couza had never been an aspirant for the high office he had held; the power which had been thrust upon him had as yet been barely tasted; and the promise that he made may well have been an act of spontaneous and disinterested patriotism, inspired by what he knew to be the wishes of his party. He was perfectly aware that (as Churchill pointed out)[2] Moldavia had elected a cause rather than a man. It was, indeed, no personal triumph in either principality. It was the longing for union which had elected him in Wallachia, and in Moldavia it was union with the reservation of eventually procuring a foreign prince. Whatever the future might have in store, Couza could not do otherwise than conciliate this feeling.

But, willing as he might seem to have sacrificed his own ambition on the altar of patriotic expediency, Couza could not well approve of the assembly's resolution, demanding that he call both chambers to Focshani[3]—obviously for the purpose of creating a single legislative body, and possibly with the intention of stampeding him into a proclamation of union. Churchill and Gödel-Lannoy accuse Place of urging Couza to take the step which his better judgement forbade; they go further, and say that Popoff, the Russian consul, who had formerly agreed with Place, was the one to dissuade him from complying with the assembly's resolution.[4] It is not, of course, impossible that Couza was tempted to mount higher on the tide of national feeling which had prompted his

[1] *Actes et docs.*, vol. viii, no. 2599.
[2] Churchill to Bulwer, no. 7, Feb. 11, F.O. 78/1443. Cf. 'It is a principle and not an individual that has been acclaimed': Place to Walewski, Feb. 20, *Actes et docs.*, vol. ix, no. 2710.
[3] Place to Walewski, Feb. 9, *ibid.*, no. 2702.
[4] Churchill to Bulwer, no. 13, Feb. 18, F.O. 78/1443; Gödel to Buol, no. 17, Feb. 22, Staatsarchiv, xxxviii/119. Place's letters give no evidence that he showed any attitude whatever. Popoff, according to Gödel, was acting under instructions from Giers, the Russian consul at Bucharest.

election.[1] When he had written of union as being 'completed' by the election at Bucharest, it is not impossible that he was feeling out French sentiment on the question. 'Show me but two lines from your government,' he told Place, 'which give me the hope that we shall be sustained, and, on coming to Bucharest, I will proclaim complete union, with all the consequences that you know.'[2] But such assurance could not be sent, and Couza could hardly have thought it could be. While to Place he testified his hope that Napoleon would now call a conference of the Powers as soon as possible[3] (Place, accordingly, telegraphed the request to Paris),[4] to the chiefs of the National Party he declared that he had carried out his pledge, but he must now wait for the action of the Powers before attempting anything further—a response which they naturally did not relish. 'Couza has quickly fallen in public esteem,' wrote Gödel, 'and seems more than ever an insignificant person who does not satisfy the expectation of any party.'[5] Yet what else could the Prince have done? Not even all Moldavians were in favour of the move to Focshani, and, if it is true that a majority of the Wallachian assembly were also opposed to the plan,[6] Couza would simply have been making himself the instrument of the extremists at a time when he needed the loyal support of all. Moreover, to have taken a step which meant no less than open defiance of the Convention—and that, too, after the meaning of that settlement had been openly challenged at Bucharest—would have incurred the risk of terminating his career at the very moment in which it was begun. More than that, it would have threatened to undo all the gain which his people had achieved by his election. However much he may have been swayed by friendly counsels,[7] it is a tribute to the coolness and judgement of the new ruler that he avoided a pitfall that might have spelled the national ruin. For, truly as he was the instrument of the national will, it was his duty to temper that national will in the interest of its ultimate triumph. Surely the most that one can say is that the prospect of the Powers sanctioning such a step would have been an even gamble. Couza, seasoned gambler though he was, did not propose to take that risk.

But, if Couza managed to escape a misstep that would conceivably have meant his country's doom, he did not let himself be bullied

---

[1] Place alleges his hesitation: Place to Walewski, Feb. 15, *Actes et docs.*, vol. ix, no. 2708.   [2] *Ibid.*   [3] Place to Walewski, Feb. 9, *ibid.*, no. 2702.

[4] Place to Walewski, Feb. 9, telg., *ibid.*, no. 2701.

[5] Gödel to Buol, no. 17, Feb. 22, Staatsarchiv, xxxviii/119.   [6] *Ibid.*

[7] Gödel declares that he was 'less prompted by his own opinions and resolutions than by foreign influences about him' (*ibid.*). The sneer was natural from the agent who had least influence. It was equally natural that Couza should listen to the advice of the French and Russian consuls, whose governments were the most friendly to the Principalities.

by any foreign representative. It may be true that he yielded to British advice to delay his visit to Bucharest in order that the present excitement might have a chance to die down [1]—but otherwise he seems to have stood his ground. After transmitting one of Bulwer's fussy messages, Churchill was forced to report that it 'had not [he was sorry to say] the least effect on him'. Couza did not disguise his hatred of the Turks or his exasperation at the doubts already raised as to the legality of his election; though he added that he relied on British justice to let the Roumans have the kind of government they wanted, and he 'would with pleasure withdraw into private life if his country were endowed with a foreign prince for the two principalities'.[2] It is hard to see how Couza could have spoken very differently. He had certainly to uphold the attitude which his people had taken, and he had been too long in the service of the militia not to feel animosity towards the ancient traducers of his country. Couza's patriotism was often to try the patience of these unwelcome foreign flunkies.

Meanwhile a deputation from Wallachia had arrived at Jassy to present Couza with the official notification of his election, and was received in state by the Prince, seated on his throne, and surrounded by deputies and officials, together with the French and Russian consuls. Rosetti read the message, which was full of eulogies of union, and violent against those Powers who were supposed to be its enemies.[3] The Moldavian assembly decided to return the compliment by sending a delegation to fraternize with the assembly at Bucharest, and it was proposed that Wallachians be elected to fill vacancies in Moldavia, and Moldavians in Wallachia.[4] Scarcely less active were the law-makers at Bucharest. Regardless of the *Règlement organique*, which prescribed a caimacamie's continuance in office until the new hospodar was invested by the Porte (the Convention, it appears, was silent on the subject), the Wallachian assembly had followed the example of the Moldavian, and invited Couza to assume the reins of government.[5] There was nothing for the caimacams to do but yield, though Mano protested that he should have received an order from the Porte, from whom he held his commission;[6] while Philippesco was probably placated by being chosen with Golesco to draw up the plan of a new cabinet and make other nominations.[7] Besides the sending of a deputation

---

[1] As Giers (through Popoff) had tendered to him Gortchakoff's advice to the same end (Béclard to Walewski, no. 160), one is tempted to believe that he, rather than Bulwer, deserves most credit for this decision.
[2] Churchill to Bulwer, no. 7, Feb. 11, F.O. 78/1443.
[3] Churchill to Bulwer, no. 6, Feb. 10, F.O. 78/1443.
[4] Place to Walewski, Feb. 9, *Actes et docs.*, vol. ix, no. 2702.
[5] Béclard to Walewski, no. 158, Feb. 16, *Aff. étr., Turquie, Bucharest*, vol. 19.
[6] Colquhoun to Malmesbury, no. 17, Feb. 7, F.O. 78/1441.
[7] Béclard to Walewski, no. 158.

to Jassy to announce the election to Couza, the assembly voted an address of gratitude to the Powers (it would seem that this sentiment was a little previous), and decreed that the day of the Prince's election should be henceforth a national fête. No one seemed to care if Stirbey chose to resign his seat, or if Bibesco returned to Vienna, or if some of the conservatives came whining to Colquhoun that they had been intimidated on the 5th of February.[1] One of the leaders of the party, Barbe Catargi, had at least the good sense to accept the invitation to retain his post as minister of the finances, and most of the party seemed still the victims of their recent stupefaction. And, in spite of certain secret misgivings on the part of some, 'the utmost confidence' was felt that the Powers would accept the result.[2] There was little, indeed, to tarnish the brightness of these days, and only the Austrian consul seemed to worry over the outcome.[3] It was perhaps natural that the Vienna government should object to celebrations among the Roumans in the border town of Cronstadt,[4] and equally natural that the Wallachians, in the hour of their triumph, should vent their feelings forcibly against the traditional foe. Few people, in the process of their redemption, have kept their heads so well, or shown a finer spirit. And everywhere there was the same spontaneous enthusiasm. Even in far-off Paris the Roumans, whom distance debarred from a more active participation, held a banquet in honour of the double election,[5] and at Bucharest the radical press was heralding the coming of the man the country was prepared with so much zest to honour.[6]

The new prince's arrival in Bucharest was awaited with undisguised impatience. It had been expected that he would come at once after his notification, but the gravity of the movement in favour of union, together with Gortchakoff's advice to wait till passions cooled, persuaded him to delay his departure till the 16th, much to the disappointment of the Wallachians. He then waited one day more, at Bratiano's suggestion, in order to arrive on the 20th, because that was Sunday, when flags always waved over the various consulates. Elaborate preparations had been made by Golesco to ensure his welcome: an arch of triumph was erected at the entrance of the city, banners waved in all the streets he was to pass through, and the garrison was massed to receive him as he entered. Innumerable crowds thronged the streets and squares. Only the appearance of the troops and police proved disappointing,

---

[1] Colquhoun to Malmesbury, no. 20, Feb. 12, F.O. 78/1441.
[2] Colquhoun to Malmesbury, no. 58, Apr. 8, F.O. 78/1441.
[3] Eder to Buol, no. 17. Eder said that excitement among the lower classes was being fostered by encouraging the fear of foreign intervention.
[4] Béclard to Walewski, no. 158, Feb. 16, *Aff. étr., Turquie, Bucharest*, vol. 10.
[5] *Actes et docs.*, vol. viii, no. 2540.   [6] *Ibid.*, nos. 2544 and 2545.

for such was the impact of the crowds that they did not keep their proper formation—a blunder quickly noted by a military man. But there was nothing really to mar the Prince's triumph. Surrounded by a troop of cavalry, he rode amid outbursts of enthusiasm to the cathedral, where a *Te Deum* was sung; then to the assembly hall, where ministers, clergy, and deputies were gathered to receive him. With becoming humility Couza took the president's chair instead of the seat reserved for hospodars, and, after taking the oath and receiving the metropolitan's congratulations, he made a short address to the assembled citizens. That evening the streets were illuminated, and Couza attended a theatrical spectacle, based on scenes in Wallachian history, composed by a native for this occasion, and pronounced by Béclard 'a great success', notwithstanding the indiscretion of the last tableau, which represented soldiers allowing themselves to be disarmed by the populace, and fraternizing with them.[1] It was, on the whole, a very promising initiation for this little-known Moldavian who must have felt that morally at least union was centred in his person. When we find Colquhoun writing that the greetings were 'cold' and 'unsatisfactory',[2] we may wonder if such observations were entirely free of spite.

Once the installation was over, however, some citizens may well have cherished misgivings over the selection of a man whose qualifications were so little known. Colquhoun writes that the day after the ceremony his house was filled with discontented members from all classes save the extreme Left, and all seemed to breathe the common prayer that Europe would take pity on their country and grant a foreign prince, as all attempts to govern with a native would end in revolution within six months.[3] Of course, the British consul was somewhat given to exaggeration; yet, if Couza had felt a certain loneliness on his new throne in Moldavia,[4] what must he have thought of his hard task of reconciling the discordant factions in Wallachia? May he not have believed that, after all, his strength lay in winning the esteem or at least the tolerance of the Powers? If he could gain the good will of Europe, he might thereby hope to earn the gratitude of his countrymen.

It was a fairly good omen that the consuls seemed disposed to give the new prince a fair test before condemning him. As soon as they were authorized by their governments, they paid unofficial visits to the palace, and, according to Béclard, there was a general feeling of satisfaction, except that Colquhoun felt some annoyance

[1] Béclard to Walewski, no. 160, Mar. 1, *Aff. étr., Turquie, Bucharest*, vol. 19.
[2] Colquhoun to Malmesbury, no. 27, Feb. 20, F.O. 78/1441.
[3] Colquhoun to Malmesbury, no. 28, Feb. 21, *ibid.*
[4] *Arhiva*, July–Aug., 1901, p. 374.

at the Prince's animus toward Turkey.[1] Giers, the Russian consul, who seems to have been his principal foreign adviser, expressed himself as satisfied with the assurance that he would rest content with the *fait accompli*. 'He will not let himself be dominated by any party, but will seek to rally all to him',[2] testified Béclard, whose interview had followed Giers's.

'I have seen Prince Couza on matters of internal administration', telegraphed Colquhoun on February 27. 'He is most rational and prudent, and apparently fully understands his position. He assures me that he will bow with all possible submission to the decision of the European conference, but he said (and thrice repeated the sentiment) that if Turkey attempts to set upon Wallachian territory, he would place himself at the head of the nation, and blood should flow; he said that he had twenty thousand men in Wallachia, and ten thousand men in Moldavia, and feared not what Turkey would do.'[3]

Eder, who was not yet in a position to call on him (since Austria did not even recognize his *de facto* authority), testified that his colleagues considered Couza 'the fittest man as hospodar to better conditions'.[4] It is undeniably true that Couza was always able to make a very pleasing impression when he made the effort, and, if his utterances sounded convincing, we need not necessarily regard them as insincere. 'Colonel Couza is frankly progressive,' was Béclard's avowed opinion, 'but he is at the same time very devoted to the principle of order. The revolutionary party, which counts here several adherents, will find him a declared adversary, instead of a docile, inert, or malevolent instrument, like Alexander Ghika';[5] and the Prussian consul told Eder that Couza had expressed his intention of relegating the men who had elected him to a sphere that would not be dangerous to the State.[6] Thus the resident agents of the Powers seemed to feel that Couza was an eminently safe choice, not at all calculated to be the firebrand of revolution.

But was not the double election itself a national act of revolution? It remained to be seen how the Porte and the Protecting Powers would view this daring distortion of the Convention. Rouman nationalism had taken a deliberate stride towards union. How would Europe regard it?

[1] Béclard to Walewski, no. 160.
[2] Béclard to Walewski, Feb. 13, telg., *Aff. étr., Turquie, Bucharest*, vol. 19.
[3] Colquhoun to Malmesbury, Feb. 27, telg., F.O. 78/1441.
[4] Eder to Buol, no. 18, Feb. 26, Staatsarchiv, xxxviii/119.
[5] Béclard to Walewski, no. 160.   [6] Eder to Buol, no. 18.

CHAPTER VIII

THE CAPITULATION OF THE POWERS

THE triumph of Couza at Bucharest, however much we may ascribe it to the play of accident, was none the less a striking manifestation of spiritual forces, as proved by the enthusiasm which was shown throughout the country. In all revolutions, or movements of a similar nature, it is always an active minority that points the way; but the really significant thing is the attitude of the nation. We do not suggest that the Moldo-Wallachians would have spilled their blood to sustain Couza—for such is one of the things that History cannot tell us; but the fact that they had consecrated their devotion to union by an act of revolution is none the less conclusive.[1] Violently opposed as it was to the spirit of the Convention, which had intended the separation of the Principalities under two distinct hospodars, the double election of Couza was the response of nationalism to the system of international control assumed by the Congress of Paris. The tutelage of the Powers, while morally preferable to the single overlordship of St. Petersburg in the old days, was no less offensive in principle to the sentiment of a people whose national consciousness had become an established fact. The Moldo-Wallachians were tugging at their chains. They did not dare, perhaps, or feel it necessary, to stake their fate in armed revolt, but they hoped, by taking advantage of the weakness of the Convention, to score a point in favour of union, with a sufficient pretension of legality to induce the Powers to accept a *fait accompli*.

The impression which the incident created in diplomatic circles was naturally one of astonishment, but otherwise the reactions of the Protecting Powers showed considerable variation. Cavour, whose interest in the Eastern Question had always been inspired by the chance of using it as a counter in his own game of diplomacy, had no hesitation in pronouncing the election legal, and imagined that Austria's attitude might lead to a welcome rupture, 'which would put an end to all our difficulties'.[2] But, of course, Sardinia was in a different position from the other Powers, who had a more direct interest in the question, and certainly more respect for public law. Malmesbury felt at once that the violation of a European settlement, so recently achieved, should not be permitted, but he was still nursing his ill humour because Ali had not asked

[1] It must be remembered that even the Wallachian *boyards* were not opposed to union, and that, while they had many misgivings in having accepting as hospodar one who was not of their party, there had been no scruples on their part about defying the will of the Powers.

[2] *Il Carteggio: Cavour-Nigra dal 1858 al 1861*, vol. ii, no. 246.

for a conference to settle electoral differences last November, and he desired, for the present, to await the Porte's initiative;[1] in the meantime he laid the case before the lawyers of the Crown, who affirmed that the double election was indeed an infraction of the Convention.[2] Walewski did not trouble himself about such a calamity, but expressed his opinion that the double election was a striking manifestation of the national will, and that it might be well to consider if satisfaction might not be rendered to the wishes of the Moldo-Wallachians—this being written to Malakoff for Malmesbury's consideration.[3] Russia expressed immediate gratification over the result, which proved to her that union was the wish of the Principalities, and, while she admitted that 'the Convention did not, strictly speaking, justify the election', she thought that 'the Powers would do well to recognize it'.[4] Austria was more guarded, though it was clear that she was not disposed to compromise. Buol wrote Prokesch that the election of Couza at Bucharest had 'crowned in a striking manner the manœuvres of the party of disorder and anarchy, acting under foreign impulse'. He gathered that the Porte would demand a conference, in which case Austria would reserve her initiative; meanwhile he demanded 'with impatience' to know what action the Porte would take.[5]

Turkey's sentiment towards her bumptious vassals can well be understood. She had brought herself to the point—before the election at Bucharest—of deciding to recognize the hospodar of Moldavia;[6] now, however, the situation had become more aggravated. Knowing, of course, that she would find a sympathetic heart at Vienna, she was prepared to submit the question entirely to Austrian counsels; and Buol's advice was to 'protest most categorically against the illegality of the proceedings'.[7] Thus encouraged, the Porte decided to denounce the election of Couza, and to request the calling of a European conference.[8]

The question of the course of action to be taken depended, of course, upon the sentiments of the Protecting Powers after sufficient rumination on the subject. Impressed by favourable reports from Churchill, Malmesbury moderated his rancour for the moment,

[1] Malakoff to Walewski, no. 16, Feb. 8, 1859, *Aff. étr., Angleterre*, vol. 702. Malmesbury had telegraphed at once to Cowley to learn Walewski's opinion: Feb. 6, F.O. 96/26.
[2] Malmesbury to Bulwer, no. 108, Feb. 9, F.O. 78/1422.
[3] Walewski to Malakoff, no. 25, Feb. 9, *Aff. étr., Angleterre*, vol. 702.
[4] Chateaurenard to Walewski, no. 11, Feb. 6, *ibid., Russia*, vol. 218; Crampton to Malmesbury, Feb. 21, telg., F.O. 65/354.
[5] Buol to Prokesch, no. 1, Feb. 6, Staatsarchiv, XII/66.
[6] Lallemand to Walewski, no. 15, Feb. 16, *Aff. étr., Turquie*, vol. 339.
[7] Buol to Prokesch, Feb. 7, telg., Staatsarchiv, XII/66.
[8] Prokesch to Buol, Feb. 7, telg., *ibid.*, XII/65; Lallemand to Walewski, Feb. 7, telg., *Aff. étr., Turquie*, vol. 339.

and telegraphed Bulwer that Couza was evidently better than most candidates, and that he did not 'think it desirable' to oppose his elevation, provided he did not 'play into the hands of the unionists'.[1] Such a view of the situation was not at all to Bulwer's liking, for the ambassador had expressed his wish for a conference as soon as he heard of the results at Bucharest,[2] and had joined Prokesch in advising the Porte to that effect; he accordingly responded,

'I place but little confidence in the reports you have of Couza, if they lead to believing he will or can permit things to take a quiet course. He is not the head but the tool of a party. However, the best solution would be leaving him to Moldavia, if he gave up Wallachia, and I would get the Porte to agree to this. I doubt very much if he [Couza] would agree.'[3]

The following day Bulwer convinced himself that the Principalities, urged by the French, Prussian, and Russian consuls, were bent on independence.[4] However faulty may have been Sir Henry's powers of observation, he was always sure of his own mind—which is more than can be said of Clarendon or Malmesbury.

The suggestion that the incident at Bucharest may have had a deeper significance than at first supposed seems to have had weight with Malmesbury; for he concluded that it was deliberately planned to upset the Convention, and, according to Malakoff's inference, the British government was not at all pleased with the reflection that the Roumans had thought to force the hands of the Powers.[5] To Cowley Malmesbury declared that Great Britain must reserve her opinion till she had learned the Porte's views, but that, if she (Great Britain) were to accept the *fait accompli*, it would be only as a special concession to the wishes of the Roumans and the need of a stable government in the Principalities, and not because she could view the double election as, in any sense, a legal proceeding.[6] The fact, however, that Great Britain was willing to consider the possibility of recognizing Couza shows that Malmesbury's indignation was perceptibly cooling. Walewski had no such difficulties with his conscience.[7] He admitted (or at least so Cowley understood him) that the election of Couza was a violation of the Convention, but it was a delicate situation, for, if the election were annulled, the

---

[1] Malmesbury to Bulwer, Feb. 9, telg., F.O. 78/1422.
[2] Bulwer to Malmesbury, Feb. 5, telg., F.O. 78/1428.
[3] Bulwer to Malmesbury, Feb. 10, telg., *ibid*.
[4] Bulwer to Malmesbury, Feb. 11, telg., *ibid*.
[5] Malakoff to Walewski, no. 20, Feb. 11, *Aff. étr.*, *Angleterre*, vol. 702.
[6] Malmesbury to Cowley, no. 215, Feb. 12, F.O. 27/1280.
[7] To the French chargé d'affaires at Constantinople Walewski adopted the curious logic that the Convention itself had intended to meet the wishes of the people, and, since it had availed to procure tranquillity, would it not be well to seek means of preventing its disturbance? Walewski to Lallemand, no. 13, Feb. 11, *Aff. étr.*, *Turquie*, vol. 339.

assembly would simply do the same thing over again, as the Principalities plainly wanted union, which, as a matter of fact, France had wanted for them. Thus did the French minister put his cards on the table. 'It is useless to conceal from myself and from Your Lordship', wrote Cowley to his chief, 'that he will do all in his power to obtain the recognition of Colonel Couza's double election.' The only consolation afforded the ambassador was Walewski's promise to consult Great Britain before making any decision;[1] but it was possibly France's frank espousal of the Rouman cause that moved Malmesbury to greater circumspection. Indeed, the Powers were on the horns of a dilemma. Suppose they wished to enforce the Convention: how, after all, was it to be done? By authorizing intervention by Turks, or by Russians, or by Austrians, or by all three? Walewski affirmed that Napoleon would never concur in the use of force; France would leave it to the rest of the Powers to take so grave a responsibility.[2]

The expedient of a conference to settle the question seemed unavoidable. Indeed, the Porte wished it, and France signified her willingness to call one.[3] Cavour alone was reluctant, for he had valued the double election as useful diversion of attention from his own schemes in Italy, and a conference might meddle with his affairs.[4] Yet no Power seemed moved to raise an objection;[5] and Malmesbury was now anxious that the Porte should accept the result in Moldavia—which would slightly simplify the situation.[6] On the assumption that a conference was in the air, there was naturally much discussion at Constantinople as to the kind of solution that should be imposed upon the fractious provinces. An idea of Bulwer's that Couza might be induced to renounce Wallachia in return for the assurance of Moldavia was communicated to Churchill, who was instructed to sound Couza. A few days later the consul replied that the Colonel seemed much impressed, and had, accordingly, put off his departure for Bucharest[7]—a very doubtful inference, to say the least! On this basis, however, Bulwer, Prokesch, Ali, and Fuad held a meeting, February 15, at Bulwer's instance, to decide what the European conference should wisely do. After considerable discussion Fuad made the suggestion that the

[1] Cowley to Malmesbury, no. 223, Feb. 8, F.O. 27/1290; cf. Walewski to Malakoff, no. 27, Feb. 14, *Aff. étr., Angleterre*, vol. 712.
[2] Cowley to Malmesbury, no. 245, Feb. 11, F.O. 27/1290.
[3] Walewski to Lallemand, no. 13.
[4] *Carteggio*, vol. ii, no. 248.
[5] Malmesbury to Bulwer, Feb. 13, telg., F.O. 96/26.
[6] Malmesbury to Bulwer, Feb. 14, *ibid*. To this pressure, Bulwer replied, 'The Porte dislikes to confirm Couza's election for Moldavia without settling something for Wallachia': telg., Feb. 15, F.O. 78/1428. The Porte then devised the plan of a caimacam for Wallachia.
[7] This correspondence, which Prokesch tells us was discussed at the meeting, is not to be found in the British archives.

Porte should be empowered to name a caimacam on a limited tenure in Wallachia; but this, of course, raised the question of the form in which the Powers should intervene, if necessary, to bring that about. Prokesch said that various considerations, such as the impending war in Italy, would prevent any direct action on Austria's part, and he thought it advisable for the Sultan to exercise coercion in his capacity as suzerain. Neither of the Turkish ministers was anxious, however, to shoulder so much responsibility, and Bulwer agreed with them that at least commissioners of the Powers should be present with an army of occupation.[1] It was finally agreed that Bulwer should continue his pressure upon Couza, and that this plan of collective intervention should be referred to the British and Austrian governments with the recommendation that the Conference should adopt it.[2] Simultaneously it was reported that various contingents of Turkish troops were sent to occupy certain points on the Danube.[3]

Nevertheless, with Austria alone counselling resistance,[4] and Great Britain rather dubious towards the plan of a caimacam in Wallachia,[5] it is obvious that the Porte had little chance of contesting the elections. Malmesbury, for his part, had evidently decided to make a virtue of necessity; for it seems to have been agreed between Paris and London that the Convention should be modified to accept the double election on the understanding that only personal union would be tolerated.[6] He accordingly telegraphed Bulwer to learn whether the Porte would accept such an arrangement, expressing also his opinion that 'every moment she loses complicates the difficulty'.[7] On receiving no satisfaction,[8] and, on learning that Russia, like France, would not take part in any measure of coercion, even if a conference should favour it,[9] Malmesbury went further, and instructed Bulwer to 'persuade' the Porte to 'recommend [to] the Powers to allow her [*sic*] to recognize Couza as an exceptional case, with positive declarations that no foreign prince shall be allowed, that two assemblies shall continue,

---

[1] This would mean invoking article xxvii of the Treaty of Paris.

[2] Prokesch to Buol, no. 13 B, Feb. 16, Staatsarchiv, XII/65.

[3] Lallemand to Walewski, Feb. 12, telg., *Aff. étr., Turquie*, vol. 339.

[4] Buol to Prokesch, Feb. 11, telg., Staatsarchiv, XII/66.

[5] Malmesbury to Bulwer, Feb. 19, telg., F.O. 96/26.

[6] Cowley to Malmesbury, no. 253, Feb. 14, F.O. 27/1270; Walewski to Malakoff, no. 27, Feb. 14, *Aff. étr., Angleterre*, vol. 712; Malakoff to Walewski, no. 22, Feb. 18, *ibid.* Malmesbury had wished to sound Walewski on the question of a conditional recognition of Couza as far back as Feb. 7, and Cowley had telegraphed an encouraging reply. But Malmesbury was only considering possibilities; for he also desired to know Walewski's opinion of a joint advice to Couza to decline the hospodariate in Wallachia. The *entente* between the two ministers developed out of subsequent discussion.

[7] Malmesbury to Bulwer, Feb. 14, telg., F.O. 78/1423.

[8] Bulwer to Malmesbury, Feb. 15, telg., F.O. 78/1428.

[9] Cowley to Malmesbury, no. 279, Feb. 18, F.O. 27/1290.

and [that] the rights of the Sultan remain untouched. This will inevitably be resolved upon', warned Malmesbury, 'and therefore the Porte will consult its dignity by taking the initiative and making the proposal.'[1] 'I shall, of course, obey your instructions,' replied Bulwer sadly, 'but please remember that other demands will follow the acceptance of Prince Couza's double election. . . . Yielding, bit by bit, to the Principalities . . . must end by establishing a confederation under French and Russian protection on the banks of the Danube.'[2] Malmesbury responded to this rather weakly that, inasmuch as Austria alone was in favour of holding out against the acceptance of the election, 'the effect of being publicly outvoted would be worse than any other complication to England'.[3] Meanwhile Walewski, like Malmesbury, was declaring that it would be to the advantage of the Porte to take the initiative in offering concessions.[4]

It would doubtless have eased the minds of diplomats, already worried over the approaching war in Italy, if Turkey had accepted the inevitable, and agreed upon the recognition of Couza as a basis for some amendment of the Convention. But Turkish statesmen are never in a hurry, and they would perhaps have been rather stupid if they had not sought to take advantage of the war-clouds arising in the West. The Porte declined to admit Walewski's arguments that the Principalities could not and should not be coerced, and to the suggestion that some guarantee might be devised to prevent further infractions of the Convention, Fuad merely asked how any guarantee could bolster up an instrument so fragile.[5] Malmesbury had—rather indiscreetly—telegraphed Bulwer that, whereas two hospodars could not be forced upon the Principalities, he believed that, if the Porte should refuse to accept the decisions of the Powers, Great Britain would quit the Conference.[6] In the meantime, the Sultan's ministers, knowing that a conference was to meet, were in no hurry to render its task easier. 'They foresee the necessity of resigning themselves to some accommodations,' wrote the French chargé d'affaires, '[but] have not the courage, or perhaps the power, to propose it.' Already a Moldavian deputation, empowered to request investiture of Couza from his

---

[1] Malmesbury to Bulwer, Feb. 20, telg., F.O. 78/1423. Cavour, remembering that Malmesbury had twice denounced the double election to D'Azeglio, refused to believe a statement of Musurus that the British statesman would now sustain it. 'The English are perfidious,' he declared, 'but they are not liars': *Carteggio*, vol. ii, no. 339. Naturally irresolution was something which Cavour could not comprehend or properly analyse.

[2] Bulwer to Malmesbury, Feb. 22, telg., F.O. 78/1428.

[3] Malmesbury to Bulwer, Feb. 26, telg., F.O. 78/1423.

[4] Walewski to Lallemand, no. 14, Feb. 18, *Aff. étr.*, *Turquie*, vol. 339.

[5] Lallemand to Walewski, no. 17, Feb. 23, *ibid.*

[6] Malmesbury to Bulwer, Mar. 6, telg., F.O. 78/1423.

suzerain, had been in Constantinople three weeks, and now an
analogous mission had arrived from Wallachia.[1] Of course, the
ceremony of investiture must now await the issue of the Conference,
but the Porte was well aware by this time that its battle had yet to
be fought.   Even Austria, who alone had seemed to share Turkey's
views, was now bidding her recognize Couza under certain conditions—the privilege of using force, if the Convention were again
violated, and the right to name a caimacam at whatever capital
Couza did not make his residence.[2] Prokesch told Ali frankly that
intervention was, at present, out of the question, since Russia
would not hear of it, and France had adopted Russia's view;[3] and
it was evident that Austria, convinced as she was of having to go
to war with Sardinia, and possibly France as well, over Italian
affairs, was not disposed to allow a crisis to develop in the Near
East.   Moreover, Malmesbury had warned Bulwer, even before
the election of Couza at Bucharest, that an attempt would probably
be made to incite the Christian provinces of Turkey to revolt, and
any government was more desirable than revolution.[4] It is no
wonder, then, in view of these facts, that the Porte decided not to
insist on the annulment of the double election, fearing, indeed,
that, if the Conference should adjourn without result, Couza might
dispense with investiture altogether, and declare the Principalities
independent.[5] All the Turks felt called upon to do at present was
to dig in and wait.

It is clear enough that, if Turkey hoped to gain by the impending
war in Italy, so also did the radicals in the Principalities, who
looked upon Couza as their tool, and would have liked him (if
Austrian reports are true) to join in a general movement for the
liberation of oppressed peoples in the East. Before the election in
Wallachia D. Bratiano had made a tour of the West, enjoying an
audience with Cavour and Prince Napoleon; but it was well known
that the Emperor's cousin would not lend himself to intrigues to
plant him on the throne of the Principalities;[6] and hence the
radicals were driven back to the policy of consolidating their power
in Wallachia—a project not easy of achievement for a minority
party. Couza, while not at all in sympathy with an element of
unrest at a time when his own position was still far from secure, was
as yet indisposed to break with the men who had elected him. Out
of the seventeen prefects, he made new appointments to fourteen, and nine, according to Colquhoun, were 'men of the most

[1] Lallemand to Walewski, no. 21, Mar. 9, *Aff. étr.*, *Turquie*, vol. 339.
[2] Buol to Prokesch, Mar. 21, Staatsarchiv, xii/66.
[3] Prokesch to Buol, no. 25 A, Mar. 30, *ibid.*, xii/65.
[4] Malmesbury to Bulwer, Feb. 1, telg., F.O. 96/26.
[5] Lallemand to Walewski, no. 23, Mar. 16, *Aff. étr.*, *Turquie*, vol. 339.
[6] Eder to Buol, no. 18, Feb. 26, and no. 23, Mar. 18, Staatsarchiv, xxxviii/119.

revolutionary opinions'.[1] Both France and Great Britain had got their agents to communicate counsels of moderation to the new hospodar;[2] and Colquhoun won assurances from all the consuls that they would support the British view that for Couza to assume anything but a quiet waiting attitude pending the European conference would be an insult to the Powers and thereby render his position insecure.[3]

But Couza was not, as he assured the conservatives, disposed to 'throw himself, *à tête baissée*, into the arms of the revolutionary party'.[4] Whether it is true or not that the radicals were still active among the peasants[5] (a weapon which had proved lately so effective), a project of agrarian reform was fairly symptomatic of their policy; and, much as Couza might have enjoyed an attack upon the economic power of the *boyards*, the present was not the time for a social revolution. Furthermore, although these *boyards* were a tame lot, 'lacking the courage to express openly their views',[6] Couza could not overlook the fact that they were the majority, and could cause him embarrassment if they chose. We may well believe his statement that he intended, as soon as practicable, to 'relegate the radicals to a safe sphere of activity',[7] and he was already talking of introducing a body of the Moldavian militia to keep order in Bucharest.[8] More worthy of his judgement was the appointment of an able conservative, Barbe Catargi, as minister of finances, to balance the presence of Golesco and Bratiano in the ministry; and he knew, besides assuming the apathy of a party that had lost its self-respect, that he could count on the *boyards'* avowed devotion to union to prevent any suggestion that his election was illegal.[9] On the whole, Couza seems to have gauged his situation with not a little acumen. Yet one might wish that he had mingled more familiarly with the magnates of this land, and utilized this chance of gaining personal popularity; but, apart from his natural diffidence, he was ill during the greater part of his first visit as prince; and what should have been the gayest season in Bucharest was said have to been the dullest. It is a curious fact that the aftermath of victory was general discontent.[10] The problem was now to allay it.

[1] Colquhoun to Malmesbury, no. 35, Feb. 28, F.O. 78/1441.
[2] F.O. to Colquhoun, Feb. 18, telg., *ibid.*; Walewski to Place, Feb. 26, *Actes et docs.*, vol. ix, no. 2711.
[3] Colquhoun to Bulwer, no. 49, Feb. 27, F.O. 78/1441.
[4] Colquhoun to Malmesbury, no. 36, Mar. 1, *ibid.*
[5] Eder to Buol, no. 17, Feb. 22, Staatsarchiv, xxxviii/119.
[6] Colquhoun to Malmesbury, no. 49, Mar. 11, F.O. 78/1441.
[7] Eder to Buol, no. 18, Feb. 26, Staatsarchiv, xxxviii/119.
[8] Colquhoun to Malmesbury, no. 36. Colquhoun says that this had the effect of reassuring the conservatives to some extent.
[9] Eder to Buol, no. 16 B, Feb. 18, Staatsarchiv, xxxviii/119. Eder remarked that neither Stirbey nor Bibesco contested his election, as they understood only too well the sentiment for union.   [10] Iorga, *Mihail Kogălniceanu*, p. 171.

Unfortunately, in neither of the Principalities could one expect anything like orderly parliamentary government or a public spirit that could rise above personalities or factional interests. It seemed vain to look for any one whose judgement could be trusted. In Moldavia Couza had wisely thought of Pano as the man to head his ministry,[1] for Pano was not only a leading member of the 'National Party', but, as a member of the late caimacamie, he had probably contributed greatly to the size of the unionist victory;[2] besides, if we are to believe Place, he was popular enough to have been chosen hospodar himself, and his failure to enter the canvass had been due to his predilection for a foreign prince.[3] Unfortunately, Pano had sought to push the Prince into a plan of *forcing* Wallachia to accept Moldavia's choice (this was before the election at Bucharest), and, as this view had also been shared by Couza's enemy, Gregory Sturdza, whose name at Pano's instance had been placed on the list of hospodarial candidates at a moment when there was some question of his eligibility, Couza naturally began to wonder if the man whom he had designated was not, after all, trying deliberately to compromise him with a view of getting him supplanted by his rival. In any event, Pano's impetuous scheme received its merited reward, and, as no understanding could be reached between the two, Couza chose another member of the late caimacamie, Vasili Sturdza, as his premier.[4] Whatever Pano's designs, it was doubtless that yearning for a foreign prince, with which he and others were credited, that lessened Couza's chances of becoming popular in his native country. The Moldavians might well have appreciated the selection of one of their number as the first ruler of 'Roumania', but, when they thought of him in that light, it was rather as an instrument to execute a programme, and, at worst, as simply an unwelcome stopgap. The Prince's refusal to summon the assemblies to Focshani to proclaim union had left his countrymen sullenly critical;[5] and, during the two months that Couza was absent in Bucharest, not a single constructive measure was passed by the Moldavian assembly, though it emphasized its mood by turning out the ministry. Couza himself showed no great fondness or aptitude for public business (even if we may discount Gödel's charge that he neglected his duties and plunged back into his old habits), but he decided, under pressure from Giers, the Russian consul,[6] and, after seeking the approval of France, to begin execut-

[1] Gödel to Buol, no. 6, Jan. 20, Staatsarchiv, xxxviii/119.
[2] See page 191.
[3] Walewski to Place, Feb. 9, *Actes et docs.*, vol. ix, no. 2702.
[4] Xénopol, *Domnia lui Cuza-Voda*, vol. i, pp. 74–6.
[5] Gödel to Buol, no. 19, Feb. 22, Staatsarchiv, xxxviii/119. Gödel says that Couza, perceiving the reaction against him, became morose and unfriendly: no. 23, Mar. 16, *ibid.*
[6] Gödel to Buol, no. 28, Apr. 3, Staatsarchiv, xxxviii/119.

ing the Convention as though his position were already assured. To that end he exercised his prerogative of appointing the members of the central commission which were to have been chosen by the hospodars. The immediate sequel was the refusal of the Moldavian assembly to provide salaries for its own delegation on the ground that the central commission was a useless encumbrance in the task of obtaining union.[1] The new premier, John Ghika of Samos, was a skilful politician, but he was a stranger in Moldavia, and seems never to have been able to manipulate the assembly.

Returning once more to Bucharest, early in April, Couza found matters even less to his taste. The conservative members of the cabinet could not, or would not, get along with their radical colleagues, and a contest over authority between Golesco and Catargi had thrown the whole administration into disorder. The Austrian consul had seemed to feel that Couza, whose position had not yet been legalized by the Powers, would find it impossible to hold his own between the contending parties;[2] but none of the foreign observers had yet taken accurate measure of the Prince, who was eventually to show that he never allowed a party to retain power long enough to get the upper hand. Learning now that the assembly had passed a vote of want of confidence in the ministry —a measure deliberately aimed at the men of '48, who were known to be planning their agrarian *coup*—Couza decided to rid the ministry of Golesco and Bratiano (the former went willingly, and was rewarded by being made an aide-de-camp), and then, as if to soften the fall of the radicals—or perhaps it was because he distrusted the old *boyards*—he forced the resignations of Philippesco and Catargi. Couza then tried to induce the Moldavian, Pano, to form a new ministry (which would have meant a Moldavian in Wallachia and a Wallachian in Moldavia), but, for some reason, Pano rejected the offer; and the post was finally conferred upon Nicholas Cretzulesco.[3]

Such measures purchased peace, at least for the moment, but hardly had a bearing on fundamentals. We have dwelt on the peculiar position of the Prince, and are aware that so far he was hardly in a position to tackle his country's problems. One of the greatest needs of the Principalities was capital; but uncertainty of the future had made the business element—at best a limited group— unusually averse from risking the little it had. During the Golesco ministry the Left had urged the government to establish facilities of credit, but the proposal rapidly foundered on the simple but irrefutable fact that the Ghika administration had left an ex-

[1] Place to Walewski, Apr. 6, *Actes et docs.*, vol. ix, no. 2718.
[2] Eder to Buol, no. 20, Mar. 5, Staatsarchiv, xxxviii/119.
[3] Béclard to Walewski, no. 166, Apr. 10, *Aff. étr., Turquie, Bucharest*, vol. 19; Colquhoun to Malmesbury, no. 57, Apr. 8, F.O. 78/1441.

hausted treasury. As it happened, the prevalent depression was most acute in agriculture, for magazines in the larger cities were full of products of the soil which could not find a market. It appears that during the Crimean War, when crops in the rest of Europe had shown a shortage, the Principalities had enjoyed a very unusual, though inflated, prosperity. The result was over-production, an inevitable revival of the usual competition from outside, rapidly falling prices, and a serious diminution of the export trade. Leasers of farm lands were naturally unable to meet their obligations, and the landowners, largely the *boyards*, were seriously embarrassed.[1] What was obviously needed was a national bank or similar agency to provide the necessary credit for coping with such an emergency, but only through the intensive development of industry with the aid of foreign capital could the perilous overbalance of an agricultural economy be adequately redressed. For the present, the national wealth was so obviously constricted that to open the vicious circle and try in some way to alleviate the processes of recovery was beyond the government's power. It was Couza who later set himself to find that opening. For the present, however, the problem was insoluble, and very probably the political unrest was largely the reflex of a painful period of economic adjustment.

None of these events in the Principalities had much bearing upon the deliberations of the Powers; for, unless Couza were to be criticized for constituting the central commission—and surely the Convention could not be left indefinitely a dead letter—there was no ground for feeling that the moderate counsels of the Powers had been seriously neglected. In any event, the accumulation of several months' argument and counter-argument among the chancelleries had resulted in a general recognition among all the Powers (apart from the Porte) that the double election must be legally confirmed. It is true, Malmesbury still insisted, to save his dignity, that the Convention as a basis should be explicitly upheld, and that departure from its spirit should be looked upon as a special concession to the wishes of the Principalities;[2] but, once this quibble had been adopted, Great Britain was as zealous as France in trying to bring the Porte to terms. Bulwer was saying now that recognition of Couza was advisable, if only the Porte were given some better guarantee for the future than was afforded by the Treaty of Paris; and Lallemand, the French chargé d'affaires at Constantinople, asked Walewski if he might give some such assurance.[3] As a matter of fact, this sort of compensation had already been discussed among the Powers.

[1] Eder to Buol, no. 19 B, Mar. 1, Staatsarchiv, XXXVIII/119.
[2] Malmesbury to Cowley, no. 268, Mar. 16, F.O. 27/1281.
[3] Lallemand to Walewski, no. 24, Mar. 29, *Aff. étr.*, *Turquie*, vol. 339.

Apparently, the sop to be offered the Porte was the dubious hope of being able to put down by force of arms the next violation of the Convention. Article xxvii of the Treaty of Paris had prescribed that

'. . . if the internal tranquillity of the Principalities should be menaced or compromised, the Sublime Porte shall concert with the other contracting Powers as to the measures to take for maintaining or reestablishing the legal order. No armed intervention can take place without a previous agreement between the Powers. . . .'[1]

But this was clearly not broad enough to cover a violation of public law, and one might feel that to strengthen the suzerain's hand was the only palpable remedy. Would it not be well to let the Porte take individual action, if either of the Principalities should refuse to listen to reason? Russia declared no, most emphatically. Gortchakoff would have no modification of the Treaty of Paris, he told the British ambassador;[2] it would simply mean that whatever Power happened to sway Turkey would be using the suzerain's prerogative to serve her own end[3] (certainly, one may remark, Russia knew that game herself), and the government of St. Petersburg would oppose any such intervention without previous concert between the Powers.[4] The Russian minister had been very active lately in preventive diplomacy over Italy, and was eager that a conference should dispose of the Principalities before a projected congress should meet to settle Italian affairs.[5]

Great Britain was no less urgent in pressing for a conference, and Cowley, who had been visiting London, was sent back to his post to hurry the matter up. But Malmesbury seemed for the moment impressed by Russia's misgivings, and expressed the conviction that 'should the Powers hereafter agree to any armed interference, that measure ought to be carried out by the forces of the Porte, but accompanied by a military commission from each of the Powers'—a necessary precaution to protect the inhabitants from a 'fanatical or vindictive soldiery'.[6] Unfortunately, for some reason these restrictions upon the Porte were omitted from the memorandum[7] which Cowley handed Walewski as embodying British views; and the French minister, primed by Russia's objections—not to mention France's own—while he was willing to accept the principle of intervention, insisted that a preliminary agreement was necessary in accordance with the Treaty of Paris.[8]

[1] Holland, *The European Concert in the Eastern Question*, p. 252.
[2] Crampton to Malmesbury, Mar. 9, telg., F.O. 65/534.
[3] Crampton to Malmesbury, no. 84, Mar. 15, *ibid*.
[4] Chateaurenard to Walewski, no. 23, *Aff. étr., Russie*, vol. 218.
[5] Crampton to Malmesbury, no. 96, Mar. 23, F.O. 65/535.
[6] Malmesbury to Cowley, no. 268.
[7] Cowley to Malmesbury, no. 324, Mar. 25, enc.
[8] Walewski to Malakoff, no. 46, Mar. 28, *Aff. étr., Angleterre*, vol. 712.

Presented with this objection, Malmesbury was ready to approve in general the concurrence of the Powers, but contended that, as time should not be wasted in this hypothetical crisis, the representatives of the Powers should be empowered to advise the Porte when a *casus interventus* had arisen.[1] Walewski then raised the question whether a majority among the representatives should suffice for a decision;[2] and Russia responded that unanimity should be necessary.[3] It was evident that neither France nor Russia really wanted any measure that would make intervention probable.

As five of the Powers were already deliberating over the Italian question, which was sufficiently distracting,[4] and, as the month of April opened with the other question still unsettled, Walewski declined to summon the Conference until France and Great Britain had reached a preliminary decision.[5] Meanwhile the Porte's instructions to Musurus, its plenipotentiary for the conference, were vehement in condemnation of the double election, and suggested that the Porte was the proper one to intervene (annulment was not mentioned, but that was presumably the intention), the Turkish army being accompanied by commissioners of the Powers.[6] Evidently the Porte still chose to stand on its legal rights, though Bulwer and Lallemand suspected that there might be secret instructions allowing concession;[7] and, indeed, the Porte was really considering the step of recognizing Couza on condition of his being represented by a caimacam at Jassy and a guarantee being provided (similar to what had been proposed) against future violations of the Convention.[8] But it was not for Turkey to decide what her pride would allow her to accept. By April 7, Great Britain, having learned that Walewski had proposed a formula, sufficiently strong, on the integrity of the Convention, reached an understanding with France on the action to be taken at the Conference.[9]

The Conference opened on April 7, and held but two meetings. European opinion was now considerably excited over the impending breach between France and Austria over the Italian question, and the Court of Vienna, while supporting the views of Turkey,[10]

[1] Malakoff to Walewski, no. 37, Mar. 29, *Aff. étr., Angleterre*, vol. 712.
[2] Cowley to Malmesbury, no. 365, Apr. 1, F.O. 27/1293.
[3] Cowley to Malmesbury, no. 399, Apr. 8, *ibid.* Oddly enough, Kisseleff, the Russian plenipotentiary, had proposed that the *limitrophe* Powers be the mandatories to intervene, when occasion required. Naturally such an idea found no favour.
[4] Malmesbury to Bulwer, Mar. 24, telg., F.O. 78/1423.
[5] Cowley to Malmesbury, no. 365.
[6] Annex to Lallemand's no. 20, *Aff. étr., Turquie*, vol. 339.
[7] Lallemand to Walewski, no. 27, Apr. 5, *ibid.*, vol. 370.
[8] Prokesch to Buol, no. 29 B, Apr. 13, Staatsarchiv, XII/65.
[9] Cowley to Malmesbury, no. 399, and enc.; F.O. to Cowley, no. 406, Apr. 9, F.O. 27/1282.
[10] Hübner to Buol, no. 45 C, Apr. 15, Staatsarchiv, IX/61. This was at the opening of the second session.

took but little interest in the Conference. The first meeting was made the occasion for a statement of Turkey's position, which took the form of an arraignment of the Principalities, and left no opening for compromise.[1] At the second meeting, April 13, Walewski introduced the prearranged pact, and five Powers (France, Great Britain, Russia, Prussia, and Sardinia) registered their adhesion in the protocol. The Porte was asked to confer investiture upon Couza as 'hospodar of Moldavia and Wallachia', but it was understood that in event of any infraction of the Convention (if so considered by the representatives of the Powers at Constantinople), the suzerain Power might be authorized to send a commissioner (accompanied by a representative of each of the Powers) to request the previous condition restored, and, if not successful, the representatives of the Powers might advise the Porte to take coercive measures.[2] Unfortunately, discussion of these proposals was, of course, cut short by the war crisis and the withdrawal of the Austrian representative, and, manifestly, without the adhesion of Austria and Turkey, the protocol could not be viewed as part of the public law of Europe.

The immediate question was whether the Porte would bow to the will of the majority of the Powers. Walewski expressed the hope that, in view of the effect which delay might have upon the situation in the Principalities and the state of Europe, the Porte would adhere to the decision of the Powers,[3] and Malmesbury telegraphed Bulwer in much the same tone, declaring that the Turks would be mad if they refused, and that Austria, embroiled in war, could not help them.[4] Yet it was evident that the Porte, notwithstanding its earlier vacillation, was determined not to adhere to the Protocol of April 13. It is not impossible, of course, that the Turks were simply bluffing in the hope of gaining further concessions while Europe was racked by war, but Bulwer, who had now the uncomfortable role of reversing his former position, was quite distracted by the obduracy he met, and warned the Porte that not only would Couza be liable to declare his independence, but it was not unlikely that Russia (whom he suspected of being over-friendly to the Porte) would see an opportunity for intervention.[5] Lallemand heard that Bulwer had communicated some very threatening language to the Turks, implying that the whole question of their treatment of the Christians might be taken up, but 'the stratagem, which consists of frightening the Turks with the

---

[1] Hübner to Buol, no. 41 E, Apr. 7, enc., Staatsarchiv, IX/61.
[2] *Arch. dip.*, 1866, vol. 2, pp. 162 ff.
[3] Walewski to Lallemand, no. 30, Apr. 29, *Aff. étr., Turquie*, vol. 340.
[4] Malmesbury to Bulwer, no. 246, Apr. 30, F.O. 78/1423. This was in reply to a telegram of Bulwer's, Apr. 29, inquiring whether the Porte should accept the Protocol or not. [5] Bulwer to Pisani, Apr. 29, F.O. 78/1431.

complaints and the needs of the Christians and the demands of
Europe on their behalf in order to obtain some concession from
the Porte on important occasions—a strategem which succeeded
sometimes in the case of Lord Stratford—has not the same success
in the hands of Sir H. Bulwer, who does not know how to act
tragedy, and whose character is little adapted to inspire terror.'
It was to this intrigue that Lallemand ascribed his inability to get
Bulwer to concur in a meeting of the ambassadors to plan a
combined pressure upon the Porte.[1]

It was certainly unfortunate that so much mutual suspicion
clouded the work of the diplomats in the face of so exasperating
a problem. One may easily guess that Lallemand was a bit jealous
of his colleague, whom he admits had been the divan's 'almost
only counsellor for a month'.[2] Judging from his own dispatches,
Bulwer was trying in his laboured way to bring the Porte to terms,[3]
and, more than likely, in acting separately from his colleagues, he
was striving to get the Porte to understand his change of front, and
to get back his personal prestige. He, in turn, it appears, suspected
Vienna of being the deterrent influence.[4] Now it is perfectly true
that Austria had lately been encouraging the Porte's delay;[5] but
the war in Italy was complication enough for the present, and
Prokesch was careful to observe a strictly neutral attitude.[6] To
Austria's recommendation 'not to touch the *status quo*' (she was
doubtless hoping for greater freedom of action when the war was
over) Fuad responded by a statement in which he recognized that
the Principalities might declare their independence and that a
congress following the war might actually sanction it; yet neither
he nor Ali could bring himself to accept the proposals of the five
Powers as they stood, and the most that could be expected was
a conditional acceptance.[7] It must be confessed that, with Bulwer
insisting that failure to accept the Protocol would cause a proclamation of independence, and the Austrians saying that the double
election was only a deliberate step towards independence, it is not
surprising that the Porte should have been rather bewildered.
Indeed, every one seemed to be at cross-purposes. Russia wanted
the conferences at Paris to continue without Austria (this was discountenanced in London); while Malmesbury, whose honesty as
a diplomat was only equalled by his clumsiness, was trying to

---

[1] Lallemand to Walewski, no. 37 *bis*, May 17, *Aff. étr., Turquie*, vol. 340.
[2] Lallemand to Walewski, no. 43, June 3, *ibid.*
[3] Bulwer to Malmesbury, no. 303, Apr. 29 and May 4, telg., F.O. 78/1431.
[4] Bulwer to Malmesbury, May 4, telg.
[5] Buol to Prokesch, May 1, Staatsarchiv, XII/66.
[6] Prokesch to Buol, no. 34 B, Apr. 29, *ibid.*, XII/65. Writing of Bulwer's efforts
to get the Porte to recognize Couza, Prokesch wrote, 'I have no intention either
of associating myself with the *démarches* of Sir H. Bulwer or of opposing them.'
[7] Prokesch to Buol, no. 36 A–F, May 11, *ibid.*

impress the Turks with the fact that he had really wanted a stronger guarantee than the Protocol had granted.[1] Only France seemed to know her own mind. Walewski declared himself mystified by the Porte's delay[2] in responding to the Powers' proposals, and felt that any demand for their modification, in view of Austria's withdrawal from the European conference, was tantamount to rejection.[3] Were there grounds for fearing, as Prokesch did, that France and Russia might forthwith accept a *fait accompli*?

Late in May the Porte decided—possibly on learning that the Conference was to be resumed[4]—to propose a substitute for the Protocol.[5] It was willing, finally, to grant investiture to Couza but only on specified conditions; and to some of the Powers at least this 'counter-project' was wholly unacceptable. France noted with disfavour that it avoided the proper designation of the Principalities, demanded that Couza should come to Constantinople to be invested, and wanted his separate investiture for each office;[6] while Russia rejected the idea of his being represented by a caimacam at Jassy;[7] and there was a fairly general disapproval of the idea that Turkish troops should necessarily be employed for the 'coercive measures' specified in the Protocol. Bulwer, not to be deprived of his diplomatic triumph, was more lenient towards the Porte's new manœuvre, but it may be true that he was nervously trying to banish the bogy of Russian ascendancy, of which the coming visit of the Grand Duke Constantine seemed to be the manifestation.[8] At all events, the *ex parte* negotiations of Bulwer,

[1] F.O. to Cowley, no. 580, May 4, F.O. 27/1283.
[2] Lallemand declared that the delay was chiefly due to Bulwer, who 'while making of a collective affair a personal affair, had spoiled it by complaisance', and, having sided with Turkey early in the controversy, was deeply embarrassed when she chose to draw profit from that fact: Lallemand to Walewski, no. 40, May 28, *Aff. étr., Turquie*, vol. 340.
[3] Walewski to Lallemand, no. 36, May 20, *ibid*.
[4] Prokesch to Schlechta, May 9, annex to Prokesch's no. 26 of May 11, Staatsarchiv, XII/65.
[5] Lallemand to Walewski, no. 43, June 3, *Aff. étr., Turquie*, vol. 340.
[6] Lallemand to Walewski, no. 46, June 22, *ibid*.; Walewski to Lallemand, no. 38, June 8, *ibid*.
[7] Bulwer to Malmesbury, June 2, telg., F.O. 78/1431.
[8] Lallemand to Walewski, no. 43 *bis*, June 7, and no. 44 *bis*, June 14, *Aff. étr., Turquie*, vol. 340; Prokesch to Rechberg, no. 45 B, June 15, Staatsarchiv, XII/65. There is much that is not clear in the French and Austrian dispatches, and the British are almost silent in the matter, but apparently the Grand Duke (a brother of the Tsar) was accorded a sumptuous reception at Constantinople on his way home from a visit to Paris; and, according to Lallemand, Bulwer, having failed to circumvent Russian influence, persuaded the Turks to strengthen their armaments and promised a loan—on terms which, however, proved too onerous. Since Lallemand suspected Bulwer of intriguing to get rid of Ali, and Prokesch suspected France and Russia of the same design, one is impressed with the atmosphere of gossip and suspicion that reigned at Constantinople. A little humour was lent to the present situation, however, when to Prokesch Ali 'expressed the conviction, not without melancholy, that all this display of money and attention [on the Grand Duke] was "a total loss" '.

whatever their motive (and one knows his appetite for compromise), had apparently proved a poor device for making Turkey walk the plank.

Meanwhile the long uncertainty of whether investiture would ever be granted, or, if such concession were made, whether the conditions would involve a fresh slight to provincial autonomy, was making the position of Couza increasingly difficult. Was he, after all, the man to command respect from the factious *boyards* or the over-exacting signatory Powers? Would he be able, now that he had parted with his dubious friends of the Left, to make a position for himself independent of the circumstances of his elevation? Politically, no ruler could have been more alone. While his enemies at home viewed him either as an unhappy accident to be removed as soon as possible, or else as an unprofitable speculation because he could not at once achieve union, the Court of Vienna was adding to his embarrassments by treating him as a sort of bastard prince, without even *de facto* recognition.

The attitude of Austria had always been that of opposing the idea of union even when its application had been of the most trifling character. In the days of the *caïmacamie intérimaire* the Austrian consul had refused to visa Wallachian passports if they bore the inscription 'The United Principalities of Moldavia and Wallachia', contending that this expression could be used only on a document which related to the joint business of the Principalities.[1] After several months of such gratuitous embarrassments (even Austrian residents suffered when the Principalities retaliated by refusing to issue any passports at all), the government of Vienna finally yielded;[2] though the very fact of yielding was liable to lead to further trouble, first by making it more than ever anxious to humble the Roumans, and, secondly, by leading the Roumans themselves to believe that with persistency they might always gain in the end. The fact, indeed, that there were something like 100,000 Austrian subjects and protégés in the Principalities gave the Moldavian and Wallachian governments a distinct advantage in dealing with a Power that was helpless in the last resort to use coercive measures. We have already noticed that Baron Eder was not allowed by his government to extend even a *de facto* recognition to Couza; and this meant, of course, a complete severance of his relations with the two governments, even in the case of the lowest officials. Such conduct, as a matter of fact, reacted very grievously on the interests of Austrian subjects in the Principalities. All suits brought by Austrian residents against the natives were suspended because Eder could not exercise the supervision to which a consul was

[1] Place to Walewski, Nov. 17, 1858, *Actes et docs.*, vol. vii, no. 2175.
[2] Buol to Eder, Feb. 25, 1859, Staatsarchiv, XXXVIII/119.

entitled, and, similarly, an Austrian, arrested on a criminal charge, was without the customary protection.[1] Finally, Couza made up his mind to gratify his resentment by treating all Austrian nationals as being amenable to the local courts on an equal footing with his own subjects. For the moment, the advice of the French consul stayed his hand, and Austria availed herself of the offer of the Prussian consul to exercise temporarily the functions of her own consul. But about the middle of May Couza carried out his threat, and the Wallachian minister of foreign affairs issued a circular to the effect that all Austrian residents should be submitted to local jurisdiction.[2] This reprisal had its desired effect. Austria made haste to put herself on the same footing as other Powers, and granted Couza *de facto* recognition.[3]

The attitude of the new ruler was symptomatic of a new determination on the part of the Principalities to make their autonomy a reality in the eyes of Europe. Naturally, the Capitulations were the favourite point of attack, for the rights of extraterritoriality accorded to foreigners were exceedingly galling to the new-born patriotism of the Moldo-Wallachians, and hatred of the foreigner seemed to coincide with the exsurgence of this sentiment. There were also tangible grounds for this resentment; for, whatever may be said of the jealousy which the superior technique of the Austrian artisan may have evoked,[4] the immunity which foreign merchants enjoyed from paying for licences (and Austrians had acquired other exemptions as well)[5] gave the natives a distinct disadvantage in competition. It was charged, moreover, that the right of consular protection was extended over many who really had no claim to it, and that sentences imposed on foreigners by a local court in criminal cases, and left, in accordance with the Capitulations, to a consul to carry out, were all too often unexecuted.[6] On the other hand, suits brought by foreigners against natives received little consideration, though, if a foreigner were prosecuted, he was liable to almost any kind of indignity. Victor Place declared that native opinion was bitter against the Convention because it confirmed the subjection of the Principalities to treaties contracted between the Powers and the suzerain court, and both he and his Austrian

---

[1] Béclard to Walewski, no. 168, Apr. 19, 1859, *Aff. étr., Turquie, Bucharest*, vol. 19.

[2] Béclard to Walewski, no. 172, May 18, *ibid.*

[3] Buol to Eder, May 11, telg., Staatsarchiv, xxxviii/119.

[4] Gödel to Rechberg, no. 45, July 3, *ibid.* Gödel-Lannoy also mentions the temptation of subordinate officials to regard foreign enterprises as an object of plunder.

[5] Circular of the Moldavian minister of foreign affairs, Oct. 10, annexed to Béclard's no. 181, *Aff. étr., Turquie, Bucharest*, vol. 19.

[6] Green to Bulwer, no. 25, Dec. 5, F.O. 78/1442. Green wrote that all he could do in such cases was to send the condemned to Malta to be tried over again.

colleague charged Couza with being the soul of the resistance.[1] Unhappily for foreign interests, the consuls, instead of combining in their defence, were often at cross-purposes,[2] and hence Couza left his ministers a free rein.

The interests of all the Powers suffered, those of Austria the most, though for a time the French fared little better. Some French millers who opened a bakery, which gave the natives, it was said, their first taste of good bread, were continually harassed until finally their shop was pillaged and the bread distributed to people in the street. Two French engineers received like indignities, and no redress could be obtained. 'I can multiply analogous facts regarding all the consulates', wrote Place.[3] Though British residents were less numerous than the French, they included natives of the Ionian Islands, who were then under British protection, and seemed to have a knack of getting into trouble with the authorities. Oftentimes they were punished without any notice being sent to the British consul.[4]

In June a measure was taken which seemed to force the Powers to attempt some official action. Prompted by a ministerial decision, and as a means of getting money for the army, Couza issued a decree, commuting a peasant *corvée* into a direct tax on all classes, including foreigners. Fundamentally, the measure was to be commended, as it was in line with the abolition of privilege, proclaimed by the Convention itself; but the government had no right to invade the immunity of foreigners from the operation of personal taxes, and, incidentally, the act was in violation of article xxv of the Convention, which vested the taxative power in the assembly rather than the executive. The Prince being absent from Jassy, Place remonstrated with the premier, Iepouriano, and warned him that he was only making trouble for himself in the assembly, but the only reply he received was that the assembly was made up of numsculls, and that if it caused embarrassment Couza's intention was to dissolve it and call another.[5] Tired at length of having their complaints persistently ignored, several of the consuls at Jassy agreed to present identical notes (June 29) recalling the privileges which foreigners were supposed to enjoy by treaty, and demanding that they should no longer be disregarded.[6] The government took its time about replying, and vexations were in no wise lessened in the meantime. The minister's answer—after

---

[1] Place to Walewski, June 16, *Actes et docs.*, vol. ix, no. 2735; Gödel to Rechberg, no. 45.

[2] Place to Walewski, June 16; Churchill to Bulwer, no. 27, June 29, F.O. 78/1442.

[3] Place to Walewski, June 21, *Actes et docs.*, vol. ix, no. 2736.

[4] Churchill to Bulwer, no. 27, June 29, F.O. 78/1442.

[5] Place to Walewski, June 21.   [6] Churchill to Bulwer, no. 27 enc.

thirteen days of reflection—proved entirely uncompromising: as Moldavia had had no share in making the treaties which granted extraterritoriality to foreigners, she could not consider herself bound by them until an enactment of her own legislature made them valid, and, in the meantime, she could not recognize any jurisdiction other than that specified in the Convention, which, in the native opinion, abrogated all these treaties. It is, of course, true that the Convention dealt with this subject only in the most general terms,[1] but the official attitude of the Moldavian government amounted to a repudiation of the Capitulations.[2] 'If there is no remedy,' said Place, 'the country will become uninhabitable for foreigners'; and Couza was said to have frankly admitted that the Roumans wanted foreigners to get out.[3] Churchill, aghast at hearing that British subjects were forced to pay the new tax, wrote to Downing Street that he would have to resign his post unless his government would support his authority.[4]

To the consulates, battling for the protection of rights confided to their care, the apparent indifference, or at least slowness, of their governments must sometimes have seemed unpardonable; whereas the cabinets themselves, immersed in questions of *haute politique*, looked upon these matters as too trifling to require more than a casual notice—a circumstance of which the Principalities were well aware. Churchill's action in the concerted move, mentioned above, was at least sustained by Bulwer[5] (though his threat to resign roused only ill humour at home),[6] but Lobanoff, the Russian minister at Constantinople, declared that Popoff, the Russian consul, had exceeded his instructions. No doubt the Powers disliked exceedingly to have their hands forced, and, when they found themselves compelled to take some action, were tempted to put the blame on their own suffering agents. But there was also the growing conviction that many of the privileges enjoyed by foreigners were unsound in theory and unworkable in practice. Such, indeed, had been the admission of most of the members of the international commission which had reported to the Paris

[1] Article ii, which confirmed the autonomy of the Principalities, ascribed this status to the Capitulations, and recalled these treaties as 'réglant leurs rapports avec la Sublime Porte', and article viii stated that 'as in the past, international treaties, concluded by the suzerain court with foreign Powers, will be applicable to the Principalities in everything that does not attack their immunities'. It is obvious that the autonomy of the Principalities was much more emphasized than the restrictions which had been placed upon it.
[2] Churchill to Russell, no. 23, July 12, F.O. 78/1445.
[3] Place to Walewski, June 29, *Actes et docs.*, vol. ix, no. 2942. Gödel, like Place, felt that the chief impulse came from Couza: Gödel to Rechberg, no. 45, July 3, Staatsarchiv, xxxviii/119.
[4] Churchill to Russell, no. 32, Aug. 7, F.O. 78/1444.
[5] Bulwer to Russell, no. 48, July 19, F.O. 78/1433.
[6] F.O. to Bulwer, no. 25, Sept. 7, F.O. 78/1426.

Conference of 1858, and, but for jealousy of Russia, the Conference might have studied the problem as it should have done.[1] Lobanoff was of the opinion that the whole question of foreign rights should be taken up with a view of thoroughgoing revision,[2] and Bulwer, while admitting that the corruption of the native courts made some degree of extraterritoriality indispensable, reminded his government that much of the trouble came from the fact that 'the grossest abuses are practised under the shield of consular power, and, as long as this power exists, and is abused as it is, a native jurisdiction is deprived in a great degree of its legitimate authority'.[3] Also in the matter of taxation, it was not fair, as Bulwer admitted, that foreign artisans resident in the Principalities should be in a more favoured position than natives.[4] All such points at issue should, of course, be decided by a conference of the Powers, and in the meantime (Bulwer thought) it was sufficient to confine oneself to protests against infractions of the treaties.[5]

There is no evidence to show that the British government was impressed by this suggestion, but at least it was not unwilling to consider proposals for revision.[6] The French government, while determined to resist encroachments upon its rights, gave its consul to understand that revision would be desirable as soon as the Moldo-Wallachian courts could give sufficient guarantees.[7] In order to clarify the issue, Walewski prepared a memorandum, made up largely of citations from the report of the European commission. All the commissioners, save those of Turkey and Austria, had admitted that in some matters, like the pretension that cases between foreigners and natives should come exclusively before a consul, the rights of foreigners under the Capitulations had been stretched beyond what was legal. The same commissioners had believed that foreign merchants should no longer be exempt from taxes, but be placed on the same footing as natives. Especially significant had been the admission by the same commissioners that 'consular jurisdiction is an anomaly in a Christian state'. This meant, of course, that rights of extraterritoriality had been originally intended as a shield against Moslem law at a time when the Turks were in actual control of the Principalities. Historically the argument was sound, but Walewski did not press it too far. It would not do, perhaps, for consular jurisdiction to be immediately abolished, but as soon as the court of cassation, decreed by the

[1] See above, p. 177.
[2] Thouvenel to Walewski, no. 62, Aug. 31, *Aff. étr.*, *Turquie*, vol. 341.
[3] Bulwer to Russell, no. 48, July 19, F.O. 78/1433.
[4] Bulwer to Russell, no. 82, Aug. 4, F.O. 78/1434.
[5] Bulwer to Russell, no. 114, Aug. 24, F.O. *ibid.*
[6] F.O. to Cowley (no number), Aug. 19, F.O. 27/1285.
[7] Walewski to Béclard, no. 12, Oct. 11, *Aff. étr.*, *Turquie, Bucharest*, vol. 10.

Convention, should be established, this jurisdiction might be conveniently revised.[1] Such might be called a definite opening of the question, and with these views the British government expressed itself in accord.[2]

The import of the memorandum—especially as its substance became known—might be to caution the consuls against abuses of their own jurisdiction, and to constitute a sort of gesture of conciliation. It is to be noticed also that the Principalities were already prepared to meet the Powers half-way. A circular of the Moldavian minister of foreign affairs to all the consuls went so far as to acknowledge that the question was at least open to discussion,[3] and Couza was responsible for the constructive suggestion that a new arrangement be drawn up, based on article viii of the Convention.[4] It was foreseen at once that this would raise the embarrassing question of proposing a situation in the Principalities different from that of other provinces in the Ottoman Empire, and that Turkey would probably demand as great a freedom from restriction for the rest of her domains. 'This pretension,' said Walewski, 'which would be scarcely justified in the present state of the Turkish administration, would render difficult the solution of the question which has been proposed to us by Prince Couza.'[5] Thus the question rested for the present; and, obviously, the problem in its fundamentals was still unsolved. But, at least for a while, there were fewer complaints of invasions of consular jurisdiction—which is, perhaps, partly to be explained by the fact that Couza's own status was in course of time settled.

Whatever his treatment of foreign Powers, Couza's attitude towards the Porte showed little disposition to alter the direct relations of the Principalities with their suzerain. Certain initial measures of defence were natural, since one could not be sure that Turkey would not intervene to suppress the double election, and scarcely deserved the Austrian sneer that the war spirit rose in proportion to the conviction that no intervention would be permitted by the Western Powers.[6] Austrian suspicions were, of course, always on the *qui vive*. While the consul at Jassy persuaded himself that Couza was only waiting for his confirmation to proclaim union and even independence,[7] his colleague at Bucharest seemed convinced that the central commission would move to Bucharest and proclaim union, after which Couza would assume

[1] Note verbale, Oct. 10, *ibid.*
[2] Note on Cowley to Russell, no. 46, Oct. 16, F.O. 78/1303.
[3] Annex to Béclard's no. 181, *ibid.*
[4] Place to Walewski, Oct. 14, *Aff. étr., Turquie, Jassy,* vol. 9.
[5] Walewski to Thouvenel, no. 76, *ibid., Turquie,* vol. 342.
[6] Gödel to Buol, no. 21 B, Mar. 8, Staatsarchiv, xxxviii/119.
[7] Gödel to Buol, no. 28, Apr. 3, *ibid.*

the role of dictator.[1] One remembered the vehemence with which
he spoke of defending the country in the event of a Turkish invasion,[2] and credited him with the plan of forming with Russian
aid a federation of the Christian peoples of the Balkans.[3] But such
schemes find no mention in other than Austrian sources, and may
be attributed to the nervousness of a Power which was then
engaged in foreign war, while constantly harassed by the fear of
revolution at home, and unable, in consequence of these distrac-
tions, to play its normal role of bullying the Balkan peoples.
Turkey herself seemed to have felt no such alarm; and, though
occasionally Ali spoke apprehensively of the danger of Rouman
independence, if Couza's position were confirmed, there were no
apparent complaints of the Prince's conduct in the interval.
When the Prince, in contemplating a uniform monetary standard
for the Principalities, desired to assume the right of mintage, he
was advised by France to take the matter up directly with the
Porte,[4] though, for some reason that we do not know, the plan was
never pursued. A more urgent matter, which was directly involved in the anomalous position of the dual hospodariate, was the
question of whether Negri, the newly appointed kapou kiaya at
Constantinople, should represent the 'United Principalities'.
Couza asked Place to put the matter before the French ambassador,[5] and, the point being referred to Paris, he was advised that
this joint representation could hardly be considered a violation of
the Convention, and that, if Negri were presented separately for
each province, the Porte could hardly object to such an arrangement.[6] The question came up after the position of Couza had been
legalized, and logically there could not well be objection to a joint
hospodar having a joint representative. In any event, Couza made
no move to force the issue; and really, apart from the fact that he
was prince at Bucharest and Jassy, and wanted to be invested as
such, Couza gave the Porte no ground for regarding him as other
than a loyal vassal.

No doubt some of the misunderstanding of Couza's motives
was due to an ambitious plan of concentrating the militias of the
two principalities to form an armed camp at Ploïesti, about ten miles
from Bucharest. It is not necessary to believe that he looked upon

---

[1] Eder to Buol, no. 38, Apr. 29, Staatsarchiv, xxxviii/119.
[2] As late as April Couza is reported to have said that he wanted money for
war with Turkey (Eder to Buol, no. 34 B, Apr. 16), but the circumstances of the
occasion do not warrant our taking the remark too seriously.
[3] Gödel to Buol, no. 28, Apr. 3, *ibid.*
[4] Thouvenel to Walewski, no. 63, Sept. 7, *Aff. étr.*, *Turquie*, vol. 341; Walewski to Thouvenel, no. 63, Oct. 13, *ibid.*, vol. 342; Walewski to Béclard, no. 11,
Oct. 11, *ibid.*, *Turquie*, *Bucharest*, vol. 19.
[5] Annex to Thouvenel's no. 72, Oct. 12, *ibid.*, *Turquie*, vol. 342.
[6] Walewski to Thouvenel, no. 68, Oct. 21, *ibid.*

himself as a bulwark for the defence of the Ottoman Empire (as he implied to Churchill);[1] and it is not improbable that he had the notion of being ready to cast his lines in case the Italian war should lead to the collapse of the Habsburg Empire, for we know, as we shall notice later, that he was flirting with agencies outside, which wanted his connivance for the promotion of such designs; but, after all, a new prince—and especially one whose status is in question—has more reason to think of dangers that immediately threaten him than of the chance of playing an ambitious role; and at present his chief concern was with his enemies at home.[2] But Austria naturally thought otherwise. The location of the camp, so near the Transylvanian frontier, coupled with the knowledge that Italian and Hungarian agents were trying to use the Principalities as a field of agitation, led Eder to regard it as a demonstration against Austria,[3] and his colleague at Jassy believed that Couza not only counted on Russian aid for something sinister, but had been promised an auxiliary force.[4] Couza himself declared emphatically that he had no understanding with Russia, and accused that Power of wanting an excuse for intervention, which he (Couza) would not hesitate to oppose with all the forces at his command.[5] It is probable that Austria occasionally cherished the fear that Russia would gobble up the Principalities during the painful interval while her back was turned and her eyes focused on Italy. It is also true that the influence of the Russian consul, who was still Couza's chief friend among the agents, might easily be exaggerated. But it was the first appearance of that long-continued suspicion of Russian leanings with which Couza had to contend throughout his reign.

In any event, the Prince was not diverted from his purpose. No doubt he was mindful of a statement of Napoleon's, reported from Paris by the Prince's agent, Alexandri, as far back as February: 'The Rouman nation, after having taken so gigantic a step forward, ought to hold to it, and constitute its military forces in order to be in readiness to profit by events.'[6] It was in France that Couza

---

[1] Churchill to Malmesbury, no. 28, May 20, F.O. 78/1443.

[2] 'The object of this camp, according to Prince Couza, is to enforce order and control the intrigues of the various parties who always combine against that which for the moment holds authority': Colquhoun to Malmesbury, no. 399, June 1, F.O. 78/1432. Colquhoun seemed to feel there was no mystery about it. Place felt that Couza had thus provided 'for his own defence in case of revolution': to Walewski, May 30, *Actes et docs.*, vol. ix, no. 2728.

[3] Eder to Rechberg, no. 48, June 4, Staatsarchiv, xxxviii/119. Eder was not reassured by hearing that France and Russia had warned Couza to refrain from complications that might threaten the stability of Turkey.

[4] Gödel to Buol, no. 35, May 9, *ibid.*

[5] Churchill to Malmesbury, no. 28; Bulwer to Malmesbury, no. 399, June 1, F.O. 78/1432.

[6] Alexandri to Couza, Feb. 25, *Arhiva*, May–June, 1901, p. 516.

expected to purchase the guns which he required, and a special emissary (Balatchano, his prefect of police) was accordingly sent thither for that purpose.[1] The new hospodar was shrewd enough to realize that a country that possesses a strong right arm is less likely to be flouted when a situation arises involving its vital interests.

Couza's initial problem was to find money to equip his army; for arms were sadly needed, and even the barracks were inadequate to house the troops beyond the summer.[2] Both assemblies were asked to vote a loan of 8,000,000 piastres (about 3,000,000 francs), and both followed the Prince's bidding,[3] though at Bucharest the Right showed a disposition to distrust the handlers of the funds; and it was said that the large majority, obtained for the loan, was a personal triumph for the Prince.[4] But it is one thing to vote a loan, and another thing to cover it. So acute was the financial depression in the Principalities, due to conditions which we have already noticed,[5] and perhaps, in part, due to a long period of haphazard government, that only a small fraction of the amount found subscribers,[6] and Victor Place was sounded as to the prospect of raising a loan in France[7]—for which purpose Bratiano was sent to Paris.[8] It was also to find money for the army that the peasant *corvée* was transformed into a new tax, to be levied on all classes.[9]

Meanwhile, regardless of the problem of financing the camp (a problem never but partially solved), there was the further difficulty of obtaining troops. The combined militia numbered less than 8,000, and Couza was said to have contemplated an army of 20,000[10]—a figure which could be reached only by further mobilization of the reserves. He decided to make up the balance by calling on the frontier guards, but the execution of this plan proved more hazardous than it was worth. These guards by custom were not supposed to leave the proximity of the border, and, as they were made up of peasants of these border towns, they felt it an unwarrantable hardship to be removed so far from their fields; moreover,

[1] Annex to Lallemand's no. 44, June 3, *Aff. étr.*, *Turquie*, vol. 340.
[2] Béclard to Walewski, no. 129, Sept. 25, *ibid.*, *Turquie, Bucharest*, vol. 19.
[3] Bulwer to Malmesbury, no. 200, Mar. 29, F.O. 78/1429; Place to Walewski, May 19, *Actes et docs.*, vol. ix, no. 2725.
[4] Catargi to Couza, Mar. 1, *Arhiva*, Mar.–Apr. 1901, nos. 3 and 4.
[5] Page 224.
[6] Eder to Rechberg, no. 46 B, May 28, Staatsarchiv, XXXVIII/119. Though Bratiano was given authority to negotiate with the Paris money-market, Couza himself was not very sanguine, as uncertainty whether the Powers were going to recognize him made subscription a rather hazardous experiment: Churchill to Malmesbury, no. 27, May 19, and no. 29, May 31, F.O. 78/1443.
[7] Place to Walewski, May 19, *Actes et docs.*, vol. ix, no. 2725. Ten to twelve thousand was the number finally provided for.
[8] The minister of foreign affairs to Walewski, May 31, *Aff. étr.*, *Turquie, Bucharest*, vol. 19.   [9] See page 232.   [10] Place to Walewski, May 19.

since their places had to be filled by other peasants, the order was looked upon as involving a double draft on the village population. In some places the order was defied, and at Focshani a riot lasted for two days, costing the lives of several mutineers. Wise after the mistake had been committed, Couza withdrew the questionable order, but the affair had subjected his government to a good deal of bitter criticism, and the ruler was driven to pretend that Russian intrigues had been responsible for the mutinies.[1] Meanwhile an enactment looking towards conscription required all of Cogalnitchano's ingenuity to make it palatable to the peasants.[2]

Victor Place (who was not yet in the Prince's confidence) came to the conclusion that Couza was conscious of having lost ground at home, and was counting on the camp at Ploïesti, as well as the still-awaited investiture, to enable him to establish a dictatorship.[3] But such a conjecture was based, not so much on any direct evidence of any sort, as on the conviction that parliamentary government in the Principalities had broken down, and that Couza lacked the qualities required to fill the breach. It is undoubtedly true that the Prince had shown little capacity as a constitutional ruler; one may believe, too, that he had not shaken off his old habits of frivolity, and (even allowing for some exaggeration from the pen of an Austrian critic) showed more fondness for Jamaica rum than for affairs of state.[4] Yet it is too much to charge him (as Place does) with lacking the force or intelligence to hold the reins effectively.[5] He had energy enough to try to equip an army— which was, after all, his only solid prop—and he had, at least, intelligence enough to resist the dangerous tendencies of his countrymen, even though, in doing so, he forfeited his only chance of popularity. It is probable that he was to blame in not at once outlining a constructive policy; yet, without recognition from the Powers, he could not afford to challenge vested interests, and he knew that the politicians with whom he had to deal were as inexperienced as he, and most of them unworthy of his confidence. In Wallachia the most stable element was the old *boyarie*, most of whom cordially hated this *parvenu* prince, whose very rule was the proof of their own timidity. Without, indeed, the courage to oppose him openly, they hoped, it was said, to compromise him by forcing him to execute another *fait accompli*.[6] In Moldavia the

---

[1] Place to Walewski, May 21, *Actes et docs.*, vol. ix, no. 2726; Churchill to Malmesbury, no. 27, May 19, and no. 20, May 20, F.O. 78/1443.
[2] Rosetti, *Penetru ce s'au râsculat ţăranii*.
[3] Eder to Buol, no. 34 B, Apr. 16, Staatsarchiv, xxxviii/119.
[4] Gödel-Lannoy wrote that he had lost thereby the esteem of every person who had believed that he saw in his frivolous manner a sort of superior endowment (eine Art höherer Begabung): Gödel to Buol, no. 28.
[5] Place to Walewski, June 9.
[6] Eder to Rechberg, no. 48, Staatsarchiv, xxxviii/119.

movement for union was more sincere, but hardly less embarrassing. Having failed to accomplish their first plan, the extreme nationalists schemed to have union proclaimed by the central commission—a manœuvre which the Prince was bound to frustrate if he could. When the resolution, moved by Cogalnitchano and approved by the premier, John Ghika, was passed by the Moldavian assembly, declaring for a foreign prince,[1] Couza, who was then at Bucharest, hurried to Jassy, and forced the resignation of the ministry.[2] The situation in Wallachia, where conservatives were stronger, and radicals more reckless, was inherently more serious—an attempt was made on the Prince's life in April[3]—but Couza had finally taken the step of placing two battalions of Moldavians in Bucharest, while detachments of the Wallachian militia performed a similar service at Jassy.[4] It was much more the device of a military man than of a constitutional ruler, but the act was not without a measure of political justification. If Couza had any hope of maintaining himself, it could only be by preventing excesses, and thereby earning the benevolence of the Powers.

In the midst of all the manifold uncertainties of his position Couza pinned his faith mainly on France. While there is no evidence to show that any French agent had a part in securing his election at Bucharest, it is not impossible to believe that Bratiano or Golesco had received unofficial encouragement from France, and we know that Poujade, a former consul at Bucharest, had telegraphed congratulations to Bratiano, when the news of February 5 had reached Paris.[5] That Couza himself was quick to make the most of France's sympathy with the national cause, and to obtain, if possible, her aid in the work of rehabilitation, is shown by the sending of his friend, Alexandri, to Paris, as soon as he learned of his election. Writing on February 25, Alexandri had told his chief that he had received a most cordial welcome from Walewski, Thouvenel, and others, all of whom had expressed highest regard for the new hospodar. 'Your Excellency can count strongly on French support on all occasions,' Alexandri had written, 'and, whatever are the difficulties which your double election will encounter . . . the Emperor will warmly defend the *fait accompli.*' After counselling his master against any breach of the Convention, Alexandri had fallen victim to his optimism. 'In a month', he said, 'you should consider yourself prince of the two states on the same footing as the king of Norway and Sweden.

[1] See page 222.
[2] Churchill to Russell, no. 33, Sept. 1, enc., F.O. 78/1444.
[3] Colquhoun to Malmesbury, no. 60, Apr. 13, F.O. 78/1441.
[4] Eder to Buol, no. 32, Apr. 12, and to Rechberg, no. 57 A, July 23, Staatsarchiv, xxxviii/119.
[5] Béclard to Walewski, no. 159, Feb. 24, *Aff. étr., Turquie, Bucharest,* vol. 19.

Organize your government in order to await quietly the decision of the Conferences.'[1] While Walewski was alleged to have declared that the double election was not only legal but a 'most unexpected realization of union', the time was not yet propitious (in the opinion of the French minister) for a *coup d'état*—an indication that perhaps Couza had sounded Napoleon on the feasibility of following in his footsteps. Meanwhile Alexandri received the Emperor's advice to organize the military resources of the country, and the agent had deftly offered to place 50,000 men at Napoleon's disposal.[2] We have already said that Couza looked to France for military experts, loans, and ammunition, and we have alluded to the visit of the prefect of police, Balatchano, to Paris and Turin during the month of June.[3] It was France, too, from whom Couza had sought advice, as we have noticed, on questions touching his relations with the Porte.[4] With Béclard, the French consul at Bucharest, the Prince's relations were cordial, if not intimate, but it was not till the end of the year that Victor Place dropped his tone of carping criticism. The fact that Place had supported another candidate for hospodar of Moldavia,[5] together with the prestige which the Russian consuls seemed momentarily to enjoy, may furnish the explanation;[6] but so ardent a champion of Rouman nationalism could not afford to sulk indefinitely. In the meantime the Prince imagined that he enjoyed a direct avenue to the Tuileries, and was at times almost naïve in his role of the little brother. He rejoiced, as far as a neutral Power could rejoice, at the success of French arms in the war with Austria, and he would have been glad to see his subjects volunteer in the French army, if Napoleon would have permitted it.[7]

Distracted by the constant pressure of his countrymen to achieve complete political union, Couza thought once again that, if France would countenance it, he might be willing to take the plunge. It was not that he believed that such a measure, so initiated, was really practicable, but he had—or, at least, was credited with having—a conscientious feeling that if the national demand for union were truly unanimous, he must not show entire indifference

[1] Walewski transmitted the same advice through Place: *Actes et docs.*, vol. ix, no. 2703.
[2] Alexandri to Couza, Feb. 25, *Arhiva*, May–June, 1901, p. 280.
[3] Page 238. [4] Page 236. [5] Page 190.
[6] It was at Russian instigation, and against Place's advice, that Couza had constituted the central commission (Place to Walewski, Apr. 3, *Actes et docs.*, vol. ix, no. 2716). It might be noted also that Place had been accused of being over-zealous in his support of Gregory Sturdza, and Walewski had warned him against meddling (Walewski to Place, Feb. 19, telg., *ibid.*, no. 2709); and in June he wrote Walewski that ever since Couza's election he had been scrupulous not to mingle in internal affairs or seek confidences (*ibid.*, no. 2736). Naturally, the Prince's treatment of foreigners had served to widen the breach.
[7] Place to Walewski, May 16, *ibid.*, no. 2724.

or hostility to the plan.[1] On May 29, when Balatchano was starting
out for his trip to the West, Couza entrusted him with a personal
letter to Napoleon, in which he presented at some length the sentiments of his people, and allowed himself to imagine the different
means by which their goal might be attained.

'Complete, definitive union', he wrote, 'is more than ever the need
of the two Principalities. This idea has so penetrated the innermost
consciousness of the Roumanian people that it regards it as the first
condition of its existence. It absorbs [their] minds to the point that it
renders them impervious to the best projects of reorganization, which
seem, by comparison, mere incidentals. Each time a proposal has been
made for union, it has received a unanimous vote, while, on the contrary,
every question of purely internal administration has been received with
a coldness that has rendered its execution impracticable. There is,
then, no [cause for] illusion; to wish to reconstruct the social edifice in
the Principalities on the precise plane traced by the Convention of
August 19, but without giving it union for a basis, is to attempt an
impossible task. When, on the part of an entire people, a conviction
has acquired that degree of *énergie*, and it is resolved, *coûte que coûte*,
to obtain what it regards as its sole means of salvation, discussion has
become useless.'

It was a question, rather, of avoiding disaster, '*en régularisant sa
marche vers la réalisation légitime de ses vœux*'. The Prince then
went on to say that there were three alternative ways by which
union might be achieved. The first was by his own decree (his
actual language was much less direct),[2] which would necessitate
his being 'armed with certain powers for some time' (this, of course,
meant a dictatorship); the second was by co-operation between the
Prince on the one hand, and the central commission and assemblies
on the other, but here there was the evident danger of agitation in
the assemblies, and the work of reorganization, which must follow
the proclamation of union, might encounter difficulties that would
not occur if everything were mapped out in advance by a 'single
will'; finally, if neither of these alternatives were tried, the inevitable recourse would be union by the route of disorder. Of the
three hypothetical courses Couza avowed himself in favour of the
first—that is, union through a dictatorship. It was to Napoleon,

[1] Béclard to Walewski, no. 174, June 14, *Aff. étr., Turquie, Bucharest*, vol. 19.
[2] 'Dans la première hypothèse, qui me paraît la meilleure, la mesure se prépare
avec discrétion et s'exécute sans secousse. Il m'est alors possible de diriger une
nation qui m'a déjà donné de si grandes preuves de sa confiance et de la maintenir,
dans tous ses actes, sur le terrain du droit et des traités. Les mauvaises passions,
contenues par le pouvoir, n'ont plus chance de compromettre notre cause et je
puis enfin mettre en application les grands principes, posés par la Convention du
19 août. Je sais, et tout le monde reconnaît aujourd'hui, que la Convention n'est
pas, pour le moment, applicable dans toutes les parties, mais les principes
libéraux qu'elle a établis sont devenus notre patrimoine et ce serait précisément
pour en hâter l'application, dans le pays, qu'il me paraît nécessaire d'être armé
de certains pouvoirs, pendant quelque temps.'

who had shown so striking an interest in him and his people, that Couza presented their case, and it was the Emperor's intervention that he invoked.[1]

There is no apparent evidence that either the Emperor or his minister made any direct reply to this appeal, and we do not have Balatchano's experiences on record, but, about two months after the letter was written, Walewski addressed a letter to Béclard and Place, enclosing the Prince's communication, and requesting that Couza be told that the plans for which he sought support seemed to the Emperor 'dangerous', 'impracticable', and fraught with 'fatal consequences'.[2]

It was not, of course, to be expected that France would assume the responsibility of conniving at a new *fait accompli*, much less a *coup d'état*, but Couza was doubtless right in his diagnosis of the prevailing apathy of the assemblies and the absorption of the public mind in the dream of achieving union. If only the Prince had reaped the fruit of his moderation, and had secured investiture from the Porte, he might have acquired a personal credit that would enable him to use the whip-hand over his countrymen; but, as Lallemand pointed out, months had passed without receiving the expected reward, and the conditions which the Porte had offered had weakened rather than strengthened his authority.[3] Perhaps, moreover, the somewhat misdirected impatience of the Roumans can in a measure be condoned, if it is realized that acute economic depression prevailed in the land, the *boyards* having to borrow at extortionate interest for their daily needs, while in Bucharest every business house was tottering.[4] Much of the trouble was, no doubt, due to the scarcity of facilities for credit, which might have tided the country over such a crisis; as it was, peasants, *boyards*, and business men were involved in a common wave of misery, which naturally found its outlet in political agitation.[5] To Moldavia Nature was no more kind than the Powers; for the crops of Indian corn and hay both failed during this year, owing to the dryness of the season and a plague of locusts. The peasants still toiled with the implements which had been used for farming three hundred years ago, and, consequently, were unable to compete with their more enterprising neighbours in Hungary. 'Commerce', wrote Churchill, 'is at a standstill, and will, I am sorry to say, continue so, so long as the present state of things remains unchanged.' The British consul gives a sorry picture of the state of the administration in Moldavia—the prisons filthy, law-suits left suspended, the

[1] Couza to Napoleon III, May 29, *Aff. étr., Turquie, Bucharest*, vol. 19.
[2] Walewski to Béclard and Place, July 28, *ibid.*
[3] Lallemand to Walewski, no. 44, June 8, *ibid., Turquie*, vol. 340.
[4] Bulwer to Malmesbury, no. 309, June 1, F.O. 78/1452.
[5] Eder to Buol, no. 19 B, Mar. 1, Staatsarchiv, XXXVIII/119. See p. 224.

finances in a muddle, public works uncared-for, public instruction of the poorest sort, and reckless disregard for both the Convention and the Capitulations.[1] Place writes in the same tone—nothing but inertia in both ministry and assembly, and, if Couza had any thought of improving matters, it was only by himself becoming dictator, though Place doubted if he had the science to govern.[2] 'I can assure your excellency', wrote the British consul at Bucharest, 'that leading men of all parties in Wallachia are unanimous in regretting the unfortunate events which have given them Prince Couza, and they seem to consider that he will not be able to hold the position to which he has been elected by an intrigue.'[3] It is doubtful, indeed, if any Rouman could have cleaned the 'Augean stables' in a year, but, when one is prince, one must expect to be the target of all complaints.

But whether or not the Powers would accept him, there were no indications that Couza's position was in any danger at home. That there was widespread discontent was reported on all sides, and there was no apparent effort on Couza's part to allay it,[4] but, as the same British observer remarked, 'A Wallachian never does anything for himself if he sees a remote prospect of any one doing it for him. It is the national character, and they have been so accustomed to have their political problems solved abroad that they are not likely, I think, to carry their opposition at home beyond words.'[5] It was, perhaps, a just reflection on the *boyarie*. The conservatives, who might, at least, have toppled over the ministry, if they had so desired, had decided to let it alone in the fear that the deadly minority, the 'Reds', might once more assume direction.[6] It is seldom one reads of so spineless a group of men as these *boyards*. Except occasionally clamouring for union and a foreign prince, the only way they hoped to get rid of Couza was by waiting for an Austrian victory in the Italian war.[7]

Partly because of the lack of a settled régime, and partly because of the political defects of the nation, the various organs of government, when they functioned at all, wasted time over trifles, or enacted measures that were not permissible under the Convention. In June the Wallachian assembly busied itself with trying to expose the defunct Ghika administration, which, having filled its private pockets, had left an empty treasury; and, when the budget came

[1] Report on the Principality of Moldavia, Sept. 1, with Churchill's no. 33 to Russell, F.O. 78/1444.
[2] Place to Walewski, May 19 and 31, *Actes et docs.*, vol. ix, nos. 2725 and 2728.
[3] Green to Bulwer, no. 7, Aug. 5, F.O. 78/1442.
[4] Place said that Couza believed that certain men, who had been excluded from power, had schemes for his overthrow: Place to Walewski, May 31.
[5] Green to Hammond, Aug. 12, F.O. 78/1442.
[6] Balatchano to Couza, May 16, *Arhiva*, Mar.–Apr. 1901, nos. 3 and 4, p. 115.
[7] Eder to Buol, no. 39, May 3, Staatsarchiv, xxxviii/119.

up on the 18th of the following month, all accounts from the time of Stirbey's administration were overhauled with a view to exposing official corruption. It was, in fact, a common thing for each administration in either principality to impugn its predecessor, but Couza himself seems to have disapproved of such vindictiveness, and no final action was taken.[1] During the Prince's absence in camp, or while he was visiting his other capital, the Iepouriano ministry (which had succeeded that of Ghika at Jassy) undertook to govern without reference to the assembly, and treated the Convention with open contempt.[2] The circumstances of the commutation of the *corvée* have been mentioned; likewise, the plan for the central commission to proclaim the union of the Principalities. Even the Prince himself showed at times a lamentable ignorance of constitutional usages. When the Wallachian ministry proposed a measure, restricting the press, and the assembly rejected it, Couza congratulated the deputies for their action.[3] The fact that the double election had been so far treated with impunity seemed to Eder an encouragement to further illegalities.[4] 'The experiment of letting these states govern themselves', remarked Place, '. . . has not succeeded.'[5] One might suppose that the central commission could have occupied a balancing role between executive and assemblies, and it is true this body lectured Couza over the illegal conduct of his ministers;[6] yet the central commission itself was ready to depart from the Convention, preparing the project of a constitution, the first article of which declared for union and a foreign prince.[7] Eder was not far from wrong when he pointed out that the Convention, being middle ground between union and separation, and tending in neither direction far enough to satisfy any party, held in itself the 'germ of embarrassments'.[8] It was really a question whether the confirmation of the double election would materially better things, for all the chiefs of the *boyarie*, many of whom had been Couza's defeated rivals, would never bury their hatred,[9] and Couza himself would find it hard, if not impossible, to rule under such an instrument as the Powers had devised.

For the deplorable chaos in the Principalities the Protecting Powers were, in part at least, responsible. Apart from the question

[1] Eder to Buol, no. 19 B, Mar. 1, *ibid.*; Colquhoun to Malmesbury, no. 79, June 21, F.O. 78/1442; Bulwer to Russell, no. 72, July 25, F.O. 78/1433.
[2] Churchill to Russell, no. 33, Sept. 1, enc., F.O. 78/1444.
[3] Place to Walewski, June 30, *Actes et docs.*, vol. ix, no. 2739.
[4] Eder to Buol, no. 34 B, Apr. 16, Staatsarchiv, xxxviii/119.
[5] Place to Walewski, June 21, *Actes et docs.*, vol. ix, no. 2736.
[6] Churchill to Russell, no. 34, Sept. 5, enc., F.O. 78/1444.
[7] Green to Bulwer, no. 10, Aug. 26, F.O. 78/1442.
[8] Eder to Bulwer, no. 45, May 21, Staatsarchiv, xxxviii/119.
[9] Bulwer pointed out that they would sooner have a foreign prince, as 'less galling to their pride': Bulwer to Russell, no. 158, Sept. 14, F.O. 78/1435.

of the practicability of the Convention, they had left the Roumans for six months without any certainty of whether their chosen leader would be accepted or unseated. After all, whatever its faults, the present régime was better than anything that had preceded it, and, even if one doubted (as Bulwer did)[1] the wisdom of confirming the double election, it was becoming more and more necessary, as the British ambassador himself urged repeatedly, that the Powers should meet again to take some common action.[2] But the war in Italy had undoubtedly been one cause for the delay, and British statesmen had also their difficulties at home. In June the Derby ministry was overthrown, and Lord John Russell became foreign secretary in the place of Lord Malmesbury. It would possibly have been better if Clarendon had resumed his accustomed post, but Russell had a greater claim on Palmerston, and insisted on the foreign office—a post for which he was not particularly fitted, and for which he could gather experience only with time. Of the Principalities he had, of course, but little knowledge, and he wished that these troublesome charges could be confided to an Austrian prince.[3]

As British policy was certain to be rather hesitant for the present, it was France, the accustomed champion of Rouman nationalism, who must more than ever take the lead in securing for the Principalities the realization of their hopes. Couza, always centring his hopes upon Napoleon, had taken the occasion of a letter of congratulation on the outcome of the war to remind him that union was still the end of all his efforts, though he assured his august patron that no action on his part should contravene the Convention. In the meantime he was busy studying the means of promoting the material welfare of his country, and was anxious that French specialists should be occupied in furthering this work. To this end he begged the Emperor's patronage; 'for a reverse [*une échec*]', he added, 'in the critical circumstances we are in would be for us a disaster'.

This letter of Couza's shows, perhaps better than any of his other acts, the kind of political acumen in which he excelled. The appeal to the imperial benevolence was inspired, certainly in part, by a knowledge of the peculiar psychology of the man with whom he was dealing. Then, the hint that without French aid the Principalities might lapse into anarchy was a deliberate piece of subtlety in which Couza was particularly adept. And finally, was it altogether an accident that he closed the letter by reminding Napoleon that 'Roumania' was a sort of outpost of the Latin race,

---

[1] Bulwer to Russell, no. 158, Sept. 14, F.O. 78/1435.
[2] Bulwer to Russell, no. 72, July 26, F.O. 78/1433.
[3] Russell to Bulwer, Sept. 4, Russell Papers, G. and D, 22/116 Pub. Rec. Off.

intended by its geographical position to be the intermediary between the Orient and the civilization of the West? 'To fulfil this role, we are sensible how necessary is the constant [and] efficacious support of the nation which has always been favourable to us, and which possesses the most affinity to us.'[1]

As a matter of fact, it was France who had already put the most effective pressure on the Porte. Great Britain's part in the negotiation was purely secondary, though Malmesbury had felt that Turkey should subserve her position to the 'state of Europe',[2] and Russell, going further, advised 'immediate, unreserved adoption of the suggestions of the 13th of April'.[3] As for Austria, her support of Turkish views was hardly more than nominal,[4] for defeat had dulled her energies for the moment. It is said that the Turks themselves had come to the conclusion that French success in Italy had made further resistance hopeless.[5] At all events, the month of July had been spent in whittling down the Turkish counter-project until even the demand that the agreement, with its doubtful guarantee, should be an *acte additionnel* to the Convention was finally rejected.[6] Characteristically obstinate in trifles, yet helpless to defend itself without the usual succour from Vienna, the Porte had yielded virtually everything, and Prokesch lamented that France and England would not 'save for her the little satisfaction of form, demanded in the interest of her dignity'.[7]

It had been arranged that the Conference should reopen in Paris, since the Porte's suggestion of Constantinople as the place of meeting had been vetoed by Russia,[8] and there was no logical reason for any other alternative capital. Now that peace was made in Italy and the Porte had yielded to the wishes of the Western Powers, there were no longer any grounds for delaying; and the Conference accordingly met, on September 6, and accomplished its work in a single session. Besides two minor matters—one of them a decision regarding the dedicated monasteries—the protocol registered the confirmation of Couza as 'hospodar of Moldavia and Wallachia', and was signed by all the plenipotentiaries.

The Protocol of September varies but little from that of April 13.

[1] Couza to Napoleon, Aug. 26, *Aff. étr.*, *Turquie, Bucharest*, vol. 19. On Aug. 15 Napoleon's 'name day' had been celebrated as usual: Béclard to Walewski, Aug. 16, *ibid.*
[2] Malmesbury to Cowley, no. 697, June 7, F.O. 27/1283.
[3] Russell to Bulwer, July 15, telg., F.O. 78/1425.
[4] Rechberg to Prokesch, July 20, Staatsarchiv, XII/66.
[5] Prokesch to Buol, no. 45 A–C, June 15, *ibid.*, XII/65.
[6] Walewski to Lallemand, no. 46, July 8, *Aff. étr.*, *Turquie*, vol. 340; Walewski to Lallemand, Aug. 5, *ibid.*, vol. 341; Lallemand to Walewski, no. 53, July 27, *ibid.*; Bulwer to Russell, July 21, telg., F.O. 78/1425.
[7] Prokesch to Buol, no. 53, July 13, Staatsarchiv, XII/65.
[8] Crampton to Malmesbury, May 24, telg., F.O. 65/536. Gortchakoff's preference was Berlin.

In one respect it was even more moderate than its predecessor, for the declaration that 'the double election . . . did not conform to the Convention of August 19' was not repeated.[1] On the other hand, it stated that 'every future investiture and election' must so conform, and, 'in order to maintain the principle of administrative separation, on which the said Convention reposes', two firmans of investiture were to be issued, one for Moldavia, the other for Wallachia.[2] The guarantee on which the Porte had agreed to recognize Couza was conveyed in the following words:

'As the Signatory Powers of the Convention of August 19 have resolved not to suffer any infraction of the clauses of this Convention, the Sublime Porte, in the case of a violation of this act in the Principalities, after having taken steps [*démarches*] and requested the necessary information from the hospodarial administration, shall bring this circumstance to the knowledge of the representatives of the Protecting Powers at Constantinople: and, once the fact of infraction is verified [*constaté*] by them, the suzerain court shall send to the Principalities a commissioner *ad hoc*, charged with requiring that the measure which constituted the infraction should be withdrawn; the commissioner of the Sublime Porte shall be accompanied by delegates of the representatives at Constantinople, with whom he shall proceed in concert and in common accord. If this demand is not granted [*fait droit*], the commissioner of the Sublime Porte and the delegates will signify to the hospodar that, having observed his refusal to obey it, he will be advised of the coercive measures to be employed. In that case, the Sublime Porte will come to an agreement without delay with the representatives of the Protecting Powers on the measures to be taken.' [3]

The only important change from the analogous statement in the former protocol was the right conferred on the Porte of taking the initiative in pointing out a possible infraction of the Convention. Since, however, the Powers must all agree on the *casus interventus* and on the measures to be taken, it is obvious that the guarantee was merely a sop to Turkish *amour-propre*, and none but Turkey was likely to take it seriously. Russell seemed to imagine that, apart from the obligation of paying tribute, the Principalities were virtually made independent, though he solaced himself with the belief that 'Couza cannot last long'.[4] Sir John's insight into this problem was not, however, very profound.

Since agreement had been reached before the Conference had

---

[1] This may have been due to the fact that Malmesbury, who had been a stickler for this declaration, was no longer in office.

[2] Since Walewski had considered two investitures 'entirely unacceptable' (Walewski to Lallemand, no. 38, June 3, *Aff. étr.*, *Turquie*, vol. 340), this was obviously a French concession.

[3] *British and Foreign State Papers*, vol. 49, pp. 457 ff., or Martens, *op. cit.*, vol. xvii, part 2, pp. 82 ff., or *Arch. dip.*, 1866, vol. 2, pp. 166 ff.

[4] Russell to Palmerston, Sept. 6, Russell Papers, G. and D., 22/30, Pub. Rec. Off.

met, Walewski had instructed Thouvenel (who had returned to his old post at Constantinople) to bid the Porte prepare the firmans of investiture,[1] and, when the news of the Protocol had been received, Thouvenel promised to see that they conformed to its provisions.[2] Such, however, were only matters of form, for the settlement had been reached, and the Prince was invested without delay, as we shall notice later.[3] It is a strange commentary on the statesmanship of the Powers that it took them eight months to reach a logical and inevitable denouement.

But, whatever the limitations of an international protectorate, the Principalities had gained one more step on the march to union. The determination of the Moldo-Wallachians to have a single ruler to govern them had triumphed over the doctrinaire Convention by which the Powers had sought to hedge them in; and, to all appearances, nationalism had won a victory on the Danube hardly less significant in principle than its triumph a month earlier on the Po. True, as yet, a personal union was the most that this Balkan people had acquired; and the much-desired corollary of union, namely a foreign prince, was scarcely yet visible on the horizon of their future. But the elevation of Colonel Couza to the joint rule of the Principalities marked, at least, the commencement of a period of transition, if not perhaps a permanent solution of the problem. The Roumanian people were to try—as long as it pleased them—the experiment of union under a native prince.

[1] Walewski to Thouvenel, no. 54, Aug. 26, *Aff. étr.*, *Turquie*, vol. 341.
[2] Thouvenel to Walewski, no. 63, Sept. 7, *ibid.*
[3] In testifying his gratitude to Napoleon, and begging his continued support, Couza remarked: 'The firmans relating to my double election in Moldavia and Wallachia have just been sent. Thus, the last formality, which *retenait encore l'essor des Principautés*, appears accomplished': Couza to Napoleon, Oct. 8, *ibid.*, *Turquie, Bucharest*, vol. 19.

CHAPTER IX

THE EXPERIMENT OF A NATIVE PRINCE

THE recognition of Couza's double election was of twofold significance. First of all, it showed that an international protectorate was too hollow to withstand a vigorous demonstration of nationalist self-assertion, even though that demonstration was unaccompanied by some of the usual features of revolution. The lesson would surely not be lost on the Moldo-Wallachians, or, at any rate, on Couza himself. If the hand of the Powers could be forced once, it could be forced again; and the Principalities were still without effective political union, and a long way from the privilege of choosing a foreign prince. Looking forward to the opportunity of attaining the first of these ends, it was, manifestly, to the advantage of the Prince to uphold the national dignity at all costs, while, at home, he preserved, at least, the semblance of a stable government; for on his conduct especially, now that he was the accredited spokesman for all the Moldo-Wallachians, would depend the readiness of the Powers to be coerced again. In the second place, the recognition of the Powers brought to Couza the realization that he might now consider himself indefinitely the ruler of his country. If there still lingered the desire for a foreign prince, it was his task to combat it, and prevent its developing into a movement fatal to himself. To this end, he might strive to conciliate his people, and seek to acquire that popularity which had so far eluded him; or he might try to amass a personal strength that would enable him to wear the iron glove in the treatment of his enemies. Perhaps he would do both. On the success of this native prince would depend the ultimate destiny of that corollary of union—namely a foreign prince—to which he himself had felt forced to subscribe in the days of his political immaturity. For the moment, anyway, his position was immensely strengthened. The 'illegitimate offspring of the two Principalities', as the British consul called him,[1] had been legitimatized.

Couza was too staunch a patriot, however, to relish the feeling that he owed his status to the Powers. When the firmans of investiture were received, and, according to custom, publicly read in the assemblies, the Prince deliberately refrained from allowing the ceremony to take on the character of an occasion for public rejoicing. In Bucharest the hall was almost empty, only the ministers, aides-de-camp, consuls, and the Turkish representative being invited to attend; and it was noticed that the Prince did not kiss the firman, according to custom. The whole affair lasted little more

[1] Green to Bulwer, no. 13, Sept. 13, F.O. 78/1442.

than a quarter of an hour; and at Jassy not even the consuls were invited to be present. Such simplicity was, it is true, characteristic of the man. It is also probably true, as Béclard suggests, that he looked upon his reign as beginning with his election, and the firmans as matters simply between himself and his suzerain. Yet the absence of the accustomed pomp which had formerly graced such occasions may well have disappointed the Moldo-Wallachians.[1] One may wonder if Couza had not learned during his early days in the West a certain spirit of independence and a contempt for the trappings of power that perhaps unfitted him to make capital out of the foibles of his fellow countrymen. If this humble soldier were to be respected as a prince, he must pander a little to the vanity of a young and essentially oriental nation.

Unfortunately, Couza lacked that political talent—so often the art of the demagogue—of rousing a public sentiment to popularize his leadership. He needed to ferret out new blood both in and outside of politics; he needed, no doubt, to apply a measure of his personal force to bring it to light. In leaving in office moderate liberals, John Ghika in Wallachia and Iepouriano in Moldavia, he is doubtless to be commended, but this, in view of the factious conduct of the Left and Right, was hardly enough to give him a solid enough support. Doubtless he was right in distrusting the political attainments of his people, and doubtless he was wise in engaging certain Frenchmen to improve the public service;[2] but higher standards of probity must generally begin at home, and thus far none of his acts had really reached the core of the problem. The chief immediate need was the nucleus of a middle party in both the provincial assemblies, backed by the Prince's favour and the more intelligent circles of the two capitals, and capable of holding at bay both the *boyards* on the one hand and the extremists on the other. Seemingly Couza had to gain his experience slowly, and perhaps he was too habitual an opportunist to see his pathway clearly. But few rulers, it must be confessed, have had a position so inherently unstable. If it is true that he allowed his ministers to flounder as best they could on the pleas of 'ministerial responsibility',[3] one must also appreciate the fact that he had two governments to look after, and doubtless it seemed to Couza that the one immediate requisite was the assurance of domestic peace. It was to that end that he resorted to disciplining Rosetti and the *Roumanul* for an attack on one of his ministers,[4] and not only nipped

---

[1] Béclard to Walewski, no. 180, Oct. 11, *Aff. étr., Turquie, Bucharest*, vol. 19.

[2] Eder to Rechberg, no. 76 A, Nov. 12, Staatsarchiv, XXXVIII/119. The principal ones were a financial expert, a military expert, a director of the post- and telegraph, and a superintendent of means of communication: Xénopol, *Domnia lui Cuza-Vodă*, vol. i, p. 127.

[3] Eder to Rechberg, no. 72 A, Oct. 22, Staatsarchiv, XXXVIII/119.

[4] Green to Russell, no. 10, Oct. 11 and to Bulwer, no. 17, Oct. 14, F.O. 78/1442.

in the bud the plan of a public demonstration,[1] but promptly
established batteries overlooking the Wallachian capital to guard
against a possible effervescence of revolution.[2] The Prince may
not have been politic but at least he could show his vigour. The
Austrian consul, on the other hand, accuses him of constant vacillation: he had the ashes of the men of '48 who had died in foreign
lands brought to Bucharest for burial, while he still kept some of
the living members of that cult behind bars.[3] But such a view
rather fails to distinguish between an abstract good and a concrete
evil; and the worst that can be said of Couza is that he had not yet
developed a clean-cut domestic policy. Was he awaiting the
inspiration of the central commission? One was tempted to forget
this artificial instrument; sometimes, indeed, the assemblies ignored
it altogether, passing measures which should have been initiated
by the common organ,[4] now preoccupied with matters—as we shall
note—of a very dubious character. Perhaps, after all, the bewildered
Prince chose to stand for the present on the anomalies of the Convention, and meanwhile—to get a momentary respite—he let the
deputies wrangle over the accounts of former hospodars.[5] It was
not wholly Couza's fault if this mongrel régime was far from being
a success; nor was it altogether to his interest to try to make the
best of it.

It was only in his position in Europe that Couza took manifest
interest. He was anxious that his friend, Costin Negri, should be
accepted as kapou kiaya for both principalities, and he obtained
his wish.[6] He was equally anxious that he should be represented
by accredited agents at foreign courts; and, though Great Britain
refused to confer a privilege that might compromise the position
of the Sultan, France had accepted Alexandri in this capacity as
far back as February, and by autumn his position there was given
a permanent character. Though a motion actually passed the
Moldavian assembly for agents to be sent to all the Protecting
Powers, Couza ventured the explanation that Pano, its mover, had
'gone beyond his [Couza's] intentions', and that he had merely
asked for provision for sending them to Paris, London, and Turin.[7]
Apart from France, Sardinia was the only Power willing to be thus
honoured. Efforts were, meanwhile, repeated to procure a loan

[1] Béclard to Walewski, no. 180, Oct. 11, *Aff. étr., Turquie, Bucharest*, vol. 19.
The plan was to present a petition against the minister at a public gathering
and the police eventually broke up the attempt. Béclard, who was disposed to
think well of Couza, said that this act of vigour made a good impression.
[2] Eder to Rechberg, no. 72 A, Oct. 22, Staatsarchiv, xxxviii/119.
[3] Eder to Rechberg, no. 76 A, Nov. 12, *ibid.*
[4] Xénopol, *Domnia lui Cuza-Vodă*, vol. i, p. 120.
[5] Béclard to Walewski, no. 182, Dec. 12, *Aff. étr., Turquie, Bucharest*, vol. 19.
[6] Prokesch to Rechberg, no. 96 B, Dec. 23, Staatsarchiv, xii/65.
[7] Hory to Thouvenel, no. 36, June 30, 1860, *Aff. étr., Turquie, Bucharest*, vol. 20.

from foreign countries, the money to be used for relieving proprietors whose estates were heavily mortgaged and for raising the salaries of public officials,[1] as the Prince had already begun to consider means of improving the personnel of his administration. Had he also begun to ponder the question of persuading the Powers to modify the Convention? He told Eder in October that two separate administrations made his position untenable, as he spent half his time in travelling between Bucharest and Jassy.[2] It was, of course, primarily the duty of the central commission to revise the *Règlement organique*, but much must necessarily depend on the skill of the Prince's diplomacy. He knew that he was expected to go to Constantinople to pay his respects to his suzerain, but, though he talked of going before the end of the year,[3] he seemed to have formed no definite plan. On the whole, one gets the impression that Couza was largely feeling his way. Perhaps his duty was, first of all, to show his fitness as an administrator.

It was on this ground, perhaps, that Couza bestirred himself in November to consider a thorough-going reform of the administration; for little could be accomplished without an efficient public service. The era of political agitation was over, he told Place, and he felt that now one should take up the work of reorganization. Whatever could be done, then, within the clumsy scope of the Convention, he would do. 'The Powers', he said, 'have pronounced irrevocably on our destinies. It is, therefore, upon their decision that we ought to hold to the Convention of 1858. It is this Convention and this alone that we ought to strive to translate into facts.' Deluding himself with the belief that new elections might furnish a new set of men to work in unison with him towards this desirable end, he planned a speedy dissolution of both the central commission and the assemblies.[4] It may have been some inkling of his intention that was soon to cause his plans to be suddenly interrupted.

Couza was no doubt aware that one thing which he must certainly avoid was that of giving the Protecting Powers the impression that the Principalities were a prey to faction, and that he himself could not effectually control them. A better opportunity for proving the point could not have been afforded at this juncture; for in December a crisis took place, which put his governing capacity to the test, and he met it without hesitation. For some time it had been known that the central commission (which had not heretofore bestirred itself to show much interest in public questions) had been planning a constitution which assumed as bases political union and a foreign prince. When it seemed evident

[1] Churchill to Russell, no. 1, Jan. 9, F.O. 78/1516.
[2] Eder to Rechberg, no. 72 A, Oct. 22, 1859, Staatsarchiv, xxxviii/119.
[3] Béclard to Walewski, no. 180, Oct. 11, *Aff. étr., Turquie, Bucharest*, vol. 19.
[4] Place to Walewski, no. 37, Nov. 24, *Aff. étr., Turquie, Jassy*, vol. 9.

that the Powers would recognize Couza, the plan had, for the moment, been relinquished;[1] but later we find its recurrence,[2] and it was evident that at least a majority of that body wished to force the perilous issue.

There was certainly little benefit to be got from such a source. 'The central commission's project', remarked Eder, 'had been put together with the greatest secrecy, and, when finally made public, it looked more like a political manœuvre than a serious constitution'.[3] Providing as it did for organic union and a foreign prince, as well as altering the name of the State to 'The United Principalities of Roumania', it departed so far from the Convention as a basis as to be clearly *extra legem*; and, while the central commission was retained (with somewhat enlarged functions),[4] the clauses providing for a general assembly to complete the work of revision not only convict the authors of political immaturity[5] but lead one to suspect that the central commission was not seriously concerned with the task which the Convention had confided to it. Such, then, with a strange irony, was the scheme which the Prince was requested to place before the assemblies.[6] Churchill remarked keenly that the purpose of the project was simply to place Couza in an impossible position. If he accepted it, he would be an accomplice in an attack upon the Convention, and so compromise himself before the Powers; if he refused, he would be represented as going back on his professed willingness to yield to a foreign prince, and would injure himself with the general public.[7]

Couza met the move with a degree of judgement and energy that did him credit. His retaliation, in short, was the dissolution of the assemblies, and of the central commission as well. His message to the assemblies was judiciously worded, and his statement that the time of political turmoil should now give way to a work of reconstruction made a favourable impression.[8] In a separate message to the central commission he affirmed his perpetual attachment to the principle of union, but he warned them that by too much haste they compromised the cause, and he bade them occupy themselves less with politics, and become more concerned with the improvements which the country urgently required; of

[1] Eder to Rechberg, no. 63, Sept. 3, Staatsarchiv, xxxviii/119.
[2] Green to Bulwer, no. 13, Sept. 13, F.O. 78/1442.
[3] Eder to Rechberg, no. 76 B, Nov. 5, Staatsarchiv, xxxviii/119.
[4] The central commission should judge disputes between administrative or judicial authorities, and should be authorized to receive petitions from individuals.
[5] Severe penalties were to be imposed on ministers who did not call the general assembly within the specified time, and that body might meet wherever it saw fit.
[6] Extracts of the 'Constitution des Principautés Unies de la Roumanie' may be found enclosed with Churchill's no. 46 to Russell, Dec. 16, 1859, F.O. 78/1444.
[7] Churchill to Russell, no. 46, *ibid.*
[8] Place to Walewski, Feb. 2, 1860, *Aff. étr., Turquie, Jassy*, vol. 10, no. 3.

the time for bringing up the question of constitutional revision, he declared himself the best judge.[1] Consul Green called the Prince's message 'a well-merited lesson, which that body will not forget in a hurry'.[2]

The dissolution of the assemblies which had elected Couza to his position might be regarded as something more than a political manœuvre (though that, indeed, was its motive) or as an example of Russian influence[3]—which is extremely doubtful. Obviously, as the great work of these assemblies—the work for which they had been called—had at last been duly consecrated, it belonged to a new set of men to write another page in the history of the Roumanian people. Couza told Gödel-Lannoy that experience had convinced him that his country was not fitted for a constitutional régime, but, for his own part, he would set about industriously the suppression of party strife and the solution of domestic problems.[4] It would not be long before the sincerity of his statement would be put to the test.

During the interval between the sessions of the old legislature and the new, the first anniversary of Couza's election at Bucharest was celebrated, on February 5. Couza issued from Jassy a decree of amnesty to quash the prosecution of those arrested for the demonstration of October, but he did not himself arrive in the city until the night of February 4, and it was only with difficulty that he could be induced to attend the fêtes. Despite the Prince's dislike for celebrations, however, he was greeted with much enthusiasm, and Baron Eder, acting in the name of all the consuls, gave him a toast at the public banquet in the evening.[5]

The election to the new assemblies were held on February 29 and the two succeeding days. There was little change in the personnel, except that the conservatives were perhaps even stronger than before.[6] Couza's speeches in opening the session were well received,[7] but no adherence to principles or expressions of good intentions were any guarantee of legislative harmony. Both ministries were undeniably shaky.[8] In Wallachia Ghika acknowledged that he could not rely on half a dozen votes, and he told Green that there existed a combination of the upper classes whose fixed determination was to overthrow the Prince.[9] Of course, as long

[1] Churchill to Russell, no. 46, Dec. 16, 1859, F.O. 78/1444.
[2] Green to Hammond, Dec. 26, F.O. 78/1442.   [3] *Ibid.*
[4] Gödel to Rechberg, no. 63, Dec. 24, Staatsarchiv, xxxviii/119.
[5] Hory to Thouvenel, no. 5, Feb. 6, 1860, *Aff. étr., Turquie, Bucharest,* vol. 20.
[6] Green to Russell, no. 4, Mar. 5, F.O. 78/1516; Green to Russell, no. 8, Mar. 25, *ibid.*; Churchill to Russell, no. 6, Mar. 9, F.O. 78/1518.
[7] Place to Walewski, no. 5, Mar. 19, *Aff. étr., Turquie, Jassy,* vol. 10; Green to Russell, no. 6, Mar. 13, F.O. 78/1516.
[8] Churchill to Russell, no. 6, Mar. 9, F.O. 78/1518; Green to Russell, no. 8.
[9] Green to Bulwer, no. 16, Apr. 20, 78/1516.

as the *boyards* felt the issue of agrarian reform to be hanging over their heads, they were suspicious of any ministry that they did not themselves control, and, as the Prince's appointments to the central commission were men of lower station, some anxiety was felt lest such a measure might be drafted by that body.[1]   In Moldavia the situation was somewhat improved when the collapse of the ministry gave way to the appointment of Cogalnitchano as premier—a man of superior ability, whose radicalism was far more patient than that of the former exiles from Wallachia; but at Bucharest the agony of the dying ministry was somewhat longer. In May a well-known 'forty-eighter', Nicholas Tell, caused a hub-bub by declaring in the assembly that the government had tried to engage him for a *coup d'état*, and, though the reputation of the accuser was not such as to lend credence to the charge, the ministry was so startled that it sought to escape a vote of censure by trying to incriminate the Prince.[2] It was only a question of time when the storm of opposition from Left and Right would engulf the premier. Couza wished to keep him in power at least during his visit to Constantinople, as he distrusted the extremists too deeply to wish them to handle the session in his absence;[3] but Ghika was person-ally unpopular (Green attributed it to his flippant manners), and, as the price of bread and meat was inexcusably high—due, it was said, to the 'corrupt influence of the authorities'[4]—there was no chance of the government's receiving sympathy from the public. It soon became evident that Ghika was powerless to get his projects even considered by the assembly,[5] and early in June the ministry tendered its resignation. With unfeigned reluctance[6] Couza consti-tuted a ministry from the Left, headed, as before, by Nicholas Golesco.

No doubt, in casting his fortunes to the Left, Couza thought he was taking the lesser of two evils, as he would not be bullied by his old enemies, the *boyards*, as long as he could prevent it. He had to 'choose between traitors and fools', he said, and, of the two, he preferred the latter, but 'do not suppose [he told Green] that many days will pass without their committing some desperate act of folly, which will lead to their dismissal; at all events, I shall not leave them in power during my absence in Constantinople. I shall reappoint the Ghika ministry; and, meanwhile, the lesson to the *boyards* is a good one.'[7] The elevation of the radicals did give their

[1] Green to Bulwer, no. 17, Apr. 22, F.O. 78/1516.
[2] Green to Hammond, May 8, *ibid*.
[3] Hory to Thouvenel, no. 27, May 26, *Aff. étr., Turquie, Bucharest*, vol. 20.
[4] Green to Hammond, May 19, F.O. 78/1516.
[5] Hory to Thouvenel, no. 27.
[6] Hory to Thouvenel, no. 31, June 11, *Aff. étr., Turquie, Bucharest*, vol. 20.
[7] Green to Bulwer, no. 23, June 7, F.O. 78/1516.

rivals a scare, since now the agrarian question seemed more than ever imminent;[1] but Couza was right in his prediction of the new ministry's fortunes. Weakened by inner dissensions,[2] distrusted by the Prince himself, and reckless in their demands for dismissals, not only from the administration but even from the army, they no longer had the least ground for existence—not even public favour. When they sought to coerce the Prince by resigning in a body, Couza accepted their decision with alacrity, July 17,[3] and appointed a ministry of moderate liberals, whose accession, we learn, was 'in general well received by the public'.[4] It may be conjectured that the Prince decided on reflection not to reappoint Ghika, whose ambition might be perilous during his absence. The strongest member of the new ministry[5] was a certain General Floresco (a son-in-law of Prince Bibesco) whom Couza, contrary to his wont, had deliberately won over from the ranks of his enemies. But none of the repeated changes seemed to bring good government.[6] When Tillos, the French consul-general, reproached him for calling mediocrities to office, Couza demanded to know whom he (Tillos) would suggest in their place, and the consul was obliged to seek shelter in the excuse that he had not been in the Principalities long enough to be familiar with personalities.[7] Just now the Prince was probably satisfied with a stopgap, while his mind was centred on his coming trip to Constantinople.

Yet there is little doubt but that Couza was, at best, severely handicapped in his opportunities for choosing the right sort of ministers. The ablest element was the old *boyarie*, but we can hardly blame him for holding such inveterate enemies at bay. Manifestly, he did not consider himself bound to choose his ministers with any reference to the complexion of the chamber, but it is hard to see how Couza could have worked with a conservative cabinet, and it is doubtful if any sort of leadership would have been able to contend against the factionalism and self-interest that characterized the assemblies. It was not merely a nation's lack of political experience. The taint of political corruption, coming down from the old phanariot days, had so permeated the body politic that lamentably few men in public life were sound enough

---

[1] Green to Russell, no. 26, May 11, *ibid.*

[2] Rosetti and the two Bratianos wanted a national guard instituted, but the majority of the ministers were opposed, and Couza intervened to prevent the measure from being considered in the assembly. The minority had also demanded a dissolution of the assembly, but here again Couza had discovered the want of unity in ministerial councils, and there was no moving him.

[3] Hory to Thouvenel, no. 29, July 21, *Aff. étr., Turquie, Bucharest*, vol. 20.

[4] Hory to Thouvenel, no. 41, July 27, *ibid.*

[5] The premier was Kostaki, a Moldavian.

[6] Eder to Rechberg, no. 1, Jan. 3, Staatsarchiv, XXXVIII/123.

[7] Tillos to Thouvenel, no. 12, Dec. 5, *Aff. étr., Turquie, Bucharest*, vol. 21.

in political morals to pursue an honest course, and matters of
public interest were subordinated to the opportunity for private
enrichment or quarrels over the spoils. John Ghika had confessed
to Green that judicial decisions were openly sold, and if laws,
indeed, were needed, it was doubtful if competent men could be
found to carry them out.[1] All initiative in the way of reform should
come, of course, from the Prince himself, and he, to his credit, had
attempted a house-cleaning soon after his accession, but with only
partial success. When he indicted seventeen prefects, they were
acquitted by the courts, and, when he discharged the refractory
judges, he was himself guilty of an evil, that of attacking the
independence of the bench. 'Besides,' as one critic remarked,
'judges and functionaries have champions in the assemblies, and
ministers, who lent themselves to these attempts at discipline, were
themselves threatened. . . . The press points out with vigilance
the peculations that come to its knowledge, but, obeying rather the
spirit of party than a sentiment of public duty, it attacks certain
names without attacking the evil itself.'[2] 'Assuredly the Moldo-
Wallachians are endowed with some estimable qualities, but one
would say that a malevolent fairy has smitten them with barrenness
and condemned them to do nothing for themselves. All their
history testifies to it.'[3]

It is in view of these conditions—the fact of being called upon
to rule a people without parliamentary experience and permeated
with the low political morality of the East—that one must judge
Couza as a statesman not of the same calibre as one might hope to
find in the West, but, after all, more high-minded and more disinterested than the great mass of his countrymen. Harshly as he
was criticized by foreign consuls, who expected him to bring order
immediately out of chaos, he was by none of them accused of using
his office for private gain. He was notoriously simple in his habits
and indifferent to luxury. Whether he had come as yet to cherish
political ambition is hard to say. Military in his antecedents, and
an intense admirer of Napoleon III, he had no doubt an *a priori*
prejudice against parliamentary institutions, and the experience
he had already acquired as a ruler convinced him that constitutional government was not adapted to the level of civilization which
his countrymen had attained. One may criticize him for not making
a greater effort to carry on under the conditions that he encountered,
but at least he had a constructive policy in one direction. Couza
was determined that the Principalities should become a compact
nation with a workable government, disturbed as little as possible

[1] Green to Bulwer, no. 16, Apr. 20, F.O. 78/1516.
[2] Tillos to Thouvenel, no. 7, Oct. 2, *Aff. étr., Turquie, Bucharest*, vol. 21.
[3] Tillos to Thouvenel, no. 12, Dec. 15, *ibid.*

by legislative restrictions. The Convention had cursed him with two ministries, three legislatures, and three capitals. At least, the Convention should be modified or abolished in the interest of domestic harmony. And it was to obtain this boon that he looked upon his coming visit to Constantinople as not without prospective value.

Though the time of going had been put off from month to month, there never had been any real doubt that Couza would pay a ceremonial visit to the Sultan.[1] While such a duty was not actually imposed by the Protocol of September, it will be remembered that the Porte had wished to make it obligatory, and, in view of Turkey's unqualified surrender on the question of investiture, the new hospodar's visit was practically dictated by the need of preserving friendly relations with his suzerain.[2] But, unhappily, for many months, the factious conduct of politicians at home had been enough to make the Prince's absence seem a hazardous experiment. Moreover, Couza was very sensitive to any suggestion that his position of vassalage should be emphasized on such an occasion, and the Porte's intention of compelling him to wear the fez was as futile as it was impolitic.[3] During the spring the relations between suzerain and vassal were conspicuously unfriendly; for Couza felt that Turkey had no right to conclude a telegraphic convention with Russia, involving as it did the construction of lines across Moldavia, without consulting the Moldavian government, and there was also complaint that Turkey had occupied some islands in the Danube, in alleged violation of the Peace of Adrianople, as well as the whole course of the Kilia mouth, thereby interfering with the fishing rights of the Moldavians;[4] and, the question being referred to French opinion, Thouvenel upheld the Principalities on the ground that article lxxxiv of the Convention did not give the Porte the right to conclude such a convention, and that the Peace of Adrianople had fixed the *thalweg* of the Danube as the boundary line.[5] While these matters were pending, the Porte refused to allow its ambassador at Paris to visa Moldavian passports on the plea that only Ottoman passports should be employed by Couza's

---

[1] Couza had so assured the French *gérant*: Hory to Thouvenel, no. 13, Mar. 11, *ibid.*, vol. 20. Cf. Churchill to Bulwer, no. 38, Aug. 7, F.O. 78/1518.
[2] Thouvenel had urged more direct relations with the Porte at the time when Negri was to be sent as kapou kiaya: Thouvenel to Place, annex to his letter of Oct. 12, 1859 to Walewski, *Aff. étr., Turquie*, vol. 342.
[3] Lallemand to Thouvenel, no. 12, Mar. 14, *ibid.*, vol. 343; Thouvenel to Lallemand, no. 22, Mar. 20, 1860, *ibid.* It was pointed out that, if precedents were needed, neither Alexander Ghika nor Michael Sturdza had worn the fez when they were presented to the Sultan.
[4] Lallemand to Thouvenel, no. 16, Apr. 4, *ibid.*; Churchill to Russell, no. 32, July 4, F.O. 78/1518.
[5] Thouvenel to Lallemand, no. 31, Apr. 27, *ibid.*

subjects,[1] and again, as in the case of the convention with Russia, the administrative independence of the Principalities seemed to be challenged. The conduct of the Porte may have been due more to the habit of straining its rights over the Principalities than to vexation because of the delay of Couza's trip; but such controversies were evidence enough that a more cordial intimacy between suzerain and vassal was essential to a better understanding between the two. In May Cogalnitchano declared that Couza would go to Constantinople, even if he had to pay the expenses of the journey from his own purse;[2] but the trip was then put off until July, at which time it was expected that the assemblies would have terminated their session.[3] Couza was also offended because La Valette, the French ambassador at Constantinople, had declined (in response to a sounding) to encourage Couza in the belief that the Convention might be modified.[4] *'Cette cause est aujourd'hui nettement dévoilée'*, said La Valette; '. . . he estimates that a simple trip of courtesy to the end of offering homage to the Sultan would lower him in the eyes of his fellow citizens, and he refuses to make it under these conditions. But he hopes that the justice and benevolence of the Powers, authors of the Convention of August 19, will condescend to recognize and repair the error which they have committed, as he thinks, in maintaining the separation of the assemblies and ministries in the Principalities, while decreeing administrative union of the two provinces.'[5] The French ambassador's sarcasm was undoubtedly right in its diagnosis in so far as it stated the ulterior object of the Prince's prospective visit, and Cogalnitchano had said as much in other words. Moreover, Couza probably saw the strategic advantage of delay. But it is also to be noticed that Russia was not only unfavourable to Couza's hopes but was suspected of being opposed to any trip at all.[6]

The relations of Couza and Russia are always particularly interesting in view of the fact that the representatives of other Powers were ever ready to believe that he had some mysterious understanding with St. Petersburg, and the historian has not yet

---

[1] Place to Thouvenel, no. 1, May 18, *Aff. étr., Turquie, Jassy*, vol. 10.

[2] Churchill to Russell, no. 10, May 25, F.O. 78/1518.

[3] Green to Hammond, June 30, *ibid.*; Eder to Rechberg, no. 32, June 9, Staatsarchiv, XXXVIII/123.

[4] Green to Russell, no. 30, June 27, F.O. 78/1516. Couza told the French *gérant* at Bucharest that he would rather retire than encounter the complications he foresaw if the Powers did not come to his aid, but, without encouragement from Constantinople, he felt that the trip would be too great a risk, since, were he to return without having received any concessions, it would give a handle to his enemies: Hory to Thouvenel, no. 35, June 28, *Aff. étr., Turquie, Bucharest*, vol. 20.

[5] La Valette to Thouvenel, no. 17, July 9, *Aff. étr., Turquie*, vol. 345.

[6] Green to Hammond, June 30, F.O. 78/1516, &c. Couza later made the positive assertion that the Russians were trying to dissuade him from making the trip: Green to Russell, no. 45, Aug. 26, F.O. 78/1517.

the opportunity of delving into the Russian archives. During the year 1860, Russia was especially active in the cause of the oppressed Christians in the Ottoman Empire, and was pushing Great Britain (much against her will) into a movement to investigate the chronic condition of Turkish misrule in the outlying provinces of the Empire.[1] It is beyond the scope of our study to enter the complications that ensued but it was certain that Russia's interest was not confined to Asiatic Turkey; her patronage of Servia and Montenegro was well known; and it was suspected that if she could draw the Principalities into her net, she might bring about a general uprising in the Balkans. It is true that Gortchakoff denied all thought of 'political adventures of any sort', and placed his action emphatically on a disinterested basis,[2] but such assurances were only given in diplomatic channels, and, when it was learned that two army corps were concentrated on the Dniester, the Principalities went through one of their periodical spells of fear of a Russian intervention.[3] Couza, when questioned by Churchill as to his relations with Russia, positively denied any understanding, said that he would resist invasion if it occurred (he would even appeal to the Turks if necessary), and he was not aware that Russia had asked, as was alleged, for the means of provisioning such an army.[4] For some reason, however, Couza disclosed on that occasion much less than he might have done; for a week later he told Green that Russia had asked him to allow an army to pass through the Principalities in plain clothes (their arms being sent through in boxes) and that he had positively refused.[5] While Green had no faith in such assurances,[6] the French agent at Jassy doubted if Russia had ever made such a demand;[7] and it is not altogether certain that Couza was not simply emphasizing his hostility to the Power with whom he was supposed to be in collusion. How much the Principalities were really a prey to Russian intrigues is of course difficult to say. Many of the *boyards* were long suspected of being hirelings of Russia[8]; and Green affirmed his belief that Russia was deliberately organizing agitation in the country in order to prove that the Principalities were unable to govern themselves.[9] But it is hard to resist the feeling that some, at least, of the foreign agents were the victims of hallucinations.[10]

[1] Persigny to Thouvenel, no. 58, May 25, *Aff. étr., Angleterre*, vol. 717.
[2] Napier to Russell, no. 82, Apr. 13, and no. 93, May 5, F.O. 65/552.
[3] Churchill to F.O., May 9, telg., and June 4, telg., F.O. 78/1518.
[4] Churchill to Russell, no. 13, May 30, *ibid.*
[5] Green to Bulwer, no. 23, June 7, F.O. 78/1516.
[6] Green to Bulwer, June 13, *ibid.*
[7] Cartaing to Thouvenel, no. 11, June 4, *Aff. étr., Turquie, Jassy*, vol. 10.   [8] We have noted Couza's denunciation, p. 256.
[9] Green to Russell, no. 20, May 23, F.O. 78/1518.
[10] A French agent even thought that the Russian consul was partly responsible,

The best evidence that Couza was not an instrument of Russia is to be found in his open and persistent disregard for her interests. In May he had freed an editor who had been successfully prosecuted for a libellous attack on two Russian diplomats;[1] and his apparent indifference on the question of the dedicated monasteries,[2] coupled with his firm attitude on the subject of the Bulgars of Bessarabia,[3] constituted even more eloquent proof of his patriotic animus. Such circumstances may perhaps explain why Russia did not care to see Couza strengthen himself by a visit to Constantinople (Couza himself made the statement that the Russian consul had tried to dissuade him);[4] but, unless it is true, as Couza believed, that Russian intrigues were responsible for the Crajova riots in the autumn,[5] it cannot be said that she did Couza much injury. Towards the close of the year, the disgrace of the Moldavian primate, who suffered just deprivation because of his peculations, but was charged with treason on less substantial evidence, marked one more grievance of the Court of St. Petersburg against the new ruler of the Principalities.[6]

It may be conjectured that Couza felt some uneasiness about the project of his trip to Constantinople while his relations with Russia were so fraught with disagreeable incidents; but it is undoubtedly true that his main reason for delaying his visit was the chance it afforded him of bargaining for some changes in the Convention—in particular, the granting of complete legislative and administrative union. In June he prepared and sent to Negri a *mémoire*, explaining his position and ideas, and desiring him to put it before the Porte and the representatives of the Powers. It cannot be said that the omens were very favourable. Although Russell was said to be favourable to some revision of the Convention,[7] it appears that Thouvenel had counselled him not only not to go for such a purpose but even to announce publicly that his only object was to render homage to the Sultan.[8] Doubtless, if Couza still

not only for the recent change of ministry in Moldavia, but for the recent elevation of the radicals in Wallachia: Hory to Thouvenel, no. 33, June 16, *Aff. étr., Turquie, Bucharest*, vol. 20.

[1] Green to Russell, no. 20, May 23, F.O. 78/1516.

[2] Couza refused at this time to execute the protocol of 1859 respecting the dedicated convents: Green to Russell, no. 39, July 27, F.O. 78/1516.

[3] See below, page 265.

[4] Green to Bulwer, no. 23, June 7, F.O. 78/1516. Churchill heard that Russia disapproved of the visit as a 'mark of submission to the Porte': Churchill to Bulwer, no. 62, Nov. 25, F.O. 195/643.

[5] Green to Bulwer, no. 65, Dec. 10, F.O. 78/1517.

[6] Place to Thouvenel, no. 23, Dec. 9, *Aff. étr., Turquie, Jassy*, vol. 10.

[7] Green to Bulwer, no. 23, June 7, F.O. 78/1516.

[8] La Valette to Thouvenel, no. 53, Aug. 27, *Aff. étr., Turquie*, vol. 346. Thouvenel assured Couza, however, that his reception would be honourable and friendly. La Valette denied to Negri that France was influenced by Russia, as Couza had suspected: La Valette to Thouvenel, no. 23, July 17, *ibid.*, vol. 545.

made up his mind to go, it was because it behoved him to accede to the wishes of the Powers, and because the trip might enable him to sense the atmosphere at Constantinople, and, by making a personal impression on the ambassadors, to lay the groundwork for some future action. Finally, it should be realized that, having lately prevented another attempt to make union from within,[1] Couza could not well refrain from trying the alternative method of getting it from without. Before leaving Jassy for Bucharest, during the third week of August, he publicly made announcement of his intention to make the journey.[2]

The only detail which had to be arranged before going was the expense. It was understood that the Porte expected no presents, and, perhaps because it was sensitive on the question of its good faith, it had objected to the plan of asking the assemblies for an appropriation to cover the trip; but Couza told the French agent at Bucharest that the sum he would ask for was designed only to pay for the journey and the sojourn at Constantinople, and that it would not be more than a tenth of what had been customary on such occasions.[3] Despite some prediction to the contrary, a generous sum was voted,[4] and thus Couza had the nominal support of his people in the enterprise. Some persons might feel that perhaps the mission itself was unworthy of that new-born sense of national self-sufficiency; but, once he had been assured that he would be treated with proper dignity, the Prince was not afraid of criticism at home. 'I have by no means met in Prince Couza', declared Place, 'that narrow spirit of pretended nationalism, in which a goodly number of his compatriots pride themselves.'[5] After a few days' delay, owing to an attack of fever[6] and a request from Bulwer to wait until he had returned from the ceremony of inaugurating the Constanza railroad,[7] Couza took his departure, early in October, with a retinue of some sixty persons. In order to placate public sentiment, he had left behind an announcement to the effect that he had decided to go to Constantinople for a short time to 'enforce Roumanian interests'.[8]

We shall leave to another chapter the matter of whether Couza succeeded in fulfilling his purpose. He had asked Negri to make

[1] Pages 253–5. See also p. 240.
[2] Place to Thouvenel, no. 15, Sept. 1, *ibid.*, *Jassy*, vol. 10.
[3] Hory to Thouvenel, no. 35, June 28, *ibid.*, *Bucharest*, vol. 20.
[4] Green to Russell, no. 58, Sept. 20, F.O. 78/1517.
[5] Place to Thouvenel, no. 15.
[6] Green to Hammond, Sept. 29, F.O. 78/1517.
[7] Ludolf to Rechberg, no. 71 C, Oct. 3, Staatsarchiv, XII/69. This was a line to connect Tchernavoda on the Danube with Constanza on the Black Sea. The contract, which the Porte had granted in 1857, as well as interesting discussion of the project, is found in Forester, *The Black Sea and the Danube*—evidently by one personally interested in the enterprise.
[8] Green to Russell, no. 60, Oct. 1, F.O. 78/1517.

the necessary arrangements, and he depended upon the French and British embassies to smooth out the difficulties.[1] But, if there were any difficulties at all, they are not apparent from any diplomatic correspondence on the subject. Nor did the discovery of an attempt upon his life (by a Polish refugee)[2] detract from the impressions of the visit. A Turkish warship had come to Sulina to take the Prince on board, and, when the party reached the palace, which, overlooking the lovely Bosporus, had been prepared for Couza's use, he was solemnly received by several of the Sultan's caïks, while guns were fired, and then, as one of the party has described it, 'two lines of Turkish soldiers, presenting arms, were formed to allow space for the Prince to pass'. The palace (formerly a possession of Reshid Pasha) had been set aside solely for the reception of members of reigning dynasties, and the last one to occupy it had been the Grand Duke Constantine during his visit of the previous year. Since no expense had been spared to give the Prince a royal welcome, a sumptuous luncheon was in readiness for the party when it arrived, and they had scarcely risen from the table when secretaries were announced, bringing greetings from the embassies. On the following day Couza received his formal audience with the Sultan. As he entered the palace, the imperial guard presented arms, and he was then met by the Grand Vizier, who escorted him into the presence of the Sultan.[3] According to Bulwer, 'his reception . . . was of the most flattering description'.[4] He had been presented to his suzerain in European dress, as he had stipulated, and, before the audience was over, he received a handsome present.[5] After a stay of eleven days Couza departed from Constantinople on October 17.[6] It is interesting to notice that the French, British, and Austrian representatives all agree that he had made a most favourable impression. It was certainly a memorable episode in his life. While still a vassal prince, Alexander John had come to assume an importance almost tantamount to that of an independent ruler.

Couza's fortunes on his return were by no means happy. In November a new tax, passed by the Wallachian assembly, roused a discontent which flamed into a small rebellion at Crajova and nearby towns. When the ringleaders were arrested, a mob attacked the prefecture and even some of the garrison, and it was not till after two days of struggle and a number of the inhabitants had been killed that the disturbance was finally quelled.[7] The Wallachian

[1] Green to Russell, no. 45, Aug. 26, F.O. 78/1517.
[2] Ludolf to Rechberg, no. 69 G, Sept. 26, Staatsarchiv, IX/69.
[3] Bolintineano, *op. cit.*, pp. 181–4.
[4] Bulwer to Russell, no. 68, Oct. 16, F.O. 78/1512.
[5] La Valette to Thouvenel, no. 79, Oct. 9, *Aff. étr., Turquie*, vol. 347.
[6] Bulwer to Russell, no. 68.
[7] Churchill to Bulwer, no. 61, Nov. 23, F.O. 195/643.

government was apparently in straits for money, and it is seldom that people take a dispassionate view of financial requisitions. A sudden determination to make the revenue-farmers pay up their arrears[1] and the extension of the new tax to foreigners caused a great deal of hostile criticism, the first, domestic, the second, foreign. It was reported that the Wallachian government owed a large sum to Austria for telegraph service, and since the money was not available the service had to be discontinued.[2] Couza was not responsible for these financial difficulties, and only indirectly for the remedies applied; but for a simultaneous crisis in Bessarabia he took full responsibility. The Bulgar inhabitants of this region, who had been Russian subjects previous to the Treaty of Paris, had been allowed three years in which to decide whether they would stay and transfer their allegiance to Moldavia, it being understood that in that case they must bear the duty of conscription along with the Prince's other subjects, or would emigrate to Russia. No decision was taken, however; for, as the year 1859 passed without any action on the part of the Moldavian government, the Bulgars thought to let well enough alone. The attempt now to enforce conscription (on the ground that the Bulgars had apparently elected to remain subjects of Moldavia) led to a riot and a resultant clash with the military.[3] Couza charged Russia with having financed the demonstration—an accusation, bitterly resented by the Russian consul.[4] Meanwhile the Prince was having the usual difficulties with his political enemies, who now represented his mission to Constantinople as a futile humiliation,[5] and with his friends who wished to push him prematurely into proclaiming union.[6] But all of the above difficulties were of slight importance beside the crisis which shook the Principalities during the month of December —an affair which arose not out of the domestic trials of the Principalities but out of their geographical position and the manner in which Couza and some of his contemporaries viewed it.

The chance of the Principalities being drawn into the maelstrom of the revolution in Italy can well be discerned. If Austria had to fight to retain her position in that peninsula, it is obvious that a Power with so many enemies would be threatened in other quarters. One of her weakest spots, undoubtedly, was Hungary, where not only the Magyars were disaffected, but there existed more than a million and a half Roumans, who had always been imbued more or less with the desire to be united under the same sceptre with

[1] Tillos to Thouvenel, no. 11, Nov. 26, *Aff. étr., Turquie, Bucharest*, vol. 21.
[2] Tillos to Thouvenel, no. 10, Nov. 23, *ibid.*
[3] Churchill to Bulwer, no. 61, Nov. 23, F.O. 195/643.
[4] Tillos to Thouvenel, no. 12, Dec. 5, *Aff. étr., Turquie, Bucharest*, vol. 21.
[5] Green to Hammond, Oct. 27, F.O. 78/1517.
[6] Tillos to Thouvenel, no. 12.

Moldavia and Wallachia. The opportunity did not escape the notice of that consummate opportunist, Cavour, when, in 1859, he was pushing on his preparations for a war with Austria. 'I consider the Hungarian insurrection', he wrote in February, 'as an essential element of the complete and prompt success of our plans.'[1] Already General Klapka, who had played an important part in the Hungarian revolt of 1849, was making some soundings at Turin and Paris, and, though the more sceptical Kossuth felt that France was only too liable to leave them in the lurch, his compatriot was convinced that the Italian statesman was bent upon driving the Austrians out of Italy;[2] and for a struggle of such dimensions Magyar aid seemed indispensable. Then the double election of Couza seemed an omen which neither Cavour nor the Hungarians could neglect. 'It is the triumph of the policy of France and Sardinia in the East',[3] exclaimed Cavour in high glee. 'The double election of Colonel Couza', he wrote to Klapka, who was still languishing in the Emperor's antechamber, 'is a fact of the highest importance; it assures us of the support of the governments of Moldavia and Wallachia. I think you have the means of putting yourself in direct communication with him.' What Cavour meant was that he was sending to Klapka one of his secretaries, whom he expected to dispatch to the Principalities to work for the common cause.[4] Of special importance, however, was the co-operation of France, who was needed to supply the arms and foot the bills. To this end it was important that Napoleon should appreciate the importance of the role which the Principalities could play in the coming war. Thanks partly to the good offices of Cavour's confederate, Prince Napoleon, the Emperor not only saw Klapka but promised that he would send Couza some arms, as soon as he should demand them, and it would then be arranged that part of the weapons should be placed at Klapka's disposal.[5] We do not know who prompted Couza in the matter[6]—it was certainly not his agent, Alexandri[7]—but, at all events, Couza's demand was soon

[1] *Il Carteggio Cavour-Nigra*, vol. ii, no. 244.
[2] Kossuth, *Souvenirs et écrits de mon exil*, pp. 79–80.
[3] *Carteggio*, vol. ii, no. 246.
[4] *Ibid.*, no. 245.   [5] *Ibid.*, no. 262.
[6] Since we learn so positively that Alexandri was not the medium of any confidential communication, and as the official correspondence of the French consuls in the Principalities is completely silent on the matter, it is evident that Couza was reached through a private channel, either Hungarian or Italian. Possibly the emissary whom Cavour mentioned was entrusted with the commission.
[7] 'Signor Alecsandri,' wrote Nigra, the Sardinian minister to Paris, 'from what the Emperor tells me, has not been informed of our plans in Italy and Hungary. He was only told that the Emperor had supplied Prince Couza with the arms that the latter had requested of him': *Carteggio*, no. 321. Obviously, even if Alexandri had been the one to present the demand, it must have been some one else who had given Couza some notion of the part that he was to play—unless, indeed, we are to assume that Alexandri had been simply invited to com-

presented, and Napoleon agreed (so he said himself) to send 10,000[1] rifles to the Principalities.[2] Meanwhile Klapka, with some sort of assurance from the Emperor, embarked, March 3, 1859, for Constantinople.[3]

While Cavour was bending his efforts to getting a Hungarian legion organized to fight under the banner of Victor Emmanuel, and trying to arrange with France for the transportation of the muskets to the Principalities,[4] Klapka reached Jassy, and not only saw Couza, but seems, according to a Hungarian source,[5] to have concluded two conventions with him. According to one of these instruments, Couza promised to allow the Hungarian patriots to establish depots of arms in the Principalities and to ask the French emperor for 30,000 rifles, of which 10,000 should be destined for the Moldo-Wallachian militia and 20,000 for the Hungarian insurgents;[6] in the second it was agreed that in event of Hungary becoming independent, the Roumans of Transylvania should have autonomy if they wished it. A year later, when questioned by Eder, Couza denied that he had made any promises whatever, having even refused to agree that arms for the Hungarian *émigrés* might be deposited on his territories. For the nationalist aspirations of the Magyars he had been willing to express some sympathy, but he had told Klapka that there was no analogy between the case of these desperate fugitives and that of the Principalities, to whom he acknowledged his first duty, and which, he felt, must not be compromised. 'The Principalities', he had told the general, 'had not achieved all they hoped to achieve, and wanted their position to be in no way suspect; for their newly-attained status, if it did not correspond to all just demands, was at least deemed a great improvement over the lamentable past . . . he could not endanger the future of these lands by any hazardous step.' Couza then propounded to Eder all his conclusive argument for acquittal. 'Fundamentally', he said, 'a rift separates us from these Asiatics. We are of quite

---

municate without explanation the Emperor's generosity. We know that Napoleon had urged Couza to strengthen his army (see p. 241). Yet I am inclined to believe that, in order to prevent possible misunderstandings, some word must have been sent to Couza of the conspiracy on foot and the fact that part of the arms was intended for Klapka.

[1] Cavour said later that 100,000 had been promised: *Carteggio*, no. 303.
[2] Hauterive, *The Second Empire and its Downfall*, p. 122.
[3] *Carteggio*, nos. 274, 279, and 281.
[4] *Ibid.*, no. 299. The retirement of Prince Napoleon from the Emperor's cabinet was a source of some disquiet to Cavour, who wondered now if he should deal directly with the Emperor in the arms intrigue.
[5] Kossuth, *op. cit.*, pp. 236–67.
[6] As Klapka had left for the East on Mar. 3 and Napoleon's letter, stating that he had promised arms (*supra*, n. 2) was dated Mar. 18, it is hardly probable that this was the occasion when Couza was invited by the Emperor to ask for arms as a condition of receiving them. Couza told Eder that Klapka spent forty-eight hours in Jassy, but we do not know the exact days.

another race and blood. We sympathize with all nationalist tendencies, but our sympathies do not go so far as to sacrifice our interests to the Hungarians, with whom we have nothing to do, and will have nothing to do.'[1] Such was the apology which Eder elicited—quite in the Prince's characteristic manner. Nevertheless, it is hard to believe that Couza was telling the truth. He may have felt an aloofness from the Hungarians; he may have wondered whether such a conspiracy really promised advantages that would compensate him for the hazards involved; he may, indeed, have refused to put his signature to either of the alleged conventions; but, if our information is correct, Klapka had represented himself as a secret emissary of Napoleon,[2] and Couza could not afford, with his status still unrecognized by the Powers, to disoblige entirely his only friend among the sovereigns. It is not improbable that Couza was willing to allow his country to be a repository of arms and a gathering place for rebels, waiting in the meantime for the reverberations which the war in Italy might produce across the Transylvanian Alps. If it is true, as Eder came to believe, that the camp at Ploïesti was part of the Prince's plans for a descent upon Hungary,[3] then one may gather that Couza wished to be in readiness to strike,[4] if his patron gave the signal.

But the signal did not come. Cavour thought that it was all arranged: Napoleon was to make a present of the arms, and Sardinia was to see that they were conveyed by sea to Galatz;[5] and, if Austrian reports are correct, some arms were actually sent by land to Wallachia, though they could not well be used, since they arrived after the Truce of Villafranca.[6] The truth of the matter seems to be that Napoleon was satisfied with his conquest of Lombardy, and, not wanting a long war, he had no need to tread the slippery path of fomenting insurrection in Hungary. Even before Villafranca his conduct had been suspect; for Klapka complained to Cavour that Walewski had disavowed the whole affair[7]—

---

[1] Eder to Rechberg, no. 33 B, June 13, 1860, Staatsarchiv, xxxviii/123.

[2] Lallemand to Walewski, June 6, 1859, *confidentielle, Aff. étr., Turquie*, vol. 340.

[3] Eder to Rechberg, no. 16 A, Mar. 18, 1860, Staatsarchiv, xxxviii/123. Eder also suspected that Balatchano's mission to Paris and Turin (see p. 241) had some connexion with the plan, and it is not improbable that Couza was checking up on Klapka.

[4] It appears that Russia was much disquieted by the reports of Couza's military activities and of the sending of agents to stir up trouble in Hungary. Gortchakoff feared that such complications might lead to a Turkish occupation, which, in turn, would force Russia to resort to arms, and then Great Britain would probably seize Constantinople: Montebello to Walewski, no. 40, Mar. 19, 1859, *Aff. étr., Russie*, vol. 219.   [5] *Carteggio*, nos. 303 and 304.

[6] Eder to Rechberg, no. 17 A, Apr. 3, 1860, Staatsarchiv, xxxviii/123.

[7] Klapka to Cavour, June 18, 1859, 'L'Italie libérée: lettres et dépêches de Victor-Emmanuel II et du Comte de Cavour au Prince Napoléon', *Revue des deux mondes*, série 7, vol. xv, pp. 858 ff.

a fact of which we have the proof from the minister's own dispatches to Constantinople.[1] Under these circumstances it may well be true that France persuaded Couza not to involve himself in dangerous complications by widening the area of the struggle.[2] But, while it is a well-known fact of history that Sardinia had been betrayed, it cannot be said that Couza had seriously compromised himself. If the French had changed their plans, he had, after all, staked nothing on the enterprise, and it is even doubtful if he had ever signed the pacts with Klapka. It was his two accomplices who had lost by the failure of these intrigues. The only satisfaction which Cavour had got from his flirtations with the Hungarians was the development of the legion (Klapka himself was made commander),[3] which seemed to him (though not to Kossuth) more important than the plan of an uprising in Hungary; but he lamented that France was not backing Couza, as she should, and he remarked that the latter's hand would be freer if he rid himself of 'an absurd and impossible constitution'.[4] At all events, the neutrality of the Principalities was not seriously involved during the war of 1859, and Cavour's schemes for striking Austria in the back had made no headway.

Until after Villafranca Sardinia had, of course, to follow more or less the will of Napoleon III, but, now that France had assumed a position of neutrality in Italy, Sardinia was much freer to continue her manœuvres against Austria, who not only sought to block the Italian schemes in central Italy, but also possessed Venetia, still the object of Italian hopes. So, in 1860, the plots and intrigues in the Principalities were resumed. Strambio, the Sardinian consul at Bucharest, seems to have been the centre of them;[5] he admitted to Eder that his role was a political one, and the Austrian consul remarked to his chief that Sardinia's commercial interests in the Principalities were hardly sufficient to call for the ordinary business of a consul. He almost wondered if Garibaldi and his friends were not preparing for an attack upon Hungary in the event of a European conflagration that might make such a move appear promising.[6] But the plot soon thickened. In June

---

[1] Walewski to Lallemand, no. 39, June 10, 1859, and no. 40, June 14, *Aff. étr., Turquie*, vol. 340.

[2] Eder to Rechberg, no. 10, Feb. 29, 1860, Staatsarchiv, xxxviii/123.

[3] *Carteggio*, no. 456.

[4] *Lettere di Camillo Cavour* (ed. Chiala), vol. vi, no. mdcxlvi.

[5] Eder to Rechberg, no. 31, June 7, 1860, Staatsarchiv, xxxviii/129. Strambio had been one of the 'conspirators' at Paris during Klapka's negotiations with Napoleon of the previous year. He was then chosen as consul to Bucharest, where Sardinia had not previously possessed a consulate: *Carteggio*, vol. ii, no. 275.

[6] One of Klapka's objects may have been to recruit men for the Hungarian legion, as Couza said that he had been engaged in this mission on his previous visit: Eder to Rechberg, no. 42 B, Aug. 3, Staatsarchiv, xxxviii/129. But it is probable that he was also engaged in an effort to incite his countrymen in Hungary.

it seems that Klapka reappeared in Moldavia and crossed the mountains with two compatriots into Hungary.[1] When Eder first heard of the general's visit (this was early in July) he sounded Couza in an endeavour to find out if the Prince had seen him. Couza feigned great surprise, said he could not believe without proof that Klapka had been there, though his ministers might possibly have knowledge of the affair (one may note a line of retreat), and, while he could not set the Principalities on end in virtue of a rumour that was probably unfounded, he said that, if Austria learned of the general's presence, he would see that he was compelled under escort to cross the frontier; 'I have promised you', he assured Eder, 'that I would not tolerate his coming; be convinced that I have kept my word, and will always keep it.'[2] Eder came to believe, in fact, that the whole story of Klapka's visit was a mere invention; and, towards the close of July, Couza, who often disarmed suspicion by his amazing frankness, showed the consul some letters he had received from Cavour, one of which had finished with the words, 'votre cause est en Italie'.[3] But he did nothing to clear up the mystery of the shadowy emissary's visit. Again one might raise the question of how much the Prince was concealing.

Actually, according to information derived from the Russians, a convention had been concluded at Turin between Couza and Victor Emmanuel, Balatchano acting in the name of the Principalities, and Klapka had brought it to Jassy for Couza's ratification. The alleged agreement was to the effect that Couza should cooperate with Sardinia in an attack upon Hungary during the winter, and should receive Bukovina as his reward (though Balatchano had tried in vain to get Transylvania as well); Sardinia, on her side, should provide arms for the equipment of 30,000 men (mostly *émigrés*, of course), and Couza would at the right moment proclaim union, and announce a war for the liberation of his oppressed brethren across the mountains.[4] A later report said that the convention was actually ratified by Couza in July, and that he and Klapka arranged the final details of the scheme. Prokesch, who picked up the story in Constantinople several months later, expressed the belief that Couza changed his mind after his visit to the Sultan's capital, which 'gave his position a legal basis' and (in Prokesch's opinion) convinced him that the favourable attitude of the Porte and the Powers towards his aspirations made it inexpedient for him to try to get union by more hazardous means.[5]

---

[1] Eder to Rechberg, no. 38, July 9, Staatsarchiv, xxxviii/123.
[2] Eder to Rechberg, no. 39, July 10, *ibid*.
[3] Eder to Rechberg, no. 41 B, July 28, *ibid*.
[4] Prokesch to Rechberg, no. 92 B, Dec. 14, *ibid*., xii/69.
[5] Prokesch to Eder, Dec. 19, annex to Prokesch's no. 93 B to Rechberg, *ibid*.

Such a view may be compared with that of Eder, who was not naturally suspicious, and had believed—before the crisis of December—that Couza, however unreliable, was mainly interested now in securing his position, and would therefore oppose any movement that might be calculated to compromise him.[1]

While it is true that the Austrians were soon to learn that the Prince was far from innocent of all mischief, the story of the convention must be looked upon with caution. It seems somehow far from plausible that so acute a statesman as Couza should have expected to obtain union more easily by a conspiracy that was almost certain to produce a European crisis and possibly foreign intervention than by giving the Powers who were his sponsors the proof of his ability to rule the Principalities with wisdom and moderation. Reports of this sort have often a foundation of fact, but it is usually a mistake to take them at face value. It is highly probable, in view of what we know of the impending arms controversy that Couza did give some sort of assurance of co-operating (at least passively) in an attack upon Hungary in return for the right to possess Bukovina, if he could procure it.[2] He would not have been the astute Oriental he was, if he had not taken some delight in fishing in troubled waters; but he was also keen enough to realize that he must keep one foot securely on the land. That is why it is doubtful if he went so far as to ratify the agreement which he may have authorized Balatchano to draw up.[3] Even Eder, when he came to hear of the understanding, did not believe that Couza intended to look upon it as binding.[4] If Couza did outwit Cavour, there is certainly one of his achievements of which he could fitly boast.

[1] Eder to Rechberg, no. 57, Sept. 28, *ibid.*, xxxviii/123.

[2] In Prokesch's words 'es sei in den ersten Tagen des verflossenen Juli in Turin eine Convention zwischen Fürsten Cuza und Sardinien unterzeichnet worden'. Clearly the Convention must have taken place earlier in the year, if Klapka, who was commissioned to get Couza's ratification, was in Moldavia in June. One might reasonably ask if the Convention were not signed during the previous year when we know that Balatchano was sent on a mission to Turin; and Eder himself says (no. 79 B of Dec. 19) that an understanding existed between Couza and Sardinia during the Italian war, and that it was 'probably' negotiated by Balatchano (Eder did not know of the Klapka conventions of that year). But the chief difficulty in the way of believing this is the word 'verflossenen', which, as Prokesch was writing in December 1860, must certainly refer to the previous July. Then too it was in 1860 that Sardinia made her serious effort to carry out her part in the conspiracy. Finally, Kossuth, who ends his recollections in 1859, but describes the intrigues of that year at length, and gives us the Klapka conventions verbatim, makes no mention of the Convention of Turin. There is, of course, the possibility that the Turin Convention was merely a distorted account of the other agreements, but here again we are confronted with the word 'verflossenen'.

[3] In a telegram to Rechberg (Dec. 20) Eder frankly expressed his doubt of the existence of such a convention.

[4] Eder to Rechberg, no. 79 B, Dec. 19, Staatsarchiv, xxxviii/123.

At all events, there is little doubt that Couza was ready enough to let his country become the base for an invasion, and that he was prepared to give Sardinia a large measure of encouragement. Besides the accrediting of a resident agent at the court of Turin, he sent certain of his officers to enrol under Victor Emmanuel to learn the art of war, and an agreement was discussed whereby certain Moldo-Wallachian youths should go to Turin to complete their education.[1] He and some of his officers were also decorated by the King of Sardinia,[2] and the public enthusiasm, evoked on the occasion of Victor Emmanuel's birthday was genuine and outspoken. In November an agent of Sardinia, a certain Cerutti, made an ostensible visit of inspection to the consulates of his government in Turkey, and, of course, included Bucharest in his operations—whether because some doubt was felt of Couza,[3] or (as also believed) in order to get some expected arms shipped into Hungary[4] is a matter for speculation. Meanwhile large sums had been voted by the Wallachian assembly for the purchase of arms and ammunition, and Couza had even thought of asking the Porte for some guns on the plea that the Principalities should be strengthened as a barrier against Russia; while the union of the war ministries of the two provinces,[5] the establishment of conscription[6] (this was what had caused trouble in Bessarabia), and the actual landing of some munitions at Galatz in August[7] were so many symptoms of the Prince's determination to be prepared for any emergency.

It is not to be wondered that Austria began to feel some apprehension. The fact that the Principalities had been the base of a conspiracy the previous year meant that such a danger could recur, and it was well known that the *émigrés* were continually plotting and that the Moldo-Wallachian radicals were in some way in collusion. In October, when the Vienna government had made formal protest against the permission accorded to certain of its subjects to cross the Principalities *en route* to Italy to enter the Hungarian legion, the Moldavian government had refused to withdraw the protection on the basis of the right of sanctuary.[8] After his return from Constantinople Couza told Eder that he was convinced that union could not be got by this means[9]—meaning, of course, diplomacy—though whether he merely wanted to

[1] Place to Thouvenel, no. 12, July 16, *Aff. étr., Turquie, Jassy*, vol. 10.
[2] Churchill to Russell, no. 33, Dec. 6, F.O. 78/1518.
[3] This might be implied by the story of the repeated pressure of the Sardinian agents: Prokesch to Eder, Dec. 19, annex to Prokesch, no. 93 B of Dec. 19, Staatsarchiv, XII/69.
[4] Prokesch to Eder, Dec. 10, annex to Prokesch's no. 91 A of Dec. 12, *ibid.*
[5] *Infra*, p. 301.   [6] Churchill to Russell, no. 33.
[7] Eder to Rechberg, no. 45, Aug. 17, Staatsarchiv, XXXVIII/123.
[8] Annex to Place's no. 24 of Dec. 10, *Aff. étr., Turquie, Jassy*, vol. x.
[9] Eder to Rechberg, no. 67, Nov. 13, Staatsarchiv, XXXVIII/123.

frighten Austria into a more favourable attitude is hard to say. Consul Green believed that without a doubt a revolutionary Hungarian committee existed at Bucharest, adding that Couza's government seemed alarmed at these undercurrents of activity; but he also expressed the opinion that, if it came to be necessary to use coercion, 'the Wallachian army would scamper like a flock of sheep before real fighting men'. 'It is difficult to form a conception', he added, 'of the supineness and incapacity of the government. From the Prince downwards, there is not the slightest reliance to be placed on any assurance.'[1] There is much truth in the latter part of the statement, but, if Couza were really hoping to see a conspiracy succeed, with himself as the innocent but powerless spectator, then one must take a somewhat different view of the supineness of the government. Nevertheless, on the ground of this inertia, whatever the cause, it was doubtless true, as Green said, that it was dangerous to allow arms to be imported into the Principalities.

Whatever may have been the part which Couza was expected to play in the intended revolution in Hungary, all doubt was soon removed of the existence of such a plot. In November Garibaldi is said to have arranged with a certain General Türr, a highly trusted officer in the service of Victor Emmanuel, that arms should be dispatched from Genoa on five Sardinian vessels and landed at the port of Galatz, some hundred miles up the Danube in Moldavia.[2] Whether the Sardinian government was behind, or connived at, his scheme, is not clearly established. Sir James Hudson, the British minister to Turin, did not think so. He learned on later inquiry from the British consul at Genoa that, the arms being dispatched as commercial merchandise, and having paid the customary export duty, the government could not legally refuse to allow their exportation;[3] and he went so far as to infer that Garibaldi was trying to entrap Cavour into an act that would compromise his position.[4] Meanwhile Strambio, fully apprised of their intended dispatch, had left Bucharest for Galatz on the plea that his presence was needed by the Danube commission, which had its head-quarters there;[5] and, shortly afterwards, Cerutti appeared at the same port with a letter of credit on the local bank for 100,000 francs—supposedly (so the British consul thought) for the payment of the freight on the vessels, which were consigned

---

[1] Green to Hammond, Dec. 18, F.O. 78/1517. Bulwer believed that Couza was sincere in his representation of having nothing to do with the *émigrés'* intrigues: Bulwer to Russell, no. 841, Dec. 11, F.O. 78/1514.
[2] Tillos to Thouvenel, no. 14, Dec. 17, *Aff. étr., Turquie, Bucharest*, vol. 21.
[3] Consul at Genoa to Hudson, Jan. 3, 1861, F.O. 45/3.
[4] Hudson to Russell, no. 275 A (*sic*), Dec. 6, 1860, F.O. 67/259. Cavour himself explained to Hudson that Garibaldi had given the arms to 'a friend' to use: Hudson to Russell, no. 477, Dec. 9, *ibid.*   [5] Tillos to Thouvenel, no. 14.

to a certain Gerbolini.[1] Later Cerutti, in company with Negri (who had been absent from his post on a furlough—or perhaps it was to consult Couza on these matters) went to Constantinople,[2] and it was said that they offered the Turks a bribe of 4,000 ducats to close their eyes when the vessels should arrive.[3] 'Not having been paid for fourteen months and yet live', as Bulwer later remarked (of the Turkish customs officials), 'would any Turk have done otherwise?'[4] In any event, the evidence against the Sardinian government was, at least, pretty grave.

The Austrians were naturally the first to get wind of these events. In October they had believed that Türr intended a landing on the coast of Bosnia (we know from Kossuth that Servia was involved in this imbroglio),[5] and a request was made to the Porte to allow Austrian troops to assist in preventing it.[6] Whether or not this was granted, Ali himself telegraphed the military authorities on the Adriatic coast to resist such an attack, and the Turkish *chargé* at Turin was instructed to warn the Sardinian government of the Porte's intention.[7] Meanwhile the Austrian vice-consul at Galatz, Dr. Becke, had much to say on the mysterious activities of a certain one-legged Hungarian of distinguished bearing, who was said to be an agent of Garibaldi's and showed great intimacy with the officers of the Moldavian militia. It was believed that something was on foot—probably a sort of mobilization of the *émigrés*—and Couza was asked about the mysterious stranger, of whom, of course, he denied any knowledge whatsoever.[8] Nothing more was said of Garibaldi's expedition, which had probably been intended as a feint to screen the major operations, but at last the veil began to be thrust aside. On December 1 the report was confirmed by a telegram from Becke that two vessels, the *Unione* and the *Mathilde*, both flying the Sardinian flag, were unloading arms at Galatz under the eyes of the Moldavian authorities. Such, apparently, had been the meaning of the one-legged visitor. Without delay the Austrian consul at Jassy was ordered to lodge a protest with the Moldavian government.[9]

The news of the actual arrival of arms in the Principalities meant that affairs had reached a crisis. Couza was certainly not taken by

[1] Powell to Russell, Dec. 12, F.O. 195/643. British and Austrian reports spell the name with one 'l', the French with two.
[2] Prokesch to Rechberg, no. 95 B, Dec. 26, Staatsarchiv, XII/69.
[3] Tillos to Thouvenel, no. 14.
[4] Bulwer to Russell, Apr. 17, 1861, Russell Papers, G. and D., 22/89, Pub. Rec. Off.
[5] Klapka had paid a visit to Belgrade in 1859, and found that Prince Michael lent a ready ear to his plans: Kossuth, *op. cit.*, pp. 251–63.
[6] Ludolf to Rechberg, no. 72 B, Oct. 5, Staatsarchiv, XII/69.
[7] Prokesch to Rechberg, Nov. 5, telg., *ibid.*
[8] Ludolf to Rechberg, no. 74 G, Oct. 12, and annex from Becke, Oct. 4, *ibid.*
[9] Rechberg to Prokesch, no. 3, Dec. 2, *ibid.*, XII/70.

surprise, for during his visit to Constantinople he had told the French ambassador confidentially that Sardinia was sending arms to Hungary by way of Galatz, and that he himself must shut his eyes to the transaction and pretend that they were articles of commerce.[1] Yet, when Eder questioned him about the matter (this was before the arms had actually arrived), the Prince met his inquiries with well-feigned astonishment. How could arms be sent there without his authorization? Did the report emanate from the Principalities, or from some foreign country? Eder replied that it came from a foreign country. 'Well,' said Couza drily, 'Sardinia must conduct her affairs very prudently, when an Austrian official is informed of the sending of these arms before their actual arrival in the Principalities.' Eder then obtained his promise to sequester the weapons, if they were really there, and to prevent any incursions of *émigrés* from without. Though the Prince's manner was less friendly than usual (attributed by Eder to the unpleasantness over the telegraph),[2] the Austrian consul seemed to believe that he could trust him.[3] The most serious aspect of the whole affair was that large numbers of *émigrés*—many of them members of the Legion—were known to be in the Principalities, while others were congregated on the south bank of the Danube. With Hungary in ferment, a raid already organized, abundant arms at hand, and a government that might or might not be solicitous of its neutrality, it is no wonder that Austria was keenly on the alert.

In the meantime three more Sardinian vessels, presumably with arms on board, were at Sulina (at the mouth of the Danube), and Cerutti had gone to Bucharest with the alleged intention of seeing to the transportation of the arms into Hungary. Austria, therefore, redoubled her precautions. While Ali, it is true, had sent a request to Couza to sequester the munitions landed at Galatz, Prokesch felt that both the Porte itself and its officials on the Danube had been wofully negligent in allowing the *Mathilde* and the *Unione* to reach Galatz. On December 8 he took the matter up with Ali, protesting that the Porte's right to stop the landing of arms within the Ottoman Empire was incontrovertible, and 'the condescension of the Sublime Porte towards Sardinia . . . was in the highest degree regrettable'. Ali admitted his negligence, promised to punish the Turkish officials of whom Prokesch complained, and assented to the internuncio's request to detain the three ships at Sulina and examine their cargoes. With regard to Sardinia's official connexion with the affair, he was willing to protest to the Sardinian

---

[1] La Valette to Thouvenel, no. 81, Oct. 16, *Aff. étr., Turquie*, vol. 347.
[2] See page 265.
[3] Eder to Rechberg, no. 74 A, Dec. 3, Staatsarchiv, XXXVIII/123. He said that he thought it might not be impossible to get the Wallachian government to hold them in custody.

legation at Constantinople and to address a circular to Turkish representatives at the courts of the Great Powers,[1] protesting against the movements in the Ottoman Empire designed to aid revolution, but he declined to inform the Sardinian embassy that he would demand the right to visit all ships arriving at Constantinople under the Sardinian flag; this, he said, would not be granted, and plenty of arms and volunteers could equally well arrive on French and British vessels; besides, the right of visitation could only be imposed when the flags and names of incoming ships were already known—information which both Austria and Turkey might do well to seek through their consuls in Italian ports. Prokesch could not gainsay this reasoning, but he seemed to believe that the Grand Vizier would have taken the matter more seriously but for the indifference of the French and British ambassadors, whose respective governments were, of course, very friendly to the Italians.[2] Trying, however, to make amends, the Porte was soon engaged in a spirited controversy with Durando, the Sardinian minister, the former pointing out that according to a commercial treaty of 1854 between Sardinia and the Porte, arms might not be imported or sold in the Ottoman Empire, whereas the latter contended that the treaty applied only to certain specified weapons, and, anyway, the idea that these ships contained contraband was the 'simple denunciation of a malevolent person or of some over-zealous or badly-informed functionary'. Durando agreed, however, that the ships and their cargoes should be returned to the Mediterranean; and, soon afterwards, the three vessels were sent back to Constantinople under the escort of a Turkish man-of-war.[3]

But all this had no bearing on the disposition of the arms already landed at Galatz. Duly informed of Gödel's action, protesting against the landing of arms, Couza sent him a communication to the effect that he would have no share in any plots against Austria, and that, if weapons were imported, he would confiscate them, though he would not touch them if they remained on board. But such assurances were deemed unworthy of confidence in view of the conduct of the prefect at Galatz in allowing the stores to be landed,[4] and Austria decided that there was nothing to do but to insist on sequestration, and to hold the Moldavian and Wallachian governments strictly responsible for any moving of the arms from the coast. As a matter of fact, Couza was beginning to be aware

---

[1] This was sent Dec. 12, and protested against the clandestine importation of arms and the security afforded by the Sardinian legation: annex to Prokesch's no. 91 A–B, Dec. 12, Staatsarchiv, XII/70.

[2] Neither Bulwer nor La Valette were as well informed as Prokesch on the matter, and it was perhaps for that reason that the initiative was left to him.

[3] Prokesch to Rechberg, no. 91 A–B, Dec. 12 and annexes, Staatsarchiv, XII/69.   [4] Rechberg to Prokesch, Dec. 16, no. 1, *ibid.*, XII/70.

that the game was up, though he did not relish the imputations that he had been privy to the affair, as was generally suspected. Indeed, all things considered, it is probable, in view of his attitude towards the *émigrés*, that Couza would have yielded fairly gracefully if his national pride had not been challenged. When Eder approached him on the question, the Prince reminded him of his assurances to Gödel, and is reported to have said: 'My loyal conduct deserves to be trusted. Instead of trusting me, the affair is made the subject of an unpleasant negotiation. I have assured you that these arms will be shipped away from the Principalities, and confiscated. To examine the ships and send them back, I am not able. But do not forget that I am not an organ of the imperial government, and that I have other Powers' interests to consider; they do not want me to undertake the functions of an Austrian corporal. The statement that a part of the arms has already slipped away is incorrect.' Then he went into the fact of his connivance at the importation of arms during the preceding year, excusing it on the plea that Austria had not recognized his position, which was then only *de facto*; to-day he and the most sensible of his countrymen realized that the dissolution of the Austrian Empire was not a desirable thing. 'Give us union', he added. 'Let us develop naturally. Free us from the fetters which in Paris were put upon our progress, and which make the firm establishment of our position impossible.'[1] It is not impossible that Couza's whole connexion with the arms episode was a subtle move to force Austria to give her consent to union. At any rate, there were evidences that the national spirit was being aroused.[2]

But, whatever aims he had in view, Couza chose to adopt for the present an attitude of injured innocence. 'Without informing themselves of the measures we are going to take,' he wrote to Negri on December 13, 'without even requesting of us the least explanation, foreign agents have addressed to my government notes, or rather protests, imputing to our authorities a concurrence which has no ground whatever, and seeming to attribute to us a connivance, the supposition of which was quite gratuitous.'[3] This letter was doubtless aimed to enlighten the ambassadors; but to the consuls he talked in much the same vein. 'I am accused on all sides', he told Green (who had received a telegram from Bulwer, demanding the sequestration of the arms), but he would do his duty, he said, whatever the consequences, even if it meant that he were killed in the streets of Bucharest; and he then complained

---

[1] Eder to Rechberg, no. 75, Dec. 8, *ibid.*, xxxviii/123.
[2] Green wrote that preparations were made to receive Couza *en route* from Jassy to Galatz, as if he were a royal personage: Green to Hammond, Dec. 22, F.O. 78/1517.
[3] Bulwer to Russell, no. 80, Jan. 29, 1861, enc., F.O. 78/1566.

that he was expected to expel all the refugees who were found without passports,[1] though Austria and Turkey had been quite well able to prevent their coming in the first place.[2] When Tillos went to demand an explanation, he assumed an attitude of confidential candour, declared that he was foreign to the whole affair, and blamed the *légèreté* of the Sardinians, who had expected the same cordial co-operation they had received a year ago, but 'I cannot', he said, 'compromise myself and my country by projects that have not the approval of the Emperor.'[3] One can hardly blame Couza for his enforced submission, though it is equally easy to understand the bitter aspersions which Kossuth, as he wrote his memoirs, was moved to cast upon his sincerity.[4] When gamblers fail, it seldom happens that they look back upon the hazards. Tillos wrote that Strambio had come back to Bucharest to raise obstacles and recall promises, once made, and that the Wallachian government was evidently embarrassed.[5] But naturally Couza's ministers did not know all the expedients to which his resourceful brain would have to resort; and it now remained to be seen whether the Prince would be able to effect a retreat with the honours of war.

Certain it is that Couza, as he said, was getting it 'from all sides'. Even Russia seemed now to be very indignant over the enrolment of Moldo-Wallachian officers under Victor Emmanuel (it was reported that they were to be admitted to his staff)[6] and Thouvenel emphatically supported Russia on the impropriety of the proceeding.[7] Since Prussia was also of the same mind, Couza had cause enough to reflect. He refused all satisfaction to the Prussian consul, resenting his imperious tone, and declared that he would not allow foreign consuls to dictate to him, but he finally promised Green that he would order the recall of the officers, 'as one imputes to it', he added to Eder, 'a significance I did not want to give it.'[8] More serious, of course, was the question of the treatment of the *émigrés*. On December 17[9] Couza promised Eder that all suspicious characters should be deported;[10] but this, of course, was not preventing their incursions. Hence the Vienna government instructed

[1] According to Eder, Couza had given such instructions to Cogalnitchano, then premier of Moldavia: Eder to Rechberg, no. 80, Dec. 20, Staatsarchiv, XXXVIII/123.

[2] Green to Russell, no. 89, Dec. 19, 1860, F.O. 78/1517.

[3] Tillos to Thouvenel, no. 14, Dec. 17, *Aff. étr., Turquie, Bucharest*, vol. 21.

[4] Kossuth, *op. cit.*, p. 250. Kossuth's second volume was to have told this story, but it was never written.

[5] Tillos to Thouvenel, no. 14.

[6] Eder to Rechberg, no. 78 B, Dec. 18, Staatsarchiv, XXXVIII/123.

[7] Thouvenel to La Valette, no. 100, Dec. 6, *Aff. étr., Turquie*, vol. 347.

[8] Eder to Rechberg, nos. 83 c, Dec. 28 and 84 A, Dec. 31, Staatsarchiv, XXXVIII/123.

[9] The date is fixed by a letter of Prokesch's (annex to no. 94 B), which evidently answers a letter of Eder's.

[10] Eder to Rechberg, no. 77 B, Dec. 17, Staatsarchiv, XXXVIII/123.

Prokesch to advise the Porte that the Hungarian legion was supposed to be at different points along the Danube, and to see that it was expelled [1]—a request to which the Porte assented.[2] Whatever may have been the whereabouts of Türr, Klapka, Cerutti, and the other conspirators, they do not come to the surface at this time, notwithstanding the numerous rumours of their spectral activities.[3] Sometimes one wonders if the Austrians were not conjuring up nightmares. When telegraphic communication was cut between Bucharest and Giurgevo (thus delaying messages from Vienna to Constantinople), Prokesch believed that it was the act of conspirators[4]—and perhaps, after all, it was. Meanwhile reports came from Galatz that six more vessels, laden with arms and men, had left Italian ports on their way to the Principalities, and the internuncio had his hands full, arranging that these questionable ships should be detained and inspected at Constantinople.[5] There was small chance now that any more legionaries would come, but one may reasonably doubt if the Turks really took any steps to clear the neighbourhood of the Danube. It was said, in fact, that the *émigrés* at Galatz were multiplying daily, and were in quite sufficient force to seize the sequestered arms.[6] It was once again true that all the threads of policy led back to Couza.

If, in fact, it were deemed unsafe to leave the arms in the Principalities, what should be done with them? Eder told Green that the Moldavian government had exclusive right to confiscate any contraband which had come within its jurisdiction, and that foreign consuls had no ground for claiming the right of supervision.[7] The opinion did honour to the Baron's breadth of view, but the Vienna government very soon took the position that, in view of the unreliability of the Moldavian government, it was imperative that the consuls should exercise this custody.[8] While this question was pending, the Porte decided that the best way of solving the

[1] Rechberg to Prokesch, Dec. 18, telg., *ibid.*, XII/70.

[2] Prokesch to Rechberg, no. 94 B, Dec. 21, *ibid.*, XII/69.

[3] Both Klapka and Türr were said to have been in Constantinople some time in December. It was reported that Türr went from there to Athens, where he was supposed to be engaged in trying to incite the Greeks to invade Thessaly— a rumour which prompted Prokesch to request the Porte to take renewed precautions against a probable effort on the part of Garibaldi to break through Bosnia into Hungary: Prokesch to Rechberg, no. 96 C, Dec. 28, *ibid.* It was later reported that Klapka was on his way to Naples: Prokesch to Rechberg, no. 8 E, Feb. 1, *ibid.*, XII/71.

[4] Prokesch to Rechberg, no. 91 A–B, Dec. 12, *ibid.*, XII/69.

[5] Prokesch to Rechberg, no. 94 B, Dec. 21 and annex and no. 95 D, Dec. 26, *ibid.* Three of the ships flew the Sardinian flag; the other three were British, Greek, and American respectively.

[6] Abstract of reports, with letter of Prokesch to Bulwer, Dec. 22, annex to Prokesch's no. 95 B, *ibid.*

[7] Eder to Rechberg, no. 80, Dec. 20, *ibid.*, XXXVIII/123.

[8] Rechberg to Prokesch, Dec. 23, no. 1, *ibid.*, XII/70.

problem was to get the arms to Constantinople, and hold them there; and both Bulwer and Prokesch supported this proposal.[1] Accordingly, Bulwer immediately instructed Green to that effect, while Prokesch telegraphed Eder that he should give Couza the alternative of consular control or the delivery of the arms to the Porte.[2] As Eder already knew (from Couza's own lips) that the former demand would never be granted,[3] and as most of his colleagues were without definite instructions, he got the consuls (Strambio, of course, excepted) to come to a meeting at the Austrian consulate, and as objection was made to going to the Prince in a body,[4] it was decided, in spite of evident reluctance on the part of Giers and Tillos, that Green should present Bulwer's demand to Couza in the name of all the consuls. The interview which resulted showed that neither the autonomy of the Principalities nor the dignity of its ruler was easily overridden. 'Prince Couza', wrote Green, 'was evidently much astonished at the nature of the communication. He explained that it was impossible; if he gave up the arms to Turkey, he should be stoned in the streets; that his right to retain possession of the arms was incontestible; that such a demand was an infraction of the rights and autonomy of the Principalities.' He would rather abdicate, he concluded, than yield to such a demand. 'The Prince', added Green, 'spoke, as he usually does, with considerable ability.'[5] Green, of course, reported the futility of his mission to the other consuls. According to Eder's version of the British consul's recital, Couza had said that the arms were now his, to do with as he pleased. The point is interesting, for evidently this ingenious prince had come to believe that he might really get something out of this imbroglio after all. If he could keep the arms himself, he would be able to show his people some profit out of the controversy, and strengthen his armaments as well. When Eder saw the Prince on the evening of the same day, it was this point which Couza stressed. He had a perfect right to the arms, and there was no law to restrain him. He could get them either by purchase or confiscation. He would *not* give them up, and, if this were insisted upon, he would bring the matter before the assemblies, who would certainly sustain him. If the Powers finally compelled him to give them up, he would simply show his people that the strong were imposing upon the weak. There was nothing, at present, to be said to this, for the

[1] Bulwer to Russell, Dec. 27, telg., F.O. 78/1574. Rechberg had already telegraphed this demand to Prokesch on Dec. 15.

[2] Prokesch to Eder, Dec. 24, telg., annex to Prokesch's no. 95 B, Staatsarchiv, XII/69.

[3] Eder to Prokesch, Dec. 21, telg., annex to Prokesch's no. 95 B, *ibid.*

[4] Tillos wrote that Eder made this proposal, but that he (Tillos) objected: Tillos to Thouvenel, no. 16, Dec. 27, *Aff. étr., Turquie, Bucharest*, vol. 21.

[5] Green to Bulwer, no. 73, Dec. 25, F.O. 78/1517.

consuls lacked authority for any further step, and it was known that Russia disapproved of the proposal to surrender the arms to Turkey.[1] Green, who alone was fully instructed, repeated his demand a few days later, but without avail. Couza insisted even more vehemently that the question was no concern of Turkey's; the arms had been landed in the Principalities in contravention of law, and he had a perfect right to confiscate them; if legally liable for their cost, he was ready to pay for them. He also let out that Tillos had told him that the consular demand was not really a demand but a recommendation.[2]

We have here, perhaps, the first hint of the usual want of accord among the Powers in dealing with the Eastern Question. While La Valette (who was no friend of Couza's) had approved Tillos's step in joining in the demand that the arms should be sent to Constantinople,[3] and it was understood in Paris that Bulwer would no longer insist on the delivery of the arms to the Porte,[4] Thouvenel subsequently adopted the view (Cowley hints that Napoleon had dictated it) that the arms might best be sent back to Genoa.[5] Such a plan unfortunately clashed with the British conviction that the suzerain's authority should be supported,[6] and still more with the Austrian contention that nothing would do but for the Turks to confiscate the arms.[7] Ali had formally demanded that Couza deliver the arms to his government, and, so far, Couza had not even deigned to return an answer.[8] It was France—very probably Napoleon—who took steps to bring matters to an issue. The essential thing, as La Valette declared, was that the arms should leave the Principalities; to ask Couza more than that would be to appear to sacrifice the autonomy of the Principalities to the Porte.[9] Satisfied now that he could not hope to keep the arms, and only anxious now to extricate himself with dignity, Couza assented to his proposal to ship them away.[10] 'I yield', he told Tillos with an

[1] Eder to Rechberg, no. 83 a, Dec. 28, Staatsarchiv, xxxviii/123. Couza told Tillos the following day that he was willing to give Austria guarantees that he would oppose the *émigrés*, but he wanted to keep the arms: Tillos to Thouvenel no. 16.
[2] Green to Russell, no. 95, Dec. 27, F.O. 78/1517.
[3] Green to Russell, no. 96, Dec. 28, *ibid*.
[4] Thouvenel to La Valette, no. 108, Dec. 28, *Aff. étr., Turquie*, vol. 347.
[5] Cowley to Russell, no. 1699, Dec. 29, F.O. 27/1351.
[6] This feeling is evident enough in Bulwer's letter of Jan. 9 to Russell: no. 25, F.O. 78/1565. Russell telegraphed Bulwer, Dec. 27: 'If sent to Constantinople, they [the arms] can be restored and sent back to Genoa, if the Sublime Porte thinks fit': 78/1502.
[7] Rechberg to Prokesch, Jan. 7, 1861, telg., Staatsarchiv, xii/74.
[8] Bulwer to Russell, no. 25.
[9] Bulwer decided that 'it was pretty evident from the remark . . . "that Prince Couza would never consent" that the French embassy would have taken care that he did not consent': Bulwer to Russell, no. 241, Apr. 3, 1860, F.O. 78/1569.
[10] La Valette to Thouvenel, no. 3, Jan. 8, *Aff. étr., Turquie*, vol. 348.

impetuous flourish, 'to the good counsels of France, and not to the threats of the others.'[1] A probable explanation of Couza's open change of front was that he expected the Powers to see that Turkey would return the arms to Genoa.[2] Actually this problem was still to be threshed out at Constantinople.

The Porte, apart from sustaining its dignity, had really no interest in the question of what should be done with the arms, so long as they were safely out of Ottoman territory; but Austria was vigorous in her opposition to sending them back to Genoa, for, once the arms were back in Italian hands, they would more than likely be used against her again. Prokesch besought all his colleagues not to consider such a plan, but he found his efforts to no purpose. La Valette pointed out wisely that it would not do to weaken Couza's position by supporting the unpopular demand to ship the arms to Turkey, and both he and the Russian and Prussian ministers held that the autonomy of the Principalities protected them against such a measure.[3] Bulwer himself, though more inclined to side with Prokesch, finally admitted that to request Couza to allow the Porte to confiscate the arms would be only adding to the Prince's difficulties; and, as his attitude tipped the balance in favour of compromise, all but Prokesch[4] seemed to agree that Couza should be asked to send away the arms, on the understanding that the Turks should let the vessels which conveyed them pass through to the Mediterranean.[5] Pressed by Bulwer to take this step, and feeling particularly grieved against the British,[6] Couza reluctantly prepared to comply[7] (he was even reported to have suggested that the weapons should be placed on English ships), but, on learning later that Prokesch was still insisting that the Porte should confiscate the arms, and that some or all of the ambassadors were sustaining his position, he stipulated that they might be delivered to the Turks if they would come and get them, but on condition that they were

[1] Tillos to Thouvenel, no. 18, Jan. 1, *Aff. étr.*, *Turquie*, *Bucharest*, vol. 21. According to Tillos's account, Couza tried to make him believe that he thought that France had concurred in the sending of the arms to the Principalities. When Tillos asked him if he still believed so, Couza exclaimed, 'Then you advise me to export the arms?' On Tillos's assenting, Couza made his theatrical surrender.

[2] We unfortunately lack the letter which La Valette must have written to Tillos or Couza, advising that the arms should be shipped out on the understanding that they should be returned to Genoa. Besides one's natural inference, Prokesch heard that such an overture had been made to Couza: Prokesch to Rechberg, no. 1 A–B, Jan. 2, Staatsarchiv, XII/71.

[3] *Ibid.* La Valette wrote that Gortchakoff had given orders to Lobanoff to support Bulwer and Prokesch, but presumably the instruction was delayed: La Valette to Thouvenel, no. 3, Jan. 8, *Aff. étr.*, *Turquie*, vol. 348.

[4] Rechberg decided, however, to leave the initiative to Great Britain: Rechberg to Eder, Jan. 8, Staatsarchiv, XXXVIII/126.

[5] Bulwer to Russell, no. 25, Jan. 9, F.O. 78/1565; Prokesch to Rechberg, no. 4 A–D, Jan. 11, Staatsarchiv, XII/71.

[6] Churchill to Russell, no. 1, Jan. 9, F.O. 78/1584.

[7] Churchill to Russell, Jan. 7, telg., *ibid.*

conveyed in the name of the Principalities.[1] It is probable that Couza assumed too readily that the French proposal had been adopted, and, when one finds that Bulwer had wanted to keep hidden the question of confiscation 'until the arms were fairly off',[2] one has cause to feel that trickery is not confined to orientals. As the Prince was much too shrewd to be caught in such a trap, it is scarcely to be wondered that he put out a new screen for his country's dignity. Bulwer naturally considered his proposal 'insulting to the sovereign authority',[3] though Prokesch seriously thought that the Porte should take Couza at his word, sending armed authority to Galatz to seize the arms, and see to their embarkation. But Austria got really no satisfaction beyond the sequestration of the ships which had been brought to Constantinople from Sulina.[4] If the arms were, after all, sent back to the Mediterranean, she 'would have won little or nothing of the essential thing'.[5]

The apprehensions of Austria were now reasonably increased by the intervention of climate in these proceedings. Navigation was suddenly closed on the Danube by the freezing of the river, and the Austrians were fain to believe that Couza had been playing a waiting game all along, knowing that the arms would have to be left in his hands for several months.[6] There was really nothing to do but to trust to Couza's good faith. The Prince had finally consented that as soon as the ice had thawed, he would send the arms to Sulina, provided it was explicitly agreed that they should be sent on to Genoa;[7] and Bulwer took occasion to remind him of his promise—a manœuvre that angered the Prince but drew from him the reply that he would stand by his word.[8] Austria saw by this time that there was little hope of preventing the return of the arms, though she thought that if the vessels which conveyed them were accompanied by war-ships, it might at least be possible to

[1] Bulwer to Russell, no. 64, Jan. 22, F.O. 78/1566.
[2] Bulwer to Russell, no. 25. He also said as much to Prokesch: Prokesch to Rechberg, no. 4 A–D.
[3] Bulwer to Churchill, Jan. 25, enclosed with Bulwer's no. 80, Jan. 29, F.O. 78/1566.
[4] Prokesch to Rechberg, no. 4 A–D.
[5] Rechberg to Prokesch, Jan. 15, Staatsarchiv, XII/74.
[6] Rechberg to Prokesch, Feb. 10, ibid.
[7] Prokesch to Rechberg, no. 9 B, Feb. 18, ibid., XII/71. Prokesch and Bulwer had only asked (so Prokesch wrote) that the arms should be delivered to Sulina. But, obviously, Couza could not see that this was any less an unconditional surrender to the Turks, who would possess themselves of the weapons at Sulina, and presumably do with them as they chose. The most that he would concede was that, if the ice still prevented navigation, he would somehow get the arms to Sulina but only on condition, as we have noticed, that they were shipped off in the name of the Principalities, whose neutrality had been violated: Place to Thouvenel, no. 27, Jan. 8, *Aff. étr., Turquie, Jassy*, vol. x. As the suzerain Power and its friends were not likely to accede to this, they had no recourse but to guarantee that the arms would be sent back to Genoa—the course which France had recommended. [8] Bulwer to Russell, no. 98, Feb. 6, F.O. 78/1566.

keep them from being employed on the Adriatic.[1] As the apparition of Klapka was again stalking abroad,[2] it was not at all impossible that a new plot was afoot. Towards the close of February,
therefore, it seemed imperative that definite measures should be
taken for the exportation of the arms.

It was, of course, Austria who felt the most immediate concern
over the matter, and took the lead in trying to devise a settlement.
First, Prokesch plied Ali to agree to provide an armed escort for
the ships (this had been done in the case of those detained at
Sulina); but, apparently because of financial straits, Ali was unwilling to comply with the demand. Then word came from Eder
that Couza, adopting a proposal of La Valette,[3] intended to employ
the ships, already at Galatz, to perform this service, and Prokesch
was outraged at the 'scandal' (as he called it) of having the return
of the arms confided to Gerbolini.[4] As a matter of fact—though
Prokesch did not know it yet—the Italian exporter had already
made arrangements to send the vessels back with quite a different
cargo;[5] but, for the moment, the internuncio was chiefly worried
over the prospect of the arms being let loose upon the world. He
therefore asked Bulwer if it would not be possible for an English
ship to undertake the commission.[6]

Sir Henry was not only willing to consider the proposal, but
became so enamoured of the idea that he gave no credit whatever
to Prokesch in his dispatches on the subject. Having procured
Russell's consent by telegraph[7] (besides assuring himself that
Couza was still favourable to this expedient), he chartered a
British man-of-war, the *Banshee*, to undertake the re-embarkation
of the arms. He then, according to his own story, put the matter
before his colleagues at Constantinople. None of the ambassadors refused assent except La Valette, who, besides some petty
objections, declared that he was without instructions to cover the
situation.[8] Bulwer was much annoyed. 'The French embassy',
he declared to Russell, 'has certainly manifested a conduct with
regard to the whole of this affair which is somewhat equivocal';
and he went so far as to suggest that the studied indifference
of the Italian minister, Durando (who was apparently bitter over
the failure of his country's plans), was the result of La Valette's
ill humour.[9] As a matter of fact, the ambassador was acting

[1] Rechberg to Prokesch, Feb. 10, no. 1, and Feb. 17, Staatsarchiv, XII/74.
[2] See above, page 279, note 3.
[3] La Valette to Thouvenel, no. 3, Jan. 8, *Aff. étr., Turquie*, vol. 348.
[4] Prokesch to Rechberg, no. 13 C, Feb. 22, Staatsarchiv, XII/71.
[5] Bulwer to Russell, no. 248, Apr. 3, F.O. 78/1569.
[6] Prokesch to Rechberg, no. 13 C.
[7] F.O. to Bulwer, Feb. 20, telg., F.O. 78/1569.
[8] Bulwer to Russell, no. 152, Feb. 27, F.O. 78/1567, and no. 248.
[9] Bulwer to Russell, no. 241, Apr. 3, F.O. 78/1569.

chiefly on a point of dignity. According to the account which he wrote to Thouvenel, he had supposed that the whole question was slumbering when a British vessel steamed up the Bosporus, and he was expected to give an immediate approval of Bulwer's impatient manœuvre;[1] he felt that France ought to have been consulted in the first place, and a French ship associated in the enterprise (Couza was supposed also to hold this view); and finally he accepted Durando's statement that Gerbolini had been engaged by Couza to ship the arms.[2] Since Bulwer himself could get no definite assurances from Durando, the British ambassador decided to proceed with the matter, regardless of his French and Sardinian colleagues;[3] and hence the *Banshee*, with the aid of a British merchant vessel, brought the arms to Constantinople.[4]

Only one point had now to be settled, but it was not an immaterial one, and that was: who should pay the freightage? The exporter of the arms, in agreeing to receive them back, refused to bear the charge, and, of course, there was no use to apply to the Sardinian government, which had explicitly denied all complicity in the affair. If responsibility attached to the Power that received the contraband, then the honours might be divided between Couza and the Porte, and whichever claimed to be responsible for the neutrality of the Principalities might be considered the more accountable. But suzerainty and autonomy are much more apt to be symbols of rights than of duties, and Prokesch and Bulwer agreed that there was small chance of exacting payment from either party.[5] Bulwer, it is true, made an effort to get Couza to promise payment, threatening otherwise to hand the arms over to the Porte, but the proposal only met with an indignant refusal.[6] Morally speaking, it was perhaps Austria who ought to have paid the freightage, since she was unquestionably the one who had most at stake; but the Vienna government likewise flatly refused to assume the burden, and felt that it was the Porte who ought to bear the charge.[7] In any event, the cost of conveyance to Constantinople was not in question[8] (that was the affair of the British government), and a happy solution was worked out by Bulwer, whereby the Porte held

[1] This hardly tallies with Bulwer's statement that he had asked the several ambassadors if they 'would like to assist in any way in the operation', as he 'had no wish to take any exclusive part in the affair': Bulwer to Russell, no. 152. It is probable that the French ambassador was so indignant at seeing the initiative snatched from him that he exaggerated his wrongs.

[2] La Valette to Thouvenel, no. 27 *bis*, Feb. 27, *Aff. étr.*, *Turquie*, vol. 348.

[3] Bulwer to Russell, no. 239, Apr. 2, F.O. 78/1568.

[4] Bulwer to Russell, Apr. 22, telg., F.O. 78/1570.

[5] Prokesch to Rechberg, no. 13 C.   [6] Bulwer to Russell, Apr. 22, telg.

[7] Rechberg to Prokesch, Mar. 3, no. 3, Staatsarchiv, XII/74.

[8] It was understood by the British merchantman, *Psyche*, that the freight would be paid by the one to whom the cargo was delivered, but, presumably, the British government had to stand for this.

the arms in deposit to be ultimately delivered to any shipper who should prove his right to their possession and would pledge himself not to land them anywhere in the Ottoman Empire.[1] This arrangement could not reasonably be unacceptable to any Power, even Austria. What became of the arms is one of History's little jokes. In June 1862 the Italian chargé d'affaires at Constantinople made the statement that Gerbolini was trying to get his government to bring a suit for damages against Couza, on the ground that after sequestering the arms, he had failed to restore them to their owners; and it was then strongly suspected that the Turks could tell, if they pleased, how the arms had been disposed of.[2]

With the removal of the weapons (calculated, Bulwer heard, to equip a force of 15,000 to 20,000 men),[3] the conspiracy against Austria fell to the ground. It is not improbably true that ninety-five cases of arms found their way into the interior before sequestration was ordered,[4] and Green believed that, together with those sent the previous year,[5] there must be 40,000 muskets in the Principalities not destined for the use of the local militia.[6] But this was hardly material enough for starting a revolution, and there was not much chance now for the *émigrés* to concentrate with any hope of success. Before the end of December Churchill had telegraphed Russell that, while the right of sanctuary had been proclaimed, as a protest against demands for the delivery of the fugitives to Austria, measures had been taken to send all of them out of the country, and most stringent orders had been issued not to allow any more to come in.[7] When Couza had found it necessary to recede in the matter of the arms, it was not difficult for him to give satisfaction on the other question.

On the whole, it may be said that Couza came out of this unpleasant imbroglio pretty well. He naturally incurred the distrust of the consuls (except, curiously enough, Eder), because it was through them that the will of the Powers had been communicated, and for a time he had shown anything but a meek and submissive attitude. But Bulwer had on the whole preserved a friendly attitude, and we have shown that some of the ambassadors had sided

[1] Bulwer to Russell, no. 316, May 1, F.O. 78/1570.
[2] Moustier to Thouvenel, no. 83, June 3, 1862, *Aff. étr.*, *Turquie*, vol. 354. Still, as late as October, 1862, the Porte was apparently disposed to comply with a request of Italy to surrender to her the arms (Erskine to Russell, no. 25, Oct. 23, 1862, F.O. 78/1658); so it may be that they were returned to Genoa in the end.
[3] Bulwer to Russell, no. 227, Mar. 30, 1861, F.O. 78/1568.
[4] Prokesch to Rechberg, no. 96 c, Dec. 28, 1860, Staatsarchiv, XII/71.
[5] See p. 268.
[6] Green to Russell, no. 95, Dec. 27, F.O. 78/1517.
[7] Churchill to Russell, Dec. 28, telg., and no. 42, Dec. 29, F.O. 78/1518; Eder to Rechberg, no. 1 A, Jan. 3, 1861, Staatsarchiv, XXXVIII/126. Cf. Cogalnitchano's speech to the Moldavian assembly, Dec. 29, 1860: *Arch. dip.*, 1861, vol. i, pp. 253 ff.

with him on the question of handing over the arms to Turkey. Only in the case of La Valette did Couza feel a measure of chagrin when he heard of his ally's ill-humour in the affair of the *Banshee*; and, knowing full well the importance of retaining French sympathies, he wrote the ambassador a personal letter of explanation and apology.[1] As to the larger issues at stake, Couza's impatience under dictation and his successful refusal to surrender the arms to his suzerain were a vindication of his position and of the autonomous rights of the Principalities, as he had interpreted them. It is unlikely that he cared very much whether the conspiracy itself succeeded or not; the failure was not his failure; and he had for several months made the Principalities play a critical role in European affairs. Probably his only disappointment was his inability to secure the arms for the benefit of his own army; he had laid great stress at first upon his right to confiscate them, and preparations had even been made to distribute them where needed.[2] It would almost have seemed too good to be true, if the Principalities had been able to retain a prize, which an unexpected fortune had, for the moment, placed within their reach; and Couza himself must have been keen enough to see that his own conduct had made such an alternative too dangerous to permit. At all events, the neutrality of the Principalities had apparently weathered the crisis; and the bitter resentment of Durando[3] and Strambio[4] not only pointed to their government's guilt but showed how keen was its disappointment. If Couza had maintained his dignity against Austria and Turkey, he had also refused to be a martyred instrument of Cavour.

It was in foreign affairs that Couza had shown his force of character. Whatever may be said of his indifference to consular rights, he had, at least, lost nothing by such exhibitions of national dignity, and towards Russia we have noticed that his attitude was consistently defiant. He was shrewd enough to know that, in the long run, he could not wisely disoblige France and Great Britain, and it is probable that it was France's gentle pressure, more than anything else, that persuaded him to compromise on the arms question. In his domestic policy there is more ground for cavil,

---

[1] Couza to La Valette, Mar. 21, 1861, annex to La Valette's of Apr. 10 to Thouvenel, *Aff. étr.*, *Turquie*, vol. 349.

[2] Eder to Rechberg, no. 1 A, Jan. 3, Staatsarchiv, xxxviii/126.

[3] Bulwer to Russell, no. 241, Apr. 3, F.O. 78/1569.

[4] When Tillos had asked Strambio what his government had expected of Couza, the Sardinian consul had answered that he had been 'only desired to shut his eyes and let arms be shipped in as merchandise without any one in any country having knowledge of it, and he should put no obstacle in the way of the assembling of the Hungarians, who, armed in Moldavia, might have suddenly broken through the Oitos Pass': Eder to Rechberg, no. 8 A, Jan. 27, Staatsarchiv, xxxviii/126.

since internally the Principalities, apart from certain military measures, had made but little progress. Yet one must be fair to the driver of two such ill-yoked steeds. At least it can be said that he had steered a middle course between the extremist parties; and, in subserving every question to that of obtaining union, he was seeking the essential thing towards the attainment of domestic harmony, as far as it could be insured by a more stable form of government. So far, the experiment of a native prince had not been altogether vain.

CHAPTER X

THE EVE OF UNION

THE arms controversy was only an interlude in the long struggle for union, but it showed in a sense that the United Principalities of Moldavia and Wallachia were subject to the 'growing pains' which frequently afflict a young nation on the way to the full development of its logical destiny. Viewed from that angle (and not from the standpoint of public law or tradition), it might be felt that Couza had lived up to any reasonable criterion of what a man, placed in his position, should have done. We have already noticed —more particularly in connexion with the Capitulations—that the nationalist spirit was beginning to be strong enough to resent the tutelage of the Great Powers, as before it had chafed under the domination of Russia. And it was this growing resentment, this awakening of national consciousness, that Couza led and typified. It was he who knew exactly the status of his country. Of the precise limits of Moldo-Wallachian autonomy, no better proof could be found than the Convention itself, which had shaped a new régime for the Principalities. It was the Powers who had given them their constitution, and the Powers who had decreed that they should have a new electoral law. Externally they were part of the Ottoman Empire, whose treaties they must respect; and that, of course, meant tolerating the special rights of foreigners resident in their land. If occasionally the Principalities made an effort to play a separate role in European affairs, the ever-watchful eyes of the ambassadors were certain to detect it and to remind them of their vassalage. Especially galling to the ruler was the role of the foreign consuls.

The political role of the foreign consuls in Servia and the Principalities is in some respects unique in public law. Apart from their ordinary consular duties and the functions which the application of the Capitulations had imposed upon them, these resident officials were the ever-active exponents of the European protectorate, assumed at Paris in 1856. It was through their vigilance, their advice, and occasionally their interference that the Principalities were to be kept to the straight and narrow path. Any deviation from the terms of the Convention or the stipulation of a treaty was their duty to report, and, if possible, to correct. While their action in most matters was largely dictated by their instructions, there is scarcely any doubt that they looked upon themselves as the mentors of the ruler. He could not escape them by going from Bucharest to Jassy, as several Powers were represented in both places, and it was actually at Jassy that France possessed her keenest agent, the irrepressible Place. At Bucharest the ablest members of the consular corps were Giers and Eder, who respectively represented the governments of St. Petersburg and Vienna. The former was serving his apprenticeship in a long career that was destined to be crowned by the position which Gortchakoff now occupied. It is unfortunate that, in lieu of his own dispatches, we have to view him generally through the eyes of his colleagues, who were inclined to believe that he was perpetually intriguing. That he enjoyed Couza's confidence is doubtful, but he seems to have supported the Prince on occasions, while equally ready to give ear to his enemies; and it seems probable that the very uncertainty of his policy—if, indeed, Russia had a policy—gave his influence considerable weight. Eder's methods were quite different. He was always straightforward in dealing with Couza, and remarkably fair in reporting his conduct. It is noticeable in most of his dispatches that he gave little space to his own observations to the Prince, but devoted more attention to reporting the latter's views, and, with the possible exception of Giers, he was much the best informed among the consuls on conditions in the Principalities. Not burdened with many instructions from his government (in itself a testimony to his ability), he was generally able to use his judgement as he saw fit, and it is an evidence of his tact that, in spite of the unpopularity of his country, he had more weight with the Prince than any other agent at Bucharest. Neither Green, the British consul, nor Tillos, his French colleague, was conspicuous for tact; nor did they ever seem to acquire any sympathy for the people with whom they were resident. Green appears to have been a man of mediocre capacity; he generally acted in accordance with instructions from Bulwer (who dearly loved the role of a disciplinarian), and showed little personal initiative; while Tillos was too much blinded by his dislike of Couza to capitalize the affection which that ruler felt for France. At Jassy Churchill was somewhat more adaptable than Green, and Place obtained for a time the Prince's confidence; but none of the consuls at the Moldavian capital enjoyed the responsibility which rested on their colleagues at Bucharest. The agents of Sardinia and Prussia played unimportant parts. It was the consuls of Russia, Austria, France, and Great Britain who symbolized the yoke of the European protectorate. Hedged in by these unwelcome monitors, Couza tugged at his fetters, and sought every now and then to act as if he were an independent ruler. It was he, indeed, whose duty it was to make his people respected. But it was manifest that Couza had not yet satisfied the nationalist yearnings—for union was the burning issue; and, apart from any question of whether he was fitted for his role, there was the inevitable question of whether or not the régime, introduced by the Convention, had stood the test of its initial years.

In some respects the Convention had not been given a fair trial. It is true that the Prince had made some use of the latitude allowed him and had engaged the services of French experts in the administration of the army, of the finances, and of public works; it is also true that the central commission had been launched, and that the Prince faithfully divided his time between his two capitals, and in the main lived up to the requirements of a constitutional prince. But the fact remains that the country had never been placed squarely under the régime of the Convention, and some of its assumptions had been consistently ignored. Naturally, in as sketchy a constitution as the Convention provided (and it had not even wholly replaced the *Règlement organique*), there was much left to be solved by legislative enactment or governmental decree; and it seems clear that the administration of both provinces still remained very largely a hit or miss affair. The ministers' spheres of competence overlapped one another, with the result of causing friction and very general confusion; the functions of the different officials were so indefinitely understood that not only ministers but prefects and even sub-prefects issued resolutions with but little regard for the law; while the police were often charged with executing civil judgements and even with the collection of imposts. In the administration of the finances there was hardly less confusion. Assessment was left in the hands of fiscal agents without adequate control from above or below, and so little note was taken of the relative urgency of appropriations in the budget that sometimes there was no money to pay official salaries.[1] In general, it may be said that the Principalities were still limping along under the vague provisions of the *Règlement* which had never really provided for the concentration of responsibility, and that the only efforts Couza had made to improve the administration had been solely in the direction of improving its personnel—a worthy design, as far as it went, but obviously not reaching to the root of the trouble, and even that recourse has been doomed to failure, as we have seen.[2] It is true, of course, that Couza had invited the central commission to draft a project, constituting a court of cassation, as the Convention had ordained, but, when the measure came before the assemblies, it was amended by each chamber in an opposite direction, and things thus remained as before; accordingly, in March 1861, it was stated that thousands of trials were awaiting a final solution.[3]

[1] Place to Couza, Aug. 6, 1861, annex to Place's no. 42, *Aff. étr., Turquie, Jassy*, vol. 10.
[2] See p. 258.
[3] Place to Thouvenel, no. 29, Mar. 6, 1861, *ibid.* In February 1861, Couza invited the central commission to prepare a bill to be submitted to the assem-

Finally, there had been no revision of the electoral law as the Convention had intended; for the only attempt in this direction had been the arrangements contained in the project of a constitution brought forward by the central commission in the fall of 1859, and this whole plan had foundered on the demand for a foreign prince. Thus the temporary scheme, provided by the Convention, was was still in force, continuing the anomaly of choosing some deputies by direct election and some by indirect, and giving much too great a predominance of power to the *boyards* in comparison with large cities like Bucharest.[1] One may well understand that so thorny a question would probably never receive a satisfactory solution at the hands of parties so vitally interested in extending or retaining their power, and to the *boyards* electoral reform threatened not merely their political but their economic power. For here is where we touch the most difficult question in the Danubian Principalities—the question of the fundamental relations of landlord and peasant.

It was understood that some measure of agrarian reform must be enacted sooner or later. The Convention itself had decreed that 'attention will be given without delay to the revision of the law which regulates the relations of the proprietors of the soil with the cultivators in view of ameliorating the condition of the peasants'.[2] We have already noticed that the peasant was in a state of economic bondage to the lord, or, worse still, to some *fermier* who had leased the lord's estate; and that, after making his various payments in labour and in kind, he had hardly been able to eke out even a tolerable existence. The more liberal element in politics, as represented by Cogalnitchano, had contended ever since 1848 that only by severing all extra-legal relations with the landlord and making the peasant a free proprietor of the soil he cultivated could any real amelioration of his lot be obtained;[3] but naturally the *boyards* did not relish the diminution of their estates, and they were loath to give up the *corvées* without the means of assuring themselves of a plentiful supply of labour—the more necessary now that foreign markets were increasingly available. Finally convinced, however, that it would be better to carry through some palliative than to wait for the possible enactment of a radical reform, such as Couza and the radicals would devise, the central commission prepared, during the summer of 1860, the project of a new rural law,[4] designed to represent the sentiment of the chastened, though unconverted,

blies, providing for the right of habeas corpus, as well as the introduction of trial by jury: Churchill to Russell, no. 12, F.O. 78/1584.
[1] Cretzulesco, *La Roumanie en 1859*, pp. 57–8.   [2] Article xlvi.
[3] Boeresco, *Amélioration d'état des paysans roumains.*
[4] The project is printed in full in *Tacmelile agricole in România: legi și proiecte*, pp. 268–73.

boyarie. The essence of this reform was that the peasant should be given in full ownership (one might better say occupancy) his house, garden, and vineyards, as well as accorded the use of certain common lands for pasturage, in return for all of which he should pay to the lord a fixed annual rent; and that the *corvée* might now, if desired, be commuted into a payment in money or kind. Nothing was said of the land, which, according to law, was still supposed to be placed at the peasants' disposal—namely two-thirds of the estate; though it was explicitly stated that the peasant might enjoy his present tenure if he wished,[1] and that, if he required more land for grazing or other purposes, he must enter into new contracts with the lord. From these new conditions it may be assumed that the landlord intended to withdraw more and more land from the customary two-thirds of his estate, cultivated heretofore by the peasants, and to force them by the limitation of their area for tillage, as well as by the increased need of grazing land, to enter new contracts,[2] which, in return for new allotments of land, would provide him with the labour which he required.[3] It amounted, in short, to the establishment of a new system of *corvées*. It was in vain that with a show of generosity the State was authorized on specified conditions [4] to sell certain portions of its lands to the peasants, as the privilege was clogged by clauses which might be interpreted as necessitating special legislative as well as administrative approval of each transaction.[5] It should also be noted that the *corvées*, fixed by law, were still so excessive that their commutation was but a scant relief, while it still further diminished the peasant's economic freedom. He was not only not a free proprietor in the proper sense of the term, but he would be placed by the operation of this law in a more onerous subjection than ever to his lord. Such was the insidious reform desired by the *boyards*—which was, indeed, nothing less than a new form of economic bondage, masked under the appearance of a reform. As a matter of fact, political struggles and the movement to obtain union prevented the measure

[1] For administrative purposes the totality of peasants on a landlord's estate was constituted by this proposed measure into a village community or 'commune'. It was to the commune that this pasture land was allotted, the total extent being figured on the basis of a hectar per family in the plains and half a hectar in the mountains.

[2] It is obvious that this pressure would be all the greater as the peasants' families increased, and the younger peasants required new land to till or to use for pasture.

[3] The peasant, being in general unable to pay the new rental, would have to 'work it out'.

[4] The State was to sell these lands on condition of holding a mortgage until the purchase price was paid, and, in order to facilitate payment of this mortgage, rural banks were to be established.

[5] Article xxxi stipulated the 'approval of the legislative powers' and article xxxvi invoked as necessary an 'understanding with the ministers of worship and finances'.

from being considered by the two assemblies, and it was not until 1862 that it was presented, in substantially the same form, for legislative action. If a really liberal project of agrarian reform were ever to see the light, it was necessary that the *boyards* should cease to control the legislative bodies. To that end, the fundamental requirement was a new electoral law which should offer a very considerable representation to the masses. It is an interesting fact that during these earlier years of Couza's reign the agrarian issue remained rather conspicuously in the background, but every one was aware that in the electoral question was involved not only the immediate political dominance but the whole economic future of the Moldo-Wallachian *boyarie*. And here, too, the Conference of Paris had expected the Principalities to initiate some reform.[1]

One can hardly accuse Couza of lack of interest in this problem. There was no doubt whatever of his hostility to the *boyards* and his longing to scotch their power at its roots. Place is probably right in imputing much of the personal enmity to the prince to the fact that he might at any time give the radicals their opening for tampering with the electoral question.[2] But Couza was too circumspect a politician to stake his position on an alliance with a small and turbulent minority (credited, moreover, with aiming at national independence)[3] until his personal power had become considerably enhanced. To that end, he must, first of all, weld the Principalities into a single compact nation. As Baron Eder pointed out in one of his keen analyses of conditions, Couza had been given a mandate by his double election to secure union and, if he did not obtain it, he had no *raison d'être*,[4] while, conversely (we may add), if he satisfied the national longings, he might hope to win that prestige among his countrymen which he had not so far acquired. The impatience of a section of public opinion to force his hand[5] was surely all that he needed to remind him of his mission, and it is not absolutely certain that an address of Cogalnitchano to the Moldavian assembly in favour of union in May 1860[6] did not win his secret approval, as a means of conveying a useful warning to the Powers. During the summer of 1860 he told Eder that, unless union were granted, he would not reign six months,[7] and there was even talk—but nothing was cheaper in the Principalities than talk —of a movement to displace him in favour of Prince Bibesco.[8]

[1] Protocol no. 9, July 10, 1858.
[2] Place to Thouvenel, no. 38, June 5, 1861, *Aff. étr., Turquie, Jassy*, vol. 10.
[3] Green to Bulwer, no. 14, Apr. 15, 1860, F.O. 78/1516.
[4] Eder to Rechberg, no. 10 A, Feb. 8, 1861, Staatsarchiv, xxxviii/126.
[5] Page 253. [6] Churchill to Russell, no. 13, May 30, 1860, F.O. 78/1518.
[7] Eder to Rechberg, no. 34, June 15, Staatsarchiv, xxxviii/129. Couza need not necessarily have believed this. He might have felt that Austria would prefer anything to the possibility of a revolution in the Principalities.
[8] Eder to Rechberg, no. 43, Aug. 11, 1860, *ibid.*

It is perhaps too much to say that Couza's position was as yet critical; but ample evidence has been shown that he had steadily lost ground since his half-welcome elevation; and he himself declared later that the chief ground of dissatisfaction was the fact that union had as yet been unattained.[1] Clearly enough, the Prince needed the moral value of such an achievement; and it is also true that, if his authority were centralized by a radical revision of the Convention, he might hope to initiate many measures, which, under present conditions, would have been lost in the maze of party strife. The way for Couza was therefore clear. He must try to persuade the Powers to grant his people union.

While he had frequently complained to the consuls of the inconveniences of the hybrid constitution under which he was expected to govern, Couza's first direct move, looking toward modification, was made in March 1860, and was directed against the weakest point in the present system, namely, the central commission. With characteristic tact, Couza addressed his complaint to his suzerain. Under instructions from the Wallachian minister of foreign affairs, the faithful Negri was to represent the difficulty of having the seat of the central commission at a distance from both capitals and at a place where ordinary comforts were so scarce that even lodging facilities were difficult to obtain; hence it was almost impossible to induce capable men to accept membership on that body; and, as the prospective court of cassation was also to sit there, such difficulties would naturally be aggravated. Negri was to impress upon the Porte, and the ambassadors as well, the necessity of changing the seat of both these institutions to Bucharest.[2] It would have been difficult to find a more astute agent to handle delicate matters than the kapou kiaya. He concluded that it would be unwise, on the whole, to address a formal request to the Porte at this time, since Couza had a better chance, himself, of securing this boon when he came to Constantinople. But he sounded some of the ambassadors on the merits of the desired change,[3] and it is not improbable that he talked with Ali,[4] though we have no certain evidence of the fact. Anyway, Austria was so opposed to the step, which she seemed to fear might be sanctioned by the Porte without first consulting the Powers,[5] that the outlook was far from promising.

No doubt Couza felt, himself, that his prospective visit to

---

[1] Eder to Rechberg, no. 10 A, Feb. 8, 1861, Staatsarchiv, XXXVIII/126.

[2] Alexandri to Negri, no. 11, Mar. 4, 1860, enc., F.O. 78/1576. Green remarked that there were no libraries, archives, or printing establishments in Focshani, and that much time was wasted by having research done elsewhere: Green to Russell, no. 11, Mar. 30, F.O. 78/1516.

[3] Lallemand to Thouvenel, no. 16, Apr. 4, *Aff. étr.*, *Turquie*, vol. 343.

[4] Fuad mentioned it to Prokesch: Prokesch to Rechberg, no. 33 C, May 23, Staatsarchiv, XII/67.

[5] Rechberg to Prokesch, May 8, *ibid.*, XII/70.

Constantinople was the best opportunity of realizing his hopes. 'I sincerely trust', he is reported to have said to Churchill, 'that my journey to Constantinople will have for effect the obtaining of some sort of concessions from the Porte towards the unification of the administration of the Principalities, without which my position becomes day by day more and more difficult, and I myself more and more unpopular.' Couza then added the assurance that if the Principalities insisted upon bringing about union themselves, he would sooner abdicate than seem to break faith with the Powers, and bade the consul 'not to listen to the reports of people interested in depriving him of the support of England'.[1] About a week later he went into the difficulty of his position with Green, and said that he meant to utilize his coming trip as a means of trying to secure concessions. There is little doubt but that he hoped to enlist British sympathies for his project, and he now found confirmation of a statement, reported by Negri, that Russell was in favour of some change in the Convention.[2] To obtain such an admission from Great Britain was certainly a great gain, but France was even more explicit. Thouvenel not only favoured the transference of the central commission and court of cassation to Bucharest (though he preferred that the former should meet alternately in each capital),[3] but he told Cowley later that he felt that the government of the Principalities should be unified, even if the legislatures remained separate.[4] Strange to say, even Russell expressed the opinion that 'the removal of the commission from Foxchani [sic] would be desirable rather than otherwise'.[5] Unfortunately Couza did not know of the Emperor's benevolence; and no assurance came from La Valette, who merely wrote the French agent at Bucharest that Couza must not think of asking for changes in the Convention.[6] This warning, coupled with a similarly discouraging statement of Bulwer to Bolantineano some months previous, made Couza decide for the moment to postpone his trip. He could not afford to let his people think that he would secure some mitigation of their lot, and then return from his mission empty-handed.[7]

Nevertheless, Couza had meanwhile decided upon a step which would enable him to feel out the Powers more fully, and, if the reaction were at all favourable, would lead him to believe that

[1] Churchill to Russell, no. 13, May 30, F.O. 78/1518.
[2] Green to Bulwer, no. 23, June 7, F.O. 78/1516. Russell's official dispatches to Bulwer reveal no such statement as early as this, but he may have written something in a private letter which Bulwer felt justified in disclosing to Negri.
[3] Thouvenel to Lallemand, no. 31, Apr. 27, *Aff. étr.*, *Turquie*, vol. 343.
[4] Cowley to Russell, no. 741, June 14, F.O. 27/1339.
[5] Russell to Bulwer, no. 169, Apr. 23, F.O. 78/1496. As Russell cited Thouvenel's opinion, he was probably acting upon it.
[6] See p. 260.
[7] Hory to Thouvenel, no. 35, June 28, *Aff. étr.*, *Turquie, Bucharest*, vol. 20.

something might be gained by going to Constantinople. In June he penned an elaborate *mémoire* to Negri, entering fully into the political condition of the Principalities, the hardships imposed upon them by the Convention, and the need of union as the obvious solution. The *mémoire* began by recalling how the expectations, called forth by the Treaty of Paris and by the remarkable display of sentiment in the *divans ad hoc*, had been disappointed by the Convention of 1858. The dualism created by that act made unified progress impossible, as it would have been necessary to secure co-operation between two separate governments and two separate legislatures—a feat quite beyond the capacity of the central commission, which had been invented to attain that end. After a painful experience with this mongrel system, the two assemblies had chosen the same hospodar, and even desired to effect the complete union of the Principalities. Couza had had 'the courage to resist' this almost unanimous pressure of his compatriots, and 'resolved to await with confidence' the decision of the Powers. He felt that he deserved credit both from them and from his people for having maintained order and tranquillity when the temptation was so general of involving the East in the struggle which was going on in Italy; but his elevation to the hospodariate in both Principalities signified the expectation that he would procure union for his people, and, if he failed to achieve that end, he might run the risk of forfeiting that confidence. Moreover, the Prince's defeated rivals for the hospodariate had an interest in cherishing their rancour, and the long period of waiting for his investiture had encouraged many persons, especially those who had lost privileges through the operation of the Convention, to create embarrassments for the new order; and, while some were opposed to all reform, others were in favour of excesses. The project drawn up by the central commission was the best proof of the latter, and the Prince had been obliged to dissolve the assemblies which had placed upon his head the crown of the two Principalities. The position of the ruler was further complicated by contradictions in the Convention itself, such, for example, as to whether the 'concurrence of the ministers' gave the hospodar considerable latitude, or whether ministers were supposed to be responsible to the chambers; and the chambers themselves either exercised their functions over trifles (utilizing frivolously the privileges of interpellation and censure) or else lapsed into inertia and futile debates. Such persons accused the Prince of bad faith in not introducing the reforms which the Convention prescribed, but made it impossible for him to do so. Could it be astonishing, in view of the repeated ministerial crises, that the more capable men should retire from public life? A further contradiction in the Convention, which had caused trouble, had been the electoral system. Although the Convention had done so much for social equality, the suffrage was so restricted that deputies were chosen almost exclusively from the former privileged classes, thus rendering almost hopeless the enactment of social reforms. Some of the electoral provisions had proved unworkable, or even ridiculous, in practice. It is true that the Powers had suggested the need of revising the system, but they could not have understood the insurmountable difficulties in the way of effecting reform in the Principalities. If he were to realize the hopes which were confided in him, the Prince must have the means of accomplishing his great task. These means were not to be found in the existence of two governments, subjected to the action of legislative majorities, which might be at variance with each other; nor could he find them in the existence of two separate assemblies, nor in an electoral system which gave preponderance to the elements opposed to social progress.

'The union of the Principalities', argued Couza, 'is imperiously demanded by the logic of the double election, which the high signatories of the Convention of August 19 have to-day recognized. It is indispensable to render my government strong and united, and to put it in a position to accomplish the reorganization of the State. For this strength and this unity will never result from a governmental action, decentralized and partitioned among several centres of gravity, Bucharest, Jassy, Focshani, subjecting the hospodar to an eternal and inconvenient oscillation between three separate residences.'

But the necessary corollary to the union of the governments was the union of the chambers, for endless delays and confusion were now produced by the necessity of submitting a project of the central commission to the two chambers, who might amend it—if they acted at all—and send it back to the central commission for further deliberations. And a third need was the revision of the electoral system—not for the purpose of introducing new elements into the assemblies, but rather to the end of reducing the preponderance of those who were hostile to all reform and unwilling to co-operate with the executive; since these men could not be expected to 'commit political suicide', there was 'no means of expecting electoral reform' from the system at present constituted. But a final argument for union was that it would fulfil the national aspirations of the Roumanian people, who gravitate towards no foreign Power, but want only to be Roumanians, and have never sought independence from the Porte which they look upon as the 'palladium of their nationality'. Let the Powers, who have given the Principalities so much proof of their interest, continue to help them![1]

[1] Couza to Negri, June 1860, enclosed in Churchill's no. 35, F.O. 78/1518. It is printed in *Arch. dip.*, *1866*, vol. ii, pp. 179 ff. and it is there stated that it was

While it might be too much to say that the *mémoire* was a brilliant or entirely objective exposition of conditions in the Principalities under the Convention, one can hardly deny that Couza made a good case for its revision. It was a conscious appeal to the justice and the sympathies of the Powers, but even more to their reason. Although he adduced the national aspirations of his people as an argument, even pointing—by implication—to the injustice of disappointing hopes, deliberately roused, Couza did not fall into the error that so many of his countrymen would have committed—that of waving unduly the banner of Rouman nationalism. He did bring out, however, the historical justification of fitting the political system to the actual recognition of himself as joint ruler; and he made it appear, at least, that the political chaos in the Principalities was entirely due to the anomalies and unworkable features of the Convention. The avowed loyalty of the Principalities to Turkey and the assurance that he was not recommending too democratic a change in the electoral system were, no doubt, designed to meet the argument that the Principalities were immoderate in their pretensions; and the point that no desirable change in the electoral system could be expected under existing conditions could only lead to the inference that the Powers themselves must lay down at least the bases of electoral reform. Thus, indeed, union and electoral reform were set down as indispensable to the national progress.

It was perhaps unfortunate that Negri was instructed to show this *mémoire* first of all to La Valette;[1] for the French ambassador was smarting under the criticism of Cogalnitchano, who had inferred that France had relaxed in her benevolence towards the Principalities (this was in view of La Valette's recent unwelcome advice),[2] and the unamiable Frenchman repeated his conviction that Couza had not given the Convention a long enough test, besides having exaggerated the extent of liberal sentiment in the Principalities. Beyond showing it to Prokesch and probably to Ali, Negri seems, therefore, to have decided to hold the document in reserve.[3] Thouvenel was, however, of the opinion that the Powers ought to consider modifications of their work, though he laid great stress (this was to La Valette) on the fact that Couza himself should not initiate any changes.[4] After the general purport of the *mémoire* had reached Vienna, Count Rechberg, the Austrian

transmitted to the minister of foreign affairs on May 1, 1861. It is, however, quite clear that its tenor was known long before that.

[1] Hory to Thouvenel, no. 35, June 28, *Aff. étr.*, *Turquie, Bucharest*, vol. 20.
[2] Page 296.
[3] La Valette to Thouvenel, nos. 17 and 23, July 9 and 17, *ibid.*, *Turquie*, vol. 345; cf. Prokesch to Rechberg, no number, Dec. 28, Staatsarchiv, xii/69.
[4] Thouvenel to La Valette, no. 57, July 20, *Aff. étr.*, *Turquie, Bucharest*, vol. 20.

minister of foreign affairs, reminded the embassy at Constantinople that Austria was opposed to any change in the Convention.[1] Apart from the French agent at Bucharest,[2] the consulates seem only to have learned of the *mémoire* and not to have read it. Cogalnitchano told Churchill that Negri was making definite proposals to the ambassadors, and that Couza could not go to Constantinople without being first assured that some changes would be made in the Convention, for if he came back without such assurance, he 'would never again be able to assume the reins of government'. (Thus did a Moldavian give his valuation of Couza!) While confessing that he himself was in favour of proclaiming union without waiting for the action of the Powers, he read a dispatch from Couza, disapproving of the proposed meeting of the two assemblies at Focshani for the purpose of settling the court of cassation, as evidence that Couza deserved credit for moderation. Finding that Churchill was looking over his shoulder, the premier admitted that Couza had also written that if his trip were not successful, he might allow union to be proclaimed, regardless of the Powers![3] There is little doubt but that Couza's power of veto was the one thing which prevented his people from taking the law into their own hands. Even a British consul admitted that, if Turkey had not yet been confronted by a *fait accompli*, she owed it to Couza alone.[4]

Yet it is easy to conjecture that there were times when the Prince felt that the suspense was almost unendurable. It was said that Tillos, the French consul, then on leave of absence, had been deputed to bear a confidential letter from Couza to the Emperor, but that Couza was subsequently told that Thouvenel would be present when the letter should be delivered, and so the letter was brought back. Whether it is true that Couza was offering to abdicate whenever Napoleon might so desire,[5] or whether the whole story of such a letter is one of the rumours so prevalent in the Principalities is more than one can say. It would not be the first time that he had sought direct access to the Emperor, and he might conceivably think that to offer to commit political *hara-kiri* was bound to impress upon his political benefactor the urgency of his cause.

---

[1] Rechberg to Ludolf, July 10, no. 3, Staatsarchiv, XII/70.
[2] Hory to Thouvenel, no. 35, June 18, *Aff. étr.*, *Turquie, Bucharest*, vol. 20.
[3] Churchill to Russell, no. 32, July 4, F.O. 78/1518. The motion for this meeting had been made in the Moldavian assembly in consequence of two diametrically opposed amendments by the assemblies to the project of the central commission, constituting the court of cassation. Churchill feared, however, that the intention might be to utilize such an occasion for proclaiming union. This was, of course, sufficient reason for Couza to forbid the meeting, apart from the fact that it would not have been permitted under the Convention.
[4] Churchill to Russell, no. 27, Sept. 20, F.O. 78/1518.
[5] Green to Hammond, Aug. 18, F.O. 78/1517.

But, however cautious and even obsequious Couza might be in his manœuvres to interest the Powers and strengthen their confidence in him, it cannot be said that he was lacking in daring when the occasion demanded it. On passing through Focshani in August, on his way to Bucharest, he told the president of the central commission that that body must make up its mind to have a holiday this year (perhaps an allusion to his hope of getting legislative union), and that he would soon have a communication of the greatest importance to communicate to them. The enigma of this last remark was solved a few days later, when the Prince united the two ministries of war by appointing Floresco, the new incumbent of that office in Wallachia, to the post of minister of war *ad interim* in Moldavia. The central direction should be located at Bucharest, which Couza told Churchill would henceforth be his chief residence.[1] Couza reminded Eder that the Convention already allowed him to unite the militias for specific cases, and the Austrian did not seem to disapprove of this stretching of the constitution, as he remarked that it would better enable the Prince to maintain order. With engaging frankness Couza declared that he felt it his duty to 'develop union along legal lines'.[2] One wonders if he had similar views when he had lately united the administration of the post and telegraph, then the customs, and finally the medical service, all of which were now located at Bucharest.[3] None of these measures was a violation of the spirit of the Convention, inasmuch as that statute had seemed to contemplate administrative union, but only the centralization of the customs administration had been explicitly ordained; and one may conclude that Couza was taking such steps as he dared towards the fusion of the Principalities, while leaving it to the Powers to grant the essential things. It was for the latter purpose that the suggested visit to Constantinople to pay homage to the Sultan had seemed to him a feasible move.

We have already dwelt upon the evolution of this incident.[4] It would be too much to say that the *boyards* were willing to give him a chance to redeem himself in their eyes, but, apparently, there was something like a truce in the long political battle between them,[5] and the Left were at least willing, now that he had prevented the nation from making union, to let him see what diplomacy could do. The fact, however, that he was somewhat uncertain of the temper of his people may be judged from his ill-advised announcement

[1] Churchill to Bulwer, no. 19, Aug. 21, F.O. 78/1518.
[2] Eder to Rechberg, no. 52, Sept. 8, Staatsarchiv, XXXVIII/123. Tillos took a different view from Eder, for he warned Couza against departing from the Convention: Tillos to Thouvenel, no. 1, Aug. 29, *Aff. étr.*, Turquie, Bucharest, vol. 21.
[3] Churchill to Russell, no. 27, Sept. 20, F.O. 78/1518.
[4] Pp. 259 ff.   [5] Green to Russell, no. 58, Sept. 26, F.O. 78/1517.

(already mentioned)[1] that he was going to Constantinople to 'enforce Roumanian interests'.

There is no doubt that Couza laid great store on what this visit would achieve for him. If he had not responded earlier to the urgings of the diplomats to make this trip, there is reason to believe —among other reasons—that he wanted to give the Powers plenty of time to consider the problem in all its aspects, and to realize that he was not inclined to make this overture without some subsequent compensation; certainly, none of the consuls were left unacquainted with his sentiments. We have already noticed the favourable reception which he was granted at Constantinople.[2] There is no evidence to show that he talked politics to Ali; indeed, he possessed too much tact to spoil the ostensible object of his visit by displaying interested motives to the ministers of his suzerain. But to some of the ambassadors he opened his heart without reserve, pitching his key according to the requirements of each individual case. To La Valette he merely repeated his objections to the Convention, and the French ambassador showed a not-too-friendly reserve.[3] But, whatever the aloofness of this surly Frenchman, Couza found in Bulwer a receptive listener, and he went over the stories of his difficulties in some detail, though whether he received any definite encouragement is not told us.[4] His most interesting interview, however, was with the Austrian chargé d'affaires, Prince Ludolf, and the methods of persuasion he employed to overcome the prejudices of Vienna throw interesting light on his abilities as a diplomat. Union was not the genuine desire of the radicals alone, he assured the Austrian, but the demand of the great majority of quiet and moderate citizens. He was not in favour of any weakening of the tie with Turkey, but the more nearly the Principalities approximated to independence, the less likely would they become the scene of revolutionary plots, notably against Austria. (It is interesting to recall his frank confession to La Valette that Sardinia was sending arms to Galatz, and that all that he felt that he could do was to close his eyes and regard them as marketable wares.)[5] But for a strong Austria, indeed, he added, the Principalities would have been swallowed up by Russia long ago. He would not venture to stretch the constitution, if the cabinets willed otherwise, and, if the cabinets did not desire any change, he was prepared to stand or fall with the Convention. He did not even deny Ludolf's contention that the double election, rather than the Convention, was responsible for the unsettled conditions in the Principalities, but, as that act had been recognized, he hoped that

---

[1] Page 263. [2] Page 264.
[3] La Valette to Thouvenel, no. 81, Oct. 16, *Aff. étr.*, *Turquie*, vol. 347.
[4] Bulwer to Russell, no. 680, Oct. 16, F.O. 78/1512. [5] *Supra*, p. 275.

the Powers would now grant the Principalities a further indulgence. To Austria he had personal grounds for gratitude because of her kindness to him during his exile. Ludolf was so captivated by the Prince's conduct throughout his sojourn that he praised his 'tact and self-possession, as well as his adroitness, which seemed to qualify him for his present position'.[1] Whether the more sour Prokesch would have displayed a similar reaction is impossible to say.

The concrete results of Couza's mission were not as yet apparent. He had made no formal request for alteration of the Convention (obviously he could not do so on such an occasion), and, so far as we know, had secured no assurances, or even hints, of assistance. He could only hope that he had presented his case in a sufficiently favourable light to obtain some intercession on his behalf from the ambassadors to their respective governments, and that he had roused their personal interest by his pleasing and dutiful conduct. 'I have no hesitation in saying', wrote Bulwer to Russell, after recounting his interview with the Prince, 'that he is a man above the common, and with a mind which seems likely to improve by responsibility and experience.'[2] Two weeks later, on meditating the problem which had been informally presented to the Powers, Bulwer wrote to Russell that the Porte had really no longer any hope of preventing union, and that not only did the enhanced strength of the nationalist movement (partly as a consequence of the Italian War) deserve consideration, but the Convention (of which, in many ways, he had never approved)[3] was now clearly obsolete, and that, while he thought it well to preserve some of it, he hoped that the Porte would request Couza to point out its inconveniences.[4] It was from a British diplomat that the Prince was receiving at this time the readiest sympathy.

Unfortunately, Couza did not know that forces were slowly working in his favour, and, for the present, he had to play the same old wearisome game of holding back his people while he continued his overtures to Europe. None of the consuls seemed to show him any sympathy except Place, who steadfastly contended that Couza was a man of capacity, energy, and liberal aspirations, and that his enemies were always aggravating a situation that was solely due to the defects of the Convention.[5] But unhappily it is always easier to make responsibility personal, and the general public felt indignant that he had nothing to show for the homage he had paid the

[1] Ludolf to Rechberg, no. 75 D, Oct. 17, Staatsarchiv, XII/69.
[2] Bulwer to Russell, no. 680, Oct. 14, F.O. 78/1512.
[3] Bulwer to Russell, July 6, 1859, Russell Papers, G. and D., 22/88, Pub. Rec. Off.   [4] Bulwer to Russell, no. 1702, Oct. 30, 1860, F.O. 78/1512.
[5] Place to La Valette, Nov. 29, annex to Place's no. 21, *Aff. étr.*, *Turquie*, *Jassy*, vol. 10.

Sultan.[1] Nothing is more patent, indeed, than the Prince's isolation.[2] Would the hopes that he had encouraged prove futile after all? Soon after his return, he told Eder—doubtless in a moment of discouragement—that he did not believe that union could be won at Constantinople.[3] It had no doubt been a mistake to allow the public to expect that his trip would accomplish something definite, and the most that he could do was to seek to create the rather hazardous impression that, if changes were proposed, the Porte would not oppose them. The *boyards* naturally chuckled over what they regarded as the failure of his mission.[4] It was rumoured at Bucharest that union would shortly be proclaimed—though stories differed as to whether it was the assemblies[5] or Couza himself[6] who would take the step; but the Prince himself told Tillos that, though his ministers urged this action, he was not willing to be their dupe by letting the assemblies come together to declare for a foreign prince.[7] Perhaps the fear of being held to his promise of 1859 was one reason why Couza did not want to see union come from within;[8] he knew well enough, of course, that union from without would carry no such danger. Once, it is true, he explained that union was all his people really wanted, and that talk of a foreign prince was merely intended to emphasize that wish,[9] but what he did not add—though later events substantiated it—was that what the *boyards* wanted was simply to be rid of *him*. Just how a foreign prince (sincerely desired by a group of Moldavians) could be reconciled with the pretension of certain *boyards* to snatch the hospodariate for themselves is something which the logic of the situation cannot explain.

At all events, there was little to console the harassed ruler, some of whose problems we have noticed elsewhere.[10] The central commission, which might have projected something useful, sat moribund, as usual, and, as this condemned the assemblies to inertia, discontent, having no other focus, fastened itself upon the government.[11] During the month of November the public mind was agitated by the Crajova riots, the suspension of the metropolitan, and

[1] Bulwer to Russell, no. 101, Feb. 6, 1861, F.O. 78/1506.

[2] He had complained to Tillos, shortly before his trip to Constantinople, that both parties wanted to push him into proclaiming union, the Right because they wanted to compromise him with the Powers, and the Left because they would drive him into a policy of extremes. 'I spend myself without result,' he said, 'and no one helps me': Tillos to Thouvenel, no. 7, Oct. 2, *Aff. étr., Turquie, Bucharest*, vol. 21.

[3] Eder to Rechberg, no. 67, Nov. 13, Staatsarchiv, XXXVIII/123.

[4] Green to Hammond, Oct. 27, F.O. 78/1517.

[5] Eder to Rechberg, no. 68, Nov. 20, Staatsarchiv, XXXVIII/123.

[6] Green to Russell, no. 73, Nov. 21, F.O. 78/1517.

[7] Tillos to Thouvenel, no. 9, Nov. 13, *Aff. étr., Turquie, Bucharest*, vol. 21.

[8] This was Eder's view (no. 68) and also Green's (no. 73).

[9] Green to Bulwer, no. 75, Dec. 31, F.O. 78/1517.

[10] Page 265.   [11] Green to Bulwer, no. 75.

a fresh attack upon the rights of foreigners. It is not improbable that the ministries were getting out of hand. However true may have been Tillos's accusation that Couza was neglecting his duties,[1] the compulsion to divide his time between two capitals was sufficient to prevent a firm hand from being exerted at either place. Roused by an inquiry from the Porte as to the truth about the Crajova affair, Couza replied that order had been maintained, and, as if to impress the point, he entered Bucharest, December 1, with an escort of 200 gendarmes.[2] While undoubtedly an easy-going man, the Prince had a reserve of energy which he could always draw on when his patience failed.

In the meantime Couza felt that he must clinch any possible gain that he had made in the favour of the Powers, and especially France, by his recent manœuvre. Some weeks after his return from Constantinople, he penned a long letter to Napoleon, and enclosed with it his *mémoire* on the urgency of union. In his letter he reminded the Emperor that he had undertaken the journey, despite his own repugnance, because the Emperor had wished it. With a possible appreciation of Napoleon's sentiments regarding Turkey and the Principalities, he remarked that he had been struck on his arrival in Constantinople with the decrepitude of Turkey— a land from which 'young Roumania' would never be able to draw new life. He declared that he knew the principles in the Convention were too precious to Napoleon to be sacrificed (this, no doubt, in order to preclude the inference that he was denouncing any act which his august friend had signed), but that the means of putting it into execution were unfortunately deficient; he had neglected nothing in the way of making the system work, but, as it was, it was paralysing the Principalities. 'When it was a question of explaining myself with freedom,' he said (recalling, it seems, his confidences in 1859), 'to whom should I turn but to your Majesty, whom the new Europe accepts as arbiter, and who has never ceased to give us proofs of constant interest?' The solution proposed in the *mémoire* was, he assured Napoleon, completely in conformity with the spirit of the Convention, and responded to the unanimous desires of the Roumanian people. The letter closed with an appeal for authorization to modify the Convention, while giving assurance that no precipitate action would be taken.[3] Couza sent a copy of the letter to La Valette with an expression of gratitude for the gracious reception which he had received from the ambassador and an acknowledgement of the advantage which his trip had brought to himself and to his country.[4] There is no evidence that Napoleon

[1] Tillos to Thouvenel, no. 9.   [2] Green to Russell, no. 80, Dec. 3, F.O. 28/1517.
[3] Couza to Napoleon, Nov. 9, *Aff. étr.*, *Turquie, Bucharest*, vol. 21.
[4] Couza to La Valette, Nov. 6, annex to La Valette's no. 96, *ibid.*, *Turquie*, vol. 347.

replied directly to the letter (though it is not impossible that he did), but Thouvenel wrote La Valette, before handing it to the Emperor, that the ambassador should neglect no occasion to give 'counsels of prudence and moderation', but that France was ready to second any effort of the Prince to secure from the Porte the amelioration which he demanded.[1] It may be said that from this moment the assistance of France was enlisted. A few weeks later the Emperor was quoted as saying that perhaps a modification of the Convention was indispensable in some particulars.[2] And finally, pursuant to the Emperor's instructions,[3] Thouvenel penned a personal letter to Couza, in which he stated that the Powers could hardly be astonished at difficulties in executing an act which had been of the nature of a compromise; that they themselves had contemplated a change in the electoral law;[4] and that it behoved Couza now to take this question up with the Porte with a view to getting another international conference summoned. He closed his letter by acknowledging the Prince's 'constant efforts to ensure the entire execution' of the Convention, and hazarded the opinion that the Protecting Powers, in appreciating this attitude, could not fail to examine the circumstances which had led him to consider necessary the changes which he had proposed.[5] It was not exactly assent to a general revision of the Convention, but it was hinting that at least the question would be considered, and that France was on his side. So much had Couza gained by his manœuvre.

We shall notice presently that Thouvenel, as good as his word, lost no time in lending his good offices at Constantinople. And certainly they were needed. La Valette had written his chief that neither Ali nor Fuad had expressed an opinion on the *mémoire*, and he regarded their silence as indicative that they did not mean to examine it.[6] Obviously the Porte, whose formal initiative was indispensable, would only rouse itself if properly inspired. It is not impossible, as we have remarked before, that one of the motives for Couza's part in the revolutionary imbroglio was the hope of convincing Austria that there would be no peace near her borders till the question of union was settled. If that is so, the experiment probably lost him more sympathy than it gained. That Great Britain, in view of her attitude on the arms question, would hurry to join her efforts to those of France was hardly to be expected. But Bulwer, who believed in Couza's good faith, and felt that the clamour for a foreign prince would die down if it were known that

---

[1] Thouvenel to La Valette, no. 97, Nov. 30, *Aff. étr.*, *Turquie*, vol. 347.
[2] Thouvenel to La Valette, no. 103, Dec. 14, *ibid*.
[3] Thouvenel to Tillos, no. 10, Dec. 14, *ibid.*, *Bucharest*, vol. 21.
[4] Thouvenel explicitly referred to the protocol of July 10, 1858.
[5] Thouvenel to Couza, Dec. 14, annex to Thouvenel's no. 10.
[6] La Valette to Thouvenel, no. 7, Jan. 15, 1861, *Aff. étr.*, *Turquie*, vol. 348.

Couza was supported at Constantinople,[1] declared that Ali ought to give a conciliatory answer to Couza's *mémoire* (which had evidently reached the vizier's hands by this time), and should submit this answer to the Powers; the Porte might further explain to the Prince that it was only the arms crisis which had delayed the transmission of its answer.[2] The British ambassador could not but feel that the silence of the Sultan in response to Couza's mission of conciliation, coincident as it was with the stringent policy which had to be dictated regarding the arms and the revolutionary plots—a fact that did not add to Couza's popularity at home—was treating his difficulties with a singular want of sympathy and understanding.[3] Yet Russell, who had conceded the necessity of changing the Convention with evident reluctance,[4] vouchsafed no reply to these suggestions. Couza remarked sadly to Churchill that he could not feel that he had made any headway in his relations with Great Britain, with whom he was 'just as far advanced as he was two years ago, having done everything that he was advised to do without having received anything in return'.[5] As this statement was made after Couza had yielded to Bulwer's request to ship the arms, one can fairly dismiss the charge, made by Gortchakoff later, that Great Britain had promised support to Couza in return for his compliance.[6]

While in Wallachia the ministry, already discredited by its handling of the Crajova disturbance, was tottering to its fall, in Moldavia the sturdy Cogalnitchano was defending the government against the charge of connivance with Sardinia, and bravely holding the factional spirit in check.[7] Couza seems to have had the feeling that to interest the country in administrative reform might serve as a useful distraction, and the central commission had prepared projects on electoral reform and a more equitable system of taxation. Couza's speech to the Moldavian assembly (which was read in his absence) was a plea for patriotism, tempered by prudence.

'I have the consciousness of my mission', he assured the deputies. 'I know that I will by no means forget that I represent the principle of union; but the realization of this salutary principle depends, above all, upon patriotism, upon concord, upon political prudence on the part of all the organs of state, as well as upon a spirit of order, peace, and real progress, which ought to animate us and guide us in all and for all.'[8]

He asked the assembly to consider a modification of the electoral

[1] Bulwer to Russell, no. 841, Dec. 11, 1860, F.O. 78/1514.
[2] Bulwer to Russell, no. 97, Feb. 6, 1861, F.O. 78/1566.
[3] Bulwer to Russell, no. 101, Feb. 6, *ibid.*
[4] Russell to Bulwer, no. 525, Sept. 21, 1860, F.O. 78/1500.
[5] Churchill to Russell, no. 2, Jan. 10, 1861, F.O. 78/1584.
[6] Montebello to Thouvenel, May 10, *Aff. étr., Russie*, vol. 224, f. 33.
[7] Churchill to Russell, no. 42, Dec. 29, 1860, F.O. 78/1518.
[8] Place to Thouvenel, no. 25, Dec. 20, *Aff. étr., Turquie, Jassy*, vol. 10.

law, and spoke of the need of increased armaments[1]—a reflection which may be ascribed to the recent crisis. The unfortunate feature of the situation was that, when expected to enact reforms, the deputies invariably concentrated on trifles, and Couza had to intervene by telegraph from Bucharest in order to keep the peace.[2] It was the same old impossible feat of having to ride two horses at a perilous distance apart. A hasty visit to Jassy was followed by the fall of Cogalnitchano; and the new ministry, which was said to be pro-Russian, gave a pardon as well as a pension to the disgraced metropolitan.[3] In Bucharest, however, the political wrangles were more serious. Tillos felt that, in supporting the Iepouriano ministry, Couza was needlessly attracting public odium to himself,[4] but Tillos was always as ready to blame the Prince for his frequent change of ministries, and even Green thought it would be 'highly injudicious' to accept Tillos's proposal of a joint intervention to try to induce Couza to make a change.[5] 'Whatever ministry may be formed,' declared Green, 'it is not probable that it will be able to hold its ground against the intrigues of those desirous of obtaining their places, the exigencies of their party, and the opposition of the Prince's entourage.'[6] Since both Right and Left had joined forces against the ministry,[7] no doubt something had to be done. At all events, Couza himself decided the point; but, instead of ousting the ministry, he took the alternative step of dissolving the assembly.[8]

The Prince's step was, perhaps, an impulse; it certainly could not be calculated to stifle the opposition. Vigorous efforts to manipulate the elections[9] only resulted in an assembly but little differing in complexion from the old.[10] The Prince was more than ever convinced that the only way to loosen the paralysing influence of the *boyards* was by means of an electoral law that would broaden the representation.[11] For the moment, however, he could not well ignore the triumph of his enemies. Realizing that his present ministry was doomed, he called in conference Catargi, the leader

---

[1] Churchill to Bulwer, no. 76, Dec. 19, F.O. 195/643.

[2] Place to Thouvenel, no. 25, *Aff. étr., Turquie, Jassy*, vol. 10.

[3] Churchill to Russell, no. 7, Feb. 2, 1861, F.O. 78/1584.

[4] Tillos to Thouvenel, no. 19, Jan. 21, *Aff. étr., Turquie, Bucharest*, vol. 21.

[5] Green to Bulwer, no. 6, Feb. 1, F.O. 78/1581.   [6] *Ibid.*

[7] Eder to Rechberg, no. 32 A, Apr. 16, Staatsarchiv, XXXVIII/126. Eder wrote that both wanted to overthrow Couza, but differed in their motives, the Left wanting to let loose the forces of revolution against Austria, Russia, and Turkey, while the Right hoped for a Russian occupation and a return to the old days when the *boyards* ruled under Russian protection.

[8] Green to Russell, nos. 17 and 18, Feb. 13 and 14, F.O. 78/1581. The precipitating cause was an effort of the conservatives to bring about an inquiry into the Crajova riots with a view of impeaching the ministry. Couza made an overture of conciliation by inviting some of the leading deputies to a state dinner, but they declined to come.   [9] Green to Hammond, Mar. 1, 1581, *ibid.*

[10] Green to Russell, no. 32, Apr. 20, *ibid.*

[11] Tillos to Thouvenel, no. 22 *bis*, Apr. 23, *Aff. étr., Turquie, Bucharest*, vol. 21.

of the conservatives, and thought to form a broad-bottomed ministry, including a few Moldavians, to tide over the period until union should be granted. The consuls, always on the side of the *boyards* (Bulwer once complained that this was too true of British agents),[1] worked with zeal to bring this about; but Catargi's demands showed that the conservatives were bent on establishing themselves permanently in power,[2] and, rather than submit to such surveillance, Couza broke off negotiations, and looked for support from the Left.[3] 'The *boyards* expected to find a docile tool, and they found only a master.' Meanwhile the ministry was actually subjected to an impeachment,[4] and the ministerial crisis had thrown the administration into worse confusion than ever.[5] Obviously, whether one should chiefly blame Couza or the *boyards* or the anomalies of the Convention, the country could not make any progress under the present condition of politics. 'Only the Powers', declared the lugubrious Tillos, 'can save it.'[6]

The Powers, in fact, had only too much reason to survey their ward with solicitude. On April 8 the Moldavian assembly by a vote of 34 to 17 had passed a resolution that the Wallachian assembly should be invited to join them at Focshani to consider the rural question. Ostensibly the raising of this question was occasioned by a project of the central commission (the *boyards*' project, which we have analysed),[7] and by the difficulty which the two assemblies would find in agreeing on so complicated a matter. But, of course, apart from the question of whether the Convention permitted such a meeting, the revival of the idea of a union of the legislatures, even for a specific purpose, was sufficient to rouse the fear that occasion would be taken to pass a proclamation of union.[8] Naturally the consuls were thrown into trepidation, and even Couza seemed to be willing to let France expect a *coup*, for he told Place that measures were being prepared with a view to the coming reorganization, and that he was free to use the information as he chose. On the other hand, he assured his faithful friend that he would not approve the step until he had received France's approval.[9] Thouvenel informed

[1] Bulwer to Russell, no. 171, Mar. 6, F.O. 78/1567.
[2] Couza to Negri, May 24, annex to Lallemand's no. 91, *Aff. étr., Turquie,* vol. 350.
[3] The French, British, and Austrian dispatches are full of the protracted negotiations for the formation of a ministry. After much hesitation Couza took the step of appointing Catargi premier at the head of a conservative ministry, but the Prince could not, or would not, get along with him, and the ministry was dismissed May 22, after holding office nine days. Couza then appointed a ministry from the Left, without including the extremists. By so doing he detached them from their strange alliance with the Right.
[4] Green to Russell, no. 37, Apr. 28, F.O. 78/1581.
[5] Green to Russell, no. 39, Apr. 30, *ibid.*
[6] Tillos to Thouvenel, no. 21, Feb. 26, *Aff. étr., Turquie, Bucharest,* vol. 21.
[7] Page 293. [8] Churchill to Bulwer, no. 19, Apr. 9, F.O. 78/1584.
[9] Place to Thouvenel, no. 33, Apr. 9, *Aff. étr., Turquie, Jassy,* vol. 10.

Tillos that France was working for an understanding at Constanti-nople, and that such a resolution was therefore ill advised;[1] while Russell took similar action by telegraph to Green.[2] There was little doubt but that Couza felt that matters had reached a crisis. Would France really help him, or not? In his reply to the Moldavian assembly Couza studiously avoided committing himself, and merely counselled it once more to show patriotism and prudence.[3] Floresco, arriving at Bucharest from Jassy, said that the Moldavian assembly had only the rural question in mind, and that it was mis-represented when persons alleged that it aimed at union,[4] but in Wallachia there were unionist demonstrations, which Tillos insisted were 'inspired by the police' as a deliberate effort to popularize the ministry,[5] which was then trying desperately, by an espousal of the Moldavian resolution, to hold its place.[6] At all events, a dispatch from Thouvenel, saying definitely that the Porte had responded to the Prince's overture,[7] gave Couza a card to play, if he chose to play it, and despite (or perhaps because of) the favour which the ministry showed to the Moldavian proposal, the Wallachian assembly parried the manœuvre for the present. On the 26th it passed a resolution assenting to the proposal of the sister assembly, but leaving it to Couza to determine when and where the meeting should take place.[8] To the deputation, which handed him this address, Couza was said to have responded that such action might have been, some days ago, of some importance, but, as it was, he was assured from Constantinople that the efforts for union had been crowned with success.[9] In any event, the Prince had been pressed to take action.

Throughout this episode Couza had shown that he himself viewed the move for a general assembly as affording him an open-ing for a timely piece of strategy. The long period of waiting for the fruits of his visit had convinced him that it was Turkey's deliberate intention by her delays to persuade the Principalities that it was the double election, rather than the Convention, which had proved the stumbling-block to settled conditions, and thus—if this infer-ence were accepted—to promote a reaction in favour of separation.[10] If, however, the movement for union were to gain enough momen-

[1] Thouvenel to Tillos, no. 3, Apr. 13, *Aff. étr.*, *Turquie, Bucharest*, vol. 21.
[2] F.O. to Green, Apr. 27, telg., F.O. 78/1580.
[3] Tillos to Thouvenel, no. 22 *bis*, Apr. 23, *Aff. étr.*, *Turquie, Bucharest*, vol. 21.
[4] Tillos to Thouvenel, no. 22, Apr. 12, *Aff. étr.*, *Turquie, Bucharest*, vol. 21.
[5] Tillos to Thouvenel, no. 22 *bis*.
[6] Green to Hammond, Apr. 12, F.O. 78/1581. This was on the eve of the elections.
[7] Thouvenel to Tillos and Place, no. 4, Apr. 19, *Aff. étr.*, *Turquie, Bucharest*, vol. 21.
[8] Tillos to Thouvenel, no. 23, Apr. 30, annex, *ibid*.
[9] Green to Russell, no. 38, Apr. 29, F.O. 78/1581.
[10] Place to Thouvenel, no. 32, Apr. 7, *Aff. étr.*, *Turquie, Jassy*, vol. 10.

tum to be dangerous, it might force the Porte, or at least the Powers, to bestir themselves. Place had remarked keenly that if Couza came to feel that he could no longer restrain the movement, he was shrewd enough to see the advantage of putting himself at the head of it, and thus steal the thunder of his adversaries.[1] By so doing, he could also head off a demand for a foreign prince. But the matter had never gone as far as that. It was mainly a question of scaring the Powers into some action, and even now he did not propose to relinquish his weapon. While denying that a meeting at Focshani was intended to bring about union, he also warned Green that he would have to refer to the central commission the wishes of the two assemblies, and could not delay such action for more than a few weeks.[2] Thus did the Prince eke profit from the dilemma which had been forced upon him. As he had already threatened abdication[3] without avail, his wary handling of the present crisis might be looked upon as his last desperate effort to force the Powers or the Porte to take some action. It had apparently the desired effect. The news that the Porte was at last ready to consider the issue was good news indeed!

It has been noticed that the interest of France had been enlisted for the problem of getting the Convention revised.[4] The British government, rather dubious about the wisdom of 'heaping fresh favours' on the Prince at a time when the disposition of the arms at Galatz was not entirely settled,[5] was at first rather indifferent. But Bulwer was not only the staunchest friend of Couza among the ambassadors,[6] he stuck firmly to his conviction that something should be done; hence, as early as December, he had plied the Porte on the question of conciliating the Principalities,[7] and in February, fearing that Couza would either be forced to proclaim union or be overthrown because of his resistance to the movement, he repeated his endeavours.[8] In the meantime, Thouvenel, who had long since set the wheels of diplomacy in motion, approved the efforts of Bulwer and La Valette to break down the stolid indifference of the Porte, and felt for the moment that the Porte ought to

[1] Place to La Valette, Nov. 29, 1860, annex to Place's no. 21, *ibid*.

[2] Green to Bulwer, no. 29, May 7, 1861, F.O. 78/1581.

[3] Eder to Rechberg, no. 35 B, July 30, Staatsarchiv, XXXVIII/129; Green to Hammond, Oct. 27, F.O. 78/1517. Couza told Green (after the passing of the Moldavian resolution) that he was ready to retire, if he himself were deemed an obstacle to an arrangement, but that help must come soon or his position would be untenable: Green to Russell, no. 32, Apr. 20, 1861, F.O. 78/1581.

[4] Page 306.

[5] F.O. to Bulwer, no. 125, Feb. 21, F.O. 78/1559.

[6] For instance, he remarked that Couza would have been a fool if he had not manipulated the elections, and he justified the Prince's unwillingness to appoint Catargi as his premier on the ground that the conservative leader was pro-Russian.

[7] Bulwer to Russell, no. 841, Dec. 11, 1860, F.O. 78/1514.

[8] Bulwer to Russell, no. 97, Feb. 6, 1861, F.O. 78/1566.

reach some agreement with the Prince before the matter should come to the Powers for final decision.[1] Then Bulwer, it seems, grasped at a suggestion of Cowley's[2] (and it seems also to have been Thouvenel's view)[3] that whatever concessions the Porte should make might be conterminous with Couza's reign;[4] though, with La Valette rather sceptical,[5] and Prokesch opposed to any concessions whatever,[6] one can understand the difficulty of exacting any decision. Fortunately, Ali was not entirely indisposed to listen to reason. When Bulwer argued that if Couza were not given some assistance, he would probably be overthrown in favour of a foreign prince, Ali admitted that some concessions were imperative, and that the greater the delay the greater the concessions would have to be. Bulwer, who liked to speculate on possible contingencies, believed that unrest in Servia and Montenegro made it particularly advisable to conciliate the Principalities, since their geographical position was such as to give them the opportunity to throw their support to any side, as they saw fit.[7] Before a month had elapsed, even Russia was talking of the need of convoking a conference at Paris.[8]

It was certainly a hopeful sign that Turkey was willing to bend a little, and under pressure from Bulwer two meetings of the Turkish ministers discussed the contents of Couza's *mémoire*.[9] Of course, there were the usual hesitations and feverish clutching at expedients. Ali's first thought that the difficulties in the Principalities might be ended, if Couza forfeited one of his hospodariates, was too stupid to deserve comment,[10] while a sudden impulse to propose the sending of a commissioner to investigate conditions was equally discountenanced in Paris.[11] It is not improbable that Austria was encouraging the Porte to dread the consummation of union more than the failure to concede it. Prokesch expressed his opinion that union was not an end but an *acheminement*,[12] and,

[1] Thouvenel to La Valette, no. 9, Jan. 25, *Aff. étr., Turquie*, vol. 348.
[2] Bulwer to Russell, no. 762, Oct. 30, 1860, F.O. 78/1512.
[3] Cowley to Russell, no. 236, Feb. 15, 1861, F.O. 27/1385.
[4] Bulwer to Russell, no. 97, Feb. 6, F.O. 78/1566.
[5] La Valette was a little suspicious of Great Britain, thinking that perhaps Bulwer had obtained Couza's surrender of the arms at a price: La Valette to Thouvenel, no. 32 *bis*, Mar. 12, *Aff. étr., Turquie*, vol. 348. We have already noticed (p. 285) the rift between the two ambassadors over the arms question.
[6] Prokesch to Rechberg, no. 13 B, Feb. 12, Staatsarchiv, XII/71.
[7] Bulwer to Russell, no. 171, Mar. 6, F.O. 78/1567.
[8] Thun to Rechberg, no. 16 F, Apr. 9, Staatsarchiv, X/46.
[9] Prokesch to Rechberg, no. 16 C, Mar. 6, Staatsarchiv, XII/71.
[10] Thouvenel to Tillos, no. 2, Mar. 23, *Aff. étr., Turquie, Bucharest*, vol. 21. This notion, according to Apponyi, received the approval of Russell.
[11] Thouvenel to La Valette, no. 27, Apr. 5, *ibid., Turquie*, vol. 349. The Porte had proposed this plan about a year ago, when conditions in the Principalities might have been described as practically normal, and Thouvenel had then shown no disposition to take it up: Cowley to Russell, no. 627, May 25, 1860, F.O. 27/1338.   [12] Prokesch to Rechberg, no. 16 C.

having heard from Apponyi in London that Russell did not seem
to share Bulwer's spirit of conciliation,[1] he apparently used this
argument to hold back the timid vizier.[2] As a matter of fact, the
British government was leaving the matter very largely to its
ambassador's discretion.[3] On learning finally that Bulwer had the
backing of his government, the Porte, already disturbed by the
news of the Moldavian resolution, announced that it would take
into consideration Couza's *mémoire*.[4] The moment had come, in
fact, when decision was imperative; for Couza had asked La
Valette's advice in face of the Moldavian assembly's resolution,[5] and Bulwer made the point that the Porte's unfortunate
hesitation let it appear that its hand had been forced by the extreme
partisans of union—a fact which also made Couza's own position
the more critical.[6]

The situation surrounding Couza was not yet beyond the capacity
of his resourcefulness, though undoubtedly the long delay had
taxed his patience to the utmost. Some time in February he had
written Negri a letter for the consideration of the Porte and the
ambassadors, stressing his conciliatory attitude on the question of
the dedicated convents, his resistance to popular clamour for a *fait
accompli*, and his innocence of complicity in the arms conspiracy; he
wished for closer relations with the Porte, and begged once more for
the realization of the national wishes.[7] What use Negri made of the
letter we do not know, but we learn that the kapou kiaya had made
it clear that Couza could not wait much longer or he would be
forced to allow union to be voted by the assemblies.[8] The news of
the Porte's surrender may have been looked upon in the Principalities as a victory for 'revolution', but Couza could not have
failed to feel gratified that his passive connivance had been successful. It may have been true that the Right thought of union in terms of
a foreign prince, and the Left, of union by act of the Principalities,
but for the present the question hung fire, as it were, and the Moldavians who had come to Bucharest to join the Catargi ministry[9] were
astounded at the ease with which the Wallachians could engage in
factional quarrels instead of planning for the early fulfilment of the

---

[1] Apponyi to Rechberg, no. 3 A–D, Jan. 12, 1861, Staatsarchiv, VIII/60.
[2] Prokesch to Rechberg, no. 16 C.
[3] F.O. to Bulwer, no. 156, Mar. 14, F.O. 78/1560.
[4] Prokesch to Rechberg, no. 27 A–D, Apr. 12, Staatsarchiv, XII/71.
[5] La Valette to Thouvenel, no. 59, Apr. 24, *Aff. étr.*, *Turquie*, vol. 349.
[6] Bulwer to Russell, no. 312, Apr. 30, F.O. 78/1570.
[7] The letter is undated, but is annexed to Eder's no. 12 D of Feb. 16 to Rechberg, Staatsarchiv, XXXVIII/126.   [8] Prokesch to Rechberg, no. 27 A–D.
[9] Pano and Mavrogheni had come on Couza's summons to discuss the situation
with him (Green to Hammond, May 15, F.O. 78/1582), but they had refused
to take office under Catargi, whose talk of union they regarded as nothing but
intrigue and promising insufficient security for Moldavia (Bulwer to Russell,
no. 43, May 13, *ibid.*).

national hopes.[1] Perhaps it was to hold the Wallachians in check that Couza allowed a bombshell to be thrown into the camp of the conservatives.

It has already been suggested that what the *boyards* feared above all things was the question of electoral reform. If they could settle the rural question (since some solution was demanded by the Convention) while they continued to sway the assemblies, the future might be faced with calm and confidence. But they knew that Couza's attitude was scarcely to be trusted (especially now that a project was definitely before the public), and they had hoped that by throwing him headlong into a proclamation of union that they would render him so baneful to the Powers that he would have to forfeit his leadership—perhaps, indeed, his 'crown'. Class interest, not patriotism, is the clue to the *boyards'* conduct. Dreading agrarian reform, they dreaded electoral reform, which, by widening the suffrage, would lessen, or perhaps end, their parliamentary predominance. It was this, according to Place, which explains the harassing opposition which Couza had had to encounter in both principalities, 'placing him under the necessity of running now to the one capital, now to the other',[2] and demonstrating unquestionably the inefficacy of the Convention. Couza himself saw, as he had stated in his *mémoire*, that a satisfactory amelioration of peasant conditions could never be hoped for from the present composition of the chambers, and the demand of Catargi for authority to formulate such a project had been one of the causes of the failure of Couza's *rapprochement* with the conservatives.[3] As the measure which had been drafted by the central commission was hardly better than a palliative, and as it was almost inconceivable that the two assemblies would come to any agreement, the issue might wisely wait until the granting of legislative union and the broadening of the electorate. The consuls, of course, did not want any reduction of the political power of the *boyards*, and consequently wanted to see the present electoral law retained;[4] but the recent conservative *débâcle* left everything unsettled. The appointment of Nicholas Golesco to head a ministry of the more moderate radicals was sufficient to cause plenty of apprehension among the Right; and the fortunes of the ministry were not likely to be easy. Then came the news that Ali's proposed concession included a reconsideration of the electoral law—this had been requested, as one will remember, in Couza's *mémoire*—and anxiety among the *boyards*

[1] Tillos to Thouvenel, no. 24, May 14, *Aff. étr., Turquie, Bucharest*, vol. 21; Green to Hammond, May 12, and to Russell, no. 43, May 13, F.O. 78/1582.
[2] Place to Thouvenel, no. 38, June 5, *Aff. étr., Turquie, Jassy*, vol. 10.
[3] Tillos to Thouvenel, no. 26, May 23, *ibid., Bucharest*, vol. 21.
[4] Tillos to Thouvenel, no. 27, May 24, *ibid.*; Green to Russell, no. 48, May 24, and to Hammond, June 22, F.O. 78/1582.

redoubled.[1] On June 4 a resolution was passed by the Wallachian assembly declaring that any electoral project submitted to the Powers without the previous concurrence of the assemblies 'should be considered as a violation of our rights of autonomy and of the Convention which has guaranteed them to us'.[2] Such a measure of self-defence can well be understood, since Couza's electoral scheme would assuredly not be theirs and, if sanctioned by the Powers, would certainly spell their ruin. And when, a week later, Catargi offered a motion in the assembly,[3] demanding information about Couza's correspondence with the Porte,[4] one may readily divine the reason. Even if true, as Tillos supposed, that the object was to see if the Prince had kept his early promise of offering to give way to a foreign prince, one may easily perceive that discrediting their ruler was far more prominent in the minds of the Wallachian *boyards* than the need of preserving a united front in the struggle to obtain union. Fortunately the consuls were able to get the motion withdrawn. Couza was well aware that union from within was the only way his enemies desired it, and that, apart from some of the patriots of the Left, the agitation for union was hardly more than a deliberately conceived device for compassing his downfall. They knew that he wanted reform, and that even the Protecting Powers had so intended, and they dreaded what his diplomacy might entail.

It is hardly likely, of course, that Couza wanted any upheaval, political or social, while the vexing question of union was still pending, but he had seen the value of frightening the *boyards* and of thus preventing them from forcing his hand at a time when he should be free to watch affairs at Constantinople. His temporary alliance with the Left had been the first step, and repeated references to him in the press as 'sovereign' of the Principalities[5] may have shown his resolution to hold the whip over his enemies. In a momentary spirit of confidence he thought even of allowing the assemblies to unite to discuss the rural question—a move which might, in view of the friendly attitude of the Powers, do no harm (besides, the Moldavian ministry was conservative), and would pacify the Moldavian assembly, which he was very anxious to keep docile on the eve of union and while he himself was absent in

---

[1] Green to Russell, no. 51, May 29, F.O. 78/1582.
[2] Annex to Tillos's no. 28, June 25, *Aff. étr., Turquie, Bucharest,* vol. 21.
[3] This motion had, according to Tillos, emanated from Moldavia, but it seems probable, judging from Place's observations (see p. 314) that the Moldavian *boyards* were in fairly general agreement with their fellows in Wallachia, and their attitude must be differentiated from that of Pano, Cogalnitchano, and others, who genuinely wanted union and were impatient to bring it about.
[4] Tillos to Thouvenel, no. 28, June 11, *ibid.*
[5] Green to Russell, no. 48, enc.; Eder to Rechberg, no. 16 B, Mar. 2, Staats-archiv, xxxviii/126.

Bucharest.[1] But the design was quickly abandoned for a bolder stroke. On learning from Ali, as we have noted, that the Principalities were expected to initiate a new electoral law, he laid the matter before the central commission (half of whom were, of course, his own appointees), and arranged that an able friend of his, Steege by name, should be the one to draft the law. The intense interest which the Prince felt in the character of this project is shown by the fact that he telegraphed Steege that, while appreciating in advance any scruples his friend might have in the extension of the suffrage, 'this extension is, however, necessary to me, [for] the national representation of to-day puts the legislative power in the hands of those who are opposed to my principles'. Couza bade him consult Place, and bring the work to Bucharest as soon as possible.[2] When the draft-project came before the central commission, it was found that it so extended representation among the middle class and peasants that Tillos remarked that it would make suffrage almost universal, and that the rural measure which such an assembly would inevitably pass would mean the ruin of the *boyards*.[3] Couza's own nominees on the Commission, together with one Moldavian chosen by the Jassy assembly, furnished a necessary majority, and the project was thus launched. 'This sweeping reform', declared Green, 'seems to fill the landed proprietors with consternation.'[4] One can well imagine their terror. The unrest among the peasants—in some places they not only refused to pay taxes but treated the local authorities with violence[5]—was quite enough to cause alarm, and the public interest in the electoral question was shown by a petition at Bucharest, with 40,000 signatures, demanding electoral reform.[6] Mustering up their majority in a last desperate effort, the conservatives forced the resignation of the ministry.[7] But Couza had no intention of letting the assemblies debate the electoral project, if he could help it, and he purposely lingered on the way from Bucharest to Jassy in order to arrive about the time of prorogation.[8]

[1] Couza to Place, May 15, annex to Place's no. 36, *Aff. étr.*, *Turquie, Jassy*, vol. 10. Place approved of the design, provided La Valette was first consulted.

[2] Couza to Steege, annex to Tillos's no. 28 *bis* of June 25, *ibid.*, *Bucharest*, vol. 21.

[3] Tillos to Thouvenel, no. 28 *bis*.

[4] Green to Bulwer, no. 42, July 8, F.O. 78/1582. Doubtless this was also why the majority in the Wallachian assembly pressed Couza to let them take up the agrarian question at once: Tillos to Thouvenel, no. 30, July 1, *Aff. étr.*, *Turquie, Bucharest*, vol. 21.

[5] Eder to Rechberg, no. 47 C, June 29, Staatsarchiv, XXXVIII/126.

[6] Tillos to Thouvenel, no. 31, July 9, *Aff. étr.*, *Turquie, Bucharest*, vol. 21. The demonstration—which was held on the Field of Liberty outside the city—was naturally engineered by the radicals. Both Tillos and Green accused the government of conniving at the affair.

[7] *Ibid.* A vote of censure was carried against the ministry: Green to Bulwer, no. 42.

[8] Churchill to Bulwer, no. 42, July 9, F.O. 78/1584.

Such a tortuous policy was, of course, bound to lead to mis-understandings on all sides. Couza did not really feel any attach-ment to the Left, and if he consorted with them occasionally, it was only because he was groping for a counter-weight to tilt the scales against the *boyards*; but invariably such manœuvres put the consuls in a fidget, and the Powers were then puzzled to know what to do. Even Thouvenel, though favouring electoral reform, could not understand how Couza should support so radical a measure;[1] but then Thouvenel had to depend for his information upon Tillos, who, as the Prince once remarked, saw no further than his own nose. When the French consul imparted to him Thouvenel's misgivings, Couza so far abandoned his usual calm as to show considerable irritation, and threatened that, if they disapproved of his course, he would proclaim union and then retire from public life. Yet, for once, it might seem that consular intervention was almost imperative. Both Tillos and Green were much excited over the reported unrest among the peasants,[2] and, after numerous interviews, succeeded in persuading Couza to see some of the *boyards* with a view to appointing a ministry that would at least not alienate that element any more than he had done. Since the Prince attributed the fall of the ministry to consular interference,[3] it is evident that he was not a man to show personal spite; and the elevation of Demetrius Ghika[4] to head a ministry of some of the less hide-bound conservatives meant, at least, turning to the man who had inspired the double election. Besides, the Prince's health was far from good; he was at times visibly depressed;[5] and his profound distrust of both parties made him feel that no electoral reform was practicable for the present.[6] Hence, having given the *boyards* a scare, he might as well patch up a truce. That this forced *entente* was anything more than an expedient, one could scarcely believe.[7] Tillos wrote early in August that, while it was clear that Couza would be forced to proclaim union if he did not get it from the Powers, it must be remembered that he had steadily worked for this boon, and, now that he was disposed to listen to France, it would be well to end the delay.[8] After all, how could Europe expect her charge to escape

[1] Thouvenel to Tillos, no. 7, July 8, *Aff. étr.*, *Turquie, Bucharest*, vol. 21.
[2] Green to Bulwer, no. 45, July 15, F.O. 78/1582.
[3] Green to Russell, no. 68, July 21, *ibid.*
[4] Couza had first resorted to Cretzulesco, who was always easy to manage, and it was only on finding that the latter had managed somehow to disappear from view that the Prince resorted to the hot-headed Ghika: Eder to Rechberg, no. 56, July 30, Staatsarchiv, xxxviii/126; cf. Green to Bulwer, no. 69, July 29, F.O. 78/1582.
[5] Besides Eder's testimony in July, Green had noted his discouragement when he found that the elections had failed to strengthen his position.
[6] Eder to Rechberg, no. 47 C.
[7] Tillos to Thouvenel, July 21, telg., *Aff. étr.*, *Turquie, Bucharest*, vol. 21.
[8] Tillos to Thouvenel, no. 33, Aug. 8, *ibid.*

a condition of anarchy when her policy had been consistently one of dubious experiments, punctuated by long intervals of indifference?

We must now inquire into the causes of the suspense which was keeping the Principalities on the rack.

CHAPTER XI

THE UNITED PRINCIPALITIES

THERE was no reason why the Powers should not resume in 1861 the task which they had left unfinished in 1858 and give the Principalities a workable organization. Now that the Italians were at last assured an independent state from the Alps to the tip of Sicily (saving only the Patrimonio of St. Peter), it was hardly just to grudge the Roumans of the Danubian Principalities the right to form a firm and compact nation. In the interval of calm which followed the exploits of Cavour and Garibaldi the Concert of Europe could reflect upon the inroads which nationalism had wrought in the clumsy fabric which an earlier school of diplomats had propped up at Vienna, and could now give some measure of attention to the problems with which a changing age had complicated the Eastern Question. No one, of course, could well expect the British to take the lead. On one occasion when Lord Napier boasted to Gortchakoff of the sympathy which his government had bestowed on oppressed peoples, the vice-chancellor asked him why it did not espouse the cause of the Christians of the Ottoman Empire; were there, then, limits to British interest in liberal tendencies? 'These limits (*Grenze*)', answered the ambassador drily, 'are the Turkish.'[1] No such devotion to Ottoman integrity restrained either Russia or France, though Russia was hardly the patron of the Principalities. More active than any Power in the range of its political interests, France was evidently the best calculated to take the lead in that direction. Though distrust had somewhat weakened the accustomed partnership of the Western Powers, Napoleon had not yet staked his fate in the Mexican venture, and, with Bismarck still serving a diplomatic apprenticeship, there was no one as yet to challenge the primacy of the Second Empire. It was always as the arbiter of peace that the Emperor shone, and, as the storms of the present year were on the other side of the Atlantic, it was meet that the Concert of Europe should resume its placid debates, with France to direct their course. In Thouvenel the Emperor had a minister of foreign affairs far more competent than his predecessor, and more experienced than any member of a European cabinet in grappling with the intricacies of the Eastern Question. Bulwer paid tribute to his 'clear head and rapid intelligence';[2] and the patient force which he could muster in order to carry a point had been amply enough demon-

---

[1] Schlözer, *Petersburger Briefe, 1857–1862*, p. 202.
[2] Bulwer to Russell, Jan. 25, 1860, Russell Papers, G. and D., 22/88, Pub. Rec. Off.

strated in the affair of the Moldavian elections. Never, apparently, trying to sway his master's policy, he might be regarded as a brilliant subaltern, so conscientious, too, that he almost sank at times under the weight of his numerous labours, and 'while still young, he seemed like an old man'.[1] Doubtless it required a man of almost superhuman capacity to care for the manifold interests of Napoleon III, and Thouvenel was far from being a genius, but, with Palmerston past his prime, Russell, a bewildered onlooker, Gortchakoff, an uneasy meteor, and Rechberg, far less competent than his predecessor Buol, one might feel that the Emperor's minister was quite the brightest luminary on the horizon. It was he who had interceded for the Principalities at Constantinople— with the result that the Porte at last had made a move to solve their problem.

The Turkish response to Couza's *mémoire* was embodied in a circular letter, May 1, to its representatives at the courts of the Protecting Powers. The Porte began by recalling that, the organization of the Principalities having been the work of the Powers, it had now the duty of calling their attention to any departure that should be made. It then went on to say that ever since the double election the Convention had failed to function satisfactorily, and it was therefore necessary to adapt it to present circumstances. Despite its opposition to the principle, it was prepared to agree to the union of the ministries and assemblies and the abolition of the central commission, but inasmuch as Couza held his position for life only, these changes should be granted only for that duration—'this is the condition *sine qua non* of our decision'. As for the electoral law, one's recollection of the divans *ad hoc*, which concerned themselves with everything except that for which they had been called, shows that caution should be taken that it should not be too radical, and it might be advisable for Couza to draw up a project of electoral reform for the consideration of the Porte and the signatory Powers.[2] Thus it will be observed that, after nearly a year's delay, the Porte assented to the more important of Couza's demands, it being understood that union was to be regarded as coincident with his own tenure of office.

The initial step having now been taken, it remained to decide upon the means by which the Powers and the Porte should concert the prospective changes. The most palpable method of arriving at an agreement was through another conference at Paris—the method by which the Convention itself had been framed and subsequent recognition accorded to Couza's dual position. But France was of opinion—and Palmerston seems to have concurred[3]—that a meet-

---

[1] Ollivier, *op. cit.*, vol. iv, p. 380.   [2] *Documents diplomatiques, 1861*, pp. 76–7.
[3] Flahaut to Thouvenel, no. 58, May 16, 1861, *Aff. étr., Angleterre*, vol. 219.

ing of plenipotentiaries of the Powers would give the affair an exaggerated importance. Besides, there was the practical objection that only one of the Powers had recognized the king of Italy, who, as ruler of Sardinia,[1] had been represented on former occasions. In view of these circumstances Thouvenel felt—and the British view was similar[2]—that the best plan would be for the Powers to send their individual adhesion to the Porte's proposals, and then the Porte should issue a firman embodying the proposed changes. As to the electoral law, Couza might make proposals to the Porte, and the Powers could then take concerted action.[3]

Nothing could be much simpler than this procedure; and, since none of the Powers but Austria was opposed to any of the changes,[4] and since Austria, despite her present discomfiture, was not inclined to put up an isolated resistance, one might reasonably suppose that the matter could be quickly expedited.

But the Western Powers had reckoned without the carping disposition of Gortchakoff, who was disposed to argue every feature of the plan, and, by offering various suggestions and objections, led the way to a protracted controversy over non-essentials. The Russian statesman did not yearn to save the Convention, which he had often severely criticized, but he could not see that instructions to the ambassadors would lead to an agreement unless they were identical, and he felt that a conference was the only practical solution. France, he believed, had been too precipitate in assenting to the Turkish proposals, and this Russia would not do. If the Porte supposed that the Principalities would be satisfied with separation after enjoying union during Couza's lifetime, it was simply harbouring a delusion; the Principalities would expect definitive union, and, in the end, demand a foreign prince. Accordingly, it was well for a conference, if one were held, to face all the consequences of this proposal. The Russian minister impressed Lord Napier, the British ambassador, as being rather put out that France should expect him to follow her lead without demur, and he did not relish the thought that a settlement made by the Powers should be so soon upset by agitation in the Principalities.[5] It was evident

---

[1] This point was made by Thouvenel.

[2] According to a dispatch to Cowley, the British government considered that 'the more regular course would be to convoke the Conference', but felt that in view of probable complications injected by Austria and Russia, it would be better to give adhesion to the Turkish proposals, and then the Sultan could call a conference or not, as he saw fit: F.O. to Cowley, no. 617, May 20, F.O. 78/1376.

[3] *Docs. dips., 1861*, pp. 77 ff.

[4] Rechberg had recently told the French ambassador that Austria's opinion regarding union had not varied, and that Buol had been criticized for having been too mild: Moustier to Thouvenel, no. 42, Apr. 28, *Aff. étr., Autriche*, vol. 478.

[5] Montebello to Thouvenel, no. 33, May 10, and no. 51, July 13, *ibid., Russie*, vol. 224; Gortchakoff to Kisseleff, May 12, *ibid.*; Napier to Russell, no. 107, May 11, F.O. 65/574.

Y

that Gortchakoff wanted a conference,[1] and equally evident that he would make its course a hard one.

The French diplomats examined these comments with patience, but not much sympathy. Thouvenel was ready to admit the logic of these objections up to a certain point, but he seemed to feel that one should show a deeper penetration. There could be no question of a foreign prince without the assent of the Powers,[2] and any conference which considered it would certainly break up without result.[3] An article in the *Journal de St. Pétersbourg*, of which Gortchakoff admitted authorship, discussing the question of the Principalities with emphasis upon the need of autonomy for all Christian races of the Ottoman Empire, led the French ambassador to believe that Gortchakoff was demanding a conference in order to widen the programme of discussion to include Servia and Montenegro;[4] and one might feel that such an inference was not unreasonable. At all events, Gortchakoff did not readily yield his point that there should be a solemn conclave. Learning that Ali wanted now to demand some new means of coercing the Principalities, if they gave further trouble (Gortchakoff had perhaps put it into his head by an allusion to 'guarantees' in the *Journal* article), the Russian vice-chancellor declared that there could be no proper way of discussing such a point except at a formal conference of the Great Powers. Since Austria, if she had to accept the idea of a revision of the Convention, much preferred the French proposal of communications to the ambassadors, Russia's insistence upon a conference was far from popular in Vienna.[5] More serious, as we know, was the effect which these delays were having at Bucharest. 'I believe', wrote La Valette, 'there is no time to lose to come to the aid of Prince Couza.'[6]

Yet the whole month of June and most of July were wasted in this sterile discussion. Gortchakoff contended that there was too much divergence already manifested among the Powers to make any other method than a conference practicable, and he now raised a new objection to the Porte's circular; the drafting of the electoral law, he said, should be a matter of collaboration between Couza and the assemblies.[7] Such points of difference were, of course, susceptible to adjustment, but the Powers were still deadlocked over the initial step to be taken, and, as Austria had suc-

---

[1] 'No other authority than the Conference,' said Gortchakoff, 'is competent to modify or abrogate what a conference has established': Thun to Rechberg, no. 31 B, June 29, *Staatsarchiv*, x/47.
[2] Thouvenel to Montebello, no. 58, May 29, *Aff. étr., Russie*, vol. 224.
[3] Cowley to Russell, no. 745, May 18, F.O. 27/1391.
[4] Montebello to Thouvenel, no. 48, June 25, *Aff. étr., Russie*, vol. 224.
[5] Thun to Rechberg, no. 31 B.
[6] La Valette to Thouvenel, no. 81, May 27, *Aff. étr., Turquie*, vol. 349.
[7] Gortchakoff to Oubril, July 12, *ibid., Russie*, vol. 224.

ceeded in obtaining Turkey's disapproval of a conference, Russia
was more than ever responsible for holding up proceedings. One
might wonder that the caprices of a single individual, however
stubborn, should be proof against the diplomatic resources of the
majority, but, as Negri lamented, one must, in spite of the urgency
of this question, always reckon on the major interests of the
Powers, 'always preoccupied with their own affairs, as well as those
of others'.[1] Then, as if complications were not already sufficiently
numerous, a fresh cause of delay was occasioned by a change of
sultans, since it was possible that neither the present vizier nor his
policy would be retained. Lallemand (now again chargé d'affaires
at Constantinople with the retirement of La Valette) reported that
Austria and Russia were trying to get Ali to revoke his concessions
on the ground that the new monarch might have different opinions
from his predecessor, though it appeared that even the Austrian
chargé saw the humour of supposing that Abd-ul-Medjid had had
any opinions whatever.[2] Nevertheless we know that Prince Ludolf
did try to get Ali to retract on this ground the concessions which he
had offered in his circular.[3] Sorely tried by this suspense, Couza
wrote to Negri on July 18, deploring this new source of delay, and
instructing him to 'submit in the most pressing manner the inconveniences that may result'. As the Prince had asked the central
commission to rule on the question of the constitutionality of the
general assembly, desired by the two legislatures, and as its
decision would probably reincite public sentiment, the complications that might accrue from longer delay were well to consider.[4]
Since Austria had gained sufficient courage to fight union, the evil
consequences of Russia's haggling can well be understood. La
Valette had believed that the central commission would give a
favourable response to the assemblies' action, and that Couza
would be forced to proclaim union.[5]

By the end of July, however, Gortchakoff decided, much to
Austria's astonishment, to give up his insistence on a conference at
Paris—the Tsar did not want, he said, to be the only obstacle to an
accord[6]—and he proposed, instead, that the bases of common
action should be determined between the ambassadors and the
Porte. This would mean negotiations and perhaps a series of con-

[1] Negri, *Versuri, Prozǎ, Scrisori*, p. 110.
[2] Lallemand to Thouvenel, no. 117, Aug. 14, *Aff. étr., Turquie*, vol. 351.
[3] Ludolf to Rechberg, no. 68 A–B, Aug. 11, Staatsarchiv, XII/72.
[4] Bulwer to Russell, no. 525, July 26, enc., F.O. 78/1273. Rechberg, while he
approved a warning which Prokesch had sent to Jassy, seems, in spite of his
obstructive tactics, to have realized the gravity of the situation. 'It appears to us',
he said, 'that the Prince has gone too far to be able to draw back': Rechberg to
Prokesch, June 30, no. 1, Staatsarchiv, XII/74.
[5] La Valette to Thouvenel, no. 96, July 10, *Aff. étr., Turquie*, vol. 350.
[6] Thun to Rechberg, no. 34, July 25, Staatsarchiv, x/46.

ferences and would threaten new complications, as Thouvenel perceived, and France, for her part, much preferred an *entente* among the cabinets which should then be communicated to the ambassadors, following which the Porte should prepare a firman to be submitted to the Powers.[1] Unfortunately the very simplicity of such a course of procedure defeated it. It overlooked the fact that Russell himself, however anxious for an understanding with France, had likewise expressed a preference for a conference at Constantinople,[2] and it is also assumed that Russia could be readily persuaded to grant the major points in the Turkish circular. This, as a matter of fact, was already a vain hope. For Gortchakoff was now demanding that the electoral law (with all its manifold complications) should be considered first.[3] Nor was this all. The Russian vice-chancellor approved a suggestion from the Russian ambassador at London that union should be granted for only three years, after which it should receive a renewed examination.[4]

It is not to be supposed that France would countenance for a moment a proposal which would have the effect of adding to Couza's embarrassment or leading to fresh controversies three years hence among the Powers.[5] Great Britain also expressed herself unreservedly against the plan,[6] and Ali told Ludolf that he did not believe it possible to get all the Powers to agree; besides, he was himself opposed to it 'as prolonging the *tiraillements* which to-day agitate the Principalities'.[7] In view of the cool reception which his proposal had received, Gortchakoff decided not to press the matter further, and therefore wrote his chargé at Paris that he took note of Thouvenel's objections, and that he himself had never formally proposed the plan, but would simply not oppose it if the other Powers liked it.[8] It is not strange that the Austrian ambassador at Constantinople had once admitted that to him the vice-chancellor's policy was 'incomprehensible'.[9]

The proposal to decide first upon the question of electoral reform was not so easily disposed of, for Austria came out strongly

[1] Thouvenel to Flahaut, no. 115, Aug. 12, *Aff. étr., Angleterre*, vol. 720, and to Montebello, no. 82, Aug. 14, *ibid., Russie*, vol. 224.
[2] F.O. to Bulwer, Aug. 8, telg., F.O. 78/1562. Russell may have been influenced by a telegram of Bulwer's, Aug. 6, which argued that a conference at Constantinople instead of Paris would give the Porte greater influence. At all events, Russell did not seem to feel that direct negotiations between the cabinets were sufficient.
[3] Rechberg to Ludolf, Aug. 6, Staatsarchiv, XII/74.
[4] Montebello to Thouvenel, no. 53, July 25, *Aff. étr., Russie*, vol. 224.
[5] Thouvenel to Montebello, no. 82, Aug. 14, *ibid.*
[6] F.O. to Bulwer, Aug. 8, telg.
[7] Ludolf to Rechberg, no. 68 A–B and 69, Aug. 16, Staatsarchiv, XII/72.
[8] Gortchakoff to Oubril, Aug. 6, annex to Rechberg's Sept. 4 to Ludolf, *ibid.,* XII/74. [9] Thun to Rechberg, no. 16 E, Mar. 15, *ibid.,* X/46.

in favour of the proposal, contending that a revision of the electoral law in a conservative sense (one may suppose that Vienna wished only *boyards* in the assembly) would quiet the Principalities, and that it might be well to await the results of such a measure before taking up the other questions raised by Couza's *mémoire*.[1] It is not, of course, difficult to guess at the object which such a captious argument concealed. Austria wanted to block the granting of union, and was shrewd enough to see that this was a much surer way than supporting the other proposal of a three years' delay. Bulwer regarded this as a typical case of Austrian ineptitude. 'She never will look before her,' he wrote to Russell, 'nor, in opposing a measure which she deems undesirable, calculate upon the consequences which might follow her opposition.' The British ambassador went on to say that Austria had apparently never made up her mind what she would do if the Principalities decided to establish union themselves, but that Prokesch admitted privately that probably neither Austria nor Turkey could do anything. Meanwhile the wily internuncio seems to have welcomed a proposal of Bulwer's, that the Porte, while trying to placate the Principalities, should ask for some additional guarantees.[2] One may remember how greatly a proposal like this had hampered the conclusion of the Protocol of 1859.

Of course, Ali would not have been a Turk if he had not profited by all this controversy to further Ottoman interests. While he did not go so far as positively to retract the position which he had taken in his circular,[3] he seems to have concluded that, with Austria on his side, the Sultan might save himself from so complete a surrender to his vassal. First of all, he thought that a warning should be issued to the Principalities of the consequences of a new *fait accompli*, and that, next, an agreement should be reached as to what measures of coercion should be taken if the Principalities should make trouble; he would then recommend that the Powers should proceed to take up the electoral law, after which he would say that the further demands of Couza would be considered, not after three years, but 'at an opportune time'.[4]

Thus it will be seen that Russia, Austria, and now Turkey had formed, as time wore on, a sort of party of opposition to a prompt and unqualified acceptance of Couza's demands. If Austria thought more of gaining time, and Turkey considered that the first

[1] Rechberg to Ludolf, Aug. 4, *ibid.*
[2] Bulwer to Russell, no. 554, Aug. 7, F.O. 78/1574.
[3] To Prokesch, who had tried to win his assent to the Russian proposals as a means of combatting union, Ali had frankly expressed his unwillingness to go back on the concessions which the Porte had made: Prokesch to Rechberg, no. 69, Aug. 16, Staatsarchiv, XII/72.
[4] Lobanoff to Gortchakoff, Aug. 13, *Aff. étr., Russie*, vol. 224.

need was to re-enforce her suzerainty, with Russia the explanation seems to have been the over-fussiness of her minister. It must be admitted that Gortchakoff was as ready to try the patience of Austria as that of France or England. He did not agree with Rechberg that one should try to preserve the Convention or that Italy could not participate in the negotiations at Constantinople, and he had seemed to the Austrian ambassador at St. Petersburg to glory in his capacity for mystifying the diplomats.[1] One almost wonders if Gortchakoff were not quite as much the dupe of himself. He had had little compunction about recognizing Couza in 1859, and now he was ready to speak of Couza's perfectly legal overture as a new *fait accompli*, and thought that compliance with his demands was unworthy of the dignity of the Powers (this, however, after all the Russian proposals had been defeated).[2] Thouvenel seems to have believed that he was secretly opposed to union and hoped by his intransigence to induce the Porte to withdraw its original concessions.[3] If such was really Russia's view, there is no trace of it in any of the vice-chancellor's dispatches. On the other hand, one cannot vouch for the sincerity of his explanation that electoral reform, subsequent to union, would be certain to assume too radical a character.[4] The least that one can say is that Gortchakoff was hopelessly erratic. Bismarck, who was then Prussian ambassador to St. Petersburg, and who, as his Austrian colleague put it, 'seeks always to find in all things, even the simplest things, the most extraordinary explanations', had recently believed that the vice-chancellor was trying to club France into an alliance.[5] But perhaps the simplest explanation of all this bickering was that Gortchakoff resented the long-established leadership of France in the handling of the question of the Principalities, and, without having any positive policy, he found it easy to become prominent through raising hypothetical expedients.

Meanwhile, this fresh protraction of the settlement was wearing on Couza's nerves. Having decided to send a deputation to Constantinople to congratulate the new Sultan, he resolved to commission one of its members, a cousin by the name of Docan, to make careful observations of the state of mind at Constantinople. But, at the same time, he confided to Place, his leading counsellor during this period, that Docan should suggest to the Porte that the question of union might well be settled by direct negotiation; for,

[1] Thun to Rechberg, no. 33 A, July 24, Staatsarchiv, x/46.
[2] Thun to Rechberg, no. 38, Sept. 4, *ibid.*, x/47.
[3] Cowley to Russell, no. 989, Aug. 12, F.O. 27/1395.
[4] Thun to Rechberg, no. 33 A.
[5] Thun to Rechberg, no. 16 F, Apr. 9, Staatsarchiv, x/46. The remainder of Count Thun's comment regarding Bismarck is perhaps worth quoting: 'Son esprit tracassier, qui se plaît à dire et à faire des choses désagréables, lui fait toujours supposer les mêmes dispositions chez les autres.'

if the Porte would only agree to union, there need be no question of intervention by the Powers. In case the Porte's response were favourable, Couza declared that he would unite the ministries, and they, rather than the turbulent chambers, should proclaim union.[1] Judging the proposal on prima facie ground, one might feel that it was unworthy of the Prince's usual acumen; but, if the statement was only a 'bluff', thrown out intentionally as a means of putting pressure upon France, the manœuvre was characteristic. In fact, the only record we have of Docan's activities was a visit to Lallemand, in which he asked that diplomat what were really the prospects of a successful issue of the conferences. The response was favourable, and, at the same time, Lallemand warned Thouvenel that it would not do to discourage Couza to the extent that he might turn from France to Russia.[2] There is no evidence that the Prince had any such temptation,[3] but, worried as he was over the agitation in his country, he felt, no doubt, that France should be spurred to greater action. At one time he meditated sending Negri on a special mission to Paris and London.[4]

Doubtless the position of Thouvenel was more difficult than Couza fitly appreciated. The French minister deplored the injection of the electoral question and the persistence with which Russia and Austria were dragging out the negotiations, whereas France, Great Britain, and Prussia wished to reduce the matter to its simplest proportions.[5] Yet he could not well refuse to discuss a question which had been raised by the Porte itself in its circular of May 1. All the Powers seemed agreed (ostensibly at least) that any reform should carefully guard against the introduction of too radical an element into the common assembly,[6] but the question of what plan should be utilized as a basis, or what agency should be designated to initiate one, led to considerable discussion at Constantinople and elsewhere. Lallemand recommended that a project should be initiated by the central commission, after which it should be submitted to the Prince and the assemblies; he rather wished that its recent plan might serve as a basis;[7] and Bulwer, after some hesitation, appeared to adhere to this view.[8] It was understood that the Conference of

[1] Place to Thouvenel, no. 39, July 9, *Aff. étr., Turquie, Jassy*, vol. 10.
[2] Lallemand to Thouvenel, no. 117, Aug. 19, *ibid., Turquie*, vol. 351.
[3] Tillos had accused Couza of making up to Russia: Lallemand to Billault, no. 109, July 31, *ibid.*, vol. 350. But, even if that were true (and Tillos was always ready to believe the worst of Couza), there is no proof that such conduct signified duplicity.
[4] Green to Hammond, Sept. 2, F.O. 78/1583.
[5] Thouvenel to Lallemand, no. 82, Aug. 22, *Aff. étr., Turquie*, vol. 351.
[6] Thouvenel to Montebello, no. 82, Aug. 14, *ibid., Russie*, vol. 224; Gortchakoff to Oubril, Aug. 4, *ibid.*; Rechberg to Thun, Aug. 5; F.O. to Cowley, no. 682, July 5, F.O. 27/1377, &c.
[7] Lallemand to Thouvenel, no. 111, Aug. 7, and no. 117, Aug. 14, *Aff. étr., Turquie*, vol. 351.   [8] Cowley to Russell, no. 1170, Sept. 27, F.O. 27/397.

Paris had intended that the legislative arm should initiate the measure,[1] but Thouvenel felt that a plan of the central commission, if submitted to the present assemblies, would only lead to endless disagreement; it would be well, he thought, for Couza to introduce such a measure before the united assembly at its first session after union was granted. If the Prince and the legislature could reach an agreement, the Porte and the Powers could then take up the question *ab initio*.[2] Great Britain, on the other hand, favoured an immediate conference at Constantinople. The matter was too complicated to be settled by an exchange of notes, and at a conference the Porte could introduce the Prince's suggestions, as well as any views of its own on the subject.[3] Presumably Russell expected this question, as well as others, to be settled before union was put in operation. Rechberg did not believe that the two Western Powers would reach an agreement,[4] but, meanwhile, Austria was in consternation over Thouvenel's apparent approval of the central commission's project as a basis, which, according to Ludolf, must mean that France wanted universal suffrage; and the Austrian chargé thought that now Turkey would certainly dare to withdraw all her concessions.[5] At this juncture one might suppose that Gortchakoff, who had thrown this apple of discord into the camp, would take the lead towards a solution; but, as usual, the Russian vice-chancellor had so many strings to his bow that he had difficulty in sorting them. The most outspoken opponent of a radical electoral law, he expressed the opinion that such a measure should be the product of the central commission and two assemblies (which he was loath then to see abolished at once), 'in order [he said] to obtain a legal counterpoise to the intrigues of Couza'.[6] Some weeks later, however, he told the French ambassador that he thought the project should be 'elaborated . . . by Prince Couza with the co-operation of the assemblies'.[7] Since, in the meantime, an analysis of the central commission's recent plan, prepared by Giers at Lobanoff's request, revealed its 'demagogic character',[8] one might gather that Gortchakoff came to feel rather less kindly towards that perishing institution. But the greatest surprise that the Russian statesman could have created among the Powers was contained in a letter to the Russian ambassador to Paris, Count Kisseleff, in which he stated that in a desire to approximate as closely

[1] See p. 170, note 2.
[2] Cowley to Russell, no. 1170 and no. 1053, Aug. 27, F.O. 27/1395.
[3] F.O. to Bulwer, no. 519, Aug. 23, F.O. 78/1562.
[4] Rechberg to Ludolf, Aug. 25, Staatsarchiv, XII/74.
[5] Ludolf to Rechberg, no. 71 B, Aug. 23, *ibid.*, XII/72.
[6] Thun to Rechberg, no. 33 A, *ibid.*, July 24, X/46.
[7] Montebello to Thouvenel, no. 96, Aug. 22, *Aff. étr.*, *Russie*, vol. 225.
[8] Appended to a letter of Giers to Lobanoff, Aug. 25, annexed to Prokesch's no. 3 of Oct. 6, Staatsarchiv, XII/65.

as possible the views of France, Russia had renounced her demand for the priority of the electoral question in the negotiation.[1] Thus closed another chapter in the history of Gortchakoff's convolutions.

While Russia's change of front on the order in which matters should be settled was calculated to simplify the negotiation, it yet remained to be decided whether the Powers should give a common assent to the points in the Turkish circular, or whether the ambassadors should engage in an exchange of ideas—at a conference or by letters—before the replies were framed. Thouvenel had all along preferred the former procedure,[2] and Great Britain seemed to swing over to his view,[3] while Gortchakoff (who had expected the electoral question to be finally settled at a conference) contended for the latter course, since the Powers would thus not seem to be abdicating their judgement.[4] In the end, it was Gortchakoff, as usual, who gave way; though the reason was probably because Austria would not deign to meet in conference a representative of the King of Italy, whom she had not yet recognized. But, inasmuch as the long debate had had the effect of tempting some of the Powers, including the Porte itself, to modify the concessions in the circular, one might wonder if a conference could be avoided. Harassed by these interminable discussions, Couza himself was moved once more to intervene. Without knowing of Russia's action, he wrote to Negri, September 9, that the electoral law was not pressing, as it could be settled after the assemblies were united, but 'that which is truly urgent—which Roumanians await with unspeakable impatience . . . is union.'[5]

Although Couza and Thouvenel might now try to keep the suffrage question from swamping the negotiation, another vexing point had arisen which had somehow been begotten of this protracted controversy. We have noticed incidentally that the notion of requiring some specific guarantees for holding the Principalities in check had been broached several times from different quarters, and this idea had already occurred to Bulwer in the present connexion, as we have seen.[6] The Porte itself had made no mention of it in its circular, but naturally, after so much discussion had been

---

[1] Gortchakoff to Kisseleff, Aug. 30, annex to Rechberg's Sept. 27 to Thun, *ibid.*, x/47.

[2] To Russia Thouvenel artfully made the point that he feared that a conference might result in another painful disagreement with her: Thouvenel to Montebello, no. 88, Sept. 3, *Aff. étr., Russie*, vol. 225.

[3] Thouvenel to Flahaut, Sept. 19, *Docs. dip., 1861*, p. 82.

[4] Gortchakoff to Oubril, Aug. 6, annex to Rechberg's Sept. 4 to Ludolf, Staatsarchiv, xii/74; Montebello to Thouvenel, no. 96, Aug. 22, *Aff. étr., Russie*, vol. 225.

[5] Couza to Negri, Sept. 9, *Arhiva*, July–Aug. 1902, p. 386; copy annexed to Ludolf's no. 89 A–C of Oct. 18, Staatsarchiv, xii/73.

[6] Bulwer to Russell, no. 554, Aug. 7, F.O. 78/1574.

occasioned by his circular, Ali thought that he might as well seek compensation for his gracious offer of temporary union, as well as open up the possibility of ending union for all time at Couza's death. What would happen if the Principalities should attempt on such an occasion to take the law into their own hands, as they had done in 1859? Would the Powers be in a position to enforce a return to the Convention—and, more than that, a return to separate hospodars? Lallemand, to whom Ali expressed his thoughts, declared that the Protocol of 1859, which had provided machinery for dealing with infractions of the Convention, had already proved sufficient for all practical purposes;[1] but, inasmuch as the Principalities would not be likely, as Gortchakoff pointed out, to renounce union after Couza's death, unless they were compelled to, it was natural that one should question whether a protocol, assuming concerted and unanimous action by the Powers, would cover such a contingency. Gortchakoff doubted if the Protocol alone would save the situation, and, as he had always insisted that granting temporary union would mean granting it *in perpetuum*, he was apparently willing to accept a *fait accompli* in such a case.[2] None of the diplomats, however—not even Thouvenel[3]—was averse from giving the matter consideration. So Ali resolved to call a conference of the ambassadors to meet with him to decide the question. Austria was, of course, unwilling to permit her representative to attend a meeting at which the representative of Italy was present; so Cerutti (particularly obnoxious to Austria because of his part in the arms controversy)[4] was, apparently, not invited.[5] While waiting for the conference, Ali prepared a series of reservations to qualify the granting of union: (1) limitation of union to Couza's lifetime; (2) administrative separation for everything that did not concern the common interests of the two provinces; (3) a threatening communication for the benefit of agitators there; (4) maintenance of what was left of the Convention; and (5) the right of the Porte to intervene by force if all means provided by the Protocol of 1859 proved unavailing. These reservations, after some revision, were presented to the conference of the ambassadors on September 26.[6]

---

[1] Lallemand to Thouvenel, no. 128, Sept. 10, *Aff. étr., Turquie*, vol. 351. As a matter of fact, it had never been put to the test. Thouvenel, for his part, was willing to consider the Protocol applicable only to Couza's reign, and to examine anew the situation that might arise on his demise: Thouvenel to Lallemand, no. 88, Sept. 19, *ibid*.

[2] Gortchakoff to Kisseleff, Aug. 30; Napier to Russell, no. 318, Sept. 25, F.O. 65/578.   [3] See above, note 1.

[4] Ludolf to Rechberg, no. 77 A–C, Sept. 23, Staatsarchiv, XII/73.

[5] Lallemand to Thouvenel, no. 134, Sept. 18, *Aff. étr., Turquie*, vol. 351; Ludolf to Rechberg, no. 80 C, Staatsarchiv, XII/73.

[6] Ludolf to Rechberg, no. 81 B, Sept. 27, *ibid*.

The centre of discussion at the meeting was the proposed stipulation regarding intervention. The Porte proposed that 'in case of violation of the constitutional act of the Convention of August 19, which is its base, after all means provided by the Protocol of September 6, 1859, shall have been exhausted, and the necessity of resorting to coercive measures shall have been recognized, these measures should be executed by the suzerain Power, and the Protecting Powers should be represented by their respective delegates with the commander-in-chief.' Lallemand, who knew that his government wanted no permanent tightening of the Protocol, insisted that such an occasion for intervention should at least be confined to the situation following Couza's demise, but, when Bulwer revealed a letter from Green, disclosing the fact that Couza had definitely stated that he would proclaim union if the Powers did not grant it, the Eastern Powers clearly won the advantage; and accordingly it was decided that if, under the auspices of an international commission, the two assemblies should, on the occasion of Couza's death, vote for separation, their vote should be the 'point of departure', whereas, if they should choose the same hospodar, a new *entente* between the Powers and the Porte should be necessary to make it valid. There was no apparent objection to the plan of military intervention, on the understanding, of course, of a preliminary accord with the Powers, as provided by the Treaty of Paris.[1] Bulwer considered the demand 'reasonable', and recommended it to his government.[2] Lallemand's hope of thwarting it was probably damped by the revelation of Bulwer's attitude, which seemed to indicate that no accord had yet been reached between their respective governments. But all the decisions of the conference were merely tentative, as the final word rested with the governments, and as no agreement was valid without the concurrence of the Italian minister.

It was not long before Thouvenel expressed his disapproval of the result, and made it clear that he did not like any scheme of intervention beyond what had been provided by the Protocol. As for Green's information, he believed that this was simply a bluff on Couza's part to make the Powers realize the urgency of union.[3] It was evident to him, he said, that the conference had deviated from its proper course.[4] Ali was much chagrined on learning that his pet scheme had miscarried, and Lallemand told Thouvenel that the vizier feared that if he failed to carry his point the Sultan would dismiss him. Bulwer, according to Lallemand, was too deeply

[1] Ludolf to Rechberg, no. 81 A–G, Sept. 27, *ibid.*
[2] Bulwer to Russell, Sept. 27, telg., F.O. 78/1576.
[3] Thouvenel to Lallemand, no. 90, Sept. 27, *Aff. étr., Turquie*, vol. 351. This letter was in response to a telegram from Lallemand.
[4] Thouvenel to Lallemand, no. 92, Oct. 4, *ibid.*, vol. 352.

committed by his past advocacy of stringent measures against the
Principalities to gainsay them now (it was said that he had even
promised Ali his support of strong guarantees at the time when he
had plied the Porte to give in to Couza's demands),[1] and it is clear
enough that the British ambassador had not telegraphed for instructions to cover the points treated in the recent conference. On
receiving a telegram from Bulwer, recounting the situation, the
British government telegraphed him at once that it would be time
enough to consider the occasion for using troops when the contingency arose; for the present it was 'better to leave the question
as it stands in the Treaty of Paris and subsequent protocols'.[2]
Bulwer seemed still to believe that Great Britain was not excluding
the Turkish proposals,[3] but he was reputed to be disappointed that
the opportunity was not given him of devising a constitution for
the Principalities[4]—we already know his propensities along that
line—and, at any rate, he was disposed to give no more than a
half-hearted support to his government's policy. But the slackness
of British diplomacy was counterbalanced by Russia's sudden
adhesion to the French position. Gortchakoff held that the Principalities should feel perfectly free to preserve union after Couza's
death if they so desired, and if, indeed, the right of intervention
demanded by the Turks were accorded, it would be likely to lead
to some misunderstanding; he therefore instructed his ambassador at Constantinople to oppose it.[5] Thouvenel, for his part, felt
that the Powers should have full liberty of action to decide what
should be done when that critical moment arose,[6] and it is evident
that France determined that union, if not made permanent now,
should eventually become so.

The efforts of Ali and his friends to get something out of the
wreck of their hopes were becoming increasingly less promising.
The vizier had had courage enough to refuse a French demand that
union be made lasting, and, with encouragement from Bulwer and
Ludolf, he had clung to his plan of intervention as long as there was
any hope; he even discussed with the Prussian and Austrian representatives the notion of asking Couza to define in writing what he
understood by the stipulations of the Conference of Paris regarding
the source of an electoral law.[7] (Why, forsooth, should Couza be
expected to interpret the Powers' will?). But when he was apprised

[1] Lallemand to Thouvenel, no. 143, Oct. 9, *Aff. étr., Turquie,* vol. 352.
[2] Russell to Bulwer, Oct. 1, telg., F.O. 78/1563.
[3] Ludolf to Rechberg, no. 89 A–C, Oct. 18, Staatsarchiv, XII/73.
[4] Lallemand to Thouvenel, no. 147, Oct. 18, *Aff. étr., Turquie,* vol. 352.
[5] Montebello to Thouvenel, no. 71, Oct. 16, *ibid., Russie,* vol. 225; Napier to
Russell, no. 349, Oct. 22, F.O. 65/547.
[6] Thouvenel to Montebello, no. 95, Oct. 1, *Aff. étr., Russie,* vol. 225.
[7] Ludolf to Rechberg, no. 86 A–E, Oct. 11, and no. 89 A–C, Oct. 18, Staatsarchiv, XII/73.

of the attitude of Russia and Great Britain, he perceived well enough that the game was up.[1] At a meeting, held at the British legation, October 30, Bulwer confessed, albeit reluctantly, that 'his government, without contesting the competence of the Porte to use coercive measures (oh, this British reverence for Turkish suzerainty!), thinks it better not to press the point'. After Prokesch had sung the swan song of 'coercion', Lobanoff, the Russian minister, made known that he had been instructed to impart Gortchakoff's view that the Porte should merely retain the right of effecting an understanding with the Powers as to the 'occasion and nature of the means to employ'.[2] This, of course, meant standing on the Protocol of 1859. The last gasp of the 'Opposition' was uttered when Prokesch (back once more at his post) urged at a subsequent meeting that a collective warning be sent to Couza through the consuls at Bucharest;[3] but Bulwer, instructed once more to stand on the basis of the Protocol,[4] knew well enough when he was beaten; besides, he had lectured Couza himself; and was suffering now from an indisposition which suspended his attendance at the meetings.[5] 'I can only explain the resolution of Lord John', sighed Ali, who had tried to move Russell through Musurus, 'by the little faith he seems to have in the approaching future of the Porte.'[6] Thus, in the end, France, with the support of Russia and Great Britain, blocked the effort to make any coercion of the Powers effective.

While the foreign ministers debated the outlines of the settlement, and the ambassadors toiled over the details, the consular agents of the Protecting Powers had to spend their energies in trying to curb the impatience of the Principalities, and furnishing advice, sometimes welcome, sometimes otherwise, to the harassed hospodar. It is evident that most of the consuls were too much in sympathy with the *boyards*, and too fearful of democratic tendencies, to make their influence felt with Couza, who must have been genuinely wearied by their continual admonitions. But in Place he found a counsellor, who, while ready to criticize the Prince, was even more anxious to help him to find a solution of his difficulties.[7] It was Place who got the Prince to consider more seriously the problem of reorganizing the administration within the limits allowed by the Convention; and, in response to a request of Couza's, he drew up a lengthy critique of the state of the ad-

---

[1] Thun to Rechberg, no. 47, Oct. 20, *ibid.*, x/47.
[2] Prokesch to Rechberg, no. 93 B, Oct. 30, Staatsarchiv, XII/73.
[3] Prokesch to Rechberg, no. 95 C, Nov. 6, *ibid.*
[4] F.O. to Bulwer, no. 63, Oct. 22, F.O. 78/1563.
[5] Prokesch to Rechberg, no. 95 C.
[6] Prokesch to Rechberg, no. 95 A–E, Nov. 6, Staatsarchiv, XII/73.
[7] Place was even accused, according to a report of Eder to Rechberg, of having elaborated the project of the central commission: Thun to Rechberg, no. 44 D, Oct. 4, *ibid.*, x/47.

ministration.[1] Subsequently, when the two discussed the rural question, Place, again at his friend's request, composed a *mémoire* on the condition of the peasantry; and, feeling that the problem was too controversial to be treated properly by the assemblies, he advised Couza to put it before the conference of the ambassadors[2] —a proposal which did not prove welcome at Constantinople. Of more immediate interest to Couza was the question of whether the prospective abolition of the central commission should make advisable the constitution of an upper chamber; and since he was at Bucharest, and had no impulse to consult Tillos, he wired Place for his opinion. Place's opinion was adverse (just as the *boyards* quite naturally preferred an upper house), and Couza consequently decided to propose a council of state instead, this plan, together with the rural question (which Place said was the fundamental stumbling-block of all progress in the Principalities) being accordingly referred to the conference at Constantinople. Couza had already telegraphed Place, August 11, that he had decided to press the conference through Negri to drop electoral reform and give consideration to the remoulding of the governmental organs.[3] He had never, he told Negri, given the same importance to the electoral law as he did to legislative and administrative union, and to bring up the matter now before the assemblies would lead only to endless and futile discussions, whereas under union there was a chance that a moderate liberal party might be formed, around which could gather the loyal supporters of the government. He then warned the diplomats of the chance that the central commission would sanction the desire of the two assemblies to meet together on the rural question.[4] If it is true that Giers actually urged the Prince to proclaim union without waiting for the Powers[5] (such a display of bad faith would indicate some covert purpose on the part of Russia, but the story may be false), one might marvel at the courage with which Couza met temptation. Yet one must not ignore the fact that if union were proclaimed, it would not be Couza but his enemies that would reap the credit from the feat, and, quite apart from whether the Powers would accept a *fait accompli*, the Prince would undoubtedly be swept aside

[1] Place to Thouvenel, no. 42, Aug. 16, and annex, *Aff. étr.*, *Turquie*, *Jassy*, vol. 10.

[2] Place to Thouvenel, no. 43, Aug. 22, and annex, *ibid.*

[3] Place to Thouvenel, no. 43, Aug. 22, and annexes; Green to Bulwer, no. 64, Sept. 21, F.O. 78/1583.

[4] Couza to Negri, Sept. 9, *Arhiva*, anul xiii, pp. 386 ff.

[5] Tillos to Thouvenel, no. 33, Aug. 18, *Aff. étr.*, *Turquie*, *Bucharest*, vol. 22; Eder to Rechberg, no. 80 B, Oct. 7, Staatsarchiv, xxxviii/126. Eder's information came from one of Couza's ministers, and it is not impossible, of course, that the Prince invented the story as one more effort to hurry up the Powers. We shall presently notice (p. 336) that Russia was by no means trusted in the Principalities.

to make way for a foreign prince. Thus a tardy yielding to the popular pressure would have been hazardous indeed. Having determined long ago to get union from Constantinople—having, indeed, staked his position on that policy—Couza had no choice but to continue on that road. 'I cannot repeat enough', wrote Tillos, 'how urgent it is to grant union.'[1]

Certainly, if so many months had transpired without even the assurance of ultimate success, it was not the fault of Couza. There is hardly reason to doubt that the Prince's intervention contributed powerfully to the termination of the discussion of the electoral question. Indeed, after Russell had come over to the French view that that question should be left to the initiative of the Principalities after union had been granted,[2] there seems to have been no serious effort to pursue the subject further. Eventually Couza's plan of a council of state (nominated by himself, and empowered to initiate all legislation)[3] was discussed at length at a conference of the ambassadors, but no decision was reached. It was plain enough that the Prince was making a deliberate effort to strengthen his own position, and equally plain that the ambassadors, while admitting the necessity of some organ to replace the central commission, were unwilling to settle the difficult problem of its precise status.[4] Thouvenel expressed the opinion that the council of state, being a matter of internal administration, could be constituted by the Principalities themselves,[5] a solution which, of course, would not satisfy Couza's hopes. At all events, since his ministers feared that the question might produce some further delay, Couza promised not to persist with it.[6] As for the rural law, the ambassadors seemed to feel that it was quite outside their competence.[7] This was Place's suggestion, as we have noticed, and in all probability Couza himself would have preferred not to complicate proceedings by bringing up an additional problem to be solved.

To a man who saw his vital interests being overhauled, as a buzzard would pick at a piece of carrion, the suspense must have been sometimes almost intolerable. In August he had again asked Place what France would think of his proclaiming union without waiting for the Powers to finish their labours.[8] It had been generally believed in the Principalities that the prominence which Russia had given to the electoral question had been merely

---

[1] Tillos to Thouvenel, no. 35, Sept. 3, *Aff. étr. Turquie Bucharest*, vol. 22.
[2] F.O. to Bulwer, no. 570, Sept. 21, F.O. 78/1583.
[3] Couza to Negri, Sept. 4, annex to Lallemand's no. 149, *Aff. étr., Turquie*, vol. 352.
[4] Lallemand to Thouvenel, no. 149, Oct. 22, *ibid.*
[5] Thouvenel to Lallemand, no. 90, Sept. 27, *ibid.*, vol. 351.
[6] Green to Hammond, Sept. 26, F.O. 78/1583.
[7] Lallemand to Thouvenel, no. 128, Sept. 10, *Aff. étr., Turquie*, vol. 351.
[8] Place to Thouvenel, no. 43, Aug. 22, *ibid.*, *Jassy*, vol. 10.

designed to defeat the whole purpose of granting union,[1] and the Prince himself was probably unaware that Eder, much to his credit, was repeatedly urging Vienna to yield to the Porte's plan of temporary union.[2] On September 30 Lallemand wrote to Place that he had learned of new efforts to force the Prince's hand,[3] and bade him caution Couza against what would be an affront to the Powers, who were now dealing with his interests in a spirit of perfect concord; 'I can tell you, moreover,' he added, 'that the patience demanded of Prince Couza will not be long protracted.'[4] Such encouragement was doubtless needed, for both Left and Right were criticizing Couza for doing nothing, and the Prince was giving the impression that he was now quite indifferent as to what took place at Constantinople, for 'on the meeting of the assemblies in December, the union will be proclaimed'.[5] Demetrius Ghika said that the *boyards* could not afford to let the radicals snatch the leadership, and that it was 'better to be put to death at once than to die of slow fever'.[6] Roused to unwonted impatience by Green's anxious letters, Bulwer telegraphed the consul that he was to tell Couza that 'any infraction of the Convention would be repressed, if necessary even by force'.[7] This message, communicated to Jassy by Arsaki, the Wallachian minister of foreign affairs, nettled Couza considerably, especially as he had just received the communication of Lallemand's friendly encouragement; and he told Churchill that if Green had disclosed the substance of the telegram, as was probably the case, it would weaken his hold over his people; it confirmed his feeling, he said, that Great Britain had changed her policy towards the Principalities.[8] Bulwer's action was undoubtedly an indiscretion, and Russell bluntly asked him on what authority he gave such orders to the British consul.[9] But, in any event, Couza was not browbeaten. When the central commission finally gave its approval of a joint meeting on the rural question, and spoke of the 'imperious necessity of realizing definitely . . . the aspirations for union', Couza promptly congratulated them on the sentiments they had expressed;[10] and when later he summoned Arsaki to arrange with him the plan of convoking the two assemblies, Green concluded that it was intended as a threat,

[1] Green to Bulwer, no. 50, Aug. 22, F.O. 78/1582.
[2] Eder to Rechberg, no. 76 B, Sept. 22, and no. 79, Oct. 4, Staatsarchiv, XXXVIII/126.
[3] Some 'patriotic resignations' of certain Moldavian functionaries.
[4] Lallemand to Place, Sept. 30, annex to Place's no. 50, Oct. 19, *Aff. étr.*, *Turquie, Jassy*, vol. 10.
[5] Green to Bulwer, no. 66, Oct. 1, F.O. 78/1583.
[6] Green to Russell, no. 69, Oct. 14, *ibid.*
[7] Bulwer to Green, Oct. 8, telg., *ibid.*
[8] Churchill to Bulwer, no. 55, Oct. 21, F.O. 78/1584.
[9] Russell to Bulwer, no. 634, Oct. 23, F.O. 78/1563.
[10] Churchill to Russell, no. 36, Oct. 20, and enc., F.O. 78/1584.

since Arsaki had informed all the consuls of the message he had received.[1] No doubt the Prince was playing with fire; but it is not easy to find fault with him. The time had come when he could no longer prevent the joint assembly; yet he wished the Powers to know it, and take warning. When word reached Bulwer that some of the Wallachian ministry were threatening to resign, the British ambassador, acting on a comment of his government that on future occasions[2] he should concert measures with his colleagues, suggested to Moustier, the new ambassador of France, that they should address a joint letter to the Prince. The Marquis replied that he had already written to the French consuls that matters were settled at Constantinople, and that patience and prudence were required; he thus felt that no concerted action was necessary.[3] No doubt the French felt that it was time to desist from clubbing the Prince for conditions he could not help.

As a matter of fact, Couza was greatly troubled by the attitude of his countrymen on the eve of union. Whereas the Moldavian ministry had now the good sense to prefer a separate meeting of the chambers, the Wallachian ministry, on threat of handing in their resignations, demanded an immediate summons of the two assemblies;[4] and, as the granting of union was now assured and nothing remained but the issuance of the firman, Couza was pained to believe that the manœuvre of his ministers (prompted, as it was, by the Wallachian assembly) was simply a ruse on the part of the *boyards* to bring about his fall.[5] It was, indeed, the last desperate effort on the part of men who had steadily hoped to see Couza discredited, and then displaced by one of their number;[6] and nothing more clearly shows the vices of *boyarisme* than this attempt to place personal and class interests above the national cause. For dealing with men of such a stamp Couza could find no weapon but the tangible proof that his diplomacy had triumphed. He had shown consummate skill in his relations with the Powers. He had displayed ostentatious friendliness even to those whom he had reason to distrust; not only did he express his intention of visiting the Austrian Emperor,[7] but he paid a compliment to the Tsar;[8] and when a Russian major was illegally arrested, the Prince not only

[1] Green to Russell, no. 94, Nov. 19, F.O. 78/1583.
[2] F.O. to Bulwer, no. 892, Nov. 21, F.O. 78/1564.
[3] Moustier to Thouvenel, no. 163, Nov. 26, *Aff. étr.*, Turquie, vol. 352.
[4] Tillos to Thouvenel, Nov. 23, telg., *ibid.*, Bucharest, vol. 22.
[5] Place to Thouvenel, no. 52, Nov. 26, *ibid.*, Jassy, vol. 10.
[6] Tillos ascribed the movement to 'pretenders and intriguers': Tillos to Thouvenel, no. 43, Nov. 26, *ibid.*, Bucharest, vol. 22.
[7] Eder to Rechberg, no. 57 B, Aug. 1, Staatsarchiv, xxxviii/126. Once he went so far as to tell Eder that if Austria would countenance union, 'Roumania would in future look to Austria and Russia instead of to France or England': Eder to Rechberg, no. 65 A, Aug. 24, *ibid.*
[8] Montebello to Thouvenel, no. 72, *Aff. étr.*, Russie, vol. 225.

made full amends, but even changed his ministry as a testimony of good faith.[1] Without his vigilance, his tact, and his unflagging perseverance, there is no knowing if even France would have given him her aid. And now, when the prize for which he had been working seemed within his grasp, he was in danger of being thwarted by the hatred of his subjects. It was well enough for Russell to warn him that if he proclaimed union he 'would probably be deposed with the general approbation'.[2] The fact of the matter was that only a speedy dispatch of the firman could save the situation.

The work of the ambassadors had been comparatively easy, now that all the most contentious points had been settled; and France and Great Britain, knowing the critical situation in the Principalities, had done their best to speed up the preparation of the firman.[3] The last difficulty to be got over was that of obtaining the assent of the Italian minister to the arrangements made without his participation. After much delicate negotiation through the medium of the French and British embassies had brought but little result, Rechberg finally relented to the extent of allowing Prokesch to meet Cerutti in conference, if it could not possibly be avoided;[4] but Italy was satisfied in the end by the privilege of sending along with other Powers her response of acquiescence to the firman. The drafting of the firman was a matter for common deliberation, and covered all the points raised by Couza except electoral reform, of which there was no mention.[5] It suspended the central commission, and granted a single ministry and assembly explicitly for the duration of the reign of Couza. Homage was paid to the principle of separation by decreeing the creation of provincial councils for the consideration of laws of interest to the province concerned, by explicitly perpetuating the frontier between the two principalities, and by stipulating that in case of a vacancy in the hospodariate the form of procedure, prescribed in the Convention, should be followed—in other words, the convocation of an assembly in each province to elect a hospodar. The Convention was, in fact, declared to be still in force, except where modified by these temporary

[1] Place to Thouvenel, no. 49, Oct. 12, *Aff. étr., Turquie, Jassy*, vol. 10.
[2] F.O. to Green, no. 7, Oct. 23, F.O. 78/1580.
[3] F.O. to Bulwer, no. 627, Oct. 18, F.O. 78/1563, and to Cowley, no. 1119, Oct. 18, F.O. 27/1380; Thouvenel to Moustier, no. 100, Nov. 29, *Aff. étr., Turquie*, vol. 352.
[4] Rechberg to Prokesch, Nov. 17, Staatsarchiv, XII/74.
[5] Article vi stated that the elective assembly should be constituted according to new elections which will be held 'in accordance with the electoral law, which will then be in force'. The use of this phrase instead of referring specifically to the electoral law of 1858, attached to the Convention, might perhaps imply that the Principalities were free to make a new law, though it was hardly likely that such a problem would be attacked before the privilege of meeting in one assembly was acted upon.

arrangements; likewise the Protocol of 1859 'for cases which have been provided'.[1] Since the Porte had been unable to secure a more effective basis of intervention in case the Principalities determined to keep union after Couza had ceased to reign, it accompanied the firman with a note which declared that at the first vacancy in the hospodariate it would send a commissioner, accompanied by delegates of the Powers, to watch over the execution of the Convention, and that, in event of its infraction, this commissioner would be charged with executing the Protocol of 1859.[2] The import of this threat was that nothing was said, as in the Protocol, about a preliminary agreement with the Protecting Powers. Consequently, all of the Powers except Austria issued reservations, some of which referred specifically to this obligatory *entente*, and all of which, in one form or another, looked forward to the possibility on that occasion of granting permanent union.[3] The Turkish note had, of course, no legal basis according to the conception of the status of the Principalities, as evolved by the Congress of Paris, which had placed them under an international protectorate. Far more important, in fact, was the implied suggestion by five Powers that union was, after all, a permanent thing.

It was an odd fact that the firman bore the date of December 2 (that great day in Napoleonic annals), which Negri had said would be the date when Couza, 'pushed to extremes by his adversaries' and 'worn out by the delays of Turkey and the Powers', was 'resolved to convoke the chambers and proclaim union'.[4] Happily enough, the assurance which Moustier had sent to Tillos that the firman would be favourable to the wishes of the Moldo-Wallachians had enabled the French consul to show Catargi and his following the folly of their antics, and their decision on the night of November 25 brought the crisis to an end.[5] At Constantinople the conclusion of the settlement had a result that was perhaps more unexpected. Hardly was the work completed than Ali was replaced as grand vizier by Fuad; though the story that Bulwer was responsible for his fall, as Ali alleged,[6] is inherently improbable. As Ali's place was taken by Fuad, his closest political friend, and as he himself was given the portfolio of foreign affairs, we may regard this slight upheaval as one of those balms with which a sultan must solace himself when forced to part with some of his dignity.

Definite news about the firman only reached the Principalities when its publication in the Paris *Moniteur* was received and

[1] *Arch. dip.*, *1862*, vol. iii, pp. 102 ff.
[2] *Ibid.*, pp. 101–2.
[3] *Ibid.*, pp. 102 ff.
[4] Lallemand to Thouvenel, no. 158, Nov. 15, *Aff. étr.*, *Turquie*, vol. 352.
[5] Tillos to Thouvenel, no. 43, Nov. 26, *ibid.*, *Turquie, Bucharest*, vol. 22.
[6] Moustier to Thouvenel, no. 87, Dec. 18, *ibid.*, *Turquie*, vol. 352.

widely distributed.[1] Couza, now that his dream was at last fulfilled, seemed indifferent as to whether his people knew the truth. Not improbably he reasoned that his triumph would receive but little recognition from a people who disliked him, and he hesitated to publish or promulgate a document which seemed to make union only conditional on his lifetime.[2] At all events, in his speech, opening the assemblies, December 15, he made no allusion to the firman, simply mentioning his efforts to obtain fulfilment of the national wishes, and the fact that union was at last achieved.[3] Though he was present in person at the opening of the Moldavian assembly, it was noted that he was suffering from great agitation, and his hand shook as he held the manuscript of his speech, though he read it in a fairly even voice. No doubt he had been impressed by the fact that the assembly had received him in 'glacial silence', and Place heard that, as soon as the meeting was over, he retired into the country.[4] Finally, under pressure from all sides, he proclaimed union in the following words:

'Roumanians, union is accomplished! The Roumanian nationality is founded! This considerable fact, desired by past generations, acclaimed by legislative bodies, called for by our most ardent wishes, has been recognized by the Protecting Powers, and inscribed in the annals of the nations. The God of our fathers has been with our country and with us. He has sustained our efforts and guided the nation towards a glorious future.

'In the days of January 5 and January 24[5] you placed your whole confidence in the elect of the nation; you united your hopes on the head of a single prince; your elect gives you to-day a single Roumania.

'You love your fatherland; you know how to make it strong. *Long live Roumania!*

'Alexander John I'[6]

In Bucharest the pronouncement was enthusiastically received: homes were illuminated, church-bells rang, and a military band played in the streets.[7] In Moldavia there seems at first to have been some misgivings, perhaps at the sudden realization that Jassy was a capital no longer; but, when the impressions in Wallachia were communicated to the Moldavians, the tone of things changed, and the assembly voted an address of congratulation to the Prince—an overture somewhat haughtily received. The day after the proclamation the consuls were invited to add their felicitations, but,

---

[1] Green to Hammond, Dec. 14, F.O. 78/1583.
[2] Churchill to Russell, no. 44, Dec. 31, F.O. 78/1584.
[3] *Arch. dip., 1862*, vol. i, pp. 95–6.
[4] Place to Thouvenel, no. 54, Dec. 16, *Aff. étr., Turquie, Jassy*, vol. 10.
[5] These are the dates according to the Julian calendar, still officially in use in the Principalities. [6] *Arch. dip., 1862*, vol. i, p. 97.
[7] Green to Hammond, no. 105, Dec. 23, F.O. 78/1583.

as the invitation made no mention of the firman or the part which the Powers had played, Couza found it necessary to revise the wording of his message before the consuls would make their pilgrimage.[1] The consuls also had a hard time, as we shall notice, in getting the firman finally promulgated, and some exception was taken to the statement 'the Roumanian nationality is founded' in the Prince's proclamation.[2] But the representatives of the Powers might well have overlooked the exuberance of a young nation, rewarded at last by the realization of its hopes after a long period of stress and agitation. Now at last one might fairly designate the new state 'The United Principalities'. To the minds of all the people of those provinces the new creation of the Powers was 'Roumania'.

[1] Place to Thouvenel, no. 55, Dec. 16, *Aff. étr., Turquie, Jassy*, vol. 10; Churchill to Russell, no. 343, Dec. 26, F.O. 78/1584.
[2] Green to Hammond, Dec. 28, F.O. 78/1584.

CHAPTER XII

PROBLEMS OF REORGANIZATION: THE AFFAIR OF THE DEDICATED MONASTERIES

WITH the achievement of political union, the Danubian Principalities had reached a definite milestone on the road to the complete fruition of Rouman nationalism. They had not yet succeeded in founding a royal dynasty—predicated, of course, on the assumption of a foreign prince—and they were still under the not very painful suzerainty of Turkey and the very often annoying surveillance of the Great Powers. But the logic of history must dispose of both these obstacles in time. The struggle with external authority must continue until the Roumanian people were able to shape their fortunes to suit themselves. For some years to come that struggle would be centred in the personality and conduct of their prince, whose leadership, however much it may have been responsible for their recent triumph, was fraught with complications, of which there had already been a foretaste. To the Protecting Powers, who had undertaken to hold Rouman nationalism in leading strings, it might appear that time could make a suppliant vassal into a resolute and patriotic aspirant of sovereignty.

The position of Couza was not less affected than that of his people by the triumph of their common hopes. As the embodiment of union, he had been indissolubly bound to a nation which had never learned to love him, and which knew that even now the enjoyment of its newly modified status was conditional on his tenure and legally coexistent with it. The child of circumstance, he was never able to outgrow its grim exactions. To the *boyards*, who had grudged him his position from the beginning, no ruler would have been acceptable who was not actually chosen from among their number; by the general public, until he had won the object of its hopes, he was presumed to have no other policy save that he should govern with reasonable efficiency, and administer his provinces with a fair degree of equity. Partly owing to the anomalies of his position, and partly due to his own deficiencies of character, Couza had shown but little capacity as an administrator; while nothing better proves the limitations of his leadership than the ingratitude he received when union was attained. After nearly three years of political manœuvring, he had not yet succeeded in forming a party which could hold a middle ground between conservatives and radicals, ready, now that union was an accomplished fact, to work for that inner regeneration which a country, born of oriental traditions, so sadly needed. Yet, with or without the support of the men to whom the legislative power was confided, Couza must needs apply his fine intelligence and his somewhat spasmodic energy to the solution of his country's problems. He had no longer the obligation—or the excuse—of subserving everything else to one immediate issue. Union was attained; he had kept faith with his people and with himself; and he was now free to organize his government on a single unified plan. While morally weaker than he had been at his accession—for he had steadily lost ground in the public confidence, and rooted dislike is far more serious than initial prejudice—he was, nevertheless, stronger in having the seat of government concentrated at one capital, and in being able to deal with one scene of party struggles instead of two and some-times three. Granting that his people were fickle and inexperienced, and that most of the men in politics were self-seeking and factious, the future success of his government would depend in large measure upon himself. Careless of the susceptibilities of persons whom he had reason to despise, disposed to rely too much upon his own judgement on public questions, and often too indolent to give them proper thought, he was, nevertheless, a man of some determination and a great deal of natural ingenuity, and, with all his dislike of forms and ceremonies, he was not without a glowing sense of pride in his position. A very fair impression of his character has been recorded by a sojourner in the Principalities during the autumn of 1861.

'Couza', wrote this traveller, 'has certainly some genuine qualities—much finesse, a brilliant and sometimes seductive intellect, a true probity in a state in which it is rare. I believe the best praise I can give him is to say that he is certainly superior to most of the politicians in the Principalities. His conduct is easy to criticize, but, in comparing it to that of his adversaries, one arrives at the conviction that there are very few among them who could hold the reins of government in hands more skilful or prudent.'[1]

Much as they might at times distrust him, the Powers had been won by his 'finesse', and undoubtedly appreciated his 'probity' and 'prudence'. From what we know of most of his contemporaries, it would be difficult to pick a man among them better qualified for his position, even while admitting his serious limitations.

While in his dealings with his own people Couza gives the historian abundant grounds for criticism, in his relations with foreign Powers, whether it meant governments, ambassadors, or consuls, he showed himself all at times equal to the occasion. We have already mentioned the political role which the consuls had to play—that combination of adviser, censor, and spy, which kept the Principalities eternally aware of the undefined protectorate that hung over them. Every week these agents met to discuss the con-

---

[1] Annex to Lallemand's no. 145 *bis*, Oct. 16, 1861, *Aff. étr.*, *Turquie*, vol. 352.

duct of their charge and shake their heads over the endless political quarrels or the restlessness of Rouman nationalism. The generous store of gratuitous advice which they showered on the Prince was undoubtedly annoying to a man who liked to think autonomy was very nearly equivalent to independence. Yet Couza seems to have listened almost invariably with patience, was capable of lying at times when he considered them too obtrusive, but usually treated them with some degree of frankness, and, only when driven into a corner, would sometimes appeal over their heads to the ambassadors at Constantinople. Most of the members of the consular corps with whose names we are already familiar retained their posts after union was established, though the suppression of the political role of the consuls at Jassy brought to an end the close attachment between the Prince and Victor Place, whose activities are henceforth unimportant. At Bucharest Eder, Green, and Tillos remained till the end of the reign, though Giers was supplanted in 1863 by Baron Offenberg, a less mysterious figure than his predecessor, and also much less able. Tillos's health was much impaired by an apopleptic stroke in the summer of 1861, and he was at times unfitted for work. It is a little strange, in view of the importance of a certain amount of sympathy in dealing with a foreign potentate, that so persistent and so bitter a detractor of the Prince should have been allowed to keep his post for so long a period; it is still more singular that his increasingly vituperative and incoherent dispatches did not prove to the government at Paris what his colleagues readily noticed, that his mind and temper had become affected by the condition of his health. But the evidence seems to point to the fact that Moustier's opinions, after the ambassador had carefully sifted those of Tillos, were usually relied upon for judging the situation at Bucharest, just as the British government placed its chief dependence upon Bulwer. None of the other consuls had the well-balanced judgement of Baron Eder, who left all useless nagging to his French and British colleagues. It is no doubt true, however, that the role of consul in a country where the national pretensions far exceeded the national attainments was not altogether enviable; and, if most of them disliked and distrusted Couza, one might see therein an evidence that Rouman nationalism was straining at its fetters. For the most part, Couza played his difficult role with an acrobat's agility, and not only managed to live peacefully with these unwelcome friends but took their counsels no more seriously than he had to.

With his own people, unfortunately, Couza had no better method of dealing than that which he employed with these foreign 'policemen' whom it was his duty to outwit. During most of the period of his rule he had kept the peace by balancing one party against the other, or occasionally confiding his fortunes to a loosely-knit and short-lived coalition. When union had been attained, the feeling gained ground that Couza's mission was properly finished, and that the continuance of his rule would only mean the continuance of the old game of taking in and putting out. That Couza realized this is evidenced by his long delay in promulgating the firman which might give his enemies a ready handle for complaining that it was not to the Principalities but to Couza that union had been awarded. After much fretting among the Powers over the inference Couza was allowing that union was permanent and unconditional— though it must be admitted that the text of the firman was by this time well known—the consuls received identical instructions to demand the promulgation of the firman, and this collective demand, December 26, was duly communicated to Arsaki, who still functioned as Wallachian minister of foreign affairs.[1] More than a month then elapsed without result, for the Wallachian ministry was unwilling to take action unless forced to by the Prince (they even offered to resign if it were insisted upon),[2] and Couza himself was still at Jassy, suffering from an illness[3] which was probably due in part to the long strain that he had been under for so many months. Finally, on arriving on February 1 at Bucharest to open the new chamber, he promised the consuls that he would comply with their request as soon as the session opened[4] (February 5), and he kept his word. By this time the public had become used to the idea that union was in theory a temporary concession, and the wrath of the radicals had been diverted to the composition of the new ministry. After several weeks' delay Couza had chosen his first ministry for the united nation, and, with a hesitation[5] that one can fully appreciate, he composed it wholly from the Right, with Barbe Catargi at its head. Since the conservatives commanded a large majority in the united assembly, and since it had been amply demonstrated that coalition ministries, composed of elements from

[1] Green to Russell, no. 106, Dec. 27, 1861, and enc., F.O. 78/1583.
[2] Eder to Rechberg, no. 102, Dec. 29, Staatsarchiv, xxxviii/134. Golesco said that nothing would induce the Prince to publish the firman: Green to Russell, no. 4, Jan. 20, F.O. 78/1664.
[3] Tillos to Thouvenel, no. 49, Jan. 18, 1862, *Aff. étr., Turquie, Bucharest,* vol. 22. Green thought that he was deliberately tarrying in order to avoid decision: Green to Russell, no. 4, Jan. 20, F.O. 78/1664. According to Eder, he suffered much from asthma, which his manner of living aggravated, but the Austrian consul considered that the reports of his state of health had been exaggerated: Eder to Rechberg, no. 2 A, Jan. 11, and no. 3 A, Jan. 17, 1862, Staatsarchiv, xxxviii/134.   [4] Eder to Rechberg, no. 7, Feb. 2, *ibid.*
[5] Green to Hammond, Jan. 16, F.O. 78/1664. Tillos wrote that Couza got him to procure Catargi's consent (Tillos to Thouvenel, no. 51, Feb. 3, *Aff. étr., Turquie, Bucharest,* vol. 22). According to Green, Catargi nearly prevented the formation of the ministry by insisting upon the inclusion of an adherent, whom Couza particularly disliked, as minister of justice (Green to Bulwer, no. 9, F.O. 78/1664).

the Right and Left, could not work with any harmony, it was a wise move on the Prince's part to begin the new era with a stable government. Unhappily, no régime could long endure unless a spirit of co-operation were engendered between the Prince and the leaders of the parliamentary majority, and Couza distrusted his old enemies profoundly.[1] At one moment he even spoke of retirement as preferable to facing the future. And, whatever his private criticism of the Left, it was not without some satisfaction that he learned that an attack on the ministry was being engineered from the rear.[2]

The radicals could hardly have expected to compose the new ministry, but they did not propose to let their political rivals believe that their supremacy was unchallenged. Mindful of the tactics which had brought them so much success in February 1859, and eager to make their influence felt at the opening day of the assembly (which was to take place on the anniversary of the double election), they organized bands of peasants to march on Bucharest.[3] The consuls were holding their weekly meeting when they learned that 10,000 peasants were within two miles of the capital, and without delay they went to Couza and implored him to check the movement before it was too late.[4] Probably the danger was somewhat exaggerated, but the murder of a sub-prefect gave the demonstration something less than a peaceful character. At any rate, the prefects and sub-prefects were instructed to employ gendarmes to halt the approaching mob;[5] and, some of the peasants being arrested and held for months without trial, Bratiano and Rosetti resigned their seats in the assembly.[6] It was a pitiful climax of a movement intended to demonstrate the political strength of the Left.

It was while many vague and ominous rumours were floating about that the assembly opened its sessions of February 5. It is doubtful if the *boyards* felt very easy over the situation, but they could not afford to quail before their new responsibilities, and, when Couza had made his speech, closing with a reference to the 'single assembly',[7] the deputies shared in his enthusiasm, some of them even shouting, 'Long live Alexander John!'[8] After the sitting was over, the consuls repaired to the palace, and Eder, as their dean, extended their congratulations, which he repeated that night at a banquet provided by the municipality.[9] It was the last

[1] According to Eder, Couza could not forget that the party contained so many 'pretenders'. [2] Eder to Rechberg, no. 11, Feb. 11, Staatsarchiv, XXXVIII/134.
[3] Tillos to Thouvenel, no. 52, Feb. 10, *Aff. étr., Turquie, Bucharest*, vol. 22.
[4] Green to Bulwer, no. 10, Feb. 4, F.O. 78/1664.
[5] Eder to Rechberg, no. 8, Feb. 5, Staatsarchiv, XXXVIII/134.
[6] Green to Russell, no. 46, May 23, F.O. 78/1665.
[7] *Arch. dip., 1866*, vol. ii, pp. 210 ff.
[8] Eder to Rechberg, no. 9, Feb. 6, Staatsarchiv, XXXVIII/134.
[9] Green to Russell, no. 11, Feb. 6, F.O. 78/1664.

occasion when Couza's subjects, with one accord, paid homage to his leadership.

The first task of the assembly was to pass the measures necessary to make union a reality—a point which Couza's speech had plainly emphasized. Since the central commission had been laid to rest, Catargi was anxious that the assembly should have the initiative in legislation, and, to that end, he proposed that seven deputies should be chosen by the assembly to aid the government in preparing projects of legislation. It was remarked that the whole committee, thus constituted (seven ministers and seven deputies), would give the premier command of ten votes out of fourteen,[1] and it is probable that this conservative was trying to buttress his power in the event of losing office. But the plan did not meet with the approval of Couza, who saw in it an encroachment of the legislature upon the executive,[2] and the conservatives had to be content with their predominance in the ministry. The removal of the court of cassation to Bucharest was a natural consequence of the granting of union, though it had looked at one moment as though the assembly might vote for its establishment at Jassy[3]—a step which would have been backward in the direction of separation, and was thought of only as a means of allaying the discontent in Moldavia. For Moldavia, it seems, was beginning to feel that she had been swallowed by her sister, whom she now proposed to consider a 'foreign land'.[4] Such a phenomenon might be called an odd freak of Rouman nationalism. Now that union had really come, and Jassy had surrendered all its political individuality to Bucharest, there appears to have been some outcry in Moldavia against the change. Added to the loss of moral prestige, involved in fusion with Wallachia, merchants were afraid of losing business, and politicians began to fear that fewer posts would be available.[5] It had been a wise move to appoint four of the seven ministers from Moldavia. Yet the smaller province was unappeased, and some leading unionists, like Pano and Cogalnitchano, were burned in effigy.[6] Place, whose congenial role of major domo was brought to an end by the suppression of the political functions of the consuls at Jassy, became now the Prince's severest critic, and denounced the precipitation with which functionaries and archives were removed without any attempt to make inventories—thus leaving behind incalculable confusion. Everything, in his opinion, was

[1] Tillos to Thouvenel, no. 53, Feb. 18, and no. 54, Mar. 4, *Aff. étr.*, *Turquie, Bucharest*, vol. 22. The four, not counted on, were obviously the four Moldavians in the ministry.

[2] Eder to Rechberg, no. 13 A, Feb. 20, Staatsarchiv, xxxviii/134.

[3] Eder to Rechberg, no. 29, Mar. 28, *ibid.*

[4] Eder to Rechberg, no. 30 A, Mar. 31, *ibid.*

[5] Place to Thouvenel, no. 56, Jan. 31, *Aff. étr.*, *Turquie, Jassy*, vol. 10.

[6] Eder to Rechberg, no. 29.

rendered worse for the Moldavians by the shifting of the political
centre to Bucharest, the Wallachian administration being less
efficient and justice more corrupt;[1] and this waning star professed
to believe that the Moldavians would sever the tie of union were
they not afraid of foreign intervention.[2] Yet a more dispassionate
observer would have realized that transitions are seldom unattended
with confusion. While the establishment of a censorship over the
press might be viewed as a party measure, most of the government's initial programme was well conceived. Catargi hoped, in
order to simplify the administration, to create four new divisions,
two in Wallachia and two in Moldavia, under the general charge
of the minister of the interior, and Couza explained to Eder that,
as the frontier line between the principalities was preserved, the
proposal involved no departure from the Convention or the
firman.[3] Painfully, and after much deliberation, the assembly took
the steps to effect the needed consolidation. The financial and
judicial systems were unified, and the question of legislative
initiative was finally settled by allowing the ministry to appoint
temporarily a committee of deputies as a council of state to draft
the laws to be submitted to the assembly.[4] One of the most useful
acts of the assembly was that of authorizing the construction of a
railroad in Moldavia;[5] and, though the end was a long way off, the
linking of the two provinces by rail would be an immense aid in
furthering unification. Green expressed his conviction that the
Roumans were not, as so many believed, unfitted for constitutional
government, and that they would improve under the advantage of
a united legislature.[6]

It was only natural that the realization of union made the Moldo-
Wallachians feel that they could now openly call themselves
'Roumanians', and even use the designation 'Roumania' on
occasions. It is true that Wallachia had long been known in
common speech as 'Tera Romănéscă' or 'Roumania', and Eder
was not expecting the censure of his government when he referred
to the Wallachians as 'Roumanians' in the course of his speech of
congratulation to the Prince.[7] But neither Austria nor Turkey was
willing to tolerate even the most innocent implication that the

---

[1] Yet Green stated, on the contrary, 'The Moldavian governing class is far
more corrupt, immoral, and innately bad than that of Wallachia': Green to
Hammond, Sept. 17, F.O. 78/1666.
[2] Place to Thouvenel, no. 60, June 14, *Aff. étr., Turquie, Jassy,* vol. 10.
[3] Tillos to Thouvenel, no. 54, Mar. 4, *Aff. étr., Turquie, Bucharest,* vol. 22;
Eder to Rechberg, no. 14 A, Feb. 26, Staatsarchiv, xxxviii/134.
[4] Tillos to Thouvenel, no. 63, May 17, *Aff. étr., Turquie, Bucharest,* vol. 22.
[5] Green to Hammond, Apr. 13, F.O. 78/1664.
[6] Green to Bulwer, no. 17, Feb. 14, *ibid.* Tillos was less sanguine.
[7] Eder to Rechberg, no. 12, Feb. 18, Staatsarchiv, xxxviii/134; Rechberg to
Eder, Feb. 11, *ibid.*

Principalities were for all time a united nation; and, when Couza
had used this appellation in his opening speech, and after it had
been employed several times in the assembly's reply (Couza being,
in fact, designated as 'prince of Roumania'),[1] Austria was ready to
protest, and had, it seems, the sympathy of Great Britain.[2]
Thouvenel, more disposed to look at the matter in a practical way,
said that he saw no serious inconvenience in its use, provided it were
not applied to public acts.[3] The known attitude of some of the Powers
seems finally to have settled the point; for, when Cogalnitchano,
who had come to be regarded as the leader of the Left,[4] proposed that
the name 'Roumania' be made official, Catargi, notwithstanding
the tumult that ensued, was able to quash his efforts by carrying
the motion for the order of the day.[5] Of course, some incidents
are easy enough to analyse. Bulwer gauged the temper of these
people when he said 'they speak of Couza and his throne as one
might speak of that of the Emperor of Austria'.[6]

Thouvenel had remarked that, if the conservatives would only
inaugurate a series of practical reforms, he believed that they would
demonstrate that they were more capable than any other party of
directing the affairs of the Principalities.[7] After the measures
necessary for the consolidation of the government had been passed,
the most urgent questions were those of electoral and rural reform,
and it was to force a satisfactory solution of these questions that
the peasants had been induced to make their recent raid on the
capital.[8] Obviously the conservatives wished for neither of these
reforms, but they knew that the time had come when at least some
measure of social and economic adjustment was no longer to be
avoided, and it would be a distinct advantage to themselves if they
should carry through their own solution. We have already noticed
the project of a rural law which the central commission had framed
in 1860,[9] and it was this measure which now served their purpose,
and which, accordingly, was brought before the assembly, May 29,
1862. Its inadequacy as a measure of agrarian reform was, of course,
pointed out by the radicals in the spirited debate which followed.
Cogalnitchano advocated a much greater allotment of land to each
peasant than the bill prescribed,[10] and his party was in favour of
indemnifying the landlords as a means of abolishing altogether the

[1] Eder to Rechberg, no. 14 A; Tillos to Thouvenel, no. 54.
[2] F.O. to Cowley, no. 183, Feb. 19, F.O. 27/1420.
[3] Thouvenel to Tillos, no. 2, Mar. 22, *Aff. étr., Turquie, Bucharest*, vol. 22.
[4] Green to Hammond, Feb. 20, F.O. 78/1664.
[5] Eder to Rechberg, no. 33 A, Apr. 7, Staatsarchiv, xxxviii/134.
[6] Bulwer to Russell, Jan. 15, 1862, Russell Papers, G. and D., 22/90, Pub. Rec. Off.
[7] Thouvenel to Tillos, no. 3, Apr. 10, *Aff. étr., Turquie, Bucharest*, vol. 22.
[8] Green to Bulwer, no. 10, Feb. 4, F.O. 78/1664.
[9] See pp. 264–5.   [10] Green to Russell, no. 46, June 10, F.O. 78/1665.

annual rent demanded of the peasant. It was supposed that Couza himself disapproved of the measure, but the ministry determined, nevertheless, to put it through, and they had the needed majority for the purpose. When the measure was duly passed, 'every one' (so it was said) deemed it 'impracticable', and it was felt that force alone would avail to execute it.[1] But, anyway, it was doubtful if Couza would sign it if the radicals would come to his aid. Hopeless of defeating a bill in a chamber where the odds were so heavily against them, the Left had resolved to evoke a protest from the peasants themselves, and accordingly a demonstration was planned for June 23, the anniversary of the revolution of 1848, to be held on the 'Field of Liberty', not far from where the assembly held its sessions. Having got wind of the plan, the ministry ordered the prefect of police to prevent its execution.[2] Catargi expressed himself with vehemence before the assembly. He would sooner meet his downfall, he declared, than consent that his country should be brought to ruin by political intrigues. Five days later, June 13, as he was leaving the assembly-hall, he was shot and killed by an unknown hand.[3] It was more than a blow at the rural law. It confounded the conservatives, and ultimately led to conditions which made a dictatorship inevitable. But the radicals (assuming that they were at least indirectly responsible) no more foresaw the consequences of this act than the French Girondins when they brought on the war with Europe in 1792.

The murder of Catargi was a deliberate assault upon the ascendancy of the *boyards*, who had tried to stifle public opinion, first, by a censorship of the press, and then by the prohibition of a mass meeting, and were, meanwhile, seeking to impose an unpopular agrarian reform upon the nation.[4] It was the only time in the recent history of the Principalities that assassination had been resorted to as a political weapon, and the excitement was intense. The consuls, true to their habit of meddling, went to Couza to express their horror at the incident, and to urge him to take all possible means to discover the murderer. The Prince was described as being 'very calm', and criticized the prefect of police (whom he had already dismissed) for letting the murderer escape;[5] what he really thought about the crime, he probably kept to himself. Since some activity had to be shown, Rosetti and Bratiano were hailed before a local tribunal, but were speedily acquitted, and scapegoats were then

[1] Hory to Thouvenel, no. 77, July 20, *Aff. étr., Turquie, Bucharest*, vol. 22.
[2] Damé, *op. cit.*, p. 127.
[3] Eder to Rechberg, no. 52, June 21, Staatsarchiv, xxxviii/134.
[4] The French agent, in recounting the causes of the crime, included Catargi's alleged Russian sympathies: Hory to Thouvenel, no. 68, June 20, *Aff. étr., Turquie, Bucharest*, vol. 22.
[5] Green to Russell, no. 51, June 21, F.O. 78/1666.

made of the minister of justice and procurator, who were deprived of their offices. The assembly voted discretionary powers to the government, which was empowered to place any bar upon the press, and arrest any one on suspicion;[1] but the identity of the assassin was never discovered.

The effect upon the conservatives was to paralyse them as a party. 'The death of Catargi', wrote Green, 'has deprived the *boyard* party of its principal strength. The avidity they had shown for plunder has lowered them in the eyes of the whole country.'[2] They certainly showed no political sagacity at this moment, and seemed to shirk responsibility. Demetrius Ghika, when offered the premiership, declined chiefly on the ground that he did not enjoy Couza's confidence; he knew, he said, that the Prince would hold him responsible for not punishing Catargi's murderer, while, himself, doing all he could to frustrate all such efforts,[3] and he added that he had no notion of grappling with the growing deficit.[4] When others among the more influential *boyards* followed Ghika's example, Couza chose Nicholas Cretzulesco, a rather colourless person, who would, at least, not raise contentious questions. But no ministry could, apparently, count on the support of the chamber, for the conservatives had determined to wage a guerrilla warfare against the Prince. Couza accepted the challenge, told one of the consuls that if the assembly did not vote the budget, he would dissolve it,[5] and, to show his animus towards the *boyards*, he arbitrarily deprived Prince Brancovano, a leading *boyard*, of the administration of certain convents, which had long been in his charge.[6] In October Thouvenel instructed Tillos to consult with Green and see if an *entente* could be reached between the Prince and the assembly, and Russell had given similar instructions to Green,[7] but as the pressure was apparently directed entirely upon Couza, and as the Prince's back was in no way relaxed by these efforts, there was little hope of any reconciliation for the present.[8]

---

[1] Green to Russell, no. 53, June 22, *ibid.*
[2] *Ibid.*
[3] Eder to Rechberg, no. 65 B, July 27, Staatsarchiv, xxxviii/134.
[4] Green to Russell, no. 59, July 1, F.O. 78/1666.
[5] Green to Bulwer, no. 69, Sept. 21, *ibid.* According to his own statement, he instructed Negri to represent that the Convention ought under present conditions to be suspended and a provisional dictatorship established: Eder to Rechberg, no. 56 A, July 4, Staatsarchiv, xxxviii/134.
[6] Tillos to Thouvenel, no. 88, Oct. 3, *Aff. étr., Turquie, Bucharest*, vol. 22. When Tillos had warned him that this act would so exasperate the assembly that it would block the work of the government, Couza had answered, 'If that is so, I will break the assembly': Tillos to Thouvenel, no. 87, Sept. 27, *ibid.*
[7] Thouvenel to Tillos, no. 5, Oct. 11, *Aff. étr., Turquie, Bucharest*, vol. 22; Tillos to Thouvenel, no. 91, Oct. 20, *ibid.* The consuls were much worked up over the Brancovano affair. Green says that he talked to Couza, but got no satisfaction.
[8] F.O. to Green, no. 13, Sept. 30, F.O. 78/1663.

Couza had given his foes a chance, and they had not taken it; so it was obviously not his fault if they chose to be recalcitrant; and, for the moment, he had the advantage. It was said that suits could readily be brought against a great many of the *boyards*, and that the Brancovano case was intended as a warning.[1] In any event, Couza was holding the fort for the present, and, if France and Great Britain failed to move him, it was partly because the nation itself, since its union, was less amenable to guidance.

Strictly speaking, if, in the course of the work of reorganization and the quarrels which resulted, the unsolicited advice of the consuls was seldom accepted, there was, after all, little ground, as long as the Convention was observed, for their acting in a tutelary capacity. In the matter of the observance of the Capitulations, however, there was never a time when these sleuths did not have to be on the alert. The effort made by Walewski in 1859[2] to provide a temporary *modus vivendi* had quite failed to reach to the root of the difficulty, and, as the national self-assertiveness of the Moldo-Wallachians was in a process of steady growth, it would not be long before a question would arise that would call for renewed attention by the Powers. In Wallachia in 1860 a tax was levied on foreigners, as well as natives, for the upkeep of the public highways,[3] and, though the consuls duly protested, there was no apparent disposition to annul the act. At the same time the conduct of the authorities in Moldavia was said to be so arbitrary that the consuls at Jassy presented the government with a collective protest.[4] The position taken by the Moldo-Wallachians was that the Convention had guaranteed their autonomy, and, for that reason, the Capitulations, regardless of the fact that they had been confirmed in that same document, were in effect obsolete. Much of the disagreement came naturally from a misunderstanding of definitions. 'Autonomy' was an elastic term which might mean much or little, but one might judge that the Convention had expressly intended it to be limited by the observance of the rights of foreign residents, as set forth in the Capitulations, which that very instrument had confirmed. Yet it must be admitted—and the consuls themselves were constantly admitting it—that these treaties were not enforceable in all respects, some of their provisions having long fallen into disuse, while others were inapplicable to the Principalities, and still others were of their nature peculiarly susceptible to violation. While the theory was sound enough that foreigners could not be expected to bear the burdens of state while denied the advantages accorded to natives, it might seem that concessions should be made in both directions. Bulwer believed that the Powers should con-

---

[1] Eder to Rechberg, no. 85, Oct. 2, Staatsarchiv, xxxviii/134.
[2] Page 234.   [3] Page 264.
[4] Memorandum, June 23, 1860, *Aff. étr., Turquie, Bucharest*, vol. 20.

sent to yield everything but extraterritoriality[1]—that is to give up everything except consular protection in civil and criminal cases. As a matter of fact the advisibility of revising the whole code of prescriptions touching foreign rights had been recognized by the Powers for several years—it was specifically admitted in 1859— but the presence of more urgent questions and the difficulty of persuading the Porte that exceptions might be made in the Principalities, which would not be thought of elsewhere in the Ottoman Empire, rendered it only too easy to postpone the question indefinitely. In the autumn of 1860 the consuls themselves thought to improve matters by drawing up some rules of procedure (based on a practical interpretation of the Capitulations) and submitting the same to the Porte and the ambassadors;[2] but, as Russia based her rights largely on the *Règlement organique*, and Austria had some special arrangements with the Principalities touching her own peculiar interests, no concerted plan could be worked out; and when Green, at Russell's request, drew up a scheme of his own, it was regarded as much too radical to meet with his own government's approval.[3] Finally, in December 1861, the Powers managed to work out such a scheme, and presented it to the Principalities in April 1862; but disagreement among the consuls had prevented substantial concessions,[4] and even as an overture, the step received no sympathy from the Prince's government. The courts were now extending their jurisdiction even over crimes committed by foreigners against other foreigners;[5] and Couza, in answer to a complaint of Eder, declared frankly that the Principalities hoped to get rid of all foreign jurisdiction. To Green he remarked tartly that he 'had no knowledge of the Capitulations, he had never read them, and he had no intention of so doing'.[6]

Always sensitive about their national rights, the Moldo-Wallachians were, in fact, bound to become involved with the Powers over restrictions which had come down from the days when the national spirit was as yet unawakened. To obliterate such legacies of the past was but a matter of time and resolution. And, now that the Principalities, united in their strength, were beginning to attack their domestic problems, there was no avoiding the question of the dedicated monasteries—a question which not only touched the national pride, but affected the financial capacity of the State.

[1] Bulwer to Russell, no. 226, Apr. 30, 1862, F.O. 78/1650.
[2] Green to Hornsby, no. 1, Jan. 9, F.O. 78/1664.
[3] Green to Bulwer, no. 29, Apr. 8, F.O. 78/1665.
[4] On one occasion the Russian consul at Jassy had been instructed not to join the other consuls, on the ground that it was desirable not to aggravate Couza's difficulties under the new régime: Eder to Prokesch, Jan. 11, annex to Prokesch's Feb. 5, Staatsarchiv, xii/76.   [5] Green to Bulwer, no. 29.
[6] Green to Bulwer, no. 83, Sept. 13, F.O. 78/1666.

It was perhaps partly their good fortune in escaping punishment for the circumstances of the arms crisis (to be mentioned later) that disposed Couza and his compatriots to try to enforce a settlement of this question, which had more or less racked the peace of the Principalities for more than thirty years. In Wallachia and Moldavia, as in other lands where the Orthodox Church held sway, a vast amount of property was held by monasteries, which in centuries past had been endowed by some prince or private individual. In Wallachia almost a quarter of the entire acreage of the country was said to be in their possession, and in Moldavia about a third.[1] We have no reliable data on which to estimate the extent of the revenues drawn from this land, and, in any event, the amount would be subject to fluctuation, but one can readily infer that they constituted an immense proportion of the liquidated wealth of these provinces. These foundations were supposed, however, to provide schools, hospitals, orphanages, and other eleemosynary services, which, as in most of Europe before the nineteenth century, were inadequately provided by the State. It was naturally the desire of the princes to make them contribute directly to the support of the State, but, being intermittently accorded the protection of Russia, the monks were usually able to resist such encroachments. Finally, by the *Règlement organique*, the revenues of those monasteries which were under native administration were submitted to the control of the minister of worship, who farmed out the collection every five years at public auction; and the fixing of these contracts was notoriously an occasion for gross political corruption. It is also clear that less than a third of the revenues was even nominally delegated to the social and religious work for which the monasteries were founded.[2] The bulk of this wealth, since 1834, was at the disposal of the State.

A very large proportion of these foundations were not, however, under native administration, but were known as the 'dedicated monasteries'—that is, dedicated to the so-called 'Holy Places',[3] the latter designation being applied to various foundations, like the Monastery of Mount Athos, all of which were situated in other parts of the Ottoman Empire, and which drew most of their support from the Danubian Principalities. This pious alienation of landed wealth had often been the act of the founder (either a prince or some *boyard*), though more often, it appeared, the process of

---

[1] Prokesch to Rechberg, no. 31 B, Apr. 16, 1863, Staatsarchiv, XII/119.

[2] Report of the international commission of 1858, *Actes et docs.*, vol. vi, part 2, pp. 630–1.

[3] It was said that the dedication was originally inspired by the desire in an age of violence to protect these monasteries by placing them under the patronage of the Holy Places: Bengesco, *Mémorandum sur les églises, les biens conventuels, et spécialement sur les monastères dédiés de la principauté de Walachie*, pp. 10–11.

dedication had been an act of donation by some prince of a monastery which had nominally been subject to the State. In any event, it was always presumed that the local humanitarian work, for which these establishments had been founded, should receive precedence, and only the surplus should be sent out of the country to the Holy Places. As a matter of fact, the philanthropic work of these monasteries was largely a dead letter; the churches were often allowed to fall into disrepair; and the monks were prone to live a life of ease, quite regardless of the needs of the native population. The fact that they were administered by certain Greeks, known as hegumens, sent thither by the Holy Places, was an additional cause of dissatisfaction. But the chief ground for criticism was the drain of a great portion of the national wealth for the support of religious communities outside the country, and one might reasonably wonder how large a proportion of the spoil went to enrich the private purses of certain foreign ecclesiastics.[1]

After the Phanariot régime, when the Moldo-Wallachians were ruled once more by native hospodars, an effort was made to levy on the revenues of the dedicated monasteries for the support of the State, but, as this was still in the period when Russian influence was predominant, and as Russia looked upon the Greek clergy as one of the chief agencies of her power,[2] it was always possible for the monasteries to get their protector to interfere—usually through the medium of the suzerain Power. When, however, Count Kisse-leff undertook the reorganization of the Principalities, he was statesman enough to see that some concession should be made to native feeling. The monasteries must yield a quarter of their revenues for public services; and a commission was appointed (partly of monks, partly of representatives of the provinces) to work out a detailed settlement. Unfortunately no *entente* could be reached, because the monks did not want one; and even Russia could not seem to prevent the gross neglect of the work to which the monasteries had been dedicated. Then, when Bibesco tried to exact a share of these revenues (nominally for this end), he was intercepted by Russia, who decided (in 1843) that the monasteries should be given ten years' respite, during which they should be exempt from any exactions by the State, though it was expected —and the expectation was not fulfilled—that they would repair their churches and perform their social duties.[3] At the expiration

[1] It was charged that much of the money was passed into the hands of Russia during the Crimean War: Mülinen to Rechberg, no. 41 c, Oct. 1, 1863, Staats-archiv, XII/119.

[2] It was said to have been customary for the Russian government to treat the monks as Russian subjects, and to grant them the protection of her consulate: Anon., *Question économique des principautés danubiennes*, p. 80.

[3] It was understood that they were to keep their buildings in repair, devoting a quarter of their revenues for this purpose, and thereafter to expend two million

of this period Stirbey made an effort to levy on these establishments,[1] but with no better luck than his brother had experienced.
Certain private individuals benefited, however, as, ever since 1851,
the collection of the revenues were farmed out to capitalists on
nine-year leases, and, the lands being now better administered,
brought a rich return to the foundations themselves. The cessation
of the Russian protectorate brought no immediate change. The
contracts of the farmers of the revenues were customarily put up
(as had become the case with the *couvents non-dédiés*) at public
auction, and the only exercise of the State's power was applied in
giving its approval of, or modifying, the terms of the contract.
This right was, of course, never recognized by the monasteries,
and remained a bone of contention.

The really vital question was, however, still unsettled. Even
granting that a quarter of the revenues was directed to the purposes
for which they were intended, the fact remains that most of the
best lands (approximately one-eighth of the acreage of the Principalities)[2] were far from contributing to the public needs in
proportion to their wealth, and most of this immense spoil was
being reaped by a privileged class, who were not even natives of
the country. Had the patriarchs and other religious chiefs been
reasonably faithful to the purposes of the founders of these institutions and regularly expended a fair portion of these revenues on
charitable work within the Principalities, the Moldo-Wallachians,
relieved thereby of much of the responsibility of providing schools
and hospitals, might have let the matter rest; but it is evident that
these monasteries were little more than money-making agencies for
foreign corporations, which acknowledged no obligations for the
benefits they received. When it is considered that the Principalities were a backward country, whose citizens—even the *boyards*—
were relatively poor, and, when it is also realized that the administration of both principalities was nominally in the hands of men of
small experience and even smaller sense of public integrity, one
may judge of the temptation to despoil these rich establishments
for the ordinary needs of the treasury. The question had many
sides, legal, moral, and practical, and the number of interests
involved, together with the varying terms of the donations, made
the problem peculiarly intricate and vexatious.

Such a question seems on the face of it more internal than
external, but, as Russia had long made it an object of her special
interest, and, as there was danger that she might aggravate the

piasters annually on charitable work: *Arch. dip., 1864*, vol. ii, pp. 256 ff. In 1851
the Russian government gave instructions that a quarter of their revenues should
be designated to this end: *ibid.*, pp. 259 ff.

[1] Stirbey's purpose was to lessen the public debt.
[2] *Actes et docs.*, vol. vi, part 2, p. 633.

situation by intrigue, if the question were not subjected to international action, it behoved the Protecting Powers to give it some
consideration. Doubtless few of their foreign ministers had ever
heard of the vexing question until the report of the international
commission, provided by the Congress of Paris, was perused by
the plenipotentiaries who met in 1858 to grant the country a constitution. The report of this commission devoted several pages to
classifying the monasteries and, in particular, to discussing the
status of those which had been 'dedicated'.[1] The majority of the
commissioners signified their belief that, in accordance with the
terms of these foundations or donations, the prime object of the
resources of these monasteries should be the conduct of social
work, the balance of the revenues being then due to the institutions
to which they were dedicated. They even went so far as to suggest
that the State should administer all these revenues against a fixed
annual sum to be paid the Holy Places. Unhappily, the plenipotentiaries at the Conference thought they had enough to do in
adjusting the quarrels among themselves without giving much
thought to a question of which they had never heard before; and
it was at the instance of Russia that a process of adjustment was
mapped out, and embodied in protocol 13 of the Conference.[2]
This process, by which a solution of the difficulties was to be
reached, was as follows:

'The interested parties shall be invited to come to an understanding
among themselves by means of a compromise; in case they do not
succeed in coming to an understanding in a year's time, it will be settled
by means of arbitration. In case the arbiters do not succeed in coming
to an understanding, they will choose an over-arbiter. If, in turn, they
find it impossible to agree on the choice of this over-arbiter, the Sublime
Porte will confer with the Protecting Powers for the purpose of designating one.'[3]

Unfortunately, the difficult period of transition through which
the Principalities were passing during the following year prevented
any effort to put the scheme in operation. On the contrary, during
the spring of 1859, the Wallachian government proposed to levy
directly upon the monasteries the fourth part of their revenues for
the fulfilment of their duties. Of course, the hegumens were
thrown into consternation, and, when they demurred, were

---

[1] *Ibid.*, pp. 629–39.
[2] It may be mentioned that the Russian plenipotentiary at the Conference—
none other than Kisseleff himself—had recommended that the Conference
should determine the portion of the revenues to be allocated to the native social
needs, but that Hübner, the Austrian, had persuaded the Conference to have
recourse to an arbitral commission. No great heed was paid to the Commission's
report, because the Conference had been unwilling to reflect on Russia's interest
in the monasteries: Hübner to Buol, no. 79 A–B, Aug. 4, 1858, Staatsarchiv,
IX/58.   [3] *British and Foreign State Papers*, vol. xlviii, p. 105.

promptly threatened with expulsion if they did not comply.[1] Nevertheless, in deference to a protest from the Russian consul, and probably because he had too much at stake just then to disoblige the Powers, Couza refrained from sanctioning the measure;[2] and, at the meeting of the diplomats at Paris shortly afterwards, it was decided in the protocol of September 6 that, as the state of uncertainty in the Principalities had so far prevented a settlement, the year of negotiation between the litigants should be considered as beginning from the time of the Prince's investiture.[3] It is hard to see how, even now, any friendly adjustment could be expected. The Principalities had long considered that these lands were really the property of the State, and should be administered accordingly. The representatives of the Holy Places, on the other hand, held that such foundations were entirely outside of State control. If the governments of the two Principalities were to receive the revenues, even on the specific ground of allocating them to philanthropic ends, there was every reason to suppose that as much corruption would be practiced as was notoriously the case with the undedicated monasteries, whose revenues were so administered. On the other hand, the governments had every ground for charging the Holy Places with fraud and peculation.[4] In an affair where self-interest and suspicion were equally predominant, what chance was there of compromise? It is obvious that the Powers had simply begged the question.

Nevertheless, on January 22, 1860, the Holy Places were invited to choose representatives to confer with representatives of the two governments to try to effect a settlement. Then in May—before a negotiation had even been started—a crisis was suddenly precipitated, when the farmers of the revenues of monastic lands in Wallachia requested the Wallachian government that either their contracts (written for five years) should terminate, or their obligations be reduced, as, owing to economic depression, they were threatened with ruin. Couza, in spite of the Russian consul's insistence that the prince alone had the right to act in the matter,[5] allowed the Wallachian chamber to make the desired reduction, which, of course, drew protests from the hegumens that such

[1] Colquhoun to Bulwer, no. 97, May 27, 1859, F.O. 78/1442.
[2] Eder to Rechberg, no. 46 B, May 28, Staatsarchiv, XXXVIII/119.
[3] *British and Foreign State Papers*, vol. xlxix, p. 458.
[4] Even Bulwer, whose sympathies were certainly not with the Principalities in this controversy, charged a great number of the monasteries with wilfully neglecting their work and treating the income 'as if it was their own': Bulwer to Russell, no. 393, Aug. 25, 1863, F.O. 78/1738. A member of the Wallachian government declared that the Holy Places had often invoked official action against dishonest hegumens: Ghika to Tillos, Mar. 12, 1863, *Aff. étr., Turquie, Bucharest*, vol. 23.
[5] Hory to Thouvenel, no. 24, May 15, 1860, *Aff. étr., Turquie, Bucharest*, vol. 20.

action violated the rights of property.[1] But worse was to follow. In Moldavia, under the premiership of Cogalnitchano, it was planned not only to reduce rentals but to take a complete inventory of the property in dispute and to exact a fourth part of the accumulated revenues since Stirbey's abortive effort in 1853. In response to the bitter protests of the monks, Cogalnitchano merely replied that they could leave the country if they did not like his measures.[2] Since it was clear that the Principalities, influenced no doubt in some measure by the economic crisis,[3] were bent on seeking a unilateral solution of this problem, some intervention on the part of the Powers seemed imperative; and the Porte, after consultation with the ambassadors, sent a remonstrance to Couza,[4] who, while deeply resenting the interference,[5] promised finally that he would not approve the action of the Wallachian chamber, and he kept his word.[6] But when, subsequently, the same body voted to impose a tax of ten per cent. on these unwelcome foundations,[7] it was clear that the Principalities were as incorrigible as ever.

The only hope of obtaining peace in a struggle which was so far of little interest to the Powers was in the year of negotiation, as provided by the Protocol. It is true that Couza had by this time appointed delegates to represent his two governments in conference with the hegumens, but it seemed apparent that these delegates (both radicals) were in no hurry to exercise their functions,[8] and months passed without a meeting. Finally, the representatives of the monasteries tendered a formal complaint to the consular agents of the Powers that, when they arrived in Bucharest in July, as they had been invited to do, they had found no one with whom to confer;[9] and the Wallachian minister of foreign affairs surprised Green by taking the position that the Protocol was simply a record of deliberations, and was in no wise binding upon the Principalities, to which it had never been formally communicated; he added, moreover, that the recognition of the autonomy of the Principali-

---

[1] Hory to Thouvenel, no. 25, May 17, *ibid.* Had the assembly confined its action to the undedicated monasteries, it is not clear that it would have been illegal, but it knew that public opinion would be opposed to any discrimination, and so both types had been affected by the proposed legislation: Tillos to Thouvenel, no. 11, Nov. 26, *ibid.*, vol. 21.

[2] Xénopol, *Domnia lui Cuza-Voda*, vol. i, pp. 318–19. Cf. Nilos to Thouvenel, June 24, *Aff. étr., Turquie, Bucharest*, vol. 20. Cogalnitchano had already forced the auctions of the farms for collecting these revenues to be held under the aegis of the minister of worship; and, mindful of their neglected duties, he had compelled the monasteries to take charge of a public asylum for imbeciles.

[3] See pp. 243, 265.

[4] *Arch. dip., 1864*, vol. ii, pp. 165–6.

[5] Tillos to Thouvenel, no. 5, Sept. 22, *Aff. étr., Turquie, Bucharest*, vol. 21.

[6] Tillos to Thouvenel, no. 9, Nov. 13, *ibid.*

[7] Green to Russell, no. 68, Nov. 1, F.O. 78/1517.

[8] Hory to Thouvenel, no. 43, Aug. 1, *Aff. étr., Turquie, Bucharest*, vol. 21.

[9] *Arch. dip., 1864*, vol. ii, p. 167.

ties, inscribed in the Convention, guaranteed them against such interference in their internal affairs.[1] When nearly a year had elapsed without any prospect of a settlement by direct negotiation, France and Russia took the initiative in recommending that the question be referred to arbitration,[2] and on December 25, 1860 Ali invited Couza to send two delegates to serve on a commission with two representatives of the Holy Places to meet at Constantinople, it being understood that six months should be allowed them to reach a settlement.[3] But once again the result was inaction. Couza did not approve of Constantinople as the place of meeting[4]—probably because it would be outside the realm of his interference—and, in spite of a remonstrance from Ali,[5] he made no move to appoint the delegates of the Principalities on the commission. Thus the question had dragged on without result up to the time when the Principalities were united under one government.

It was Russia who brought the matter anew before the Powers at the beginning of the new year. At the instance of her minister at Constantinople, the Porte was requested by the diplomatic corps to make a final effort to bring the parties to terms.[6] A week later, on January 11, 1862, the British ambassador informed his colleagues that Negri had spoken hopefully of a compromise, and it was decided at Bulwer's suggestion that the litigants should have until the end of April to reach a friendly settlement, but that, if no accommodation were obtained by that time, the question should be referred to arbitration.[7] Of course, now that the problem of union had ceased to engross the attention of the Moldo-Wallachians, and inasmuch as questions of inner reorganization were urgently demanding action, there was reason to hope that the Principalities might be persuaded to seek a settlement. Indeed, the Catargi ministry, after some more urgent matters were disposed of, were quite willing to take a glance at the monasteries, and were reputed to be in favour of a compromise.[8] But the pride of nationalism had grown apace since the attainment of union, and the action which the government finally took scarcely savoured of a friendly negotiation. It was decided to appoint a commission to investigate the question of the monasteries, and an invitation was sent to the representatives of the Holy Places to send delegates to appear before that body, bringing with them all documents which might

[1] Green to Russell, no. 39, July 27, F.O. 78/1576.
[2] Thouvenel to La Valette, no. 100, Dec. 6, *Aff. étr., Turquie*, vol. 347
[3] Ali to Couza, Dec. 25, *Arch. dip., 1864*, vol. ii, p. 176.
[4] Green to Russell, no. 15, Feb. 12, 1861, F.O. 78/1581.
[5] *Arch. dip., 1864*, vol. ii, pp. 176-7.
[6] Prokesch to Rechberg, no. 3 A–B, Jan. 10, 1862, Staatsarchiv, XII/195.
[7] Prokesch to Rechberg, no. 33 A–B, Apr. 23, 1863, *ibid.*, XII/119.
[8] Tillos to Thouvenel, no. 52, Feb. 10, 1862, *Aff. étr., Turquie, Bucharest*, vol. 22.

be calculated to throw light on the status of the monasteries.[1] Taking advantage of the fact that the period of negotiation granted by the Powers was about to end, the religious communities declined the invitation.[2] It was said that Catargi now tried through Negri to get the period of negotiation extended,[3] but, whether or not the monks put greater pressure on the Porte, Ali proposed to the ambassadors that the period of arbitration should now commence, and that Couza should again be summoned to send his delegates. This plan was approved by the ambassadors at a meeting on May 31,[4] and the vizirial letter was duly dispatched to Couza.

Naturally enough, the sentiment of a stubborn and rather egotistical public sentiment was roused by this frustration of the government's plan; and feeling ran so high in the assembly that one of the ministers once more denounced the Protocol as not binding on the Principalities.[5] Moreover, to show that this was not an empty boast, an extraordinary tax was levied by the assembly on the lands of the dedicated monasteries.[6] Nor was this all. A month later, when it was learned that the monasteries had appointed the archimandrite, Nilos, to represent them on the arbitral commission, he was at once deprived of his post as hegumen of two of the monasteries, and Green proceeded to warn Bulwer that Couza was aiming at independence.[7] While the British consul was doubtless premature in the expression of his fears, the behaviour of the Moldo-Wallachian government and assembly might well be construed as a challenge to the Powers.

In the face of this display of nationalist self-assertion, the Powers showed little sign of uniting in any measure of coercion. Russia, it is true, wanted identical instructions to be sent to the consuls to put pressure upon Couza,[8] but, while the governments proved willing[9]—or at least nominally so—the drafting of the instructions was the duty of the ambassadors, and Prokesch hinted that Moustier prevented any decision.[10] Once again, the comedy of an international protectorate was being played before spectators that knew

[1] *Arch. dip.*, *1864*, vol. ii, pp. 180–1.
[2] *Ibid.*, pp. 181–2. The monasteries contended that this action was contrary to the protocol: Green to Bulwer, no. 35, enc., May 1, F.O. 78/1665.
[3] Tillos to Thouvenel, no. 62, May 5, *Aff. étr.*, *Turquie, Bucharest*, vol. 22.
[4] Prokesch to Rechberg, no. 33 A–B.
[5] Green to Bulwer, no. 44, June 13, F.O. 78/1666. Couza affected to deplore the attitude of the assembly, but Green suspected him and his ministry of connivance.
[6] Green to Bulwer, no. 47, June 27, enc., F.O. 78/1666.
[7] Green to Bulwer, no. 53, July 25, *ibid.*
[8] Gortchakoff to Oubril, July 5, and to Lobanoff, Aug. 10, *Aff. étr.*, *Russie*, vol. 228.
[9] Rechberg to Prokesch, Aug. 31, Staatsarchiv, XII/119.
[10] Prokesch to Rechberg, no. 33 A–B, Apr. 23, 1863, *ibid.*, XII/119.

only too well the quality of the acting. Since no protest had been made against his recent flouting of the Protocol, Couza prompted an ordinance, dated November 25, 1862, sequestering all the revenues of the dedicated monasteries, which were ordered to be deposited in the public treasury. With a pretty touch of humour, it was alleged in the decree that the patriarch and chiefs of the monasteries had complained that the hegumens had misappropriated the funds, and thus, to protect these funds, intended for holy ends (though the decree did not actually indicate these ends) was *un moyen de sûreté*.[1]

Obviously, the fact that the government had now laid hands on some of the revenues, even though they were supposed to be held in trust, was eloquent of the national determination to treat the affair as a local problem. What was more serious—it became a standing temptation to an impecunious government to resort to spoliation. When in January 1863 the assembly insisted on inscribing these revenues in the budget as part of the resources of the treasury, the issue had come to reach an acute form. We shall dwell elsewhere on the motives of the assembly. Couza, whose struggle with the conservatives was then at its height, was loath to incur the odium of flouting the chamber's will, even while deprecating its action;[2] and France blissfully declined to advise him what to do.[3] The Porte, however, took note of the situation, and dispatched a sharp protest to Couza against an act which would be 'in effect, a spoliation or seizure of the revenues of the monasteries in question' and quite 'outside the limits traced by the conferences of Paris'.[4] To back the suzerain Power, the ambassadors agreed on January 20 to send instructions to the consuls to stiffen Couza's attitude,[5] and Tillos took the credit of having persuaded the Prince to withhold his sanction of the assembly's action.[6] As, soon afterwards, the legislative session was adjourned, and the Prince's quarrel with the *boyards* took another direction, the danger seemed averted for the present. Yet the money was still locked in the coffers of the government; and France was ready now to concede the proposal of the international commission, namely that the Holy Places should renounce their alleged rights in return for a money payment. It was the most reasonable approach to a solution, though it quite overlooked the cumbersome scheme of the Powers by which a settlement was intended to be achieved.

[1] *Arch. dip., 1864*, vol. ii, pp. 187–8. In a letter to Alexandri, the Prince's agent at Paris (Dec. 1, 1862), the minister of foreign affairs dwelt at length upon cases where the Holy Places had requested the revenues to be delivered to the government for safe keeping: *Aff. étr., Turquie, Bucharest*, vol. 23.

[2] Eder to Rechberg, no. 2, Jan. 5, 1863, Staatsarchiv, XXXVIII/139.

[3] Lhuys to Tillos, no. 2, Jan. 27, *Aff. étr., Turquie, Bucharest*, vol. 23.

[4] *Arch. dip., 1864*, vol. ii, p. 186.

[5] Bulwer to Russell, no. 190, Apr. 16, F.O. 78/1734.　　[6] Lhuys to Tillos, no. 2.

For some months after this the Powers were too much absorbed in the settlement of the arms crisis—of which an account will be given presently—to expend much serious thought upon the monasteries. But on April 14, at the instance of the Porte, the ambassadors met to consider what action should be taken by way of smoothing out the situation. It was Bulwer now who took the lead in the discussion. While he could not well disparage the principle of an indemnity, since he had been one of the commissioners who had advocated this plan in 1858, the British ambassador was firm in his insistence that the protocol should be observed, since that was the law by which the Powers had undertaken to regulate the method of procedure. Drouyn de Lhuys, on hearing of his obstinacy in this matter, marvelled that he should take so much interest in a question which concerned the Orthodox Church, and pointed out that much of the wealth of the Holy Places had poured into Russian hands during the late war.[1] France had no interest in the question save a natural sympathy with Rouman national aims, and the desire 'not to disoblige the Russian government too much'.[2] What she apparently wished was that the affair should drag along until the Principalities had settled the matter themselves. Hence, when Bulwer now suggested that an order should be sent to Couza to raise the sequestration and prepare to submit the question to an arbitral commission, Moustier objected that the Prince had sent a *mémoire* to justify his action (he read it at the meeting), and that the distraint of the revenues was a salutary measure;[3] for his own part, he could not agree to such an order as Bulwer demanded, nor could he consent to the installation of an arbitral commission. Some of the ambassadors then answered that Couza was constituting himself an arbiter, and that was in flagrant opposition to the prescriptions of the Protocol.[4] But the most that Moustier would concede was that the Holy Places might, if they wished, refer to arbitration the question of the amount which they thought they should receive from the total of the revenues.[5] When the French ambassador endeavoured to substitute some plan of his own to replace the one proposed, Bulwer, much piqued, refused positively to consider it, and the question was then referred by the ambassadors to their home governments.[6]

[1] Mülinen to Rechberg, no. 41 C, Oct. 1, Staatsarchiv, XII/119.
[2] Moustier to Thouvenel, no. 15, Jan. 29, 1862, *Aff. étr.*, *Turquie*, vol. 353.
[3] Lhuys, in approving Moustier's attitude, held that the sequester was a 'provisional measure' and 'did not affect the *fond* of the debate': Lhuys to Moustier, no. 33, Apr. 24, *ibid.*, vol. 358.
[4] Prokesch to Rechberg, no. 31 B, Apr. 16, Staatsarchiv, XII/119.
[5] Bulwer to Russell, no. 190, Apr. 16, F.O. 78/1734.
[6] Bulwer to Russell, no. 191, Apr. 16, *ibid.* Moustier's account of the meeting (Moustier to Lhuys, no. 72, Apr. 15, *Aff. étr.*, *Turquie*, vol. 358) somewhat differs from that of Prokesch and Bulwer. According to his version, he said that,

It was evident (and became more so as time went on) that the fabian strategy of Moustier was quite beyond the talent of Bulwer to surmount. A few days later the British ambassador realized his mistake in letting the question pass from the more or less discretionary cognizance of the ambassadors, and he proposed that, instead of sending a peremptory demand to Bucharest, the matter of getting the sequester raised and that of persuading Couza to consent to arbitration within three months should be submitted to the collective action of the consuls. Moustier's only comment was that the proposal had come too late: the question was now before the cabinets.[1]

While the representatives of the Powers were still haggling over the question of whether arbiters should be appointed, the Principalities continued to look upon the whole position of the Church as a purely local question. In March the use of the Greek language in the Orthodox churches throughout the land had been forbidden by ordinance (the assembly having been indefinitely suspended), and the vernacular was henceforth to be used in all the churches and monasteries of the Orthodox communion.[2] In spite of Bulwer's feeling that the action, as applied to the monasteries, was merely 'spiteful',[3] the compulsory use of the Roumanian language in church services could be defended on a variety of grounds, and was typical of that spirit which Couza had done so much to develop. For the Church to try to resist the will of the State was clearly futile, as even its primate realized.[4] But nothing relaxed the obstinacy of the monasteries. When one of the hegumens refused to turn in the revenues of his monastery, he was arrested and deprived of his position, while another was similarly treated for

while he had no instructions from his government to go beyond the method of an *entente amiable* (that is, an amicable negotiation between the two parties), he was 'ready to go further and support the necessity of resorting promptly to arbitration, leaving to the arbiters the task of examining the nature and the value of the measures for which Couza had been blamed'. As Bulwer would not accept this proposal, Moustier came to the conclusion that the monks did not really want arbitration, but were simply fighting to get the sequester raised. According to his own account, moreover, Moustier did not defend the sequester, merely saying that his government had not passed an opinion on it. If it is true that he really did go so far as to consent to arbitration, Bulwer would have been wiser to have 'called his bluff'. Unfortunately for his policy, the British ambassador was never able to keep personal feelings out of the question. It is plain from his letters (no. 19 to Russell and no. 5 to Green) that he felt that Moustier wanted to snatch from him the initiative. He had also the jealous fear that France wanted to make the Principalities believe that she 'alone decides their affairs, and that they have only to look to France'.

[1] Moustier to Lhuys, no. 78, Apr. 23, and annex (Bulwer's proposals), *Aff. étr.*, *Turquie*, vol. 358.

[2] *Arch. dip.*, *1864*, vol. ii, p. 189.

[3] Bulwer to Green, no. 5, Apr. 23, F.O. 78/1735.

[4] Green wrote, indeed, that the superior of the monasteries thought it well to command obedience to the ordinance, lest the monks should be expelled: Green to Bulwer, no. 34, May 1, F.O. 78/1747.

refusing to hand over the documents of the establishment which he managed. Documents and even jewels were seized from the monasteries. Such acts were merely the beginning of a determined proscription of all the clergy who refused to adhere to the law.[1] To certain foreign statesmen, however, Couza's measures seemed nothing less than arbitrary acts of tyranny or spoliation.

'You shall endeavour', wrote Russell to Bulwer, 'to obtain justice for the dedicated convents in the Principalities. Their property has been seized; their agent, who endeavoured to obtain their rents for them, imprisoned and condemned by a corrupt tribunal; their priests ordered to conduct their worship in a language not their own. The representatives should inform Prince Couza that such proceedings are illegal, tyrannical, and subversive.'[2]

It is true that an exception might have been made in the case of services held solely for and by monks; it is true, likewise, that the sequester might be called illegal, and Gortchakoff's term, 'shameful spoliation'[3] had, indeed, some basis in reason; but to expect that Couza's government would patiently wait for arbitration to settle the disposition of so much of the national wealth was to ask the impossible of a people which had come to be nation-conscious.

It should have been evident by now that, if the Powers could not arrange an adjustment soon, the question would speedily pass beyond the range of any compromise. Russia not only wanted immediate arbitration, but deplored the interval of three months which Bulwer had recommended, holding that this would give the Principalities the excuse for further delay and impose financial loss upon the Holy Places.[4] But the Powers were not a unit, for France was not willing to take any action at all. When Bulwer suggested that a collective note should be sent to the consuls to intercede for the luckless hegumens, Moustier promptly objected that this would have the character of a demonstration, which was 'perhaps not to the taste' of all the members of the diplomatic corps.[5] Again, at a meeting of the ambassadors on June 3, it was Moustier, as usual, who prevented action. Bulwer having proposed that the question should be referred to a commission of arbitration, and that in the event that three months should pass without results an over-arbiter should be chosen, the French ambassador declared that the Principalities would not consent to this, and that it was hazardous to oppose the unanimity of a nation; in any event, he had not as yet received instructions from Paris. The inference that two months had elapsed without receiving word from

[1] Green to Bulwer, no. 58, July 13, and to Hammond, July 24, *ibid.*
[2] Russell to Bulwer, no. 281, June 18, F.O. 78/1730.
[3] Napier to Russell, no. 656, Oct. 14, F.O. 65/638.
[4] Gortchakoff to Novikoff, Apr. 25, Staatsarchiv, xii/119.
[5] Moustier to Lhuys, no. 92, May (*sic*), *Aff. étr., Turquie*, vol. 358.

France on the idea of arbitration might reasonably have been doubted,[1] and Moustier seemed well able to offer a new suggestion—namely that, inasmuch as no *entente* was possible till the monasteries had renounced the rights of ownership which they had claimed, it would be well to ask Couza on what basis he would treat.[2] This, of course, meant to push the idea of an amicable negotiation with the certainty, moreover, that Couza had won the stake before the game had really commenced. Interestingly enough, Drouyn de Lhuys had simultaneously suggested this expedient. The allowance, he said, of only three months for negotiation before referring the question to arbitration was 'completely insufficient and almost ludicrous'. Even more unreasonable was the idea of resorting to an over-arbiter. Could any of the Powers, he asked, be so unjust as to leave to an over-arbiter the question of whether a fifth part of the revenues should go to foreign monks? To begin with, he declared, the Powers should decide exactly what should be referred to arbitration.[3] Manifestly, France viewed some of Couza's demands as settled *ab initio*. On receiving this letter, Moustier was ready now to admit that his government had expressed itself, but he made it clear that the French preferred an 'amicable accord' to any resort—even yet—to arbitration. This 'amicable accord', he repeated, should be sought by asking Couza to propose a *point de départ* for the negotiation; and, to that end, he believed that Ali should apply to Couza for his views.[4]

Such a policy, if followed, would certainly score a point for the Principalities. It is interesting to notice that Negri had just discussed with Ali a division of the revenues, which would assign to Couza's government only a fourth part of the total[5]—the hypothetical proportion which had been urged in earlier days.[6] If, however, Couza were invited to state his terms, it is hardly likely that they would remain equally generous. Such a course as Moustier proposed was naturally far from meeting with Bulwer's approval, since it would simply mean gravitating towards a unilateral decision; and he remarked somewhat acidly that he was 'not aware whether this proposal . . . had been indicated by M. Drouyn de Lhuys'.[7] Nevertheless, the undaunted Frenchman put

[1] As a matter of fact, Drouyn de Lhuys had approved Moustier's conduct at the Conference of Apr. 14, and that would imply disapproval of Bulwer's plan of arbitration: Lhuys to Moustier, no. 33, Apr. 24, *Aff. étr.*, *Turquie*, vol. 358.

[2] Moustier to Lhuys, nos. 101 and 103, June 4, *ibid.*, vol. 359; Bulwer to Russell, no. 264, June 4, F.O. 78/1736; Prokesch to Rechberg, no. 45 B, June 4, Staatsarchiv, XII/119.   [3] Lhuys to Moustier, no. 43, June 5, *Aff. étr.*, *Turquie*, vol. 359.

[4] Moustier to Bulwer, June 15, annex to Moustier's no. 114, *ibid.*

[5] Moustier to Lhuys, no. 108, June 11, *ibid.*   [6] Page 355.

[7] Bulwer to Moustier, June 16, annex to Moustier's no. 114, *ibid.* Bulwer was of course mistaken, as Drouyn de Lhuys's letter of June 5 shows, though apparently Moustier had first made the suggestion (on June 3) on his own authority.

the matter at once before Ali, who said that Bordeano, the kapou kiaya's secretary, had already, before his recent departure, promised to put forth his best endeavours to get Couza to promise something. As it developed that Bordeano had gone to Bucharest for that express purpose,[1] it is reasonable to deduce that Moustier had instigated his mission. Naturally Bulwer, who saw that his colleague had stolen a march on him, could not well approve of a step, which, following the spirit of the Protocol, should only have been concerted with the ambassadors *ensemble*;[2] and it galled him, besides, to think that the Powers were being vanquished by Couza, who would undoubtedly be encouraged to greater 'pretensions'.[3] But the game was lost,[4] and any chance to apply the Protocol was now clearly out of the question. Whether or not Ali had been privy to this conspiracy, France had prompted the manœuvre which had rendered it inoperative. Austria, too, had come to believe that perhaps her interest lay in supporting the Principalities in a matter of *amour propre* (for so she regarded it), which was of small concern, anyway, to Vienna;[5] and both the Prussian and Italian ministers were apparently siding now with Moustier.[6] The French ambassador noted with pleasure that Ali had penetrated his British colleague's bad humour, which 'betrays a little the sincerity of certain protestations of which he has been so prodigal towards the Porte'.[7] Bulwer alone seemed unwilling to admit defeat, and Moustier accused him (to Drouyn de Lhuys) not only of wanting deliberately to embarrass Couza,[8] but of engaging in what might readily be called 'sharp

[1] Moustier to Lhuys, no. 114, June 18, *ibid.*

[2] Bulwer to Ludolf, June 22, Staatsarchiv, XII/119. According to Bulwer's dragoman (Pisani to Bulwer, June 18, enclosed in Bulwer's no. 294), Ali said that he could not make the request of Couza except in concert with the Powers, though, if Couza were to act on his own initiative, he was ready to consider any proposal. Moustier, on the other hand, wrote Bulwer (June 18) that Ali welcomed his idea, and said he had already begun to act on it. He (Moustier) acknowledged, however, that the Porte and the ambassadors must pass approval on Couza's proposals. No doubt Moustier was technically correct in regarding the invitation to Couza as a step in the 'amicable negotiation', which had not yet been superseded by the next stage in the protocol, namely arbitration; but there could hardly be any doubt that, once Couza had made definite proposals, there would no longer be any chance of persuading him to submit to arbitration.

[3] Ludolf to Rechberg, no. 51 A, June 25, Staatsarchiv, XII/119. A 'spoiled child' Bulwer called the Principalities: Bulwer to Russell, no. 294, June 25, F.O. 78/1736.

[4] According to Moustier (no. 114) Bulwer himself had urged Bordeano to come to terms with the Porte, but Bulwer makes no mention of this in his own dispatches. Moustier seemed to think that Bulwer's action was just a ruse to obtain the confidence of the Moldo-Wallachians, and instanced it as another example of Bulwer's duplicity.

[5] Ludolf to Rechberg, no. 51 B, June 25, Staatsarchiv, XII/119.

[6] Moustier to Lhuys, no. 103.

[7] Moustier to Lhuys, no. 116, June 25, *Aff. étr.*, *Turquie*, vol. 359.

[8] Moustier interpreted Bulwer's manœuvre as follows: if Couza consented to arbitration, he would lose credit with his own people, whereas, if he refused, he would disoblige the Powers: Moustier to Lhuys, no. 115, June 24, *ibid.*

practice'.[1] Doubtless, in point of diplomatic ethics, there was little choice between the two ambassadors, but in actual finesse the Frenchman was superior. All this bout was but a reproduction, in softer tones, of the rivalry between Stratford and Thouvenel.

Thus, with the active or passive support of the Porte and of the majority of the ambassadors, the prescriptions of the Protocol were practically cast aside, and the Prince was invited to state his own terms as a basis of negotiation. Judging from the act of sequestration, as well as the known views of the Prince, one could hardly doubt what that basis would be. In the latter part of June the kapou kiaya presented a lengthy *mémoire* of the Prince, contesting on the basis of the past history of the foundations the pretensions of the Holy Places to unrestricted ownership of these lands; and, in conclusion, the Prince denounced the Protocol as an encroachment on the autonomy of his country, declaring that the question could be solved only in the Principalities and by the Principalities, and that such a solution could only be transference (in consideration of an indemnity) of the control of these monasteries from the Church to the State.

'Despoiled of the importance which the interference of Europe gives it,' wrote the Prince, 'this question would appear in all its simplicity, and its solution would be most easy. It would consist in placing the monasteries, which appear under the invocation of the religious communities of the East, on the same basis as the undedicated Roumanian monasteries, and in conceding, for a purely pious end, to these communities, once for all, a capital sum the figure of which would be finally determined by us, as the revenue to be allocated to the eventual needs of the Holy Places.'[2]

It was not, of course, necessary for the Powers to accept the extreme position assumed by the Principalities. To give them the right of dictating the solution of this question, even of fixing the amount of a hypothetical indemnity, would be to abrogate entirely the international and intra-Ottoman character of the question and convert it into a purely local issue. But Austria and even Great Britain were willing that the period of negotiation should be extended;[3] though how any one could suppose that a fruitful negotiation between the parties was any longer practicable is difficult to fathom. Trying to save their faces, the supporters of the Protocol now discussed anew the question of a limit to this period of

---

[1] Although the matter was now before the cabinets, Bulwer, he said, had appropriated a plan of Novikoff's, which had not been discussed in conference, and which he wanted the cabinets to believe had been the case. This plan appears to have been simply another effort to fix the time for arbitration: Moustier to Lhuys, no. 115, June 24, *Aff. étr., Turquie*, vol. 359.

[2] *Arch. dip., 1864*, vol. ii, pp. 197 ff.

[3] Rechberg to Ludolf, July 9, Staatsarchiv, XII/119; Bulwer to Russell, no. 326, July 16, F.O. 78/1737.

negotiation, and Drouyn de Lhuys expressed his willingness to accept a limit, provided the tone of Bulwer's original proposal were softened.[1] But France also assumed the position that the only thing with which arbitration should concern itself was the amount of the indemnity to be paid.[2] Such a view naturally appeared to Bulwer much too arbitrary; some of the monastic property had been bought by the Holy Places and some had been granted to them, and, while he felt that most of the land which they controlled did not come under these heads but was dedicated to a specific end, the whole question of adjudication, he felt, should be settled by arbitration as the Conference of Paris had decided;[3] for that reason he would like to proceed to the appointment of an over-arbiter,[4] some Protestant sovereign being mentioned for that role.[5] The Porte also felt that the time had come to appoint an over-arbiter, and on September 10 Ali issued a circular to the Powers inviting them to come to some agreement on that point.[6]

It seems beyond dispute that on strictly legal grounds Bulwer's position was thoroughly sound. The Principalities were not an independent state which might override private contracts and summarily dispose of monastic lands, as England had done in the time of Henry VIII. In the days of the Russian protectorate the question had been within the purview of the government of St. Petersburg, and had been so treated. After the Russian ascendancy had given way to the régime of the Protecting Powers, it was quite within the competence of the Powers to take the action, feeble as it was, which they had done in 1858. Moreover, in strict equity, no one should be the judge of his own case. The position of the Principalities had been amply stated; the Holy Places had done likewise,[7] and one of their representatives, the archimandrite Nilos had visited London, Paris, and St. Petersburg to try to win sympathy for their cause; it would now seem that an impartial arbiter should examine the question *au fond*, and pronounce a judgement on the basis of his researches. Indeed, had the diplo-

---

[1] Metternich to Rechberg, no. 29 F, July 12, Staatsarchiv, XII/119. Drouyn de Lhuys went so far as to circularize the Powers in the interest of conciliation. He was particularly anxious that question of what should be solved by negotiation or arbitration should be precisely fixed: Lhuys to Moustier, no. 57, July 17, *Aff. étr., Turquie*, vol. 359.

[2] 'Pro memoria,' July 25, Staatsarchiv, XII/119. In his circular (July 17) Drouyn took the curious view that to deny the right of the Principalities to appropriate the revenues (presumably with compensation) was an attack upon their autonomy.

[3] Bulwer to Russell, no. 372, Aug. 6, and enc., F.O. 78/1737, and no. 373, Aug. 24, F.O. 78/1738.

[4] Bulwer would have preferred an arbitral board, appointed by the Powers, though he seemed quite unaware that this would be enlarging on the provisions of the Protocol.

[5] This was Russell's suggestion: Cowley to Russell, no. 1044, Nov. 3, F.O. 27/1498.   [6] *Arch. dip., 1864*, vol. ii, pp. 271 ff.   [7] *Ibid.*, pp. 274 ff.

mats at Paris expended any statesmanship on this vexing question, they would have left out all the preliminary machinery which they had devised, and placed the matter immediately in the hands of an over-arbiter. It is conceivable that in 1858 an arbitral award might have been accepted by both sides, whereas now, as Bulwer admitted,[1] it would be necessary to use force to have it respected. Moreover, as it was, France could always talk of 'the spirit, rather than the letter of the protocol',[2] as a means of contending for a longer negotiation, knowing full well that such a method of procedure would be barren of any result save to encourage the Principalities to decide the matter for themselves.

Yet it may be admitted that public law cannot stand against a revolution; and what was going on in the Principalities at this period was, in a sense, a nationalist revolution. To Couza and his compatriots the term 'autonomy', for which they held such reverence, and which the Convention had guaranteed to them, was something closely approximating to independence. Little by little, as the occasion arose, they would scrap all the restrictions on their sovereignty until they emerged—perhaps through bloodless struggles—as an independent state. Fortified now by the attitude of France, whose emperor was the staunch defender of nationalism, the Principalities intended to fight the struggle over the monasteries to a finish. Thus Negri told the Austrian chargé d'affaires that Couza's *mémoire* was 'the last word of the Moldo-Wallachian government'.

'It is not the Prince alone,' said the kapou kiaya in substance, 'but an entire people who are unwilling any longer to suffer a considerable part of the revenue of the State to be squandered by foreign priests and a third of the territory of the Principalities to be administered from without. The Powers may employ against us all their forces, but an occupation cannot last eternally, and on the first favourable occasion you can be certain we shall return to the issue, and nothing will be gained for the monks. We understand our duty to contribute to the splendour of the Holy Places, but it is not ours alone to support them. We shall be generous, I promise you, when it is a question of fixing the amount of the indemnity, but that is all that one can demand of us.'[3]

Rightly or wrongly, then, the Principalities intended to settle this matter for themselves, not on any strict basis of what precisely

---

[1] Bulwer to Russell, no. 393.

[2] Lhuys to Montebello, no. 50, July 4, *Aff. étr., Russie*, vol. 231.

[3] Ludolf to Rechberg, no. 54 A, July 6, Staatsarchiv, XII/119. Couza took a similar tone, when Green, in pursuance of instructions from Bulwer, expostulated with him for the plunder of the monasteries for documents, &c. 'So far from making any impression on the Prince,' wrote Green, 'he distinctly declared that he and the country had a duty to perform, and that no interference would prevent them from performing it': Green to Bulwer, no. 58, July 13, F.O. 78/1747.

were the rights of the Holy Places, but admitting a moral (or perhaps it was really practical) obligation of allowing them a certain fraction of their wealth, while the great mass of it should become for good and all national property. Looking at the matter from the standpoint of a self-conscious nation, suffering perennially from a large deficit, one finds it hard to criticize the conduct of the Moldo-Wallachians. To the end of honesty and justice, it would have been better if France had frankly proposed the abrogation of the Protocol instead of pursuing obstructive tactics which were designed to secure that end. But the ways of diplomats are devious, and the Powers were not wont to admit a blunder, particularly in the case of a party who is nominally a dependant. For some reason that is not entirely clear diplomacy prefers to accept a *fait accompli* than to avert it by altering legally the status quo.

While the question of arbitration was still being agitated, Negri announced on behalf of Couza (August 22) the solution which his government had enacted—not proposed—as a settlement. The 'Roumanian government' had awarded to the Holy Places the sum of ten million piasters[1] on condition that this capital should be placed under the collective guarantee of the Porte and the Protecting Powers; that the Holy Places should give an account of their expenditure of the proceeds therefrom; and that documents and other valuables which had been given to the monasteries (and subsequently purloined) should be restored to them. In addition, the government proposed to endow a school and hospital at Constantinople with the sum of ten million piasters, the organization of which establishments was then specified.[2] Needless to say, such a settlement as Negri defined was not accepted by any of the Powers, for Ali could not regard the Prince's decision as anything but a proposal,[3] and even France had not abandoned the idea of arbitration if bipartite negotiation should fail to achieve results,[4] though she would confine its application to fixing the amount of the indemnity.[5] By the middle of October Austria was ready to join France in thus limiting the scope of arbitration,[6] and, as Russia had played—curiously enough—a secondary role in the discussion, it was highly unlikely that Bulwer's lingering fondness for the Protocol would stand its ground much longer. When the latter made a visit to the Monastery of Mount Athos, Moustier strongly suspected him of wanting to take the monks under the protection

---

[1] Bulwer declared this to be the equivalent of £500,000: Bulwer to Russell, no. 393, Aug. 25, F.O. 78/1738.
[2] *Arch. dip., 1864*, vol. ii, pp. 270 ff.
[3] Moustier to Lhuys, no. 176, Sept. 10, *Aff. étr., Turquie*, vol. 360.
[4] Metternich to Rechberg, no. 40 F, Sept. 27, Staatsarchiv, XII/119.
[5] Ludolf to Rechberg, no. 77 A, Sept. 21, *ibid.*; Cowley to Russell, no. 1076, Nov. 14, F.O. 27/1498.
[6] Rechberg to Mülinen, Oct. 18, Staatsarchiv, XII/119.

of his government,[1] but, in view of the British diplomat's fixed habit of going to the bottom of things, a more plausible explanation may be hazarded. As for effective interference, there was none. Moustier observed to Prokesch that the Prince's *mémoire* 'contained a system of solution', and he believed (or so pretended) that the patriarchs would modify their refusal to consider it.[2] Bulwer, true to his principles, blamed Ali for inviting any reply from the Holy Places, and considered that the question was between Couza and the Powers.[3] He did not relish, moreover, being reminded by Drouyn de Lhuys that, as commissioner in the Principalities, he had advocated secularization with compensation, and to the end he maintained that the Protocol was 'the law'.[4]

But, after all, the affair had got beyond technical considerations. The Powers might still consider the means by which a solution could be reached, but Couza would proceed as he saw fit. Since July, no meeting of the ambassadors had been held over the question,[5] probably because unanimity was hopeless, and it was left to the governments to correspond on the matter. As two of the leading Powers had accepted the principle of an indemnity, there was every reason to expect that the Principalities would take the final step of secularizing the lands of the dedicated monasteries, and even of insisting upon the right of fixing the indemnity.

It is obvious that Rouman nationalism had won a striking victory. The collective authority of the Powers had been successfully defied. If it was left to them to settle, by arbitration or otherwise, the amount of compensation to the Holy Places, the fact remained that the Principalities were going to preserve in their own hands the administration of this vast revenue and use the bulk of it for national needs. How nearly a settlement by the Powers would have approximated to that result one can never know. But that decision should come as it did showed that Couza and his people had grown in moral power. Meanwhile, as we shall see, a controversy, much keener, and more seriously affecting the prestige of the Powers, had been raging for several months.

---

[1] Moustier to Lhuys, no. 194, Sept. 30, *Aff. étr., Turquie*, vol. 360.

[2] Prokesch to Rechberg, no. 94 D, Nov. 25, Staatsarchiv, XII/119.

[3] Bulwer to Russell, no. 429, Sept. 24, F.O. 78/1738.

[4] Bulwer to Russell, no. 449, Oct. 5, F.O. 78/1737.

[5] In December the Porte again addressed an invitation to a meeting (Prokesch to Rechberg, no. 9 B, Dec. 9, Staatsarchiv, XII/119), but there seems to be no evidence that any was held. On Dec. 23 Ali again tried to bring the representatives together (Ali to Moustier, Dec. 23, annex to Moustier's no. 235, *Aff. étr., Turquie*, vol. 360), but Moustier merely denounced the position taken by the monks, and was plainly loath to attend a conference (annex 4). The action of the Moldo-Wallachian assembly finally settled the matter.

CHAPTER XIII

THE ARMS CRISIS OF 1862: THE PLIGHT OF THE PROTECTING POWERS

THE feeble efforts of the Powers to find some workable compromise on the vexing question of extraterritoriality had been
doubtless due to the feeling that a situation, so derogatory of their
dignity, demanded some amendment. Yet one wonders if—even
before the bitter controversy over the monasteries—the Powers had
not begun a little to appreciate that growing spirit of nationalism,
which, more than anything else, was making the Principalities a
European problem. No longer could the child, which they had
allowed to grow up before their eyes, be treated with the discipline
which they had sought to administer in its infancy. To blind oneself to that truth would be to court retribution and further loss
of dignity. Towards the close of 1862 the Principalities became
the scene of an unexpected crisis which shook the suzerainty of
the Sublime Porte almost to its foundations, and taught the Powers
a lesson which they would cherish in their memories for some time
to come.

The uncertainty of Russia's relations with the Near East was a
problem which had disturbed the ease of Europe's diplomats ever
since the great Eastern Power had accepted the results of her defeat
in the Crimean War. The fact that she did not regard as permanent
the deprivation of the Black Sea for her naval power could be
readily inferred by any one with a modicum of knowledge of
geography and history, and, if tangible evidence were wanted, her
occasional efforts to evade the restrictions upon the use of her
southern outlets were clear enough omens of what might some time
be expected. Then, the repeated interest which she showed in the
welfare of the Christian subjects of the Porte, transferred, like the
Danubian Principalities, from the benevolent protection of Russia
to the corporate responsibility of the Powers which had signed the
Treaty of Paris, indicated clearly enough that Russia still regarded
the Ottoman Empire as an important sphere for the exertion of her
vigilant diplomacy. It seems beyond dispute that, if the Powers
had deprived the government of St. Petersburg of all separate right
of intervention on behalf of these harassed peoples, then it was the
duty of those Powers who had signed the Treaty of Paris to see
that the reforms, demanded of Turkey, should be faithfully
carried out. Since, as a matter of fact, this provision of the treaty
was very evidently a dead letter, it was hardly strange that Russia
should have demanded that some collective action should be taken
by the signatory Powers to procure some redress. In 1858, just

before the Conference of Paris, Gortchakoff had attempted to enlist the co-operation of France in a systematic effort to investigate the condition of the Christian subjects of the Porte. Since France had too many other interests just then, and Walewski was not the man to plunge into unnecessary complications, the overture had been deliberately discouraged. Then, in 1860, when serious unrest was known to exist in Bosnia, Herzegovina, and Montenegro, Gortchakoff made a more determined effort to interest the Powers. Manifestly, Europe could not well ignore the principles involved, and it was certainly desirable to avoid any possible action, whether by intrigue or otherwise, on the part of Russia alone; but the crux of the question was whether a Turkish commission of investigation should be assisted in its work by the consuls of the Powers. Thouvenel, who was now minister of foreign affairs, saw well that something must be done, and, though he did not go so far as Gortchakoff in demanding an organization for the Christian provinces that would furnish adequate guarantees, he was quite willing that delegates of the Powers should accompany the commission—a proposal, which, for some reason, Russia seemed unwilling to accept. The chief difficulty, however, lay in the fact that Great Britain considered the notion as an attack upon the sovereignty of the Porte. Punishment for such indifference was soon forthcoming, when the Syrian massacres occurred in July of the same year—forcing an Anglo-French intervention in that quarter. But the episode gave no hope of any drastic remedy for the trouble. Gortchakoff was utterly unable to get the Powers to extend their interest to the rest of the Ottoman Empire, and his efforts to reach an understanding without Great Britain foundered on France's unwillingness to part company with her quondam ally. Yet it must be admitted that Russia's diplomacy was not always straightforward or readily intelligible.[1] Apparently she became afraid that the Italian revolution might inculcate a spirit in the Balkans that would bring about results more serious than she cared to contemplate. And, anyway, it was doubtful if concerted action by the Powers would yield to Russia any appreciable advantage. The most that she accomplished was the tightening of the bonds of friendship between Paris and St. Petersburg[2]—a sort of set-off to

[1] An interesting account of these manœuvres of Russian diplomacy (though my own conclusions are somewhat different) may be found in Charles-Roux, *op. cit.*, book 3, chap. iv.

[2] Somewhat disturbed by a threatened *rapprochement* between Russia and Austria, Thouvenel had been willing, in Sept. 1860, to present to Gortchakoff a memorandum, professing no objection if Russia and Austria 'took measures which they might think necessary to protect the populations of Herzegovina, Bosnia, and Bulgaria', besides proposing that bases of a new organization in Turkey be concerted by the Powers; and he proposed that this should be communicated to Austria. Gortchakoff refused, however, to take the matter up with

the Anglo-French alliance, and a confirmation, one might say, of the general understanding which had taken place at Stuttgart in 1857. It did not avail to prevent the final triumph of the Italians, and it might not preclude French interference in the affairs of Poland, but it did explain the accord which France and Russia displayed during the Balkan crisis of 1862-3.

But, whatever the intricacies of Gortchakoff's diplomacy, there is no evidence that Russia had wished to stir up a situation that might be calculated to justify her intervention—either with Austria or alone. Times had changed since the Greek Revolution, and she knew it. On the whole, it must be admitted that she had not, so far, assumed any role that could not be based quite legally on the principles of the Treaty of Paris. If she was ready to take the side of the Christian vassals of the Sultan (as, for instance, Montenegro), whenever a dispute arose between these little states and their suzerain, she had yet to be proved a deliberate disturber of the peace. It was only that the realization of her wrongs, the impression created by her restless and enigmatical diplomacy, and the existence of nationalities in the Balkans, which for a century had been looked upon as the pawns and protégés of St. Petersburg, made one suspect the hand of Russia in every disturbance in that region.

The manner in which Russian diplomats looked upon the Principalities is something of a mystery which will never be entirely cleared up till the contents of her archives are disclosed to the historian. So far as one may judge from her support of union and her unwillingness to adhere to any suggestion of Turkish interference in these lands, she seems to have been willing that a reasonably strong state should be constituted on her threshold—a power strong enough, at least, to protect itself against external pressure, Turkish or European. The very fact that it was strong enough to resist these weaker forces did not, however, mean that Russia herself could not eventually assimilate it. In the meantime, until that day should come, Couza, on whose tenure union depended, was a suitable stopgap. He should be supported, Gortchakoff told the Austrian ambassador, because his downfall would inevitably mean revolution[1]—and he might have added that Russia was not yet ready for that contingency. If he were inclined to disparage Couza to foreign ambassadors,[2] it was, no doubt, because he did not wish them to suppose that Russia looked upon

---

Austria, and preferred, instead, a secret understanding with France: *ibid.*, p. 391. One may guess that Russia had no hankering for a policy that might lead Austria to share with her the right of sponsoring the interests of the Balkan states. Evidently Thouvenel had spiked her guns.

[1] Thun to Rechberg, no. 5, Mar. 1, 1863, Staatsarchiv, x/49.

[2] e.g. Thun to Rechberg, no. 38, Sept. 4, 1861, *ibid.*, x/47, and no. 3 A-B, Feb. 4, 1863, *ibid.*, x/49.

this prince as an instrument of her policy, or to imagine, in fact, that Russia had any designs whatever upon the future of the Principalities. And it cannot be said from available evidence that she had.[1] 'You may assure every one', so had said the vice-chancellor to Austria's ambassador in 1861, 'that we will never accept this crown of thorns for a Russian prince, or for any one in whom we are interested.'[2] The future might test the sincerity of that remark. In the meantime, Russia was represented by an able consul at Bucharest, and nothing was lost by waiting for events to shape themselves.

During the year 1862 circumstances were tending to make not the Principalities but Servia the centre of diplomatic gravity in the Balkans. It is, of course, too irrelevant to our theme to discuss the position of Servia in any detail, but a few facts are needed to explain the situation which linked her with the Principalities in the crisis of that year.[3] Economically and culturally Servia was quite as backward as her neighbour across the Danube. In the words of a British consul, the Servian people, mostly swineherds, 'prefer a life of sloth and intemperance in their native forests to the civilization which might result from improved industry and intelligence'.[4] Politically Servia's status was also similar to that of her neighbour. Autonomous to a certain extent, though tributary to the Porte, she, too, had been placed by the Treaty of Paris under the protection of the signatory Powers, who thereby explicitly guaranteed her 'rights and immunities' and the existing organic relations which bound her to the Porte. But the conditions of that relationship were much more onerous than any which the Principalities had to suffer, for Servia was still the victim of a military occupation. Turkish garrisons still held six Servian fortresses, four of which, including the citadel, formed the ring of the capital's defences; and it was from the citadel that much interference had come in the course of Servia's frequent domestic difficulties. Largely owing to the perennial rivalry of Obrenovitches and Karageorgevitches, Servia was much more a prey to political strife than the Principalities, and, as the weakness of her constitution had been seized upon by the Turks as a ready occasion for intrigue and often arbitrary interference, it is not unnatural that the Obrenovitches should realize that only by strengthening the power of the prince could their country's autonomy be protected. Moreover, Servia, unlike the Principalities, was still compelled to harbour a Mussulman

[1] I have gone very thoroughly through the archival material in Paris, London, and Vienna, and have discovered no evidence of such designs.
[2] Thun to Rechberg, no. 44 F, Oct. 4, 1861, Staatsarchiv, x/47.
[3] My account of the imbroglio in Servia and the resultant action of the Powers is chiefly based on British, French, and Austrian dispatches.
[4] Longworth to Russell, no. 35, Aug. 24, 1860, F.O. 78/1515.

population. While a firman of 1830 had stated that 'no Turk except those who garrison the fortresses should be allowed to inhabit Servia', a subsequent firman had explicitly excepted the Moslem quarter of Belgrade, and although the Turkish inhabitants of the other fortress towns were still supposed to leave the country, no move was made to carry this stipulation into effect. It may be true that these Moslems were, for the most part, peaceable and law-abiding communities, but their presence in the bosom of a nation which nourished the tradition of hatred of the Turk and looked upon the citadel as something like a yoke was sufficient to produce periodic discord—especially in Belgrade. Since, moreover, the Porte would not allow its Moslem subjects to be subject to Christian tribunals, any Turk who disturbed the peace must be handed over to the custody of a Turkish gendarme, and his case was then handled by the Turkish authorities under the auspices of the pasha who commanded the citadel. This dual jurisdiction was a frequent cause of trouble, since a quarrel between Serbs and Turks had often to be settled by the nearest Servian gendarme, and the subsequent intervention of the Turkish authorities, provided the Turk had been the offender, was only too liable to provoke difficulties with the Servian government. Another bone of contention was the privilege the Turks enjoyed of guarding the inner gates of the city. Since the capital had spread out far beyond these four passages, it was no longer necessary to pass through them to go into or out of the city, but the presence of these Turkish sentinels in the heart of a Servian community was naturally a constant source of irritation. Still, it cannot be said that serious disorders had been common, and if now, of a sudden, the atmosphere was to become tense, one must find the explanation in the advent of a new ruler.

Michael Obrenovitch, Prince of Servia since September 1860, was not the one to adapt himself to the fetters which his predecessors had tolerated. His life had already been a stormy one, as he had once before been occupant of the throne, from which he had been expelled, partly as a result of popular distaste for his reforming zeal, and partly through the action of the Turks, prompted, it was said, by his complicity in a Bulgarian insurrection. While his father (also once before prince and likewise expelled) was reigning in his place, Michael spent a rather indolent exile in Vienna and longed for the day when he should once more resume an active role. On his return to power with old Milosh's death, he applied himself with diligence to a reorganization of the whole administration, and from the outset he showed that he meant through his power as prince to guard both his country and his throne from any possible recurrence of the disasters he had known. Perhaps it is not unnatural if the grapes that he had eaten had put his teeth on edge. Headstrong and ambitious, Michael was not the one to take unwelcome advice—certainly not from the foreign consuls (who played a role analogous to that of the agents in the Principalities), and, in the words of the Austrian consul, he 'showed unmistakably towards a part of the consular corps the antipathy which he nourishes towards all European diplomats'.[1] It was natural, to be sure, to suppose that, in the event of any trouble with his suzerain, he could count on Russian aid, and it seems clear that Russian influence was dangerously strong at Belgrade, but Michael himself was no tool of the government of St. Petersburg, and it was not until after he had failed by direct negotiation with Constantinople to get jurisdiction over Turkish residents of his country that he turned to a foreign power—and it was France, not Russia—for arms and advice. While supplying him with arms, the French refused to give him counsel—which was perhaps a subtle way of leaving him to his own devices; and, in the meantime, a French officer was engaged to reorganize the army and raise the country's fighting strength to an unprecedented level. One can hardly say that Michael was plotting a war, but he would not have been a Servian patriot if he had not longed for the day when the last Turk, civilian or soldier, should depart from Servian soil. There is little doubt, moreover, that the failure of his diplomacy to bring the Sultan to reason had brought him to the conviction that only by rattling the sabre would he win his suzerain's respect. Since the Slavs of Montenegro and Herzegovina were then in a state of revolt, the opportunity of playing the deliberate role of *enfant terrible* could hardly have escaped him.

The year 1861 ended ominously with some legislative enactments which not only seemed to stretch the prerogatives of the prince in matters external but also provided for an augmentation of the army through conscription to more than 50,000—an innovation which clearly contravened the organic law that the size of the prince's army should be only large enough to secure domestic tranquillity, and which drew immediate but futile protests from Great Britain, Austria, and the Porte. Then followed in the spring and summer of 1862 a series of clashes between Turkish and Servian residents, culminating on June 17 in the bombardment of Belgrade. It is perhaps unnecessary here to discuss the question whether the pasha was justified in turning the guns of the citadel on a defenceless city. Fortunately—one might almost say miraculously—few lives were lost, though naturally a good deal of property was destroyed. The chief immediate result was to strike terror into the Servian population, a large portion of whom left their homes and fled from the city. Meanwhile the

[1] Borowicka to Rechberg, no. 86, Oct. 29, 1860, Staatsarchiv, XXXVIII/122.

Servian troops to the number of 7,000 erected barricades to protect the capital, and several of the consuls courageously risked their lives to prevent the dreaded renewal of the struggle. One may wonder that the Servians were not impelled to attack the citadel, and perhaps, if the Turks had not just then been worsting the Montenegrins, the intrepid Michael might not have shown such creditable self-control.

But it was evident to the Powers that some concerted action should be taken with a view of preventing another and perhaps more serious crisis. Michael himself had written letters to Napoleon, the Tsar, and Lord John Russell, invoking their sympathy for his country's plight, and it was evident that the Turks were almost equally disturbed, as they knew that their dominions were seething with discontent, and that Russia was only too likely to take advantage of their embarrassments. Yet it took the Powers a whole month to decide on their course of action. If one is astonished at a plan of Lord John Russell that Belgrade should (with the consent of the Powers) be occupied temporarily by Austrian troops, it is not improbable, indeed, that the government of Vienna thought for the moment that Lord John had taken leave of his senses. Not caring to attempt anything so hazardous (we know that Rechberg was anything but rash), and reasonably sure that such approval of the Powers was unobtainable, Austria proposed, instead, a conference of the representatives at Constantinople in conjunction with the ministers of the Porte. This proposal met with general acceptance, and, after some delay, consequent upon the necessity of obtaining further information from Belgrade, Ali proceeded to call the conference.

The Conference of Constantinople held its first meeting on July 22, and, after a good deal of diplomatic fencing, its final decisions were registered in a protocol on September 8.[1] It was noticeable from the beginning that France and Russia were in some sort of collusion. Strongly supporting the cause of Servia, they wanted the evacuation of all the fortresses including the citadel; but, when it became evident that such a drastic modification of the Porte's rights was impossible to carry, Thouvenel instructed Moustier to be moderate in his demands. Since the Russian minister's position was invariably too extreme, it is to Moustier's credit that the Servians came off as well as they did. There was to be no limitation of the Servian army, as Bulwer had desired, and the two interior forts were to be abandoned. The other four, including the citadel, were to remain in the possession of the Turks, but no Turk should reside outside these strongholds. An open space was to be cleared before the citadel in order to give it

[1] *Arch. dip., 1863,* vol. i, pp. 244 ff.

greater security, and, as a reciprocal measure of precaution, all instructions to the pasha should be previously announced. Such was the most that France and Russia could obtain in the way of protecting the Servian capital from another such catastrophe. The Conference had really staged a continuous and hard-fought struggle between Moustier and Bulwer. The French ambassador was a diplomat of considerable assurance and uncommon skill in manœuvre. Truculent when he chose to be with the Turks, he was exasperatingly urbane when facing opposition from his colleagues, and often wore them out by multiplying objections or refusing to come to a decision without further reference to Paris. One might wish that one possessed his impressions of Bulwer, for the British ambassador had much to say of his rival in his private letters, and it is quite evident that Moustier was a type so foreign to the Anglo-Saxon that even such vivid comments can hardly give one the material for drawing an accurate portrait. 'He is *par excellence* a casuist, who can never look at any matter in a plain, straightforward way, and constantly undertakes to tell you that a horse chestnut and a chestnut horse are one and the same thing.'[1] Bulwer admired his polish and wit,[2] but his 'avalanche of words'[3] was sometimes overpowering, for the Marquis would never yield a point until he had quite exhausted every resource. 'A most teasing colleague' had been Bulwer's comment, drawn from an exasperated soul during the monastery controversy.[4] Such a man proved an exceedingly efficient exponent of the Emperor's policy; but it is hardly strange that the Turks should have greatly feared him, and that few of his colleagues liked him.[5] The tactics of Bulwer were less baffling than his rival's; yet there was always a certain point beyond which he could not be budged, and none of the diplomats who struggled with the complexities of the Eastern Question was more fertile in finding expedients for disposing of petty difficulties. In the present instance he played his favourite role of arbiter with more than usual skill, and Prokesch considered that he deserved the chief laurels. 'The great and principal merit in the conduct of the negotiation', wrote the internuncio, 'belongs to Sir Henry Bulwer, whose just survey, faculty of work, wealth of conciliatory ideas, politeness of manner, and calm dignity in discussion, joined with the weight of his public character, refuted from the beginning the position of the ambassador of France and the minister of Russia, which the

---

[1] Bulwer to Russell, Mar. 16, 1863, Russell Papers, G. and D., 22/93, Pub. Rec. Off.

[2] Bulwer to Russell, Nov. 12, 1862, G. and D., 22/91, *ibid.*

[3] Bulwer to Russell, Mar. 16.

[4] Bulwer to Russell, Jan. 29, 1863, Layard Papers, Brit. Mus., Add. MSS., 39104.

[5] Lord Lyons later testified that he himself was the one exception: Newton, *Lord Lyons, A Record of British Diplomacy*, vol. i, p. 156.

exaggeration of their demands was failing to improve.'[1] Every one, however, was relieved that a peace had been patched. 'Thank God', wrote Thouvenel to the French ambassador at Vienna, 'the affair of Servia is ended at Constantinople, and I hope that the Servians will have the wisdom to content themselves with the results obtained.'[2] No one, of course, was prepared for the curious aftermath in the autumn.

Yet, notwithstanding some satisfaction with the result of the Conference, the episode left grave disquietude in London. Was Russia as innocent as Lord Napier, the British ambassador to St. Petersburg, had lately represented her to be?[3] What was the meaning of this vigorous co-operation between France and Russia at Constantinople? The existence of secret treaties is something that has always been very hard to keep hidden; and, early in August, Lord John Russell heard rumours from Paris and St. Petersburg that a secret protocol had been signed some time during the previous summer. Instructed to make inquiries,[4] Cowley taxed Thouvenel with the matter, impressing it upon him also how important it was that French and British policy should be identical in matters relating to the East. Thouvenel at once denied that any such agreement existed, and assured his questioner that France looked upon the Treaty of Paris as the basis of her Eastern policy.[5] Still, the rumour would not die, and Cowley was so convinced that Thouvenel had lied, that, when the French minister voluntarily reiterated his denial, he (Cowley) declared that if Thouvenel persisted in these assurances, he must do so 'with his eyes open to the consequences'.[6] Not content, however, with his own protestations, Thouvenel later told Cowley that Napoleon had stated—after Cowley, much disturbed, had exacted an answer from the Emperor—that, while he appreciated the fact that for several years Russia had shown greater sympathy for France than had Great Britain (he referred pointedly to the question of Savoy

[1] Prokesch to Rechberg, no. 68 c, Sept. 8, 1862, Staatsarchiv, XII/76.
[2] Thouvenel, *Le Secret de l'Empereur*, p. 383.
[3] Napier to Russell, no. 274, June 11, F.O. 65/604.
[4] Russell to Cowley, no. 821, Aug. 7, F.O. 27/1426.
[5] Cowley to Russell, no. 984, Aug. 14, F.O. 27/1444. Russell remarked that this was no assurance, as France and Russia might differ as to the interpretation of the treaty: Russell to Cowley, no. 862, Aug. 21, F.O. 27/1426. Thouvenel did admit the existence of the protocol to the French ambassador at London (he wrote as though there was no question of any denial), though he insisted that it was based on the Treaty of Paris and that no engagement had been taken which 'would remove in any way the Emperor's liberty of action'; and he excused the transaction on the ground that there had been no idea exchanged with the Russian government which had not been communicated to London: Thouvenel to Flahaut, no. 80, Aug. 14, *Aff. étr., Angleterre*, vol. 722. One can only deduce that Thouvenel was giving Flahaut information which he could use if the secret could no longer be preserved.
[6] Cowley to Russell, no. 991, Aug. 15, confidential, F.O. 27/1444.

and Nice), he had no engagements which bound him to Russia, and in questions relating to Turkey he was no less free than before.[1] If we may credit these words, communicated successively by Thouvenel and Cowley, the Emperor thus confirmed the falsehood (such a protocol having been actually signed at Paris on July 8). British persistence by no means abated, however, and Russell continued to express his certainty that such an agreement had taken place, and to instruct Cowley to that effect.[2] Parallel efforts to get the truth from Gortchakoff met with little better success. Russia had an understanding with France, he said, when it was found that Russia and Great Britain could not agree on the policy to be pursued, but there was no agreement of the nature which Great Britain suspected.[3] By September, however, the British government was in possession of the substance of the protocol;[4] and Gortchakoff, who, with all his finesse, was not a good actor, was manœuvred into admitting that something like an agreement —he studiously refused to call it a 'protocol'—had been signed. Lumley, the British chargé d'affaires, concluded with some astuteness that France had agreed to sign the protocol as part of the bargain which had induced Russia's recognition of the kingdom of Italy.[5] The secret agreement (which solely concerned Servia) was not as bad as the British had once feared, and its importance may have been somewhat magnified, but the fact that France had turned her back rather decisively on her late ally, and was co-operating with Russia in the Near East was not without its significance. The fruits of the Crimean War seem already to have decayed.

The explosion in Servia did more than demonstrate a realignment among the Powers—it produced reverberations elsewhere in the Balkans. The United Principalities had never ceased to be a part of the network of intrigue and conspiracy which Italian patriots had woven about Austria, and the fact that they were provinces of the Ottoman Empire was enough to make them sensitive to any upheavals in Servia, which was both a part of Turkey herself and a neighbour of Austria as well. Both Michael and Couza had much the same aspirations; they had both jeopardized their neutrality during the arms plot of 1860; and the presence of a resident agent from Servia at Bucharest since 1859[6] was an evidence of a closer understanding between the countries.

[1] Cowley to Russell, no. 996, Aug. 15, F.O. 27/1444.
[2] Russell to Cowley, no. 883, Aug. 27, F.O. 27/1426.
[3] Lumley to Russell, no. 105, Sept. 9, F.O. 65/607.
[4] It was an agreement on the part of the two governments to co-operate at the Conference of Constantinople in reducing the menace of the Turkish occupation of Servia and in seeking to have Turkish residents of that country placed under Servian jurisdiction: *Aff. étr., Russie*, vol. 228, fo. 76.
[5] Lumley to Russell, no. 112, F.O. 65/607.
[6] Eder to Rechberg, no. 75, Nov. 3, 1859, Staatsarchiv, XXXVIII/119.

In January 1862 Arsaki had told Green that (to quote Green's words) 'the political agitation, which has taken the form of open rebellion on the Adriatic, extends to the Black Sea', and he had admitted that his government and Servia had been in correspondence 'on these matters'.[1] When the report went abroad that some arms were being landed by the French imperial *messageries* at the port of Braïla, foreign consuls began to prick up their ears. The unloading of arms in the Principalities had once before been the forerunner of a conspiracy against the peace and neutrality of the Ottoman Empire.

There was a good deal of mystery about these weapons. The fact that they had been detained by the Wallachian customs authorities leads one to the supposition that Couza was innocent at this time of any part in a conspiracy against a foreign Power. The steamer-captain insisted that the weapons were *armes de luxe*, which, in accordance with a commercial treaty with France, might be imported by French subjects, and the French vice-consul at Braïla supported this claim. When the boxes were opened, however, they were found to be ordinary muskets.[2] The captain, on finding that he was not permitted to land his cargo, succeeded, after four chests had been secretly unloaded, in sailing off with the remainder, but he was subsequently stopped, and most of the thirty-six chests were held in the customs-house, pending inquiries.[3] Of course, the news of this affair was quick to reach Constantinople, and, while Negri was assuring the Porte that the arms had been landed in the Principalities against their will,[4] the Austrian, British, and French ambassadors began at once to make inquiries of their consuls at Bucharest. Prokesch was at first the most disturbed, having lately heard a rumour that a Garibaldian expedition had embarked for some unknown point, and that arms were on the way to the Principalities;[5] and he accordingly appealed to Bulwer,[6] whose meddlesome energy had achieved such striking results in 1860. Informed by Churchill of what was brewing,[7] this sleuth already had his suspicions. Besides questioning Green by telegraph, the British ambassador, whose temper had perhaps suffered from a recent illness, made a point of catechizing the Italian chargé d'affaires, who was 'deeply wounded', he told Moustier, at the insinuation that Italy was responsible for the affair.[8] As a matter of fact, the arms were said to be of Italian

[1] Green to Hammond, Jan. 23, 1862, F.O. 78/1664.
[2] Green to Bulwer, no. 40, May 27, F.O. 78/1665; Eder to Rechberg, no. 42 B, May 24, Staatsarchiv, XXXVIII/134.   [3] Eder to Rechberg, no. 44, May 30, *ibid.*
[4] Green to Bulwer, no. 40, May 27, F.O. 78/1665.
[5] Prokesch to Rechberg, Mar. 18, telg., Staatsarchiv, XII/75.
[6] Moustier to Thouvenel, no. 84, June 3, *Aff. étr., Turquie*, vol. 354.
[7] Bulwer to Russell, May 21, telg., F.O. 78/1651.
[8] Moustier to Thouvenel, no. 83, June 3, *Aff. étr., Turquie*, vol. 354.

'origin',[1] and Bulwer did not doubt that Italy, or at least some organization in Italy, was once more using the Principalities as the base for some attack upon Austria. The French were only concerned that they should not be thought parties to the offence, and, when the consular agent at Bucharest, acting on instructions from Moustier,[2] complained of an official pronouncement which had charged the *messageries* with culpable negligence, Couza blamed it on his ministers, whom he 'qualified by an epithet little flattering', and Arsaki was required to make amends without delay.[3] As far as circumstantial evidence goes, it points to Italy as the culprit.[4] Green heard that a private secretary of Victor Emmanuel had been in Jassy recently, and had had an interview with Couza[5]—a fact which recalled the role which Cerutti had played in 1860. The most that can be said for Couza is that the evidence is insufficient to condemn him, and that even the Austrian consul does not suggest that he was guilty. Certainly, the Prince had had his lesson in furthering the designs of Italian and Hungarian revolutionaries, and we know that he was not an instrument of the Left. On the other hand, there is little doubt that these arms had been sent for revolutionary purposes (either in Austria or Turkey), and there was doubtless some connexion between the extreme radicals and the Garibaldians which has yet to be disclosed. Eder hazarded the opinion that these Balkan firebrands, cast down by the news of Garibaldi's reverse at Aspromonte, had now acquired encouragement from the recent unrest in Greece.[6]

At all events, whatever the purpose or the outcome of this 'affair of the *messageries*', the atmosphere remained unsettled. While the *boyards* held the Prince responsible for Catargi's murder, the Prince himself attributed it to John Bratiano;[7] and, apparently, the public mind was in such a state of tension that nearly every one was fighting phantoms. In August Couza dispatched a considerable force to Little Wallachia, partly because of a rumour

---

[1] Moustier to Thouvenel, no. 84.

[2] Moustier was much exercised over Couza's charges against the imperial *messageries*, and sent a very strong dispatch to the French agent. 'I do not know', he telegraphed, 'whether it is his policy to create a merit with others by false charges against us, but, at all events, he knows that we will not tolerate it. If you are afraid to say this, lay my dispatch before Prince Couza': Moustier to Hory, July 4, telg., *Aff. étr., Turquie*, vol. 354.

[3] Hory to Moustier, July 6, *ibid.* Arsaki ascribed the mistake to the confusion following Catargi's murder. The probability is that Couza's insinuations against the French were intended to shield himself.

[4] The French, however, remained technically satisfied with Couza's forced denial that the weapons had been anything but *armes de luxe*: Moustier to Thouvenel, no. 117, July 15, *ibid.* This was obviously to clear their own skirts, and really proves nothing.

[5] Green to Bulwer, no. 40, May 27, F.O. 78/1665.

[6] Eder to Rechberg, no. 95, Nov. 4, Staatsarchiv, xxxviii/134.

[7] Green to Hammond, Nov. 19, F.O. 78/1667.

that the Turks intended to occupy a Wallachian island in the Danube, and partly to guard against an inroad of revolutionaries from Servia.[1] He had recently told Eder in a burst of confidence that he believed that a connexion had existed between the recent events in Servia and the murder of Catargi; 'it is all a train of powder', he added, 'from Nauplia to the Black Sea'. According to his view, the conspirators (whoever they were) had exaggerated the gravity of the Servian crisis, and had hastened to take advantage of it, but the attempt had been evidently premature. Eder himself believed that Michael was in the confidence of these revolutionists (an emissary of his had frequently come to Bucharest), but he did not think that there was any collusion between this prince and Couza.[2] On the contrary, the revolutionary elements seemed, according to all accounts, to look upon Couza as an enemy.[3] In November the *Roumanul*, gloating over the dethronement of King Otto of Greece (which had occurred during the previous month), published an encomium of the Greeks, which occasioned a visit of some of the consuls to Couza, led to a sentence of three months' imprisonment for the offending editor for inciting revolt, and was something of a shock to Couza.[4] It is not altogether safe to be a Balkan prince at any period, and at no time had the situation been so full of ominous signs.[5] Meanwhile, the country was overrun with Hungarian and Polish fugitives, who, having entered with French or Italian passports, could not very well be deported;[6] yet their presence seemed to show that something sinister was brewing. When a crisis did arrive, however, it had nothing to do with *émigrés*, and involved not the 'revolutionary party' but Couza's government itself.

On November 22 word reached the British and Austrian consulates at Bucharest that a long wagon-train, containing arms and military stores, had crossed the Russian frontier into Moldavia near Bolgrad.[7] Both consuls immediately informed their governments, and Green—perhaps without crediting the rumour—went to Couza to ask for an explanation. The Prince said that he knew nothing of the matter, and that 500 wagons could not pass into the Principalities unobserved by his officials; he discredited the story,

---

[1] Hory to Thouvenel, no. 83, Aug. 26, *Aff. étr., Turquie, Bucharest*, vol. 22.
[2] Eder to Rechberg, no. 56 B, July 4, Staatsarchiv, XXXVIII/134.
[3] Eder to Rechberg, no. 74, Aug. 29, *ibid.*
[4] Eder to Rechberg, no. 95, Nov. 4, *ibid.*; Green to Russell, no. 99, Nov. 2, and no. 102, Nov. 18, F.O. 78/1667. The offender was a contributing editor, not Rosetti.
[5] Couza told Green that he and his ministers frequently received anonymous letters threatening assassination: Green to Hammond, Nov. 19.
[6] Eder to Rechberg, Aug. 26, 29, Sept. 23, Oct. 10, Staatsarchiv, XXXVIII/134.
[7] Green to Russell, Nov. 22, telg., F.O. 78/1667; Eder to Rechberg, no. 99 B, Nov. 22, Staatsarchiv, XXXVIII/134. Green's information came from Ward, British vice-consul at Galatz: F.O. 78/1667.

which came from an Austrian agent, but he promised to look into the matter, and to act if necessary. Receiving instructions from Constantinople immediately afterward, Eder and Green went to Couza on the following day (November 23), and had much the same reception. The only carts conveying arms, of which he admitted any knowledge, was a requisition that he himself had made of 40 carts containing weapons that belonged to garrisons in Bessarabia, and which were being sent to Bucharest for repairs. A report of 500 wagons coming from Bolgrad was quite another story, and he was amazed that he had learned nothing of it. Moreover, the prefect of Galatz, when asked about these arms, had said that he had found no convoys except the 40 carts which were bound for Bucharest by an order from the government. He then proceeded to speculate on the question of who might be behind all this, assuming the story to be true, which it could not be. The Prince spoke with such frankness that it was difficult not to believe him.[1] Yet against his testimony was the report of Kremer, the Austrian vice-consul at Galatz, based on the evidence of several eye-witnesses, to the effect that 500 carts, containing arms, were on their way from the Russian border to Little Wallachia, with Servia as their probable destination. Moreover, Giers told Tillos, who told Eder, that Couza himself had spoken of cart-loads of arms being sent by Russia to Bulgaria.[2] Of course, this statement, while admitting that this apparition might not have been an 'apparition' after all, was calculated to divert suspicion from Servia, and to raise the delicate question of Russia's possible connexion with the episode.

But the plot thickened as confirmatory evidence poured in. A second courier arrived from the Austrian vice-consul at Galatz, who declared that he had seen the transport-train with his own eyes and that it had come from Russia. Though Green had received telegraphic instructions from Russell to send some trustworthy person to the place where the wagons were supposed to be, it was now felt that such recourse was unnecessary.[3] 'Arrival of arms from Russia', telegraphed Green to Russell, 'is beyond a doubt.'[4]

Suspicion now pointed to Couza's government with redoubled force. If the fact was well established that this long train of wagons did exist, then it would be impossible to suppose that officials on or near the frontier were unaware of it. Couza himself was begin-

[1] Eder to Rechberg, no. 100, Nov. 24, Staatsarchiv, XXXVIII/134; Green to Russell, Nov. 22, telg. 'He spoke', said Green, 'with a simplicity and apparent unreservedness, which, if I had not [had] considerable experience of [sic] Prince Couza's power of dissimulation, I should have declared it impossible for any one to assume': Green to Russell, no. 103, Nov. 24, F.O. 78/1667.
[2] Eder to Rechberg, no. 100, Nov. 24, Staatsarchiv, XXXVIII/134.
[3] Eder to Rechberg, no. 101, Nov. 25, *ibid.*
[4] Green to Russell, Nov. 26, telg., F.O. 78/1667.

ning to think that he must now accept the story as a fact, and consequently sent a message to the Porte, expressing his disapproval of the incident. Ali responded by telegraphing a request that he sequester the arms.[1] 'Support Turkey on the question of the arms,' Russell had telegraphed Green, 'but do not go beyond what the Porte wishes to be done.'[2] As Eder had received an even more explicit order, requesting him to demand the sequestration of the arms, both consuls went to Couza on the 26th and put the matter before him. There was little more satisfaction to be got from Couza on this occasion than on the previous one. His government, he said, had no knowledge of the arms; he had sent some officers of his suite several days ago to investigate, but they had not returned; if, however, they should report any wagons conveying arms, these would be sequestered.[3] It is interesting to notice that to the Porte the Prince telegraphed 'in somewhat haughty terms' that for the present he must decline to comply with its demand,[4] but, as far as the consuls were concerned, he did not yet admit that any contraband weapons existed.

But the consuls were in no wise deceived. 'The complicity of Prince Couza', wrote Green '. . . is beyond a doubt.'[5] 'Couza acted', said Eder the same day, 'as if he knew nothing of the affair. While his officials make a show of seeking these transports, these are continuing on their way in different directions, and will be lost in the country. . . . In this situation the interference of single Powers will yield proportionate results only if one can count on the sincere co-operation of Prince Couza, [and] this co-operation may be possible only if there has been no previous understanding between this prince and the agents of the Russian government. [But], had not this understanding taken place, the transports would not, indeed, have been sent to the Principalities.'[6] Eder had already made this deduction in his previous dispatch.[7]

The consuls were obviously convinced now that Couza knew more about the arms than he was willing to acknowledge. Apparently he had an interest of some sort in seeing them proceed, and by feigning ignorance as long as possible, he was simply playing for time. It was not so certain how far Russia was implicated, though it was beyond any doubt that the weapons had come from there, and the fact that Giers, the Russian consul, had lately returned from a furlough made some suspect that Couza had

[1] Erskine to Russell, no. 96, Nov. 26, F.O. 78/1660.
[2] F.O. to Green, Nov. 26, telg., F.O. 78/1663.
[3] Eder to Rechberg, no. 102, Nov. 27, and no. 103, Nov. 28, Staatsarchiv, XXXVIII/134.
[4] Erskine to Russell, no. 98, Nov. 30, F.O. 78/1660.
[5] Green to Russell, no. 106, Nov. 27, F.O. 78/1667.
[6] Eder to Rechberg, no. 102.
[7] Eder to Rechberg, no. 101.

yielded to his pressure.[1] Moreover, while Couza was found to be inaccessible on the day following the consuls' visit, Giers was also ill and equally invisible. But the question of the destination of the arms was of more immediate importance. According to Austrian advices, the wagons, after crossing the Russian frontier, were concentrated at the village of Nomolassa which was on the estate of Prince Vogorides (the late hospodar of unsavory memory); and it was further reported that part of these were then sent in the direction of Little Wallachia with Servia as their objective, while the rest were destined for Bulgaria, where Vogorides was engaged in an intrigue, it was said, to incite an uprising that would make him prince of that country.[2] British reports declared that the whole wagon-train was under the direction of a Servian, who, whenever questioned by any over-zealous official, exhibited a document bearing a large red seal, and was always allowed then to proceed.[3]

The presumption that Prince Michael was expecting the arms was a new factor to be considered; and Couza's attitude towards the question was, therefore, more than ever deserving of observation. On receiving word from Ali that he was to deliver the arms to a Turkish official (Omer Pasha, the Turkish member of the Danube commission, then resident in the Principalities), the Prince expressed himself as insulted, and declined the request on the ground that such action would be a violation of the autonomy of the Principalities, as defined by the Convention.[4] One may recall the similar position that Couza had taken during the arms episode of 1860. So far, if we may credit a statement of Giers, based on the Prince's answer to the consul's questions, he had 'taken . . . the necessary dispositions to discover the arms and effectuate their seizure; [but] some days later the Prince received from the Servian agency the declaration that these arms belonged to the Servian government, on whose order they had been bought abroad. While doing everything to guard the arms, the Hospodar questioned the Prince of Servia by telegraph in order to verify the accuracy of the declaration. Prince Michael confirmed it formally, adding that, not knowing the way which the transport had taken, he had not been able, unfortunately, to inform Prince Couza sooner of its passage through the United Principalities. In consequence of this information, Prince Couza gave orders to the local authorities to let the transports pass freely, and hastened so to inform the Prince of Servia.'[5]

[1] Tillos to Lhuys, no. 97, Nov. 28, *Aff. étr., Turquie, Bucharest*, vol. 23.
[2] Eder to Rechberg, no. 100, Nov. 24, and no. 103, Nov. 28, Staatsarchiv, XXXVIII/134.
[3] Erskine to Russell, no. 96, Nov. 26, F.O. 78/1660.
[4] Green to Russell, no. 109, Nov. 30, F.O. 78/1667; Erskine to Russell, Nov. 30, telg., F.O. 78/1660; Eder to Rechberg, no. 104, Nov. 30, Staatsarchiv, XXXVIII/134.
[5] Giers to Gortchakoff, Nov. 30, annex to Tillos's no. 97.

Whether Couza had suspected, or had had reason to know, that Servia was the destination of the arms, is a point we shall discuss later; but to the consuls who were chiefly engaged in hounding him he gave no such information as he had imparted to the Russian consul.[1] Apart from the sympathies which he may well have felt for a prince who was in a position similar to his own, and afflicted with the same enemies, Couza was probably taking delight in standing on what he conceived to be the rights of his country. He had felt compelled to back down in 1860. This time he was clever enough to get the best of the Powers, and he meant to enjoy his triumph to the full.

There was little likelihood now, as Eder regretfully confessed, that all the wagon-loads of arms could be sequestered in time to prevent their arriving in Servia to add to the dangers that were besetting the Ottoman Empire.[2] But some of them might still be detained[3]—at least to show that the consuls were not negligent of their duties! And at any rate the wily Prince might be forced to admit the existence of the arms. Since Eder had obtained some conclusive evidence from one of the drivers, an Austrian subject, who had by this time reached the neighbourhood of Bucharest, he and Green repaired to the palace on December 2, and plied Couza again. The Prince began, of course, by saying that it was all a mistake. Then Eder produced his evidence, and Couza confessed that there could no longer be any doubt that arms had been imported, and that they were reported to be for Servia. He added that the Porte had expressed regret for having communicated with him through the Turkish commissioner, Omer Pasha, explaining that it had been induced to take this action by Austria and Great Britain.[4] As to the matter of sequestering the arms, 'he pretends', telegraphed Green, 'that he will detain them, but, meanwhile, the government is facilitating their passage through the country'.[5] Eder heard that Couza had informed Michael that the arms would be sent on.[6]

Meanwhile, the governments of London and Vienna had decided to take more vigorous measures, and Eder and Green were instructed to request that the arms should not only be sequestered, but placed under the custody of the consuls. Since Eder felt, however, that it would be more effective if they asked for one thing

---

[1] Eder did not learn till later of the interchange of telegrams between the princes, as it was not till Dec. 7 that he telegraphed the fact to Vienna.
[2] Eder to Rechberg, no. 112, Dec. 14, Staatsarchiv, xxviii/134.
[3] Eder to Rechberg, no. 109, Dec. 8, *ibid.*
[4] Green to Russell, no. 110, Dec. 3, F.O. 78/1667.
[5] Green to Russell, Dec. 2, telg., *ibid.*
[6] Eder to Rechberg, no. 109.

at a time,[1] and Green believed that the latter part of the demand was likely to be refused, unless backed by some of their colleagues,[2] the two consuls decided for the moment merely to request sequestration. With this in view, Green sent a formal request to the minister of foreign affairs, and, when that met with no response (Green had expected a refusal),[3] they brought their demand direct to Couza. The most that the Prince would do was to promise orally that he would comply with the demand, and he subsequently assured them that he had done so. Arsaki, whom Eder saw the following day, told him that Couza had said that, as soon as a government had claimed ownership (one may note that Couza was not letting out any more than he had to!), he would raise the sequestration. Whether Michael had a right to buy the arms (Arsaki professed to quote his master), and to have them transported across the Principalities, did not concern him (Couza); the Powers could take that up with Michael. Eder got confirmation of all this from Couza's own lips the next day, and, when he now demanded not only distraint[4] but consular custody of the weapons, the response which the Prince made could hardly have been unexpected. 'One must not ask the impossible', was his answer. It would not only be an evidence of distrust, he said, but he could not recognize that the Porte had any such right of interference, much less, the Powers, who had placed the Principalities in no such state of dependence. Then he made it clear that even sequestration had not been ordered after all. If such a demand were made collectively by the ambassadors at Constantinople, he would sequester the arms, and there was plenty of time for negotiation, as the train could not cross into Servia until the Danube was frozen over.[5] Meanwhile to Ali Couza sent word that, the arms having now been claimed by Servia, he would not be justified in detaining them longer.[6] There is really no certainty that Couza had ever issued an order of sequestration.[7]

It was evident that if anything could be done to move Couza, and save at least the dignity of the Powers, the number of the besieging forces must be increased. Responding to pressure from London and Vienna, Drouyn de Lhuys, the new foreign minister of France, consented that Tillos should be instructed to join the

---

[1] Eder to Rechberg, no. 109, Dec. 8, Staatsarchiv, XXXVIII/134.
[2] Green to Russell, no. 111, Dec. 5, F.O. 78/1667.
[3] Green to Russell, Dec. 7, telg., *ibid.*
[4] The repetition of this request seems to show that Eder did not believe that the order had been given.
[5] Eder to Rechberg, no. 109.
[6] Erskine to Russell, no. 121, Dec.11, F.O. 78/1661.
[7] A Turkish dispatch credits him with having done so: Callimaki to Ali, Dec. 9, *Arch. dip.*, *1863*, vol. iii, p. 108–9.

others in pushing their demands.[1] It cannot be said that up to this moment France had shown much interest in the crisis, and Couza craftily made use of her reserve to convey the impression that France had some sort of understanding with Russia, and that she was not opposed to military activities in the Balkans.[2] Tillos, who was more roumanophobe than any of his colleagues, was more than glad to be instructed to associate himself with these efforts, and on December 10 the three consuls tried the experiment of three notes, framed in identical terms, to John Ghika, the minister of foreign affairs, who had up to this time ignored the communications of Eder and Green. These notes demanded not only the sequestration of the arms, but their deliverance to the custody of the Powers.[3] The effect of this *démarche* was to extract at least a response from Ghika to the previous note, but, as the latter merely wrote that he had nothing to add to what the Prince had said by word of mouth,[4] it was more than ever obvious that Couza meant to grant no satisfaction. As, in the meantime, the Prussian consul had received instructions to join in the hopeless siege,[5] and as no reply was yet forthcoming to the triple communication, the four consuls went to Couza on December 13 and demanded a categorical answer to their request for sequestration. Couza received them with his customary *sang-froid*, told them the case demanded reflection, and that, when a decision had been reached, they would hear from his government. Since, as a matter of fact the Porte had been notified that the arms were not to be held back, and since Couza had virtually admitted that they had not been sequestered, it was clear that he was simply playing with his 'guardians' till the arms had gone safely out of the country. It was in vain that Eder urged that sequestration would mean only a temporary measure till the legal question of their disposition were decided. Pressed for a more definite answer, Couza replied, 'As long as you took up the matter with me, I entered into it with you. You have applied to my government, and must now await an answer from my government.' The consuls all regarded his answer as tantamount to a refusal, and, after they had sent an identical note to the minister of foreign affairs, calling his attention to the delay in receiving a response to their previous communication, and demanding a categorical response in twenty-four hours,[6] there seems to have been a general feeling that they had done all that

[1] Cowley to Russell, no. 1368, Dec. 9, F.O. 27/1448; Metternich to Rechberg, no. 67, Dec. 9, Staatsarchiv, IX/71.
[2] Tillos to Lhuys, no. 99, Dec. 9, *Aff. étr., Turquie, Bucharest*, vol. 23.
[3] Green to Russell, no. 116, Dec. 11, enc., F.O. 78/1667.
[4] Ghika to Green, Dec. 10, enclosed in Green's no. 116.
[5] Green to Hammond, Dec. 12, F.O. 78/1667.
[6] Annex to Tillos's no. 101 of Dec. 15, *Aff. étr., Turquie, Bucharest*, vol. 23.

was in their power, and that there was nothing to do but to accept defeat.[1] It was adding insult to injury when the official reply not only evaded the question, but declared that explanations had been put before the ambassadors at Constantinople, and that the result of that overture must be awaited before an answer could be given to the demand.[2] It was not the first time that the incorrigible prince had appealed to the ambassadors over the heads of the troublesome consuls.

It was an example of the persistent failure of the consuls to take the measure of Couza's patriotism that they usually attributed his obduracy to an understanding with Russia, to whom he was alleged to be subservient.[3] 'If', said Eder, 'the efforts, taken in the name of the Powers, should meet with nothing but a negative answer from Couza, and he should suffer no ill consequences therefrom, the policy and influence of Russia would be exalted here, and the policy and influence of the other Powers would correspondingly sink.'[4] Yet even Eder, who was an exceptionally astute diplomat, had made the mistake of not inviting Giers to share their councils—a move, which might have fixed upon Russia some sort of responsibility for refusing. Giers felt bound to resent his exclusion from the meetings of the consuls (as also an investigation which the Prussian consul instituted near the Russian frontier),[5] and, when Eder tried rather lamely to excuse himself, and tardily solicited his co-operation (as dean of the consuls, he was, in a sense, their representative), Giers lost nothing by saying that his government's dignity would not allow him to take his cue from others.[6] It was, of course, clear enough—though the reason was not yet known—that Russia wanted no interference. When plied by the Austrian, French, and British governments to join in their pressure upon Couza, Gortchakoff put them off with the excuse that he had not yet received sufficient information,[7] or that the

---

[1] Eder to Rechberg, no. 112, Dec. 14, and no. 114, Dec. 16, Staatsarchiv, XXXVIII/134; Tillos to Thouvenel, no. 101, Dec. 15, *Aff. étr., Turquie, Bucharest*, vol. 23; Green to Russell, no. 118, Dec. 14, F.O. 78/1667.

[2] Green to Russell, no. 119, Dec. 15, enc., *ibid.* Russell penned on Ghika's note: 'P. Couza has throughout preserved this course. He objects first to the Porte's interference, next to the consuls', and then, after every sort of evasion, refuses point blank to comply with the Powers' requisition.'

[3] Tillos to Lhuys, no. 99, Dec. 9, *Aff. étr., Turquie, Bucharest*, vol. 23.

[4] Eder to Rechberg, no. 112.

[5] Giers to Gortchakoff, Nov. 30, *Aff. étr., Turquie, Bucharest*, vol. 23; Eder to Rechberg, no. 110, Dec. 11, Staatsarchiv, XXXVIII/134. Giers had finally attended a meeting after the triple note had been delivered, but, as he kept silent during the discussions, no one cared to quizz him: Green to Hammond, Dec. 12, F.O. 78/1667.

[6] Giers to Gortchakoff, Nov. 30; Eder to Rechberg, no. 110. Eder wrote that Giers himself had broached the subject of his exclusion, and was 'in great agitation'.

[7] Montebello to Lhuys, no. 131, Dec. 18, *Aff. étr., Russie*, vol. 229; Thun to Rechberg, no. 39 A–E, Dec. 13, Staatsarchiv, X/48.

claim of the Porte to prohibit the importation of the arms into its dominions was open to question, and that it was desirable not to irritate the Christian subjects of that Power.[1] Whether or not the arms were of Russian manufacture, he asserted positively that their importation into the Principalities was not the act of the Russian government.[2] Finally, after much pressure from the British ambassador, he stated frankly that if the arms were for revolutionary purposes, he would instruct his consul to join in the intervention of the other Powers, but that, if they were the property of Servia or of the Principalities, there would be 'no legitimate ground for interference'.[3] As a matter of fact, Gortchakoff knew perfectly well that the arms were bound for Servia, and he wished them to arrive there. This does not prove that Russia was guilty of any plot to bring about a Balkan conflagration; but it is incontestible that she wanted the little Balkan states to be stronger instruments of Russian policy, and she probably hoped that Michael would be strong enough before long to coerce the Turks into withdrawing altogether from Servian territory.

The truth about the arms was only gradually known, and even what the dispatches tell us may not be the whole truth. Prince Michael had apparently ordered a quantity of arms from Belgium, and, as there was danger that a shipment of arms via the Mediterranean would be stopped by inquisitive cruisers, he had probably arranged with the government of St. Petersburg that they should be transported across Russia.[4] The fact, which he is said to have represented to Couza,[5] that he did not know what route they would take, hardly does justice to that prince's intelligence, and may be reasonably discounted. According to French sources, he had sent an envoy to Bucharest in March, 1862 to see that passage through the Principalities might be secured, and Catargi, who was then premier, had, after much hesitation, finally yielded to Giers's pressure.[6] If this story is correct, then Couza's telegraphic inquiries (assuming that we may believe him) were merely for purposes of confirmation and not because Couza was really ignorant of the Servian transaction;[7] and, considering the fact that Couza

[1] Napier to Russell, no. 476, Dec. 11, F.O. 65/610.
[2] Thun to Rechberg, no. 39 A–E.
[3] Napier to Russell, no. 479, Dec. 14, F.O. 65/610.
[4] Tillos to Lhuys, no. 120, Apr. 29, 1863, *Aff. étr., Turquie, Bucharest*, vol. 23.
[5] The statement was made in Michael's message to Couza, already noted, page 388. That he did not know whether they would be sent overland or up the Danube is of no significance, as, in either case, it would have behoved him to communicate previously with Couza.
[6] Tillos to Lhuys, no. 120.
[7] Eder wrote in his letter of Dec. 8 that Couza told him that he did not know the owner of the arms or their destination. If, as Giers wrote on Nov. 30, Couza had told him that he had ascertained by telegraph that they were Servia's, then Couza must have been lying to Eder, if we are to credit the latter's report.

was not a person about whom assumptions could safely be made, it is reasonable to conclude that Michael had obtained some sort of understanding with Bucharest. Whether Gortchakoff's supposition that some of the arms for which Michael had contracted were old muskets from the arsenal at Kherson,[1] which had been sold to an American merchant,[2] was really true, or merely thrown out to screen the real transaction, is something we cannot settle. It is certainly not improbable that some of the weapons were purchased in Russia, and, if such were actually the case, it hardly seems quite plausible that the destination of the weapons was unknown in official circles. We know that a Russian vessel, carrying lead and saltpetre, had been stopped by the Turkish authorities in her course up the Danube, and it was believed that her cargo had also contained arms, which had been landed, before her detention, at some unknown point in Wallachia and sent thence by land to Servia.[3] Nevertheless, most of the consignment seems to have been shipped across the Black Sea to Akkerman in Russian Bessarabia, where carts were hired to take them across the frontier into Moldavia; there they were put on wagons or sledges, and carried over different roads (avoiding towns as far as possible) to Little Wallachia and Servia.[4] It was confidently believed that some of the arms were intended for Bulgaria, although held for the time being in Servia or on the Wallachian side of the Danube, lest they fall into the hands of the Turks;[5] but this argues collusion between Michael and certain elements in Bulgaria, of which there is insufficient evidence. How many muskets there were in all is also a matter on which one cannot speak with certainty. Couza was variously reported to have placed the figure at 30,000 and 40,000,[6] and Gortchakoff's estimates were similar,[7] though the consuls seemed to believe that the number was much greater.[8] Michael

[1] He had suggested Kiev to the Austrian ambassador: Revertera to Rechberg, no. 42 A–C, Dec. 27, Staatsarchiv, x/48.

[2] Napier to Russell, no. 516, Dec. 28, and no. 523, Dec. 31, F.O. 65/610. The American was said to be a naturalized Servian.

[3] Napier to Russell, no. 476; Longworth to Erskine, no. 70, Dec. 15, F.O. 78/1673. If it is true that there were arms and that they escaped in this way, it was apparently due to the negligence of the Turkish authorities at Sistova, who made a most superficial examination of the cargo, and admitted that boxes which probably contained arms had been left unopened. When the vessel, thanks to British activity, was finally stopped at Widin, the lead and saltpetre were confiscated as contraband of war: Ricketts to Erskine, no. 10, Nov. 8, and to Bulwer, no. 21, Nov. 24, F.O. 78/1673.

[4] Napier to Russell, no. 516; Green to Russell, no. 115, Dec. 10, F.O. 78/1667; Eder to Rechberg, no. 103.

[5] Eder to Rechberg, no. 118 A, Dec. 26, Staatsarchiv, xxxviii/134; Prokesch to Rechberg, Dec. 26, telg., *ibid.*, xii/76.

[6] Eder to Rechberg, no. 119, Dec. 26, *ibid.*, xxxviii/134; Bulwer to Russell, no. 25.

[7] Napier to Russell, no. 37, Jan. 22, 1863, F.O. 65/626.

[8] Green to Hammond, Dec. 15, F.O. 78/1667; Tillos to Lhuys, no. 103,

was by different persons reported to have admitted receiving 20,000, 25,000, and 30,000.[1] Obviously none of the interested parties can be implicitly believed.

In any event, Michael doubtless received the bulk of the arms which he had expected, and Gortchakoff declined to admit the British contention that Russia should not have allowed them passage, or to agree that the number of weapons were out of proportion to Servia's needs.[2] Indeed, Gortchakoff refused to believe that any suspicion should attach to Michael's intentions. It is not, of course, impossible that the contracts for the arms had been made before the Prince had settled his quarrel with Turkey,[3] and we learn that he had telegraphed Gortchakoff that they had not been ordered for warlike purposes, but 'only for the ordinary need for order and public security in my country';[4] Gortchakoff told Napier that he had reminded Michael of this assurance and felt himself to be the guarantor of his good faith[5]—an allusion to the fact that he had telegraphed Michael's message to the other Protecting Powers. Russia's strong intervention had the effect of inducing Prussia to instruct her consul to dissociate herself from further pressure upon Couza,[6] and France likewise withdrew all objection to the Servian transaction.[7] Apparently, if Michael were to slay the dragon, he was not without friends or at least benevolent neutrals. But one could hardly expect Vienna to approve of any activities that might tend to strengthen Servian nationalism or endanger in any way the status quo in the Ottoman Empire. The Austrian consul refused to consider the Prince's attitude defensive, but believed that he had sought this means, and was now awaiting the opportune moment for pursuing aggressive designs;[8] though it is an evidence of that mixture of fear and contempt that is so often the product of distrust, that the chauvinism of the Servian press led to the consul's scornful comment that '100,000 badly-armed Servians and a half-trained militia could not defend the land against even a badly-planned attack by the Porte'.[9] On December 27 the consul obtained an interview with the Prince, who spoke his mind with a vehemence and a frankness that left no doubt of his position. 'I do

---

Dec. 22, *Aff. étr., Turquie, Bucharest*, vol. 23. Tillos thought, from the number of carts, that there must have been from 80,000 to 150,000.

[1] *Ibid.*; Longworth to Bulwer, no. 70, Dec. 15, F.O. 78/1269; Bulwer to Russell, no. 25, Jan. 22, 1863, F.O. 65/626.
[2] Napier to Russell, nos. 523 and 537.
[3] Revertera to Rechberg, no. 42 A–C; Napier to Russell, no. 523. Such was also Napier's opinion.
[4] Michael to Gortchakoff, Dec. 17, annex to Thun's no. 40, Staatsarchiv, x/48.
[5] Napier to Russell, no. 523.
[6] Montebello to Lhuys, Dec. 17, telg., *Aff. étr., Russie*, vol. 229.
[7] Lhuys to Montebello, no. 89, Dec. 19, *ibid.*
[8] Wassitch to Rechberg, no. 66, Dec. 16, Staatsarchiv, xxxviii/133.
[9] Wassitch to Rechberg, no. 68, Dec. 22, *ibid.*

not see what right any one has', he declared, 'to prevent my getting these arms.' No intercession from the Powers, he continued, had availed to prevent the bombardment of his capital, and he was not going to be unprepared for another such catastrophe. 'With all due respect for the guarantee of the Powers, I prefer to apply my own means.'[1]

It would probably be too much to say that Servia had no logical right to buy arms, since neither firmans nor treaties had fixed precisely the size of her army or the extent of its equipment. If we are to contend, then, that a vassal prince had a right to arm his militia (and, of course, no ulterior object could be proved), might not another prince, who occupied the same status in the Ottoman Empire, allow the arms to be transported through his territories? The situation was quite different from that of 1860, when the arms introduced were plainly for use against Austria, thus compromising the neutrality of the Ottoman Empire. The question might perhaps be referred to the commercial treaties with the Porte, which banned arms from being introduced anywhere in the Ottoman Empire, though no such treaty with Russia seems to have been cited. Couza probably cared little for the legal question anyway. He proposed to play the role of an independent ruler— 'imagined himself to be a great Power' was Eder's comment[2]— and seems to have suggested all along that not only Russia but France was indifferent to his conduct.[3] To Eder he expressed his belief (though we know that it was erroneous) that Tillos had acted contrary to his instructions: 'This man', he said, 'does not see farther than the end of his nose.'[4] At all events, having successfully defied the consuls, he went so far as to send his own troops to protect the convoys and see them safely across the border.[5] Meanwhile, he counted on Negri to defend his cause, if necessary, with the ambassadors, to whom he had referred the question.[6]

Since, whatever the legal aspects of the case, both the Porte and the Protecting Powers had failed to bend Couza to their will, the only preoccupation left was to assuage their wounded dignity. For

---

[1] Wassitch to Rechberg, no. 69, Dec. 28, Staatsarchiv, xxxviii/133.
[2] Eder to Rechberg, no. 112, Dec. 14, Staatsarchiv, xxxviii/134.
[3] Eder to Rechberg, no. 119, Dec. 29.   [4] *Ibid.*
[5] Eder to Rechberg, no. 114, Dec. 16, *ibid.* It was also said that Couza had held a council meeting after his interview with the consuls on Dec. 13, and that it was decided to give the affair a 'national character' (both Eder and Green use that term) (Eder to Rechberg, no. 114; Green to Russell, Dec. 15, telg.), and Green later remarked upon the fact that Couza had 5,000 soldiers on the Danube: Green to Russell, no. 10, Feb. 2, 1863, F.O. 78/1746. It looked like a pretentious precaution against a Turkish invasion.
[6] Tillos to Lhuys, no. 102, Dec. 18, *Aff. étr., Turquie, Bucharest*, vol. 23. For Fuad's letter of reproach to Couza (which was communicated to the ambassadors) see *Arch. dip., 1863*, vol. iii, pp. 109–11.

a vassal prince thus to defy his superiors with impunity was unpleasantly reminiscent of the days of Mehemet Ali. It must have
seemed, indeed, as though the very existence of the international
protectorate over the Principalities had been challenged. Something, apparently, must be done; and, when it came to considering
the form of discipline which should be administered, it was natural
that some one should think of the coercive provisions of the
Protocol of 1859.[1] If the Principalities had not observed the proper
relationship with the Porte, as confirmed in the Convention, then it
might be pleaded under the aforesaid protocol that a commissioner
of the Porte should be sent thither to investigate the offence. Such,
in fact, was Rechberg's proposal, telegraphed to Prokesch on
December 18, though the dispatch, owing to heavy snows, did
not reach the internuncio until the 23rd.[2] Nothing was said about
the preliminary assent of the ambassadors, though that may have
been understood.

It remained to be seen now whether the unwieldy combination of
suzerain and guardians would agree upon any concerted action.
The Porte, which had already felt it necessary to invoke the aid
of the Powers if Couza were to be made to yield,[3] and which now
saw that yielding was out of the question, grasped eagerly at the
Austrian proposal, and sent a circular to its representatives proposing that a Turkish commissioner should be sent to the Principalities and associate himself with the consuls of the Protecting
Powers in some effort to recall Couza to his duty.[4] Russell was
also reported (by Musurus) as already favouring recourse to the
Protocol, though it was evident that he had felt that Turkey should
take the initiative,[5] and Drouyn likewise expressed this view.[6] The
attitude of France was wary, to say the least. At the time when
Tillos was instructed to join in the consular intervention Drouyn
de Lhuys had written to Moustier that, as Russia's probable
connexion with the sending of the arms made the question a
delicate one, he thought that France should avoid meddling in the
matter as far as possible,[7] and it was not hard for Moustier to
perceive that his government had mainly acted under the pressure
of circumstances and was really opposed to doing anything.
Russia was the first, however, to express unequivocal disapproval
of the proposed step. Gortchakoff said that such a measure would

[1] Page 248.
[2] Prokesch to Rechberg, no. 95 A–B, Dec. 24, Staatsarchiv, XII/76.
[3] *Arch. dip.*, *1863*, vol. iii, p. 111; Prokesch to Rechberg, Dec. 6, telg., Staatsarchiv, XII/134. [4] Prokesch to Rechberg, Dec. 24, telg., *ibid.*
[5] Prokesch to Rechberg, no. 95 A–B; cf. F.O. to Cowley, no. 1279, Dec. 17,
F.O. 27/1429. Russell confessed to Apponyi that he thought such a step rather
risky: Apponyi to Rechberg, no. 93, Dec. 24, Staatsarchiv, VIII/64.
[6] Cowley to Russell, Dec. 19, telg., F.O. 27/1448.
[7] Lhuys to Moustier, no. 98, Dec. 5, *Aff. étr.*, *Turquie*, vol. 356.

cause 'irritating discussion',[1] and he doubted—later he put it more emphatically—if the Protocol of 1859 would apply.[2] No one, of course, would have expected any different answer from Russia. But on January 1 Rechberg telegraphed Prokesch that, as France (as well as Great Britain) approved the proposal, the Porte should send its commissioner without waiting for the concurrence of the other Powers.[3] It was not the first time that Austria had tried to get the Porte to go beyond its legal powers in dealing with the Principalities,[4] and such an experiment had never been justified by the result. If France should now be moved to side with Russia, the chance of overcoming Gortchakoff's isolated resistance would be definitely lost.

As far as may be judged from the dispatches, France was playing what may be called at the very least an ambiguous role at this juncture. Count Metternich, the Austrian ambassador at Paris, had reported, December 30, that Drouyn de Lhuys had given his adhesion to the Austro-Turkish proposal, as contained in the Porte's circular;[5] and, pursuant to advices he had received, Rechberg telegraphed to Prokesch that he was assured that Moustier would be instructed to act immediately with Bulwer and the internuncio.[6] Drouyn's actual instructions to Moustier, however, gave a loophole for evasion. While he felt, he said, that he could not refuse the Porte's request, now that it had taken the initiative, and Great Britain and Austria had given assent, he had told both Metternich and Cowley that it was not yet established that the Convention had been violated, and that the Porte should have first submitted the question to the ambassadors before asking that the Protocol be applied.[7] No such objection, as a matter of fact, had been raised by the French minister, until he had found that the Porte intended, after all, to force the issue. Cowley hinted that Napoleon was responsible for the change of tone, and said that he feared that 'very vague' instructions would be sent, which 'would justify M. de Moustier's non-interference, should he be disinclined to help the Porte'.[8] Moustier, as might be expected, took his cue from Drouyn's letter and, when Ali asked him if he had received instructions regarding the sending of a commissioner, he answered that his government felt that the ambassadors should first decide whether the Protocol was applicable.[9] He made the same assertion

[1] Montebello to Lhuys, no. 9, Jan. 7, 1863, *ibid.*, *Russie*, vol. 230.
[2] Gortchakoff to Novikoff, Dec. 16, 1862, *Aff. étr.*, *Turquie*, vol. 356.
[3] Rechberg to Prokesch, Jan. 1, 1863, telg., Staatsarchiv, XII/80.   [4] See p. 59.
[5] Metternich to Rechberg, no. 70 B, Dec. 30, 1862, *ibid.* A telegram to the same effect had been dispatched from Paris on the 29th.
[6] Rechberg to Prokesch, Jan. 2, 1863, *ibid.*, XII/80.
[7] Lhuys to Moustier, no. 1, Jan. 2, *Aff. étr.*, *Turquie*, vol. 357.
[8] Cowley to Russell, no. 1479, Dec. 26, 1862, F.O. 27/1448.
[9] Moustier to Lhuys, no. 14, Jan. 15, 1863, *Aff. étr.*, *Turquie*, vol. 357.

to Prokesch, and, as if to emphasize the divergence between the spirit of his own government and that of the others, he criticized the recent action of the consuls *en fixant une terme péremptoire* for Couza's reply to their demand, adding that Couza's refusal to accede to it was not regarded at Paris as a blow to the dignity of the Powers.[1] To Ali Moustier declared, further, that he could not see the wisdom of letting Michael and Couza gain popularity by calling forth a patriotic sentiment in a controversy with the Powers. But some of his colleagues showed no such spirit of resignation as the French ambassador was manifesting. Prokesch, according to Moustier, displayed an 'anger, which exceeded the zeal of the ambassador of England', and Bulwer, for his part, would not brook the idea of standing the 'impertinences' of Couza.[2] When the internuncio heard that Couza meant to ask the Powers for a dictatorship, he was more than ever convinced that intervention was necessary.[3] 'The Principalities are a tough problem,' Lord John Russell had once said, 'whenever the question is debated.'[4]

Undoubtedly, from the point of view of the diplomats, who wished to keep the Prince in the subjection to which his position had consecrated him, the evident resolution of the Principalities to settle the question of the dedicated monasteries to suit themselves, and the fresh infractions of the Capitulations which had lately been reported, coincident as all this was with Couza's attitude on the arms question, made some action on the part of the Powers seem indispensable, if the Principalities were not to get entirely out of hand.[5] Nor should it be overlooked that Michael was still unchastened, and, if he had offended less often than his fellow prince, he had offended more seriously, since it was he who now possessed the forbidden fruit. But, for the moment, the case of Couza seemed the more serious. 'The existence of this tension', wrote Prokesch, 'between the Prince and the suzerain Power veils the danger of further friction which may break out—not, in the last instance, to the advantage of the Prince, for, if the question assumes a more serious character, no Power will in the last instance subordinate the greater interest to the lesser.'[6] There is no denying the logic of this remark, but would things work out that way 'in the last instance'? Was there any interest powerful enough to induce

[1] Prokesch to Rechberg, no. 5 A–B, Jan. 16, Staatsarchiv, XII/78.
[2] Moustier to Lhuys, no. 14.
[3] Prokesch to Rechberg, no. 2 C, Jan. 7, Staatsarchiv, XII/78.
[4] Russell to Bulwer, Sept. 4, 1859, Russell Papers, G. and D., 22/116, Pub. Rec. Off.
[5] Bulwer seemed to feel that the same commissioner should handle all pending questions: Prokesch to Rechberg, no. 6 A–C, Jan. 21, 1863, Staatsarchiv, XII/78.
[6] Prokesch to Eder, no. 6 A, Jan. 21, *ibid.*

all the Protecting powers to coerce Couza into submission? Was there anything really to be gained by sending a commissioner to investigate or remonstrate? One might hazard the guess that such a display of discipline would either rally Rouman nationalism to support the Prince (and then the situation would be at least no better than it had been), or else would give a handle to Couza's enemies, who might bring about his fall. That, of course, was the last thing that the Powers wanted.

Since, therefore, the Powers were not willing to carry their quarrel to conclusions—since, after all, the whole question of procedure had been inspired by the damaged prestige of the Porte and the flouted dignity of the Powers, the attitude of France was much more consonant with realities, much more grounded on common sense than that of the other Powers. When a conference of the ambassadors met on January 20, 1863, and Bulwer formally proposed the sending of a commissioner, Moustier stuck to his view that such a measure was impracticable. Pressed by Bulwer (who was much annoyed) to suggest some alternative, the French ambassador proposed that Couza should be asked to send a delegate to Constantinople to give the Porte explanations and satisfactory assurances. Moustier hoped that Couza might be induced 'spontaneously' to offer this atonement—by which he probably meant that, while the consuls were individually to bring the matter before him, no formal demand should be tendered by the ambassadors or the Porte.[1] The other diplomats saw that they could do no better than accept this compromise; and Prokesch and Bulwer then persuaded him to agree to identical treatment of Michael,[2] to which suggestion only the Russian chargé d'affaires seemed to demur.[3] But Russia's conduct was, after all, a mere reflection of her mercurial vice-chancellor. Gortchakoff had been more vehement than Drouyn de Lhuys in his disapproval of the sending of a commissioner to Bucharest,[4] and he had also been the stoutest champion of Michael, but the outbreak of an insurrection in Poland had convinced him that he had better not risk placing Russia in an isolated position;[5] and Drouyn de Lhuys noted with pleasure

[1] It was characteristic of Bulwer that he wrote directly to Couza: Bulwer to Russell, no. 46, Jan. 30, enc., F.O. 78/1732. The other ambassadors seem to have been content with writing to their respective consuls.
[2] Bulwer took sole credit for the idea: Bulwer to Russell, Jan. 27, telg., F.O. 78/1732.
[3] Moustier to Tillos, Jan. 21, *Aff. étr., Turquie*, vol. 357; Moustier to Lhuys, no. 18, Jan. 22, and annex, *ibid.*; Moustier to Tillos, Jan. 21; Prokesch to Rechberg, no. 6 A–C.
[4] Montebello to Lhuys, no. 1, Jan. 7, *Aff. étr., Russie*, vol. 233; Revertera to Rechberg, no. 1 D, Jan. 18, Staatsarchiv, x/49.
[5] 'You will be very prudent in regard to the Principalities and Servia', Russell telegraphed Bulwer on Jan. 27. 'Prince Gortchakoff has changed his language

that the Court of St. Petersburg had decided to concur in the arrangement.[1] The result was certainly no tribute to British diplomacy, for Russell had hectored Gortchakoff on the subject of the arms until the Russian statesman had almost lost his temper.[2] Relations between Great Britain and Russia, never friendly when the Eastern Question was under discussion, became still more alienated over the uprising in Poland. The only satisfaction to London might accrue from the fact that Napoleon threw away his newly cemented friendship with St. Petersburg by initiating the futile attempt at intervention in Polish affairs in June, 1863. But, so far, the Franco-Russian *rapprochement* had held firm, and the arms crisis had tilted the balance of victory in favour of the vassal princes.

The notion of sending a commissioner to the Principalities was not quite dead, as we shall notice presently in another question, but the idea of dispatching persons to raise a rumpus over a situation that was beyond retrieval had happily been abandoned. Couza made no trouble about sending the desired excuses, and Negri, who had happened to be in Bucharest, was sent back to his post to deliver his master's sentiments. Michael refused to send any one from Belgrade, and merely tendered his explanations through his resident agent at Constantinople.[3] The performance of this ceremony of atonement through the kapou kiayas was even less of a condescension than the Powers had expected. It was but a small scrap of satisfaction that the Porte and its friends had received after demanding so peremptorily the sequestration of the arms and discussing the expediency of punishing the culprit who refused to obey them.

The crisis of 1862-3 had, in fact, revealed the hollowness of the European protectorate over the United Principalities. The coercive stipulation of the Protocol of 1859, on which the Porte had counted so strongly, was demonstrated as a fiction, which, most likely, France and Russia had foreseen from the first. The attempt to force Couza to observe public law as Turkey and the Protecting Powers interpreted it had degenerated into a feeble effort to save the face of the suzerain, who had nothing but a nominal hold over his vassals, and to satisfy the dignity of two Powers, who, out of interest or tradition, took the protectorate[4] rather seriously. In

and become more friendly to Great Britain. The insurrection which has broken out in Poland makes the Russian government unwilling to foment rebellion elsewhere': F.O. 78/1728. It was more likely that Gortchakoff wished to avoid an intervention of the Powers in Poland.

[1] Lhuys to Montebello, no. 11, Jan. 31, *Aff. étr.*, *Russie*, vol. 210.
[2] See the Russell-Napier correspondence, F.O. 65/610 and 626; Montebello to Lhuys, no. 2, Jan. 21, *Aff. étr.*, *Russie*, vol. 230; Revertera to Rechberg, no. 3 A–B, Feb. 4, Staatsarchiv, x/49.
[3] Prokesch to Rechberg, no. 13 A–B, Feb. 18, *ibid.*, XII/78.
[4] Rechberg, in a moment of despair, raised the question of whether it might

May Negri handed Moustier a letter, in which Couza expressed his gratitude to the French embassy for the support he had received in the recent controversy.[1] Of the honour of having stultified the position of the Protecting Powers, possibly Couza and Napoleon may claim an equal share.

be well to call it ended, since unanimity among the Powers seemed absolutely impossible: Bloomfield to Russell, Jan. 22, 1863, Russell Papers, G. and D., 22/42, Pub. Rec. Off. It is a pity that so much wisdom was not uttered dispassionately.

[1] Moustier to Lhuys, no. 90, May 14, *Aff. étr.*, *Turquie*, vol. 358.

CHAPTER XIV

'THE LITTLE *COUP D'ÉTAT*'

IT is something like an historical truism that there is nothing better calculated to unify a nation that is torn by internal strife than a controversy with a foreign Power. On that assumption Couza's successful resistance to the Porte and the Protecting Powers in the arms controversy should have brought the national feeling to his aid and strengthened his position as ruler. But it is doubtful if one can apply this maxim to a nation in embryo. The patriotism of the Moldo-Wallachians was too recent a phenomenon to overcome either the pressure of class interests or the ambition of individuals who mistook a constitutional régime for machinery for enhancing their political fortunes. If the Porte had been permitted to intervene in the Principalities, it is not unlikely that the first act of the *boyards* would have been to overthrow Couza, and that any foreign prince, even a Russian, would have been welcomed as a means of consolidating the political and economic ascendancy of the *boyarie*. Yet it must be admitted that Couza had done nothing to rouse public sentiment in his favour. Having always looked to outside aid for the realization of his hopes, he had not ventured to incite a feeling that might conceivably have compromised him with the Powers. Between the alternative of rousing his people against the Powers or rousing the Powers against his people, he preferred the latter—the less hazardous, though slower and more tortuous—course. For that reason the Balkan crisis was but a passing cloud in the bitter struggle between the Prince and the *boyards*.

It has already been noticed that the weakness of the ministry and the virulence of the opposition were bringing matters to a situation wherein Couza, if he were to govern at all, must govern without reference to the assembly. He might, of course, have tried the experiment, which served him so well in 1861, of giving the ministry temporarily to the Left, and frightening his enemies by reviving the electoral question. But Couza was not sure now that he could handle so sharp a weapon. The march of the peasants in February, the murder of Catargi, and the evidences of collusion between the 'revolutionary party' and similar organizations elsewhere were enough to give him pause. 'It would be a poor system', he told Eder, 'that would drive me into the arms of the revolutionary party. If I succeeded in annihilating the *boyards* by means of the revolutionary party, I could not easily rid myself of the latter.'[1] Furthermore, like most men with a revolutionary background who have risen to a position of authority, Couza had become a

---

[1] Eder to Rechberg, no. 92, Oct. 24, 1862, Staatsarchiv, XXXVIII/134.

moderate in politics. However much he might have wished to lessen the political and economic power of the *boyards*, he had long since divested himself of the spirit of '48, and he distrusted its disciples. When the episode of the *Roumanul*'s indiscretion[1] occurred, Couza put before the consuls the question whether he might wisely employ the discretionary powers granted him after Catargi's murder. None of these agents, however, would take the responsibility of counselling him to take measures against the party which they feared,[2] and it is not improbable that the Prince was merely showing up the futility of this vigilance corps, of whose want of sympathy he frankly complained.[3] In the meantime the measures against the Left were not taken more seriously than they were intended, and, though the Prince sometimes gave way to momentary depression,[4] the episode of the arms during the winter demanded all his wit and courage.

But there was no doubting that the *boyards* were quietly biding their time and thirsting for revenge upon the man in whose service their leader had been lost. A discussion of the budget for the year 1863 gave the Opposition its first opportunity. Some weeks previously Couza had issued the decree sequestering the revenues of the dedicated monasteries. When the budget came up for discussion on January 3, some one injected into it, as part of the receipts, the revenues of these religious foundations. Manifestly, this would have been sheer confiscation,[5] and foreign complications, especially with Russia, would immediately have resulted. The ministry threatened to resign if the item were retained, but as this was just what the Opposition wanted, while even the friends of the government gloated over a chance to despoil the Church, the measure was passed by a nearly unanimous vote. It would seem now that, if Couza wished to avoid an external crisis, he had no alternative but to dissolve the assembly, and to do so without a budget would virtually mean the establishment of a dictatorship.[6] By the Opposition, on the other hand, the struggle was fostered

---

[1] Page 385.

[2] Eder to Rechberg, no. 95, Nov. 4, Staatsarchiv, XXXVIII/134; Tillos to Lhuys, no. 93, Nov. 3, *Aff. étr., Turquie, Bucharest*, vol. 23; Green to Russell, no. 99, Nov. 2, F.O. 78/1667.

[3] Tillos to Thouvenel, no. 95, Nov. 17, *Aff. étr., Turquie, Bucharest*, vol. 23.

[4] *Ibid.* In conversation with Tillos Couza threw out the idea that he might be rid of the intrigues of pretenders if the Powers would now appoint his successor. Eder heard that he talked of abdicating, but found, after a long interview with him, that he 'has not the least intention of giving up his present position': Eder to Rechberg, no. 98 A, Nov. 17.

[5] Green learned that the assembly's purpose was to get the means of exercising some control over the sums in sequester (Green to Russell, no. 1, Jan. 4, 1863, F.O. 78/1746), but he admitted the assembly's factiousness, which seems to be the most obvious explanation of this episode.

[6] Eder to Rechberg, no. 2, Jan. 5, 1863, Staatsarchiv, XXXVIII/139.

with the deliberate intention, by withholding any budget that the government would accept, of forcing the Prince's deposition.[1] But, happily, the Left was unwilling to go that far,[2] and the moment was lost before the assembly adjourned for its Christmas recess.

The interval was hardly more than a breathing-spell, however, before the battle would be renewed. 'The atmosphere', wrote the British consul, 'is so impregnated with duplicity and intrigue that it must be much easier to see clearly at a distance from the scene than in the midst of it.'[3] It was predicted that, as soon as the session opened, the assembly would utilize its reply to the Prince's address to bring forward an *exposé* of the evil condition of things, and then declare for a foreign prince.[4] Such, of course, was a convenient mask for the ambition of all 'pretenders',[5] and it is very hard to feel that this movement was disinterested. None the less, it was formidable. Couza told Green that he knew that the radicals were joining forces with the *boyards*, and that John Ghika (whom he had always distrusted) was the leading spirit of the Coalition. He himself was apparently awaiting the issue of events before making any plans, but he spoke to Green as if he were confident of meeting any emergency.[6]

The assembly opened January 22, and at once considered the Prince's address, which had been delivered on November 16, calling chiefly for consideration of the budget.[7] Manifestly, it was the part of the Opposition to take the first offensive step, and, judging from the consular reports, it appeared that almost every one was in that category. It was known that a determined effort would be made to force the Prince's dethronement, and already people were talking of his successor, the preponderance of *boyard* opinion favouring the Tsar's brother-in-law,[8] the Duke of Leuchtenberg, one of those princes whose fate it is to be mentioned whenever a throne is to be disposed of, while the more liberal element declared for Prince Napoleon. France was, of course, quick to discountenance the use of the latter's name,[9] while Russia, in spite of the equivocal conduct of her cousul,[10] was not seriously

---

[1] Eder to Rechberg, no. 1, Jan. 1, *ibid.*
[2] Eder to Rechberg, no. 3, Jan. 10.
[3] Green to Hammond, Jan. 31, F.O. 78/1746.
[4] Tillos to Lhuys, no. 109, Jan. 18, *Aff. étr., Turquie, Bucharest*, vol. 23.
[5] 'Ils demandaient le prince étranger,' wrote Cogalnitchano, 'les braves gens, mais cela non point pour l'avoir, mais pour arriver à deux princes séparatistes': Iorga, *Mihail Kogălniceanu*, pp. 175–6.
[6] Green to Russell, no. 9, Jan. 18, F.O. 78/1746.
[7] *Arch. dip., 1863*, vol. i, pp. 458–9.
[8] *Almanach de Gotha*, 1860, p. 70.
[9] Lhuys to Tillos, no. 3, Feb. 13, *Aff. étr., Turquie, Bucharest*, vol. 23.
[10] Giers, like the policy of his government, was a good deal of a mystery to his colleagues. Tillos, at one moment, accused him of working openly for Leuchtenberg's candidacy, but Green had reported that he was urging Couza to assume

suspected of plotting Couza's overthrow.[1] The focus of the battle
was the question of the reply to the address from the throne. The
original project being too mild to suit many of the assembly, a
substitute, of which John Ghika and Pano, the Moldavian, were
reputed to be the authors, was presented to the chamber with
thirty-three signatures. Though couched in respectful language,
this document was a severe indictment of the four years of Couza's
reign. The true union of the Roumanian people, so loudly
demanded, had not been attained because of inner divisions, and
because the 'government of Your Highness does not show the
desired perseverance and a sufficient vigour in its labours to
facilitate the work of regeneration and reconstitution, which it was
under obligation to accomplish'. The cause of all the evils which
the nation had suffered was attributed to the fact that a 'constitutional régime cannot produce any good in the State unless it is
applied with sincerity'. After a defence of the assembly against the
imputation of reactionary aims, and after much stress on its
devotion in voting large sums for the support of the government's
policy, the charge was made that the attempt to secure an electoral
law from foreigners at Constantinople, instead of taking up the
measure voted by the central commission, was a breach of the
national autonomy. It is 'not the constitutional régime' which had
ignored the electoral question, failed to promulatge the rural law,
neglected public works and public instruction, brought the finances
into disorder, and converted the personnel of the administration
into 'an instrument instead of that solid edifice, prescribed by the
Convention'.[2] The tirade was of great length, and its force was
somewhat vitiated by faults of composition, but, as constituting
the Opposition's case against Couza, it has some passing interest.
The Prince could easily have answered it by reminding his enemies
that he had offered the ministry to the chiefs of the conservative
party, and that they had preferred dissension to co-operation, and
intrigue to the assumption of responsibilities. Meanwhile, outside
the assembly a petition was being circulated, declaring for a
foreign prince—an act which roused the government through the
Moniteur to call on the prefects to put a stop to it.[3]

a dictatorship, and Eder said that he was trying to mediate between the contending factions: Tillos to Lhuys, Feb. 9, telg.; Green to Russell, no. 3, Jan. 6;
Eder to Rechberg, no. 5 A, Jan. 17. The probable truth is that Giers was instructed to gain the confidence of both sides, while preventing, if possible, the
precipitation of a crisis. The situation in Poland was not such as to make Russia
want a crisis at present.

[1] Certainly none of the consuls seemed to think so; and, though Tillos had
warned his chief that Leuchtenberg's candidacy would win, unless France, as he
hinted, would back Napoleon (Feb. 9, telg.), he later came to the conclusion that
Russia had no immediate plans: no. 3, Feb. 13.
[2] Green to Russell, no. 25, Feb. 5, enc., F.O. 78/1746.
[3] Green to Russell, no. 21, Feb. 3, *ibid.*

After the substitute address was tabled for further consideration, and a paragraph of the original address, expressing the nation's gratitude to the Prince, was rejected by a vote of 63 to 40, a new project, framed by a committee, of which Pano and Ghika were members, was introduced and passed by a slightly larger majority.[1] While some unimportant excisions were made in Pano's substitute, and while the admission was recorded that the more enlightened sections of the population unfortunately preferred public office to any other walk of life, thus producing a competition which prevented all governmental efforts at amelioration—'one of the principal causes of the paralysis of our society', which (note the contradiction) all rulers had failed to combat—the charges of negligence and misgovernment, made against the Prince, were allowed to stand.[2] This final project was passed on February 23 by a vote of 63 to 48.[3] It is to be noticed that even the most inveterate enemies of Couza did not offer an amendment, demanding his dethronement, but Demetrius Ghika brought up the question of a foreign prince in the course of the debate, and Gregory Sturdza, once the defeated aspirant for the hospodariate of Moldavia, made the declaration (and he professed to speak in the name of the majority) that it was time to realize the wishes of the *divans ad hoc* for a foreign prince.[4] John Ghika was also accused of openly demanding the Prince's abdication.[5]

This political chaos was naturally very disquieting to the ambassadors at Constantinople, who had hardly closed the annoying episode of the smuggled arms before they were called upon to give their attention to fresh difficulties. Prokesch suggested that, after all, a commission should be sent to the Principalities, who should '(1) examine the causes of the present threatening opposition to the government of the Prince as well as the means of remedying it, (2) regularize the application of the Capitulations and the position of foreigners in Moldo-Wallachia, and (3) conduct to an equitable outcome the question of the landed property of the monasteries'.[6] But the whole question was one of tactics, and not so easily disposed of. The consuls, who had been asked their opinion, found that Couza himself believed that the sending of a commissioner would do more harm than good,[7] and Eder got the impression that the Prince would do all he could to hinder such a

---

[1] Green to Bulwer, no. 12, Feb. 10, *ibid.*
[2] Green to Russell, no. 37, Mar. 9, enc., *ibid.*
[3] Green to Russell, no. 26, Feb. 24, *ibid.*
[4] Green to Russell, no. 30, Feb. 20, *ibid.*; *Résumé* of the debates, annexed to Prokesch's no. 16 A, Feb. 27, Staatsarchiv, XII/78.
[5] Green to Russell, no. 9, Jan. 18, F.O. 78/1746.
[6] Prokesch to Rechberg, no. 13 A–B, Feb. 18, Staatsarchiv, XII/78.
[7] Green to Russell, no. 16, Feb. 23, F.O. 78/1746.

step.[1] Perhaps it was the fear of something like this that put Couza on his guard; for Negri was instructed to lay before the Porte a description of the present state of affairs—the difficulties which the Prince encountered under the existing system of government, and particularly the unscrupulous conduct of the Opposition, which included (said Negri) twenty-seven pretenders for the throne, all of whom masked their designs under the cry for a foreign prince.[2]

Some sort of intervention might well seem desirable, but the case obviously demanded delicate handling. The kapou kiaya seemed clearly to have made an impression on Ali, who now voiced the fear that the arrival of a commissioner would have the immediate effect of encouraging the enemies of Couza to overthrow him and install a foreign prince,[3] and Bulwer, who sympathized with Couza, and felt that his difficulties were mainly due to the long period of Turkish delay in granting union,[4] seemed to share the Turkish minister's opinion that such a measure would be perilous.[5] All the ambassadors, moreover, appeared to feel that the consuls had allowed themselves too readily to be drawn into petty intrigues, and Moustier blamed Tillos severely for his bias against the Prince.[6] The French ambassador discountenanced the story of Russian designs on the hospodariate, and doubted the charge that Couza was planning to abdicate in favour of a foreign prince. Yet he fully agreed with his colleagues that, unless something were done to smooth out the present difficulties, the situation might lead to dangerous complications.[7] The Turkish minister having formally put the matter before the ambassadors,[8] the diplomats met in conference, February 26, at the French embassy to decide what course to take.

The result was hardly creditable to the judgement of these diplomats. It was readily agreed that the question must be kept, if possible, from a serious international complication—which would be the case if Couza were ousted—and it was felt by Moustier, in particular, that the consuls, instead of busying themselves with Couza's mistakes, should 'use more energetic language to the Opposition than they had done hitherto'. Bulwer then expressed the fear that taking the side of the executive against the legislature might be misunderstood in England,[9] and the decision

[1] Eder to Rechberg, no. 12, Feb. 23, Staatsarchiv, XXXVIII/139.
[2] Prokesch to Rechberg, no. 13 A–B, Feb. 18, Staatsarchiv, XII/78.
[3] Eder warned Prokesch that the coming of a commissioner, while the assembly was still sitting, would probably have this result: Prokesch to Rechberg, no. 16 A–C, Feb. 27, *ibid.*   [4] Bulwer to Russell, no. 23, Jan. 21, F.O. 78/1648.
[5] Prokesch to Rechberg, no. 13 A–B.
[6] Moustier to Lhuys, no. 26, Feb. 12, *Aff. étr.*, Turquie, vol. 357.
[7] Moustier to Lhuys, no. 33, Feb. 17, *ibid.*
[8] Ali to Prokesch, Feb. 22, annex to Prokesch's no. 16 A–C.
[9] Moustier to Lhuys, no. 36, Feb. 26, *Aff. étr.*, Turquie, vol. 357.

of the conference in the end was rather wanting in precision. The outcome of the session was a collective telegram to the consuls. The dispatch ran as follows:

'The representatives of the Powers at Constantinople, justly pre-occupied with the situation which has occurred at Bucharest, are unani-mous on the necessity of preventing any attack upon the constitution and any act of the assembly which may compromise the rights of the prince. The important point is that of preventing a local question from becoming a general question. You will concert with your colleagues a means of acting promptly and energetically to attain that end, putting aside all dissidence and every subsidiary consideration. You are like-wise to combine to inform us of your common judgement on what may contribute to give the crisis a peaceful outcome.' [1]

It is to be observed that the ambassadors had decided to give the consuls the discretionary authority to deal with the situation, and to act as they saw fit. This was hardly likely to solve the problem, as it was a foregone conclusion that the agents would put all their pressure on the Prince, and expect him to make all the concessions required by the situation. In the telegraphic reply which the consuls sent to Constantinople they severely criticized him for choosing undesirable advisers, neglecting the state of the adminis-tration, and employing political manœuvres ('the game of see-saw') which destroyed the general confidence. The advice which they had agreed to give him was that of choosing ministers from the parliamentary majority.[2]

It remained to be seen whether the Prince would accept what would amount to a defeat in the parliamentary battle. To the consuls he made it clear that he would not. He knew, he said, the instructions which they had received; and his manner and words, 'when speaking of the assembly', gave little hope that he would yield an inch. But the crux of the situation, as the consuls had pointed out in their message, was the budget. It was well known that the finances were in a hopeless muddle, that there was a serious deficit, and that for two years the government had collected revenues and expended them without any account being submitted to the assembly. Before the present crisis a proposal had been made that the minister of finance be forced to accept a committee of supervision, chosen by the legislature, but the suggestion was negatived on the ground that the Convention did not warrant such an encroachment on the executive.[3] Yet the government was equally without justification in refusing to allow its accounts to be examined. Obviously, the simplest way of making the government

[1] *Arch. dip., 1863*, vol. iii, p. 112.
[2] Eder to Rechberg, Mar. 2 and annex, Staatsarchiv, xxxviii/139. Eder wrote that the Russian consul was much displeased with his instructions.
[3] Green to Russell, no. 19, Feb. 2, F.O. 78/1746.

financially amenable to the legislature was to appoint a ministry which had the confidence of the chamber, but as this implied the acceptance of the principle of ministerial responsibility, which the Prince was not bound to accept, and as it also meant surrender to his enemies—which naturally he would not think of—the only constitutional means of redress for the assembly was to refuse to pass any budget until the state of the finances was thoroughly examined. Unhappily, the assembly was more than likely to resort to this club as a sheer political manœuvre. Moreover, such a course would probably have the effect of driving the Prince to the unconstitutional practice of contracting loans without legislative approval. Such procedure had already proved an easy way of avoiding dependence upon the chamber, and the discovery that the ministry of finance had borrowed five million piasters, instead of two million as authorized by the assembly,[1] was an offence still fresh in the public mind. If Couza could find the money to run the government without applying to the assembly, a dictatorship would be established in all but name.

Couza no doubt saw that he had reached the cross-roads. To give in to the assembly would mean to accept the yoke of the *boyards*, while to continue the struggle might enable him to get the Powers' consent to a dictatorship. A possible middle course might have been to make overtures to Ghika and Pano, who had only lately joined his enemies, and whose support might have split the Opposition; but, unfortunately, it was these men who had offended him the most deeply, and all the evidence seems to show that he meant to defy the assembly and place his case before the ambassadors at Constantinople. At the time when the consuls had advised him to choose a ministry from the parliamentary majority, Couza responded that there was no coherent majority, properly speaking, and even if there were, he would not change his ministry. In the Principalities, he told Eder, the principle of authority must be upheld above all other considerations. The conduct of the assembly had shattered this principle, and now to give it to a factious majority would be shattering it still more. The experience of the last four years had shown that the constitutional tendencies of the Convention were simply not suited to his country, and the only possible way of smoothing out the situation was to strengthen the executive power by removing the assembly altogether. For consideration of the budget a senate or some other consultative body should replace the existing legislature. 'Do you believe', he exclaimed, 'that next year, if I encounter this assembly's opposition, I will call them again? . . . I have told the so-called repre-

[1] Green to Russell, no. 3, Jan. 6, F.O. 78/1746.

sentatives of the land that ... they will know full well with whom they have to deal.'[1]

The Prince had made his decision; but of course the assembly had its bolt to deliver too. On March 10 it voted that as long as the present ministry, which did not enjoy the confidence of the assembly, remained in office, no budget should be voted, and any one who ordered taxes to be paid or collected them should be declared a transgressor of the law. It was a question, as Eder viewed it, of prestige versus constitutional rights.[2] And, so far, the outcome of the struggle was still undecided. But Couza meant to procure a respite for a time, and accordingly on March 14 he closed the session.[3]

The significance of the Prince's act did not, of course, pass unnoticed, even if Eder was a little hasty in defining it. 'While Prince Couza simply closes the assembly,' wrote the Austrian consul, 'he gives notice that he will rule without any consultation of the chamber on the budget. Thereby he puts himself outside the Convention, and arrogates to himself discretionary authority which is not recognized by the constitution.' Far from traversing the Convention, Couza himself did not, of course, recognize that his proceedings were in any way arbitrary: he had closed the assembly because it had lasted its conventional three months,[4] and, in default of a new budget, he had perfect right under the Convention to proceed according to the previous one.[5] At all events, the parliamentary struggle was ended for a time, though Green pointed out that opposition, in consequence, would take the form of conspiracy; yet as revolution was not to be expected, he continued, the only thing that could avert a dictatorship was the intervention of the Powers.[6] Cogalnitchano put it more mildly when he wrote that Couza had nine months in which to organize his authority and triumph over his enemies within and without.[7]

The immediate aftermath of the crisis, as far as the Opposition was concerned, was certainly not serious. Some fifty of that faction had abstained from voting for the final address, and Couza may have thought, like Moustier, that the intervention of the consuls

[1] Eder to Rechberg, no. 17, Mar. 8, Staatsarchiv, xxxviii/139; cf. Green to Russell, no. 33, Feb. 28.
[2] Eder to Rechberg, no. 20, Mar. 11, Staatsarchiv, xxxviii/139.
[3] Green to Russell, Mar. 14, telg., F.O. 78/1746.
[4] Green to Russell, no. 43, Mar. 16, F.O. 78/1746. Green pointed out that assemblies had frequently lasted longer.
[5] Couza to Negri, June 27, annex to Moustier's no. 134, *Aff. étr.*, *Turquie*, vol. 59. According to article xxii of the Convention, 'if the budget were not voted *en temps opportun*, the executive power might provide for the public services in conformity with the budget of the previous year'. Couza could, therefore, plead a technical justification.
[6] Green to Russell, no. 43. 'Only a declaration of the Powers can stop him and prevent catastrophe', telegraphed Tillos on Mar. 14: *Aff. étr.*, *Turquie*, *Bucharest*, vol. 23.
[7] Iorga, *Mihail Kogălniceanu*, p. 177.

had at least had the effect of intimidating the less resolute. Many of the deputies would have welcomed an investigation by a commission from Constantinople, and Eder suggested that such a mission might be restricted solely to pacifying the contending forces; but the division which existed among the ambassadors seemed to make such a plan impracticable. Whereas Prokesch, like Ali, sided with the opposition to Couza, Moustier and Novikoff, the Russian chargé d'affaires, had revealed at the meeting of February 26 that their sympathies were with Couza, and Novikoff showed plainly that he disapproved of the consuls' action—a fact which lent colour to the suspicion that the Prince was Russia's tool.[1] Meanwhile, Moustier was saying that Couza was perfectly justified in closing the session, since the failure to vote the budget was not his fault, and as the Opposition was now divided, it was but natural that the Prince should decline to change his ministry or decline to confide to its care the administration of the army.[2] Bulwer seemed to feel that the interference of the Powers would be more than justified, but that if the Powers preferred to wait until Couza had established a dictatorship, such a condition would probably be no worse than what had existed beforehand.[3] The British ambassador was apparently disposed to make a virtue of necessity.

In the meantime Couza was marking time, and, as far as can be judged, was not yet in serious financial embarrassment. Some of the more violent of his enemies formed an organization to impede the collection of taxes,[4] but even Tillos doubted of their success.[5] Since the collection of taxes had been authorized for January and February, and a loan of six million piasters obtained before the recent political battle had commenced, there was no immediate chance of the Prince's capitulating for lack of funds. If, when these resources were expended, he invoked the previous budget, he had at least a specious claim for so doing. Even with most of his people hostile, or at least lukewarm in their loyalty, Couza could still count on the army, and it was probably not without design that he held a review of the garrison of Bucharest on the day following the closing of the chamber.[6]

The question of whether he had the secret backing of Russia is one that has often been raised, and, without the evidence of Russian dispatches, cannot be conclusively settled. Moustier wrote that Novikoff had shown him some of Giers's dispatches,

[1] Prokesch to Rechberg, no. 19 C, Mar. 11, Staatsarchiv, XII/78.
[2] Moustier to Lhuys, no. 55, Mar. 19, Aff. étr., Turquie, vol. 357.
[3] Bulwer to Russell, no. 159, Mar. 31, F.O. 78/1734.
[4] Eder to Rechberg, no. 24, Mar. 27, Staatsarchiv, XXXVIII/139.
[5] Tillos to Lhuys, no. 118, Apr. 3, Aff. étr., Turquie, Bucharest, vol. 23. Tillos quoted Couza as saying if it were attempted, he would declare the peasants freed of all obligations. Probably this threat was effective.
[6] Green to Russell, no. 43, Mar. 16, F.O. 78/1746.

which gave not the least indication that Russia was pursuing any policy apart from the other Powers.[1] There is no doubt that Eder, Green, and Tillos had persuaded themselves that Couza and his government were completely under Russian influence, and the dispatches of the last two repeat the accusation *ad nauseam*. Yet one may easily suspect that these consuls, on finding that their wishes had not the least effect on the Prince's conduct, became convinced that in some mysterious way Russia had been manipulating the strings which directed the recent political drama. The statement that Couza had agreed to retire in due time in favour of the Duke of Leuchtenberg rests on Tillos's sole authority;[2] and this consul was later inspired to believe that Couza was encouraging, under Russian auspices, the separatist tendencies of Moldavia with a view of retiring thither after he had found his position in Wallachia untenable.[3] But Tillos had been ill again lately, and at such times his ravings became worse. 'The intentions one attributes to Russia,' declared Gortchakoff, 'are absurd; Tillos must have had a nightmare.'[4] Turning from the wild conjectures of the French consul and the almost equally dubious testimony of Gortchakoff, one may look for more enlightening evidence in the known activities of the Prince in any connexion in which Russia might be interested.

Late in May 1863 General Türr, whom we have met before during the arms crisis of 1860, arrived in Bucharest and had an interview with Couza. It is not unreasonable to suppose that this wily adventurer was looking over the ground to see if Couza would give some support to an uprising in Hungary that would encourage Italy to attack Venetia.[5] Judging from results, there is ground for believing that the Hungarian's mission had no success; but the consuls got nothing out of Couza, who seemed to delight in mystifying them.[6] Türr may, or may not, have been dickering with some Poles who had taken refuge in Moldavian Bessarabia.[7] When Eder reproached the Prince for allowing these transactions, and hinted

[1] Moustier to Lhuys, no. 26, Feb. 12, *Aff. étr., Turquie*, vol. 357.
[2] Tillos to Lhuys, Feb. 9, telg., *ibid.*, *Bucharest*, vol. 23; Moustier to Lhuys, no. 33, Feb. 17, *Aff. étr., Turquie*, vol. 357. Iorga makes the charge in his *Histoire des relations russo-roumaines*, p. 324, but gives no evidence to substantiate it.
[3] Tillos to Lhuys, no. 122, May 20, *ibid.*, *Bucharest*, vol. 23.
[4] Thun to Rechberg, no. 5 F, Mar. 1, Staatsarchiv, x/49. A story of Tillos that Giers was now openly working for Couza's dethronement and the installation of Leuchtenberg led Moustier to see Novikoff, who, besides denying it, passed on the story to St. Petersburg. According to Napier, Gortchakoff telegraphed to Novikoff that Tillos must have had a bad dream, and imputed the story to the French consul's intimacy with the Opposition: Napier to Russell, no. 107, Feb. 25, F.O. 65/627.
[5] Tillos to Lhuys, no. 123, May 26, *Aff. étr., Turquie, Bucharest*, vol. 23.
[6] Tillos to Lhuys, no. 125, June 2, *ibid.*; Eder to Rechberg, no. 49 A, June 20, Staatsarchiv, xxxviii/139.
[7] Tillos says that Türr tried to get them to march into Galicia to stir up trouble there: Tillos to Lhuys, May 23, telg., *Aff. étr., Turquie, Bucharest*, vol. 23.

that Russia's hand was somehow at work, Couza responded that the gratitude he owed to Russia was sufficient to keep him from conniving at insurrection. 'While you wished to drown me,' he declared, 'Russia has kept me above water.'[1] The remark deserves no more weight that we can usually attach to Couza's observations. Some weeks later, however, he became more confidential: Garibaldi, he told Eder, had recently had an understanding with Michael, and he (Couza) was designed to play a part in a new conspiracy, but not having been consulted when the scheme was hatched, he had rejected it.[2] We are told also that he sent assurances to Paris that Türr had made no definite proposals.[3] Probably the most that can be hazarded from the various rumours floating about is that this astute trimmer was keeping his eyes open but not committing himself to any policy.

Almost equally mysterious was the affair of the Polish refugees. In June a member of some Polish revolutionary organization, Miroslawski by name, seems to have had an interview with Couza,[4] but what was discussed or agreed upon we cannot say. Early in July a band of Polish exiles collected on the south bank of the Danube to a number variously reported as 350 and 600, seized a British steamer, and crossed to Wallachian territory,[5] while a proclamation, published in the *Moniteur*, besought free passage from the Moldo-Wallachians.[6] Couza was in a quandary over what he should do. He knew of Napoleon's sympathies with the Polish insurrection,[7] but to permit the passage of an armed band of outlaws through his territories would certainly involve him with Russia, whose goodwill might well be needed for his overture to Constantinople on the subject of a dictatorship. After a futile effort to get the Poles to lay down their arms, and much pressure from Offenberg (the new Russian consul) to take energetic measures against them, Couza finally sent a small body of infantry to disarm the intruders.[8] In the resultant clash about a hundred fell on each side, and the affair had no decisive result until Couza sent reinforcements large enough to apprehend and disarm the surviving members of the contingent,[9] who were afterwards most generously

---

[1] Eder to Rechberg, no. 46, June 9, Staatsarchiv, xxxviii/139.
[2] Eder to Rechberg, no. 54, July 7, *ibid.*
[3] Eder to Rechberg, no. 49 A, June 20, *ibid.*
[4] Green to Russell, no. 62, May 25, F.O. 78/1747. Rumour had it that Couza promised 6,000 muskets for a rising in Galicia.
[5] Green to Russell, July 13, telg., *ibid.*
[6] Damé, *Histoire de la Roumaine contemporaine*, p. 131.
[7] Drouyn de Lhuys's telegram (July 16) to Tillos was certainly non-committal; the Prince 'should have in the present case as much circumspection as he showed some months ago on the occasion of the transit of great convoys of arms through the Principalities.'
[8] Eder to Rechberg, no. 57, July 17, Staatsarchiv, xxxviii/139.
[9] Green to Russell, no. 29, July 17, F.O. 78/1747.

treated.[1] Green criticized him severely for not having sent a force large enough in the first place to avoid bloodshed;[2] and the affair was not only certain to embitter the revolutionary element, but might possibly compromise the Prince's relations with France. Learning shortly afterwards that there might be war between France and Russia over the rejection of Napoleon's demands on behalf of Poland, Couza expressed his intention of putting his army at the Emperor's disposal.[3] But the role of serving as an auxiliary of his illustrious benefactor was denied to him by the course of events.

Trivial as the episode was, it convinced Couza's enemies, or ill-wishers like Tillos, that the Prince was more than ever the instrument of Russia.[4] The fact that he had taken drastic measures against the dedicated monasteries should have proved that he was not a blind satellite of St. Petersburg. Moreover, the Polish imbroglio had almost certainly been an unexpected contingency, out of which the Prince could eke nothing but embarrassment. In judging his somewhat floundering way of stepping through the puddle, one may gather that all he cared about was to keep on amicable terms with the two Powers—now unhappily on opposite sides—which had shown a friendly spirit towards his country. Unhappily too, the pivotal position of the United Principalities not only placed it in perpetual danger of being used as a field for intrigue and conspiracy, but made every action of its prince an object of suspicion. When an extradition treaty was signed in June between Servia and the Principalities, it was inferred that an offensive-defensive alliance was about to be concluded against Turkey.[5] Moustier, who learned of the rumour from Tillos, was frankly sceptical about the matter, but a simultaneous order of cannon from Belgrade and Bucharest was very disquieting to Ali,[6] and had, doubtless, some bearing on later developments.

Neither the visit of Türr, nor the episode of the Polish *émigrés* had much effect on the struggle between the Prince and his enemies, which had considerably abated its intensity since the closing of the session. Hopeless of contending against Couza

[1] Moustier to Tillos, Aug. 3, annex to Moustier's no. 149, *Aff. étr., Turquie*, vol. 349. Since Couza allowed the officers to proceed into Austria, and negotiated with the Porte to receive the remainder of the contingent, Moustier acquitted him of any duplicity toward the Poles.

[2] Green to Russell, no. 79. It is possible, of course, that Couza relied on the judgement of the commander-in-chief.

[3] Tillos to Lhuys, no. 133, July 22, *Aff. étr., Turquie, Bucharest*, vol. 23.

[4] Several months later Offenberg accused Couza of giving aid to the Poles, and the Prince replied bluntly that he was not a gendarme of Russia: Tillos to Lhuys, no. 160, May 2, 1864, *ibid.*, vol. 24.

[5] Eder to Rechberg, no. 49 A, June 20, and no. 67, Sept. 4, Staatsarchiv, xxxviii/139. Couza himself denied it.

[6] Moustier to Lhuys, no. 89, Nov. 6, *Aff. etr., Turquie*, vol. 360.

while he was able to govern without them, the Opposition borrowed a leaf from his book and decided to lay their case before
the Powers; so Stirbey left on a pilgrimage to Vienna and Paris[1]—
with what result we do not know. During May and June Couza
spent much of his time in negotiating with foreign banking houses
for a loan as well as for the establishment of a national bank, from
which money could be borrowed regularly;[2] and he subsequently
granted an English company the right to construct some railways
in Wallachia.[3] All such plans, however, required the sanction of
the assembly, and as such co-operation could not possibly be
expected unless he made a show of yielding, the Prince busied
himself with the problem of appointing a new ministry to last until
these matters were safely concluded. He is said to have told his
ministers that he would have to part with them for a time, but
would reinstate them as soon as the loan was effected. After some
talk of handing the premiership to Sturdza—on the ground that an
avowed enemy was preferable to the group which had vacillated in
the recent crisis[4]—he finally entrusted the premiership to Prince
Cantacouzene, a Moldavian *boyard* of distinguished family and
rather mediocre attainments. Unfortunately, the men whom
Couza had held at bay were bent on stripping him of the one
asset which might enable him in the last instance to hold his
throne—namely, the army. When Cantacouzene (who was probably a tool of the party chiefs) insisted that the high command should
be responsible to the assembly, the chance of an accommodation
was gone.[5] Balked in his effort to score a point over his enemies,
Couza now made up his mind to put out a feeler at Constantinople
on the subject of a dictatorship, and wrote a letter to Negri, describ-
ing the failure of his 'attempts at conciliation', which he asked the
kapou kiaya to lay before the Porte and the ambassadors.[6]

The result was not exactly forbidding. Moustier's expressed
disapproval of Tillos's attitude made it clear enough that he had

---

[1] Green to Hammond, Apr. 25, F.O. 78/1747.
[2] Green to Hammond, June 6, *ibid.*; Tillos to Lhuys, no. 125, June 2, and
no. 127, June 19, *Aff. étr., Turquie, Bucharest*, vol. 123. Tillos says that Herz, who
represented the Ottoman Bank and the Credit Foncier, was pushing the project
of the bank, but a loan was already arranged with Lefevre (representing Anglo-
French interests), who expended much wine and money to put through the deal.
[3] Green to Russell, no. 78, July 15, F.O. 78/1747.
[4] Green to Hammond, June 6, F.O. 78/1747; Tillos to Lhuys, no. 125, June 2,
Aff. étr., Turquie, Bucharest, vol. 23.
[5] Green to Bulwer, no. 53, June 23, F.O. 78/1747; Tillos to Lhuys, no. 127,
June 19, *Aff. étr., Turquie, Bucharest*, vol. 23. The whole affair had been very
embarrassing to Tillos, since Cantacouzene, in deference to the radicals in the
'Coalition', had demanded the inclusion of Bratiano in the ministry, and when
Tillos, in accordance with Moustier's instructions, had been forced to advise
against Bratiano's appointment, Couza, who distrusted the radical leader and
was resolved to exclude him, said that he did so out of deference to France.
[6] Couza to Negri, June 13, annex to Moustier's no. 117, *ibid.*, vol. 359.

no patience with the *boyards*, and Bulwer's benevolent indifference was not unlikely to germinate into some tangible support for the harassed prince. As for Ludolf, who was again in Prokesch's place, he was ready to admit that between Couza's dethronement and his maintenance in power the latter was the lesser of the two evils.[1]

The failure of negotiations to form a new ministry convinced the consuls, at least, that a *fait accompli* was now impending. If Couza could not get a loan through constitutional procedure, he could only hope to obtain it by a change in the constitution, which would enable him to rule as a dictator. It was a chance, of course, that the Powers might refuse to sanction his venture, but anything was preferable to a surrender to his enemies, and it was not the first time that Couza had played for high stakes. In the meantime he made it clear that the door to compromise was closed. Towards the end of June he made some administrative changes, including the appointment of a new minister of justice and a new prefect of police, and while they may not have been the hardened criminals that Tillos brands them,[2] they were certainly not connected with the Opposition. He was now free to harass his enemies with prosecutions, and in order to give them a striking lesson in the necessity of subservience, he removed Golesco, who had voted for the declaration against levying taxes, from the position of aide-de-camp, which he had held since 1859.[3] 'Never before,' said Eder, 'have despotism and illegality prevailed in these lands, as they do to-day. As for the internal administration, it has shown in this last year a distinct retrogression.'[4]

Perhaps a wiser course than that of striking at his enemies would have been to try to find some probity and justice with which to oil the wheels of the administration and the judiciary (Green may be right in his fierce denunciation of the prevalent corruption);[5] but if Couza had any notion of conciliating the public, it was not in that way, and it is not certain that any ruler in the thick of a political struggle could have put his house in very satisfactory order. The fact that he was not a mere time-server is proved by the contracts which he granted to western capitalists for the establishment of a bank and the construction of railways in both principalities.[6] The renewal of a contract for a loan of £2,000,000 had already been consummated likewise;[7] but the problem still remained of getting an assembly to ratify these arrangements, or of finding an adequate

[1] Ludolf to Rechberg, no. 54 B, July 6, Staatsarchiv, XII/79.
[2] Tillos to Lhuys, no. 130, June 30, *Aff. étr., Turquie, Bucharest*, vol. 23.
[3] Tillos to Lhuys, no. 127, June 19, *ibid*.
[4] Eder to Rechberg, no. 61, Aug. 4, Staatsarchiv, XXXVIII/139.
[5] Green to Hammond, July 31, F.O. 78/1747.
[6] Eder to Rechberg, no. 61, Aug. 4, Staatsarchiv, XXXVIII/139.
[7] Green to Russell, no. 78, July 15, F.O. 78/1747.

substitute for the assembly. At the present juncture only the latter course seemed feasible.

There is no doubt whatever now that Couza meant to carry his struggle through to the end. Early in July he frankly stated his position to Eder. He had nothing to fear from his enemies, he said, but he frankly distrusted both Right and Left, and whilst he might have given a share of power to the former, they had shown themselves too base and cowardly to be trusted with authority; he even seemed to regret that the closing of the assembly had not occasioned a riot, which might have given him the excuse for a *coup d'état* then and there. The Convention, he declared, was obsolete and the constitution unworkable; in fact, experience had taught him that any constitution was unsuited to his country. He then talked glibly of a dictatorship, but wished it understood that he would not take such a step with the approval merely of Austria, Russia, and Great Britain, whom he regarded as neighbouring Powers (Great Britain, because of her interest in Turkey), and consequently liable to entrap him. He had considered it his duty, however, to call the attention of the Powers to the state of affairs; and the Porte had requested him to put his opinions in writing.[1] Such an assurance, if genuine, had probably come through Negri; and the Prince was evidently ready enough to act on it. He proposed, in short, to lay his whole hand on the table.

Sent in the form of a letter to Negri, Couza's *mémoire* was of great length, and consisted partly of an arraignment of the Opposition, for coping with whom the present machinery of government was inadequate, and partly of some definite suggestions by way of changing the existing order of things. The *mémoire* began, strangely enough, by deploring the suspension of the central commission,[2] which had been able to 'show the abuses that needed reforming', as well as to 'control the projects of laws, voted by the assemblies'. A senate, it is true, had been recommended by the firman, but 'how suppose, indeed, that the assembly would willingly renounce an increase of influence?' As for the legislative committee, which had been constituted to propose legislation, it had proved a singularly futile body. Since, indeed, there was no longer the central commission to enact the role of arbiter between prince and assembly, 'the executive found itself at once face to face . . . with the legislative power'. The Prince then went on to say that, while he could not repudiate the principle that sovereignty should lie with the people's representatives, he had become convinced that the assembly did not represent the people, and was

---

[1] Eder to Rechberg, no. 54, July 7, Staatsarchiv, XXXVIII/139.
[2] The central commission had been a special object of his complaint in the *mémoire* of 1860. See p. 297.

'concerned more with individual quarrels than with great questions of public utility'. The conservatives, ranged under the banners of certain pretenders to the throne, had formed with the radicals 'that monstrous coalition', which, while pretending to be the protector of constitutional ideas, had as its aim the subversion of the whole order of things, inaugurated by the double election and sanctioned by the Powers. It had sought systematically to embarrass the ministry, touched sometimes upon vital questions of foreign policy (even bringing the Porte into the discussion), had blamed the government for the financial irregularities of the past, and had, in fact, condemned it for everything.

'I recognize,' said Couza, 'that all abuses are not extirpated in this classic land of abuses, (and) that most of our aspirations towards modern civilization cannot so far even begin to give satisfaction, but can one reasonably demand for a reign of four years a work which entire generations have not been enough to accomplish in other states after centuries of investigation and experience?'

He then recounted the steps forward which he had taken (some of them, by the way, had been ordained by the Convention), and then reverted to the demand for a foreign prince, founded on his offer in 1859, and to the ambitious designs of the radicals, who, by manipulating their rivals, were threatening to bring about an armed revolt.[1] Having thus displayed the intolerable chaos of the existing régime, Couza recommended (1) a considerable lowering of the property qualifications for voters, (2) a strict definition and limitation of the powers of the assembly, (3) the creation of a senate, whose members were to be nominated by the prince for a fixed term of years, (4) a council of state to elaborate laws and defend the administration before the assembly, and (5) a court of finance to examine and control public finance. He considered, however, that the political attainments of the Principalities were insufficient as yet to warrant the immediate application of a broader suffrage, and since he could not carry on a work of reorganization under existing conditions, he recommended a suspension for five years of the elective assembly, during which interval he proposed to carry out the reforms which the country needed, including, first of all, an administrative council[2] to assist him in this work. Among his projects were the concession of a bank, contracts for building railroads, the improvement of roadways, the granting of property rights to foreigners, and, in fact, 'some sixty projects of laws, which have been presented during the last four years to the assemblies,

---

[1] Couza stated that during a recent municipal election at Bucharest the police had seized a double proclamation to the people and the army, 'which was nothing less than an appeal to arms'.

[2] Half should be chosen by the present assembly, and half by himself.

but never voted'. During this period he would be free to elaborate at his leisure a constitution for the State. Moreover, the State would gladly accept this provisional régime, for it was 'tired of enduring the caprice of a factious oligarchy'.

'The good sense of the nation is not duped . . .,' declared the Prince, 'and it is to the Prince that the populations have appealed from the errors of the assembly and the culpable intrigues of the Coalition. I accept this great role, and all the responsibilities it conveys. . . . If my ideas cannot find the immediate support that I look for, I will not hesitate to sacrifice my personal ambition and retire from the political scene. I will abdicate and will try to leave to a prince better supported the task which my isolated situation and the means of which I dispose do not permit me to accomplish.'

In conclusion, he urged Negri to bring 'this supreme resolution' before the Porte and the ambassadors, and to assure them that public order would not suffer during these urgent measures; though his own life might be forfeited, he added, that danger would not deter him from his task.[1]

A scrutiny of this document reveals in many subtle ways the efforts of an artful politician to touch the springs by which the sympathies of the Powers could be enlisted. In clarity of reasoning it is below the *mémoire* of 1860, and there is much more straining of the truth, as, for example, the implication that the Coalition wanted to undo the act of union. In the suggested basis for a new political organization he doubtless had in mind the framework of the Second Empire, the favour of whose sovereign he had most need of winning. But it is noticeable, both from the tone and from the omissions in the document, that Couza was not the suppliant that he had been in 1860. He wrote of his plan as a 'resolution', and, while he intended that it should be laid before the Powers, he made no specious plea for their gracious consideration. Drouyn de Lhuys somehow read into the letter the idea that the situation was so urgent as not to admit of waiting for the proposed changes to be formally granted by the Porte and the Protecting Powers.[2] Probably Couza did not really expect that the Powers would give him *carte blanche* to carry out his 'resolution'. He simply felt, as one may judge, that inasmuch as the overthrow of the existing order was likely to prove expedient, it was well to sound the Powers in advance on their reaction to the suggestion, and to impress them with the fact that necessity might drive him to this act willy nilly. What he demanded was an unrestricted dictatorship. It mattered not that he limited it hypothetically to a five years'

---

[1] Couza to Negri, June 27, annex to Moustier's no. 134, July 16, *Aff. étr.*, *Turquie*, vol. 359.
[2] Lhuys to Tillos, no. 5, Aug. 11, *ibid.*, *Turquie, Bucharest*, vol. 24.

time. His present hope was to be untrammelled by any sort of legislature. His sword was still sheathed, but he proposed to get it sharpened for the final battle. In short, the *mémoire* served notice to the Powers that he wanted their blessing for a *coup d'état*.

There is no reason to suppose that the Porte or the ambassadors was greatly startled by this piece of effrontery, since Couza's position on the question of the monasteries had already revealed the measure of his patriotism, and Constantinople must certainly have been aware that a desperate man is not deterred by desperate expedients when he finds himself embroiled in a life-and-death struggle. Moustier, always favourable to the Prince, had apparently no criticism to make of his proposals, and though Bulwer was more guarded (for the course of the monastery quarrel had roused his irritation), both he and Ali were inclined to accept a temporary dictatorship, designed to prepare the way for some constitutional changes. Ali's sole consideration was the fear lest the downfall of Couza would lead to anarchy and a foreign prince.[1]

No such thought occurred to Russell, whose remoteness from the scene of battle may account for that ignorance that sees no ground for compromise. 'Do not advise the Porte to sanction a dictatorship of Prince Couza,' he telegraphed Bulwer. 'Rather let him resign and the assembly elect another hospodar.'[2] Very simple indeed for Couza to get out of the way and let his foes wrangle over his mantle! Bulwer, though by no means justifying the extreme demands of Couza, pointed out to his chief that the present constitution would not work under any prince, and that, unless a dictatorship of, say, five or six months were granted Couza, things would certainly reach a crisis, and Couza would save himself only by usurping the powers he wanted. For his own part, he did not believe any of the leading men in the Principalities were preferable to Couza, and if a new hospodar attempted to govern under the present system, he would soon find himself in similar straits, as 'the present form of government is impracticable'.[3] Bulwer's final advice—inspired, no doubt, by Russell's uncompromising stand—was that 'matters should take their course'. Russell's reply showed that he was as far as ever from understanding the problem. While rejecting Bulwer's notion of a short-time dictatorship, he thought that the Principalities 'should be left as far as possible to frame their own internal government', and then threw out the suggestion that union might be dissolved and a hospodar chosen for each principality.[4] With much more penetration Drouyn de Lhuys acknow-

---

[1] Ludolf to Rechberg, no. 59 D, July 23, Staatsarchiv, xii/79.
[2] Russell to Bulwer, July 18, telg., F.O. 78/1730.
[3] Bulwer to Russell, no. 338, July 21, F.O. 78/1737.
[4] Russell to Bulwer, no. 374, Aug. 12, F.O. 78/1730. Russell would have the hospodars chosen for seven years (he did not say by whom) and would give each

ledged the need of drastic changes in the constitution, 'though one
could not . . . disguise the objections which the establishment of a
dictatorship provokes'.[1] After some correspondence with London
he finally succeeded in persuading Russell to consider the question
seriously, and they agreed that a conference might meet—either at
Paris or Constantinople.[2] Moustier hoped that the Porte would
cease to regard Couza's recommendations as a declaration of intention and try to reach an understanding with the Protecting Powers
without delay.[3]

One cannot be sure that Couza's stroke was not simply a bluff
to obtain a certain measure of the power which he had solicited.
It was something to know that Bulwer and the French diplomats
were ready to approve some changes, and if he could obtain a
system of government which, while avoiding an out-and-out dictatorship, would assure him sufficient mastery of the situation, his
object would be attained. Early in September Bordeano presented
to Ali a definite project of a new constitution, it being understood
that his former proposals had not been really official, and that only
this new plan was to be submitted to the Powers. The scheme
included a council of state to draft the laws and a senate, chosen
by the Prince, which should share with the assembly the right to
approve or reject them; and, finally, the electoral law was to be
revised in a democratic direction, though not in such a way as to
make the suffrage universal.[4] Bordeano informed Ludolf that, as
these innovations had, in principle, received the approval of the
Powers,[5] the Prince would not feel it necessary to await their further
sanction, if the negotiations should seem to entail delay and the
crisis in the Principalities should become acute. He would make
one more effort to work with the assembly; but if this proved
abortive, he would promulgate the constitution, though not apply
it for two months in order that the Powers might give it consideration.[6] Such a policy might be said to denote a qualified *fait accompli*. He would overthrow, if necessary, the existing political order,
but he was proposing in its stead—and giving due notice of it in
advance—a scheme which was supposed to have the approval of
the Powers, and he would give them the opportunity of palliating

a council of state and an elective assembly. His action against union was a strange
reversal of the position which he had taken in 1857 (see p. 140), for there was
nothing in the present strife in the Principalities to indicate a wish to go back to
separation. Indeed, so sweeping a proposal was simply begging the whole
question.

[1] Lhuys to Tillos, no. 5, Aug. 11, *Aff. étr., Turquie, Bucharest*, vol. 24.
[2] Cadore to Lhuys, Sept. 9, 1863, annex to Moustier's no. 72, *ibid.*
[3] Moustier to Lhuys, no. 166, Aug. 27, *ibid., Turquie*, vol. 360.
[4] Primary and direct electors were only those who paid certain taxes. The
plan gave representation to the cities.
[5] An allusion to the Convention.
[6] Ludolf to Rechberg, no. 74 B, Sept. 10, Staatsarchiv, XII/79.

the crime after it had been committed. The idea naturally did not meet with much approval. Drouyn de Lhuys found by communicating with the Powers that they were all willing that changes should be made in the present constitution, but none of the diplomats wanted their hands forced prematurely.[1] Gortchakoff felt that what was most needed was an *entente* between the Porte and the Protecting Powers.[2]

It remained to be seen how far the Prince would allow the Powers to advise him. Always a stickler for legality, Bulwer wrote to Negri, protesting against the notion of taking any action without the consent of the Powers and the Porte,[3] and he subsequently pointed out to him that such a senate as the Prince desired was calculated to throw all the power into his hands. The kapou kiaya merely replied that Couza might be willing to let this body be modified by the new assembly which should meet after the new constitution was put in force.[4] Soon afterwards Negri left for Bucharest, and it was believed that he went to counsel the Prince to treat the Powers with more 'prudence'.[5] At all events, when the project was formally submitted, late in October, a slight concession was made in the constitution of the senate. The British chargé d'affaires gathered from Negri that Couza would be willing to revise his plan in accordance with suggestions from the Powers, but if no proposals were made, he would act as he saw fit.[6] Ludolf, however, got from Bordeano an entirely different story. The presentation of the project to the Powers did not mean that their sanction was requested, or that its execution would depend on their approval.[7] It is not improbable that Bordeano had let the cat out of the bag, for Negri would never have been guilty of such a want of diplomatic finesse. Couza meant to wield, if not a dictatorship, at least something closely approximating to that condition. If he submitted his plan to the Powers, it was merely to strengthen his moral position—and it was possible, of course, that they would grant him what he wanted. Even Rechberg, who had thought in his blundering way that Couza had given up the game,[8] was now sure that he was planning a dictatorship, and wrote to Prokesch that the Porte would have to bring the whole crisis before the cabinets.[9]

It was finally agreed that, as the project had been submitted to

[1] Lhuys to Moustier, no. 175, Sept. 18, *Aff. étr., Turquie*, vol. 360.
[2] Gortchakoff to Novikoff, Sept. 22, annex to Thun's report of Dec. 11, Staatsarchiv, x/49.
[3] Bulwer to Negri, Sept. 27, *ibid.* XII/79.
[4] Bulwer to Russell, no. 445, Oct. 1, F.O. 78/1739.
[5] Ludolf to Rechberg, no. 81 A–D, Oct. 5, Staatsarchiv, XII/79.
[6] Erskine to Rechberg, no. 3, Oct. 27, F.O. 78/1739.
[7] Ludolf to Rechberg, no. 86 C, Oct. 22, Staatsarchiv, XII/79.
[8] Rechberg to Ludolf, Oct. 17, *ibid.*, XII/80.
[9] Rechberg to Prokesch, Nov. 5, *ibid.*

the Porte and the ambassadors, it was the duty of the Porte to place the question before the Powers. Ali, who had made up his mind that the Principalities were on the road to independence,[1] was plainly loath to take such action, and considerable pressure had to be applied[2] before he finally sent a circular on November 12 to the Turkish representatives at the various courts.[3] Yet the Powers themselves were even more guilty of dilatory behaviour; for Napoleon, viewing the discord in the Principalities as likely to produce a serious crisis in the East, had bethought himself of a congress to pacify Europe,[4] and when the opposition of Austria and Great Britain had balked this plan,[5] there was too much wrangling over the final phase of the monastery controversy to induce the cabinets to give much thought to Couza's 'constitution'. In December Moustier admitted that he did not yet know the reception which Couza's project had met with in Paris, and Ali frankly said that he believed it was a dead letter.[6] Bulwer alone seemed to find some enjoyment in analysing the situation in the Principalities and speculating about remedies. In January 1864 he took the unusual course of addressing a letter direct to Drouyn de Lhuys, giving the results of his cogitations. Moustier, to whom the letter had been given for transmission, subjected to it some critical annotations; but one opinion of the British ambassador was certainly close to the point: 'The Principalities are, in my opinion, too restricted in what concerns their real autonomy: the right of creating rights for themselves and concerning only themselves.' Thus 'a constitution, given by the Powers, can be changed only with the consent of the Powers, even in matters purely local, such as the electoral basis for a representative assembly'.[7] When one considers that the character of the existing assembly in the Principalities had much to do with the aggravated state of affairs, and that it would take the cumbersome machinery of the European protectorate to ratify any relief, even assuming that Couza alone knew the proper mode of relief, one can hardly be surprised that the torrent rushed on, unchecked by any

[1] Ludolf to Rechberg, no. 76 C, Sept. 17, Staatsarchiv, XII/79.

[2] Moustier to Lhuys, no. 217, Nov. 5, *Aff. étr., Turquie*, vol. 360.

[3] Prokesch to Rechberg, no. 94 C, Nov. 25 and annex, XII/79.

[4] It will be recalled that the chief occasion for this proposal was the ruthless suppression of the Polish insurrection (see La Gorce, *Histoire du Second Empire*, vol. iv, pp. 761–3). Drouyn de Lhuys had announced in the *Moniteur* that the Principalities would be included among the questions which the congress should settle: Lhuys to Moustier, no. 98, Dec. 11, *Aff. étr., Turquie*, vol. 360.

[5] Russell to Cowley, no. 1326, Nov. 25, F.O. 27/1483; Rechberg to Prokesch, Dec. 20, Staatsarchiv, XII/80. Couza himself was reported as very much opposed to having the question of the Principalities discussed in a congress: Eder to Rechberg, no. 96, Dec. 7, Staatsarchiv, XXXVIII/139. Doubtless, he expected to get better results from treating with the diplomats at Constantinople.

[6] Prokesch to Rechberg, no. 99 A–F, Dec. 18, Staatsarchiv, XII/79.

[7] Moustier to Lhuys, Jan. 9, 1864, annex to Moustier's dispatch of Feb. 11, *Aff. étr., Turquie*, vol. 361.

dam that could be erected from without. Once more, the Principalities were to be left, in their inexperience, to work out their own
salvation. Whether that salvation lay on the side of Couza, or in
the laps of his enemies, the next few months would show.

The summer of 1863 was simply a confused interlude when every
one was waiting and wondering how the struggle would finally end.
If the Coalition had lapsed into what seemed to be outward submission, it may have been because it hoped and believed that the
Prince would be forced by lack of funds to reconvoke the assembly.
It was, no doubt, something of a shock to learn that the man they
feared had been trying to evoke the aid of the Powers for his designs, and at a meeting on August 5 of the leaders of the Opposition,
the resolution was taken of sending two representatives to Vienna,
London, and Paris to counteract his manœuvres.[1] Later it was
decided that Pano alone should go,[2] though he did not actually do
so until six months later,[3] and what he accomplished is not evident
from the consular correspondence. In any event, Couza could not
afford to mark time. Notwithstanding the tendency of the consuls
to believe the worst of the Prince, and to harp on his growing unpopularity, there is little doubt but that it behoved him to find
some means of buttressing his position. It may or may not be true
that the army had shown some signs of discontent.[4] After all, while
Floresco was acting hetman the Prince could count on a friend who
believed in military despotism as truly as himself, and Floresco's
ability was not disputed. But Green tells us that a prosecution
which the court of cassation was conducting at the instance of one
of the ministers resulted in an acquittal despite the fact that two of
the judges had been replaced on the eve of the trial, and that the
defendant's departure from the court-room was nothing less than
an ovation, punctuated, it was said, with shouts of 'Down with the
tyrant'.[5] Such, perhaps, were symptoms of the alienation of the
public, and it was doubtless to give it something else to think
about that Couza allowed the principle of universal suffrage to be
discussed in the papers which he controlled. Eder did not believe
that either Right or Left would try to stay his hand by revolution
or that he needed even to fear an assassination plot,[6] and Green
wrote with even greater contempt of the prevalent want of courage.[7]

---

[1] Eder to Rechberg, no. 61, Aug. 4, Staatsarchiv, xxxviii/139.
[2] Green to Russell, no. 86, Aug. 13, F.O. 78/1747.
[3] Xénopol, *Domnia lui Cuza-Voda*, vol. i, p. 274, n. 41.
[4] Green to Russell, no. 90, Aug. 18. Eder wrote that the radicals had for a
long time been cementing ties with some of the under-officers, but that Couza
could still count on the loyalty of the battalion commanders and over-officers:
Eder to Rechberg, no. 75, Sept. 24, Staatsarchiv, xxxviii/139.
[5] Green to Russell, no. 97, Sept. 24, F.O. 78/1348.
[6] Eder to Rechberg, no. 75, Sept. 24, Staatsarchiv, xxxviii/139.
[7] Green to Russell, no. 90.

A more serious matter for the government was the condition of its finances.[1] Some relief could be had from the revenues of the monasteries (anticipating confiscation by the assembly) or it might still be possible to float the loan which the assembly had granted before its rupture with the Prince;[2] but there was still the need of parliamentary backing for his bank and railway schemes.[3] Was there any hope of mitigating the enmity of his foes? Or must he assume that, after all, the deadlock could be broken only by executing his contemplated *coup d'état*.

Couza resolved, as he had told the diplomats, to give the assembly one more chance to save itself. Up to this time he had made but one effort to divide his enemies (the same old game of *bascule*, of which Tillos had so often complained), but it had failed because he had tried to detach some of the *boyards*. Why not go to the other pole and seek support from the radicals? The official advocacy of universal suffrage had seemed to show what was in his mind. It was a bid for their favour—but exactly whose? Bratiano and Rosetti were too wild to be tamed by a man who would not yield an atom of his authority, and Golesco was not only a mediocre figure but only recently had felt the master's lash. There was, however, a new leader of the Left, a man whose services he had once before employed, whose principles and methods were not dissimilar to his own, and who had the requisite boldness for the part that must be played. There was Cogalnitchano.

Appointed premier on October 24, Michael Cogalnitchano was the man who was destined to share the rather unappreciated glory of the closing years of Couza's reign. In some respects his career had paralleled that of his former classmate, for, like Couza, he had studied abroad, and, like Couza, he had been one of the revolutionists of 1848. Whatever opinion one may hold of his statesmanship, Cogalnitchano was, beyond all doubt, a fervent patriot. 'I would not exchange my poor Moldavia', he had written in 1835, 'for the first throne in the world.'[4] A man of vigorous personality, he had taken a prominent part in the divan *ad hoc* and in the assembly which had elected Couza in 1859, and had been premier of Moldavia for several months during the following year. Since the establishment of union, he had been one of the leaders of the radical group, and had led the attack upon the rural project of 1862.

[1] Tillos to Lhuys, no. 138, Sept. 4, *Aff. étr., Turquie, Bucharest*, vol. 24.

[2] A further and larger loan was arranged with the London and County Bank, but the assent of the assembly was required as a condition of the transaction: Eder to Rechberg, no. 58 B, July 21, Staatsarchiv, XXXVIII/139.

[3] Couza told Green that if a ministry, chosen from the majority, should refuse to sanction these measures, they would be 'stoned by the people', and the British consul concluded that he was thinking for the moment of invoking the aid of the populace, as had been done in 1859: Green to Russell, no. 90.

[4] Cogalnitchano, *Scrisori* (1834–49), p. 38.

Though a scholar[1] and a man of keen intellect, Cogalnitchano lacked the patience for mastering the details of a problem of which he undertook the solution, and was headstrong and precipitate in striving for an objective.[2] But the quality of his statecraft was yet to be tested, and evidence to his prejudice was certainly not convincing. Naturally some of the consuls were his enemies from the beginning, partly because he was a radical, and partly because he was willing to aid Couza, for whose downfall all the foreign agents no doubt prayed in secret. Tillos, who suspected him of being just another of Russia's tools (for he was wont to see the spectre of Russia at every turn), expressed also his belief that he had accepted the premiership because, as the owner of a cloth factory, he hoped to obtain a lucrative contract with the government;[3] while the strictures of Green on both Cogalnitchano and his colleagues were ungraced by any qualification. 'It would have been difficult', wrote the British consul, 'to select men less calculated to inspire confidence. It was impossible for M. Cogalnitchano, whose principles are so notoriously wild and whose practices are so unblushingly dishonest to find any colleagues, even in these principalities, but the most complete nonentities or persons of objectionable antecedents.'[4] So sweeping an indictment can hardly be accepted, for Couza had appointed as finance minister his old friend, Steege, who had engineered the electoral project of 1860,[5] and was a conscientious and able man,[6] who had held himself aloof from party brawls. Most of the selections, it is true, might be labelled as 'nonentities'; but as a ban had been placed on the conservatives, and as even Tillos had admitted the penury of able men,[7] one can hardly see how the Prince could have done better. No doubt he pinned his faith on the personality of the premier.

Cogalnitchano's path was not likely to be easy, but he seemed at first to have decided to see what conciliation would do. Thus he was ready to admit that taxes should not have been levied without the assembly's consent; he was willing to allow the impeachment of the old ministry if such vengeance was insisted on; and various prosecutions against the liberal press were immediately quashed by government decree.[8] Then, as the government proposed to charm its enemies into submission, the assembly was reconvoked to meet on November 15.[9]

---

[1] He published in 1837 the first volume of a history of the Roumanian people, but the work was never completed.   [2] Soutzo, *op. cit.*, p. 394.
[3] Tillos to Lhuys, no. 174, Oct. 26, *Aff. étr., Turquie, Bucharest*, vol. 24. Tillos says that it was Offenberg who persuaded Couza to appoint Cogalnitchano, but as, later on, he charged Offenberg with plotting his fall, there may be as much truth in one story as in the other.
[4] Green to Russell, no. 106, Oct. 25, F.O. 78/1748.   [5] p. 316.
[6] Soutzo, *op. cit.*, p. 382.   [7] Tillos to Lhuys, no. 138.
[8] Green to Hammond, Oct. 25, F.O. 78/1748.   [9] Tillos to Lhuys, no. 144.

Of course, it was all a question of tactics. Opportunist though he was, Cogalnitchano was much too deeply committed to the programme of the radicals to forget either the rural or the electoral question. Bourgeois himself (and it was said that his private fortunes needed resuscitation[1]), he was naturally in sympathy with the Prince's plans for an industrial renascence.[2] But it would not do to open his whole quiver at once. If he could keep the assembly docile until he had settled the budget, carried through the economic programme, and solved the question of the monasteries in a way that would enhance the national revenue, he would then be ready to doff the mask and take up universal suffrage, for which his party was still clamouring. If, on the other hand, he failed to get the majority he expected, he would raise the question at once. In either case he would give the assembly its final chance to avert a *coup d'état*.

Couza seems to have had fewer illusions on the result of such tactics, and even expected an immediate breach. Shortly before the change of ministry he had once again expressed his rooted conviction that his country was unfitted for the present system of government and could only be ruled by an absolute monarch.[3] He was willing to part with all his old ministers as a concession to the assembly,[4] but he would have preferred to force at once the question of universal suffrage, hoping to obtain through its operation a constituent assembly which would organize the type of régime which he considered necessary. Cogalnitchano—with a frankness in which one may divine a subtle purpose—spoke openly of the divergence between his view and that of the Prince, and said that he had converted Couza to his plan.[5] It remained to be seen whether the premier would really hypnotize the assembly as he hoped. Already his own party was abusing him roundly for forgetting his principles, and the radical press was declaring that he could not avoid the dissolution of the assembly and a proclamation of universal suffrage. How was he to get this party's support while he pacified the *boyards*, and at the same time masked the real view which his master had in mind? His position, moreover, was the more isolated in that he was the only one of the ministers who was at the same time a deputy—the only personal link between the government and the assembly. Only the Prince, he told Tillos, had any confidence in him. Would the support which Couza promised him[6] be sufficient?

[1] Tillos to Lhuys, no. 150, Dec. 14, *ibid.*
[2] Eder wrote that Cogalnitchano hoped that his cloth factory would be purchased by the government: Eder to Rechberg, no. 81 B, Oct. 25, Staatsarchiv, XXXVIII/139.
[3] Green to Russell, no. 103, Oct. 13, F.O. 78/1748.
[4] This, according to Eder, he considered concession enough.
[5] Eder to Rechberg, no. 81 B.
[6] Tillos to Lhuys, no. 146, Nov. 9, *Aff. étr., Turquie, Bucharest*, vol. 24.

The assembly opened on November 15, and, we may imagine, was well attended. Couza appeared in person, wearing the sword of honour which had been presented to him by Prince Michael as testimony of gratitude for his aid in the arms crisis. His speech was mainly an appeal for concord, but his statement that he 'hoped that the struggle was over, but, if not, it was the last time that he should meet them'[1] was eloquent of the Prince's temper at this period. It was hardly astonishing that the assembly in its projected address in reply charged the government with innumerable offences,[2] and Couza quite frankly told Eder that he considered it more personally hostile than the project of the previous session.[3] Simultaneous with this vicious indictment of his government, the Opposition was stirred by the reading of Couza's projected constitution, which, through some one's indiscretion, had just been printed in a Paris journal.[4] Doubtless a revival of the suspicion that the Prince had been really guilty of connivance with foreign Powers for the extension of his authority was quite too serious an embarrassment to be passed off lightly, and Cogalnitchano had even threatened to resign unless the published document were labelled as apocryphal.[5] Much disturbed by the assembly's action and by an attack in the *Roumanul*, which branded him as 'the enemy in the citadel', Couza actually denied to the consuls the existence of such a project[6]—a curious step, thought Drouyn de Lhuys ('he might better explain than deny it'), though he took the charitable view that the Prince's present embarrassments atoned for his duplicity.[7] Eder believed for the moment that there was no weakening of the assembly's determination[8]—which we may assume

[1] Green to Hammond, Nov. 16, F.O. 78/1748; Tillos to Lhuys, no. 147, Nov. 16, *Aff. étr., Turquie, Bucharest*, vol. 24. Tillos wrote that the threat was appreciated. It was not felt necessary, however, to retain it in the official draft. Included in the Prince's address was the government's projected programme of reform: a rural law, an electoral law, a reorganization of the army, the establishment of free and compulsory education, and the unification of the codes of law, as well as the granting of concessions for railways and institutions of credit: *Arch. dip., 1866*, vol. ii, pp. 214 ff.

[2] The project criticized severely the closing of the last session, the unconstitutional procedure of the government since then, the violent prosecutions, and the squandering of public moneys, which was declared to have been more extensive than under any previous régime. The address was not comminatory, but was almost entirely devoted to invective. Even the 'beautiful projects of law', enumerated in the Prince's speech, received sarcastic treatment: Green to Russell, no. 117, Dec. 5, enc., F.O. 78/1748.

[3] Eder to Rechberg, no. 96, Dec. 7, Staatsarchiv, XXXVIII/139. Couza expressed himself similarly to Green and Tillos.

[4] *La Nation*, Nov. 24.

[5] Eder to Rechberg, no. 96.

[6] Tillos to Lhuys, no. 149, Dec. 7, *Aff. étr., Turquie, Bucharest*, vol. 24; Green to Hammond, Dec. 4, F.O. 78/1748. To Eder alone (in a private interview) Couza seems to have discussed the matter frankly.

[7] Lhuys to Tillos, no. 8, Dec. 26, *Aff. étr., Turquie, Bucharest*, vol. 24.

[8] Eder to Rechberg, no. 96.

was the dethronement of the Prince; but in a later letter he said that it lacked the courage to carry it through. In fact, the assembly's initial assaults were little more than a flash in the pan.[1] After the absence of the government's supporters had prevented the projected address from being considered,[2] a fairly innocent substitute was introduced and passed.[3] Had the Coalition possessed the requisite energy, one might suppose that it would have capitalized the Prince's unpopularity, of which we hear so much, and, by means of the Left, have won the support of the army. But apparently its belligerency had been sapped by the long-protracted parliamentary recess—or shall we say that fulminations in the assembly marked the limit of its courage? It would obviously take a much more determined struggle if it wished to save the assembly's legal existence.

But, after all, these were the same *boyards* who had allowed themselves to be frightened into electing Couza in 1859. Now, in spite of much grumbling and many threats, they passed a loan of 10,000,000 piastres,[4] demanded by the government, and they adopted the government's solution of the question of the monasteries. Having thus accepted the most urgent measures in Couza's programme, they were practically without defence against his batteries.

But at least the passiveness of the assembly gave it a somewhat longer lease of life. The charge that Couza was not man enough to carry out a *coup*[5] may be discounted by what we know of his character as well as the course of future events. We are aware, moreover, that he was not fond of power for power's sake, and that he was extraordinarily indifferent to its trappings. There was, therefore, no point in hastening unnecessarily to the issue, as long as the assembly did not venture to obstruct his policies. Finally, the encouragement which he had expected from Constantinople was as yet of too vague a character to make him feel that the time was yet propitious for throwing his crown into the crucible.

It was hardly strange, in view of Couza's attitude towards the *couvents dédiés*, that most of the Powers had, apparently, been rather loath to meet him half-way on the problem of reorganization. It was whispered that Bulwer had been rather curt to Negri when discussing the matter along with the question of the monasteries.[6]

---

[1] Eder to Rechberg, no. 99 A, Dec. 15, Staatsarchiv, XXXVIII/139.
[2] Green to Russell, no. 117, Dec. 5, F.O. 78/1748.
[3] Green to Russell, no. 122, Dec. 12, *ibid*.
[4] Tillos to Lhuys, no. 151, Dec. 23, *Aff. étr., Turquie, Bucharest*, vol. 24. Tillos believed that only this averted a *coup d'état*.
[5] Eder to Rechberg, no. 99 A.
[6] Rechberg to Ludolf, Oct. 8, Staatsarchiv, XII/119. Bulwer had expressed the opinion in July that the confiscation of these lands, in case the payment of taxes was refused, would enable Couza to establish a military dictatorship: Ludolf to Rechberg, no. 59 D, July 23, *ibid*.

Throughout the autumn the Powers still paid futile homage to the Protocol, no headway being made, because Great Britain could not bring herself to countenance the idea of secularization, and France, who had finally brought Austria to her side, would not hear of arbitration on any other basis. Even Ali, who had never relished the role of intermediary in a matter which but little concerned his government, had already come to the conclusion that secularization must be the eventual solution, though he hoped that a reasonable indemnity could be secured for the Holy Places.[1] It was the monks who proved the uncompromising actors in the drama. Advised by the Russians not to yield to any overture,[2] and perhaps a little encouraged by Russell's shallow obstinacy,[3] the representatives of the Holy Places rejected all suggestion of drafting a counter-project in answer to Couza's enactment,[4] and it is difficult to believe that France had ever supposed that her 'amicable accord' would ever become realized. The difference between French and British diplomacy was that the former had been fundamentally dishonest, but executed with admirable sagacity and directness, while the latter had been fundamentally sincere, but compromised by pedantry at London and rather shifty manœuvring at Constantinople. Hopeless to sway the embassies by his counsels or the Porte by his intrigues, Bulwer finally left for Paris to see if Drouyn de Lhuys would listen to his arguments. Of small avail was Sir Henry's pertinacity. Diplomacy was bankrupt, and the Moldo-Wallachians—if not also the French—had known it all along. Informed that Ali had come to accept the principle of secularization,[5] Couza simply waited for the opening of the assembly, with whom on this point at least he would certainly be in accord. On the opening day of the session the assembly formally resolved that the question of the dedicated monasteries should be decided 'in and by the State'. Then a few days later, on learning that Ali had sent another circular to the ambassadors inviting them to a meeting, the Prince's government placed the question squarely before the assembly.[6] It was a handsome Christmas gift that the nation now presented to itself. On December 25 by a unanimous vote the assembly passed the law secularizing the lands of the dedicated

[1] Ludolf to Rechberg, no. 69 B, Aug. 24, *ibid.*, XII/195.
[2] Moustier to Lhuys, no. 190, Sept. 24, *Aff. étr.*, *Turquie*, vol. 360.
[3] Ludolf was apparently right in believing that Russell had been influenced by the visit of the archimandrite Nilos to London: Layard to Russell, Aug. 4, Layard Papers, Brit. Mus., Add. MS. 38989, f. 116.
[4] Annex (Nov. 7) to Moustier's no. 235, *Aff. étr.*, *Turquie*, vol. 360. They felt that any negotiation would compromise the position which they had taken that their property rights were unassailable, and that the question should be settled by arbitration.
[5] Green to Russell, no. 128, Dec. 28, F.O. 78/1748.
[6] *Arch. dip.*, *1864*, vol. ii, pp. 326 ff.

monasteries and fixing the indemnity at 51,000,000 piastres.[1] It must have been of intense satisfaction to Cogalnitchano that under his ministry a scheme on which he had long set his heart had been finally achieved. To Couza and, in fact, to public opinion the decision signified a victory in a hard-fought nationalist struggle. No wonder a *Te Deum* was sung in celebration.[2] Yet Couza—as one may believe—was far too supple a politician to close the door completely to conciliation; and a letter of the foreign minister, addressed to Negri, explained that the Prince, 'inspired at once by his patriotism and the imminent dangers of a popular movement embracing the whole of Roumania', resolved to give his country the satisfaction which was its due.[3] This apology had been written two days before the act of secularization had been passed.

Since the question of the monasteries had been practically laid to rest—though the matter of the size of the indemnity might still be a subject of negotiation—there was nothing for the Powers to do but accept the situation as gracefully as they could—which meant, of course, to make a fuss and actually do nothing. The Porte, though rather indifferent (it was said[4]), dispatched an immediate protest to Couza's government,[5] while the representatives of Russia, Prussia, Austria, and Great Britain sent identical instructions to their respective consuls in Bucharest, bidding them inform Couza that their governments did not recognize the act which had been passed.[6] Naturally the Prince took these measures for what they were worth. 'There was a superciliousness in the Prince's bearing,' wrote Green, in relating the consuls' action, 'which under the mask of repeated declarations of respect for the governments which approve of the Turkish note, was to my mind peculiarly offensive.'[7] Viewing the affair from a distance, Prokesch expressed the gloomiest forebodings. 'Independence, which is, in truth, already at hand, will next be proclaimed, and, since France openly wishes and supports it, I see, under the present circumstances, no means of warding off this declaration.' Convinced that the monastic revenues would be spent in improving the army, the internuncio expressed his belief that this rising Roumanian state, hostile as it was to Austria, and patronized by Napoleon, would turn out a 'second Piedmont'.[8] It is hardly strange, perhaps, that

---

[1] *Arch. dip.*, *1864*, vol. ii, pp. 338 ff. The other conditions followed the resolution, already communicated by Bordeano.

[2] Haas to Rechberg, Dec. 27, 1863, Staatsarchiv, XII/119.

[3] Erskine to Russell, no. 27, Jan. 18, 1864, enc., F.O. 78/1801.

[4] Moustier to Lhuys, no. 238, Dec. 31, *Aff. étr.*, *Turquie*, vol. 360.

[5] *Arch. dip.*, *1864*, vol. ii, pp. 334 ff.   [6] *Ibid.*, pp. 335 ff.

[7] Green to Russell, no. 3, Jan. 15, 1864, F.O. 78/1810. 'The secularization of the property of the dedicated convents . . . he now looks upon as a matter of his double election and the union.'

[8] Prokesch to Rechberg, no. 3 c, Jan. 8, Staatsarchiv, XII/196.

so crushing a moral victory should seem to have for the moment an exaggerated significance. It was to Prokesch himself that Moustier flatly refused to join in his colleagues' demonstration ('the chamber, as well as the Prince, have acted in the fullness of their rights'); [1] and Drouyn de Lhuys gave him unqualified approval.[2] To the very end, France was willing that her little friends should have their way.

It now remained for the Powers to swallow the noxious pill, and try to make it a trifle less unpalatable for the monks. Drouyn de Lhuys, while admitting that the action of the Principalities had been illegal, felt strongly that it would be unwise to quarrel over the act of secularization. Thus he regarded it as inopportune any longer to consider the operation of the Protocol, but he was willing to have a conference to determine the amount of the indemnity.[3] After some hesitation Great Britain came around to this view,[4] even affirming that she would cease to consider the monks if they refused to accept the figure which a commission should determine.[5] It is interesting to notice that the plan was being accepted which a majority of the European commission on the Principalities had advocated in 1858,[6] and even Bulwer, now that the Protocol was undeniably dead and buried, resumed the position he had once taken.[7] But the British government still found it difficult to submit to Couza's *défiances* with equanimity. In his instructions to Bulwer, which were communicated to Drouyn de Lhuys, Russell concluded that he could accept the idea of secularization only if it was agreed that Couza should be severely reprimanded,[8] and that the revenues of the monasteries should be placed under a sequester, imposed by the Porte with the concurrence of the Powers. Russell then declared that it was plain that Couza was aiming at independence, and that, in view of his charge that the assembly was to blame for the friction between them, it might be well to call a national

---

[1] *Ibid.*, annex. 'We have no right', contended Moustier, 'to meddle in the internal affairs of the Principalities.' This was obviously repudiating the Protocol.

[2] Lhuys to Moustier, no. 1, Jan. 8, *Aff. étr., Turquie*, vol. 361.

[3] *Ibid.* Drouyn circularized the governments of Austria, Prussia, Russia, and Great Britain on the subject, Jan. 9, *ibid., Angleterre*, vol. 728.

[4] La Tour d'Auvergne to Lhuys, no. 22, Feb. 6, *Aff. étr., Angleterre*, vol. 728. There was still the question of whether the titles of the ecclesiastical foundations should be rigorously investigated, France contending that all rights of mainmorte were inherently unsound, while Great Britain felt that only by such an inquiry could the amount of the indemnity be equitably determined: La Tour to Lhuys, no. 8, Jan 15, *ibid.*

[5] F.O. to Cowley, no. 193, Feb. 23, F.O. 27/1517. [6] See p. 357.

[7] La Tour to Lhuys, no. 22. Bulwer had first made this concession while in Paris when he found that under no circumstances would Drouyn de Lhuys agree to even a temporary restoration of the revenues into the hands of the monks: Bulwer to Russell, Jan. 5, F.O. 78/1801.

[8] This had been urged by Bulwer: to Russell, Jan. 22, 1864, Russell Papers, G. and D. 22/93, Pub. Rec. Off.

assembly and place before it the conduct of the Prince himself.[1]
It did not, of course, take much effort on the part of Drouyn de
Lhuys to refute such a ridiculous proposal.[2] The British foreign
office never understood the Principalities, which were looked upon
as nothing but a bother, and, when given any consideration at all,
were treated as a perfectly responsible nation or (more often) as
a fractious and incorrigible dependency. In the meantime the
British government, as we have noticed, had shifted its ground to
a demand that the revenues be neutralized pending the final settlement of the indemnity.[3] Such a precaution, however sound in
theory, was manifestly impracticable, as any one with any compre-
hension of Rouman nationalism must know. France, at all events,
was realist enough to know that Couza would not tolerate such a
measure and that no one would force him to submit to it. When,
at the Porte's instance, a conference of ambassadors was opened at
Constantinople on May 9, Moustier strenuously opposed both the
idea of a collective reprimand and that of interfering in any way
with the Prince's appropriation of the revenues.[4] Despite his
efforts, the Protocol of May 28 which resulted from the last meeting
of the Conference did embody both these measures in modified
form; but in order to get the revenues deposited at Constantinople
no machinery was suggested beyond acquainting Couza's government with the decision, and one might readily have guessed that
the Protocol of 1864 would be no more respected than the one
which had been registered at Paris five years earlier.[5] All that the

---

[1] Russell to Bulwer, no. 2, Feb. 3, F.O. 78/1797. These instructions were
communicated to Paris.

[2] Lhuys to La Tour, no. 42, Mar. 1, *Aff. étr., Angleterre*, vol. 728.

[3] The British government contended that it would be useless to proceed with
any investigation as long as Couza was free to utilize the revenues as he chose
(F.O. to Grey, no. 18, Apr. 29, F.O. 27/1518). Yet it is difficult to see how the
Principalities were to be prevented from enjoying the firstfruits of secularization.
Drouyn de Lhuys had admitted the logic of the British proposal, but had de-
clared frankly that he would not permit coercion (Cowley to Russell, no. 423,
Apr. 23, F.O. 27/1528). This was, of course, the favourite French way of begging
the question.

[4] Moustier to Lhuys, no. 50, May 10, no. 59, May 18, and no. 60, June 1, *Aff.
étr., Turquie*, vol. 362. The proposal to put the revenues under some sort of
international sequester had been partly instigated by the news (not wholly
credited) that the Moldo-Wallachian government had begun to sell some of the
lands (Prokesch to Mensdorff, no. 33 B, May 16, Staatsarchiv, XII/196). After
a heated discussion it was decided at the meeting of May 21 that any alienation
should be forbidden pending the final settlement, and the principle of an international sequester was then adopted; but Moustier was still able to prevent any
action calling for the restoration of ecclesiastical utensils (Prokesch to Mensdorff,
no. 35 A, May 23 and annexes: *ibid.*, XII/82).

[5] What might seem an obvious means of bringing Couza to terms would have
been to offer him a loan on condition that he would comply with the wishes of the
Conference; but, of course, any such assistance would have required official
backing, and Russell—perhaps with a thought of parliamentary difficulties—
had expressly repudiated the idea of a loan under an international guarantee:

Conference really accomplished was to appoint a commission to classify the monasteries and to endeavour to form an opinion on the value of the rights which the Holy Places had lost.[1] But as the monks would never accept even the principle of an indemnity, notwithstanding the fact that Couza had been persuaded to treble the amount of the indemnity,[2] and as the commission could not induce them to present all the pertinent documents, no settlement seemed possible;[3] and eventually the government of the Principalities, after

Cowley to Russell, no. 126, Jan. 30, F.O. 27/1567; F.O. to Cowley, no. 78, Feb. 6, F.O.27/1555.

[1] Prokesch to Mensdorff, no. 37, May 30 annex, Staatsarchiv, XII/82.

[2] It was Bulwer, apparently, who instigated this offer of 150,000,000 piastres (Bulwer to Russell, no. 270, Aug. 29, F.O. 78/1806), and Couza seems to have come to it with considerable reluctance (his delegate, Negri, had at first offered 102,000,000); but the monks, instead of capitalizing this victory, demanded a further sum to cover their losses of the previous two years, when the revenues had been under a sequester. Couza then proposed that the monks should cancel this demand against a renunciation of a claim of his government for sums due to the State for charitable purposes, neglected by the representatives of the Holy Places. The Porte, accordingly, proposed this compromise to the monks, but they fell back, as usual, on their refusal to accept even the principle of an indemnity. Ali attributed this intransigence to Russian influence (Prokesch to Mensdorff, no. 58, Aug. 25, no. 59 C, Sept. 1, no. 65, Sept. 22, and no. 66, Sept. 26, Staatsarchiv, XII/196).

[3] Some feeble efforts at compromise were made by Russia, and seem to have been backed by Austria, since Mensdorff-Pouilly considered it to be of great political importance just then to side with the government of St. Petersburg (Mensdorff to Prokesch, Aug. 11, *ibid.*)—presumably on account of Schleswig-Holstein. Russia's major proposal was that, while the monastery lands should be given up to the Principalities in return for an indemnity, the churches and other buildings should be restored to the Holy Places (Prokesch to Mensdorff, no. 81, Dec. 7). The idea met with no favour, however, from the majority of the Powers, and was definitely rejected by the monks (Talleyrand to Lhuys, no. 4, Jan. 18, and no. 6, Jan. 31, 1865, *Aff. étr., Russie*, vol. 234). Tillos argued keenly that Russia was trying desperately to retain a little of her former influence in the Principalities by enabling the monks to remain there—a scheme which the Principalities, with their insistence upon a national Church, would certainly not accept (Tillos to Lhuys, no. 2, Jan. 24, *ibid., Turquie, Bucharest*, vol. 25). Gortchakoff, who appeared to be very much pained at the attitude of the Powers (Talleyrand to Lhuys, no. 4; Buchanan to Russell, no. 28, Jan. 18, F.O. 65/678), then brought up—again with Austrian concurrence—the question of the 'special chest', into which, according to the Protocol of May 28, the revenues were supposed to be deposited, but which had, apparently, been regarded, at least tacitly, as impracticable. Talleyrand (then French ambassador at St. Petersburg) remarked that this was a 'supreme and desperate attempt' to get a larger sum for the Holy Places, that no one expected any result from such a move, and that it was put forth in order to prove to the Greek clergy that a 'last *cartouche*' was being fired in their interest (Talleyrand to Lhuys, no. 8, Feb. 13, *Aff. étr., Russie*, vol. 235). After considerable negotiation Couza agreed to deposit 150,000,000 piastres with the Ottoman bank, and Russia accepted this amendment (Prokesch to Mensdorff, no. 20 A–D, Apr. 13, Staatsarchiv, XII/196); but the question was later reviewed and shelved when it was learned that Couza intended that payments should extend over a period of twenty years, and that such a plan also predicated the negotiation of a loan (Prokesch to Mensdorff, no. 35 A–B, June 5, *ibid.*). In any event, the monks showed no disposition to conform to any arrangement proposed; and the meetings of the commission, as well as the negotiations of the ambassadors, were cut short by the February revolution at Bucharest, and subsequent events made it quite impracticable to try again to effect a settlement.

agreeing to set aside in various instalments the amount which it had stipulated to pay, kept the lands in their possession without the cost of a single piastre. Again one is impressed with the utter incapacity of a European protectorate.

The general satisfaction with which both Couza and the *boyards* hailed the spoliation of the monasteries was sufficient to cause a truce of a few months in the political battle. There was no longer any talk of a movement against the Prince. Couza may at times have feared assassination[1]—for it is when an opposition is weakest that it is most dangerous—but there is no ground for believing that he had any longer the expectation of a project of dethronement, much less a popular revolution. The British consul, who had written so much about his waning popularity, throws significant light on the extent of his authority, as well as on the generally favourable conditions in the country. 'The authority of the government,' wrote Green, 'is indeed so great that a sub-prefect in the most distant district has but to be heard to be obeyed. A single *dorobany* (gendarme) suffices to arrest and bring in any number of prisoners. The government is all-powerful.' Neither was there turbulence nor depression. 'The country in its length and breadth', continued this witness, 'is perfectly tranquil. An isolated case of highway robbery lately led to the immediate detection of the culprits. An unprecedented large harvest has been got in. The value of land has doubled and tripled within a few years; so has the value of labour. Agricultural machinery is being extensively introduced from England. There is complete religious toleration. The numerous Jews are subjected to no persecution. The press is practically free. People sleep with open doors. In no country are the necessaries of life in greater abundance.' Then this survey goes on to say that the government is corrupt, arbitrary, and prodigal, and that the public funds, which ought to be spent on improving the means of communication, are squandered on 'an undisciplined and ridiculous army'.[2] Yet this testimony shows clearly enough that Couza's reign was not oppressive and that the people themselves had no serious ground for a change of rulers. Even the ill-natured Tillos made similar observations. 'In the midst of all this disorder', wrote the French consul (he had been discussing the state of the administration), 'the population remains indifferent. It comprehends nothing in all these subtleties which divide the executive power and the chamber. The harvests are good; employment has been on the increase; and, as in this state both evil and good are attributed to the government, the masses regard the reign of Prince Couza as fortunate. The state of the finances touches them little—

---

[1] Tillos to Lhuys, no. 149, Dec. 7, *Aff. étr., Turquie, Bucharest*, vol. 24.
[2] Green to Russell, no. 120, Dec. 11, F.O. 78/1748.

justice, not at all; the administration and the police are ordered to conciliate them. That is why Couza desires universal suffrage.'[1] Was there not ground for the Prince's feeling that, after all, the public was behind him?

It was with rare acumen that Couza, looking beyond his enemies, the *boyards*, and a middle class too meagre as yet to furnish him strength, saw as his greatest potential allies the millions of peasants, who, like him, had no love for the *boyard*, who would be sure to reward a ruler who came to their deliverance, and who would not have the political intelligence to cavil at his measures. In the course of a journey in the country during the previous spring Couza had received the most cordial welcome from the peasants, and in some districts deputations came to thank him for not having sanctioned the rural project of 1862. 'It is there', he said to one of his suite (speaking of the peasantry) 'that respect for authority has taken refuge, annihilated everywhere else. They are the State's active force. The rest do not matter, and the day an effort is made to overthrow me I shall have three million peasants with me.'[2] It is not charged in any of the consular dispatches that the peasants were yet encouraged to expect emancipation, and there is no suggestion that they were in a state of agitation, but apparently arms had been distributed in certain rural communities,[3] doubtless as a means of holding the *boyards* in check. It is hardly to be doubted that Couza meant to relieve a class from disabilities which dwarfed its economic existence, for, apart from motives of genuine sympathy, the value of the peasantry as a political weapon was fully appreciated by the man who was fighting with the *boyards* for the retention of his throne.

Of greater immediate importance was the reliance which he placed upon the army, of whose loyalty he had boasted during the crisis of the last winter.[4] As long as General Floresco was its chief, the Prince could feel that this instrument was in safe hands, for Floresco had long since parted with the Right, and his restless ambition had tied him pretty closely to the Prince's fortunes. To the strengthening of the army the Prince gave considerable attention. During November a large consignment of arms and munitions came from Marseilles by arrangement with the French contractor, Godillot.[5] As Couza had acquainted the Porte with these projects,[6] there was no ground for the suzerain's interference; yet

---

[1] Tillos to Lhuys, no. 149, Dec. 7, *Aff. étr., Turquie, Bucharest*, vol. 2.
[2] Tissot to Lhuys, no. 5, May 13, *Aff. étr., Turquie, Jassy*, vol. 11.
[3] Green to Russell, no. 113, Nov. 27, F.O. 78/1748; cf. Tillos to Lhuys, no. 144.
[4] Green to Russell, no. 15, Jan. 29, F.O. 78/1746.
[5] Tillos to Lhuys, no. 144.
[6] Moustier to Lhuys, no. 96, May 21, *Aff. étr., Turquie*, vol. 358.

the rumour that 60,000 muskets had been received and the fear that Couza was in league with Michael to engage in something mischievous [1] moved Ali to write to Couza for an explanation [2]—a step which Austria would fain have had the Powers follow up by a joint communication. [3] Couza answered that the arms were his, and were justified by the present state of Europe. [4] This, to be sure, was not very enlightening. Bulwer had feared that Couza wanted the revenues of the monasteries in order to set up a military dictatorship, [5] but Negri told Moustier that the arms were intended to equip the corps which Couza was hoping to place at Napoleon's disposal, [6] and the evidence seems to show that the Prince was still hoping for a war in which his contingent might play a role analogous to that of Sardinia in the Crimean War, and claim as his reward the completion of Rouman unity (that is, the incorporation of the Transylvanian Roumans). [7] But no war broke out, and Napoleon politely declined the Prince's offer. [8] Then the presence of some intriguing Poles in northern Moldavia proved sufficiently disquieting to Austria and Russia to cause them to concentrate some troops near the frontier, [9] and Couza could hardly be reproached for wanting to put his forces in a state of fitness to defend his country's neutrality. Unfortunately, the present atmosphere led to all sorts of forebodings. Green seriously expected a proclamation of independence. [10]

Couza's plan for the augmentation of the army included the principle that every able-bodied Roumanian should be subject to call. Of course, the *Règlement* limited the number of soldiers under arms to approximately 7,000, but it was possible to argue that this restriction did not apply to various classes of reserves, [11] and, anyway, he seems to have contemplated an active force of 18,000 men, [12] if he

[1] Prokesch to Rechberg, no. 93, Nov. 19, Staatsarchiv, XII/79.
[2] Annex to Prokesch's no. 99 A of Dec. 18, *ibid.*
[3] Rechberg to Prokesch, Dec. 27, *ibid.*, XII/80.
[4] Prokesch to Rechberg, no. 95, Nov. 27, *ibid.*, XII/79. Eder said positively that part of the arms were for the Polish insurgents (Eder to Rechberg, no. 94, Dec. 2, *ibid.*, XXXVIII/139), but the story seems inherently unlikely.
[5] p. 430, n. 6.
[6] Moustier to Lhuys, Oct. 25, telg., *Aff. étr., Turquie*, vol. 360.
[7] Tillos to Lhuys, no. 143, Oct. 22, *ibid., Turquie, Bucharest*, vol. 24.
[8] Napoleon to Couza, Dec. 20, annex to Lhuys' no. 8, *ibid.* Couza had addressed his offer personally to Napoleon.
[9] Green to Hammond, Nov. 16, F.O. 78/1748. Gortchakoff told the French chargé d'affaires at St. Petersburg that the purchase of arms and the possibility of raising a force of 125,000 men, if the contemplated military organization should be carried out, 'are disquieting to the neighbouring Powers': Massignac to Lhuys, no. 16, Mar. 20, 1864, *Aff. étr., Russie*, vol. 233.
[10] Green to Hammond, Apr. 20, F.O. 78/1810.
[11] Eder to Rechberg, no. 14, Feb. 26, Staatsarchiv, XXXVIII/139. Couza took this position in interviews with Green and Eder.
[12] Green to Erskine, no. 5, Jan. 26, F.O. 78/1810. Eder to Rechberg, no. 94, Staatsarchiv, XXXVIII/139.

could avoid being called to account by the Porte. It might be presumed that a more strenuous opposition would be encountered in the assembly, which on the ground of expense as well as danger to the constitution could not well approve of a large standing army. But the government's argument that these measures were needed for defence against foreign invasion and the fear that Couza might outstrip them in popularity finally induced the deputies to pass the money demanded for the new equipment; and so bright was the outlook that Godillot, who had recently been in Bucharest to advise the Prince, returned to France to cover additional orders. 'Everything here', wrote Green, 'smells of gunpowder.'[1] Yet the assembly did finally balk at the plan of a *levée en masse*, though, not daring to reject it flatly, it brought forward an amendment to create a national guard in every town.[2] As Couza was certain to disapprove of any measure to arm the middle class, his veto was a foregone conclusion.[3] In the meantime a demand was made of the assembly for a large sum for extra pay for the army, and preparations were undertaken for an armed camp at Focshani[4]—which may recall a similar measure in 1860. An Austrian conjecture that these armaments were wanted mainly to defend the Prince against his own people[5] was perhaps right in so far as the *boyards* were likely to observe the warning.

For a time, indeed, it seemed as if no *coup d'état* would be necessary. The assembly had saved itself, as Tillos remarked, by voting the loan of 10,000,000 piastres,[6] and though it arched its back on one or two occasions, it not only ratified a railway concession[7] and authorized a loan to pay the indemnity to the Holy Places,[8] but went so far as to vote for a council of state and a court of accounts (both to be nominated by the Prince)—two of the innovations which Couza had planned in his *mémoire* to the Powers. If it could also be persuaded to adopt a new electoral law, the political execution of the *boyards* could be carried out painlessly— by the process of slow suicide. Tillos was disgusted with the 'inanity' of the Opposition, and admitted that Cogalnitchano 'had manœuvred well up to the present'.[9] Whether or not the French consul merely imagined an alleged intrigue against the premier on

[1] Green to Hammond, Feb. 10, F.O. 78/1810.
[2] It was said that the *boyards* hoped thereby to have the means of suppressing peasant uprisings as well as to obtain an instrument to use against the government: Tillos to Lhuys, no. 157, Feb. 10, and no. 158, Feb. 16, *Aff. étr., Turquie, Bucharest*, vol. 24.
[3] Green to Erskine, no. 6, Feb. 2, F.O. 78/1810.
[4] Tillos to Lhuys, no. 162, Mar. 16, *Aff. étr., Turquie, Bucharest*, vol. 24.
[5] Ludolf to Prokesch, no. 83 B, Oct. 23, 1863, Staatsarchiv, XII/79.
[6] Tillos to Lhuys, no. 151, Dec. 23, *Aff. étr., Turquie, Bucharest*, vol. 24.
[7] Green to Hammond, Mar. 8, 1864, F.O. 78/1810.
[8] Tillos to Lhuys, no. 156, Feb. 2, *Aff. étr., Turquie, Bucharest*, vol. 24.
[9] Tillos to Lhuys, no. 157, *ibid.*

the part of some of the Prince's *entourage*, the Prince told him readily enough that he would stand by Cogalnitchano and that he felt that he could count on him.[1] However much they might differ on the ultimate form of government, both men were anxious to widen the suffrage and to relieve the peasants of some of their burdens.

It was the rural question—that question which had so long troubled the internal peace of the Principalities—that put the position of the ministry in jeopardy. On March 28 the Prince sent a message to the assembly that he had not sanctioned the measure voted in 1862 because it did not fulfil the conditions guaranteed by article xlvi of the Convention, and that he now submitted to it a new project—the chief feature of which was to make of the peasant a free proprietor.[2] Simultaneously the proposed law was published in the *Moniteur* and given the fullest publicity among the peasants. This attack from the front and the rear could hardly have been expected, and the *boyards* immediately took alarm. It was perhaps the realization that they had been trapped which induced the hitherto docile assembly to reject an item of the budget on April 1.[3] Some of the chiefs of the conservatives sought the aid of Tillos, but the French consul had been so frequently upbraided by Moustier for his bias against the Prince that for once he gave the *boyards* cold comfort, and he pointed to the article of the Convention which had declared for an 'amelioration of the state of the peasants'. Threatened on all sides (for Cogalnitchano had calculated that this would split the Coalition by winning over the Left), the distracted *boyards* did not dare to reject the bill, and could only hope to meet it by a flank movement. On April 25 the assembly passed by a vote of 83 to 36 a resolution of want of confidence in the ministry.[4] Undismayed, Couza told Tillos that he would present a new electoral law and prorogue the assembly, and if opposition continued, would not only dissolve it, but, if necessary, resort to a *coup d'état*, but that he would depart as little as possible from legality (he called it a 'limited *coup d'état*'), for the newly elected assembly would ratify his action and then draw up a new constitution.[5] One can understand his confidences, while hardly putting faith in his assurances; but, anyway, a crisis was fast approaching. In the meantime some intriguers (Tillos did not say who they were)

---

[1] Tillos to Lhuys, no. 160, Mar. 2, *Aff. étr., Turquie, Bucharest*, vol. 24.

[2] Eder to Rechberg, no. 28 A, Apr. 8, Staatsarchiv, XXXVIII/145; Green to Russell, no. 29, Apr. 11, F.O. 78/1810.

[3] Cogalnitchano had asked for a large sum for the purpose of bribing some foreign journals on the ground that the question of the Principalities was likely to come up before a congress and it was desirable to have means of explaining and defending their rights. In spite of the support of the Left, it was defeated by a vote of 33 to 30: Green to Russell, no. 27, Apr. 5, *ibid.*

[4] Tillos to Lhuys, no. 167, Apr. 27, *Aff. étr., Turquie, Bucharest*, vol. 24.

[5] Tillos to Lhuys, Apr. 26, telg., *ibid.*

came to the Prince the day after the assembly's action, and after promising to vote the credits demanded (for thus far the budget had not been passed), begged him to put off all consideration of the rural law for three years. Couza said that he viewed the overture as an ultimatum, but he held his ground.[1] Since the only conventional alternative was the dissolution of the assembly, which would merely mean the election of another of precisely the same character, Couza saw that he must bring up the electoral question,[2] and that in all likelihood a *coup d'état* was inevitable.

The contemplated electoral law would virtually establish universal suffrage.[3] In forcing the issue, Couza was frankly appealing to the nation against its formal representatives, and the project, whether voted or not, would in either case have meant the rout of the Coalition. It was now the Prince's turn to deliver an ultimatum. His enemies could escape a *coup d'état* if they would, but only at the cost of their political ascendancy. On April 28 Couza formally presented the new electoral law, and then prorogued the assembly to meet again in extraordinary session on May 14.[4] If the *boyards* had meant to defy him, the Prince had accepted the challenge.

The public mind was naturally in a state of great agitation.[5] It was said that 80,000 Russians were on the Bessarabian frontier, and it was known that an Austrian force was concentrating at Cronstadt,[6] while a Turkish army was encamped across the Danube.[7] The menace of foreign invasion seemed to hang over the land. Meanwhile every one recognized that the crisis in the political struggle had now come. It was generally believed that the Prince would promulgate the electoral law on his own authority; for the *boyards* had said that they would not vote for what amounted to a sentence of death. Driven now to the situation of clutching at straws, they made one last effort to enlist the intervention of France, urging that the Prince's agrarian policy was bound to lead to a *jacquerie*. It was vain. Tillos only told them that the rural question demanded prompt solution and that he approved of its principles;[8] of the electoral project he said nothing, presumably because he had never been in favour of a democratic reform, and his instructions did not order him to support it. Furious at the rebuff, Demetrius Ghika said that France need not be surprised if they now turned to Russia.[9] Couza, for his part, was not idle in

[1] Tillos to Lhuys, no. 168, Apr. 29, *ibid.*
[2] Eder to Rechberg, no. 31, Apr. 29, Staatsarchiv, xxxviii/139.
[3] Green to Bulwer, no. 31, Apr. 28, F.O. 78/1810.
[4] *Arch. dip., 1864*, vol. ii, pp. 351–2.
[5] Tillos to Lhuys, no. 169, May 3, *Aff. étr., Turquie, Bucharest*, vol. 25.
[6] Tillos to Lhuys, no. 167, Apr. 27, *ibid.*
[7] Green to Hammond, Apr. 20, F.O. 78/1810.
[8] Tillos to Lhuys, no. 167.
[9] Tillos to Lhuys, no. 173, May 17, *Aff. étr., Turquie, Bucharest*, vol. 25.

the interval. He tried to conciliate his dangerous neighbours by keeping careful watch over the Polish refugees, who were supposed to be the *raison d'être* of the military demonstration,[1] and he wrote to several of the Powers that the country was in danger.[2] He also made a tour of the provinces to satisfy himself that public opinion was on his side on both of the pending questions. When Tillos, in accordance with instructions from Drouyn de Lhuys, urged him to make a trip to Constantinople to defend the project of reorganization which he had submitted to the Powers, Couza sensibly pointed out that if he were to go at this moment, it would be said that he looked not to his own people but to the governments who supported the suzerain Power. He would convoke the assembly, he said, as he intended. That body would do one of three things: refuse all relations with the ministry, make the electoral law more radical by eliminating indirect election,[3] or vote for his dethronement. In event of any of these occurrences, he would call a plebiscite of the nation on the electoral law and the constitution which he had drafted, and of which, he added, Moustier had approved. Then he would go to Constantinople and ask the approval of the Porte and the Powers. Tillos could not turn him from his purpose, and marvelled at his firmness.[4] For once, indeed, the Prince had made an impression on the bitterest of his critics.

On May 14 the assembly met in extraordinary session. Every deputy was present, and despite the prevalence of a rumour of an imminent *coup d'état*, there seems to have been some doubt whether the government was in earnest.[5] On the other hand, it was said that some members of the Coalition, frightened by their own temerity, had given up the struggle.[6] Perhaps by some minor concessions could the harassed deputies manage to find escape from the fate which now hung over them. With perceptible nervousness Cogalnitchano rose from his seat, and announced that they were met solely to vote the budget and to consider the electoral law which had been presented to them. The Opposition at once combated this by an attack upon the government[7] and by carrying a

---

[1] Eder to Rechberg, no. 33, May 10, Staatsarchiv, xxxviii/145.

[2] This was, of course, invoking article viii of the Convention, which made the Porte and the Protecting Powers responsible for the defence of the Principalities against aggression from without.

[3] It is not clear why Couza should have thought of this possibility, unless he believed that the Opposition might think of altering the law in such a way as to make it still more unacceptable to the Powers.

[4] Tillos to Lhuys, no. 171, May 10, *ibid*. It is strange, in view of Tillos's own account, that Green should say that Tillos told him that Couza was very undecided in his course: Green to Hammond, May 11, F.O. 78/1810.

[5] Damé, *op. cit.*, p. 137.   [6] Soutzo, *op. cit.*, p. 392.

[7] Boeresco, as representative of the Opposition, after summarizing the complaints of his party, declared that the ministry was not representative of the chamber, and that the Prince, instead of dissolving the assembly, as he should

resolution that the assembly would not discuss anything with a ministry against whom it had passed a vote of distrust. The premier then read a message from the Prince, dissolving the assembly; and when that body retaliated by pronouncing itself in permanent session, Cogalnitchano called in a body of soldiers, who summarily cleared the chamber.[1] The Prince had carried his fight to a conclusion, and the rout of the *boyards* was complete.

The way was now cleared for the *coup d'état*, and on the same day (May 14) the citizens[2] of Wallachia and Moldavia were asked to vote yes or no on the electoral law and the new constitution, both of which were submitted simultaneously. A special proclamation was issued to the army (a dictator is not without appreciation of his main pillar of support), congratulating it for having shown 'immovable firmness' and for having contributed 'by its loyal and energetic attitude to give liberty to the State'; while another one was addressed to the citizens of Bucharest—that benevolent middle class, who were to 'preserve order' and 'aid the government in fulfilling its great mission'. Also an ordinance appeared, reviving the press law of 1859, which had created a species of censorship. Until the new constitution was promulgated, it was announced that the Prince would govern by ordinance.[3] All this was very reminiscent of December 2, 1851.[4] No wonder the wits called the affair 'the little *coup d'état*'.[5]

have done, had taken the part of his ministers. This, he said, was contrary to constitutional usage. It was a mistake, moreover, to represent the assembly as opposed to the rural law; it only asked for time to consider it. As for the electoral project, it would discuss such a measure only with a constitutional cabinet: Damé, *op. cit.*, p. 137. The claim of ministerial responsibility was not, of course, justified on the basis of the Convention, and had not been generally respected. The explanation regarding the rural law is hardly convincing, and the decision not to consider the electoral project had evidently been taken in the beginning.

[1] Green to Russell, May 14, telg., F.O. 78/1810; Tillos to Lhuys, May 14, telg., *Aff. étr., Turquie, Bucharest*, vol. 25.

[2] All were privileged to vote who could meet the requirements for communal elections.

[3] *Arch. dip., 1864*, vol. ii, pp. 382 ff.

[4] The famous *coup d'état* of Louis Napoleon, afterwards Napoleon III.

[5] Eder to Rechberg, no. 36, May 16, Staatsarchiv, XXXVIII/145.

CHAPTER XV

A BENEVOLENT DICTATORSHIP

THE *coup d'état* of May 14, 1864, with its inseparable accompaniments, the new electoral law and the agrarian reform, was the climax of a five-year struggle between the vested interests of the landed aristocracy and the idea of a strong national leadership, based on more or less arbitrary interpretations of the public welfare. The inauguration of a dictatorship, but thinly shrouded in constitutional forms, looking for its support to a loyal army and a contented populace, and standing for social reform according to the approved standards of the nineteenth century, signified the creation of a sort of replica of the Second Empire. Like Napoleon III, whom he slavishly admired, Alexander John was to try the role of an eighteenth-century despot, touched by some of the enlightenment that Europe had received from the French and Industrial Revolutions. There was, in fact, more ground for such a régime in the United Principalities than in western Europe, for the transition from landed aristocracy to economic liberalism was only in its beginnings in these lands. The history of continental Europe had always revealed the need of a benevolent despot to crush the old order before a more liberal political philosophy could usher in the new. Thus Couza is a landmark in the history of Roumania. How well he would play the role for which History had cast him, and which he had deliberately assumed, was soon to be determined. The result would be the gauge of his insight and character. He had at the outset the advantage of the passive approval of a large section, albeit the less articulate section, of his people, and it now behoved him to secure the active co-operation of the embryonic middle class, which looked rather to the future than to the past. But, first of all, he must make his peace with the Powers.

The overthrow of the Convention in a *fait accompli*, which, unlike that of 1859, had not the least shadow of legality, was the greatest act of defiance which Rouman nationalism, now embodied in its chief, had ever yet hurled at the European protectorate. While it is noticeable that ever since union was proclaimed the consular corps had produced increasingly little influence over the ruler who was in their charge, the *coup d'état* may be said to have practically terminated their role as informal advisers. They had utterly failed in the task which the ambassadors had confided to them in February 1863. They had been powerless to prevent the *coup d'état*. Even Eder, the ablest of them all, had been wrong in his calculations, for he had said that neither side had the courage

to pursue its aims to a finish. Green found his only consolation in
continuing his malevolent strictures upon all the Prince's acts, even
hoping that the loan that Steege was negotiating in London would
fail in the end to materialize—a result which might force despotism
to capitulate to bankruptcy.[1] The dispatches of Offenberg are not
available to tell their tale, but it appears that the Russian consul,
who had none of his predecessor's ability to keep abreast of political
struggles while earning a reputation for potent villainy, could think
of nothing now but ventilating his spite.[2] Finally, Tillos had been
placed in the awkward position of benevolent neutrality. While
Drouyn de Lhuys had finally expected him to prevent a *coup d'état*,
Moustier, on the other hand, had instructed him to let Couza have
his way, if he (Couza) were willing to take the responsibility.[3] This
was, of course, not opposition, and Couza had thus known that at
least he was not alienating the country on whose aid he had always
counted in an emergency. When Tillos told him that France
declined responsibility for his acts, Couza promptly gave his
approval of such a decision, as it would not look well, he said, for
the *coup d'état* to be ascribed to foreign influence.[4] The United
Principalities had, in fact, taken a stride of their own volition, and
wished to walk alone. When the ministers came in visible agitation
to tell him of the dissolution of the assembly, the Prince alone was
calm. It was, after all, his victory—his, and—in a sense—the
nation's.[5]

While most of the consuls were aware that the whole affair was
beyond their capacity, Strambio, at Offenberg's instance, invited
them to a meeting on May 17 to decide what should be done.[6]
Nothing, of course, happened, beyond a decision to send the fullest
information to the governments and await instructions.[7] On
Saturday, May 20, the Prince was, as usual, at home to the consuls;
but though Offenberg would have had them all absent themselves,
there is no evidence that any of them did so but him. On one
ground, indeed, the consuls enjoyed a sort of moral triumph, for,
without the endorsement of the Powers for his act, Couza could
not well afford to admit its arbitrary character. When he ventured
to assure Green that he had not violated the constitution, because
the Powers were the ones in the last instance to decide the matter,

[1] Green to Hammond, June 14, F.O. 78/1811.
[2] Montlong to Rechberg, no. 37, May 17, Staatsarchiv, XXXVIII/143.
[3] Green heard that Tillos had finally told Couza to avoid a *coup*, 'if possible':
Green to Hammond, May 11, F.O. 78/1810.
[4] The sceptical Demetrius Ghika remarked that that was all very well, but
that Couza never did anything without the consent of France: Tillos to Lhuys,
no. 173, May 17.
[5] Tillos to Lhuys, no. 173, May 17, *Aff. étr., Turkey, Bucharest*, vol. 25.
[6] Montlong to Mensdorff, no. 37.
[7] Green to Bulwer, no. 31, May 17, enc., F.O. 78/1810.

the British consul pointed out that the proclamation had stated that the new constitution and electoral law were to be final if the plebiscite approved them. The Prince then took refuge in the statement that he could use no other language to his people, who were jealous of foreign interference.[1] One may judge, oneself, who were the intended victims of the Prince's frank duplicity.

Nothing served as yet to mar the good impressions of the victory. The most incorrigible of the *boyards* confined themselves to gathering in small circles, and cursing the Prince, or complaining that France had betrayed them. None of their many *mémoires* and brochures had availed them, and they lacked the courage now even to make a protest to the Porte.[2] On the other hand, as Tillos tells us, 'a number of people, hardly very hostile, to be sure, have gone to the Prince to make honourable amends. The result is (continued the French consul) that I hear on all sides that the Prince has done well, but that he ought to make use of other instruments. That means that each one would have wished to make the *coup d'état* with him in order to profit by it.'[3] Evidently, while the *boyards* —or, at least, most of them—sulked in their tents, and the people awaited the plebiscite, some of the politically ambitious, as always on such occasions, had begun to seek the rising star. Meanwhile, something had come from the suzerain; for Ali had written to the Prince a formal letter, denying his right to change the constitution. Yet, inasmuch as it also promised immediate consideration of 'existing difficulties',[4] one may agree with Couza that the protest was a mere form, and that he would probably receive a gracious reception at Constantinople.[5] Any brightening of the outlook drew the British consul's sarcasm. 'Unless', Green declared, 'the Porte is prepared to have an independent Roumania, the best thing it can do is to keep this restless, ambitious gentleman on the Bosporus when he gets there.'[6]

The Prince was, of course, under the political necessity of going to Constantinople to be shriven by the Porte and the representatives of the Powers; but he could not well do so, as he told Tillos, until after the plebiscite had been held.[7] Not only was it desirable to show the Powers that the 'little *coup d'état*' had the approval of the nation, but the Prince would scarcely dare to leave the country until his victory was complete. So this Napoleonic artifice was

[1] Green to Russell, no. 44, May 22, F.O. 78/1810. Couza made a similar statement to Tillos: Tillos to Lhuys, no. 175, May 24, *Aff. étr., Turquie, Bucharest*, vol. 26.
[2] Montlong to Rechberg, no. 36, May 16, Staatsarchiv, XXXVIII/145.
[3] Tillos to Lhuys, no. 175.
[4] *Arch. dip.*, 1866, vol. ii, pp. 228–9.
[5] Tillos to Lhuys, no. 175 *bis*, May 31, *Aff. étr., Turquie, Bucharest*, vol. 25.
[6] Green to Bulwer, no. 33, May 20, F.O. 78/1810.
[7] Tillos to Lhuys, no. 175 *bis*.

duly carried out in the last week of May, and resulted, as any one
might have predicted, in an overwhelming approval of the two
propositions: the amended constitution and the new electoral law.
The vote stood 682,621 to 1,307. It was spread abroad from
sources which the British consul credited that many of the peasants
had so misunderstood the whole manœuvre—which they believed
to be a census for fiscal purposes—that they went into hiding,
rather than vote.[1] Green also rejoiced in the fact that 52,520[2]
qualified voters had failed to register any opinion.[3] Yet, without
grudging this consul any comfort that he might derive, it must be
said that in a country where the electorate was normally 200,000
the plebiscite had made a creditable showing. When the returns
were finally announced, a salute of twenty-one guns was fired, and
the night was spent in joyous celebration, in which the army was
conspicuous.[4] 'When I go to Constantinople,' said Couza, 'I shall
place my homage at the feet of the Sultan, my suzerain, but supported by the wishes of my country.' Tillos felt that with his arts
the Prince would know how to succeed.[5]

But the eloquent endorsement of the *coup d'état* was a noxious
mouthful for the consuls. Neither Green's story of the frightened
peasants nor the more reliable reports of government pressure
could alter the fact that the great majority of the nation, whether
ignorant or otherwise, were in favour of the new régime. It is easy
to understand that the peasants would look upon Couza as their
friend, but the fact that Bucharest and Jassy gave a large affirmative
vote signified that, after all, the dictatorship of Couza seemed to
respond to a national need. While admitting some pressure from
the government, Tillos asserted that, even without that, 'the result
would have been very much the same'.[6] Yet Offenberg expressed
the opinion at a meeting of the consuls that they ought to report
the results to Constantinople as improperly obtained, and the
British and Prussian consuls were disposed to support the notion.
Fortunately, Tillos, who had learned at last to take his cue from
Moustier, objected that they had already decided to await instructions, and he thought that they should send no collective report,
unless requested, as in February 1863. Though the Russian
consul lamented that Couza would give a false picture to the
ambassadors, it was obvious that most of the agents had lost their
zeal for meddling, and even the myoptic Tillos had the sense to see
that it was useless to disparage so overwhelming a majority for the
government. It was said that the Russian consul had wanted to

[1] Green to Bulwer, no. 37, May 27, F.O. 78/1810.
[2] This figure was later corrected to 70,220: Green to Russell, no. 50, June 3,
F.O. 78/1811.   [3] Green to Bulwer, no. 39, May 31, F.O. 78/1810.   [4] *Ibid.*
[5] Tillos to Lhuys, no. 175 *bis*, May 31, *Aff. étr., Turquie, Bucharest*, vol. 25
[6] *Ibid.*

furnish his embassy with the ammunition to be used at Constantinople, and, when thwarted in this ruse, he had spread the report that Couza would not go to the Sultan's capital.[1] In any case, it was clearly not the consuls but the ambassadors who must unravel the difficult knot.

There seems to be no evidence that Constantinople was astonished or greatly disturbed by the news of the *coup d'état*. Such an event had long been foreshadowed; and the reception which the Porte and the Protecting Powers themselves had given to Couza's proposals during the previous year had made them to a certain extent accomplices before the fact. If the matter could have been consummated in such a way as to respect their collective susceptibilities, there would have been no question of resting Couza's programme on legislative approval. When it had become evident that Couza and his legislature were gripped in a hopeless deadlock, Moustier had stressed to the Prince the urgency of a visit to Constantinople; he should prorogue the assembly and 'come without losing a minute'.[2] It may have been that Couza really intended to comply, but the assembly's resistance to dissolution had virtually forced the *coup d'état*.[3] Yet it must have cheered him to know that France at least was on his side, and it was to Napoleon, who was represented as approving of the contemplated trip,[4] that he appealed for vindication.[5] The situation was not without its dangers. Though Couza did not know it, Russell had gone so far as to telegraph to Bulwer that Great Britain would not object if Turkish troops should enter the Principalities, provided that the other Powers concurred,[6] and Bulwer forthwith took the matter up with Ali.[7] Quizzed by Moustier as to what he would do, the Turkish minister merely remarked that the events of 1857 had taught Turkey a lesson as to the amount of confidence to be placed in British assurances.[8] Nevertheless, regardless of the timid prudence of the Porte, it was not impossible that a crisis might be brewing; for Russian and Austrian troops were still encamped on the frontier,[9] and though Couza assured the Porte that he could

[1] Tillos to Lhuys, no. 176, June 4, *Aff. étr.*, *Turquie, Bucharest*, vol. 25.

[2] Moustier to Lhuys, no. 47, May 5, *ibid.*, *Turquie*, vol. 362.

[3] Bordeano, the Prince's chargé d'affaires, was reported to have made this statement: Bulwer to Russell, no. 106, May 18, F.O. 78/1803.

[4] Tillos to Lhuys, no. 171, May 10, *Aff. étr.*, *Turquie, Bucharest*, vol. 25.

[5] Moustier to Lhuys, no. 47.

[6] Russell to Bulwer, May 18, telg., F.O. 78/1798.

[7] Bulwer brought it up at one of the sessions called to consider the question of the monasteries.

[8] Prokesch to Mensdorff, no. 35 c, May 23, Staatsarchiv, XII/81.

[9] Napier to Russell, no. 291, June 2, F.O. 65/650; Massignac to Lhuys, no. 26, May 15, *Aff. étr.*, *Russie*, vol. 233; Mensdorff to Metternich, May 13, Staatsarchiv, IX/79. Both Austria and Russia explained that the measures were precautions against the movements of the *émigrés*. Nevertheless some disquiet was felt both at Paris and at London.

answer for the safety of his State,[1] he must have known that he was really at the mercy of these Powers. Suppose, after all, that they should find in the present crisis that oft-discussed *casus interventus*! Perhaps it was that—especially Russia's ominous behaviour—that may explain the Prince's remark to Tillos that he knew the risks he had undertaken, but that, even if he himself were sacrificed, he believed that the Emperor would save the State —which was, after all, the essential thing.[2] Moreover, as might be expected, the air of Constantinople had appreciably changed since the Prince had rested his case on the approval of his people. It was one thing to hurry to Constantinople and beg the Porte's adhesion in advance to a *coup d'état*, and quite another matter to expect the suzerain Power to sanction a *fait accompli*.

It was just this question of dignity that made the Porte regard the Prince's prospective trip with some disfavour. If Couza had only come when he first intended, then, as Ali told Moustier, he would have been marvellously well received, but now, as Ali implied, the situation was different. It was in vain that Moustier argued that the Powers had stretched their *tutelle* over the Principalities, and were really not prepared, when the occasion arose, to enforce it.[3] It was evident enough that Turkey did not relish her vassal's conduct, and possibly other Powers might be found to think as she did. Gortchakoff, who hated Couza,[4] and did not seek to disguise the fact, remarked to the British ambassador that Couza 'will arrive at Constantinople with a heavy purse and a flexible back', and he quite agreed with Austria that the step should be discouraged.[5] Prokesch said that, in Ali's place, he would refuse to receive the Prince, and he, himself, would like to see a commissioner dispatched to the Principalities on the ground that the Convention had been broken.[6] But Bulwer, though he vehemently denounced the Prince (in fact at first he was in favour of a collective summons to the Prince), was not prepared to go that far. He was willing that Couza should come, provided he suspended his new decrees; but, if he should come without having done so, then, as he declared to Moustier and Ali, he (Bulwer) would turn his back on him. 'In that case,' said Moustier, 'I will tell him not to come,'

---

[1] Tillos to Lhuys, no. 175, May 27, *Aff. étr., Turquie, Bucharest*, vol. 25.

[2] Tillos to Lhuys, no. 176, June 4, *ibid.* The remark was made when Tillos had told Couza of Offenberg's story that he (Couza) would not go to Constantinople.

[3] Moustier to Lhuys, no. 54, May 16, *Aff. étr., Turquie*, vol. 362.

[4] 'The United Provinces', Napier had written from St. Petersburg in April, 'are regarded here as the last and most dangerous arsenal of sedition. Prince Couza is looked upon as an ungrateful, rebellious, and impious renegade (this was, of course, an allusion to the secularization issue). . . . The correspondence, conversation, and policy of Prince Gortchakoff breathe the most decided animosity against Prince Couza': Napier to Russell, no. 188, Apr. 5, F.O. 65/659.

[5] Napier to Russell, no. 269, May 25, F.O. 65/659.

[6] Prokesch to Mensdorff, no. 34, May 16, Staatsarchiv, XII/81.

whereupon Ali, much disturbed, declared that it was necessary that he should come; and Bulwer said no more.[1] Despite the efforts of Bulwer to prejudice the Porte,[2] it was evident that Ali had gradually become convinced that only by some agreement could the inevitable be legalized and the authority of the Porte be properly restored. To this end, it was necessary that the Prince should make his visit. According to the French ambassador, all the Porte really asked for was a 'convenient line of retreat'.[3]

It is interesting to notice that neither Austria nor Russia—the Powers most affected by events in the Principalities—had any effect upon the decisions of the Porte. It was Moustier and Bulwer to whom Ali looked for advice, and if these two could reach an agreement, the visit would be expected, and a settlement attempted. Bulwer's ill humour was partly inspired by the feeling that Moustier was 'running the show', and partly due, no doubt, to his reverence for the law as made by the Powers and to the distaste which he felt at seeing their hands forced by a man whom he now regarded as only fit to be deposed.[4] He would act cautiously, he telegraphed Russell, but he was 'resolved not to let the Prince have his way'.[5] To the British ambassador's prejudices Moustier replied with such logic as the situation allowed. Couza was, after all, he said, 'the instrument of circumstances'. Even the Convention had intended a revision of the electoral law, and since it had also expected the wishes of the nation to be consulted, the Prince had, at least, observed the spirit, if not the letter, of that instrument. What was necessary, he told his colleagues, was to safeguard the dignity of the Porte, and at the same time to see that Couza was not discredited on his return from Constantinople. After much discussion, the two ambassadors arrived at a tentative agreement.[6] It was then proposed that the Porte and the ambassadors should dispatch identical telegrams, inviting Couza to Constantinople, and Bulwer finally consented on condition that the Prince should also be requested to make the journey *before* promulgating the new

[1] Moustier to Lhuys, no. 58, May 23, *Aff. étr.*, *Turquie*, vol. 362.
[2] Moustier to Lhuys, no. 57, May 22, *ibid.*
[3] Moustier to Lhuys, no. 58.
[4] Bulwer to Russell, no. 144, June 8, F.O. 78/1804.
[5] Bulwer to Russell, May 20, telg., F.O. 78/1803.
[6] This memorandum was signed by Ali, Moustier, and Bulwer, and its substance was as follows: (1) Couza had a right to dissolve the assembly; (2) he was right in feeling that the Convention should be modified, both by reason of its lacunae and because that instrument had intended a new electoral law; (3) he was right in bringing the matter before the Porte after consulting his own people; (4) the Porte and the ambassadors cannot enter into the motives of Couza in departing from the letter of the Convention; and (5) acts in the Principalities which should depart from the tenor of the treaties cannot bind the Porte and the Powers, to whom alone belongs the right of revising the treaties and the duty of maintaining them: annex to Moustier's no. 58.

decrees.[1] Unfortunately, this plan of 'summoning' Couza (as
Bulwer was pleased to call it), was rejected by Prokesch and
Novikoff, who believed, according to Bulwer, that anything to
which Moustier had assented must be favourable to Couza.[2] In the
end, only Moustier sent the telegram,[3] though Ali sent the Porte's
invitation through the Prince's chargé d'affaires.[4] Urged by
Prokesch and Novikoff, who, unable to prevent the visit, wanted it
regarded as a mission of atonement, Ali coupled the invitation with
a request that Couza should write a letter explaining that he had
broken the Convention, though forced by circumstances to do so.[5]
One can readily imagine how eagerly the Porte had grasped at a
means of salving its dignity. But Couza avoided the trap. In
a courteous note he bade his agent tell Ali that the latter's invitation
was contrary to the plans of 'His Royal Highness', but that he
hoped that the Porte did not doubt that the end of his acts had
been to restore the State to proper order, and he was 'disposed to
give the suzerain court the new proof of the deference which it
requests of him'.[6] According to Tillos, he telegraphed to the Porte
that he would arrive in Constantinople as soon as the results of
the plebiscite were known, and that nothing would be put in
execution until his return.[7] With such assurances the Porte had to
be satisfied. It was not as a 'mission of atonement' that Couza
would make his pilgrimage.

Having consummated his *coup d'état* by evoking the approval of
the nation, Couza had no longer any ground for putting off his
visit, and there is every reason to suppose that he was anxious to
have it over. But, unless he were merely acting, it would appear
from an interview which he gave the Austrian agent (Eder was
then on furlough) that he was satisfied with the moral strength
that he had acquired and confident in the issue.

'I will not hesitate to declare at Constantinople', he is reported to
have said, 'that I alone, as prince, know the true needs of this land. . . .

---

[1] Moustier to Lhuys, no. 58, May 23, *Aff. étr., Turquie*, vol. 362.
[2] Bulwer to Russell, no. 173, June 28, F.O. 78/1804.
[3] Moustier bade Tillos counsel Couza to 'come without delay to Constantinople in order to give explanations of his late acts before putting them into
execution': annex to no. 58.   [4] Moustier to Lhuys, no. 58.
[5] Moustier to Lhuys, no. 62, June 1, *Aff. étr., Turquie*, vol. 362.
[6] Couza to Bordeano, May 24, annex to Moustier's no. 58.
[7] Tillos to Lhuys, no. 175. Couza's answer to the vizirial letter of protest
(p. 446) was more deferential. In defending the *coup d'état*, he acknowledged that
the Porte might be expected to want an explanation, and as he had for some time
intended to go to Constantinople to pay his respects to the Sultan, he would take
that occasion to 'furnish . . . all the explanations, calculated to justify the measures
. . . taken'. He did not doubt, he said, that he would be able to convince the
Sultan that, far from having violated the Convention, he had been fortunate
enough to save both the public order and the collective work of the Porte and
the Powers: annex to Moustier's no. 63.

In my opinion, it is entirely the part of the Powers, and especially of the Porte, to decide whether to keep unchanged the political position of the Principalities, but it is not theirs to trouble themselves with the internal organization of these autonomous lands. It will be seen that the land will prosper with the direction which I shall give it. That the land is satisfied, the unanimous adoption of the plebiscite proves. Should I express my fundamental opinion? I make no disguise of the fact that I do not consider the land ripe for constitutionalism.'[1]

Thus Couza was satisfied with his accomplishment, and meant to stand by it. Moreover, nationalism was demanding the right to settle its own affairs. On June 2 he departed for Constantinople.[2]

It seems odd that the Porte and the representatives had as yet no plan in mind of what they were going to grant their visitor, or might reasonably exact in return. Count Mensdorff-Pouilly, who had succeeded Rechberg in 1863 as Austria's minister of foreign affairs, regretted afterwards that Couza's trip had not been deferred until these preliminaries should have been settled.[3] But possibly the ambassadors realized that no agreement with Moustier was possible. Drouyn de Lhuys, while ready enough to denounce the *coup d'état*, was no less ready to admit that perhaps it had been necessary, and he seemed quite to approve of its results.[4] Russell, for his part, was little concerned; he told the Prussian ambassador that the *coup d'état* was much like that of Louis Napoleon, and quite incompatible with the Sultan's suzerainty,[5] but he seems to have allowed Bulwer to exercise his judgement. And, of course, Sir Henry had his views. The idea of convoking a constituent assembly in the Principalities, to be attended by commissioners of the Powers and the Porte,[6] would perhaps have staggered his colleagues, if they had not been used by this time to his singular proposals. Prokesch felt that the way to proceed was to hear the Prince's desires and then expect the Porte to draw up a *contre-projet*.[7] Such, in fact, would seem a reasonable form of procedure.

Couza arrived at Constantinople on the 7th, and was, possibly we may say, adequately received; for accounts certainly differ. The Sultan had prepared for his sojourn one of his own palaces—

---

[1] Montlong to Mensdorff, no. 43 B, May 31, Staatsarchiv, xxxviii/143.

[2] Green to Russell, June 2, telg., F.O. 78/1811. Tillos gives us the 5th as his date of departure (Tillos to Lhuys, no. 177, June 7, *Aff. étr.*, *Turquie*, *Bucharest*, vol. 25), but this would hardly have enabled him to reach Constantinople on the 7th.   [3] Mensdorff to Prokesch, June 2, Staatsarchiv, xii/82.

[4] Lhuys to Moustier, no. 32, June 3, *Aff. étr.*, *Turquie*, vol. 362.

[5] Bismarck to Werther, June 9, annex to Mensdorff's letter of June 16 to Prokesch, Staatsarchiv, xii/82.

[6] Prokesch to Mensdorff, no. 39, June 6, Staatsarchiv, xii/81.

[7] Prokesch to Mensdorff, no. 38, June 2, *ibid.* This was endorsed by Mensdorff: to Prokesch, June 9, *ibid.*, xii/82.

'a thing never done before, even to a royal prince'—and he decided that, as this plan had been announced, it would not do to change it.[1] Presumably it was the *coup d'état* which had moderated the welcome. Bulwer declared that the Sultan absented himself from his capital rather than receive his guest on the day of his arrival, and that, when he did receive him (after keeping him waiting for some time), his manner was 'civil but cold'.[2] Prokesch wrote that his reception was 'courteous', but that the Sultan lectured him on his duty to respect the treaties.[3] One gets a different impression from Moustier's account:

'The Prince was received by the Sultan on the day after his arrival with very great honours. . . . He was introduced into the reception hall of the great palace by the great door, leading to the sea, reserved for His Majesty alone. The Sultan took his hand, and made him sit on the divan beside him—an honour which is reserved for sovereigns, and which the Sultan awards to none of his subjects. Prince Couza told His Imperial Majesty that he had come to place at his feet his own homage and that of the whole Rouman nation, and he explained in a few words the motives of his late acts. The Sultan made no personal objection, and merely said something about the engagements of Turkey with other Powers, but without insistence, or any tone of reproach. The conversation lasted a half hour, and turned principally on the progress of the Turkish army.'[4]

It is possible that the ill humour of some of the ambassadors led them to believe too readily whatever might be disparaging to the Prince, and equally possible that Moustier had received a coloured account from Couza's own lips. In any event, there was much ill-feeling because the French ambassador, as Bulwer complained, 'seemed disposed to take the Prince forthwith and ostentatiously under his particular protection'.[5] It was Moustier, who had first sent his dragoman to receive him,[6] and it was Moustier, who, without consulting Bulwer, the dean of the diplomatic corps, had invited the Turkish ministers and the ambassadors to a dinner in the Prince's honour. Most of the ambassadors, including Bulwer, declined to attend it.[7] We shall not dwell on the various courtesies shown the Prince. Even Bulwer testified to his agreeable manner,

[1] Bulwer to Russell, no. 145, June 8, F.O. 78/1804.
[2] Bulwer to Russell, no number, June 19, 'very confidential', *ibid.*
[3] Prokesch to Mensdorff, no. 41 A–C, June 13, Staatsarchiv, XII/81.
[4] Moustier to Lhuys, no. 69, June 15, *Aff. étr.*, *Turquie*, vol. 362.
[5] Bulwer to Russell, June 19.
[6] Moustier to Lhuys, no. 64, June 7, *Aff. étr.*, *Turquie*, vol. 362. Couza then expressed his gratitude for the support of the French embassy.
[7] Bulwer to Russell, June 19; Moustier to Lhuys, no. 69; Prokesch to Mensdorff, no. 41 A–C. Ali and the Prussian minister attended. Fuad sent his regrets, being prostrated by the death of a son. Novikoff would not come because Couza did not consider it proper to return the call of a chargé d'affaires. Moustier wrote that Couza blamed Bulwer for not arranging these matters of etiquette before his arrival; but no one, naturally, had anticipated the French ambassador's dinner.

and when as host at a dinner in Couza's honour, he dwelt upon the errors which the Prince had made, his guest took the observations, as Bulwer remarked, 'in perfect good humour'.[1] Certainly there was much said that might be calculated to tax the visitor's patience. Prokesch took occasion to scold him for 'following counsels of vulgar ambition' and 'sacrificing the beautiful role, for which Providence had destined him, to dreams which, if they were fulfilled, would for ever compromise the future of his state'—to which remarks Couza replied that, since Austria had never helped him, he did not feel that Austria had cause to complain of his conduct.[2] But even Prokesch did not criticize the Prince while he was entertaining him at dinner.[3] It had taken the pedantic Bulwer to spill pepper into the sweets.

All this bode rather ill for an agreement when the business of the visit came at last to be discussed. Couza wished, and seems to have assumed, that the Porte and the Protecting Powers would give his decrees an entire approval; and as discussion with Ali had led to nothing definite, he made known that he was preparing his departure. Bulwer was frantic at the thought that, after all, the Prince might 'have his way'. Learning from Ali that nothing had, in fact, been settled, he went with Prokesch to Couza, and besought him to put off his departure. When the Prince objected that the Turks were always so slow that they never reached a result, Bulwer took it upon himself to promise action, and the following day he managed with Ali and Fuad to work out a scheme (the result of an all-night session) which entailed certain changes in the Prince's programme.[4] Unfortunately, when the Turkish ministers took it up with Couza, he refused to yield an inch, and not even the threat of a Turkish occupation (if we may credit Ali's account) availed to turn him from his purpose. Not till the sedulous Bulwer had again besieged Couza and he and Prokesch had tried their blandishments on Negri did they get the Prince to yield just enough to save their faces.[5] Every one was tired when the matter was finally settled, and once, indeed, the choleric Prokesch had flown into a rage at Bulwer.[6] Between Couza's calm effrontery and the Porte's fear of a rupture, while Bulwer, Prokesch, and Moustier fought (with different motives) for a compromise, it is almost to be wondered that any settlement at all could be achieved. Distracted

[1] Bulwer to Russell, no number, June 19, F.O. 78/1804.

[2] Prokesch to Mensdorff, no. 41 A–C, June 13, Staatsarchiv, XII/81.

[3] Prokesch to Mensdorff, no. 42, June 16, *ibid*.

[4] The concessions most insisted upon were a moderate qualification for electors and some restriction upon the choice of some of the senate by the Prince.

[5] Prokesch to Bulwer, June 19; Prokesch to Mensdorff, no. 43 A–B, June 20, Staatsarchiv, XII/81; Moustier to Lhuys, no. 70, June 22, *Aff. étr., Turquie*, vol. 362. Bulwer wrote that while the arrangement was 'not what I should wish', it could be 'accepted without humiliation'.

[6] Bulwer to Russell, no. 158, June 17, 'confidential', F.O. 78/1804.

by his ignorance, Russell wrote that, after all, the Powers had conceded that some changes should be made, and how did any one know what the Principalities required?[1] But at Constantinople it was *amour-propre* which had all but caused a rupture.

If, indeed, these threatening clouds had failed to bring on a storm, it was Ali's sense of realities which not a little contributed to averting such a catastrophe. All that he had expected was that Couza would make some changes in his decrees that would enable the Porte to feel that it had not simply assented to what its vassal had ordained. But, once the Sultan's dignity had been assuaged— and the Porte was not exacting—Ali felt it to be a matter of in- difference how Couza ruled his subjects.[2] It was all very well for Russia to demand a Turkish occupation of the Principalities. Ali knew that France would never assent to such a step, and that, once the point was reached, the British government, whatever it might have said, would not tender its support. It was singular indeed, Ali remarked, that while nothing had been done to punish Michael, who had acted as if treaties never existed, whom Russia herself had furnished with arms, and who had never had the courtesy to come, even on invitation, to Constantinople, a great hubbub should be made about Couza, who had twice come spontaneously to render homage to his suzerain.[3] Thus did weakness find some logic in its defence; and perhaps, indeed, if Bulwer had not stubbornly inter- vened, the Turks would have capitulated entirely. In the end the Porte was said to be content with the result.[4] The Prince had allowed the suzerain Power to make some slight amendments, and its dignity had been saved.

The final agreement was adopted by the Porte and the am- bassadors at a meeting on June 28,[5] and the new constitution was called, as homage to the dear defunct, *L'Acte additionel à la Convention de 1858*. In the final article it was stated that 'all dispositions of the Convention of Paris, which are not modified by the present act, are once more confirmed, and remain in full and entire vigour'; but whatever was really left of the Convention was scarcely more than a shroud to give it decent burial. The new instrument, when analysed, reveals a veiled dictatorship. The Prince, with the aid of a council of state, was to have the sole initiative in legislation. Laws should be voted upon by the as- sembly and an upper house, known as the senate, composed partly of certain officials *ex officio* and partly—indeed chiefly—of the

[1] Russell to Bulwer, no. 175, June 16, F.O. 78/1798.
[2] Bulwer to Russell, no number, June 19, F.O. 78/1804.
[3] Prokesch to Mensdorff, no. 44 B, June 23, confidential, Staatsarchiv, XII/81.
[4] Prokesch to Mensdorff, no. 44 A–D, June 23, *ibid.*
[5] Moustier to Lhuys, no. 73, June 29, *Aff. étr., Turquie*, vol. 362. There was little discussion, Moustier says, at this last and formal meeting.

Prince's nominees.[1] All laws, as formerly, required the Prince's sanction. At the close of each session the two houses were each to appoint a commission, which should jointly submit to the Prince a report on the work of the preceding session and a statement of any conditions that seemed to demand reform. In one important particular Constantinople went beyond the Prince's decrees in strengthening his position: while the houses were not in session the Prince was privileged to enact laws, which he had only to explain when the legislature convened. It was the electoral law on which the contest between Couza and his guardians had been chiefly waged. Couza had wanted universal suffrage and a representative in the assembly for every 25,000 people. The Porte, however, had stipulated for a *cens* of 400 ducats, which, after some negotiation, had been reduced to 100 ducats, and this was finally accepted. As the Porte had also objected to the lumping of the cities and districts, it was finally agreed that 'deputies should be named by the cities and districts in a proportion corresponding to the importance of these cities and districts'. Moustier remarked to his chief that it would be 'easy to say later that the proportion will be one deputy for 25,000 inhabitants, (for) the word "importance" will, in effect, be understood only in the sense of the importance of the population'.[2] Thus the only concession worthy of mention which the Powers had wrung from Couza was a small electoral qualification. On the other hand, his right of issuing decrees when the houses were not in session was the strongest buttress of the new dictatorship. Finally, of great importance to the Principalities was the amazing stipulation that they (the Principalities) 'may henceforth modify or change the laws which regulate their internal administration . . . without any intervention'.[3] It was no wonder that Couza, when he published these modifications of his decree, underlined this last phrase, for, by such a provision, the *Acte* was simply consigning itself to destruction. One may hazard the guess that Ali was getting tired of these local problems.[4] But, manifestly, the *Acte additionel* was a landmark in developing the autonomy of the Principalities.

Such were the main features of the new constitution, which, in its essence, had already been accepted by the people of the Principalities. Bulwer remarked that it was not a bad one, but he doubted if it would be observed in a 'country where there are found many amiable qualities but little morality, judgement, or civic

[1] In Couza's decree the Prince was to choose 64 members from among persons possessed of a certain income. In the *Acte additionel* this number was reduced to 32, the other 32 being chosen by the Prince from lists presented to him by the districts. One can readily see that his control of the senate was but little affected by the modification.

[2] Moustier to Lhuys, no. 70, June 22, *Aff. étr.*, *Turquie*, vol. 362.

[3] *Arch. dip.*, *1866*, vol. ii, pp. 230 ff.; printed also in Martens, *op. cit.*, vol. xviii, p. 161.   [4] See Bulwer's views, already noted, p. 424.

courage'.[1] The internuncio consoled himself with thinking that, after all, if the constitution were violated, it would not be difficult *then* to get the Powers at last to agree on intervention.[2] How weak, indeed, is the lens through which a diplomat sees the future! Meanwhile, the Prince bade his adieux, and returned to enlighten his people.

Having bent the Powers without difficulty to his will, Couza could now feel free to carry out the work of political reorganization and social reform on which he had set his heart. It soon became evident that he had no intention of risking any possible opposition, even from an assembly which would not be under *boyard* domination. Thus the task of drafting the rural law was submitted only to the newly constituted council of state, after which it was to be promulgated by the Prince's own authority. Instead of publishing the *Acte additionel* in full—which might, perhaps, have cast some reflection on his decrees—he issued a lengthy proclamation, explaining the need of getting the Powers' assent to the changes approved by the plebiscite, and explaining that the modifications adopted at Constantinople in no way touched the existence and the fundamental bases of the institutions approved by the nation, and that 'these modifications are only provisional; they can be transformed and completed by the legislative bodies in their approaching sessions'. He then appended a list of the 'modifications' to which he referred, though omitting, it may be noted, the article which related to the Convention[3]—a ruse in which Green seemed to see an ulterior motive.[4] Whatever the reason for such an omission (and it may have been simply a wish to seal up the past), Couza determined to take advantage of his rights under the *Acte*, and until the legislature convened in December, he proposed to rule by ordinance—partly for the sake of expedition, and partly because some of the measures that he intended, such as granting property rights to foreign residents, would be unlikely to pass any assembly as prejudiced as any body of Roumans at this period.[5] In the meantime, apart from the official *Moniteur*, two papers, the *Bucamul* and the *Voix de Roumanie*, carefully enlightened public opinion, while Rosetti's paper, the *Roumanul*, was summarily sus-

[1] Bulwer to Green, no. 4, June 20, F.O. 78/1804.
[2] Prokesch to Mensdorff, no. 44 A–D, June 23, Staatsarchiv, XII/81.
[3] *Arch. dip.*, *1866*, vol. ii, pp. 234 ff.
[4] Green to Bulwer, no. 49, July 18, F.O. 78/1811. Green suspected that he wanted to avoid calling the legislature in December, as would be required under the Convention; but surely the Prince had plenty of time to enact his reforms without thus needlessly offending public opinion. It is more likely that Couza wanted to give the impression that an entirely new order had come into being.
[5] Couza had said as much to Green: Green to Russell, no. 44, May 22, F.O. 78/1810.

pended.[1] The *Bucamul*, which was edited by an able adventurer, César Bolliac,[2] had taken as its motto: 'universal military service, universal suffrage, emancipation of the peasants, and an hereditary throne'.[3] How seriously the Prince regarded the idea of founding a dynasty is rather hard to say. Eder wrote that he had once broached the subject, but that, as he had no legitimate children, the Austrian consul was uncertain of his plans.[4] It is not improbable that he wished, at least, that the Principalities should get accustomed to the idea, just as he was quite willing that the *Bucamul* should occasionally call him 'sovereign'.[5] No longer had Couza any fear that the consuls would berate him about such trifles.

Of all the measures of reform initiated at this period, the one of most interest and importance was the rural law, of which Cogalnitchano was the author, and which emanated from the council and was finally promulgated by the Prince, August 26, 1864. The law was more drastic than the *boyard* project of 1862, for it made the Moldo-Wallachian peasant a free proprietor. He was given in full ownership two-thirds of the land which he had been cultivating, and in order to ensure the stability of the peasantry, he was prohibited from selling or mortgaging it for thirty years except to another peasant or to the commune. The *corvée*, the tithe, the obligation of gratuitous transport of the landlord's produce, and all similar services, were for ever abolished. For getting release from these burdens he was to pay an annual sum to the government, roughly in proportion to the number of oxen he owned; while the landlord, in return, was to receive a proportionate compensation in the form of treasury bonds, bearing ten per cent. interest, for a period of fifteen years. We shall not dwell here on the working or the defects of the law, which in some particulars seems to have followed the emancipation edicts recently enacted in Russia.[6] The peasants were jubilant on learning of their deliverance from ancient obligations, Couza being greeted with enthusiasm when he toured the country explaining the features of the new law,[7] while Cogalnitchano received also his meed of praise.[8] Less

[1] Green to Hammond, May 29, F.O. 78/1810. This suspension wisely took place before Couza's trip.

[2] Tillos accused Bolliac, who had been a 'forty-eighter', of having stolen from Kossuth the Hungarian crown jewels. On his reproaching Couza for choosing the instruments he did (such as Bolliac, Cogalnitchano, Floresco, and Marghilomann, the prefect of police), the Prince replied that 'in time of a crisis one had to employ men that would not do in normal times'. 'It is the Prince's misfortune,' commented Tillos, 'that he has not been able or willing to attach some worthy men to himself': Tillos to Lhuys, no. 177, June 7, *Aff. étr., Turquie, Bucharest*, vol. 25.

[3] Eder to Mensdorff, no. 72, Aug. 29, Staatsarchiv, XXXVIII/143.

[4] Eder to Mensdorff, no. 47 A, June 10, *ibid.*

[5] Green to Bulwer, no. 48, July 12, F.O. 78/1811.

[6] Cioriceanu, *La Roumanie économique*, p. 77.

[7] Green to Russell, no. 63, Oct. 14, F.O. 78/1811.

[8] Eder to Mensdorff, no. 72, Aug. 29, Staatsarchiv, XXXVIII/143.

striking, but hardly less important in its results, was a law of public instruction which had been introduced by Cogalnitchano and passed by the chamber before the *coup d'état*, but subsequently submitted to the council of state and modified in certain particulars. Education, as provided by the State, was henceforth to be gratuitous, and primary instruction declared to be obligatory. True, the number of schools was never sufficient to give the measure its full application, and the compulsory element was therefore not enforced; but no reform in Roumanian history has contributed more to the advancement of a backward people. The widening of the suffrage, the agrarian reform, and the reorganization of the educational system marked the beginnings of a social revolution, the course and outcome of which no one could foresee.

The reforming energies of the government did not abate with the recasting of the political institutions and the great agrarian and educational reforms. In Nicholas Cretzulesco, minister of justice, the Prince found a man thoroughly imbued with the ideas of the West and hardly less active than Cogalnitchano in giving shape to the Prince's programme. Besides an active collaboration in the educational reforms, he promoted the establishment of a conservatory of music and of a school of fine arts and gave ardent encouragement to science, being himself the author of a manual on anatomy. He had also much to do with planning and preparing the judicial and administrative reforms which followed close upon the more radical measures which we have mentioned.[1] The Napoleonic Code was introduced, with slight modifications, and every effort made to give the judiciary improved standards. Trial by jury was introduced in a limited form, and the inviolability of the home was guaranteed. The civil marriage was made obligatory, and the privilege of granting divorce transferred from the Church to the State. Religious equality became the law of the land, and the Orthodox Church was made, as we have noted, administratively free, while bishops were henceforth to be chosen by the State. Some measures which were of great importance to business were the adoption of the Gregorian calendar (in the teeth of the Church's opposition, financed, it was said, by Russian influence), the proposed introduction of the metric system (this was eventually rejected), the granting to foreign residents of the right to own land, and the creation of elective chambers of commerce in the towns, though the exclusion of foreigners from electoral privileges and membership was unfortunate in a country where most of the export trade and larger industries were under foreign management.[2] Some efforts were also taken for a more systematic collection of the

[1] Xénopol, 'Nicolae Kretzulescu', *Analele Acadamei Române*, seria 2, tomul xxxiv, pp. 740–1.   [2] Green to Russell, no. 70, Nov. 10, F.O. 78/1811.

revenues, and salt and tobacco were made government monopolies without compensation to the dealers in those commodities.[1] If certain of these measures seemed unfair to foreign interests, perhaps, apart from national prejudice, one may reasonably ascribe them to Couza's evident wish to build up, as far as possible, a native middle class.

One of the major features of Couza's programme, as we have noticed, was the enlistment of foreign capital in the development of his country. A concession had already been granted for the building of railway lines in Moldavia, and a similar enterprise in Wallachia was still the subject of negotiation. A beginning was made in the improvement of the roads, and a British company was under contract to construct a number of iron bridges.[2] Already negotiations were under way for the establishment of a national bank. Of course, the rapidity with which public works could be extended or improved must depend on the financial soundness of the government, but it is indisputable that the country was possessed of immense national resources, and the chief immediate problem was to balance the budget and dispense the revenues in the treasury with intelligence and economy. The Moldo-Wallachian government had for years been shouldering a deficit, and the floating of large loans gave only a false impression of prosperity. It was this problem, unhappily, which Couza's government never solved.

Yet the inauguration of this programme of moral and material improvement seemed to show—for the time being, at least—that the *coup d'état* had justified itself. No such reform spirit had animated the old assemblies, torn as they were by factional strife or hostility to the Prince. It was by virtue of his benevolent dictatorship that Couza gave the momentum to a social transformation that was to bring Roumania to the level of a modern state.

It must not be supposed, however, that a rather placid people were particularly thrilled by all this work of regeneration. The new calendar and the new system of weights could be adopted only gradually, and must overcome a wealth of popular prejudice. It would take time to operate the agrarian reform; the money for education would be found with difficulty; the courts had yet to assimilate the benefits of the new codes. When Eder cautioned Cogalnitchano against such swift and sweeping changes, the premier answered that the government could not afford to take half-measures, which would only have the result of arousing

---

[1] This brought protests from some of the consuls, as some foreigners were thereby ruined: Tillos to Lhuys, no. 29, Aug. 11, *Aff. étr.*, *Turquie*, *Bucharest*, vol. 26.

[2] Green to Russell, no. 83, Dec. 31, F.O. 78/1811.

opposition.[1] Certainly, for the time being, at least, opposition was practically non-existent—partly, no doubt, because it was dazed. The *boyards* had no nerve to continue the struggle, and were mainly concerned with studying their position, as affected by the rural law.[2] Two insignificant members of the class were arrested for plotting treason,[3] but the bulk of the aristocracy were incredibly inert. The radicals, for their part, had no complaint against the adoption of so many of their projects, but it piqued them that they could not enjoy the political power which they felt to be their due.[4] Only Cogalnitchano seemed to reap any glory, though such prominence in the service of a despot had its dangers too. Public opinion—if one might use such a term—had apparently succumbed to the new leadership, and stretched itself in silence. The new legislature was, of course, not presumed to possess any importance, and it is hardly strange that little interest was displayed in the elections. When the session opened on December 18, it was found that only seven members of the old assembly had seats in the new one, and three of these were now satellites of Couza, while the other four were said to be nonentities.[5] Couza's speech to the assembly was full of gratification over the new political order, and consisted chiefly of a record of his achievements since the *coup d'état*.[6] There was not a single discordant note in the assembly, whose docility was as marked as that which had characterized the legislatures in Paris during the early days of the Second Empire. Couza gloated over his triumph. 'You remember, Monsieur l'Agent,' he said to Tillos, 'how you said, three weeks after your arrival in Bucharest, that my measures were a veritable campaign against the Convention?' 'Yes,' answered Tillos, 'and now I say they are directed against the suzerainty of the Porte and for the promotion of independence.'[7]

There was really little justification for so ill-natured a retort, though it may have been intended as a warning. Some fresh violations of the Capitulations had sufficed to press the point that the Principalities were still resolved to stretch them, regardless of the consequences.[8] It was said that Couza had himself styled 'sovereign' in several public documents, and there were rumours of a plan for

[1] Eder to Mensdorff, no. 70 A, Aug. 20, Staatsarchiv, XXXVIII/143.
[2] Tillos to Lhuys, no. 188, Oct. 31, *Aff. étr., Turquie, Bucharest*, vol. 25.
[3] Eder to Mensdorff, no. 48, June 14, Staatsarchiv, XXXVIII/143.
[4] Green to Russell, no. 72, Nov. 21, F.O. 78/1811.
[5] Green to Russell, no. 74, Dec. 11, *ibid*.
[6] *Arch. dip.*, *1866*, vol. ii, pp. 259 ff.
[7] Tillos to Lhuys, no. 194, Jan. 18, 1865, *Aff. étr., Turquie, Bucharest*, vol. 25. Green had insisted before the *coup d'état* that Couza would proclaim the independence of 'Roumania': Green to Hammond, Apr. 20, F.O. 78/1810. He repeated his fears in a letter of May 29.
[8] Tillos to Lhuys, no. 190, Nov. 15, 1864, *Aff. étr., Turquie, Bucharest*, vol. 25.

an order of knighthood and of a project for a separate national coinage[1]—an innovation that was really much needed. It is undoubtedly true, moreover, that Couza dreamed of founding a dynasty, for he had not concealed his hopes, and it is a fact that one of his henchmen introduced an amendment to the assembly's address, proposing that, as a measure of stability, the principle of heredity should be adopted.[2] This, of course, was entrenching on the firman of 1861, which had fixed the terms of Couza's position, and while it could be alleged that only in this manner could the safety of the State be ensured against pretenders (another leaf from the Bonapartes!), it was believed that Couza wished to invoke the national approval before placing his request on the knees of the Powers. But none of these signs, nor even the growing importance of the army, was seriously indicative of a design to establish independence. Indeed, this none-too-popular prince would have enough to think about in fortifying his dictatorship without seriously aspiring to royal sovereignty. A single false step might unsettle its foundations.

While most of Couza's difficulties are to be ascribed to the lack of certain qualities requisite in a ruler—in other words, due to sins of omission of one sort or another—the dismissal of Cogalnitchano in February was a serious error of judgement. Granted that this stalwart Moldavian was vain and domineering—'a necessary evil', Couza called him[3]—he had that indomitable driving power which Couza himself so sadly lacked; and if his patriotism was not unmixed with gross self-interest, he was at least a man of ideas and, what is more, a man of action. Couza needed him to carry the work of reform to a successful conclusion, and to have one to share with him the responsibility of pacifying the public if anything went amiss, and of holding in check the venal appetites of the hospodarial *entourage*. But for several months jealousy had been operating to undermine the premier's position. During the previous year Cretzulesco, who was minister of justice, had tried to supplant him, but at that time the Prince had stood by Cogalnitchano,[4] and the intrigue had not only failed, but Cretzulesco and Steege[5] were both dismissed from office. But on February 5 a more than usual celebration of the double election was held,

---

[1] Green to Russell, no. 83, Dec. 31, F.O. 78/1811.

[2] Tillos to Lhuys, no. 194, Jan. 18, 1865, *Aff. étr., Turquie, Bucharest*, vol. 25.

[3] Tillos to Lhuys, no. 188, Oct. 31, *Aff. étr., Turquie, Bucharest*, vol. 25. The rest of Couza's comment was deleted by the censor at the Archives des Affaires étrangères.

[4] Eder to Mensdorff, no. 80, Oct. 11, Staatsarchiv, xxxviii/143.

[5] Steege was an able man, as even Tillos admitted, but he seems to have been implicated in the intrigue: Tillos to Lhuys, no. 188. Green wrote of Cretzulesco that he was 'opposed to everything and everybody, and his colleagues in particular': Feb. 17, F.O. 78/1866.

which seemed a symptom that the reforming premier was no longer needed.[1] Apart from the fact that certain of Couza's confidants had long been trying to get the Prince to oust him, it is probably true that Couza felt himself to be overshadowed by a stronger character.[2] The immediate cause of the premier's disgrace was a quarrel with the council of state, in the course of which Cogalnitchano had threatened them all with dismissal; they thereupon went in a body to Couza, who amiably dismissed the offender.[3] The fall of Cogalnitchano was something of a portent. Though the fact was not apparent at first, the tranquil days of the dictatorship were now permanently at an end. The shadows of coming disaster would soon begin to appear.

The change of premiers did, at least apparently, arrest the orgy of legislation in which Cogalnitchano had been steadily engaged;[4] and it is probable that the country had its surfeit of reform. Some laws, it was said, had been good in themselves, but quite inapplicable to the Principalities, while others were simply difficult to execute.[5] What, unhappily, was most needed was administrative talent. The new premier, Boziano by name,[6] was said to possess one of the best legal minds in the Principalities, but he was not a man of political experience, and neither he nor his colleagues gave promise of much stability.[7] Couza himself was much too fond of his leisure to acquire the secret of political leadership, and, unwilling to fill the breach left by the fall of his powerful minister, he became less and less accessible to ministers and consuls alike. 'By shutting himself up entirely from the world,' wrote Green, 'or by allowing none to approach him but a handful of devoted followers, who would be the last to tell him the truth and the first to abandon him; above all, by having suppressed all the newspapers, (he) has deprived himself of all the means of learning the feelings of the population.'[8] For a few weeks the ill-built ship of state seemed to rock along without encountering serious storms, for Eder wrote at the end of February that Couza's position

[1] Green to Russell, no. 11, Feb. 7, 1865, F.O. 78/1866.
[2] Eder to Mensdorff, no. 15 A, Feb. 10, Staatsarchiv, XXXVIII/143. Tillos wrote that just before his fall Cogalnitchano had come to him and inquired if it would be opportune to ask France for the order of the Legion of Honour for Couza. The French consul's comment was that Cogalnitchano, who had just boasted of his own achievements, was evidently seeking the honour himself: Tillos to Lhuys, no. 5, Feb. 7, *Aff. étr., Turquie, Bucharest*, vol. 25.   [3] *Ibid.*
[4] Towards the end of December, Cogalnitchano had boasted that he had ready forty-five new laws, which he intended to have promulgated without consulting the legislature: Eder to Mensdorff, no. 103, Dec. 23, Staatsarchiv, XXXVIII/143. One can begin to understand why the council of state had rebelled against his dictation.
[5] Eder to Mensdorff, no. 42, May 8, 1865, *ibid.*, XXXVIII/145.
[6] He had been minister of the interior and vice-president of the council of state.   [7] Tillos to Lhuys, no. 5.
[8] Green to Russell, no. 15, Feb. 21, F.O. 78/1866.

seemed more secure than ever,[1] and the Prince himself talked of making a tour of the West during the summer,[2] for which he expected an appropriation from the legislature. Difficulties with the consuls over the Capitulations and with the ambassadors over the interminable convent question were but clouds 'which (so ran an Austrian report) could be boldly swept away by his personal influence at different courts'.[3] What Couza had in mind in planning such a trip can only be conjectured. One is tempted to wonder if he were not hoping to sound his great protector on the question of a dynasty. His government had been modelled on that of France; the whole character of his reign was a copy of the Second Empire; only one last step, and he would emerge a miniature Napoleon III!

But Couza's trip was yet to be taken, for the present state of the treasury did not justify the expense.[4] The deficit, in spite of Steege's ingenious figuring, had never been made up, and a special grant to repair the damages done by floods was far more urgent than the Prince's triumphal tour. In any case the situation of the country was not such as to make the Prince's absence advisable. Bad weather and poor roads had caused a scarcity of provisions in the cities, and the prices of necessities had doubled and even trebled.[5] Worse still, the state of agriculture was rapidly growing serious. For some unknown reason[6] the government was inexcusably dilatory in executing the rural law. No division was as yet made of the land between the peasants and the proprietors, and the former, not knowing positively what belonged to them, refused to plant their wheat.[7] 'The consequence is', wrote Green, 'that the whole country has remained practically uncultivated. It is said that, setting aside all question of having corn for exportation, a sufficient quantity of land has not been sown to meet the requirements of the population. In making this statement, I am putting in the mildest form the predictions, which reach me from every quarter, of an imminent famine.'[8] It was an odd commentary on this great liberating reform that the government should now be forced to order the prefects to compel the peasants to till their fields.[9]

[1] Eder to Mensdorff, no. 20, Feb. 28, Staatsarchiv, xxxviii/145.
[2] Green to Russell, no. 24, Mar. 11, F.O. 78/1866.
[3] Montlong to Mensdorff, no. 31, Apr. 11, Staatsarchiv, xxxviii/145.
[4] Montlong to Mensdorff, no. 36, Apr. 25, *ibid.*
[5] Tillos to Lhuys, no. 9, Apr. 11, *Aff. étr., Turquie, Bucharest,* vol. 26.
[6] Boziano complained of Couza's indulgence to the *boyards* (*ibid.*), and it may be that the Prince was waiting for this class to adapt itself to its new status. But clemency to the *boyards* was not characteristic of Couza, and it is more likely that Boziano was trying to shift responsibility for his own weakness.
[7] Montlong to Mensdorff, no. 36. Tillos wrote that only a tenth of the arable land in Wallachia had been sown this year (1865): Tillos to Lhuys, no. 23, *Aff. étr., Turquie, Bucharest,* vol. 26.
[8] Green to Russell, no. 41, May 9, F.O. 78/1866.
[9] Tillos to Lhuys, no. 15, May 10, *Aff. étr., Turquie, Bucharest,* vol. 26.

The immediate troubles which arose from the rural law were undoubtedly due to the delays of the government and the machinery with which the law was executed. But the law itself had serious defects. To assign so much land to a peasant of a certain means overlooked the fact that the value of the land varied considerably in different parts of the country, and, conversely, the indemnity which the proprietor should receive might or might not be proportionate to his losses,[1] though it is probable that, in general, the indemnity was too high.[2] Apparently no exhaustive survey had been made before determining the division of the land, and—possibly due to corrupting influences—the poorest land was usually awarded to the peasantry.[3] Though formerly the proprietor had placed at the disposal of his *corvéeables* an adequate amount of land, he had now attained a freedom, more effectual in fact than the theoretical freedom of the peasant, and it may well be true that it was the *boyards*, whatever their present outcry, who gained the most immediate profit from the law.[4] The measure also failed to make provision for the future growth of the peasant population, for the division of the land through successive generations would result in progressive impoverishment.[5] Whether the growth of industry would be rapid enough to absorb this surplus population was a question for the future to decide. But at least it could be said that, if the agrarian problem was not now solved, it could well become a subject of subsequent study and further legislation.

But, apart from faults of statesmanship, it is undoubtedly true that it takes time and patience to achieve a social revolution. And if history has shown that a people cannot be quickly transformed by legislation, it is equally true that an oriental government cannot readily learn new ways, or change its habits in a moment. The new codes of law were certainly needed. 'Already bound, they make a fine showing in the national library,' remarked Eder, 'but where are the judges to awaken the(se) dead books to life?'[6] Where were the financiers, he might have added, who might grapple with the deficit, and liquidate for the treasury the accumulations of stored-up capital? And where were the men who would turn over to the treasury all the revenues which they had collected? 'Instead of the earlier simple and cheap, as well as bad administrative system,' wrote Eder, 'one has developed a system, complicated, costly, and no less bad.' The growing needs of the army, Eder went on to point out, and the projected improvement of public works,

---

[1] Eder to Mensdorff, no. 74, Sept. 9, and no. 79, Oct. 4, 1864, Staatsarchiv, XXXVIII/145.　　　　　　　　　[2] Cioriceanu, *op. cit.*, p. 81.
[3] Evans, *The Agrarian Revolution in Roumania*, p. 41.
[4] Cioriceanu, *op. cit.*, pp. 81–2.
[5] Cartaing to Lhuys, no. 29, Oct. 2, *Aff. étr.*, *Turquie, Jassy*, vol. xi.
[6] Eder to Mensdorff, no. 41, May 2, 1865, Staatsarchiv, XXXVIII/145.

which required heavy guarantees from the government, considerably increased the government's already heavy burdens. It was all very well to talk of developing a new system of taxation on the model of those in operation in other lands, but in the Principalities agriculture—prostrated now by the rural law—was practically the only existing source of revenue.[1] One gets the impression, indeed, that the administrative personnel was unequal to the transition that Couza was attempting. While the government was faced with a deficit of 40,000,000 piastres,[2] it was admitted that neither the customs nor the export trade were yielding their normal return,[3] and such was the want of cohesion and discipline in the ministry that the minister of war refused to concur in the minister of finance's demand for economy.[4] Meanwhile neither army nor functionaries were being paid, and the immediate effect of disclosing the state of the finances in the assembly was the inability of holders of treasury *mandats* to cash them at any price.[5] Part of the difficulty came from having to pay a share of the indemnity to the Holy Places, only part of which was covered by a loan.[6] It also appears that the treasury officials had difficulty in applying a new method of collecting the taxes, and much revenue was, accordingly, in arrears. No wonder Couza said that he had momentarily given up his plan of a trip to the West, as his presence was urgently demanded at home.[7]

The desperate state of the finances moved even a docile legislature to make an investigation. According to article xii of the statute, the senate and assembly had the privilege of appointing a joint commission to suggest projects of improvement to be submitted to the government and the council of state. Such a commission now took into consideration the state of both the finances and the judiciary, and tendered their complaints direct to Couza, with some recommendations for economy, chiefly bearing upon the army. It had been proposed in the body of the commission that the Prince should be reminded of his offer, long ago, to retire, when called upon, in favour of a foreign prince; but the final decision of the

[1] Eder to Mensdorff, no. 100 A, Dec. 12, 1864, *ibid.*, XXXVIII/143. Eder noted the unfavourable effect of the agricultural depression upon business (no. 42, May 8, 1865, *ibid.*, XXXVIII/145), and he had predicted that the raising by 5 per cent. of the government's export tax was bound to react unfavourably upon trade with Austria, which represented half of the volume of the Principalities' foreign commerce (no. 78, Sept. 27, 1864, *ibid.*, XXXVIII/143).
[2] Eder to Mensdorff, no. 42; Tillos to Lhuys, no. 14, May 5, 1865, *Aff. étr., Turquie, Bucharest*, vol. 26.
[3] Green to Russell, no. 43, May 10, F.O. 78/1866.
[4] Tillos to Lhuys, no. 14. Tillos wrote that the minister of war depended on a third of the annual revenue for the army: no. 25, July 18, *Aff. étr., Turquie, Bucharest*, vol. 26.
[5] Tillos to Lhuys, no. 17, May 16, *ibid.*
[6] Eder to Mensdorff, no. 52 B, May 23, Staatsarchiv, XXXVIII/145.
[7] Tillos to Lhuys, no. 17.

body was against including so provocative a proposal.[1] The tone of the report was neither disrespectful nor exceptionally severe, but it found some fault with the administration of the taxes and it even hinted at graft in connexion with the recent outlay on public works.[2] There was evidently an impression that the government was in straits, and something should be done about it. 'As regards sentiment at present,' wrote Eder, 'I learn that in all circles and in all classes the greatest discontent prevails. But that any outbreak will take place is not to be feared.'[3] Evidently, however little the government was esteemed, there were as yet no signs of an incipient revolution.

It was clear enough, however, that neither Couza nor his ministers were equal to the situation. The Prince himself went for several weeks into retirement, partly perhaps because he was puzzled and depressed over a state of things for which he must now, since the *coup d'état*, shoulder the major responsibility. He also suffered a severe recurrence of his old malady, asthma, and was probably at times too ill to give his attention to public affairs. 'One might liken Prince Couza to the Thibetan dalai lama,' remarked Eder, 'if women's feet were accustomed to tread the latter's holy of holies.'[4] None of the consuls could obtain access to him, and it was said that he sought relief by playing with tame bears[5]— surely a more soothing diversion than listening to foreign jackals! Yet the formal adoption of an illegitimate son as Prince Alexander and the resumption of his plan of journeying to Paris, presumably to ask Napoleon's consent to the founding of a dynasty, showed that Couza could still dream of further triumphs. Emerging finally from seclusion, Couza made one feeble effort to retrieve the situation. The Boziano ministry was dismissed, and Cretzulesco, pliable, but not endowed with much political capacity, was once more elevated to the premiership, while Floresco, the most valuable of the Prince's intimates, became minister of war. When Tillos saw the Prince shortly afterwards, he was told that the ministers had been dismissed chiefly because of their attitude towards foreigners[6]—a rather strange excuse, since Couza himself had

[1] Eder to Mensdorff, no. 41, May 2, and no. 42, May 8, Staatsarchiv, XXXVIII/145; Tillos to Lhuys, no. 16, May 13, *Aff. étr., Turquie, Bucharest*, vol. 26.
[2] 'We believe ourselves obliged to call the attention of Your Highness's government particularly to the agents of public works, who consume important sums without the works being executed in proportion to the sums': Green to Russell, no. 60, July 14, enc., F.O. 78/1867.
[3] Eder to Mensdorff, no. 42.
[4] Eder to Mensdorff, no. 63, June 12, Staatsarchiv, XXXVIII/145.
[5] Eder to Mensdorff, no. 66, June 19, *ibid.*
[6] Tillos to Lhuys, no. 24, July 11, *Aff. étr., Turquie, Bucharest*, vol. 26. Boziano was reported to have said that the consuls were the 'scourge of the State', and that he would have no communication with them: no. 9, Apr. 11, *ibid.*

shown persistent unwillingness to force his officials to observe the Capitulations.[1] As far back as the Cogalnitchano ministry the complaints of the consuls had been so numerous that the ambassadors had held several meetings over the question (the initiative had come from Austria), and in March had sent a joint remonstrance for the support of the harassed agents.[2] The expulsion of foreigners on the ground of plotting sedition[3] without any notice to the consul in question,[4] the ignoring by the courts of the consuls' representatives, and the general levelling of foreigners to the position of natives[5] were abuses which had become so common that, if Couza's government were not forced to mend its ways, the Capitulations would soon cease to have any weight at all.[6] This, however, was the least of Couza's cares, and the shifting of responsibility was one of his besetting sins. The true reason for the change of ministry was undoubtedly the fact that in the present state of confusion and incipient unrest Couza needed more pliable instruments on which he could rely. Cretzulesco had served him in 1863 during the breach with the *boyards*, and Couza had retained him against all attacks; while Floresco in office was a hostage for the loyalty of the army. But the change of ministers gave no signs of better relations with the legislature, which, in spite of that subservience which the *Acte additionel* had been calculated to ensure, was revealing the first signs of open resistance to the dictatorship. An intrigue of John Ghika was said to be responsible for the failure of a new railway project to be considered.[7] Still more serious was the inability of the government to get legislative sanction for the projected national bank, for which an Anglo-French banking interest, represented by a certain Mr. Hertz, had lately obtained the concession,[8] and which various hostile interests were determined to defeat. Superstitious fear of paper money,[9]

[1] On one occasion Couza had shown an unwonted spirit of defiance in answering a complaint of Eder's. 'As long as the Principalities are not occupied by troops,' he declared, 'I will not permit foreign rights in Roumanian lands to be decided over Roumanian interests': Eder to Mensdorff, no. 72 A, July 7, 1865, Staatsarchiv, XXXVIII/145.   [2] Mensdorff to Eder, May 12, *ibid.*

[3] Green to Russell, no. 8, Aug. 31, 1864, enc., F.O. 78/1811.

[4] Tillos to Lhuys, no. 6, Feb. 21, *Aff. étr., Turquie, Bucharest*, vol. 25.

[5] Couza frankly said on one occasion that the introduction of foreign capital made it necessary that foreign interests should be identified with native: Tillos to Lhuys, no. 8, Mar. 21, 1865, *Aff. étr., Turquie, Bucharest*, vol. 25.

[6] The ambassadors at Constantinople held a number of conferences during the spring and summer of 1865, looking towards a revision of the Capitulations, but when the consular intervention failed, there was a general feeling that no accommodation on the subject was realizable. Drouyn de Lhuys told Cowley that no consular intervention would be effective without coercion, and since that would probably lead to Couza's abdication and revolution, he considered the problem hopeless: Cowley to Russell, no. 697, June 13, 1865, F.O. 27/1573.

[7] Tillos to Lhuys, no. 24, July 11, *Aff. étr., Turquie, Bucharest*, vol. 26.

[8] Tillos to Lhuys, no. 6, Feb. 21, *ibid.*, vol. 25.

[9] Tillos to Lhuys, no. 38, Oct. 13, *ibid.*, vol. 26.

the alleged opposition of Austria and Russia,[1] the prejudices of local bankers, who feared to lose their privilege of charging extortionate rates of interest,[2] the venal appetites of government officials, who tried to induce Hertz to line their pockets,[3] and, finally, the rooted want of confidence in the government—all these circumstances combine to explain the failure of a measure, of which the Principalities stood in serious need. But, with all his easy-going indifference to the details of administration and his reputed neglect of public duties, Couza was far too persevering to give up one of his plans for the modernizing of his state. He told Tillos that he intended to introduce the bank project again at the next session, and, if it encountered the same opposition, it would prove to the Powers that an elective legislature was 'too complicated a wheel' to operate with the government; whereupon the French consul concluded that despotism wished to be free of all checks of any sort.[4] Green remarked upon the fact that the government could do nothing even with a chamber composed of 'rabble', a senate of 'bureaucrats', and 'both exclusively consisting of the Prince's nominees'.[5]

Was it true, then, that Couza could govern only when his will was entirely unfettered? Was it impossible for him to obtain co-operation even from men who were supposed to be his creatures? Did all his reforms and all his efforts to raise the material condition of his country mean nothing? There is no denying that his 'benevolent dictatorship' had failed to win the confidence and the sympathy of the nation. Even the peasants were in a state of bewilderment over the provisions of the rural law, and, in any event, the goodwill of such a class could scarcely be translated into action. An uprising of peasants against the legislature could hardly be attempted without an issue that the peasants could understand; and the Prince's government had now nothing to point to but its record. The alienation of the *boyards*, the corruption and inefficiency of the administration, the inability of the ministers to reach a *modus vivendi* with the legislature; worst of all, the hopeless muddle of the finances—all this furnished a problem which Couza, and only Couza, had the authority to settle. Could it be supposed that he would govern more effectively without a legislature? Why was the Prince unable to use the power which his good fortune, not to mention his own ingenuity, had already placed in his hands?

The answer is necessarily complex, and to seek it wholly in the ruler's incapacity would be too simple an explanation. Granting

---

[1] Tillos to Lhuys, no. 23, July 4, *ibid.* The charge is made repeatedly, and may well be true, but it should be added that there is nothing in Austrian dispatches to support it. [2] Tillos to Lhuys, no. 47, Dec. 26, *ibid.*
[3] Tillos to Lhuys, no. 24, July 11, *ibid.*
[4] *Ibid.*   [5] Green to Russell, no. 57, July 3, F.O. 78/1867.

certain patent defects, all the reforms and innovations which Couza had attempted were amply justified. Unhappily, in a country where not a tenth of the population were literate and most of the educated classes were narrow and venal, where parliamentarism had failed to take root and patriotism was manifested in hatred of the foreigner, where few men were experienced enough to handle intricate political and social changes, and still fewer were honest, it would take a man of genius, combined with extraordinary energy and political sagacity to pilot the ship of state through so swift a transition as Couza had intended. Alexander John was something of a Joseph II. He appreciated the enlightenment of the West, and he wanted to transplant it bodily to a backward country, still in a quasi-feudal stage and wrapt in an oriental somnolence. But he lacked the unflagging energy of Joseph II, while he was no less a doctrinaire, and no less deficient in the arts of conciliation. Lacking not only in the qualities of political leadership but also in that indomitable driving power which benevolent despotism needs if it is to get along without recourse to moral suasion, Couza was perhaps foredoomed to fail. He was a ruler with ideas but without the other requisites of statesmanship.[1] Perhaps his most patent fault had always been that of unduly despising the qualities of his countrymen. There were men like Ghika, Cogalnitchano, and Steege, who might conceivably have proved the instruments through whose guidance executive and legislature might have been brought to march along a fairly even road of progress. But Couza would not trust them, and (if we except Cretzulesco, whose honesty and idealism hardly balanced his political faults) he preferred, instead, to turn to third-rate intellects, whose only virtue was that of blind devotion to himself. As we survey his reign as a whole, we may agree that the Prince had vision and a certain pertinacity in carrying out a resolution (as witnessed by his work for union), but in his utter incapacity for visualizing the concrete requirements of the changes which he inaugurated and in his inability to develop in his service a sense of public duty and to attract to it that administrative talent in which he himself was lacking, Couza gave himself no chance of atoning for his own limitations as an executive. He aspired to become a Napoleon III by the methods of a Joseph II. But he had neither the country nor the qualities that would make the hope attainable.

[1] Though scarcely doing justice to Couza's vision, an estimate by the French consul is perhaps worth quoting. 'I do not impugn the intentions of Prince Couza,' wrote Tillos, 'but the qualities of organizer and administrator are completely lacking in him. He is a man of expedients, very clever, but he is not a statesman. It is the more regrettable in that he knows his country perfectly, and the population is very easy to handle': Tillos to Lhuys, no. 9, Apr. 11, *Aff. étr.*, *Turquie, Bucharest*, vol. 26.

One asset Couza had had, and that was the inertia of his people —that *mollesse*[1] which foreign consuls had so often ascribed to the Moldo-Wallachians. 'Every *boyard*', wrote a British observer, 'says that he has no intention of doing anything that will put his person or his property in the smallest possible danger.'[2] Already more than a year had passed since the *coup d'état* without the sound of even the distant rumbles of revolution. As long as the elements of opposition made little attempt to coalesce and the army remained loyal, nothing, indeed, but the interference of the Protecting Powers seemed likely to terminate this orgy of misgovernment. Yet nothing but the dread of revolution would be likely to move these guardians. Who, then, could predict the end?

The political atmosphere in the midsummer of 1865 was deadly calm but sultry. Some of the more bitter enemies of the Prince (both *boyards* and radicals) held a meeting to ventilate their hope of his removal, but so far no programme had been formed.[3] Couza himself decided, finally, to make his trip to the West. It was thought by some of the consuls that he intended to see Napoleon and to try to get his permission for some further political changes,[4] but, ostensibly at least, he was going for his health, and this was what he announced in an official proclamation to his people. The statement that he had become worn out by 'seven years of labour in the interest of the State' caused some hilarity, it was said, in Bucharest;[5] for though the Prince's duties had often imposed upon him both anxiety and strain, his lapses into idleness were equally well known. How much these intervals of inertia had been due to the curse of asthma the public did not know. But there was no doubt that the state of his health practically necessitated the trip. In his proclamation he made it clear that he confided the country to the 'sentiment of order and sagacity', which he did not doubt would prevail notwithstanding the fact that he himself would be far distant. 'I do not doubt,' he said, '. . . that you will be proud of showing the world that you are worthy of the future to which you aspire.'[6] Was there a slight note of uneasiness in this fatherly leave-taking?

Suffering acutely from asthma, and perhaps a little depressed, Couza left Wallachia, late in July, to take the water at Ems.

[1] e.g. Tillos's letters of Oct. 6, 1865, and Jan. 29, 1866. Green's similar impression has already been quoted; Eder seems to have had much the same opinion.
[2] Dalyell to Clarendon, Feb. 6, 1866, F.O. 78/1930. (The date of this letter is significant.)
[3] Eder to Mensdorff, no. 71, July 5, 1865, Staatsarchiv, xxxviii/145.
[4] Eder to Mensdorff, no. 73, July 13, *ibid.*
[5] Tillos to Lhuys, no. 26, July 25, *Aff. étr., Turquie, Bucharest*, vol. 26.
[6] Green to Russell, no. 61, July 20, enc., F.O. 78/1867.

CHAPTER XVI

INTO THE ABYSS

ON August 15, 1865, while a *Te Deum* was being sung in honour of the Emperor's name-day, the sound of gun-shots broke the accustomed calm of Bucharest.[1] Some vendors of fruit and vegetables had objected to a new municipal ordinance requiring the rental of wooden booths for the display of their produce instead of allowing them, as heretofore, to hawk it about in the market-place. Before the police could interfere the booths were burned, and presently a crowd, composed of some of the dregs of humanity, and armed with sticks, stones, and a few pistols, made an attack upon the municipal buildings. After half an hour the military appeared and quelled the tumult. About twenty persons were killed and a great number were wounded (there were no casualties, it appears, among the soldiers), and the day closed with some two hundred arrests and a thoroughgoing patrol of the city, which resulted in indignities to a great many excited but law-abiding citizens.[2] As a riot, it was apparently a rather meaningless affair, easily put down, and indicative of nothing but the presence of those undesirable elements which are to be found in any European capital. But was there not a deeper significance in this street fight than was apparent on the surface?

It is not easy to connect this market scrimmage with politics; yet there are some circumstances which indicate the threads of a conspiracy. According to Tillos, 'for a dozen days one had been speaking of an approaching revolution'.[3] Placards and anonymous letters had, in fact, proclaimed its coming, and the government had been sufficiently disturbed to take extraordinary military precautions.[4] Offenberg had heard the report and credited it, though doubted if any movement would succeed as long as Couza's government was supported by the army.[5] At any rate, the absence of the Prince had seemed a fitting occasion for testing the popular temper and especially for ascertaining whether the loyalty of the army could be shaken. Some negotiations had taken place between the *boyards* and the radicals, the former wishing to start an uprising

---

[1] Tillos to Lhuys, no. 30, Aug. 16, *Aff. étr., Turquie, Bucharest*, vol. 26.

[2] Eder to Mensdorff, no. 83, Aug. 16, Staatsarchiv, xxxviii/145.

[3] Tillos to Lhuys, no. 30. Green had also testified—three days before the embroglio—that the talk of conspiracies in both principalities had become increasingly prevalent, and 'form the subject of general conversation among all classes'. He declared that the government had increased its unpopularity by establishing a tobacco monopoly, which, if it raised the price of tobacco, would naturally embitter 'a smoking population': Green to Russell, no. 65, Aug. 11, F.O. 78/1867.

[4] Eder to Mensdorff, no. 81, Aug. 12, Staatsarchiv, xxxviii/145.

[5] Eder to Mensdorff, no. 80, Aug. 11, *ibid.*

against the Prince and needing the aid of their political rivals, who were closer to the populace. It was said, however, that the radicals had doubted of their ability to incite the peasants, as the rural question had now ceased to be an issue, and that efforts to buy over Floresco in order to secure the army had come to nothing.[1] Nevertheless, if Eder was correct, a meeting of some of the chiefs of the two factions had been held on the night before the riot, and, as on former occasions, the question of how to get rid of Couza and whom to install in his place had formed the *raison d'être* of the conference. No agreement was reached, however, because the Left had desired the question of Couza's successor left open—presumably they still wanted a foreign prince—while some of the *boyards* insisted that one of their number become hospodar. Apart from the fact that they planned a general uprising, no project seems to have been formed for bringing it about.[2] There is certainly no evidence that the radicals plotted a riot on the morrow. Nor, on the other hand, is there any proof that the police (as hinted later by John Ghika[3]) deliberately trumped up the disturbance. Finally, the statement of Green that 'the movement may be described as a spontaneous protest of the people against bad government'[4] is clearly an exaggeration. It may well be true that, had not the riot been quickly and effectually suppressed, a more general uprising would have immediately occurred,[5] but there was nothing in this sudden, ill-organized *émeute* to suggest a 'spontaneous protest of the people'. There was, doubtless, discontent, but on this occasion it was local rather than national, and though there was plotting in the background, such an explosion—even from the standpoint of the plotters—was decidedly premature.

[1] Tillos wrote that the radicals offered Floresco their support for seizing the government and holding a plebiscite designed to make him hospodar, but that he distrusted them and refused, though he was actually disloyal to Couza and was intriguing with the *boyards*. He further wrote that the general had been transferred to the ministry of the interior 'to break his neck': Tillos to Lhuys, no. 30.

[2] Eder to Mensdorff, no. 86, Aug. 19, and no. 93 A, Sept. 4, Staatsarchiv, XXXVIII/145.

[3] Ghika's circular to representatives of the Protecting Powers, Mar. 4, 1866, *Arch. dip., 1866*, vol. ii, pp. 289 ff. A somewhat different version is given by Eder (no. 93 A), who says that Librecht, minister of post and telegraph and Couza's chief confidant, had been delegated to watch the government during the Prince's absence, and had brought about this brawl in order to show up the malcontents and test the loyalty of the ministers. Green retails much the same story, and writes that the municipal authorities of Bucharest publicly accused the police of instigating the riot (no. 72, Aug. 29). The story is inherently unlikely and savours of the kind of gossip which was always prevalent during internal crises in the Principalities. Ghika's charge may well have been a deliberate invention, as he was not above that sort of thing, and his circular was a sweeping indictment of Couza's government.

[4] Green to Russell, no. 68, Aug. 15, F.O. 78/1867.

[5] Eder to Mensdorff, no. 90, Aug. 26, Staatsarchiv, XXXVIII/145.

Probably the most that can be said is that there were disloyal elements clandestinely plotting revolution, but as yet there was no programme. The mob which ran amuck on the 15th had apparently no leaders or plan and was for the most part unarmed.[1] The episode was not without its import, however, as it proved to the Opposition that the army was still loyal to the present régime. The government naturally made the most of this, and heaped praises on the officers who had directed the suppression of the riot.[2] When it came to finding scapegoats for the calamity, it was easy to blame the radicals (Rosetti and Bratiano being, as usual, included among the numerous arrests), while the *boyards* were annoyed with some of the consuls for reporting to their governments the trivial character of the affair, instead of representing it as a great popular protest.[3] Somehow, instead of staging tragedy the enemies of Couza came very near making themselves figures in comedy.

The comic aspects of the affair were not, however, a monopoly of the disappointed *boyards*. As it was always thought good policy to ascribe an ebullition of discontent to foreign intrigue, and, as in former times, 'nothing (to quote Eder) ever happens here without foreign co-operation', the ever-active Floresco, lately transferred to the ministry of the interior, published a proclamation on August 18, alleging that the Austrians had introduced from Switzerland an inflammatory brochure (printed in the Roumanian language), which was distributed widely throughout the Principalities. As excitement had by no means died down, the incident caused a great sensation. The truth of the matter seems to have been that two letters from Switzerland, delivered by the Austrian post, had contained such a pamphlet. There was, of course, no ground for the inference that Austria was trying deliberately to provoke a revolution, or for believing that the government at Vienna had anything to do with the affair. Eder took the matter up with the premier and the minister of foreign affairs, and insisted that the content of the proclamation should be corrected.[4] Apparently,

[1] Eder to Mensdorff, no. 86. Tillos seemed to believe (no. 30) that a conspiracy was at the bottom of it, but the plan miscarried. He adduced no proof, however.
[2] There had been some fear that the soldiers might fraternize with the rioters, but it appears that most of the garrison had been made up of Moldavians, and it was said that the government took every means to incite the soldiery, Eder hinting that perhaps that would account for the drunkenness of so many of them and for the resultant outrages: Eder to Mensdorff, no. 90.
[3] Tillos to Lhuys, no. 30. The consuls, of course, held a meeting as soon as they learned of the disturbance, and there was some talk of sending a concerted communication to Constantinople, but no agreement could be reached on the question of its content. All that the consuls did, therefore, was to seek explanations from the ministers and report details of the riot to their respective governments.
[4] Eder to Mensdorff, no. 85, Aug. 18 and annex, Staatsarchiv, xxxviii/145.

the ministry, as a whole, had been unprepared for this little drama, enacted by Floresco with the connivance of Librecht, the director of the post, and was willing to make amends if the result were not too painfully embarrassing to the government; and, after some toning down of the language, a refutation, written by Eder, was published in the *Moniteur*, together with an official 'explanation' of the error.[1] Offenberg told Eder that Librecht had sent a secret circular to all his subordinates in the postal and telegraph service, bidding them get up popular protests against the riot of August 15, which should be attributed to Austro-Russian influence.[2] Among so many intrigues, accusations, and counter-accusations it is, of course, hard to sift falsehoods from the truth. But there is no certainty that the affair of August 15 was any more than a market brawl, out of which both the government and its enemies were seeking to make capital.

Yet the government was weakened by the incident, for the severity of the soldiery (some of whom had almost certainly been drunk) left a train of bitterness,[3] and its relations with the Powers, already aware of misgovernment in the Principalities, were marked, as we shall notice presently, by an unpleasant aftermath. Couza, who received the consuls on his return, entertaining them to 'coffee, sweets, and cigars according to the custom of the country', had little to say of the incident, though, in spite of having formally thanked the army, he gave the consuls to understand that he highly disapproved of certain features of its conduct.[4] Naturally the Prince deplored the handle which had been given to his enemies, of whose activities he must certainly have been informed.[5] The elements of opposition seemed encouraged by the outbreak of a crisis which they had not anticipated, and at last the two discordant factions were able to coalesce. Out of an earlier association for the defence of constitutional government a society was secretly formed, which had as its avowed aim the overthrow of Couza and the elevation of a foreign prince. Thus had the *boyards* finally yielded their class-interest to the broader vision of their rivals. Among the prominent members of the organization were the Golesco brothers, Rosetti, John Bratiano, John and Demetrius Ghika, and two Moldavians, Mavrogheni and Lascar Catargi. It was Rosetti's task to prepare a revolution at home, while Bratiano was to undertake a mission to foreign courts to tell the painful truth about Couza

[1] Eder to Mensdorff, no. 87, Aug. 20, *ibid.*
[2] Eder to Mensdorff, no. 89, Aug. 24, *ibid.* It seems that Librecht told Tillos that Offenberg had been in the plot. But, of course, some one always accused Russia of complicity whenever disturbances occurred in the Principalities.
[3] Eder to Mensdorff, no. 80, Aug. 11, *ibid.*
[4] Green to Russell, no. 74, Sept. 7, F.O. 78/1767.
[5] The premier had gone to meet him at Raginusa: Green to Russell, no. 72, Aug. 29, *ibid.*

and to look over the available material for a foreign prince. It is hard to say how much success this stalwart radical obtained. He published a brochure on his arrival at Paris, scintillating with invectives against Couza and his government,[1] and evidence was soon to appear that the French government became gravely critical of its former protégé. But no government, save Russia, really desired the fall of Couza, and such an event must come, if come at all, as the voluntary act of his people. For the present, one only noticed symptoms of unrest.

The news of the affray of August 15, even though the affair could hardly be looked upon from a distance as a grave disorder, might well have been viewed as the premonition of revolution. The Protecting Powers, who may have hoped, ever since the arms crisis, that they had earned an interval of rest from the obligation of watching over the Principalities, were somewhat brusquely made aware that the problem was still with them. France, while deploring the outcome of her confidence in Couza, was as yet unwilling to consign him to extinction, but it is interesting to note that Russell seriously conjured up the plan of giving the Principalities to Austria on the understanding that Venetia should be ceded to Italy.[2] Palmerston seemed favourable to the principle, but saw that neither Russia nor Austria would consent to its execution. 'In the meantime,' he added, 'Couza laughs at us all. He knows that nothing can be done unless the Five Powers are agreed upon it, and he knows pretty well that such is not likely to happen.'[3] The matter was taken more seriously at Constantinople. The Porte, ever anxious to display its fatherly attitude towards the most precocious of its children, telegraphed to Couza that he should return without delay. Of course, no such instruction was needed by the Prince, who, apprised of what had happened, was already on his journey homeward, but he sent word to Ali that he would investigate the matter as soon as he had returned, and would then inform the Porte of the true state of affairs.[4] Neither Moustier nor Bulwer seemed as yet much disturbed, and, until Paris and London had received full particulars, there was a chance that the whole affair, as far as Europe was concerned, might speedily blow over.

But a storm suddenly appeared from an unexpected quarter. For some time Gortchakoff had been irritated by what he was

[1] Damé, *op. cit.*, pp. 148–51.

[2] This plan seems to have been urged by Italy in January 1864, but Palmerston had taken the position that its success required the consent of too many parties, and that anyway the Schleswig-Holstein question was enough to bother about just then without any further complications: Palmerston to Russell, Jan. 7, 1864, Russell Papers, G. and D. 22/15, Pub. Rec. Off.

[3] Palmerston to Russell, Aug. 29, 1865, *ibid.*

[4] Vetsera to Mensdorff, no. 51 A–B, Aug. 28, Staatsarchiv, XII/83.

pleased to regard as the predominance of France at Constantinople.[1]
The prominence of Moustier in the arms crisis and his evident
partiality to the Principalities in the affair of the monasteries had
given Russia the impression that the success of her interests was
dependent upon the nod of Napoleon's ambassador. She had been
deliberately retarding a settlement of the monastery question (that
is, the settlement of the indemnity due to the monks),[2] and it was
fairly evident that the appointment of the pan-slavist General
Ignatieff as minister to Constantinople had been intended as the
first step in restoring Russian influence in that quarter;[3] for
Ignatieff, fresh from his triumphs in China, and at home 'the man
of the hour',[4] was the first forceful diplomat she had sent to Turkey
since the Crimean War. While the Porte, on learning of the affair
at Bucharest, was pondering what measure it should take, Ignatieff
proposed the sending of an Ottoman commissioner.[5] It was the
old device, provided by the Protocol of 1859, which had been so
often invoked, and always set aside—usually because France had
never intended it to be effective. Twice in 1863, as we have already
noticed, Moustier had frustrated such a proposal. But Moustier
happened at present to be absent from his post, and if only Ignatieff could get Bulwer to consent, the proposal might be telegraphed
to the Powers and hurriedly approved, while France's mind was
fixed on something else. But unfortunately for his Russian colleague, Bulwer had already received notice of his recall. There had
been a feeling in the British cabinet that his intrigues had been
more damaging than profitable to British interests[6] ('I have the
greatest distrust of Bulwer', Russell had written to Palmerston in
July),[7] and his failure to hinder the French project of cutting the
Suez canal had led Clarendon to believe that 'if he had remained
at his post, there would have been an explosion in Parliament'.[8]
As the British ambassador had probably no notion of attempting
something which he could not carry through, the most that he
would promise was that he would discuss the matter with Ali; and
the Turkish minister, though flattered by an insinuation from
Ignatieff that an Ottoman commissioner might be chosen, did not
care to risk so hazardous an experiment, especially as Bulwer
thought that the matter called for reflection. Just what Ignatieff
had in mind by telling his British colleague that now was the time

---

[1] Napier to Russell, no. 35, Dec. 21, 1863, F.O. 65/663.

[2] See p. 435, n.3.

[3] Napier had been much disquieted by his appointment: Napier to Russell,
no. 219, May 16, 1862, F.O. 65/603.

[4] Thun, *Erinnerungen aus meinem Leben*, p. 145.

[5] Vetsera to Mensdorff, no. 50 B, Aug. 31, 1865, Staatsarchiv, XII/83.

[6] 'The embassy has long been a scandal' was Clarendon's comment.

[7] Russell to Palmerston, July 12, Russell Papers, G. and D., 22/30, Pub.
Rec. Off.   [8] Clarendon to Russell, Aug. 2, *ibid*.

for getting rid of Couza[1] is hard to fathom. There is some reason to suspect that he was deliberately planning a crisis which would furnish Gortchakoff with an opportunity of testing Russia's strength in the Principalities. But, of course, without knowing the content of the Russian dispatches, one can do no more than hazard a conjecture.

Though the idea of foreign intervention in the Principalities was, as usual, a chimera, Fuad and Ali seem to have felt that some action, showing the authority of the suzerain on this occasion, was desirable. A message from the Moldo-Wallachian minister of foreign affairs to the kapou kiaya, making light of what was called 'a market riot' and expatiating at length upon the vindictiveness of the Prince's enemies as well as upon the general contentment over the 'social and financial regeneration of the State',[2] was not communicated to the Porte before Fuad had dispatched to Couza a letter which was intended to be the Turkish solution of the present problem. After testifying to his anxiety over an affair which, he said, must be due to 'a general discontent, of which we do not know the causes', Fuad bade the Prince not only inflict such punishments as these disturbers of the peace deserved but 'render the seditious efforts of these disturbers unfruitful as far as the population is concerned by the adoption of measures calculated to extirpate every germ of dissatisfaction'.[3] The language of the dispatch was, of course, full of those courteous phrases to which the French language lends itself, but the document none the less bore the character of a lecture. The Austrian chargé d'affaires expressed approval of the dispatch,[4] and Ali confessed that Ignatieff's advice had not wholly failed[5]—a statement which might be interpreted to mean that the Russian diplomat had something to do with this action.[6] Such was, in fact, the inference of the French chargé d'affaires, who protested to Ali against the formal character of the dispatch; and Bordeano was so indignant that the Porte should have gone back on its promise of a year ago not to meddle in the affairs of the Principalities, that he declared that Couza, his position weakened by such manœuvres, and abandoned by the Powers, would be driven to ask for the protection of Russia. It is curious how logic under the influence of anger will sometimes turn

[1] Vetsera to Mensdorff, no. 50 B.
[2] Balanesco to Negri, Sept. 15, 1865, *Arch. dip., 1866*, vol. ii, pp. 267 ff.
[3] *Ibid.*, pp. 266-7.
[4] So did Russell: Russell to Bulwer, no. 165, Sept. 30, F.O. 78/1854.
[5] Vetsera to Mensdorff, no. 53 A-B, Sept. 8, Staatsarchiv, XII/83.
[6] Couza seems to have felt that Russia had something to do with it, as he expressed his conviction that Turkey was on this occasion under the 'influence of a neighbouring Power': Eder to Mensdorff, no. 111, Dec. 7, *ibid.*, XXXVIII/145. Such appears to have been the view at Paris; *Annuaire des deux mondes*, 1866, pp. 627-8.

full circle. Interestingly enough, we learn that the Russian minister had said to Bordeano: 'Go and tell France, who protects you, and we shall see what you obtain. Believe me, you will only really live, when you return to us.'[1] But Russian diplomacy was rather too ingenuous to deceive any one; and perhaps the agent of Couza was just attempting a bit of bluff.

It was Couza himself, however, who administered the vitriol, which he felt that Fuad's scolding letter merited. After deploring the publicity of the vizierial dispatch—it had been printed in the official organ of the Porte before reaching the Prince's hands— Couza recalled to the vizier the right which the Principalities enjoyed according to the Convention (signed, he added, by Fuad himself) of managing their own affairs; and then reminded him that 'if the august suzerain court has the right to instigate measures of public order in Roumania (*sic*), it is necessary, in the first place, that order should have been compromised, and, in the second place, that there should first have been an entente between the Sublime Porte and the Protecting Courts'. The riot, Couza declared, was inspired by some sanitary measures analogous to those taken at Constantinople on the appearance of cholera, and it was not to his knowledge that any international understanding had been established on the question. 'I seek in vain what may be the motive and the aim of Your Highness's letter.' He then went on to say that such language as Fuad employed 'engendered . . . difficulties which you have not suspected', for the letter implied the existence of a revolution and mentioned a 'general discontent'. The affair had been exaggerated; the Roumanian people had rejected with indignation an attempt against the plebiscite, and why suppose that the government should not take measures against the rioters? The letter closed with some amiable reflections on the desirability of mutual tact and intimate relations between 'Roumania' and the Porte.[2] It might have been better if Fuad had ignored it, but, fearing probably that silence might denote that he had been vanquished, the vizier replied at length in a letter the substance of which was that he had been cruelly misunderstood. 'The motive and aim' of his former letter had been to obtain information on an affair to which the press had attributed alarming proportions, and it was the press, not the Porte, which had imagined that there could be 'general discontent'.[3] It is unnecessary to follow the vizier further in his contortions. The original letter had been the greater mistake. We may well believe that it roused the Prince's irritation.[4] But it is also probably true that this cunning oriental saw a

[1] Bonnières to Lhuys, no. 121, Sept. 13, *Aff. étr.*, *Turquie*, vol. 366. This was told to Bonnières by Bordeano himself.

[2] *Arch. dip.*, *1866*, vol. ii, pp. 272 ff.   [3] *Ibid.*, pp. 277 ff.

[4] Green to Russell, no. 11, Dec. 12, F.O. 78/1867.

chance of appealing to the patriotism of his countrymen at a time when his government was morally discredited.[1]

Could the Prince, in his present situation, have saved himself by picking a quarrel with his suzerain or by showing a menacing attitude towards one of the neighbouring Powers? Was there any chance of rallying patriotism around the throne?[2] One has only to reflect on the negative effect of his patriotic role in the arms question or in the secularization of the Church lands in the face of Russia's disapproval to realize how hopeless it was to make a public issue out of an external struggle. In one of his carefully reasoned surveys of public sentiment in the Principalities Eder gives us a very clear impression of the apathy and pessimism which permeated theoretically the whole of the population. Even that enthusiasm for union, which had once been so marked, he said, had disappeared since its attainment. The more intelligent section of the population have no longer any hope that any regeneration can come through a native ruler, and, while a foreign prince was still the expressed desire, 'no one believes that the Powers will make this concession to the Principalities'. It may be (continued the Baron) that a land which has not the vitality to exist by itself will fall a prey to either Russia or Austria; and Eder felt, naturally enough, that union with Austria would be the best panacea for the moral and material development of the country. As for national feeling, it had never been existent except in the upper classes and a certain section of the intelligentzia, and Couza's victory over the former had doomed them to sink into insignificance. The fact also, he added, that the population belongs to the Greek Church makes it possible for Russia to depress a national feeling that 'is not made of hardy stuff'.[3] Such an analysis seemed to contain a large element of truth. The patriotism of the Roumans had always been the possession of a limited social stratum, and ever since the aspiration for union had been realized the dominance of class interests had overbalanced all zeal for the future of 'Roumania'. The shallow-minded *boyards*, no longer able to struggle with the Prince (whose deposition in their eyes was far more important than the national interest or prestige), had lapsed into lethargy or arm-chair conspiracies, while only a few benighted radicals seemed to look for better things in any direction.

In contrast to the inertia or the petulant obstructiveness of the

[1] Tillos to Lhuys, no. 44, Nov. 24, *Aff. étr., Turquie, Bucharest*, vol. 26.

[2] Tillos, who retailed all the rumours he heard, credible and otherwise, wrote that Couza had sent officers into the provinces to sound the people as to whether a declaration of independence would win popular support: Tillos to Lhuys, no. 43, Nov. 16, and no. 44, Nov. 24, *ibid.* According to Eder, thousands of copies of Couza's letter to Fuad were distributed in the Principalities, and the Prince received deputations from some of the districts, congratulating him on his attitude: Eder to Mensdorff, no. 112, Dec. 9, and no. 114, Dec. 12, Staatsarchiv, XXXVIII/145.

[3] Eder to Mensdorff, no. 92, Aug. 30, *ibid.*

men around him, Couza stands forth as one of the country's few patriots. He it was who had seen the necessity of union without revolution; he it was who had envisaged the national need of a free and prosperous peasantry and had appreciated the importance of foreign capital to tap the vast resources of these lands. Unhappily, while he strove for the greater things, he underrated the lesser. For the humdrum work of administration he had neither the energy nor the talent, and, as a national leader, he lacked the subtle persuasiveness that might have melted opposition and the tone of conviction that might have stimulated the men with whom he worked. Was there, then, no hope that he could retrieve himself? If he could not inculcate patriotism in his people, could he not intimidate so mild an opposition? 'The Prince has force at hand,' groaned Tillos. 'Why does he not employ it to reorganize, and govern honourably?'[1] It is not exactly clear what Tillos wanted; but as long as Couza had the devotion of the army, he might still hope to live somewhat longer—by his wits.

But Couza's wits seemed somewhat dulled by the hopelessness of his situation. Prodded by Tillos, he did, indeed, grant the concession for a national bank by decree while the legislature was enjoying a recess. The government also began, with the little money at hand, to pay the first instalment of the indemnity due to the landowners.[2] Best of all, perhaps, the Prince addressed a letter to his premier, demanding an improvement in the personnel of his administration.[3] But nothing but a fearless and ever-vigilant eye could have purified the bureaucratic machine, and, if his own probity had set a salutary example, he did not prevent the pillaging of the State by his henchmen.[4] Green probably put it mildly when he said, 'The Principalities would be quite as well governed were there no government at all.'[5] When the legislative session opened on December 18, the Prince's sense of failure was astonishingly revealed in his opening address. After dwelling at length upon his government's achievements, and denouncing in vigorous language the Porte's imputation that a revolution was brewing, he declared that his sole ambition was to possess the affections of his people, to be truly useful to his country, and to assure its prosperity.

'Be convinced', he said, 'that I would not want any power that rests only upon force. Whether at your head or by your side, I would always be with the State (and) for the State, and for the State without any other motive than the national will and the great interests of Rou-

---

[1] Tillos to Lhuys, no. 36, Oct. 6, *Aff. étr.*, *Turkey, Bucharest*, vol. 26.
[2] Tillos to Lhuys, no. 41, Oct. 31, *ibid.*
[3] Tillos to Lhuys, no. 44, Nov. 24, *Aff. étr.*, *Turquie, Bucharest*, vol. 24.
[4] Tillos to Lhuys, no. 36. 'Never', wrote Tillos, 'have robbery . . . (and) traffic in employments and all enterprises been practised with such effrontery.'
[5] Green to Lyons, no. 11, Dec. 12, F.O. 78/1867.

mania. I want it to be well known that never will my person be an obstacle to any event which would permit consolidating the political edifice of which I have contributed to lay the foundations. In Alexander John Couza, Prince of the Roumanians, the Roumanians will always find Colonel Couza, who, member of the assembly *ad hoc*, then of the elective assembly of Moldavia, proclaimed the memorable act which contains the great principles of the regeneration of Roumania; the same Colonel Couza, who, already chosen prince in Moldavia, declared officially to the Great Protecting Powers, on receiving the crown of Wallachia, that he would accept this double election as the expression, incontestable and immutable, of the national will in favour of union, but which he would accept only as a sacred trust. Senators, deputies, the legislative session of 1865–6 is open. God bless your work! God protect Roumania!'[1]

This solemn offer to redeem his pledge of 1859 and retire in favour of a foreign prince might almost be regarded as an invitation to revolution. Was it a presentiment? asked Paris.[2] The desire for a foreign prince had already been on many lips, but no one had expected that the Prince himself would raise the question. Did it show that Couza's patriotism was always greater than his ambition, or was he merely ready to give up a losing cause? Later one found among his papers a copy of the letter he wrote to Napoleon early in October 1865, arguing the impossibility of a native prince for the Principalities and expressing his willingness to abdicate in favour of a foreign prince.[3] It is not unlikely that self-sacrifice had long been in his mind; and a few days before the reading of his speech he had intimated to Green that he was tired of his people's ingratitude and might decide to abdicate.[4] No doubt, if Couza had satisfied his people, or if he had managed to develop a more efficient administration, he would have wanted to reign until his death and to have left a dynasty to succeed him. But he knew that he had failed; not even his ambition could blind him to that fact; and there is no reason to doubt that, with all his indolence and cynicism, he had at heart his country's welfare. It would be idle to suggest a lack of courage. When a man has made a hard fight and surrenders to conditions which he cannot overcome, the readiest explanation is that he has shown a real sagacity. In Couza's case we believe that this quality was blended with a sense of patriotic duty. At all events, the fact is none the less curious that during these autumn months of 1865 the spectre of revolution had appeared both from above and from below.

One consideration which had perhaps influenced the Prince's decision was the attitude of France. As long as Napoleon had been

[1] Annex to Tillos's no. 46 of Dec. 19, *Aff. étr., Turquie, Bucharest*, vol. 26.
[2] *Annuaire des deux mondes*, 1866, p. 628.
[3] Green to Clarendon, no. 31, Mar. 4, 1866, F.O. 78/1920.
[4] Green to Lyons, no. 11, Dec. 12, 1867, F.O. 78/1867.

with him, Couza had always felt that he might ignore his people's sluggish sensibilities and defy his numerous enemies both within and without. He had refashioned the Principalities on the model of France herself, and, to Tillos's despair, had insisted to all his critics that he had complied with France's wishes. It was France who had helped him through every pitfall—the complications of the double election, the crisis over union, the controversies over neutrality and secularization, even the dubious experiment of the *coup d'état*. In his present distress he had as usual turned to France, only to find to his despair that it was common report that France wished to replace him by the younger Bibesco, that Bratiano had been well received in Paris, and finally—and this was only too true—that the *Moniteur* had published an article, reflecting severely on the conduct of his government. Commenting on the riot of August 15, this paper had declared that it was 'assuredly the symptom of a regrettable malady. Numerous criticisms are directed against the administration of the hospodar. They are not devoid of foundation. It is just, however, not to forget the difficulties which the government has had to surmount and the obstacles which it has had to encounter in the profound demoralization into which the State had fallen under former régimes.'[1] The extenuating sentence hardly sufficed to excuse the publicity of this frank indictment; but it was a second article, a month later, warning him that 'it would not be without peril to his power to count too much on the embarrassments of the cabinets',[2] which seemed to convey the message that France might even join with other Powers in bringing about his fall. Had the friend who had fought his battles lost faith in him at last? No wonder he took the step of sending a special courier to Paris, protesting his devotion and lamenting the Emperor's coldness in his regard. Moreover, others besides Couza had noted the change of temperature.[3] Russia, quick to see the opportunity of transferring him to her patronage, had capitalized to the full this alleged betrayal by his patron. Ignatieff and Offenberg were working hard to convince him that his government was a failure and that only Russia could save him from the abyss. While the Russian consul sent Gotchakoff lurid stories of the 'daily outrages on the part of an undisciplined and licentious soldiery', the widespread discontent, the withdrawal of all respectable men from the service of the State, and the misrule of a horde of 'unprincipled and

[1] *Moniteur universel du soir*, Aug. 22, 1865.
[2] *Ibid.*, Sept. 21.
[3] Metternich to Mensdorff, no. 8 A, Feb. 22, 1866, Staatsarchiv, IX/81. According to Drouyn de Lhuys, as reported by Metternich, Napoleon was anything but pleased by the letter, and instructed his minister to tell him that after the support he had given him on the monastery question and on a thousand other occasions he could do no more. Some such reply may have been handed to Cantacouzene, the Prince's messenger.

needy adventurers',[1] this sedulous agent was said to be in constant attendance at the palace, prolific in advice,[2] and urging Couza to cease sacrificing his country to 'latinism' but to 'realize that Napoleon, disturbed by his Mexican policy and revealing his real attitude in the *Moniteur* article, had neither the power nor the will to lend him aid. It was said that Couza was tired of being regarded as the tool of either France or Russia, when in fact he was 'neither French nor Russian nor Austrian, but was a Roumanian and nothing but a Roumanian'.[3] Manifestly, the difficulty of Couza's position and his penchant for balancing opposing forces had fairly earned the impression that he was always a foreign instrument, but it has been abundantly shown that he used France rather than served her, and there is no reliable evidence that he ever had a secret understanding with St. Petersburg. The most that can be said at present is that Couza hoped, by affecting to draw closer to Russia, to create some slight alarm at Paris, which might lead to a revival of its sympathy. In this he partially succeeded.

In the meantime much communing took place among the cabinets over what should be done with Couza—whether he should be sacrificed or merely admonished to mend his ways. Soon after the August riot Drouyn de Lhuys had sounded the cabinets,[4] and from London he learned that Russell was in favour of keeping Couza.[5] It was, of course, a vastly annoying situation; but, in truth, not one of the cabinets was willing to bring on a crisis prematurely, and even Gortchakoff's language was studiously 'correct'. As if conscious of a suspicion that Russian policy might be viewed with some distrust, he told the British ambassador that the Czar would not countenance the candidature of Leuchtenberg,[6] though later, it must be confessed, he greatly astonished Buchanan by saying that if Couza were deposed, there was no necessity for union to be maintained[7]—a statement which might indicate the wish that somehow things might come to the worst. But on this as on all occasions wherein the Principalities were concerned, the action of the Protecting Powers awaited the initiative of the cabinets at London and Paris. Great Britain, for her part, seemed to feel that a dose of strong medicine was preferable to surgery, and a visit of the younger Bibesco to the Western capitals did not spell the end of Couza. Clarendon, who replaced Russell as British

[1] Buchanan to Russell, no. 280, Sept. 14, F.O. 65/681.
[2] Tillos to Lhuys, no. 40, Oct. 20, *Aff. étr., Turquie*, vol. 26. Tillos also accused Offenberg of trying to get Floresco to resign, but he added that the wily soldier was making too much money to consider such a step.
[3] Cretzulesco to Bordeano, Oct. 22, *ibid.*, fo. 312.
[4] *Les Origines diplomatiques de la guerre de 1870–1*, vol. vii, no. 1555.
[5] Baude to Lhuys, Sept. 7, *ibid.*, no. 1557.
[6] Buchanan to Clarendon, no. 318, Oct. 25, F.O. 65/681.
[7] Buchanan to Clarendon, no. 375, Dec. 5, F.O. 65/682.

foreign secretary, told the Austrian ambassador that he doubted if conditions were as bad as Bibesco had represented them; that the case of Greece showed how difficult it was to get a satisfactory foreign prince; and that it would be highly imprudent to get rid of the present régime unless one knew that one could improve upon it.[1] Mensdorff thought it futile to desire Couza's overthrow,[2] and he doubted very much if France's interest in Bibesco should be taken seriously; she would want to keep Couza, who has 'heretofore assured her predominant influence in these countries'.[3] There is certainly no evidence that France wanted Couza's deposition, but her attitude towards his interests seemed to lack its former precision. Beyond the laconic statement, 'Maintain him' (imparted to Moustier on his departure for Constantinople in November),[4] the Emperor himself was doubtless too deeply engrossed in other directions to give much thought at this time to his little protégés in the East, and his minister had never displayed the interest in the Principalities that Thouvenel or Moustier had manifested. Drouyn de Lhuys's letters to Tillos were mildly critical, mildly benevolent towards Couza, though he could hardly ignore Tillos's warning that the Principalities, if deserted by France, would probably swing to Russia.[5] Metternich, the Austrian ambassador, told his court that he did not believe that the French minister had any thought of contributing to the fall of Couza.[6] Yet how shall we explain the gratuitous thrusts of the *Moniteur*? 'In what concerns Prince Couza personally,' Drouyn de Lhuys had written to Tillos, 'if we show less interest in him, it is that we attach so much greater price to seeing him accomplish with success the task to which he was called by the unanimous vote of his compatriots.'[7] It is not impossible that France felt that Couza's unpopularity was compromising the cause of union itself. Hence, if the *Moniteur*'s warning was unheeded, he had only himself to blame if he succumbed to revolution. There could have been a worse solution than Bibesco. But perhaps there was a better one.

At all events, the symptoms of unrest in the Principalities had seemed to suggest the wisdom of some concerted action. Moustier had apparently been the first to suggest that the Powers should come to some understanding in the matter, and, apparently at his

[1] Kalnaky to Mensdorff, no. 41 B, Nov. 24, Staatsarchiv, VIII/73.
[2] Mensdorff to Prokesch, Nov. 12, *ibid.*, XII/85. Cf. Gramont to Lhuys, Oct. 20, *Origines*, vol. vii, no. 1634. Mensdorff replied similarly to Metternich, Dec. 28, in direct reply to Drouyn de Lhuys's inquiry: Staatsarchiv, IX/79.
[3] Mensdorff to Revertera, Nov. 18, Staatsarchiv, X/52.
[4] Prokesch to Mensdorff, no. 62 C, Nov. 17, *ibid.*, XII/83.
[5] Tillos to Lhuys, Oct. 13, *Origines*, vol. vii, no. 1613.
[6] Metternich to Mensdorff, no. 49, Dec. 2, Staatsarchiv, IX/80.
[7] Lhuys to Tillos, no. 8, Oct. 21, *Aff. étr., Turquie, Bucharest*, vol. 26.

instigation, Ali had written a letter to Safvet, now Turkish minister at Paris, urging that 'the Great Powers interested' should take some action to 'render the duration of his (Couza's) administration possible'.[1] Soon afterwards Lord Lyons, the new British ambassador to the Porte, had summoned Green to Constantinople to learn of the situation in the Principalities, and both Moustier and Prokesch[2] had talked with him. After imparting his views to Lyons, the British consul wrote them down in the form of a report, which could be then dispatched to the Foreign Office. Green felt that revolution in the Principalities was imminent, and that if such a catastrophe took place, the 'red republicans', such as Rosetti and the Bratianos, would control the new régime. The only possible way of averting such a catastrophe would be some concerted action by the Powers—not the sending of a commissioner, as Fuad suggested (shades of the Protocol again!), but through the direct intervention of the cabinets, though he was not certain, to be sure, that such action would not do more harm than good. Green rather doubted if even good government would save the Prince from downfall, since the prevalent spread of corruption had created a vested interest which no one could safely challenge;[3] and he did not believe, as he told Moustier, that any one of the Prince's subjects was capable of taking his place.[4] It is curious how timidity restrained the British agents from recommending the logical solution for the Principalities; once it was union, and now a foreign prince. But the talk of 'red republicans' was not unlike the proverbial red rag, if we may metamorphose the august British lion into a bull.

Instigated both by the Porte's letter and by the pessimistic report of Green, Clarendon decided to put forth a determined effort to save the rule of Couza, and though he applied first for France's co-operation,[5] he later directed a circular to the other Powers.[6] Nothing loath to try a consular intervention—which was the essence of Clarendon's plan—Drouyn de Lhuys agreed to follow suit by instructing Tillos to act in concert with his British colleague (who by this time had returned to Bucharest).[7] Accordingly, Clarendon told Green to inform Couza that he 'would no longer be permitted to disregard existing treaties' (with a strange want of insight he had put the emphasis on breaches of the Capitulations), as well as to urge him to 'correct the errors of his

[1] Ali to Safvet, Nov. 16, annex to Prokesch's no. 65 A–D, Staatsarchiv, XII/83.
[2] As to Lyons and Moustier, so to Prokesch Green deprecated any change of ruler: Prokesch to Moustier, no. 65 A–D, Dec. 8, Staatsarchiv, XII/83.
[3] Lyons to Clarendon, no. 53, Dec. 5 and enc., F.O. 78/1862.
[4] Moustier to Lhuys, no. 146, Dec. 6, *Aff. étr., Turquie*, vol. 366.
[5] Clarendon to Grey, no. 95, Dec., F.O. 27/1565.
[6] Clarendon to Ellis, no. 24, Dec. 27, F.O. 7/1565, enc.
[7] Lhuys to La Tour, Dec. 21, *Origines*, vol. vii, p. 249 n.

administration';[1] and in a private dispatch he ordered the consul to consult with Tillos on the evils of which the two governments had cause to complain, and to hold identical language.[2] The instructions which Tillos received were conceived in the same spirit, though much less definite in character.[3] As a result of these parallel communications, the two consuls talked the matter over at length, but were plainly pessimistic about the result, and Tillos told Green, who was to see the Prince first, that the latter was certain to fall back on his desire for a foreign prince.[4] Green saw Couza the following day, and read him Clarendon's dispatch. Couza remarked that the note appeared to him like a sharp remonstrance, whereas he had understood from Tillos that he was to get support. Green answered that it was intended as a friendly but serious warning. Couza then explained that his character was misunderstood, and that he was ready to retire, not as a coward but in favour of a foreign prince, chosen by the Powers. This, of course, did not satisfy Green, who urged him to adopt the expedient of ministerial responsibility—a suggestion which the Prince regarded as hopeless.[5] Couza told Eder afterwards that he had offered to allow the consuls to choose his ministers, understanding that they should take the responsibility for the result, but that Green had replied that he and Tillos had agreed to refrain from discussing personalities.[6]

The failure of the interview—of which Green was painfully conscious—showed clearly enough the futility of the international protectorate in handling such a problem. The Powers shirked the responsibility of making practical recommendations, and the consuls lacked the authority and the courage to do it themselves. Couza could thus take refuge in bandying generalities with generalities, and the only benefit to be seen from this manœuvre was to show that two of the Powers were at least acting in common. Nothing was better calculated to disarm his interviewers than the offer to retire in favour of a foreign prince.[7] If they could not, or would not, show him a practical way out of his difficulties, he was ready to let his mentors try their luck with another ruler.

Tillos was, of course, no more successful than his British colleague. Couza took, in fact, a higher tone in talking to the French consul, denied the stories of discontent, and seemed quite to resent the guardianship which England and France were apparently assuming.[8] It had been hoped that all the consuls would put similar

---

[1] Clarendon to Green, no. 7, Dec. 20, F.O. 78/1867.
[2] Clarendon to Green, Dec. 20, *ibid.*
[3] Lhuys to Tillos, no. 10, Dec. 22, *Aff. étr., Turquie, Bucharest*, vol. 26.
[4] Tillos to Lhuys, no. 2, Jan. 6, 1866, *ibid.*, vol. 27.
[5] Green to Clarendon, no. 2, Jan. 5, F.O. 78/1920.
[6] Eder to Mensdorff, no. 3, Jan. 9, Staatsarchiv, XXXVIII/148.   [7] *Ibid.*, etc.
[8] Tillos to Lhuys, no. 3, Jan. 9, *Aff. étr., Turquie, Bucharest*, vol. 27.

pressure upon Couza, in order that it might appear that all the Protecting Powers were acting now in concert, and, in fact, all but the Prussian consul did receive instructions to take part in the experiment.[1] But Tillos felt, for his part, that they had erred in laying the emphasis on different points; he himself thought that they should support Couza against revolutionists and pretenders, whereas Green seemed to prefer to press reforms upon the Prince by collective intimidation, and Eder thought most of the protection of foreign residents, among whom the Austrians were naturally the most numerous. No one, of course, knew what Offenberg had said, but Tillos suspected that all he was working for was the appointment of a pro-Russian ministry,[2] and he accused him in one of his dispatches not only of patronizing the *boyards* but of sending vendors of images as agents for spreading propaganda among the peasants.[3] To some subtle warnings from Green against russianizing the government, Offenberg answered that, apart from her interest in the Church, Russia had no separate views regarding the Principalities.[4] One must not overlook the current propensity for seeing Russian intrigue in every nook and corner; and yet one wonders if the Prince's subtle manœuvres were not in some degree responsible for deluding all the Powers—even Russia—at this juncture. If Couza did not scruple to flirt with Russia, it is probable that he was prompted by his pique at discovering that France had become less friendly to his interests and by the hope that by such manœuvring he could somehow bring her back. It would not be the first time that this wily oriental had played one Power off against another.

But, unhappily, Couza was no more able than formerly to handle his own people. The weakness of his position lay in the fact that he was now confronted with a parliamentary opposition not composed as heretofore of pretenders and their henchmen, but, as Eder believed,[5] of men who were really concerned over the deplorable misgovernment, and who saw no hope of relief as long as Couza reigned. The very fact that these men had been chosen as satellites of the governments made their conduct all the more significant. While it may be true that the practical object of the Opposition was to force a change of ministry, it is hardly to be denied that Couza's speech had stirred the embers of old fires; for even the fairly docile senate had ventured in their reply to welcome the idea of a foreign prince.[6] Granting the narrowness of vision and tendency to faction on

[1] Eder to Mensdorff, no. 14, Jan. 31, Staatsarchiv, xxxviii/148.
[2] Tillos to Lhuys, no. 6, Jan. 29, *Aff. étr.*, *Turquie, Bucharest*, vol. 27.
[3] Tillos to Lhuys, no. 7, Feb. 1, annex, *ibid.*
[4] Green to Clarendon, no. 9, Jan. 22, F.O. 78/1920.
[5] Eder to Mensdorff, no. 1, Jan. 1, Staatsarchiv, xxxviii/148.
[6] Eder to Mensdorff, no. 2, Jan. 2, annex, *ibid.*

the part of the average Roumanian politician, one can hardly blame the legislature for looking askance at ministers, who either could not, or would not, cure the financial ills of the government, and at a prince who deigned to give his confidence only to men of doubtful repute.

Naturally, then, Couza found his relations with the legislature no smoother than they had been during the previous session. A concession to the assembly of the right of interpellation[1] (this was before the intervention of the consuls) had proved as futile a resource as the same concession at Paris two years later when the Prince's great protector was tottering to his fall. The chamber was in no mood to help him extricate himself, and criticized him unsparingly for issuing the decrees establishing a national bank as well as making other grants for public works while the legislature was not in session.[2] When the Prince disclosed his plans for introducing the metric system, both houses rejected the measure, and the senate went so far as to pass a vote of censure—an act which Green declared to be 'incomprehensible', seeing that the Prince's henchmen really controlled that body.[3] But the session had never been anything but stormy. The assembly's reply to the address was very caustic and received a tart rejoinder from the Prince.[4] But the projected reply of the minority was not only a sweeping indictment of the government but an exposure of graft and corruption on a gigantic scale.[5] 'What if the counter-project of the minority had passed!' exclaimed Tillos.[6] But, after all, the publicity which it received could not but do the government serious damage. Tillos urged the Prince to prorogue the assembly for three months, use the interval for making an honest report of the finances, and purge his ministry of liars; then perhaps the assembly would meet him in a better spirit. But Couza saw no hope in such advice, and after some hesitation merely sacrificed Floresco and another minister who were then the principal targets of the public hatred.[7] Later, when he talked of giving the premiership to Morousi, an able man but said to be a satellite of St. Petersburg, Tillos combined with Eder to protest against what appeared to them a surrender to Russian influence. Couza hotly denied it, and intimated that he was tired of being accused of being the tool of this or that Power, and that he was forced to look for support where he could get it.[8] These protests were the last instance of consular intervention during the reign of Couza. Dimmed as were

[1] Tillos to Lhuys, no. 47, Dec. 26, *Aff. étr.*, *Turquie, Bucharest*, vol. 26.
[2] Green to Clarendon, no. 10, Jan. 22, 1866, F.O. 78/1920.
[3] Green to Lyons, no. 10, Feb. 6, F.O. 78/1920.
[4] Tillos to Lhuys, no. 7, Feb. 1, *Aff. étr.*, *Turquie, Bucharest*, vol. 27.
[5] Annex to Tillos's no. 7.   [6] Tillos to Lhuys, no. 6, Jan. 29, *ibid.*
[7] Tillos to Lhuys, no. 9, Feb. 12, *Aff. étr.*, *Turquie, Bucharest*, vol. 27.
[8] Eder to Mensdorff, no. 19, Feb. 18, and no. 20, Feb. 20, Staatsarchiv, XXXVIII/148.

his eyes, the lonely prince must surely have seen the ever-lengthening cloud. A rumour had been current that the revolution would break out on February 5, and even in the palace itself some one had posted a handbill which declared that the place was 'to be let' on that date.[1] While it is true that the day passed without a semblance of disturbance, the celebration of this national fête was a sad mockery of the glad event which had given the Prince his double crown, and one may well imagine his feelings as he rode on horseback through his capital, glancing at placards, 'Down with robbery!' 'The official rejoicings', wrote Green, 'went off with more than their usual melancholy.'[2] 'Nothing whatever has been done by the Prince,' he added later, 'calculated to improve his position. He will probably hesitate to take a decided course until it is too late.'[3] Green himself had no illusions on the dangers of the situation.

The time had come, certainly, when Couza was merely living from hand to mouth, and the end could not be far off. Possibly ruling by decree would have enabled him to surmount many difficulties for the moment, but the desperate state of the finances was an evil beyond his power to cure. At the time of the consular intervention in January Couza had frankly acknowledged that, if the government could not get the funds to meet its current expenses, the administrative machine would stand still, and everything must collapse.[4] Nearly all of the available revenue—and there is little doubt that much of it was plundered[5]—was required to pay the interest on government loans, or to cover the rural and monastery indemnities. An effort to secure permission for a new loan of 40,000,000 piastres from the chamber foundered on the rock of legislative hostility, and the most that it would do was to sanction one for 6,000,000—a loan which, after local bankers had proved refractory, had been advanced by the new national bank.[6] But to a government so needy such was far from proving an escape from its dilemma. No money could be had except at extortionate rates of interest,[7] and the government's credit was so low that a loan had been refused in London because of insufficient security.[8] Treasury

[1] Eder to Mensdorff, no. 15, Feb. 4, Staatsarchiv, xxxviii/148.

[2] Green to Lyons, no. 10, Feb. 6, F.O. 78/1920.

[3] Green to Clarendon, no. 17, Feb. 12, *ibid.*

[4] Eder to Mensdorff, no. 14, Jan. 31, Staatsarchiv, xxxviii/148. Couza had also spoken of his financial difficulties to Tillos.

[5] Not trusting its own officials, the government had decided to put the collection of taxes in the hands of the communes: Tillos to Lhuys, no. 1, Jan. 1, *Aff. étr., Turquie, Bucharest*, vol. 27.

[6] Tillos to Lhuys, no. 47, Dec. 26, *ibid.*, vol. 26, and no. 3, Jan. 9, and no. 5, Jan. 22, *ibid.*, vol. 27.

[7] Eder to Mensdorff, no. 10, Jan. 27, Staatsarchiv, xxxviii/148.

[8] Eder to Mensdorff, no. 15, Feb. 4, *ibid.* Green wrote that the minister of finance appealed to the Imperial Ottoman Bank and other establishments but without success: Green to Clarendon, no. 12, Feb. 2, F.O. 78/1920.

bonds had greatly depreciated in value[1] (on January 9 we learn that they had not been honoured for fifteen days),[2] and on February 2 Green testified that official salaries had not been paid for months. Worst of all from the standpoint of Couza's political interests, the troops were neither regularly paid nor fed, and an artillery officer was said to have declared that he could no longer be responsible for his men.[3] It is this revelation which enables us to understand why Couza lost his last prop, the army. It must surely have been a hopeless *impasse* when the Prince let go his one hope of warding off his downfall. It was, in fact, the pinch of want that drove the officers of the palace guard to Rosetti and his compatriots of the Left.

It is a proof of the blindness or confusion in government circles that neither Couza nor his intimates was aware that a conspiracy was on foot. For a month or more a revolutionary committee had been plotting the Prince's overthrow, gathering in adherents, and discussing the proper method of rousing the nation. If the police were cognizant of such activities, they certainly kept the information to themselves; for no arrests were made, and even the keen-scented consuls knew nothing of such a plot. It is not unlikely that some of the ministers themselves had been suborned, and that treason had eaten so deeply into the vitals of the government that those who might have warned the Prince were overcome by momentary despair. Looking behind the scenes, as one may do after the event, one finds that prominent men of all factions had joined Rosetti's movement, and that the brain that was bringing it to a head was that of Couza's old enemy, John Ghika.[4]

For some reason we do not know the night of February 22-3 was selected for the execution of the design. A *coup de main* was to be executed, and then the nation could be relied upon to approve the removal of a prince of whom it was weary. The palace guard was commanded by a Moldavian, named Lecca, who was already in the plot; but, in order to make success doubly sure, the higher officers of the other regiment, cantoned in the capital, were likewise won over. Couza, it seems, was warned at nine o'clock in the evening that something was on foot, but he refused to allow his confidence in the army to be shaken, and he went, as usual, to the house of his mistress, Princess Obrenovitch, with whom he returned to the palace at two in the morning. It has often been observed that a woman has a keener sense of danger than a man, and Obrenovitch

---

[1] Eder to Mensdorff, no. 10, Jan. 27, *Staatsarchiv*, XXXVIII/148.
[2] Tillos to Lhuys, no. 3, Jan. 9, *Aff. étr., Turquie, Bucharest*, vol. 27.
[3] Green to Clarendon, no. 12, Feb. 2, F.O. 78/1920. Cf. Tillos to Lhuys, no. 11, Feb. 4, *Aff. étr., Turquie, Bucharest*, vol. 27; Eder to Mensdorff, no. 2 B, Jan. 2, *Staatsarchiv*, XXXVIII/148.
[4] St. Pierre to Bismarck, no. 11, Feb. 25, *Reichsarchiv, Turkei*, vol. 30. Cf. Tillos to Lhuys, no. 11, Feb. 24, *Aff. étr., Turquie, Bucharest*, vol. 27.

was not quite easy in her mind when Couza mentioned to her the warning he had received. She therefore persuaded her lover to take some precautions, and, to please her, he summoned Baldimen, the prefect of police; but, as Baldimen gave satisfactory assurances, the Prince and his lady retired to bed. At four o'clock the conspirators gathered, and at half-past four about forty persons, including several officers, broke into the royal bed-chamber. Couza sprang out of bed,[1] while Obrenovich, trembling, concealed herself behind its draperies. The Prince asked his assailants what they wanted at this hour of the night, and was told that, while his life was not in peril, people were tired of his rule, and that both the nation and the army demanded his abdication. Confronted with a paper, containing the renunciation which he was expected to sign, and perceiving the number of armed conspirators in the doorway, he hesitated but a few moments, and then signed his abdication. (In recounting the episode afterwards, he recalled with satisfaction that he had signed the document on the back of one of his captors.[2]) He was then permitted to dress (as was also his mistress, one of the officers protecting her from the gaze of the bystanders), and he was then escorted out of the palace under guard to a private residence in one of the suburbs of the city. The Prince was calm throughout the episode, and, when he saw that resistance was hopeless, displayed an indifference as to his fate.[3] We have already noticed that he had perceived his fortunes to be sinking, and if the end had come sooner than he expected and in a somewhat different way, he was too much of a patriot as well as too shrewd not to give in gracefully. There is no evidence that he expressed regret at his downfall, and he announced later that he would make no protest to the Powers.[4] Granting all his mistakes, Prince Alexander John had played a decisive role in the remoulding of his country. But the time had come when the Roumanian people needed another hand to guide them, and it was not to be the hand of a Roumanian. Couza knew that—knew, in fact, that the pledge, made in 1859, was now to be redeemed.

[1] According to a brief account of the episode which Couza later gave to an Austrian officer, he first heard footsteps in the hall-way, and accordingly rose and bolted the door, then seized a pistol and looked through the keyhole, spying some officers to the number of about fifteen. When he refused to open at their command, they got a palace-guard to force an entrance. They then held the Prince under fire: Kriegsarchiv, 1866, vol. 33, no. 4.

[2] *Ibid.*

[3] The most detailed consular report on the episode seems to be that of St. Pierre (already cited), who got his story from one of the conspirators. Eder's report (no. 22, Feb. 23) gives some additional information and is in substantial agreement. Tillos, who wrote only a brief account (no. 11, Feb. 24) of the Prince's deposition, heard that the conspirators 'put a pistol to his throat in demanding his abdication'. Green confined himself to a telegraphic report.

[4] Eder to Mensdorff, no. 24, Feb. 25, Staatsarchiv, xxxviii/148.

Though we are told that everything had been put in readiness at Bucharest for an uprising,[1] the complete success of the palace revolution gave its promoters every cause for confidence in the issue. In any event, there seems to have been general rejoicing. As the news of acts of violence travels quickly, it was still early morning when spectral figures paraded the streets, flags waved, and music blared.[2] Naturally the army was particularly popular on this occasion, and all classes fraternized with the troops.[3] It is a matter of conjecture whether the Moldo-Wallachians would have risked shedding their blood to get rid of Couza, but they had sufficient sense of the dramatic to enjoy a change, and certainly no reason for early misgivings.

Indeed, as in most revolutions, it was a group of leaders who had pointed the way, and if the general public were satisfied with the work of subversion, it was likely to be in a receptive mood about the consequences. In the act of abdication, which had been prepared for him, Prince Alexander John had 'placed the reins of government to-day, February 23, 1866, into the hands of a *lieutenance princière* and a ministry, chosen by the people'.[4] The functions of the *lieutenance princière* were assumed by three of the conspirators, Nicolas Golesco, Nicolas Haralambi (an officer in the army), and Demetrius Sturdza, who was acting for Lascar Catargi; and it was also these three who signed the proclamation which was communicated to the people who thronged the streets on the 23rd.[5] This document was partly an indictment of Couza's rule and an announcement of its termination, and partly it was a revelation of what was to come. 'Roumanians', it declared, 'by the election of a foreign prince to the throne of Roumania all the wishes expressed by the divans *ad hoc* become an accomplished fact.'[6] This harking back to the declaration of the elected assemblies of 1857 was a clever device, for it made the election of a foreign prince a national issue. It was evident also that the *boyards* had accepted the radical programme as a requisite of success.

It was the general appearance of harmony that constituted the nation's best hope of winning this boon from the Powers. It is also true that the personnel of the provisional government, consisting of some of the most prominent figures in the country, not only gave prospect of the stability of the new régime but further emphasized the sincerity of the national sentiment. The *lieutenance princière* was merely a council of regency which acted as makeshift until the choice of a new prince, the real authority being wielded by the ministry which it had constituted. John Ghika, who headed

[1] Goerling to Bismarck, Feb. 24, *Reichsarchiv, Turkei*, vol. 31.
[2] Eder to Mensdorff, no. 22, Feb. 23, Staatsarchiv, xxxviii/148.
[3] Tillos to Lhuys, no. 11.   [4] *Arch. dip., 1866*, vol. ii, p. 282.
[5] Eder to Mensdorff, no. 22.   [6] *Arch. dip., 1866*, vol. ii, pp. 282–3.

this cabinet and was likewise minister of foreign affairs, was probably the shrewdest politician in the Principalities. He had been one of the men of '48 who, like Couza, had become a moderate on his return to public life, being much too ambitious to waste his opportunities, like Rosetti, in pressing a radical programme for his country. Having been made Prince of Samos in 1854, he was declared ineligible for the hospodariate in 1859 on the ground that Turkish service was 'foreign service', which, according to the Convention, was a bar to candidature. Such an interpretation was scarcely just, but Ghika wisely refrained from taking his disappointment too keenly. He served Couza on various occasions during the years that followed, but the Prince, knowing his ambition and habits of intrigue, never trusted him, and soon came to detest him.[1] He was a leading member, as we have noticed, of the coalition which tried ineffectually to oust the Prince in 1863 and was among the first to head the new opposition which developed in 1865 and which precipitated the Prince's downfall. Though at one time patronized by the British,[2] Ghika never won the confidence of Bulwer. 'I am not one of this person's enthusiastic admirers,' the British ambassador had written in 1861. 'Under an appearance of modesty he nourishes an inordinate ambition. Under an appearance of straightforwardness, I look upon him as an artful and determined intriguer, and under the air of equity and moderation he but ill conceals an implacable spirit of hatred and revenge.'[3] A Frenchman, whose keen delineation of Couza has already been quoted, declared Ghika to be a man of capacity but 'of a duplicity great enough to be remarked upon even in the Orient'.[4] Yet it was perhaps this very unscrupulousness that enabled him to cope with men who were merely less adept than himself in practising the same arts, and his shrewdness, combined with undoubted force of character, had enabled him to head the movement which now made him the Warwick of Roumania. Whether he would be true to any one but himself, the future was to show; probably he himself was merely aware that he was trimming his sails to the winds, confident that in the end he could be master of the storm. Thanks to his prominence in the late conspiracy, as well as his influence over Golesco, Rosetti was also a member of the government as minister of worship and public instruction. Demetrius Ghika, a nephew of the late caimacam, and an important figure during the events of the late reign, was made minister of the interior; though restless and impulsive, he

---

[1] Couza long ago suspected that Ghika wanted to supplant him: Tillos to Thouvenel, no. 31, July 9, 1860, *Aff. étr., Turquie, Bucharest*, vol. 21.
[2] He had been Stratford's preference for the caimacamie in 1856.
[3] Bulwer to Russell, no. 171, Mar. 6, 1861, F.O. 78/1567.
[4] Annex to Lallemand's no. 145 *bis*, Oct. 16, 1861, *Aff. étr., Turquie*, vol. 352.

was an able man and an eloquent speaker. Mavrogheni and Demetrius Sturdza, men above the average in intelligence, were respectively minister of finances and minister of public works, while Lecca, as representative of the army, held the portfolio of war, and Cantacouzene, an honourable but rather mediocre *boyard*[1] and nephew of John Ghika, was minister of justice. Moldavia was represented by Catargi[2] on the *lieutenance* and Mavrogheni in the ministry. A scrutiny of these personages shows the general complexion of the new régime to have been moderately liberal, though it might not be easy to tame the doctrinaire, Rosetti, and it was still uncertain whether the personal ambition of the new rulers, many of them ex-candidates for the hospodariate,[3] would merge itself with the welfare of the nation. Doubtless it was as much for the sake of internal peace as for anything else that John Ghika had made up his mind to propose a foreign prince.[4]

For the present, anyway, there was nothing to mar the serenity of the occasion. At noon on the 23rd the senate and chamber convened in joint session, and Golesco read to them a message of the provisional government, announcing the abdication of Alexander John and urging them to 'sanction the will of the nation, which in 1857 was manifested with so much fervour and firmness'.[5] The members of the *lieutenance* then left the hall, and John Ghika, after an appeal to the patriotism of the law-makers, proposed the election of Philip, Count of Flanders, as hospodar of Wallachia and Moldavia. It is not clear why this nephew of the King of the Belgians was the first choice of the government—or possibly of Ghika.[6] But the advantage of selecting a member of an inconspicuous dynasty is evident enough on the surface, and the King of the Belgians was supposed to enjoy friendly relations with the Court of St. James. At all events, the assemblage was only interested in the fact that he was a foreign prince. Without any opposition he was acclaimed lord of Roumania as Philip I,[7] and the entire assemblage broke out in cheers. One of the deputies, with the general approval, pulled

---

[1] St. Pierre to Bismarck, no. 12, Feb. 27, *Reichsarchiv, Turkei*, vol. 31.

[2] Lascar Catargi was a son of Constantin Catargi, who had been the objectionable minister of the interior under Balsche, and was a nephew-in-law of Demetrius Ghika.

[3] Golesco, Cantacouzene, and the two Ghikas had been candidates for the hospodariate of Wallachia in 1859; Mavrogheni and Catargi had aspired to the corresponding position in Moldavia.

[4] Eder to Mensdorff, no. 22, Feb. 23, Staatsarchiv, xxxviii/148.

[5] *Arch. dip., 1866*, vol. ii, p. 283.

[6] The choice of Philip had probably been made before the conspiracy was carried out, as the proclamation to the people invoked their support for all public liberties, &c. 'as one practices in all civilized states and especially in Belgium'. Green remarked upon 'what at first sight appears to be an uncalled-for allusion to Belgium': Green to Clarendon, Feb. 22, telg., F.O. 78/1720. In 1857 a Belgian consul, Blondeel, had been very conspicuous for his intrigues at Bucharest, and may have made useful connexions.   [7] *Arch. dip., 1866*, vol. ii, pp. 284–5.

down the draperies of the empty throne (they bore the name of the late prince in gold), and trampled them under foot.[1] After the oath of allegiance had been administered to all,[2] the session closed with the appointment of a deputation to make the formal offer of the crown to the Count of Flanders, and likewise to solicit the approval of the Protecting Powers.[3]

It was still some days before this nation in revolution would worry over the attitude of the Protecting Powers, and for once the consular body, mute under the spell of these astounding events, refrained from offering any advice. At ten o'clock on the morning of the 23rd Eder, as dean of the consular corps, had called a meeting of his colleagues to discuss the situation.[4] It was agreed that without instructions they could do nothing which should indicate their attitude, but, at Green's suggestion, it was decided to request the *de facto* government for an audience with the Prince to whom they had been accredited as a means of determining if his abdication (published in the *Moniteur*) was genuine.[5] As soon as this was agreed upon, Eder took the step of sending word to Ghika, asking that a member of the government should call upon him. Ghika answered the message in person, and, when acquainted with the consuls' desire, said he would consult his colleagues; in the meantime, he added, they could be assured that the late prince would be treated with all respect.[6] Subsequently Eder received word that the consuls might interview Couza, but not in a body.[7] Tillos, it seems, had, meanwhile, received a message from Couza expressing a wish to see him,[8] and at a second meeting of the consuls—presumably for the purpose of reporting what Ghika had said to Eder,[9] and before the government had announced its final decision—the French consul declared that he would insist on seeing Couza immediately, even if he had to force his way through the guard. He spoke with contempt of the provisional government, and made Green suspect that he was hoping for a counter-revolution.[10] According to his own account, however, Tillos when consulted by an officer loyal to Couza, made nothing but evasive replies, and when he succeeded at length in getting access to the prisoner, Couza assured him that he had yielded to no compulsion, but really

[1] St. Pierre to Bismarck, no. 10, Feb. 24, *Reichsarchiv, Turkei*, vol. 31.
[2] Green to Clarendon, no. 20, Feb. 24, F.O. 78/1920.
[3] St. Pierre to Bismarck, no. 10. Miss Wambaugh incorrectly states (*op. cit.*, p. 121) that a plebiscite was held on the nomination of Flanders.
[4] Eder to Mensdorff, no. 22.
[5] Green to Clarendon, no. 24, Feb. 25, F.O. 78/1920.
[6] Eder to Mensdorff, no. 22; Green to Clarendon, no. 20.
[7] Green to Clarendon, no. 24.
[8] Tillos to Lhuys, no. 11, Feb. 24, *Aff. étr., Turquie, Bucharest*, vol. 27.
[9] One may judge that this was the purpose of the meeting from the fact that Eder did make such a communication to the assembled consuls.
[10] Green to Clarendon, no. 24.

wanted to end his reign. On hearing that Tillos had forced an entrance while the matter was still pending, the government withdrew the permission it had granted, and even Eder was denied access to the prisoner.[1]

One cannot reasonably criticize the precautions of the government, but the materials for a counter-revolution were almost ludicrously lacking. Apart from the one officer who had sounded Tillos (and he soon quit his command),[2] the only outspoken regret for the ex-Prince was to be found among the officials and garrison of Galatz,[3] where Couza had made his home, and, as most of his entourage had been merely time-servers,[4] there was no evidence of a serious plot in his favour. Couza himself, whose life had probably been spared by the success of the *coup de main*, was too sensible to look for such relief, and was only anxious to take refuge in exile. On the day after his dethronement he wrote Golesco, endorsing the plan of bringing in a foreign prince (for which end he affirmed that he had always laboured), and remarked that, as a new government was now constituted, he supposed that there would be no opposition to his departure. Probably to ensure his safety, the deposed Prince had been removed to his summer residence at Catroceni,[5] where he was joined by his wife; and a few days later Colonel and Madame Couza crossed the frontier *en route* to Vienna and Ems.[6] Gramont, the French ambassador, who talked with Couza at Vienna, was struck with the fact that he seemed to bear no rancour; placed on the throne by accident, he said that he felt no regret in having to leave it. He testified his gratitude to Napoleon for his kindnesses, and begged him to continue to serve his country's cause.[7] Whatever his faults, Couza was, first of all, a Roumanian.

The safe passage of the ex-Prince out of the country was, in fact, an evidence that the Moldo-Wallachians were not a bloodthirsty people and allowed their revolutions to take a placid course. Apart from the Couza family there were not more than three arrests,[8] and, if we except a prison sentence,[9] the worst fate that befell the worst of these culprits—Couza's henchman, Librecht—was the

[1] Tillos to Lhuys, no. 11, Feb. 24, *Aff. étr., Turquie, Bucharest*, vol. 27.

[2] This officer, a certain Colonel Salomon, had told Tillos that he was ready to attempt a rising against the government, but, before beginning civil war, he wanted Tillos's opinion. Apparently he regarded the French consul's answer as insufficient encouragement.

[3] Kiparissi to Mensdorff, no. 12, Feb. 26, annex to Mensdorff's dispatch of Mar. 7 to Metternich, Staatsarchiv, IX/83.

[4] We learn that some of these actually rejoiced at his downfall, ready apparently to look to new sources of enrichment: Goering to Bismarck, Feb. 24.

[5] St. Pierre to Bismarck, no. 10, Feb. 24, *Reichsarchiv, Turkei*, vol. 31.

[6] St. Pierre to Bismarck, no. 12, Feb. 27, *ibid*.

[7] Gramont to Lhuys, no. 30, Mar. 14, *Aff. étr., Autriche*, vol. 490.

[8] Green to Lyons, no. 16, Feb. 27, F.O. 78/1920.

[9] Librecht, a naturalized Belgian, was eventually released through French influence.

compulsion to disgorge his ill-gotten riches.[1] When a commission,
deputed to examine Couza's papers, found his secretary reluctant
to hand over his own papers on the ground that some of them
might perhaps belong to his master, the commission was said to
have refrained from reading them.[2] The new government was in
all respects conspicuous for its moderation, and Eder affirmed his
belief that neither foreign influence nor personal ambition had had
anything to do with the movement which had placed it in power.[3]
Equally striking was the self-restraint of the public at large. 'I am
happy to be able to record on the fifth day', wrote Green, 'that
there has not been a single act of disorder reported throughout the
Principalities.'[4]

Yet, notwithstanding the ease with which the opening phases of
the revolution had been executed, a government having its origin
in violence is bound to find some troubles in the transition. The
treasury was empty, and it was doubtful if the project of a patriotic
loan, though underwritten by some of the banks, would find the
requisite number of subscribers.[5] Few revolutions, after all, have
met the test of financial generosity from its supporters. But the
situation was grave, for the army was still unpaid and, consequently, mutinous,[6] and, but for the chance of employing it on the
frontier to repel possible invasion,[7] a serious crisis might have
resulted. It is doubtful, indeed, if the present assembly was really
competent to consider a budget[8] (certainly the talk of impeaching
Couza's ministers did not warrant much faith in its judgement),[9]
and now that the opposition minority had become, by virtue of the
revolution, the majority,[10] the members of the Left, led by Rosetti
(whose presence in the ministry was itself a menace to harmony)
were only intent upon a programme of radical reconstruction. At
the same time, while the ambition of the several members of the
provisional government was creditably hidden, some of the younger
politicians, who had participated in the revolution, were dissatisfied
with their present share of the fruits,[11] and ready, doubtless, to

[1] Eder to Mensdorff, no. 29, Mar. 2, Staatsarchiv, xxxviii/148. Eder called
the director of the post 'the right hand of Couza, and a person whom public
opinion branded with the guilt of all the defalcations here. No concession could
be made (he added), no government contract concluded without Librecht getting
a rake-off for the transaction.'

[2] Green to Clarendon, no. 31, Mar. 4, F.O. 78/1920.

[3] Eder to Mensdorff, no. 31, Mar. 5, Staatsarchiv, xxxviii/148.

[4] Green to Clarendon, no. 29, Feb. 28, F.O. 78/1920.

[5] Eder to Mensdorff, no. 29.

[6] Green to Clarendon, no. 46, Mar. 28, F.O. 78/1920.

[7] Colonel Haralambi of the *lieutenance princière* had taken special pains to
rouse their patriotism: St. Pierre to Bismarck, no. 20, Mar. 24, *Reichsarchiv,
Turkei*, vol. 31.

[8] St. Pierre to Bismarck, no. 21, Mar. 31, *ibid*.

[9] Green to Clarendon, no. 46.

[10] St. Pierre to Bismarck, no. 21.   [11] Green to Clarendon, no. 46.

follow any current of dissension. Speaking, in general, of the assembly, Ghika was doubtless correct when he told Eder that a body composed in large part of the henchmen of the late prince, having no longer any hope of being rewarded for its services, was determined not to submit itself to the leadership of the present government.[1] Perhaps also some of the trouble came of the fact that Europe had not yet given its sanction to the new régime, and the assembly, holding over from the days of Couza's rule, regarded these usurpers with mingled jealousy and contempt. At all events, faction, intrigue, and emotionalism were rapidly becoming the order of the day. It is, unhappily, an historic fact that a revolution seldom sustains its initial moral level.

Such being the temper of the assembly, it was not strange that the provisional government was quite unable to guide its course. Especially to be questioned was its cancellation of the contracts which Couza's government had made for the new bank of circulation and the railroad from Bucharest to Giurgevo. This, of course, affected foreign interests, and both Green and Tillos felt called upon to protest.[2] The French consul, who persisted in distrusting the government and seemed even to hope for its speedy downfall, cherished the suspicion that it had connived at the breach of these contracts;[3] but though it appears that public opinion had been thirsting to glut its hatred of the foreigner,[4] it is hard to believe that the government itself was in favour of a step which might alienate the Powers at the very time when their goodwill was so essential. It was remarked, too, that the government's plight was partly due to the fact that some of its members had opposed these very concessions at the time when they were trying to embarrass Couza.[5] But, in any case, the assembly had the ministry at its mercy. Helpless to stem the tide, the government, under pressure from the radicals, sent the once-famed project of a constitution, drafted by the central commission of 1859, to the council of state for revision applicable to the present situation, and Rosetti's pet proposal, the creation of a national guard, was then adopted.[6] It is almost a truism that political inexperience breeds legislative

---

[1] Eder to Mensdorff, no. 44, Mar. 31, Staatsarchiv, xxxviii/148.

[2] Green to Clarendon, no. 42, Mar. 22, F.O. 78/1920.

[3] Tillos to Lhuys, no. 19, Mar. 27, *Aff. étr.*, *Turquie, Bucharest*, vol. 27.

[4] Eder to Mensdorff, no. 39, Mar. 19, Staatsarchiv, xxxviii/148. Eder said that the Russian consul was supposed to be fomenting this agitation, but that he himself did not believe it. Tillos affirmed that it was due to the rooted hatred of foreigners (Tillos to Lhuys, no. 19), though he was said to have attributed some of the trouble to Ignatieff. Here again, without the Russian dispatches, we cannot test the truth of the accusation, but the well-known distrust of foreign enterprise seems explanation enough.

[5] Green to Clarendon, no. 42.

[6] Tillos to Lhuys, no. 16, Mar. 16, *Aff. étr.*, *Turquie, Bucharest*, vol. 27. See p. 257, note 2.

haste, but it is not improbable that the radicals were deliberately taking steps to capture the revolution while the moment seemed opportune. At all events the government could fairly plead that the legislature, as constituted, had never been representative; and even the factional leaders, whether 'pretenders' of the Right or hot-bloods of the Left, came to believe that the present assembly was too uncertain to serve their interests;[1] and when the rumour became current that that body had the intention of forcing the downfall of the government, some of the saner minds in authority no longer hesitated, and on March 30 the legislature, which had fathered the revolution received notice of its dissolution. Though a few of the startled deputies made some effort at resistance,[2] the hammer had effectually fallen, and Couza's 'rabble parliament' was no more.

The provisional government had thus struck a blow for its own security, and, incidentally, had avoided further embarrassments with the Powers. We shall not deal here with the attitude of those guardians who seemed not at all to appreciate the wisdom of the measure. In any event the trials of the provisional government were by no means ended. Its chief difficulties were still unsolved, and were, in fact, more deeply inherent in the situation. Apart from the unsolved financial tangle, there was the unknown attitude of Europe, and—what was immediately more serious—the question whether union itself would survive the crisis.

The attitude of Moldavia was the problem which gave the provisional government the greatest anxiety. It is true that Moldavia was no less gratified than Wallachia at the downfall of her native son, and the event was celebrated by three nights of illumination at Jassy. But there had long been soreness over the feeling (scarcely justified) that Moldavia had been sacrificed to her sister province ever since union had been consummated, and now that Couza's fall had reopened the whole question—for the firman, it will be remembered, had sanctioned union only during his lifetime—the opportunity of returning to a separate status was not lost on persons who wished to indulge either their grudges or their vanity. It is interesting in this connexion to note the characterization of these people by the Prussian consul at Jassy. 'The Moldavian', wrote Goering, 'is naturally inclined to intrigue, and finds pleasure in political broils. His penchant for idleness and for bodily and spiritual comfort leads him to shun serious work and strained activity. His vanity and presumption drive him to play, at least in appearance, a weighty role. Without vigour and energy, without principle and virtue, without higher zeal and fervour, there are no noble and elevated aims to which he sets his strength, no great

---

[1] St. Pierre to Bismarck, no. 21, Mar. 31, *Reichsarchiv, Turkei*, vol. 31.
[2] Eder to Mensdorff, no. 44, Mar. 31, Staatsarchiv, xxxviii/148.

battles in which he ventures. The narrowest egoism possesses him, as well as avarice, frivolity, and often the lust for intrigue alone and the hope of fishing in troubled waters. To such a character a time like the present is welcome. It says to him, "There are parties to build, plans to formulate, counter-plans to frustrate; artfulness, deceit, and falsehood to pit against those qualities in opponents." He considers himself weighty because others make an effort to win him, and in that case he thinks to utilize the opportunity for the best advantage to himself.'[1] There is little doubt but that Moldavia saw her strategic advantage and was ready to play with it. Though one may demur at so sweeping an indictment of a people, and adeptness at intrigue was probably no more characteristic of Moldavians than Wallachians, yet the spirit of the Moldavian politicians was decidedly factious at this juncture, and the habit of intrigue was never more conspicuously shown.

The fact that union was to be combated in Moldavia was not at first apparent. Lascar Catargi, the Moldavian who had a seat on the *lieutenance princière*, was much respected in his native province, and his weight was naturally thrown in the scale for union.[2] The majority of the official class, made up of young men who had got their training in foreign countries, were also ardent supporters of union and a foreign prince, and this party, it was said, was at present in the ascendancy. But the danger lurked in elements beneath the surface. Two influential Moldavians, Mavrogheni (himself a member of the ministry at Bucharest) and Gregory Sturdza, whom Couza had routed in 1859, were supposed to be candidates for the hospodariate, and knew that union under a foreign prince would for ever dispel their dreams. From the dissatisfaction of all classes with what they were pleased to regard as Wallachian rule and from a suspicion that the provisional government was supporting the Count of Flanders as a shield for private ambitions, these politicians might reasonably hope to eke profit. Sturdza, who was expected home from Paris, was a man of wealth and reputed ability, and already possessed an extensive influence over the clergy.[3] Whether the conservatives would go to pieces over rival candidates as they had in 1859 was yet to be seen. The separatists were organizing at all events, and, though we may discount the Russian consul's statement that 'almost all classes of the Moldavian population with the exception of certain exalted ones desire separation',[4] there was no doubt that a reaction against union was already under way.

[1] Goering to Bismarck, no. 175, Feb. 28, *Reichsarchiv, Turkei*, vol. 31.
[2] Kiparissi to Mensdorff, no. 12, Feb. 26, annex to Mensdorff's dispatch of Mar. 7 to Metternich, Staatsarchiv, xxxviii/148.   [3] Goering to Bismarck, no. 175.
[4] Oubril to Gortchakoff, Feb. 25, *Reichsarchiv, Turkei*, vol. 31.

The government at Bucharest was not unaware of the danger, and proposed at once to meet it. An extraordinary commissioner, named Cozadini, was sent to Moldavia with full powers to see that union was maintained;[1] the old prefects were replaced by new ones who could be trusted; and Wallachians were placed in command of the army.[2] Then, because his fidelity to union was in doubt, the new prefect at Jassy was succeeded by a Wallachian, and changes were made in the personnel of some of the courts.[3] When, as early as the evening of February 23, a petition to Constantinople was got up by the *boyards*, invoking the application of the Convention, the government took stringent measures to prevent its circulation, though the end was soon accomplished through the formation of local clubs.[4] However justified may have been these measures of the government, they were not calculated to win the devotion of the Moldavians, and Goering affirmed that, if a free expression of opinion were elicited, it would tell heavily against union.[5] The petition we have noted was duly dispatched to Fuad, proclaiming the right of Moldavia to elect her own prince in accordance with the Convention.[6] The activities of the separatists, carried on largely in secret, were not confined to a group of *boyards*, but, according to the British consul, were largely stimulated by the business men of Jassy, who had never ceased to deplore the removal of the capital to Bucharest.[7] On April 3 a proclamation was placarded in the streets of Jassy to the following effect:

'The Moldavians will no longer tolerate a Wallachian in the affairs of Moldavia or in the administration of justice, army, and church.

'Let the Wallachians return, unmolested, whence they came, and let the Moldavians assemble where they have always stayed in our fatherland, because, by the authority of the Convention, we want to govern ourselves, as we have done for a hundred years.

'This is the voice of the Moldavian people in answer to the proclamation of the provisional government and its ministry at Bucharest. . . .'[8]

The Austrian consul wrote that sentiment at Jassy was 'very much in earnest', and it was prophesied that an outbreak would take place at Easter.[9]

The calling of a new assembly for the Principalities was pretty likely to bring on a crisis. To the separatists no such assembly would be acceptable, since it implied the maintenance of union, while to the men at Bucharest, whose one aim was the installation

[1] St. Pierre to Bismarck, no. 12, Feb. 27, *Reichsarchiv, Turkei*, vol. 31.
[2] Oubril to Gortchakoff, Feb. 25.
[3] St. Clair to Green, no. 4, Apr. 5, enclosed in Green's no. 54, F.O. 78/1920.
[4] Haas to Mensdorff, no. 12, Mar. 6, Staatsarchiv, xxxviii/148.
[5] Goering to Bismarck, no. 175.
[6] Haas to Mensdorff, no. 22, Apr. 13, Staatsarchiv, xxxviii/148.
[7] St. Clair to Green, no. 4.
[8] Annex to Haas's no. 22.   [9] Haas to Mensdorff, no. 22.

of a foreign prince for the united realm, the outcome of the elections was a matter of great importance. Much concerned by the news of anti-union agitation in Moldavia, two of the *lieutenance princière*, Golesco and Cartagi, repaired to Moldavia to carry on a propaganda in that country which should ensure the election of a unionist assembly. Arriving on April 7, they called together a meeting of prominent citizens of Jassy, and ordered that clubs should be formed which should instruct electors to vote only for candidates who 'had declared without reserve for the revolution of February 23 and its consequences'. It was designed to have the candidate sign a *mandat*, as in 1857, proclaiming his principles. The formation of clubs for carrying on the canvass was duly carried out; but such material was combustible, and it speedily burned the fingers of the men who had devised it. While the 'National Party', whose original standard had been 'Moldavia for the Moldavians', now took as its watchword 'Union under a Foreign Prince or Separation from Wallachia', even the avowed unionists, who declared for a constituent assembly, were extremely sensitive about the position of Moldavia. When Catargi undertook to harangue the leading unionist club, he found that most of its members were far more excited over the wrongs of Moldavia, and his appeals for harmony were met with the cries, 'Down with Wallachia! We will not be schoolmastered by the gipsies!' When the club held an election of a steering committee, Golesco made the blunder of asking for a patriotic loan, and it was only with some difficulty that he and Catargi escaped being mobbed. In the end, amid a torrent of invectives against Wallachia, the separatists succeeded in stampeding the assemblage, and a certain Rosnovano, one of the most rabid of the anti-unionists, was chosen president of the directing committee which should undertake the supervision of the elections. Simultaneously, the co-operation of the clergy was secured, and there was nothing to relieve the decisive defeat of the government.[1]

Yet one may really doubt if the separatists were as strong as they appeared. Jassy was not Moldavia, and there were no indications that other towns were willing to go so far as to repudiate a foreign prince. Tillos considered that, whatever the grievances of the Moldavians, the more intelligent among them realized that their country had gained more than it had lost by union.[2] The news that a new candidate for prince had been found in place of Flanders (who had declined acceptance of the honour) and that a plebiscite was to be held on the question of his nomination seems to have led

---

[1] Haas to Mensdorff, no. 24, Apr. 13, Staatsarchiv, xxxviii/148; Oubril to Gortchakoff, Apr. 1. The Russian consul wrote that there were four sessions of the club, the last one being the most stormy. One person who spoke for union under a foreign prince was forced to leave the hall.

[2] Tillos to Lhuys, no. 19, Mar. 27, *Aff. étr., Turquie, Bucharest*, vol. 27.

the separatist leaders to believe that their best resource was a demonstration—an idea which Russia probably abetted, and may have inspired. The occasion for this effort was Easter Day, when the city was normally crowded with outsiders, and when brandy was plentiful. At ten o'clock on that day (April 15) the metropolitan, who was one of the leading separatists, harangued a crowd before his palace against union, and undertook to lead them to the house of Rosnovano, where most of the separatist chiefs were holding conclave. The crowd had hardly begun their course thither—amid cries of 'Down with union' 'Long live Moldavia', 'Long live the Convention'—when the police interfered, and, in the scuffle which followed, the metropolitan was wounded. Some one then shouted, 'Our brothers are being murdered; our fathers are being killed,' and there was a general rush for the Russian consulate. The military was now called out to disperse the mob, but the public authorities were so anxious to avoid bloodshed that the troops were forbidden to fire or even to charge with the bayonet. The result was a rather unequal struggle, the soldiers being charged and pelted with stones and clubs, while barricades were being raised in the streets near Rosnovano's house. The separatists had hoped to seize the municipal buildings and proclaim a provisional government, and through the connivance of the clergy the church bells were rung to call out the citizens. As far as we may learn, however, only a rabble—largely from out of the city—was engaged in the riot, the majority of the citizens remaining quiet; and, in the end, two battalions of infantry were able to repel the rioters, remove the barricades, and restore order. The struggle had lasted about three hours. Some twenty of the rioters had been killed and about sixty wounded, while only two soldiers had lost their lives, though a large number had suffered from contusions.[1] Over two hundred arrests were made, including Rosnovano and the primate, though the chief plotter, Constantin Morousi,[2] a brother-in-law of Rosnovano, was able to hide himself in the Russian consulate, and to escape soon afterwards to Russia. Incidentally, one may remark that the conduct of the Russians was, to

[1] These figures are the French consul's. Goering wrote that 150 of the rioters were killed and 50 or 60 wounded, while the loss of the military was about 60; Eder estimated 30 to 40 deaths and 80 wounded among the insurgents, but does not mention losses on the other side. It is easy, however, for the number of casualties to be exaggerated at first. Moreover, reports of brutalities on the part of the military (to which Haas gives credence) can easily be explained by the fact that some of the fleeing citizens were mistaken for rioters.

[2] According to Tillos, he was a Russian subject who owned lands in Moldavia, and had been sent thither with a confederate to work up a movement against union: Tillos to Lhuys, no. 22, Apr. 13, *Aff. étr., Turquie, Bucharest*, vol. 27. (Tillos also makes the extraordinary statement that Morousi directed secretly the double election of 1859, being convinced that Couza would not have the stability of character to hold Moldavia.)

say the least, suspicious, but if they actually had been in the plot, they had done either too much or too little to make it successful. One gathers that the chief reason for the failure of the conspiracy was the enlistment of a hoodlum element, which did not serve to invite the co-operation of the citizenry.[1]

The collapse of the *émeute* of April 15 marked the passing of the crisis. Whether or not it is true that bitterness against Wallachia was enhanced by this affair, and that another outbreak was seriously expected,[2] there is apparently no evidence of any further trouble. The Moldavians were not possessed of that tenacity which will stand up under a losing fight, and the country districts were alienated by this senseless recourse to violence. One cannot say whether the separatists would have swept the elections if the incident had not occurred, but such a result would not have been improbable. As it was, the pendulum was now in full swing back to union. Moldavia was not to have her own prince, but would remain an integral part of the United Principalities.

There was still the problem of making the revolution acceptable to Europe. Though it may be held that the statute of 1864 had given the Principalities the right to make such changes as they desired, yet by no stretch of the imagination could this have been intended to give them the privilege of scrapping the Convention and the firman of 1861.[3] On March 4 Ghika issued a moderately toned circular to the consuls, which was a sort of apology for the revolution (made necessary, he declared, by Couza's misrule) and an appeal to the expressions of the divans *ad hoc* of 1857 in favour of a foreign prince.[4] Most of the consuls seemed to feel that the Principalities were determined upon this solution, and Eder believed that, if they were thwarted, various candidates for the throne would try a popular uprising,[5] while Green thought that, if frustrated, the State would proclaim its independence.[6] Eder himself would have liked to see a caimacam nominated by the Porte—a temporary solution which he believed would enable the forces of separation to operate until union was quietly dissolved.[7] The idea was characteristic of the Baron's subtlety and resource, but it overlooked the strength of the movement which had managed to

---

[1] Interesting accounts of the riot of Apr. 15 are given by Goering (no. 15, Apr. 16, *Reichsarchiv, Turkei*, vol. 31), by Cartaing (no. 33, Apr. 15, and no. 34, Apr. 17, *Aff. étr., Turquie, Jassy*, vol. 11), and by Haas (no. 26, Apr. 17, Staatsarchiv, xxxviii/148). St. Clair, the British consul, gives a rather coloured account (to Green, no. 5, Apr. 20, F.O. 78/1920) and charges the soldiers with being drunk and exceptionally brutal.

[2] Haas to Mensdorff, no. 26, Apr. 17, Staatsarchiv, xxxviii/148.

[3] This was, however, Tillos's contention: Tillos to Lhuys, no. 16.

[4] *Arch. dip., 1866*, vol. ii, p. 287.

[5] Eder to Mensdorff, no. 28, Mar. 1, Staatsarchiv, xxxviii/148.

[6] Green to Clarendon, no. 40, Mar. 16, F.O. 78/1920.

[7] Eder to Mensdorff, no. 31, Mar. 5, Staatsarchiv, xxxviii/148.

have its way in Europe during the past seven years. The Moldo-Wallachians did not really know what to expect from their Protectors, but they meant to face them with one more *fait accompli*. It was a critical period—this interval when a new prince was being sought, the national integrity in jeopardy, and the attitude of Europe in doubt. Would the revolution really achieve its end? The time had come when the Principalities were demanding the full realization of their national programme. Would the Powers grant them a foreign prince?

CHAPTER XVII

A FOREIGN PRINCE

THE revolt of Rouman nationalism against the series of inter-national instruments which had determined the legal scope and limits of its operation had now reached a stage where a nation that was nominally a dependency was deliberately grasping the initiative in settling for itself the most cherished of its problems. To combat its determination to have a foreign prince and to insist that only the collective will of Europe could mark the course which it should follow was the plain duty of the Powers who had taken that nation under their protection. Now, more than ever before, in the tangled history of the Roumanian problem, was the prestige of the Concert of Europe at stake. Would it reveal the unity and practical statesmanship required to meet this crucial test? Would a Europe, which had invested a king of Italy, be strong enough to blackball a prince of Roumania? Could a public law which had proved unavailing against a Bismarck operate with any more effectiveness on the Danube than on the Baltic? Already the more imaginative ears could detect the distant rumbles of the coming war between Austria and Prussia; yet that institution which watched over Europe's peace was like a leaky derelict, tossed by the winds. How impotent it was to deal with nationalism, when strength and will had underlain that force, had only just been demonstrated; and, as an eminent historian has rightly said, the war with Denmark, with its wanton disregard for a European settlement, had 'smashed the Concert of Europe into fragments'.[1] Now, if the broken fabric were to be mended, it was only against a weak state that its forces could be marshalled with any prospect of success. And yet experience had shown that at no critical juncture in the history of the Danubian Principalities had the Concert of Europe maintained a united front. Would it be able to grasp the present occasion to recover its stability and to revive its own faith in its fundamental *raison d'être*? Clearly the European areopagus must prepare to meet the challenge which Couza's pupils had delivered.

Once the news of Couza's fall and the nomination of a foreign prince had sped by telegraph to the various courts of Europe, the unwieldy mechanism of diplomacy began in rather jerky fashion to put itself in motion. Constantinople was, of course, the most immediately affected, and, at Ali's request, the representatives of the Protecting Powers came together on February 26 to consider with him what action should be taken. Ali himself had no hesitation in the matter. Now, as never before, was the case an occasion

[1] Robertson, *Bismarck*, p. 184.

for the application of the famous Protocol of 1859. In other words, a Turkish commissioner, with delegates of the Powers, should be sent to Bucharest to staighten matters out.[1] Prokesch and Ignatieff responded cordially to the idea, saying that they were authorized to support anything which the Porte should deem necessary. Lord Lyons, the British ambassador, having as yet no instructions, remained silent. Moustier remembered that his government had withheld the right to reconsider the whole question in the event of Couza's demise, and accordingly declared that he must reserve to his government the interpretation of its reservation to the firman of 1861.[2] It was finally decided, on his proposal, to ask the cabinets at home for instructions, based on the Porte's demand;[3] and meanwhile 'identic' instructions were sent to the consular agents to have no official relations beyond what were strictly necessary with 'the authorities of the moment'.[4] Such was, after all, the most that Constantinople could do.

It was idle, of course, to speculate on the causes of the 'calamity', which Prokesch was inclined to attribute to French intrigues. Every one knew that such a crisis had been foreshadowed, no matter how much shock had been the actual occurrence, and even Prokesch himself admitted that Moustier had shown surprise.[5] Like the double election of 1859, the revolution was fundamentally a spontaneous affair, and little time was wasted in trying to explain it. But, naturally, the Principalities were placed on the defensive, and Ghika had at last found time to write to Bordeano a kind of official apology to be communicated to the Porte: the new situation had been prompted by necessity, and was a proof (he added) of a desire to 'serve the great political interests of the Porte'.[6] Naturally the Porte did not hold so charming a theory. Sorely troubled by an explosion in this particularly combustible portion of its realm, it now proposed to make such a catastrophe an occasion for some international action. It only remained to be seen whether the Powers would grant assent.

The Powers were not greatly astonished either by the Porte's

[1] Ali adduced the curious argument that the election of a foreign prince who was not a vassal of the Sultan was a violation of the integrity of the Ottoman Empire, which the Powers had guaranteed. He was then called away from the Conference, and, when he returned, he announced that Flanders had declined the election.

[2] Brassier de St. Simon to Bismarck, no. 16, Feb. 27, *Reichsarchiv, Turkei*, vol. 30.

[3] Moustier to Lhuys, Feb. 28, *Arch. dip., 1867*, vol. i, p. 242.

[4] Lyons to Clarendon, Feb. 26, telg., F.O. 78/1921. The consuls, as we have noticed (p. 496) had already taken this decision, pending the reception of instructions.

[5] Prokesch to Mensdorff, Mar. 2, private, Staatsarchiv, XII/84.

[6] Ghika to Bordeano, Feb. 27, annex to Moustier's no. 22, *Aff. étr., Turquie*, vol. 367.

demand or by the crisis which had occasioned it. St. Petersburg had long been prepared for the collapse of Couza, and Gortchakoff told the Turkish minister that 'now it was for the Porte to show Europe whether it still had *couilles* or not'.[1] The British government was wary of expressing an opinion for the moment. Clarendon was said to be not unfavourable to the election of Flanders,[2] if a foreign prince had to be (for the court of Brussels was closely related to that of Windsor), but, on second thoughts, the Count's refusal of the honour was hailed with some relief[3]—the British being never long detached from an established policy. Drouyn de Lhuys had shown at once that he did not approve of Flanders's election,[4] and the reason was not far to seek. The Count was related to the House of Orleans—the one family which Napoleon had always kept at a safe distance. There is a story that Flanders, on the pretext of being on his way to Nice, had paid a hasty visit to Napoleon, and had then been told that he was not to accept the proffered throne;[5] but the evidence seems conclusive that the Count had given his definite refusal before he took his departure from Brussels.[6] Anyway, this preliminary difficulty being cleared away, France proposed to face the problem in a generous spirit. Apprised of the Porte's demand by telegraph from Moustier,[7] Drouyn de Lhuys at once put his veto on any application of the Protocol,[8] and, of course, without unanimous consent this ill-fated instrument was quite inoperable. Already, indeed, without waiting to hear from Constantinople, the French minister had communicated with the governments of all the Protecting Powers, proposing a conference to deal with the question of the Principalities.[9] As an international conference was already in session at Paris, treating the question of the Danube navigation, it was only necessary for the governments to widen its scope and to send full powers to their respective representatives.

[1] Redern to Bismarck, no. 12, Feb. 27, *Reichsarchiv, Turkei*, vol. 30.
[2] La Tour to Lhuys, Mar. 23, *Origines*, vol. viii, no. 2923.
[3] La Tour to Lhuys, no. 33, Feb. 24, *Aff. étr., Angleterre*, vol. 736.
[4] Cowley to Clarendon, no. 315, Feb. 25, F.O. 27/1612.
[5] Bamberg, *Geschichte der orientalischen Angelegenheit*, p. 346.
[6] Hügel to Mensdorff, no. 22, Feb. 28, Staatsarchiv, XXII/24. Earlier it had been reported: 'Assurément que S. Altesse Royale ne reviendra pas sur son refus et pour ne pas faire naître des suppositions erronées le Prince, qui quitte Bruxelles demain pour l'Italie, ne compte pas s'arrêter à Paris: Hügel to Mensdorff, no. 24, Feb. 21, *ibid.*
[7] Moustier to Lhuys, Feb. 26, *Origines*, vol. vii, no. 1797.
[8] Cowley to Clarendon, no. 231, Feb. 27, F.O. 27/1612. Cf. Bismarck to Goltz, Mar. 8, *Reichsarchiv, Turkei*, vol. 31. To the Turkish ambassador, who insisted that the Porte would participate in the Conference only on condition that all existing treaties should be respected and that the question of a foreign prince should not be raised, Drouyn de Lhuys tactfully replied that all questions should be equally reserved to the Conference: Lhuys to Moustier, Mar. 2, *Arch. dip., 1867*, vol. i, pp. 240–1.
[9] Lhuys to diplomatic agents, Feb. 25, *Origines*, vol. vii, no. 1793.

There was no objection from any quarter to this proposal. Manifestly, as the firman of 1861 had made no provision for union beyond Couza's lifetime, and as some of the Powers had explicitly reserved their right at that time to re-examine the whole question on the termination of Couza's reign, there was now the obligation, incumbent upon them all, of convening once again and of reaching a collective decision on the question. Since, moreover, the whole problem was now complicated by the strong sentiment in the Principalities in favour of a foreign prince, it hardly seemed feasible, despite the Porte's expressed preference,[1] to attempt to effect a settlement through the diplomats at Constantinople. So the conference, as on three former occasions, would sit at Paris, and consist of the various ambassadors, acting, of course, as plenipotentiaries, with the French minister of foreign affairs as director of proceedings. Great Britain and Austria were anxious that it should meet without delay, but Prussia and Russia responded with less alacrity, and it was not expected that Budberg, the Russian plenipotentiary, would arrive before March 11.[2] The delay at least gave the French and British governments the opportunity of trying to concert a plan to present to the Conference, as they had done in 1859.[3] Though Clarendon seemed at first inclined to support the Turkish proposal of intervention,[4] he did not press the matter strongly, and while claiming—with doubtful justification—that the fall of Couza had vindicated British disapproval of union, he was ready to support its continuance if the people really wanted it.[5] With that much spirit of conciliation in London, there seemed no reason for borrowing trouble in Vienna or St. Petersburg. Yet one cloud rose over these first pourparlers between the cabinets, which might, had it waxed more louring, have produced a considerable storm.

It has been noticed that at various times the idea of giving the Principalities to Austria, who should in turn yield Venetia to Italy, had formed a subject of discussion at Paris and London. The Italian government had more than once tried to interest the British

---

[1] Lhuys to Moustier, Mar. 2. Cf. F.O. to Lyons, no. 75, Feb. 28, F.O. 78/1903.

[2] Redern to Bismarck, no. 15, Mar. 7, *Reichsarchiv, Turkei*, vol. 31.

[3] Clarendon said that Great Britain would take no step without France's concurrence (F.O. to Cowley, no. 203, Feb. 26, F.O. 27/1601), and Drouyn de Lhuys had already given a similar assurance (Cowley to Clarendon, no. 215, Feb. 25, F.O. 27/1612).

[4] F.O. to Cowley, Feb. 27, telg., F.O. 27/1601; La Tour to Lhuys, Mar. 16, *Origines*, vol. vii, no. 1859. Clarendon, as he informed Cowley, had telegraphed Lyons that he would support the Porte's proposal if France concurred. Drouyn de Lhuys, on being apprised of this by Cowley, said that there was no reason for such action, as there was no disorder in the Principalities, and the sending of a commissioner would do more harm than good: Cowley to Clarendon, no. 224.

[5] F.O. to Cowley, no. 275, Mar. 8, F.O. 27/1602.

cabinet in the idea, and Russell, in spite of Palmerston's scepticism,[1] had consulted Drouyn de Lhuys very earnestly in November 1864 about its practicability.[2] The French minister had apparently welcomed the notion, provided he were assured that the Moldo-Wallachians would be satisfied, but he felt strongly that Great Britain should take the initiative, since 'the victors of Solferino would show bad grace in demanding of Austria new territorial sacrifices in Italy'.[3] Even then Russell did not drop his pet plan, but got Lyons to sound Ali on the idea—an overture which the Turkish minister, after some hesitation, decisively rejected.[4] Meanwhile Napoleon, after the British cabinet decided that it could not take the initiative,[5] decided himself to press the matter, and it was only after finding that Austria was very sensitive on the point that he promised Metternich 'not to raise the question again'.[6] Thus nothing whatever resulted from all these pourparlers, and Austria's 'repugnance'[7] to the idea might have settled the question definitely, had not Couza's downfall definitely reopened it. Their hopes raised by the sudden crisis, the Italians now brought up the question again, and in addition to some soundings in London, the Italian minister to Paris made the suggestion boldly to Napoleon. The Emperor was ready enough, to be sure, to accede to the idea, but he doubted, he said, if Austria would consent to it unless she feared that otherwise Italy would join Prussia in the impending war over Schleswig-Holstein.[8] Nevertheless, as a feeler, he took the step of sounding the Austrian government—not, it is true, mentioning the Principalities, but raising the question of whether Austria would be willing to consider Bosnia and Herzegovina by way of compensation for Venetia. As the Austrian answer was sufficient to discourage further overtures,[9] the Emperor now resorted to another roundabout method.

[1] La Tour to Lhuys, Dec. 13, 1864, *Aff. étr., Angleterre*, vol. 731.
[2] Russell's scheme (Russell to Cowley, Nov. 1864, Russell Papers, G. and D. 22/15, Pub. Rec. Off.) is very curious. It suggested among other things that Italy should pay a large enough sum (say, £50,000,000) to indemnify the Porte for its loss of tribute, Couza for the loss of his throne, and 'the *boyards* and the Greek clergy for the property of which they had been despoiled'. Since the peasants were supposed to have been satisfied by the land law of 1864, Russell seemed to feel that all parties would acquiesce in the arrangement; though, as he made no mention of a plebiscite, his plan, from the standpoint of international morality, is perhaps somewhat below Napoleon's handling of Savoy and Nice. It is, at least, a curious commentary on how a contemporary statesman measured Rouman nationalism.
[3] La Tour to Lhuys, Nov. 29, *Origines*, vol. v, no. 1065.
[4] Lyons to Russell, Jan. 4 and 18, 1865, Russell Papers, G. and D., 22/92, Pub. Rec. Off.
[5] Russell to Cowley, Nov. 26, Russell Papers, G. and D., 22/16, Pub. Rec. Off.
[6] Metternich to Mensdorff, Mar. 22, Oncken, *Die Rheinpolitik Kaiser Napoleons III*, vol. i, pp. 115 ff.
[7] Rothan, *La Politique française en 1866*, p. 85.
[8] Ollivier, *op. cit.*, vol. viii, p. 42.
[9] Mensdorff to Metternich, Apr. 26, Staatsarchiv, IX/83.

Prompted by Drouyn de Lhuys (since Napoleon had promised that Italian minister that he would take up the matter with London,[1] and Drouyn believed that a proposal of this kind would really come more acceptably from there), La Tour d'Auvergne, the French ambassador at London, asked Clarendon if he thought Austria would consent to the exchange, and was answered plainly in the negative. Clarendon would, indeed, be very glad to see such an arrangement (so La Tour represented); in fact, he told some one later that it 'would be an excellent scheme if it could be carried out';[2] but he felt sure that Austria would never consider it (he doubted if she would take the Principalities 'as a gift'), as it would rouse the enmity of Russia, which would be far more serious than that of Italy.[3] With somewhat more scruples than Russell, Clarendon pointed out that the Principalities could not be bartered without their consent—which would certainly be unobtainable; furthermore he felt sure that Turkey would not agree to 'an act of spoliation'. Naturally the British government had been approached by Italy, and with no better result.[4] To the Austrian ambassador Clarendon showed an unwonted bluntness when he declared that 'Austria already had enough semi-barbarous people to govern without piling up four millions of savages which she did not want, and who, for their part, were in no wise ambitious to be incorporated in her empire.'[5] Such language was obviously not backing Napoleon's manœuvre. Since Italy herself had come by this time to perceive the hopelessness of her scheme, and as she had felt some pangs of conscience (that is, the pangs of conscience which are sensitive to appearances) over the rights of the Moldo-Wallachians in the matter,[6] the British minister at Florence quoted La Marmora as saying that 'the Italian government would not ask for or expect that the Danubian Principalities would be made over to Austria if the transfer should be contrary to the wishes of the people'.[7] Yet Napoleon, who had so long played the role of Italy's fairy godmother that he was not above sacrificing the Moldo-Wallachians in her interest, actually instigated the Empress to argue the question with Metternich—an overture which only met with a categorical rejection.[8] Whatever advantage such an exchange

[1] La Marmora, *Un peu plus de lumière*, pp. 132–3.
[2] Clarendon to Layard, Mar. 10 (or 16?), Layard Papers, Brit. Mus., Add. MS. 38992.   [3] La Tour to Lhuys, Mar. 9, *Origines*, vol. vii, no. 1865.
[4] Clarendon to Cowley, no. 292, Mar. 12, F.O. 27/1602.
[5] Apponyi to Mensdorff, no. 20 C, Mar. 20, Staatsarchiv, VIII/74.
[6] La Marmora, *op. cit.*, pp. 131–2.
[7] Elliot to Clarendon, no. 98, Mar. 21, F.O. 45/85. Bismarck believed, from information he derived from Florence, that Italy would rather get Venetia as the result of a war than run the risk of incurring Russia's opposition to the exchange plan: Bismarck to Goltz, Mar. 20, *Die gesammelten Werke*, vol. v, pp. 267 ff. It was obviously to Bismarck's own interest that Italy should seek it through war.
[8] Metternich to Mensdorff, no. 12 B.

might ordinarily have had for Austria (and it was a question whether a stronger geographical position would compensate for an aggravation of her racial problem), one may judge that, apart from the Austrian Emperor's unwillingness to part with any of his subjects, neither he nor his ministers were fools enough, at this critical juncture, to cast their ship of state on a sea of such uncertainty. In the meantime, as these frequent discussions could not fail to reach the ears of all the cabinets, it is interesting to note some of the distant reverberations. Bismarck told the Prussian ambassador at Paris that he could only give his consent on condition that Prussia should have the Duchies, and that, of course, raised the question of satisfying all the Powers. But Russia, as Bismarck found, saw no basis for even a compromise.[1] Notwithstanding a suggestion of Talleyrand, now French ambassador at St. Petersburg, that Russia was in no position to oppose the plan, it was very soon evident that something like a premonitory storm was approaching from that quarter. When inklings of the discussion had come, at last, to Russian ears, the Czar was reported to have written a notation on a dispatch, 'Inadmissible jusqu'à la guerre'. Whether he meant 'up to' or 'including war' was a matter of conjecture in diplomatic circles;[2] but there is little doubt that Russia would, if necessary, display sufficient aversion from the proposal to deter Austria from adding one more enemy to her list. As a matter of fact, there is no evidence that Austria was seriously tempted by the suggestion.

Meanwhile, the Conference opened on March 10,[3] and it was at once agreed that no definite decision could be taken until the Russian plenipotentiary had appeared, but the Conference listened to Turkey's proposals, the high point of which was that all consideration of the question of a foreign prince should be excluded from the discussions. The Turkish plenipotentiary, Safvet Pasha, gave it to be understood that only on that ground would the Porte consent to participate in the Conference. Although discussion was naturally adjourned on this issue, it was clear enough already that this feast of corporate reason would not be without this sourest apple of discord. Thus Count von der Goltz, the Prussian ambassador, felt convinced that dissension would break out in the Conference, and he hoped that France and Austria would become divided on the question—in which case, if Austria followed her usual practice of rallying to Turkey's views, she might end in

---

[1] Bismarck to Goltz, Mar. 20, *Die gesammelten Werke*, vol. v, pp. 267 ff.

[2] Bismarck had sounded Oubril, the Russian ambassador, on the question of dividing the Principalities—Wallachia to Austria and Moldavia to Russia—but Oubril argued that this would give Austria much the greater advantage.

[3] The protocols of the Conference will be found in Martens, *op. cit.*, vol. xviii, pp. 166 ff., or in *Arch. dip., 1867*, vol. 2, pp. 611 ff.

becoming isolated among the Powers. Yet he admitted that Austria was supposed to be willing that union should be maintained (which did not look like violent recalcitrancy), and if she were opposed to a foreign prince, it might be that she wanted to avoid what would block her eventual absorption of the Principalities.[1] It was, doubtless, this feeling that London and Vienna could not be relied upon that so dispirited the Turks—'very unhappy', wrote Lyons, 'and ridiculously afraid that they will be thrown over at the Conference'.[2] After all, from the Turkish point of view, there was much ground for fear, for the Protocol was dead before the Conference had met, and the question of a foreign prince was very much alive. In the meantime, the only positive action which the Conference had taken was the resolution, at Cowley's suggestion, of sending an identical telegram of warning to Bucharest.[3]

There is no denying the fact that most of the Powers, if not all, were fully informed of the determination of the Principalities to have a foreign prince, and even Russia later admitted that Moldavia's alleged desire for separation was only inspired by the thought that the prime wish of the Principalities would not be countenanced.[4] To a telegram of Clarendon, stating that the Conference would not agree on sanctioning a foreign prince, and inquiring what effect this refusal would have on the Principalities,[5] Green responded that in that case the provisional government was expected to proclaim the national independence.[6] Such information had no effect on Clarendon, however. He seemed convinced that it would be impossible to secure Russian assent to a foreign prince, declared that it would lead to the dismemberment of the Ottoman Empire, and expressed the opinion that, if the Principalities were not assured of some support in the Conference, they would at once become calmer. La Tour d'Auvergne pointed out shrewdly that a foreign prince would be just as much under the suzerainty of the Porte as a native, but Clarendon found shelter in the belief that no scion of any princely house in Europe would accept the position of a vassal.[7] No doubt, the fear that, if his assumption were not correct, the Principalities would be led by an ambitious foreigner to declare their independence had a certain logic to justify it, but the fact is still manifest that Clarendon discounted unduly the force of public sentiment at Bucharest, and it is noticeable once again that Great Britain consistently placed

[1] Redern to Bismarck, no. 17, Mar. 12, *Reichsarchiv, Turkei*, vol. 31; Goltz to Bismarck, no. 99, Mar. 13, *ibid.*
[2] Lyons to Layard, Mar. 4, 1866, Layard Papers, Brit. Mus., Add. MS. 39119.
[3] Protocol no. 1.
[4] Cowley to Clarendon, no. 363, Mar. 20, F.O. 27/1613.
[5] F.O. to Green, no. 6, Mar. 18, telg., F.O. 78/1919.
[6] Green to Clarendon, Mar. 19, telg., *ibid.*
[7] La Tour to Lhuys, Mar. 23 and 27, *Origines*, vol. viii, nos. 1933 and 1952.

the legal rights of Turkey above the welfare of the Principalities. Yet one wonders how a person of even Clarendon's mentality could not grasp the simple fact that native rule in the Principalities —which would mean the rule of some *boyard*—was demonstrably impracticable.

Nevertheless, the stubbornness of Great Britain had undoubtedly much to do with the attitude which France, in turn, had assumed. As a matter of conviction, France was just as much in favour of a foreign prince as she had been in 1858, and Napoleon himself made this clear in a conversation with Cowley.[1] But in 1866 France had neither the feeling of assurance nor the perception which had served her at an earlier period (one must never overlook the fact that Napoleon's health was failing), and there was less disposition to push Great Britain into following her accustomed leadership in the East. Naturally Drouyn de Lhuys, who had not had the experience of manœuvring for the Emperor during the greater part of the period since the Crimean War, was somewhat less insistent than his sovereign on the virtues of a foreign prince;[2] he had impressed Cowley with the belief that, if the Principalities could not serve the cause of Italy, he was not greatly interested in their fate: they might 'struggle on as best they could'.[3] On the other hand, it may reasonably be suspected that he had learned during his four-year tenure of office that by hedging or dilly-dallying on a question which was of vital interest to the Principalities France would in the end ensure the precipitation of a *fait accompli*, and that then, by blocking, as a single Power could, any attempt at coercion, she would enable the Principalities in the end to have their way.[4] Such tactics merit none of the admiration which one accords to Bismarck's assaults under a carefully prepared smoke-screen or to Palmerston's diplomatic *coups de main*, but the game of international politics affords practical resources to a wide range of talent, and Drouyn de Lhuys might be classed as a brilliant second-rate diplomatist. Having carefully sounded the British position,[5] he concluded that the wisest course for France was to assure himself of British co-operation in resisting Russia's campaign to disrupt the moral union which the firman of 1861 and the experience of five years of consolidation had been able to accomplish. Indeed, he could hardly have done less in view of the

[1] Cowley to Clarendon, no. 451, Apr. 12, F.O. 27/1615.
[2] Goltz to Bismarck, no. 99, Mar. 13, *Reichsarchiv, Turkei*, vol. 31.
[3] Cowley to Clarendon, no. 215, Feb. 25, F.O. 27/1612.
[4] As the discussions wore on, Goltz came to the conclusion that it was the intention of 'the dominant party, encouraged by France' to 'strive to set up a foreign prince and to weary the Powers by constantly reverting to it': Goltz to Bismarck, no. 131, Mar. 25, *Reichsarchiv, Turkei*, vol. 31.
[5] Cowley to Clarendon, no. 312, Mar. 13, F.O. 27/163; Lhuys to La Tour, Mar. 16 and 19, *Origines*, vol. viii, nos. 1893 and 1913.

previous attitude of his government, and if he had talked of a foreign prince, one might feel that he was thinking chiefly of the *quid pro quo*.[1] For these reasons (as we may judge) he was now prepared—and he stated it more than once—to give up all thought of a foreign prince in return for the assurance that the union of the Principalities would become a permanent fact.[2] If Napoleon yielded to this plan, it was doubtless because, as he intimated to Goltz, he thought more of the 'general peace'; and Drouyn de Lhuys had already said that no one was ready at this time for a revival of the Eastern Question.[3]

There was no Power to whom this statement more clearly applied than to Austria. As Mensdorff expressed it, 'the new complication in the Danubian Principalities is from the point of view of Austria the more regrettable in that it comes at a moment when our attention ought to be directed above all things on the affairs of Germany in which the adventurous policy of Count Bismarck threatens to provoke a crisis'.[4] It was all very well for Prokesch to urge his government that now was the occasion to 'strike the nationalist humbug on the head';[5] the government of Vienna faced problems far more formidable than the chance of setting a Balkan state in order. Confronted by the probability of war with Prussia over Schleswig-Holstein and the possibility that Italy would lend adhesion to Bismarck's policy in order to play the ghoulish role of seizing Venetia from her helplessness, Austria could not well afford to make unnecessary enemies, and must, as Mensdorff frankly stated to Metternich, pursue an attitude of cautious conciliation.[6] If France was resolved to perpetuate the union of the Principalities, then Vienna, despite her long career of opposition to the principle and her literal adhesion to the firman of 1861, must now accept that principle as a point of departure. But how far did France mean to go? asked Mensdorff of Metternich.[7] Much as Austria needed to keep Napoleon passive during her present struggle with Prussia, she could not afford, by seconding his plan of a foreign prince, to make an unnecessary enemy of Russia. In fact, if the truth were told, Austria did not want French

---

[1] Goltz deduced that his expressions in favour of a foreign prince had, in fact, the object of making sure of union: Goltz to Bismarck, no. 111, Mar. 18, *Reichsarchiv, Turkei*, vol. 31.

[2] Cowley to Clarendon, no. 343, Mar. 20, F.O. 27/1613, and no. 397, Mar. 31, F.O. 27/1614. His first declaration to that effect was made at the session of Mar. 19. He said, however, that he would not agree to the exclusion of the question from the Conference without knowing its ultimate decisions. This, of course, would keep the way open for a reconsideration of the question.

[3] Goltz to Bismarck, no. 111.

[4] Mensdorff to Prokesch, Mar. 4, Staatsarchiv, XII/84.

[5] Prokesch to Mensdorff, Mar. 2, private, *ibid.*

[6] Mensdorff to Metternich, Mar. 1, no. 1, *ibid.*, IX/83.

[7] Mensdorff to Metternich, Mar. 1, no. 2, *ibid.*

policy to triumph, but only that she herself might not be thought in any way as trying to obstruct it. Accordingly, 'being able to combat union only indirectly', she would fain submit the question to a vote of the Principalities and thus avoid a possible break with France;[1] while Metternich (going beyond his official instructions) went so far as to say that union might be tolerated.[2] At the same time, Mensdorff secretly encouraged Russia to second the Turks in standing on the Protocol[3]—a move which, if successful, would realize Austria's wishes, while another Power, more able than she to assume the responsibility, would pluck her chestnuts from the fire. It was, of course, a vain hope, since France, as we have seen, had easily squelched the Turks; and so Austria was doomed to remain a passive and troubled witness of events she could not prevent.

It is interesting to notice that Prussia's view of the problem was somewhat analogous to Austria's. Bismarck had long ago remarked that Prussia had no interest in the Eastern Question,[4] and in this respect she had the advantage over Austria, but, like her rival, she viewed the Conference as merely a sort of side-show to the spectacle in central Europe. For both Powers the stake was always French neutrality, but Austria's role was purely negative, while Bismarck, not having any interests on the Danube, and never averse from fishing in troubled waters, was consequently much more ready to align himself with the Emperor[5]—a policy which Prussia had steadily pursued ever since 1856 and which had borne its fruit in the famous interview of Biarritz. 'Say that we are ready for anything,' he telegraphed to the Prussian ambassador on March 14, 'and we are actually so as soon as a Prussian interest becomes involved.'[6] In a letter which he wrote the same day the minister president explained that it was 'not under the circumstances to our interest that the Conference should come to an end quickly and unanimously'.[7] Perhaps, indeed, he could use the crisis as a diversion against Austria. 'We must manage,' he telegraphed on the 15th, 'that she will not dare to withdraw all her troops (from the Roumanian frontier). Manœuvre with foreign prince and (the principle of) heredity in such a manner as will appear to you to attain that end.'[8] But Bismarck cautioned Goltz not to grasp the

[1] Mensdorff to Metternich, Mar. 22, telg., *ibid.*
[2] Goltz to Bismarck, no. 115, Mar. 19, *Reichsarchiv, Turkei*, vol. 31. Cf. Metternich to Mensdorff, no. 14 (error for no. 11), Mar. 20, Staatsarchiv, IX/81.
[3] Mensdorff to Revertera, Mar. 29, *ibid.*, x/53.
[4] Bismarck to Brassier, no. 35, Dec. 10, 1865, *Reichsarchiv, Turkei*, vol. 31.
[5] Bismarck to Goltz, no. 75, Mar. 8, 1866,*i bid.*
[6] Bismarck to Goltz, Mar. 14, telg., *ibid.*
[7] Bismarck to Goltz, Mar. 14, *Die gesammelten Werke*, vol. v, pp. 403 ff.
[8] Bismarck to Goltz, Mar. 15, telg., *ibid.*, p. 405.

initiative;[1] and when his minister reported that Drouyn de Lhuys had told him confidentially that France would declare for a foreign prince and hoped for Prussia's support,[2] Bismarck told him he must be on his guard, as this might simply be a 'conference manœuvre', and the best way to meet it, he told the ambassador, was not to show Prussia's hand, but to express the wish that a Prussian interest might be considered in reciprocity.[3] This meant, no doubt, that if Drouyn de Lhuys meant to press the question of a foreign prince Bismarck would hedge a little until he had time to fathom the French design and sense the reaction of the other Powers to it. Of course, the whole range of Bismarck's reasoning pivoted on the question of how the Powers would view his quarrel with Austria over the Duchies. He must therefore be on his guard against taking a position that would have the effect of offending Russia, and, on that ground, it was important that he should know what France intended.[4] Pursuant to these instructions, Goltz would gladly have done what he could to lengthen the debates and accentuate the friction at the Conference, but he told Bismarck frankly that he could not oppose what would be in the general interest without putting his government in 'the awkward position of seeming intentionally to cause complications', and that anyway the effort would be fruitless.[5] If Goltz failed to exert an appreciable influence on the Conference, he at least carefully noted the groupings of the Powers,[6] and gave to France that restrained support which was intended. He told the Emperor that Prussia would support him up to the point of a foreign prince, but that, if this should involve her unpleasantly with Russia, she would expect a reciprocal favour. When, however, he learned that Russia was decidedly more opposed to a foreign prince than France was in favour of such a scheme, he merely followed the policy of seconding Drouyn's moves.[7] It was, on the whole, a moderate policy and a waiting one; and though Goltz cannot be said to have shown conspicuous acumen, he at least displayed that quality of reserve which Bismarck always required before he planned a decisive stroke.

The policy of Russia was, as usual, hard to fathom, since Gortchakoff was generally opportunist, but so violent in his feelings that one never knew how much was a passing mood. Bismarck seemed to feel that Russian policy would have been best served by union,

---

[1] Bismarck to Goltz, Mar. 14, *Die gesammelten Werke*, vol. v, pp. 403 ff.
[2] Goltz to Bismarck, Mar. 12, telg., *Reichsarchiv, Turkei*, vol. 31.
[3] Bismarck to Goltz, no. 92, Mar. 14, *ibid*.   [4] *Ibid*.
[5] Goltz to Bismarck, no. 112, Mar. 18, *ibid*.
[6] Goltz to Bismarck, no. 93, Mar. 11, *ibid*.
[7] Goltz to Bismarck, no. 117, Mar. 19, *ibid*. Napoleon had said his attitude was 'correct': Goltz to Bismarck, no. 111, Mar. 18, *ibid*.

since a strong state would be founded, which would naturally be expected to gravitate towards Russia;[1] but no such practical view seemed to enter Gortchakoff's mind. With unblushing inconsistency he completely reversed the position which he had taken so conspicuously at the Conference of 1858. Not only did he become the most determined opponent of a foreign prince, but he plainly desired, by emphasizing the alleged separatist tendencies in Moldavia—which his government was strongly suspected of fomenting—to bring about the dissolution of union.[2] It was only too clear that he had wished the application of the Protocol, and Clarendon was convinced that 'Russia is determined even at the risk of war to oppose the appointment of a foreign prince'.[3] Looking at the matter less gravely, the Prussian ambassador noted a marked distrust of Napoleon, as well as a regret that the Conference was holding its sessions in Paris, since the Emperor, with his usual 'tenacity' (so St. Petersburg read him!), was likely to prolong its meetings and obtain a solution which would not be to Russia's interest.[4] Without the Russian dispatches to aid us, one can only conjecture the motives of Russian policy, but it would seem that if Gortchakoff wanted to reduce the Principalities to the position which had been granted them under the Convention, it was because he hoped that by their disruption to revive Russian influence—an object which, under union, had proved quite unattainable in competition with France. And as he was not quite daring enough to try to get a Russian chosen for the vacant throne at Bucharest, it was obviously contrary to Russia's interest to allow any prince to be installed whom Austria or the Western Powers might seem to favour. Even when Bibesco was later suggested, at a moment when some of the Powers were talking of a native prince, Gortchakoff vetoed the selection as a satellite of Vienna.[5] It is difficult, on the whole, to escape the conclusion that Russia would have welcomed a state of anarchy in the Principalities, which might, if war broke out between Austria and Prussia, enable her to enforce her interests in these lands with a strong hand.

[1] Bismarck to Goltz, Mar. 20, *Die gesammelten Werke*, vol. v, pp. 267 ff.
[2] To Talleyrand he said that he had never been an enthusiastic partisan of union, but had yielded to it merely to show his 'amiable disposition', and that the circumstances were now very different from what they had been in 1858. Talleyrand believed that his opposition to union was inspired by the fear that the Venetia exchange plan might be pressed: Talleyrand to Lhuys, Mar. 21, *Origines*, vol. viii, no. 1927.
[3] Clarendon to Layard, Mar. 10 (or 16?), Layard Papers, Brit. Mus., Add. MS. 38992.
[4] Redern to Bismarck, no. 21, Mar. 15, *Reichsarchiv, Turkei*, vol. 31.
[5] Redern to Bismarck, Apr. 15, telg., *ibid.* Austria became a partisan of this candidate, probably in the hope of heading off a foreign prince, but Goltz doubted if the favour which Napoleon was supposed to have accorded his candidature was really sincere: Goltz to Bismarck, no. 169, Apr. 12, *ibid.*

But, whatever the clue to Russian policy, the government of St. Petersburg was not long in revealing its attitude towards the paramount questions. At the second meeting of the Conference, March 19, the Russian plenipotentiary proposed that the Convention be regarded as the basis of deliberations. Goltz and Drouyn de Lhuys promptly objected on the ground that the Convention had been nullified by subsequent acts, and the French minister reminded the Conference that Russia herself had been a party to the reservation to the firman of 1861—thus assuming that the whole question would be re-examined at the close of Couza's reign. Cowley remarked that that was, in fact, why the Conference had met; and Budberg thereupon called up the Turkish proposal which had been made at the previous meeting. This meant, of course, that the question of a foreign prince would be aired, though Budberg went back to article xii of the Convention, which had stipulated the choice of a native as hospodar in each province. Safvet, for his part, was uncertain whether he ought to take part in the debates, inasmuch as Turkey's participation in the Conference was conditional on the exclusion of a foreign prince, but he seemed finally to come to the conclusion that he might at least take its decisions under advisement. The question of a foreign prince having thus been injected into the debate, Drouyn de Lhuys read a letter from the resident agent of the Principalities, stating that the Principalities wanted a foreign prince, and that two commissioners had been appointed to receive a hearing at the Conference. Although this privilege was speedily denied by the Conference, and little weight was attached to the import of the agent's message, the plenipotentiaries of France, Prussia, and Italy were all agreed that the inhabitants certainly wanted union, and when Drouyn de Lhuys affirmed that, in view of the opposition to a foreign prince, his government would not insist upon this measure, provided only that union were retained, the Conference agreed at once to postpone further discussion of the weightier question. This opened the way for a consideration of the principle of union itself. When Safvet thereupon demanded that union should be considered as dissolved by the dethronement of Couza, Budberg declared that his government wished that the populations of the Principalities should have a chance to vote on the question, and affirmed that in his opinion the great majority of Moldavians were in favour of separation. Drouyn de Lhuys expressed his opinion that a vote was unnecessary, as the populations had already expressed themselves more than once, and he artfully quoted the arguments for union to be found in that Russian instrument, the *Règlement organique*. Since the majority of the plenipotentiaries seemed, however, to favour a fresh expression of the wishes of the

Moldo-Wallachians, Drouyn de Lhuys did not persist in his disapproval; but the Conference only found itself slipping more deeply into the mire, as the question now arose: how was the sentiment of the Principalities to be consulted?[1]

The question of what the Principalities really wanted and how their wishes could become known had already been a subject of discussion between French and British diplomats. Cowley had suggested that, as the Convention had given each principality the right to choose its own hospodar, one could soon ascertain whether they wanted the same man. Drouyn de Lhuys had, of course, no difficulty in responding to this point by simply recalling that the mechanism of two assemblies had long since disappeared. The British ambassador then rejoined that if a single assembly elected the hospodar, the Moldavians would be in a minority, and a Wallachian would therefore be chosen—probably against their will. This contention raised the whole question of how the Moldavians might freely express themselves. When Drouyn de Lhuys shifted his ground and offered to support any candidate whom Great Britain should nominate, provided that she, in turn, would support union, Cowley replied that his government 'could not undertake so responsible and so invidious a task'.[2] There was apparently no escaping the alternative of giving the Moldavians the special privilege of registering their wishes; and the present undercurrent for separation in that province was the basis of Russia's hopes. Budberg now proposed at the present meeting that either the Moldavian members of the present assembly should move to Jassy for a poll on the question of union, or that, if that were disapproved of, two separate assemblies should be elected to that end. Goltz then suggested that new elections should be called for a single assembly (Metternich had wanted the Conference to set up a new provisional government to conduct them),[3] but as no unanimity seemed at present possible, it was decided at Drouyn's instance to refer five alternatives to the various cabinets: (1) Should the present assembly be allowed to divide for voting purposes if the Moldavians desired it? (2) Should this procedure be followed without ascertaining the wishes of the Moldavians? (3) Should the Moldavians repair to Jassy for this poll? (4) Should new elections be called for a single assembly to meet at Bucharest? (5) Should two assemblies be convoked, one at Bucharest, and one at Jassy?[4]

[1] Protocol no. 2; Goltz to Bismarck, no. 117, Mar. 19, *Reichsarchiv, Turkei*, vol. 31.

[2] Cowley to Clarendon, no. 312, Mar. 13, F.O. 27/1613.

[3] This proposal had been made just before the session (the circumstances are not told), but it was decisively opposed by Drouyn de Lhuys, Goltz, Cowley, and Budberg: Goltz to Bismarck, no. 112, Mar. 18, *Reicharchiv, Turkei*, vol. 31.

[4] Protocol no. 2; Cowley to Clarendon, no. 323, Mar. 20, F.O. 27/1613; Goltz to Bismarck, no. 117.

Metternich seemed to prefer the second proposal, as the poll could then be undertaken under the supervision of the consuls[1] (and this, of course, would obviate the uncertainty of a new election); Bismarck adhered to the fourth, since, judging from Goltz's reports, he believed that it would not be eventually opposed by France, and that Russia seemed likely to favour it.[2] Drouyn de Lhuys had, indeed, expressed assent to a new test of the sentiments of the Principalities—the assembly, if necessary, he said, could meet in a neutral place; but Goltz had deduced from the conversation that if repeated polls should be insisted upon, France would then demand that the question of a foreign prince should be submitted to a vote as well.[3] It is easy to see that French patience was beginning to show a strain; and it is hard to see how six Powers could be expected to unite on any one of the five alternatives. In the meantime, nothing had been done to dispose of the actual bogy. While Clarendon was regretting that the Principalities had not been told that the Powers were unanimous against a foreign prince,[4] Budberg was declaring that under no circumstances would Russia consent to such a scheme, and when Goltz asked him what she would do if the Principalities installed one in defiance of the Conference, he answered that she would not hesitate to 'occupy them militarily'.[5] Making full allowance for a Russian bluff, one can fairly well discern on what thin ice the Powers were skating.

But the question of what method should be employed in consulting public sentiment in the Principalities was speedily decided in an unexpected manner. The provisional government resolved to dissolve the existing assembly, and gave as its reasons the imperious and obstructive conduct of the deputies and the need to prevent the country from falling into anarchy.[6] The Prussian consul gave as the real explanation the dissatisfaction of the Left, who felt that their plan of a new constitution would not succeed in going through the present assembly, and the selfish interests of the Right, among whom there were many pretenders to the throne who doubted if they could get a sufficient following from a legislature chosen under Couza.[7] But the fact had been evident for some time that the government could not work with the assembly, and it was probably true that the government itself was too heterogeneous to work for harmony. What was evidently needed was a strong hand to prevent the ship of state from foundering on the rocks of radical experiments or private intrigue. And it is hard

---

[1] Metternich to Mensdorff, no. 12 D, Mar. 22, Staatsarchiv, IX/81.
[2] Bismarck to Goltz, Mar. 29, telg., *Reicharchiv*, vol. 31.
[3] Goltz to Lhuys, no. 121, Mar. 20, *ibid.*
[4] Clarendon to Cowley, no. 351, Mar. 22, F.O. 27/1603.
[5] Goltz to Bismarck, no. 115.   [6] See p. 500.
[7] St. Pierre to Bismarck, no. 21, Mar. 31, *Reichsarchiv, Turkei*, vol. 31.

to believe that any one but a hospodar from without could play that difficult role.

At all events, the dissolution of the chambers was hardly to be condemned, and no one as yet divined its ultimate purpose. It is also to the credit of the government's desire for peace that the King of the Belgians was urged—though, unhappily, quite in vain—to persuade the Count of Flanders to change his mind.[1] Perhaps the crisis was more serious than onlookers realized; for Eder credits the statement that the Left had even in mind to proclaim a republic, with Golesco or Bratiano at its head, though subsequent events were fortunately to change their plans.[2] In the meantime, whether it is true (as Green reports) that Rosetti and his party were now masters of the situation, it was evident that the Left was still determined that the time had come for liberalizing the State, and immediately after the dissolution of the legislature Rosetti announced that the new assembly to be chosen would be a constituent body.[3] Doubtless, the programme thus implied seemed ominous for the moment; but, assuming that the new assembly had been legally called in the first place, there was nothing to prevent its altering the constitution (the *Acte additionel* having clearly granted such a right), and, anyway, it was not at all certain that the Left would win the elections. A far more serious danger was from an unpaid soldiery, for the 'patriotic loan' having failed to yield results, the treasury was still in dire straits.[4] Perhaps the only thing that prevented a military revolt was the government's policy of taking steps to avert the danger of invasion, a Turkish corps of 30,000–40,000 men having already encamped across the Danube.[5] Hearing that the Turks were concentrating their forces for an invasion, Clarendon sent a warning telegram to Constantinople.[6] But there was no evidence that the Porte ever seriously thought of defying the protocols and acting without the concurrence of the Powers, and the sending of forces to the Danube had probably no other object than to give these bumptious vassals a sight of the suzerain's teeth and perhaps to scare the Conference into taking drastic measures. At all events, in giving the provisional government a chance to invoke the national spirit and set the

[1] Balan to Bismarck, no. 34, Apr. 3, *ibid.* The King refused to grant an official audience to the deputation sent to make this request, and told its members that his brother's decision was as free as it was decisive, and that it would not be well, anyway, to anticipate the Conference's decisions.

[2] Eder to Mensdorff, no. 55, Apr. 15, Staatsarchiv, xxxviii/148. Their plans were ultimately changed, Eder said, by a message from Paris that Napoleon suggested Charles von Hohenzollern as prince.

[3] Green to Lyons, no. 26, Apr. 10, F.O. 78/1921.

[4] Green to Clarendon, no. 46, Mar. 28, F.O. 78/1920.

[5] St. Pierre to Bismarck, no. 20, Mar. 24, *Reichsarchiv, Turkei*, vol. 31.

[6] F.O. to Lyons, Mar. 4, telg., F.O. 78/1903.

army to work, the Porte was really doing the Principalities a service.

None the less, the present uncertainty of the drift of political currents in the Principalities was ground enough for anxiety at Paris. Much disturbed by the communication of a particularly gloomy telegram from Green[1] (dispatched before the news of the provisional government's decision), Cowley advised Drouyn de Lhuys to call an immediate meeting of the Conference instead of waiting until April 2, as had been planned.[2] So a session was called together on March 31; and Drouyn de Lhuys was able to acquaint the diplomats with the definite fact of the assembly's dissolution. Judging from Cowley's account of the meeting, deliberations were somewhat strained. Budberg said that he was waiting for new instructions, and Drouyn de Lhuys felt that further delay was inadmissible. Though no one was found to approve the un-authorized action of the provisional government, Drouyn de Lhuys affirmed frankly that the Conference itself was to blame for having come to no decision,[3] and he then took occasion to harangue the assembled diplomats on the merits of a foreign prince. There were, he said, three courses open to the Conference: to let the Moldo-Wallachians dispose of their own fate (this would be France's own preference), to treat the dissolution as a *fait accompli* and continue discussions, or to enforce the resolutions of the Conference—a step which would open the way to dangerous complications.[4] Later he told Cowley that it was a choice between assuming that the provisional government had simply forestalled the Conference's decision (in which case the Conference might go on with its deliberations) and adjourning the Conference and letting matters take their course.[5] In any event, as Budberg and Cowley were without instructions, no decision of any moment could be reached at the present meeting. Though most of the diplomats seemed not unwilling to accept, at least tacitly, what they could not help, Cowley insisted that any such attitude was much too great a derogation of dignity.[6] Accordingly the Conference adjourned till April 4.[7]

Undoubtedly the action of the provisional government had fairly brought it home to these doctrinaire diplomats not only that a

[1] This was Green's telegram of Mar. 19, already noted (p. 514).
[2] Goltz to Bismarck, no. 142, Mar. 30, *Reichsarchiv, Turkei*, vol. 31.
[3] Cowley to Clarendon, no. 397, Mar. 31, F.O. 27/1614.
[4] Protocol no. 4.
[5] Cowley to Clarendon, no. 406, Apr. 2, F.O. 27/1614.
[6] Cowley to Clarendon, no. 397. After the meeting Cowley set to work on the draft of a pronouncement which he hoped to induce his colleagues to accept, and which, to that end, should 'necessarily be vague', but, according to his plan, should be accompanied by an 'identic' dispatch to the consuls: Cowley to Clarendon, no. 409, Apr. 3, F.O. 27/1614.   [7] Protocol no. 4.

revolution was in progress, but that somehow distance greatly diminished the sanctity with which the Conference was supposed to be regarded. If, as Drouyn de Lhuys heard, the assembly at Bucharest had been deposed because it strove to be constituent, it was perhaps equally true, as others heard, that the new assembly, in turn, was to be entrusted with the making of a constitution. If such were the case, the august Protecting Powers were even more eloquently snubbed. Whether or not the news from Bucharest had a sobering effect, Goltz seemed to feel that Budberg was less opposed to a foreign prince, for in the course of the debate on this expedient he had asked—'What foreign prince?'[1] When, finally, the Russian diplomat received his instructions, he was authorized to state that, while Russia would on no account favour a foreign prince, she would not object to union under a native if the Principalities desired it. This proviso signified, of course, that the new assembly should divide, in order to let the Moldavian contingent vote at Jassy; but Cowley, to whom Budberg imparted his instructions, did not believe that the Russian plenipotentiary would insist upon this point in the face of the opposition it would encounter.[2] While it may be suspected that the government of St. Petersburg was still counting heavily on the effect of its encouragement to the separatists in Moldavia, it was nevertheless significant that Russia was contemplating a possible acceptance of the principle of union. Was it perhaps that Gortchakoff was concentrating all his forces to defend his last trench? Clarendon, who had never openly fought the retention of union, was as much as ever opposed to a foreign prince, and felt that the Conference should make its authority felt at Bucharest. But the only means he could think of to bring this desired result was to suggest that the Conference should send some admonitory message to the provisional government.[3] As this had been tried before, one may conclude that Clarendon's statesmanship was bankrupt for the moment. When the Conference met on April 4, Cowley had no other advice to offer than to leave to the provisional government the responsibility of its acts and to send an 'identic' telegram to the consuls. We shall not dwell on the debates of what was the longest and most futile session of the Conference. The British proposal was adopted, and in six 'identic' telegrams the Conference shook its warning finger at the Principalities.[4]

The weakness of the Protecting Powers was never more fully

[1] Goltz to Bismarck, no. 146, Mar. 31, *Reicharchiv, Turkei*, vol. 31.
[2] Cowley to Clarendon, no. 412, Apr. 3, F.O. 27/1614. Cowley was certainly right in his prediction. Budberg proposed this separation; Drouyn de Lhuys declared that such a proposal was too late; and Budberg accordingly yielded.
[3] La Tour to Lhuys, Apr. 3, *Origines*, vol. viii, nos. 1997 and 1998.
[4] Protocol no. 5.

manifested than in the resolution of the Conference to adjourn pending further tidings from Bucharest and in the demand of one or another of the plenipotentiaries to reconvene. Cowley signified his utter hopelessness of any decisive action being taken when he wrote in a private letter, 'I am not arguing for a foreign prince, but, the more I bear the question in mind, the more I become reconciled to the idea; (for) all I can say is you cannot prevent its being entertained'.[1] Only his sympathy for the Porte seems to have curbed the British diplomat's official conduct, but no one could put faith any longer in the Conference. Instead of seeking any longer to enact a settlement or to guide the course of events, the Powers were simply delivering the initiative into the hands of the Principalities. When the Porte, considerably agitated, demanded to know the reason for the suspension of the sessions, Cowley reminded Safvet that 'the Conference was not master of the situation and (that) it was far better, therefore, to remain a spectator than to attempt to act'.[2] In some quarters, however, it was felt that time was working to the advantage of France and the Moldo-Wallachians. Though Mensdorff regretfully accepted the *fait accompli*, Metternich sharply blamed Budberg, whose opposition to union had resulted, he said, in strengthening France's desire for a foreign prince.[3] Of course, the Power most dissatisfied was the Porte; and Ali, on hearing Drouyn's arguments for a foreign prince, told Moustier that while the Powers might impose this evil on the Porte, the Turks themselves would have nothing to do with it, and instead would withdraw from the Conference.[4] We do not know, of course, whether Drouyn's revived interest in a foreign prince was prompted from some underground channel, but for a few days longer the world was without suspicion that France had stacked the cards—nor can we actually prove that as yet she had really done so. Doubtless it was to make a show of moderation that Napoleon hit upon the idea of recommending the election of a native hospodar for four years[5] (he expressed his preference for Bibesco, who was an officer in the French army),[6] and went so far as to send a new consul, Baron d'Avril, to Bucharest to make this recommendation.[7] Yet he must have known that he was demanding

---

[1] Cowley to Layard, Apr. 9, Layard Papers, Brit. Mus., Add. MS. 39119.
[2] Cowley to Clarendon, no. 443, Apr. 9, F.O. 1615.
[3] Metternich to Mensdorff, no. 15 E, Apr. 9, Staatsarchiv, IX/81.
[4] Moustier to Lhuys, Apr. 11, *Doc. dip.*, *1866*, p. 149.
[5] Cowley to Clarendon, no. 451, Apr. 12, F.O. 27/1615. As the idea found favour with Austria, Goltz was somewhat worried for fear she had suggested it to Napoleon, in which case the two Powers might be in closer relations than Prussia liked to contemplate: Goltz to Bismarck, no. 169, Apr. 12, *Reichsarchiv*, *Turkei*, vol. 31.
[6] *Ibid.*
[7] Lhuys to Avril, Apr. 13, F.O. 27/1619. These instructions (also found in the French archives) were communicated to the British government.

the impossible, and it was the possible and probable that France really wanted. As we have already remarked, the game was in the hands of the Moldo-Wallachians, and they were more than ever convinced of it. The *Roumanul* published a telegram from Paris that the Conference had left it to the Principalities to work out their own salvation. Were they then, after all, to have a foreign prince?[1]

There is still some obscurity shrouding the origins of the Hohenzollern candidature to the throne of the Principalities, but there is no reason to doubt the story that it originated in Paris. However much Bismarck may have welcomed the prospect of a Hohenzollern ruling on the other side of Austria, there is not the least trace of any attempt on his part to put it into the heads of the Moldo-Wallachians or to place it even by indirect channels before Napoleon. From evidence that can hardly be doubted it appears that the idea was first proposed by Madame Cornu, an intimate friend of Napoleon, to the Wallachian emissary, Bratiano, who, as we have noticed, had gone to Paris in 1865 to find a candidate for the throne from which it was planned to expel Couza.[2] Bratiano could not well have wanted the younger Bibesco, and it is doubtful if he had anything to do with the desultory interest in that *boyard's* aspirations. It is rather doubtful, in view of Napoleon's attitude, if he had suggested the Count of Flanders as the possible successor of Couza. Ghika said later that, in nominating Flanders, the provisional government had been mainly concerned with espousing a principle, and, manifestly, there had been no assurance beforehand that the Count would accept the doubtful honour. During most of March there is no hint that the provisional government, apart from renewed efforts at Brussels, had any candidate in view; and the plight of the Moldo-Wallachians began to assume a comic aspect. Several obscure persons applied for the job of ruling the Principalities—a shoemaker of Munich, who would fain be content with a very modest civil list, and a French captain, who would promise to relieve a people in distress, and so on.[3] Then on March 24 came a telegram from Balatchano, the Moldo-Wallachian agent at Paris, that a likely candidate had been found—a fact which was confirmed two days later by a telegram from Bratiano.[4]

The circumstances, as revealed in Madame Cornu's letters, are as follows. Madame Cornu appears to have been closely attached to the Sigmaringen branch of the Hohenzollern family, represented by Prince Anthony and his three sons, Leopold (afterwards famous for his candidature to the throne of Spain), Charles, and Anthony.[5]

---

[1] Green to Lyons, no. 26, Apr. 10, F.O. 78/1920.   [2] pp. 475–6.
[3] Tillos to Moustier, Apr. 11, annex to Moustier's no. 44, *Aff. étr., Turquie,* vol. 367.   [4] Damé, *op. cit.,* p. 156.
[5] It is interesting to notice that a daughter of Anthony later married the Count of Flanders, erstwhile nominee for the throne of the Principalities.

On meeting Bratiano in the cosmopolitan society of Paris, and having learned the object of his mission (which by this time was possibly official), she suggested that a member of this family would be the fittest choice. They were closely allied to the Emperor (Prince Anthony had married a Beauharnais[1]), and he was very fond of them. It was true that neither Anthony nor his eldest son would want to become a vassal of the Sultan, but the second son would doubtless be willing to make the sacrifice. She did not deem it expedient, she said, to broach the subject to the Emperor, who, 'being a member of the Conference, would answer me by a refusal'. 'But, if you anticipate him,' she continued, 'he will strive —I do not doubt—to prevent the Conference's resistance from being carried to extremes.'[2] Much impressed with the lady's proposals, Bratiano went at once to Düsseldorf to woo the heart of a Hohenzollern.

The Hohenzollern-Sigmaringens were a branch of the Hohenzollern family who reigned at Berlin. Up to 1849 Anthony had been a petty duke of the little principality of Sigmaringen in southern Germany; but he was possessed of such a deep devotion to Prussia that in 1849 he ceded its sovereignty to his kinsman, Frederick William IV, elder brother and predecessor of the present king, William I. Soon after this astonishing renunciation he entered the service of Prussia, and became for a time the president of the Prussian ministry. Despite his marriage with an adopted daughter of Napoleon I, he was not by any means animated by sympathy with France, and was one of the most ardent members of that patriotic German society, the *Nationalverein*. Unlike most Prussian officials, however, he was fairly liberal in his sentiments, and if his connexion with France did not affect his personal affiliations, they were at least something of an asset at the present juncture. And Anthony was certainly ambitious. Having secured a Portuguese princess for his eldest son, would he not regard it as a welcome stroke of fate that a throne should be offered to 'young Karl'?

Charles von Hohenzollern was a soldierly youth, just under twenty-seven years of age. While not a person of exceptional attainments, he had been given the usual advantages accruing to a scion of a royal house, and had applied himself in whatever he had undertaken with exemplary industry. With his natural diligence, in addition to a sturdy body and martial tastes, he became a capable artillery officer and served with distinction in the war with Denmark. Visits to Italy, Portugal, and Algeria gave him personal knowledge of some of the world outside the radius of

---

[1] Stéphanie de Beauharnais, daughter of the late Duke of Baden and adopted daughter of Napoleon I. [2] Ollivier, *op. cit.*, vol. viii, pp. 71–2.

Prussia's interests, while the prominence of his father in Prussian official life brought him somewhat in touch with politics and its problems. Not his least important experience was a visit to France, where the Emperor admitted him to the circle of his intimates; and the stalwart young officer had his taste of the seductive culture of the Second Empire. One might always say of Charles that he possessed a strong sense of duty and a patience and tenacity that never allowed either a blunder or a misfortune to turn him from his path. But Time, of course, was yet to test his mettle. 'It is so difficult to be a prince!' Thus the young Charles had written when, a child of nine, he had heard of the revolutionary movement in Sigmaringen[1]—the movement which had probably contributed to his father's abdication. Was he now to test the truth of these words by personal experience?

Whatever the qualifications of Charles for the office for which he was designated, he was no more than a name to the people of the Principalities—to most of them a name soon to be heard for the first time.[2] At the time when the assembly was dissolved and when it was announced that the elections would be held April 9–12, no mention had been made of the choice of any prince, though it is reasonable to infer that Bratiano had had authority to tell Anthony that the government had the intention of placing his son in nomination. The final decision to nominate Charles appears to have been taken on April 11 on the return of Bratiano to Bucharest.[3] Bratiano had, no doubt, related the fact that he had paid his visit to Düsseldorf; that he had been fortunate enough to find Prince Charles himself there; that no decision was taken,[4] though it was evident that the proposal had been cordially received; and that Balatchano had been told in an audience with Napoleon that France was partial to the choice.[5] This was about as much as Bratiano could have told, though he may well have exaggerated the degree of France's interest and the prospect of the Prince's acceptance. On the 11th Ghika telegraphed to Balatchano, inquiring whether Charles accepted the offer—in which case his nomination would be submitted to the country; and the same day (it looks as if an answer had not been awaited) a proclamation was issued, calling the nation to vote in a plebiscite on the nomination of Charles Louis of Hohenzollern, 'who will reign under the name of Charles I'. The proclamation was cleverly worded. It pretended

---

[1] Lindenberg, *König Karl von Rumanien*, p. 12.

[2] Eder to Mensdorff, no. 54, Apr. 14, Staatsarchiv, xxxviii/148.

[3] *Charles I, Roi de Roumanie: Chronique, actes, documents* (ed. Sturdza), vol. i, p. 80. (This will be henceforth cited as 'Sturdza, *op. cit.*')

[4] See Charles I, *Aus dem Leben*, vol. i, pp. 3–4.

[5] Eder to Mensdorff, no. 55, Apr. 15, Staatsarchiv, xxxviii/148. Eder seemed to believe that the government was overborne by Bratiano.

that the Powers had approved greatly 'the incident of February 23',
and that the same Powers demanded a strong, not a weak and
demoralized state, on the Danube, and that the nation had already
demonstrated that it wanted a foreign prince as a means of consolidation.[1] One might feel that the form of its wording was
designed for a double audience.

It cannot be said that this pronouncement was a bolt out of a
clear sky, as Balatchano's account of Napoleon's assurances had
become known, though few but the initiated had given it much
weight.[2] Up to this time, however, the government had guarded
the secret of its activities so jealously that even the Prussian consul
had not known of them. Both he and Green now believed that
fear of an imminent crisis in Moldavia (this was just before the
Easter riot) had induced the government to make the proclamation
when it did.[3] The suggestion is plausible, and such may have been
the chief motive of the government in picking this particular
moment for the plebiscite; but it is obvious that, having called a
general election, it may well have felt that this was the appropriate
occasion for placing a programme before the nation; indeed its
position was hardly strong enough to warrant its facing the
electorate without one.[4] It is true that Charles had not yet accepted
the proffered honour, but surely the prospect of its acceptance
would be stronger when the nation had acclaimed him through a
plebiscite. In all such tactics one may divine the shrewd judgement
of John Ghika. It was assumed that Charles *would* accept the
throne,[5] and the proclamation had been worded in that sense.
Meanwhile, doubtless in order to sustain the national spirit, a
most bellicose attitude was taken towards the myth of danger from
invasion, though to competent observers the actual condition of
the army made such action seem ridiculous. There were, finally,
of course, the sensibilities of Europe to reckon with, but that was
nothing new. From the broad standpoint of carrying on the
national revolution, the announcement of the plebiscite was simply
one more crossing of the Rubicon. The nomination of Flanders
had signalized a challenge to the European protectorate, and the
present government would have lost its *raison d'être* if it had not
found another foreign prince. There was at times a little anxiety
over what the Powers might do, but, after all, if it were really
certain that Napoleon was on their side, the collective will of the

[1] Sturdza, *op. cit.*, vol. i, pp. 80–1.
[2] St. Pierre to Bismarck, no. 25, Apr. 14, *Reichsarchiv*, vol. 31.
[3] *Ibid.*; Green to Clarendon, Apr. 13, telg., F.O. 78/1920.
[4] Eder said that the government did not really want Charles, because too many
of its members were candidates themselves, but that the reason why it allowed
itself to be manipulated by Bratiano and a small group of radicals was a combination of weakness, fear, and cowardice: Eder to Mensdorff, no. 54, Apr. 14,
Staatsarchiv, XXXVIII/148.   [5] *Ibid.*

Protecting Powers was of no moment. Moreover, had not the *Roumanul* stated that the Conference had left the Principalities to their fate?[1] Certainly, if these lands were likely to become a pawn on the European chess-board, such a fear seems never to have entered the heads of Ghika and his colleagues. All they thought of was the solution of the national problem and the safe passing of a grave political crisis. Eder, who sniffed at the idea that so disorganized a nation could be of any peril to Austria, even if placed under a Prussian prince, declared that 'none of the conditions existed for playing seriously a role in the trumped-up adventure of Herr von Bismarck'.[2]

It is now time to inquire what had been the fate of the Hohenzollern candidature, and what really had been Prussia's connexion with the affair. Charles had frankly told Bratiano that he would not let the suzerainty of the Porte become a hindrance, but that he could give no definite answer till the King of Prussia, as head of the family, had been consulted.[3] With that assurance Bratiano returned to Paris and subsequently to Bucharest. Meanwhile Goltz telegraphed to Bismarck that Balatchano had wished the matter to be brought secretly to the attention of the King of Prussia, stating that a formal offer of the crown would be made as soon as it was established that the King would give his consent, and adding that Napoleon seemed to prefer Charles von Hohenzollern to any other German prince.[4] Bismarck's reply was cautious: the King, as head of the family, had written to Anthony to learn his decision, and meanwhile it was scarcely likely that the Prince would take the plunge on his own responsibility.[5] At the same time he sent, without comment, to Anthony (he stated that it was at the King's request) the substance of Goltz's communication.[6] Glad of an opportunity to take the matter up in earnest, Anthony now wrote to Bismarck, assuring him that the candidature had been entirely uninspired by himself or any of his family, and that of course in this matter he must defer to the King.[7] He then wrote a long letter to William to plead his son's cause. He had been surprised, he said, by Bratiano's overture, and had told him that the King,

---

[1] See p. 527. Tillos had written (to Moustier, Apr. 11) that the news that the Conference had resumed its sessions had caused some perturbation. But it was after this that weight was attached to the statement that the Conference had left matters in the hands of the Principalities.

[2] Eder to Mensdorff, no. 55.   [3] *Aus dem Leben*, vol. i, p. 4.

[4] Goltz to Bismarck, Apr. 2, *Reichsarchiv, Turkei*, vol. 31.

[5] Bismarck to Goltz, Apr., *ibid.*

[6] Bismarck to Anthony, Apr. 3, *Die gesammelten Werke*, vol. v, p. 431.

[7] Anthony to Bismarck, Apr. (day omitted), *Reichsarchiv, Turkei*, vol. 31. He said that he appreciated the fact that the King would not want the glorious name of Hohenzollern cheapened (this was doubtless an allusion to the suzerainty of the Sultan), but that the case would be somewhat different if his (Anthony's) second son were to take the throne.

as head of the family, must exclusively decide the matter. He was
assured by Bratiano that only with the express approval of Napoleon
had this matter been broached, and that there was every probability
that Charles would be acclaimed by the Principalities, since they
meant to show the Conference that they were determined to have
a foreign prince. Anthony did not overlook the difficulty of
vassalage to the Porte or the need of battling with Russian or
Turkish influence in the Principalities; but it was a great and noble
task, the fruits of which would reflect credit on the dynasty, and
the country had undoubtedly a great future. Furthermore, the
opportunity was not wholly a personal one, as Prussia would come
to have a cultural influence over these lands, and the new
relationship would redound to her business advantage. Would
the King sanction the proposal, or consider it *non avenue*?[1]
There was no doubt whatever that Anthony and Charles were
ready for the venture, and nothing but the King's scruples and
Bismarck's caution would prevent the undertaking. In the meantime father and son made fresh soundings in Paris by reaching
Drouyn de Lhuys through an indirect channel.[2] It was desirable,
of course, that France should *know* that the Hohenzollerns were
willing!

It was not long, indeed, before France began to send Prussia
a more direct encouragement. Informed by Benedetti of the King's
hesitation, Drouyn de Lhuys sent word that while France could
not herself take the initiative, yet if Prussia could succeed in
modifying the attitude of the Powers, the French government
would support her action.[3] It was also clear that he was lukewarm
on the question of the four-year hospodar (considering it merely an
'expedient' which he would not press upon the Principalities),
and he would vehemently oppose any suggestion of two assemblies.[4]
But Bismarck was not disposed to commit himself—as yet. A more
appropriate course for Charles, he responded to Benedetti, would
be to try to obtain Russia's consent, rather than to engage the King
in a matter in which Prussia could not exert the decisive influence.[5]
The inference was fairly clear. Let France try her blandishments
with Russia. As it was apparently on the following day that

[1] Anthony to William, Apr. 4, *Reichsarchiv, Turkei*, vol. 31. In closing, he
declared that 'all this is in case the chamber at Bucharest should bring one
of my sons as candidate for the crown before the Conference in Paris—which
proposal, however, should be made without any effort and co-operation on my
part'. Though part of this interesting letter is printed in Charles's memoirs, the
arguments of the writer in support of his son's candidature are, curiously enough,
omitted.

[2] *Aus dem Leben*, vol. i, p. 7.

[3] Lhuys to Benedetti, Apr. 13, *Origines*, vol. viii, no. 2054.

[4] Goltz to Bismarck, Apr. 18, *Reichsarchiv, Turkei*, vol. 31.

[5] Benedetti to Lhuys, Apr. 18, *Origines*, no. 2081.

Bismarck made his decisive move, this sidelight on his diplomacy is not devoid of interest.

Perhaps it was the news from Bucharest which had induced Napoleon to take a slightly bolder course.[1] The plebiscite had proceeded according to orders, and no one seemed to have the least doubt of the result.[2] On April 15 a mass meeting was held on the Field of Liberty, and Bratiano had then made a speech, urging the reasons for supporting Charles, among which was the fact that Napoleon was behind him, and that the young Prince belonged to a family which (here Clio hid her face!) had given to France such heroes as Napoleon I and Napoleon III.[3] To give greater solemnity to the occasion, the tribune had been dedicated by a bishop, and the relics of St. Demetrius had been taken from the metropolitan church to be displayed. But although the *Roumanul* had imprudently declared that union must be capped by independence,[4] there was nothing revolutionary in the conduct of the citizens,[5] who thronged, in conformity with Couza's liberal law,[6] to cast their votes. Green remarked upon the fact that no police or soldiers were to be seen anywhere near the voting booths, and that there was no effort whatever to influence the voters.[7] It may or may not be true that the conservatives were dissatisfied and hoped for the intervention of the Powers.[8] Whatever the *arrière-pensées* of those whose self-interest was always greater than their patriotism, there was no evidence of such feelings on the surface. On the other hand, Bratiano was a trifle hasty when he telegraphed to Anthony on the 15th that 'five million Roumanians acclaim Prince Charles, son of your Royal Highness, as their sovereign',[9] for this zealous Wallachian must have been thinking of the total population. Yet in spite of the fact that many of the Wallachian *boyards* had stayed away from the polls,[10] the total number of votes was sufficiently impressive; and when the official figures were finally published it was found that Charles had been acclaimed by 685,969 votes, with only 224 in opposition.[11] In announcing that a deputation was

[1] The proclamation of the plebiscite was, in a sense, an answer to the French proposal of a short-term native hospodar, and it is not unlikely that Napoleon saw that the movement for a foreign prince might now be stealthily taken as a basis for negotiation.
[2] St. Pierre to Bismarck, no. 25, Apr. 14, *Reichsarchiv, Turkei*, vol. 31.
[3] Eder to Mensdorff, no. 59 A, Apr. 21, Staatsarchiv, xxxviii/148.
[4] Eder to Mensdorff, no. 55, Apr. 15, *ibid.*
[5] Eder wrote that Bratiano had warned Rosetti by telegraph before his return that there must be no revolutionary incidents in the Principalities (*ibid.*). A great demonstration had been planned for his reception (Green to Clarendon, no. 50, Apr. 5, F.O. 78/1920), but was apparently called off.
[6] Goering to Bismarck, no. 17, May 7, *Reichsarchiv, Turkei*, vol. 32.
[7] Green to Clarendon, no. 60, Apr. 16, F.O. 78/1920.
[8] Eder to Mensdorff, no. 55, Apr. 15, Staatsarchiv, xxxviii/148.
[9] *Aus dem Leben*, vol. i, p. 9.
[10] Goering to Bismarck, no. 17. [11] Sturdza, *op. cit.*, vol. i, p. 119.

appointed to acquaint him with the result, a proclamation of the minister of the interior declared that the news from abroad 'gives us reason to maintain anew, with full conviction, that the Roumanian nation has only to persist with dignity . . . and firmness . . . and soon its will will be . . . respected'.[1] Yet, in spite of this significant demonstration the British foreign office instructed Green to tell the provisional government that the result was unacceptable, as it would lead to independence, and surely there must be some native with as much honesty and capacity as any foreign prince.[2] As far as having the slightest effect on the course of events in the Principalities was concerned, this brilliant message may be considered the British government's swan-song.

In fact, as far as the question of the Principalities was an issue of international politics, the whole affair may be considered as a contest between France and Russia, with Prussia occupying a pivotal position. One may well believe that Bismarck's decision in the matter would be decisive, but we know enough of that states-man's methods to know that he was in no hurry to show his hand, and that he intended to be in full *rapport* with the international situation before he took a decisive step. Moreover, as was well demonstrated later in the case of the Hohenzollern candidature to the throne of Spain, Bismarck had no easy task in coping with his sovereign's dynastic interests. For the present, certainly, the King held the key to the situation. When it was known that the pro-visional government had placed Charles in nomination (the news somewhat surprised Charles, and seemed to indicate that Bratiano had made sure of Napoleon's backing), there was still no word from Potsdam.[3] But a few days later William wrote him a brief note to the effect that he would do well to remain wholly passive, as Russia and the Porte were opposed to a foreign prince. On the same day Bratiano's telegram arrived, and one can well imagine the emotion with which it was received. To his sovereign Charles wrote a courteous and non-committal answer, but to his father he said that he was resolved to accept the throne, even were it against the will of the Conference.[4] The decision did credit to the young Prince's courage and ambition, but it was perhaps a little impulsive. On the 14th the King had at last broken silence, for Anthony received by special messenger on the 16th the answer to the letter which he had written on the 4th. William explained his delay on the ground that he had been awaiting developments at Paris and Constantinople, and that Bismarck did not deem it necessary to

---

[1] St. Pierre to Bismarck, no. 38, Apr. 28 and annex.

[2] F.O. to Green, no. 11, Apr. 17, F.O. 78/1919. The dispatch wrote of the news of Charles's election having been received.

[3] Anthony received indirect word, however, that William was awaiting news from Paris: *Aus dem Leben*, vol. i, p. 8.   [4] *Ibid.*, pp. 7–10.

hurry a response. No decided action was even now appropriate, the King said, until a formal offer of the crown was received. For his own part, he questioned whether a position of vassalage to the Porte was befitting the dignity of a Hohenzollern. Then there was the effect it would have upon Prussia.

'I understand perfectly,' he said, 'your political conception of the question, namely that Prussia, by not being directly concerned in the question, is the most fitted for allowing a member of its house to be called to the Roumanian rulership without rousing the jealousy of the Great Powers directly concerned. But such a summons would mean that in the future Prussia's position would be assailed by every oriental complication, and could no longer remain neutral, as heretofore.'

And then one really must consider, above all, the attitude of the Powers represented in the Paris Conference. Both the Porte and Russia might be forced unwillingly to assent, but if Russia should unwillingly assent, she would employ ceaseless intrigues in the Principalities; and, in short, however favourable France's attitude might be, the Prince's position would be untenable without Russia's concurrence.[1] The inference was that William was not favourably disposed as a Hohenzollern, and, as King of Prussia, he felt it to be a hazardous and questionable venture. On receiving this letter, Anthony wrote to his son that acceptance, on the score of family discipline, was impracticable.[2] Yet it is interesting to note that the King pencilled a statement on a telegram of Goltz's, dated the 18th, to the effect that the deputation, when it arrived to tender the crown, had better go to Paris rather than Berlin, since the principal question was to be decided by the Conference; 'yet, eventually,' continued the King, 'I can be questioned as head of the family'.[3] This would seem to be the first indication that William was willing to see a way out of the difficulty.

It was now that Bismarck felt able to spring into the breach. Caution had thus far marked his attitude all along. He had telegraphed to St. Pierre on April 14 not to support the candidature of Bibesco, but to take no notice of any demonstration for Charles and to decline to be the recipient of any communication to him.[4] He had likewise waited patiently to make sure of Napoleon's attitude. Finally, on learning of Russia's suspicions, he telegraphed to the Prussian ambassador at St. Petersburg that the King had written to Anthony that Prussia had no interest in the affair, and

---

[1] William to Anthony, Apr. 14, *Reichsarchiv*, vol. 31, printed (with some slight differences in phrasing) in *Kaiser Wilhelms des Grossen, Briefe, Reden und Schriften*, vol. ii, pp. 116 ff., and in *Aus dem Leben*, vol. i, pp. 11–13. Extracts are quoted in Whitman, *Reminiscences of the King of Roumania*, pp. 15–17.

[2] *Aus dem Leben*, vol. i, p. 14. Anthony wrote another letter to the King, however, repeating his arguments and begging him to give his assent: *ibid.*, pp. 14–15.

[3] *Reichsarchiv, Turkei*, vol. 31.   [4] *Ibid.*

that, personally, he could only advise him not to lend himself to anything without the assent of Russia.[1] But by April 29, if not before, Bismarck came to the conclusion that with France on his side and with King William refusing the request of the Turkish minister to forbid acceptance,[2] it would be safe to let matters take their course, and even to assist them to reach the desired conclusion. Of Napoleon's neutrality in the Austro-Prussian conflict he had already assured himself, and Russia, if provoked at the idea of a Hohenzollern at Bucharest, might be appeased by the request for the hand of a Russian princess for the new hospodar. Since already Bismarck had signed the offensive-defensive alliance with Italy, and war was only a question of a few months, it would be manifestly a fine stroke of politics to force Austria to keep an army on the Moldo-Wallachian frontier. With Hohenzollerns on either side of her, the enemy's strategic position would be weaker than ever. Accordingly, when Charles, at the minister president's own request, paid a visit to him on the 19th, Bismarck bade him take the plunge. 'You have been unanimously elected by a whole nation,' he declared with redundant emphasis. 'Obey the summons. Proceed at once to the land, to whose government you have been called.' Amazed, no doubt, at the sudden turn of events, Charles demurred that he could not do so without the King's consent.

'All the more reason (for going),' exclaimed Bismarck. 'In this case you have no need for the direct permission of the King. Ask leave of the King—leave to go abroad. The King—I know him—will understand this and penetrate your intention. You will, moreover, take the decision out of his hands—a most welcome relief to him, as politically his hands are tied. From abroad resign your commission. . . . When once Your Serene Highness is in Roumania, the question will soon be solved; for, if Europe sees herself confronted by a *fait accompli*, the interested Powers will, of course, protest, but a protest stands on paper, and the fact cannot be undone.'[3]

Bismarck's frank exhortation, repeated later on the 23rd (and

[1] *Reichsarchiv, Turkei*, vol. 31.

[2] Karolyi to Mensdorff, no. 31, Apr. 21, Staatsarchiv, iii/93.

[3] Bismarck had also much to say on the attitude of the Powers, among whom only the Porte and Russia (he said) were likely to protest, and since Prussia could not afford a rupture with Russia, Bismarck, as Prussian minister, could not favour the enterprise. All would be well, however, if the Prince took independent action; then the King would be spared a painful situation. According to Bismarck's own account of the interview, as reported by the American minister, to whom Bismarck had told the story, Charles showed a good deal of hesitation. 'The Prince,' said Bismarck, 'came to me with the question whether he should go to Bucharest. I said to him, "How does it strike you? Have you the courage to take the risk?" He hesitated, and said he would speak to the King. "If you speak to the King," I said, "the King will arrest you." Still he hesitated.' Then Bismarck declared, 'You run no danger. The time is past when princes' throats were cut and they were subjected to mistreatment': *Süddeutsche Monsatsheft*, Feb. 5, 1930.

once again on May 5) did not clinch matters, however; for though the furlough had been graciously granted, Charles hesitated on learning that the King still disapproved of his cherished project. On the 27th a deputation came to Düsseldorf, and presented to Anthony what amounted to a formal offer of the crown; it was even represented how serious it would be for the country if Charles should finally decline. After a long consultation the emissaries were told that Charles was ready to accept, provided the King would give his consent. Not discouraged by the King's reply to a second appeal which he had written to him[1] Anthony came to Berlin, and after an interview with Bismarck he sought an audience with the King. It was then, at last, that William declared that he would not exert any direct influence upon Charles, but would let the *fait accompli* take its course.[2] How much Bismarck had had to do with influencing the monarch's decision, we do not know. The affair affords an interesting illustration of the weight of family discipline in Prussia.

One can imagine the suspense which prevailed all this time at Bucharest. The deputation had returned, convinced that Charles wanted to accept the honour, but they had to admit that his condition had not yet been met. Then, when the matter was finally settled, Bratiano (who had gone back to Paris) and Balatchano learned on coming to Düsseldorf that Charles was now free to give his acceptance,[3] and on the following day, May 8, the details of the journey were arranged. On the 11th Charles took his departure for Roumania.[4] Whatever the views of collective Europe, it now appeared that the Moldo-Wallachians were to have their 'foreign prince'.

[1] Page 535, note 2.
[2] *Aus dem Leben*, vol. i, pp. 16–28.
[3] Sturdza, *op. cit.*, vol. i, pp. 157, 159.
[4] *Aus dem Leben*, vol. i, pp. 28, 31.

CHAPTER XVIII

'ROUMANIA' IS MADE

IF time were to be measured by the number of vicissitudes which men encounter in following its course the Moldo-Wallachians might be deemed to have traversed a cycle of their history between the beginning of their subjection to a European protectorate in 1856 and the decisive national revolt against that protectorate in 1866. When the Congress of Paris benevolently granted a Balkan people the right to voice its wishes on the question of its reorganization, it did not foresee that the time would come when that people would proceed *sua sponte* to convert its wishes into fact. The calling of a foreign prince and his answer to the summons were the formal challenge to the protectorate. If that challenge failed to stir the sluggish Powers into really effective action, 'Roumania' would be made. The *Acte additionel* had given the Principalities the right to make their own constitution. It was now their expressed intention to carve for themselves a constitutional monarchy of their own choosing. United, self-governing, and now installing an hereditary dynasty—yes, 'Roumania' was soon to take her place in the European system.

But, so far, the Concert of Europe was unconvinced that nationalism was capable of freeing itself from bondage. However unwilling to make their guardianship effective, the Protecting Powers could not bring themselves to regard their role as any less important than of old, and they did not apparently see that a merely obstructive attitude was simply sealing the doom of the European protectorate. When, at last, France—of all Powers!—had suggested something constructive, as a possible means of warding off a foreign prince, one might readily assume that such a move would come too late. Indeed, one wonders if this proposal of a hospodar for a limited period were not simply an amiable gesture to pacify the British, and perhaps, withal, a screen to cover the Emperor's tacit encouragement of the Hohenzollern candidature.

At all events, even a feeble manœuvre was welcome in a Europe so confounded. Whether Baron d'Avril had private instructions from Napoleon, we cannot say. His formal instructions, while covertly intimating that union under a native prince might, after all, be compromised, quite honestly threw out the suggestion of a temporary hospodar[1]—a compromise which would 'conserve (to the Moldo-Wallachians) the advantages acquired up to the present without requiring of them the abandonment of those principles for

[1] 'The duration of this government might be fixed at from four to five years' was the way Drouyn de Lhuys phrased his proposal.

the future'; after trying this experiment (the argument continued), they would be in a better position to get a definitive arrangement in accordance with their wishes; and Drouyn de Lhuys expressed his certainty that the proposed plan would gain the assent of the majority of the Powers.[1] These instructions were shown to Clarendon, who promised to write in similar vein to Green,[2] and expressed the conviction that even Charles's acceptance of the crown—now widely rumoured—should not deter them from taking such a step.[3] At Paris the reports from Düsseldorf kept some, at least, of the diplomats in a state of grave uneasiness. Goltz begged Bismarck to come to a decision quickly, since if he were to oppose the compromise plan before Prussia's attitude were known, it would naturally create distrust.[4] But the Turks were the most excited. On hearing of Charles's acceptance, Safvet told Cowley that the Conference should meet and take such action as would prevent his installation. Cowley refused to believe the news, however, and deprecated a meeting of the Conference, which, he said, could only be of advantage to those who favoured a foreign prince; better leave the Principalities to themselves, for they would soon find themselves so helpless that they would have to propose something acceptable to the Conference.[5] Such a view was hardly worthy of that diplomat's sagacity, but his dread of another meeting of the Conference was not devoid of insight. In the present state of Europe it was manifestly conceivable that France might try to persuade the other Powers to give the Roumanian question the easiest solution.

It was not France, however, but Russia who instigated another meeting of the Conference on April 24. It seems that Gortchakoff was much provoked at Budberg for not having taken a firmer stand at its recent sessions,[6] and as for that diplomat's requiring further instructions—'he was saturated with them!' growled the Vice-Chancellor.[7] On April 5 the vociferous Russian had published a defence of his country's policy since 1856,[8] and to the Austrian

---

[1] Lhuys to Avril, Apr. 13, 1866, F.O. 27/1639.

[2] He did so: Clarendon to Green, no. 11, Apr. 17, F.O. 78/1919. Mensdorff wrote similarly to Eder, Apr. 27: Staatsarchiv, xxxviii/148.

[3] La Tour to Lhuys, Apr. 18, *Origines*, vol. viii, no. 2084. Clarendon seems, however, to have distrusted France's impartiality, not, it is true, suspecting any encouragement of a foreign prince, but believing that French influence would be thrown to Bratiano for the hospodariate: Clarendon to Cowley, no. 492, Apr. 17, F.O. 27/1604.

[4] Goltz to Bismarck, Apr. 21, telg., *Reichsarchiv*, vol. 31.

[5] Cowley to Clarendon, no. 499, Apr. 19, F.O. 27/1615.

[6] Buchanan to Clarendon, no. 162, Apr. 9, F.O. 65/698; Revertera to Mensdorff, no. 11 B, Apr. 7, Staatsarchiv, x/53.

[7] Buchanan to Clarendon, no. 169, Apr. 11, F.O. 65/698.

[8] 'Résumé historique de la question des Principautés depuis 1856 jusqu'à 1866' in *Journal de St. Pétersbourg*, Apr. 5. Gortchakoff admitted the authorship. Yet, even furnishing his own interpretations (he made much of his opposition to the plan of temporary union in 1861 as creating future complications), he cannot

ambassador he fumed and raged over the impotence of the Conference: 'Europe, constituted *en aréopage*, gives the air of following the impulse of a little state of the third order!'[1] But when more explicit instructions were sent to Budberg on April 16,[2] one wonders if Gortchakoff were not largely prompted by the news of what had been happening in Moldavia. In virtue of the failure of Russia's machinations at Jassy—her connivance in the Easter riot was boldly stated in the press[3]—he might feel that, now that the revolution could not be made to collapse from within, the only hope of quashing it was by Europe's intervention. At all events, Budberg repeated his demand for separate assemblies, and stated that Gortchakoff had insisted that the Conference should declare unequivocally that it would not permit a foreign prince. 'What if the government of the Principalities refused to annul the recent elections?' Cowley queried. 'In that case,' Budberg retorted, 'one should apply the Protocol of 1859.'[4] Since this obviously implied a resort to force, neither Cowley nor Drouyn de Lhuys would signify their assent, and the most that the Conference decided was to refer to the cabinets a declaration which was intended to be submitted separately by the consuls to the provisional government.[5] The week's delay before the Conference could meet again did not alter the situation, though it gave time for fresh explosions at St. Petersburg. Gortchakoff now complained that the Moldavians were subjected to a régime of terror, which consequently nullified their vote in the recent plebiscite. He was willing, he said, to support the French project of a temporary hospodar, provided the Conference desired it; but it was evident that the Vice-Chancellor regarded it as a second-best expedient.[6] Yet notwithstanding the anxiety of the provisional government,[7] the Russian policy of coercion had not the slightest prospect of success. The only thing that was certain was that collectively the Powers would not accept—as yet—a *fait accompli*. Meeting again on May 4, the Conference passed its declaration in final form. We quote it entire:

'The provisional government in Bucharest, in bringing about through a recent plebiscite the nomination of a foreign prince, has contravened the Convention of August 9, 1858, which, according to article xii, vests the hospodarial election in the assembly. The Conference decides, in referring to its resolution of the 4th of this month, that the task of

be said to have revealed a very impressive record of Russia's policy towards the Principalities.

[1] Revertera to Mensdorff, no. 11 B, Apr. 17, Staatsarchiv, x/53.
[2] Gortchakoff to Budberg, Apr. 16, *Arch. dip.*, *1868*, vol. i, pp. 277 ff.
[3] *Le Constitutionel* (Paris), Apr. 18.
[4] Cowley to Clarendon, no. 521, Apr. 24, F.O. 27/1615.
[5] Protocol no. 6.
[6] Talleyrand to Lhuys, Apr. 29, *Origines*, vol. viii, no. 2183.
[7] Avril to Lhuys, Apr. 28, *ibid.*, no. 2167.

solving the question of the maintenance of union should be left to the assembly which is going to convene. If the majority, either of Moldavian or of Wallachian deputies, request it, they should have the right of voting separately. In case the majority, either Moldavian or Wallachian, pronounce against union, the vote should have as a consequence the separation of the two Principalities.

'This question disposed of, the assembly shall proceed to the hospodarial election, which, according to article xiii, ought to fall only on a native.

'The consuls are entrusted with watching in common accord over the free conduct of the voting, and with signalizing immediately to the Conference any assault which may be made on it.'[1]

The Principalities were not anticipating this reprimand, but they knew that the Conference was still resolved that they should have a native prince, and both Avril and Green had duly communicated the 'compromise' proposal.[2] Ghika told Green that this question of a short-term hospodar was for the assembly to decide, for the government 'could not possibly' take the responsibility of proposing what would annihilate the wishes of the country. With characteristic finesse he ventured the opinion that the assembly would not only reject such a proposal but might in despair proclaim the independence of the State.[3] No doubt Ghika readily judged that it would be far more serious for the provisional government to renounce the results of the plebiscite than to evade the wishes of the Powers. An effort on the part of a faction to overthrow the government had just been brought to light, and, apart from the discontent of an unpaid and restless soldiery, the object of the conspirators seems to have been to ensure the preservation of union and the choice of a foreign prince.[4] It was reported, on the other hand, that Demetrius Ghika was reckoning up the number of his adherents in the coming assembly with the hope of obtaining the election.[5] As the great majority of the deputies would be conservative, it was possible that the Left might lose its leadership, and that Charles would, in

[1] *Arch. dip., 1867*, vol. i, pp. 254-5.
[2] Avril's counsels of prudence (Avril to Lhuys, Apr. 8, *Origines*, vol. viii, no. 2166) were not credited by Eder, who, in reporting to Vienna, charged him with having told the Moldo-Wallachians that, if they persisted in their resolution, they would get a foreign prince (Eder to Mensdorff, no. 69 B, May 5, Staatsarchiv, xxxviii/148).
[3] Green to Clarendon, no. 73, Apr. 28, F.O. 78/1920. Ghika further argued that a foreign prince was not incompatible with the suzerainty of the Porte, and that a native prince was more likely to declare his independence—which Couza, he alleged, had been about to do. Avril likewise found the provisional government averse to the idea of a short-term native hospodar (Avril to Lhuys, May 2, *Origines*, vol. viii, no. 2213).
[4] Eder to Mensdorff, no 65, Apr. 28, Staatsarchiv, xxxviii/148. Some officers—among them, Couza's friend, Captain Salomon—were arrested, and one regiment was divided into small detachments and sent into the country: Eder to Mensdorff, no. 66, Apr. 30, and no. 79, May 20, *ibid*.
[5] Eder to Mensdorff, no. 66, Apr. 30, *ibid*.

consequence, be repudiated before he had finally published his decision. No wonder, then, that Ghika steered a wary course. Would these cautious Hohenzollerns ever make up their minds?

Then, slightly anticipating a message from the consuls, acquainting the government with the Conference's declaration of May 2, came a telegram from Davila (one of the deputation which had communicated to Charles the outcome of the plebiscite), declaring: 'Success certain. Firmly maintain your position.' Later in the same day equally encouraging telegrams were received from Bratiano and Balatchano, who were also at Düsseldorf. Inspired by these assurances, Rosetti took the bold step of publishing in the *Roumanul* that Charles had accepted the crown.[1] Perhaps, in view of the action of the Conference and of the more insidious danger of certain yawning political appetites at home, the announcement was not a bad stroke of policy. As a matter of fact, it was not until May 7 that Charles acquainted Bratiano and Balatchano that he would respond to the national appeal, but as Bismarck himself had telegraphed to St. Pierre on the 3rd, alluding to the Prince's journey as a settled fact (though carefully pointing out that Prussia would take no notice of the step),[2] it is hardly strange that there was general expectation of this outcome before it was positively determined.[3] In the meantime, though its substance was generally known, the government refrained at first from publishing the Conference's declaration.[4] There was now scarcely a doubt that the assembly, when it should meet, would ratify the outcome of the plebiscite; and such a thrust at Europe would be really much more stunning than the double election of Couza in 1859.

The assembly opened on May 10. There had been some talk of the Moldavians meeting at Jassy and there electing Sturdza as their hospodar instead of answering the summons to Bucharest;[5] but when the session opened, forty-two out of the forty-eight Moldavians were present, and some of those who were absent sent telegrams, supporting loyally the outcome of the plebiscite. Moreover, the deputation from the smaller province had met

---

[1] Eder to Mensdorff, no. 68, May 3. According to Goltz (to Bismarck, no. 221, May 2, *Reichsarchiv, Turkei*, vol. 32), Balatchano had written that Charles had accepted the throne, with the reservation that his action should be approved by the majority of the Powers. Charles himself, however, makes no mention of this qualified acceptance in his memoirs. One must realize that these Moldo-Wallachian diplomats were doing their best to force the issue.

[2] Bismarck to St. Pierre, May 3, telg., *ibid.*

[3] Avril also heard that the provisional government had learned on May 2nd or 3rd of the qualified acceptance, mentioned above: Avril to Lhuys, May 5, *Origines*, vol. ix, no. 2250.

[4] Eder to Mensdorff, no. 70 B, May 7, Staatsarchiv, xxxviii/148. Green ascribed to himself the credit of getting it finally published: Green to Lyons, no. 38, May 19, F.O. 78/1931.

[5] Eder to Mensdorff, no. 71, May 9, Staatsarchiv, xxxviii/148.

and declared that they would not request the privilege of voting separately.[1] The message of the *lieutenance princière* to the assembly, apart from some discussion of the monastery question, was confined to a brief summary of the national movement for a foreign prince and of the attitude of the Powers thereto, not omitting an appeal for perseverance in the programme undertaken. The assembly in reply, without dissenting vote, pronounced 'Roumania' one and indivisible, and proclaimed Charles hereditary prince of the united State. Naturally, the declaration of the European conference, though it was read to the assembled deputies, had no apparent effect on their enthusiasm, and the legislature's response merely proclaimed anew the maintenance of the union of the Principalities, with Charles as hereditary Prince of Roumania.[2] There was some debate on these propositions, but, with a few neglible exceptions, all present were similarly minded. All voting was loud, since no one had asked for a secret ballot, and when the result was announced many of the deputies shouted, 'Long live Roumania! Long live Charles I!'[3] The day closed with a great celebration (including ovations before the French and Prussian consulates[4]), the members of both the government and the legislature attended a public dinner, while the streets were illuminated, bands played, and every one seemed prepared to make merry. Green testified to the entire harmony between Moldavians and Wallachians, and declared that nothing but force could check this national demonstration.[5]

To most of the Protecting Powers the action of the assembly was no less and no more impressive than the plebiscite or the formal offer of the crown to Charles. Russia, who had been the most vigorous opponent of Roumanian aspirations, seemed now to show less interest in the matter, and it is not unreasonable to conjecture that Gortchakoff had come to fear that France, in proposing a provisional hospodar for four years, had really in mind Bibesco, who, as the Vice-Chancellor complained, 'would govern the Principalities as a French prefect'.[6] It was only the Porte who looked upon the crisis in the Principalities as a matter of vital import. Not content with the action of the Conference on May 2, the suzerain Power had sent a vizirial letter to the Provisional Government, insisting that the assembly should choose a native hospodar, and that the Moldavians should be given the right to vote against union if they wished. 'Any attempt to repeat the choice of a foreign prince,

[1] Green to Clarendon, no. 81, May 14, F.O. 78/1921.
[2] Sturdza, *op. cit.*, vol. i, p. 161–70.
[3] *Ibid.*, p. 178–9.
[4] St. Pierre to Bismarck, no. 50, May 16, *Reichsarchiv, Turkei*, vol. 32. St. Pierre testified to the great enthusiasm fo Charles manifested in the assembly.
[5] Green to Clarendon, no. 81.
[6] Buchanan to Clarendon, no. 238, May 15, F.O. 65/699.

and to carry through a plan which the Protecting Powers, like the Sublime Porte, have decisively and unanimously rejected (the pronouncement added), would only end in compromising your state.'[1] The letter itself was in no way offensive, but a few days earlier Ali had told the kapou kiaya that, if the Principalities broke the treaties, any Powers who dissented from the decisions of the Conference as a whole might feel justified in dispensing with the preliminary accord legally necessary for undertaking a military occupation. Although Ali had made it clear that he was not alluding to his own government, since the Porte had every reason to uphold the Treaty of Paris, one still has ground for suspecting that the minister had taken this method of circumlocution to hint that Turkey herself might become a 'dissenting Power'. The Porte's constructive proposal was the one which had been brought forward by France, and the kapou kiaya wondered if Charles himself could be assigned to that provisional capacity.[2] At all events, these cryptic admonitions, coupled with the rumours of the march of troops in the direction of the Danube, were quite enough to give the Provisional Government some very anxious moments. Green believed that Ghika had taken the assembly into his confidence during the secret session which had preceded the discussion of union, and that that was one reason for the assembly's unanimity.[3] If so, one can once more note an occasion when an action of the Porte had been tactically at fault. The Provisional Government's reply to the vizirial letter consisted merely of a polite defence of the step which the assembly had taken and an assurance of fidelity.[4] But nothing but Avril's assurances availed to quiet its apprehensions.[5] As a matter of fact, though Turkish troops were reported in readiness to march,[6] one could not yet be certain that the Porte, even in the presence of the distracting struggle in central Europe, would be bold enough to defy the restrictive clauses of the Treaty of Paris by attempting intervention alone. Certainly one needs more evidence than Prokesch's statement that 'the Porte, in case the Prince comes to Bucharest to be installed, seems resolved to invade the Principalities and to force him to leave the land'.[7]

In any event, the Porte chose, for the present, the safer course of appealing to the Conference. At a meeting of that body on the 17th, called to consider the navigation question,[8] the Ottoman plenipo-

---

[1] Sturdza, *op. cit.*, vol. i, pp. 158–9.
[2] *Ibid.*, vol. i, pp. 152 ff.
[3] Green to Lyons, no. 37, May 6, F.O. 78/1921.
[4] Sturdza, *op. cit.*, vol. i, pp. 189 ff.
[5] Eder to Mensdorff, no. 78, May 18, Staatsarchiv, xxxviii/148.
[6] Moustier to Lhuys, May 19, *Origines*, vol. ix, no. 2384.
[7] Prokesch to Mensdorff, no. 27 A–C, May 15, Staatsarchiv, xii/84.
[8] The question of the Principalities was taken up when Drouyn de Lhuys presented a communication of Ghika's, announcing the result of the plebiscite

tentiary proposed the nomination of a native hospodar by the Conference for an interval of six or seven years. Much discussion followed, in which Goltz played for time, Budberg found fault with the proposal, and Drouyn de Lhuys evidently floundered in the morass into which his recent veering to Charles had plunged his government's policy. He now took pains to make clear that the French plan of a provisional hospodar was not designed to be obligatory, but was only a suggestion,[1] which, if adopted by the Principalities, would avert a Russo-Turkish intervention;[2] he was bound, he said, to stand by the treaties, though he believed more than ever that the best solution was a foreign prince—a 'funeral oration', wrote Goltz to Bismarck, 'which the next yellow book will embellish'. In spite of a suggestion from Drouyn de Lhuys that the Porte might come to terms with the Principalities (bearing in mind, of course, the restrictions imposed by the treaties), it was a singularly futile meeting. 'One has resolved to do nothing', wrote Goltz, 'that is calculated to end the present *provisorium*.'[3] So far, then, the Porte had quite failed to move the Protecting Powers into anything like a decisive action. And meanwhile the relentless logic of events was speedily bringing matters to a crisis.

We have noted Charles's departure on May 11. The itinerary chosen was through Switzerland and Austria, then via the Danube to Wallachia. It must have been with curious emotion that the Prince had received, after his departure, an order to return to his regiment, for the King had signed on May 9 the order for the mobilization of the Prussian army. The journey was covered, however, by the furlough which the King had granted; and in the company of Werner, a member of the Prussian cabinet, he made his way to Switzerland. At Zürich he wrote a letter to Napoleon, pleading that he could not decline the mission which Providence had imposed upon him; one to the Czar, begging for that sovereign's august protection; and finally one to the Sultan, assuring him of his fidelity to the obligations incumbent upon a Roumanian prince. At Salzburg he dispatched his resignation from the Prussian army, and once his resignation was accepted, as undoubtedly it would be, the Prince would have definitely severed his connexion with his *Geburtsland*.

It was a hazardous moment for a Prussian to set foot on Austrian soil, for already the Austrian army was being mobilized for war, and it was well known that Charles was on his way to Bucharest.

and begging the Conference to accept it. The Conference met this appeal by standing firm on its resolution of May 2.

[1] Protocol no. 8.
[2] Goltz to Bismarck, May 17, telg., *Reichsarchiv, Turkei*, vol. 32. This statement is not found in the protocol, so may have been made outside the Conference.
[3] Goltz to Bismarck, no. 275, May 18, *ibid.*

But his passport, made out for a certain Herr Hettingen, bound for Odessa, successfully passed the scrutiny of the Austrian customs officials, and though once he narrowly escaped recognition, it was evident that Fortune was smiling on his exploit. Bratiano joined him en route down the Danube, but out of respect for the secrecy of the journey, he carefully refrained from recognizing his sovereign. Once in the course of a steamer conversation the Prince heard some one remark, 'The new prince will make himself as impossible as Couza.' The newspapers were saying that Turkey was on the point of invading Roumania.[1]

But it was too late for Charles to regret his adventure, and we have no evidence that he did so. At Turnu-Severin, the first Wallachian port where the steamer docked, Charles made ready to step on shore, where arrangements had been made for his arrival. When the captain stopped him to ask why he should want to leave the boat when his destination was Odessa, Charles replied that he merely wished to go ashore for a few minutes. Once ashore, he was promptly joined by Bratiano, who hurried him into a carriage, and —except for a word of explanation to the prefect—his identity was still concealed on account of the nearness of the Turks, encamped across the Danube. But the moment he left the gangplank, Charles had heard the captain exclaim, 'By God, that must be the Prince of Hohenzollern!'[2]

Charles was not much impressed with the squalid little oriental town which constituted his first acquaintance with the land of which he was now the ruler. Nor did his first inspection of a Roumanian regiment at Crajova meet with the exacting standards of a Prussian army officer. But the heartiness of the greetings which he received on his three-day journey to the capital atoned for many defects which this backward land presented. Golesco and Ghika had ridden to meet him at Ploïesti, and it was in their company that he signed his first official act—a pardon to the metropolitan who had participated in the Easter riot at Jassy. At Ciocanati, where the party was joined by Demetrius Ghika, the Prince exchanged his travelling clothes for a Roumanian uniform. The arrival at Bucharest was marked by a truly royal welcome. Long files of troops lined the broad avenue which brought him into his capital, while beyond stood the throngs of cheering spectators, and as he entered the town many a woman leaned from her window to shower her new sovereign with flowers. Seeing a building a little larger than the others, the Prince turned to Golesco, and asked, 'What is that house?' 'That,' replied Golesco, 'is the palace.' 'But where is the palace?' pursued the Prince. The minister's embarrassment confirmed his previous answer. Without pausing for better acquaintance with this unregal domicile, the Prince went on to the cathedral, where the metropolitan presented him with the cross and bible to kiss; then, to the strains of a *Te Deum*, sung in the rather nasal tones of the Greek ritual, he came to the assembly hall, where, in the presence of the deputies and the judges of the high court, he took the oath to observe the laws, maintain the rights, and preserve the integrity of Roumania. Then, in response to an address of welcome from the president of the assembly, Charles delivered a brief speech in French. '. . . Citizen to-day;' he said, 'to-morrow, if necessary, soldier, I will share with you good and bad fortune. From this moment all is in common between us. Believe in me, as I believe in you. . . .' Almost in one breath, in response to his closing words, 'Long live Roumania!' came the hearty refrain, 'Long live Charles I!'[1] That night the capital was illuminated, and all classes seemed to vie with one another in testifying their joy.[2] Green wrote that Charles had made a most favourable impression, his dignity and urbanity being something of a contrast to Couza's unregal bearing and habitual aloofness.[3] On the whole, the Moldo-Wallachians thought well of their 'foreign prince'.

And perhaps, indeed, they also thought well of themselves. They had got their 'foreign prince'—in spite of Europe's decrees!—and, though his position would be untenable if he were not recognized—a fact which only those who knew the state of the treasury perhaps realized—the feeling was undoubtedly general that nothing but *force majeure* should force them to yield their prize. 'No one thinks', wrote the French consul, 'any longer of submitting to the injunctions of the Conference, and one envisages with calm, even with resolution, all the consequences of a refusal.'[4]

Well—now that the event which Europe had for some time anticipated had become an actuality, the moment had come for the Protecting Powers to reflect on their complicity—whether passive or active—in the success of the enterprise. Drouyn de Lhuys was still loud in his insistence that France had had no part in the elevation of a foreign prince,[5] but Napoleon is said to have laughed at Charles's letter, particularly a statement that the writer was following his example in accepting a duty to which he had been called, and was then reported as adding that things

[1] *Aus dem Leben*, vol. i, pp. 50–3.
[2] Avril to Lhuys, no. 22, May 23, *Aff. étr.*, *Turquie, Bucharest*, vol. 28.
[3] Green to Clarendon, no. 86, May 23, F.O. 78/1921. Green had been simply a spectator in the crowd, as the consuls had felt compelled to ignore the official invitation to attend the ceremonies.
[4] Avril to Lhuys, no. 23, May 23, *Aff. étr.*, *Turquie, Bucharest*, vol. 28.
[5] Lhuys to Talleyrand, May 23, *Origines*, vol. ix, no. 2420.

must take their natural course.[1] Naturally the finger of responsibility was pointed more squarely at Prussia. In a letter to London and Vienna Drouyn de Lhuys remarked that Prussia had disavowed all connexion with the affair, but he could not see how Charles could possibly have carried out his venture without that government's connivance.[2] Meanwhile, to Benedetti, Bismarck expressed elaborate astonishment that Charles had left the King's service without obtaining an assurance of that sovereign's good will, and persistently denied that the Prince had consulted the King at all.[3] According to Clarendon's reported account, the Prussian ambassador had told the same story in London,[4] and both the Russian ambassador at Berlin[5] and the Russian government itself were given unqualified statements of Prussia's innocence.[6] To the Prussian minister at the Porte, Bismarck wrote,

'The Prince has entered upon his undertaking without the knowledge of the King's government, which, true to its declarations at the Conference, cannot approve the Prince's enterprise. The personal relations of the Prince to the King's house were without any influence on the position of the King and of the King's government in relation to the affair.'[7]

It is obvious that, when Bismarck chose to lie, he left no room for qualification. Naturally, the most disturbed was poor Goltz, who never had received word that Bismarck and even the King had been accomplices in the plot. When questioned by his colleagues, he was forced to protest his government's innocence, but, though his assurances were received in polite silence, he noted that 'several of these gentlemen gave a certain impression of

---

[1] Goltz to Bismarck, no. 301, May 26, *Reichsarchiv, Turkei*, vol. 32. One must not take too seriously Metternich's evidence to the effect that Napoleon had told him that he had discouraged this 'escapade', as he called it, which he ascribed to Bratiano and the encouragement which his (Napoleon's) entourage had given him behind his back, and that he spoke of the Prince's 'ridiculous letter' (the words are Metternich's): Metternich to Mensdorff, no. 28, May 23, Staatsarchiv, ix/81.

[2] Lhuys to La Tour and Grammont, May 21, *Origines*, vol. ix, no. 2392. According to Loftus, he 'said emphatically that he had no wish that Prussia should be involved in a "second Kingdom of Greece" ': Loftus to Clarendon, no. 138, Apr. 21, F.O. 64/593.

[3] Benedetti to Lhuys, May 22, *ibid.*, no. 2412.

[4] La Tour to Lhuys, May 23, *ibid.*, no. 2426.

[5] Benedetti to Lhuys, May 21, *ibid.*, no. 2393.

[6] Bismarck to Redern, &c., May 21, telg., *Reichsarchiv, Turkei*, vol. 32. This telegram of denial was sent to all the Protecting Powers. In a letter to the Prussian ambassador at St. Petersburg (no. 147, May 30, *ibid.*) Bismarck entered into a lengthy explanation, expressing complete astonishment at the way the Prince had utilized his furlough, and explaining that, only out of consideration for the Hohenzollern name, had the King brought himself to accept his resignation from the army. He insisted that Prussia had no interest in Charles's action. Gortchakoff seemed, in the end, to acquit the Prussian government of complicity: Buchanan to Clarendon, no. 279, June 6, F.O. 65/700.

[7] Bismarck to Brassier, no. 42, May 22, *Reichsarchiv, Turkei*, vol. 32.

indignation'.[1] In a letter which he ventured to write direct to the King he remarked that

'one finds difficulty in believing, and it is scarcely desirable that one should believe, that he (Charles) has acted against Your Royal Majesty's will. . . . One will expect a decisive disavowal from Your Majesty and a command to the Prince to return. If Your Majesty does not give such a command, then your government will be suspected on all sides of taking in the Conference only a sham position and of actually combatting the resolutions of the Powers. . . . I believe that in our present situation it is expedient to avoid such suspicions and reproaches'.[2]

But little did these passing irritations penetrate Berlin. When, with British bluntness, Lord A. Loftus, the British ambassador at Berlin, had told Bismarck that the King should disavow Charles publicly, the Prussian statesman, while ostensibly disturbed by the Prince's insubordinate conduct, merely answered that the King could not be expected to impose a public censure upon him, and that Prussia would give satisfactory assurances to the Conference.[3] There is often a world of difference between a carefully composed official apology and the manœuvering which generally takes place behind the scenes. But Bismarck had known perfectly well how to play his cards. The Prince had gone to Bucharest with Napoleon's tacit blessing; he would probably never know (and it did not matter if he did) that he was now being branded as an unruly subject; and, while Bismarck covered his tracks by casting the family mantle over his roguery, he, Bismarck, was perfectly aware that no possible proof of his own encouragement to Charles or of the King's reluctant assent was available to the Powers. Moreover, he doubtless reflected that the coming war with Austria would soon put Roumania in at least temporary oblivion.

But the Porte, as we have said before, was in no wise persuaded that the convulsion in central Europe was any reason for expecting her surrender to the Roumanians. While still willing to promise that he would not act without the assent of the Powers, Ali plainly wanted an occupation of the Principalities, though, when the question came to be debated by the council, it failed, in spite of its indignation, to come to any decision.[4] One gathers that it was not so much the fear that a foreign prince would jeopardize the integrity of the Ottoman Empire that upset the mental equilibrium of Constantinople, but, rather, the familiar feeling that the dignity of the suzerain had been flouted. 'Why had Prince Charles made the mistake of not passing by Constantinople?'

[1] Goltz to William, no. 287, May 22, *ibid.*   [2] *Ibid.*
[3] Benedetti to Lhuys, May 26, *Origines*, vol. ix, no. 2455.
[4] Moustier to Lhuys, May 23, *Docs. dip., 1866*, p. 159.

Ali had complained. 'It might have embarrassed us greatly, and the Sultan would have recognized him.'[1] One may infer that underneath the criticism of Charles's tactics lay the wish that he had given his suzerain that previous homage. Even the Prince's letter had quite failed to assuage the Turkish ruler's *amour propre*.

In the meantime, once again, the Porte had taken the step of placing the vexing question before the Conference. At a meeting called at Turkish instance on May 25 Safvet inveighed once more against Charles's accession, which he declared to be illegal, and, on his own account, reserved to his government the right to use 'the privilege, given it by the treaties ... of restoring the legal order of things in the Principalities'. There was, however, no disposition on the part of the plenipotentiaries to consider intervention, and it was hardly solving the question at issue when the Conference decided to take no action which implied the recognition of Charles I.[2] Probably the Prussian plenipotentiary had least cause to enjoy this particular session. It was in vain that he gave the assurance—in response to queries—that Charles had acted on his own responsibility, and that he had resigned from the Prussian army. He was forced to admit that such resignation had no value until it was sanctioned by the King; 'so that at this moment,' remarked Cowley, 'the Prince is a deserter, and that, too, at a time when there is imminent danger of war'.[3] Goltz was evidently much piqued by a cross-examination which he felt to be unwarranted; but though he acknowledged that the furlough could not have been granted to the Prince for the purpose of going to Roumania,[4] he was able, by his very ignorance of what had gone on at Berlin, to mask his government's complicity. All this was, however, of small interest to the Porte. In the course of the meeting Safvet had gone so far as to recall a telegram from Ali,[5] announcing his decision to send troops immediately to occupy the Principalities (Clarendon had also received the same information from Lyons),[6] but, when questioned whether this statement

---

[1] Moustier to Lhuys, May 26, *Origines*, vol. ix, no. 2457.

[2] Protocol no. 9. On Budberg's motion the Conference decided to forbid the consuls to have any official relations with the new Prince.

[3] Cowley to Clarendon, no. 694, May 25, F.O. 27/1617.

[4] Goltz to William, no. 300, May 25, *Reichsarchiv, Turkei*, vol. 32. Clarendon seems to have ruminated on the idea of having the Conference request William to call Charles back to his 'military duties': Clarendon to Russell, May 24, 1866, Russell Papers, G. and D., 22/16, Pub. Rec. Off.

[5] See Ali to Safvet, May 24, *Origines*, vol. ix, no. 2434.

[6] Lyons to Clarendon, May 24, telg., F.O. 78/1910. Clarendon's remark in this connexion seems curiously beside the mark. 'If Charles I is left alone,' he wrote, 'he is very likely to succumb from intestine difficulties. If he is attacked, his power in the Principalities will be consolidated': Clarendon to Layard, May 30, Layard Papers, Brit. Mus. Add. MS. 39120.

was intended for the Conference (if not, Budberg advised a formal request for concerted action), or whether it was simply private information, the Turkish plenipotentiary could give no satisfactory explanation.[1] One gathers that Ali was attempting a little bluff, and that Safvet was unequal to the task of putting it over. The Porte had, in fact, sent this message to its agents at the courts of all the Protecting Powers;[2] and, a few days later, what appeared to be an effort of the same kind was repeated. There was no longer any threat of 'immediate occupation' (probably Ali had been informed that the Conference had been chilly), but Safvet told Drouyn de Lhuys that, according to his new instructions, the Porte could see no other recourse than a military occupation, and would be disposed to try it of its own accord, if, within a period of fifteen days, the Conference had not imposed respect for the treaties.[3] There was even a report in the press that a Russo-Turkish army had already invaded Moldavia.[4]

It is impossible to say to what extent, if at all, Russian influence at Constantinople was being used to push the Porte into this attitude of belligerency. The kapou kiaya asserted that this pressure was a fact, whatever might be stated to the contrary;[5] and Moustier had also the conviction that Ignatieff was secretly responsible for the Porte's behaviour.[6] We know, as a matter of fact, that Gortchakoff had again become explosive; for he told the French ambassador that Charles had insulted the Protecting Powers, and that, while Russia alone would not engage in any punitive action, such was certainly the manifest duty of the Conference, and that, if that body decided to accept the *fait accompli*, Russia, for her part, would withdraw from the Conference.[7] Budberg talked in similar vein to Cowley, who tried to persuade his colleague that the best way of punishing the offender was to ignore him.[8] But, for the moment, Russia's wrath was not to be appeased, and at a meeting of the Conference on June 4, called at Budberg's instance, the proposal was made of sending a commission of the Powers to the Principalities in accordance with the Protocol of 1859. As such a wedge for the promotion

[1] Goltz to Bismarck, no. 301, May 26, *Reichsarchiv, Turkei*, vol. 32.
[2] Mavrogheni to Balatchano, May 29, *Origines*, vol. ix, no. 2484.
[3] Lhuys to Moustier, June 1, *ibid.*, no. 2525.
[4] *Le Constitutionel* (Paris), May 24.
[5] Mavrogheni to Balatchano, May 29.
[6] Moustier to Lyons, June 12, *Origines*, vol. x, no. 2649.
[7] Talleyrand to Lhuys, May 28, *ibid.*, vol. ix, no. 2475. Other reasons for Gortchakoff's disapproval of Charles's accession, as Talleyrand reported later (to Lhuys, June 6, *Aff. étr., Russie*, vol. 237), were the fear that the radicals, who were instrumental in bringing Charles into power, would have too great an influence and also the uncertainty of a Catholic ruler's attitude towards the Orthodox religion.
[8] Cowley to Clarendon, no. 748, June 2, F.O. 27/1618.

of a military occupation naturally met with no support, Budberg
could only say that he believed that his government would retire
from the Conference.[1] What this threat might mean could only
be surmised. But, as usual, Gortchakoff's truculence was only
a bit of bluff, and Europe had no reason to take it seriously.
Though it was reported that the Czar did not welcome Charles's
letter[2] (Gortchakoff called him 'a Filibuster'[3]), and it is probably
true that a deputation from the Principalities, sent to appease
that ruler's wrath, was at first coldly received,[4] the Russian
government was evidently not disposed to assume the responsibility of disciplining Roumania. It was, in fact, more characteristic
of Russian policy to try to persuade the Porte to bear the onus of
separate action.

It was in consequence of disquieting news from Constantinople
that an order was issued for the mobilization of the Roumanian
army, while Balatchano was instructed to bring the situation
to Napoleon's attention and to invoke his intervention.[5] Inasmuch
as these steps were taken on May 23, and Charles had only been
in power twenty-four hours, one may judge of the strain to which
he was subjected from the outset of his rule. He had wisely
begun by selecting a ministry from representatives of all factions,
including not only the trimmer, Demetrius Ghika and Mavrogheni,
the late aspirant for the Moldavian hospodariate, but Cantacouzene,
the wealthy *boyard*, and, naturally, John Ghika, Bratiano, and
Rosetti. For premier, he had wisely chosen the most trustworthy
of Moldavians, Lascar Catargi, whose qualities he highly esteemed.
Though the consuls were prohibited from any official relations
with the Prince, all of them—the British consul, last of all[6]—
accepted his invitation to an 'unofficial' audience, and there was
no apparent disposition on the part of any of them to criticize the
new ruler's conduct. Anyway, for the present, the danger of
invasion precluded any serious consideration of internal problems.
On the 28th the assembly voted a credit of 8,000,000 piastres,
though, as a loan was out of the question, one might wonder where
the money was to be obtained. Charles himself was sick at heart
when he contemplated his means for repelling invasion. The
military establishments were sadly lacking in the implements of

---

[1] Protocol no. 10. Safvet naturally supported Budberg's proposal.
[2] Talleyrand to Lhuys, May 28, *Origines*, vol. ix, no. 2475.
[3] Buchanan to Layard, June 6, Layard Papers, Brit. Mus. Add. MSS. 39120.
[4] Green to Clarendon, no. 110, July 5, F.O. 78/1921.
[5] *Aus dem Leben*, vol. i, p. 59.
[6] Green wrote to Clarendon on June 2nd that, as he was the only agent who
had not received an audience, his situation was awkward. Clarendon objected
that even an unofficial audience was an indirect recognition (telg., June 5), but,
as he later relented (telg., June 7), Green had an audience with Charles on June 7
(Green to Clarendon, no. 98, June 8, F.O. 78/1921).

war, and there was hardly enough powder to supply a small contingent. Worse than that, the frontier battalions mutinied (on the ground that they were not supposed to be employed for offensive manœuvres), and the morale of the whole army was far from satisfactory.[1] The problem was particularly difficult for the Prince because he could not try to rouse enthusiasm by a martial proclamation without jeopardizing his chances of recognition and perhaps, for all he knew, goading the Turks into action. Green announced on the 8th that 10,000 soldiers were marching from Bucharest towards the Danube, adding, however, that if they put up any serious resistance to the invaders they would 'astonish themselves as much as their enemies'.[2] Perhaps it was a case of 'whistling to keep their courage up' that the troops, when they reached the Danube, engaged in feverish activities—even firing on Turkish river craft—with the natural result that the Turkish forces across the river were much annoyed by such 'bravado'.[3] The danger of a frontier 'incident' was manifest, and it might have gone hard with these raw recruits if the Turks had crossed the river. At all events, the month of June was undoubtedly a period of grave anxiety in the Principalities, the more so because of that very consciousness of military inadequacy.[4] Charles himself, though he could not afford to neglect the national defences, had really more hope of obtaining his country's salvation by prompt appeal to the Powers; and on June 7 one of the ministers sent a circular to the consuls, 'indicating unequivocally' (as Green expressed it) the intention of the Turks to invade Roumania.[5]

Fortunately, Turkey never came quite to the point of deciding to send her forces across the Danube.[6] If she had failed to induce the Russians to take action, she had likewise lacked the courage, or the folly, to become the docile instrument of Gortchakoff. As it was, the Porte's hesitation was Europe's opportunity. Oppressed by the fear that Russia, who had proposed the closing of the Conference,[7] would find an opportunity of bringing greater pressure on the Turks,[8] Clarendon advised the Porte through

---

[1] *Aus dem Leben*, vol. i, pp. 63, 68.

[2] Green to Clarendon, no. 98, June 8, F.O. 78/1921.

[3] Dalyell to Clarendon, no. 13, June 13, F.O. 78/1930.

[4] Eder to Mensdorff, no. 93, June 20, Staatsarchiv, xxxviii/148. Eder himself was still hoping for a military occupation: Eder to Mensdorff, no. 89 A, June 10, *ibid*.

[5] Green to Clarendon, no. 98 and enclosure.

[6] Moustier asserted also that the Porte was not ready for the emergency; that 'there were not 8,000 men in condition to cross the Danube': Moustier to Lhuys, June 13, *Arch. dip., 1867*, vol. i, pp. 261–2. Whatever the number, however, the British consul at Rustchuk wrote of the Turkish soldiers on the Danube as 'well equipped, in perfect order, and in first rate discipline': Dalyell to Clarendon, no. 13.

[7] Gortchakoff to Budberg, June 12, *Arch. dip., 1868*, vol. i, pp. 280 ff.

[8] Characteristically, Gortchakoff refused to join Clarendon and Drouyn de

Lyons to acknowledge Charles 'as successor to Prince Couza', it being understood that the new Prince would recognize the customary obligations which the hospodars owed their suzerain.[1] As Drouyn de Lhuys had already given the same advice to Safvet,[2] one is impressed with the fact that Turkish belligerency was proving the wedge by which the Powers were likely to come to the point of recognizing the *fait accompli*. Pursuant to their instructions, Moustier and Lyons saw both Ali and the vizier, and the former used every argument he could think of to dissuade the Turks from taking military action.[3] In spite of Safvet's announcement that Turkey would occupy the Principalities until satisfaction were obtained,[4] Moustier wrote on June 13 that he believed that the crisis was over.[5] The Sultan had never sanctioned the project of an invasion, and Ali's dispatch to Safvet was evidently unauthorized. Indeed, Ali confessed now that the whole motive of these armaments was 'moral', and he announced in confidence that the Porte had responded to an overture from the Principalities, and was now negotiating with Ghika,[6] who had been sent to Constantinople for the purpose.[7] It seems that 'on the suggestion (wrote Green) of persons favourable to Charles's success', the government at Bucharest had taken, though rather tardily, the wise step of formally asking the Porte for his investiture.[8]

If Charles had not been astute enough to take this resolution on his own initiative, he is at least to be commended for his handling of his country's internal problems. Few rulers have had so discouraging a task thrust upon them at the commencement of their occupancy of a throne. The greatest need of all was to obtain money; for Couza had left a public debt of 55,000,000 piastres,[9] and most officials, as well as even the army itself, had received no pay for six months.[10] There was no chance of a loan until the Powers were willing to grant recognition, and, since the cost

Lhuys in asking the Porte to accord Charles recognition; and he told the British ambassador that, while he had not advised it, he thought that the Porte should have entered the Principalities without consulting the Conference: Buchanan to Clarendon, no. 288, June 14, F.O. 65/700.

[1] F.O. to Lyons, no. 208, June 6, F.O. 78/1904.
[2] Lhuys to Moustier, June 9, *Origines*, vol. x, no. 2608. According to Drouyn de Lhuys, he (Drouyn) had done so before Clarendon asked for France's co-operation at Constantinople.
[3] Moustier to Lhuys, June 12, *ibid.*, no. 2649. Moustier said that Lyons's co-operation was only passive; but it is possible, of course, that the French ambassador was deliberately taking most of the credit to himself.
[4] Lhuys to agents, June 14, *ibid.*, no. 2681.
[5] Moustier to Lhuys, June 13, *ibid.*, no. 2690.
[6] Moustier to Lhuys, June 16, *ibid.*, no. 2712.
[7] *Aus dem Leben*, vol. i, p. 71.
[8] Green to Clarendon, no. 104, June 17, F.O. 78/1921.
[9] Report of the finance minister, Sturdza, *op. cit.*, vol. i, pp. 223 ff.
[10] *Aus dem Leben*, vol. i, p. 64.

of living was lamentably high,[1] it was hardly to be expected that the Prince's new subjects would be able to fill the breach. Bratiano tried in vain to persuade the assembly to take the dubious step of an issue of paper money;[2] and, for several months, the government lived from hand to mouth. To make matters worse, there was an epidemic of cholera in Moldavia and—what was more immediately embarrassing—an outbreak of anti-semitism in that province. The occasion for this disorder—which rapidly spread to Bucharest —was the course of the debate on the project of a new constitution. All the efforts of the progressives to procure the emancipation of the Jews proved quite unavailing against the tide of public senti- ment, and the burning of a synagogue in Bucharest induced the Jews themselves to ask for the withdrawal of the measure.[3] From the outset, as might well be assumed, the drafting of the new constitution[4] was the scene of bitter quarrels, and it was apparently only through the patient insistence of the Prince[5] that agreement was finally reached and a constitution finally adopted on July 11. Charles himself had stood inflexibly for the right of the crown to impose an absolute veto on legislation, and, in the end, won his point.[6] The constitution was not illiberal, compared to the organic laws of other countries, but it is noticeable that the suffrage was so restricted as to exclude most of the peasants whom Couza had enfranchised.[7] But the groundwork of the monarchy had been laid. And, though many vital problems were yet unsettled, the making of a constitution by the Moldo-Wallachians was another landmark in the national evolution.

Still, one must not misinterpret its immediate valuation. In declaring for a hereditary monarchy, the constitution went beyond the legal power vested in Roumanian autonomy, and it remained to be seen whether this position would be accepted by the Porte, and consequently by the Protecting Powers as well. For the legal status of the Principalities was still unchanged as long as Europe's recognition of the new régime remained a matter of doubt. We have noticed that France and Great Britain were ready to grant that favour, but it was equally clear that they felt that the initiative should be taken by the Porte, and that it was for the Porte to settle

---

[1] *Ibid.*, p. 62.

[2] As foreign capital would inevitably have suffered from any attempt to defray obligations with depreciated currency, Eder was ready to instigate consular intervention, if the plan had carried: Eder to Mensdorff, no. 89 B, June 10, Staatsarchiv, XXXVIII/148.

[3] *Aus dem Leben*, vol. i, pp. 75–7.

[4] This step was taken on the basis of the preamble of the 'Acte additionel' of June 28, 1864: Green to Clarendon, no. 104, June 13, F.O. 78/1921.

[5] *Aus dem Leben*, vol. i, p. 93.

[6] *Ibid.*, pp. 79–80.

[7] The constitution is printed in the appendix to Damé, *op. cit.*

the question by direct negotiation with Bucharest. The Conference at Paris had signally failed to solve the problem (on June 4 Clarendon had telegraphed to Cowley, 'I look upon the Conference as at an end'[1]), and there was no point in continuing useless discussions while central Europe was being rapidly engulfed in war.[2] Apart from Turkey, the only Power which sustained her interest in the Principalities was Russia, and Russia, as we have noticed, had abandoned all hope of using the Conference to suit her ends. How much trouble would come from Russia must depend, of course, on Gortchakoff. Though one cannot take his statements or his overtures too seriously, it is noticeable that his coldness toward the Roumanian deputation considerably thawed before their mission was concluded. Assuming that the Conference was very soon to be terminated, he said that Russia would reserve her liberty of action, and that she would then be disposed to recognize Charles.[3] The inference that the Conference had thus prevented Russia from displaying her generosity is rather amusing, but, judging from the statement of one of the other ministers, who was said to share the vice-chancellor's confidence, this sudden friendliness may partially be explained. If Charles should agree to marry the Princess of Leuchtenberg (Talleyrand, it was said, was privately urging this at St. Petersburg[4]) one might meet Russia's objection to his rule on the score of religion.[5] Still, the suggestion was, perhaps, no more than a feeler, and Russian intrigues at Constantinople amply justify the belief that Gortchakoff was, as often, following mutually contradictory courses of action, and that, in all probability, his policy was undetermined.

Nevertheless, when Russia had brought the Conference to an end, and Budberg had formally announced that each Power should recover its liberty of action, there was not a little perplexity as to what Gortchakoff intended. Ali, who had felt disposed to go on with the negotiations[6]—temporarily blocked because the Porte was too exacting in its demands[7]—was now hesitating in fear of this uncertainty. According to information, which apparently came

[1] Clarendon to Cowley, June 4, telg., F.O. 27/1606.
[2] It was on the 6th that Clarendon had telegraphed to Cowley, raising the question whether, in view of international complications, it might not be well to recognize Charles, on the assumption that he would recognize the Sultan's suzerainty.
[3] Gotchakoff's only stipulations were that he must be assured of the maintenance of public order and of the removal of all risk to the national religion.
[4] Buchanan to Layard, June 6, Layard Papers, Brit. Mus. Add. MSS. 39120.
[5] Talleyrand to Lhuys, June 8, Origines, vol. x, no. 2604.
[6] Moustier to Lhuys, July 5, ibid., no. 2872. Prokesch intimates that Austria's military defeats in the war with Prussia was a factor leading the Porte to consider recognition of Charles: Prokesch to Mensdorff, no. 39 A–B, July 10, Staatsarchiv, XII/84.
[7] Avril to Lhuys, June 20, Origines, vol. x, no. 2762.

from Ignatieff, the Porte was led to believe that Russia, in breaking up the Conference, had gone so far as to denounce the Treaty of Paris. This unfortunate misapprehension was speedily corrected,[1] but it is fairly safe to assume that a certain lurking dread of Russia had something to do with the continuous protraction of the negotiation. Another cause of delay was a sudden change of viziers, the Sultan having decided to make a scapegoat of Fuad for the failure of Turkish policy. As the dominant note in Turkish circles was the necessity of defending the honour of the Empire, the wary Ali, who narrowly escaped disgrace along with his friend, had every reason to temporize. Finally, in spite of Charles's assurances to Ali, that he was not an instrument of Bismarck's,[2] the Porte was led by Austrian statements—so it was alleged—to believe that the Prince had been sent to Roumania to incite a rebellion in Hungary; in any case, one might wait to see the outcome of the war, as the importance of Austria could then be gauged.[3] Sensing, perhaps, the uncertainties of the future, Drouyn de Lhuys, when the Conference met for the last time to be dissolved, had raised the question of the meaning of the Russian declaration, which would substitute for the principle of the common *entente* the right of the Powers, neighbouring on Roumania, to pursue what course they chose. The representatives of Turkey, Prussia, Italy, and Great Britain adhered to France's view that the Protecting Powers were still bound to come to some *entente*, and Metternich merely reserved his government's liberty of action in the event that deliberations should arrive at no result.[4] By so doing, Drouyn de Lhuys felt that he had spiked the enemy's guns.[5] Austria certainly could not afford to break her pledges, and Russia would think twice before she undertook alone to defy the public law of Europe.

While the Porte was somewhat assured by this information from Paris, the conduct of Charles during the struggle in which his native land was engaged was perhaps the best evidence of his sanity as a statesman and of his patriotic judgement as Prince of Roumania. We have no evidence to suppose that Bismarck ever tried to induce him to break his own neutrality.[6] It was enough

[1] Moustier to Lhuys, no. 79, July 11, *Aff. étr.*, *Turquie*, vol. 368.
[2] Eder to Mensdorff, no. 84, May 28, Staatsarchiv, xxxviii/148.
[3] Moustier to Lhuys, no. 77, July 4, *Aff. étr.*, *Turquie*, vol. 368.
[4] Mensdorff had not put it in quite that way to Metternich. He had said merely that Austria's own point of view agreed with that of Russia (Mensdorff to Metternich, June 15, no. 3, Staatsarchiv, ix/83). But then it is noticeable that Mensdorff seldom displayed critical judgement, and seemed to leave a good deal to the discretion of the ambassadors.
[5] Lhuys to Moustier, no. 44, July 6, *ibid.*
[6] Eder's belief was that the most that Bismarck expected of Charles was to stir up an insurrection in Transylvania: Eder to Mensdorff, no. 114, Aug. 15. Examination of the consular correspondence in the Reichsarchiv reveals no trace of

that Austria was forced to watch her border.[1] But, in any event, it is doubtful if Charles would have succumbed to the temptation. Though the fear of invasion by the Turks had now subsided,[2] the Prince had had too painful an experience not to profit by its lesson. When that perennial adventurer, Türr, came to Roumania to seek his co-operation in fomenting an insurrection in Transylvania, Charles refused without qualification to engage in such intrigues.[3] Whether or not it is true that the radicals were guilty of encouraging such a conspiracy,[4] Charles had taken the opportunity of parting with these firebrands. As Bratiano and Rosetti had broken with Catargi,[5] and since the latter, on resigning, advised the Prince to choose a homogeneous ministry,[6] Charles decided to appoint one from the Right and chose as its head John Ghika, because (according to his own explanation) that statesman seemed to enjoy the confidence of the Porte.[7] Though Austria had never felt sure of Charles's behaviour as long as the Left had been in office, her feeling had been chiefly due to the fear that a ruler, so weak, would find himself unable to resist its pressure. Such a fear could now be largely allayed. Eder, for his part, though refusing to credit Charles with any sagacity,[8] felt that, after all, the best guarantee that this son of Prussia would refrain from mischief was the internal condition of his state,[9] and it is certainly true that bankrupt Roumania was in no position to engage in foreign adventures.

The time was coming, indeed, when, if his government could manage to escape economic collapse, Charles would probably reap the reward of his patient waiting. The obduracy of the Porte was, after all, largely a matter of habit, and history had proved that under pressure it would nearly always yield. The only indis-

---

any conspiracy against Austria; and assuredly if Charles had moved any forces to the Austrian frontier, the other consuls would have noted it.

[1] A study of the Akten der militarischen Kanzlei des Kaisers, 1866, in the Kriegsarchiv shows that Austria sent no additional troops to the border, but, in response to urgent solicitation from Field Marshal Prince Montenuovo, commander of the forces in Transylvania, the Emperor allowed him to take all measures of defence that he deemed necessary 'without further questioning and without regard to cost'. This order is dated July 17.

[2] Green to Clarendon, no. 105, June 23, F.O. 78/1921.

[3] Aus dem Leben, vol. i, p. 89.

[4] Eder to Mensdorff, no. 111, Aug. 2, Staatsarchiv, xxxviii/148.

[5] According to Damé (op. cit., p. 170) they resigned because they were unwilling to leave it to Catargi to supervise the new elections, necessitated by the dissolution of the assembly. Charles does not mention in his memoirs the cause of their disaffection, but implies that financial difficulties had brought about the crisis (Aus dem Leben, p. 90). According to Eder, Charles would like to have retained Bratiano (Eder to Mensdorff, no. 111).

[6] Eder to Mensdorff, no. 111.   [7] Aus dem Leben, vol. i, p. 90.

[8] Eder to Mensdorff, no. 111. He called him 'a complete nullity' and declared that he had not 'grown to the task'. It was not often that the Baron was so prejudiced in his judgements.   [9] Eder to Mensdorff, no. 114.

pensable requirement was the aid of some disinterested Power; and, engrossed though he was in affairs of greater moment, Napoleon was too genuinely interested in the Roumanians to abandon them in the hour of need. Early in July Balatchano had sent the cheering news that the Emperor had said that he would soon extend his recognition, and to that end he promised his good offices at Constantinople.[1] It was felt in French circles that Charles should voluntarily go to Constantinople to seek investiture;[2] but suzerain and vassal were still too far apart to make so marked an overture quite practicable—especially when it was known that the Porte, departing from the treaties, was now demanding this visit as one of its conditions. Ali had, in fact, drawn up a statement of the Porte's terms, which must be accepted as the price of recognition. This document[3] was handed to Ghika, who was reported to have said that he believed that the conditions would prove, in the main, acceptable,[4] and thereupon departed for Bucharest to submit them to his government.

The result was a prompt rejection; and, when we come to examine the terms of the Porte's project, we can only wonder that Ghika should have shown so little patriotism or insight. The most objectionable of the Porte's conditions were: (article 4) that the princely dignity should remain elective, (article 8) that the Porte should be represented by a resident agent at Bucharest, (article 10) that the tribute, due to the Porte, should be increased in proportion to the present resources of the Principalities, (article 12) that the Prince should be debarred from coining money or awarding decorations, and (article 3) that his administration would have no legal status without preliminary investiture and that he should come immediately to Constantinople to procure it. It is patent enough that article 4, if granted, would have placed the foreign prince on the same basis as Couza, and have signified an abandonment of a condition, inseparable from his position—namely, hereditary rule. The other articles, above-mentioned, were a departure from or extension of existing treaties; another (article 7), which forbade the publications of journals of a nature to disturb the peace, was reviving a question which had been a bone of contention once before;[5] and still another (article 5), restricting the size of the army in accordance with existing treaties, was naturally an impediment to the national ambition; finally, it was keenly felt by the government that the Principalities should not be debarred (as article 6 seemed to imply) from forming alliances with foreign Powers with or without the Porte's consent, and that

[1] *Aus dem Leben*, vol. i, p. 78.
[2] Lhuys to Avril, July 13, *Origines*, vol. xi, no. 2971.
[3] Printed in Sturdza, *op. cit.*, vol. i, pp. 302–5.
[4] Lyons to Clarendon, no. 260, July 12, F.O. 78/1911. [5] See p. 186.

they should be allowed at least to make treaties of local import with neighbouring Powers.[1] In fact, not one of the conditions of the project received the unqualified approval of the prince or his council.

On July 17 the council of ministers drew up a counter-project[2] in response to the Porte's demands. The prince would pledge himself to go to Constantinople, but not until recognition had been granted (article 3), the Prince's rule should be hereditary (article 4), the army might be increased without a preliminary *entente* with the Porte (article 5), the amount of tribute should be increased but fixed at some future time (article 10). The article of the Turkish project imposing a censorship on journals, as well as those providing for a Turkish agent and forbidding the privilege of coining money or conferring decorations were suppressed entirely in the counter-project; likewise, a provision (article 11) that the question of the monasteries should be settled in conformity with the protocols. In place of the flat demand from the Principalities to defend, when necessary, the general interests of the Empire (article 6), the counter-project limited such a requirement to aid against foreign aggression. Some contentions of the Roumanian government were based on pride rather than practical expediency. Objection was made to the article in the Turkish project which had defined the legal relations of the Principalities to the Ottoman Empire and also to the expression 'firman of investiture', which the counter-project replaced by 'act of recognition'; and, instead of the present denomination of the state, which the Porte desired (article 2), the counter-project substituted 'Roumania', or the 'Roumanian Principalities'.

It is easy to see that so decided a divergence in the standpoint of the two parties would demand considerable discussion. Both sides were striving to obtain a position which went beyond what suzerainty or autonomy, as the case might be, had heretofore warranted; and, certainly, on the part of the Principalities, much was asked, for the fulfilment of which a more promising moment would have to be awaited. Drouyn de Lhuys (by Napoleon's order) again urged Charles to go to Constantinople, promising the Emperor's assistance to his cause, but the Prince felt strongly that the terms of the Porte's project did not as yet justify the venture.[3] Fortunately, Ali had given Lyons to understand that he was willing to consider changes, provided that the essential points in his project were maintained,[4] and to Golesco, the Rou-

---

[1] *Aus dem Leben*, vol. i, pp. 119–20.
[2] The counter-project is printed parallel with the project, article by article in Sturdza.
[3] *Aus dem Leben*, vol. i, p. 92.
[4] Lyons to Clarendon, no. 267, July 17, F.O. 78/1911.

manian kapou kiaya, he suggested that, if the Roumanian government were to conclude a military convention with the Porte for
common defence against assaults upon the Empire, it would have
the effect of inducing concessions on the part of his government.[1]
Moustier, who had learned from Avril some of the points to
which the Roumanians objected,[2] replied by telegraph that some
articles were susceptible to misunderstanding through faults of
composition, and that the Porte had not only given up the
monastery provision but had decided (though apparently this
was an error) to admit the hereditary character of Charles's
rule.[3] To Drouyn de Lhuys Moustier telegraphed on July 30,
'I believe that all present difficulties are in the Principalities';
he went on to say that the Porte was piqued that no mention
had been made in the constitution of the suzerainty of the Sultan,[4]
and then advised that the Prince should, above all, notify the Porte
that the rights which had been vested in him by the constitution
should be held as only within the limits of the treaties.[5] At the
close of July the outlook appeared so dark that Charles felt it
necessary to reinforce the army. Yet the strain on the depleted
treasury was more than it could bear, and Charles had to draw on
his civil list to defray the cost of his new armaments. 'Only a loan
can save us to-day,' he wrote in his journal on July 28. 'We are
negotiating with bankers, but the conditions are more than hard.'[6]
No ruler could have been more tireless in his devotion to public
duty. He had snatched every available day to become better
acquainted with Wallachia, but he had not yet been able to spare
the time to visit Moldavia. His confidence in the present ministry
led him, apparently, to the belief that the worst days were over,[7]
but actually the economic state of the country was becoming
daily more acute. On August 17 he wrote a personal letter to
Napoleon, impressing upon him the vital importance of having
the Porte's recognition. 'The entire state, especially Moldavia,'

[1] *Aus dem Leben*, vol. i, p. 91.
[2] Avril to Moustier, July 17, annex to Moustier's no. 83, *Aff. étr., Turquie*, vol. 368.
[3] Moustier to Avril, July 23, telg., *ibid.*
[4] It appears that this was deliberate on the part of the framers. Avril, who remarked that the assembly, which had passed this Act, had 'often shown more *enfantillage* than practical sense', tells us that they really had 'the dangerous idea of separating their country from the Porte', and that the only deputy who wished to discuss the rights of the Sultan was refused the floor: Avril to Lhuys, no. 58, Aug. 10, *ibid., Turquie, Bucharest*, vol. 28.
[5] Moustier to Lhuys, July 31, *Origines*, vol. xi, no. 3235; and Aug. 1 (no. 84), *Aff. étr., Turquie*, vol. 368.
[6] *Aus dem Leben*, vol. i, pp. 93–4.
[7] This entry was on Aug. 11: *ibid.*, p. 98. Charles had probably in mind the termination of the political quarrels at Bucharest. It may be added that *Aus dem Leben* is compiled partly from a diary and partly from private correspondence; see Witte, *Quinze Ans d'histoire*, pp. 13–14.

he wrote, 'is threatened with famine. . . . The sole means of coming to the succour of the people is to secure a loan.'[1] The only hopeful change in the situation was that the Porte had finally yielded on the question of heredity in the main line,[2] though it stubbornly insisted on the right to have an agent, like other Powers, at Bucharest;[3] on most questions, indeed, such as the relations of the Principalities to the Empire, the Turks felt that Charles should be more generous.[4] Lyons and Moustier had come to the opinion that now was the propitious time for the Prince to make his visit, and they had sent identical telegrams to their consuls to that effect.[5] But Charles felt that he could not leave during an epidemic of cholera,[6] and that, anyway, he should first have received his firman of investiture—seeing that such had been the procedure in the case of his predecessor; even his request, he complained, had never been acknowledged.[7] Of course, he must have realized that previous investiture was quite impossible until the contentious points had been removed, but he was probably right in feeling that the Porte had much to concede before he could wisely make the journey. For his own part, he was willing to bend a little. While he did not want to be restricted as to the number of his troops, he told Avril that he intended out of economy to cut the army to half its size, and that he would never think of attacking his suzerain or his neighbours.[8] Finally, after a regrettable delay, he brought himself to comply with Moustier's wise suggestion, and wrote to Ali that he would not exercise the rights conferred upon him by the constitution save within the limits of the treaties and his obligations to the suzerain Power.[9] Unhappily, the Porte was little mollified by the Prince's 'interpretation';[10] and, while the Prince's request for investiture was now, at last, 'received', Ali complained both of its tardiness and of its tone, which was 'that of one sovereign to another';[11] he did not think, on the whole, that the present moment was the time for the Prince's trip.[12] And so the deadlock continued throughout August; and Charles, not seeing any progress in the negotiation, made his long-intended

[1] *Aus dem Leben*, vol. i, pp. 99–100.
[2] Lyons to Stanley, no number, July 31, F.O. 78/1912.
[3] Lyons to Stanley, no. 305, Aug. 15, *ibid.*
[4] *Aus dem Leben*, vol. i, pp. 99–100.
[5] Avril to Lhuys, no. 55, Aug. 4, *Aff. étr., Turquie, Bucharest*, vol. 28.
[6] Avril to Lhuys, no. 54, Aug. 1, *ibid.*
[7] Avril to Lhuys, no. 58, Aug., *ibid.*
[8] Avril to Lhuys, no. 55.
[9] Iorga, *Correspondance diplomatique roumaine sous le roi Charles I*, p. 11. He now said that he was ready to go to Constantinople as soon as the Sultan granted him recognition: Stirbey to Balatchano, Aug. 11, *Origines*, vol. xii, no. 3380.
[10] Lyons to Stanley, no. 305.
[11] Moustier to Lhuys, no. 86, Aug. 14, *Aff. étr., Turquie*, vol. 368.
[12] Lyons to Stanley, no. 305.

journey to Moldavia—a step which was amply repaid by the heartiness of the welcome.[1]

Yet, thanks to Moustier's efforts at conciliation, the month had not been wasted. Charles's government now begged that negotiations should not be severed,[2] and the easy-going Ali was really anxious to please the Powers, if only the Sultan's dignity were properly respected.[3] Pressed by Lyons and Moustier, who promised to make one further effort to bring Bucharest to reason,[4] Ali drew up a second project, which he declared to be his government's last word,[5] and he told Moustier that he felt that the Porte had made great concessions.[6] As a matter of fact, the hereditary principle had not been granted for collateral lines, and the Porte maintained its former position regarding minting and decorations, the size of the army, the augmentation of tribute, the summons to Constantinople, and the establishment of a resident Turkish agent at Bucharest. Charles felt that he could not accept such hard conditions, and, in spite of renewed pressure from Napoleon, who thought that he might smooth out these points of difficulty in Constantinople, he resolved not to make the trip until the desired recognition had been extended.[7] Yet he seems to have given Avril to understand that he would accept whatever Moustier advised, and he talked of making the journey as soon as the quarantine against cholera, which had been established against Moldavia, should permit.[8] In order to facilitate an understanding, two of the ministers, the younger Stirbey and Demetrius Sturdza, were sent to Constantinople to conduct some further *pourparlers*. After much effort on the part of Moustier and of the chargé d'affaires, Bonnières (after the former had been called to succeed Drouyn de Lhuys as foreign minister), the Porte had given up its not unreasonable demand for a resident agent at Bucharest.[9] It was also decided that the army should be fixed at 30,000 men—a figure which signified a considerable augmentation over the establishment Couza had enjoyed. In the matter of minting, the Porte had already expressed its willingness to extend this privilege, provided a symbol of Turkish suzerainty were stamped on all coinage; and this compromise was eventually accepted. But the point which seemed to cause the greatest difficulty was the statement in the

[1] *Aus dem Leben*, vol. i, chap. viii; cf. St. Clair to Green, no. 20, Sept. 3, F.O. 78/1922.
[2] Lyons to Stanley, no. 320, Aug. 29, F.O. 78/1912.
[3] Moustier to Lhuys, no. 86, Aug. 14, *Aff. étr., Turquie*, vol. 368.
[4] Lyons to Stanley, no. 325, Sept. 5, F.O. 78/1913.
[5] Moustier to Lhuys, Aug. 29, *Origines*, vol. xii, no. 3822.
[6] Moustier to Lhuys, Aug. 29, *Docs. dip.*, *1867*, p. 172.
[7] *Aus dem Leben*, vol. i, pp. 119–20.
[8] Avril to La Valette, Sept. 5, *Origines*, vol. xii, no. 3556.
[9] Bonnières to Moustier, Sept. 26, *ibid.*, no. 3631.

Turkish project that the Principalities were an 'integral part of the Ottoman Empire'. For some reason Charles seemed to feel that the word 'integral' had an invidious connotation. On September 30 a special meeting of the council of ministers, to which certain prominent leaders outside the government had been called, pronounced itself opposed to most of the Turkish conditions;[1] and, if the Prince himself were not disposed to show himself more yielding, it was difficult to see how even the friends of the Principalities could help them to a solution.

But the time had come when Hohenzollern pride and Roumanian patriotism must bend to circumstance. It was reported that Napoleon was much irritated by Roumanian recalcitrance, and Ghika told his master that under present conditions his ministry could go on no longer.[2] With much reluctance Charles consented to make the trip to Constantinople before some of the minor points were settled, but he insisted that to the expression, 'integral part of the Ottoman Empire' should be added the words, 'within the limits fixed by the Capitulations and the Treaty of Paris'. It was somewhat the same douche as that which had enabled the constitution to become purified; and to this amendment Ali consented.[3] Only the form of the agreement had now to be determined; for, while the Porte had expressed itself as willing to send the firman,[4] Charles had wisely decided, once he should have received recognition, to go to Constantinople to be invested. At a happy suggestion of Moustier's it was decided to register the agreement by an interchange of letters—a device which would avoid the cold formality of 'projects', as well as convey the desired recognition; and, accordingly, after the sending of the final conditions in a vizirial letter and their acceptance by an immediate reply,[5] Charles was free to undertake his mission of homage.

On October 22 Charles left with a numerous retinue for Constantinople.[6] His reception was as cordial as could be desired, and he was granted three audiences with the Sultan, who presented him with a sabre, richly-studded with diamonds.[7] But his proud

[1] Aus dem Leben, vol. i, pp. 119–20.
[2] Ibid., p. 120. Lyons to Stanley, no. 325, Sept. 5, F.O. 78/1913.
[3] Bonnières to Moustier, Oct. 11, Origines, vol. xii, no. 3669.
[4] According to his own account, Charles, on receiving a telegram from Sturdza that Ali still held out for the journey before recognition, instructed Sturdza to threaten Roumanian aid to the Cretans, who were then in revolt. One is rather inclined to smile at this bravado.
[5] Charles gave in on the question of conferring decorations, and left the fixing of the tribute and some details respecting the minting question to future arrangement. He also promised to keep his dominions free of trouble-makers and to conclude an understanding with the Porte for the protection of imperial interests. The vizirial letter and Charles's adhesion are given in Aus dem Leben, vol. i, pp. 132–5.
[6] Charles himself gives the best account of his visit: Aus dem Leben, vol. i, chap. x.   [7] Bonnières to Moustier, no. 106, Oct. 31, Aff. étr., Turquie, vol. 368.

soul revolted against any token of vassalage. Disregarding a gesture of the Sultan to occupy a stool at his feet, he deliberately selected a seat on a sofa beside his suzerain, and, when the firman was handed him, he passed it, unopened, to one of his ministers. Nevertheless, the Prince was said to have made a most favourable impression (one may judge so from the fact that he won his point both as to minting and as to the granting of honorary orders); and the conditions of the investiture, while involving some minor concessions on the part of a vassal state, and forcing it to retain the cumbersome title bequeathed to it by the Convention, gave, in truth, to 'Roumania' a status which justified the name by which her people proudly hailed her.

On the day before the Prince's departure the consuls, with the single exception of Offenberg, received an audience with the Prince and congratulated him on the conclusion of his settlement with the Porte. 'Therewith', wrote Charles in his diary, 'is expressed the European Powers' official recognition.'[1] Yet the Prince was slightly anticipating the legal act by which the Powers acknowledged his right to the Roumanian throne. Although there was no doubt of the outcome, a delay of some months ensued over the form in which the intended recognition should be extended. France and Great Britain desired that the Conference of Paris should reconvene and send a collective sanction of the firman; Russia, on the other hand, characteristically raised objections, persisting in her contention that the Conference was dead and buried.[2] Perhaps the only significance of a dispute, which on the surface was undeniably petty, was the palpable implication that the role of the Protecting Powers had now properly come to an end. As a solution of the dilemma, Great Britain, France, Austria, Prussia, and Italy sent practically identical dispatches to the Porte, conveying a ratification of the settlement;[3] and already Russia had given her separate adhesion. By 1867 all the Protecting Powers had tendered their recognition,[4] and one may fairly assert that 'Roumania' had been 'made'. An immediate result of the national triumph was the conclusion of a loan at Paris. Roumania could now feel that her worst trials were over.

We shall now end our story of the making of Roumania, leaving to another to tell of the steps by which Charles was able to get rid of the hated Capitulations, secure the independence of Roumania

[1] *Aus dem Leben*, vol. i, p. 136. Offenberg later tendered his congratulations: Green to Hammond, Nov. 8, F.O. 78/1923.
[2] Beust to Miilinen, Dec. 18 and 24, Staatsarchiv, IX/83.
[3] Prokesch to Beust, no. 5 A–C, Feb. 1, 1867, *ibid.*, XII/85. A copy of the French dispatch is printed in *Doc. dip.*, *1867*, pp. 178–9.
[4] *Arch. dip.*, *1867*, vol. ii, p. 706. Shortly afterwards Austria granted the request of the Principalities to receive an accredited agent at Vienna: *Collectiune de tractatele romaniei* (ed. Mitilineu), p. 132.

in the Treaty of Berlin, and elevate his principality to the status of a kingdom. Independence, while often thought of as the ultimate destiny of this nation, had never been a paramount object of Rouman nationalism during the critical and formative years which we have described. It was by realizing the aspiration of uniting the two principalities, Moldavia and Wallachia, and eventually securing for them the right to be ruled by a foreign prince that the Roumanian people had hoped to found their state securely on a basis that would enable them to face the future and feel that it was theirs. Through the moral strength of their cause they had won the indispensable assistance of the Emperor Napoleon III. Somewhat grudgingly—because the aspirations of these strange people seemed less cogent than the long established rights of the suzerain Power—Great Britain had usually seconded the good offices of France. It was undoubtedly by virtue of the prestige of the Western Powers that the Danubian Principalities were saved from becoming the arena of Ottoman intrigue and allowed to seek their fortunes untrammelled by the intrusive interference of their neighbours. If the triumph of these people was so long delayed, the reason may be sought in the more than dubious experiment of an international protectorate. Yet it is often with heavy and laboured tread that History attains her ends.

BIBLIOGRAPHY [1]

PRIMARY AUTHORITIES
Unpublished

Archives du Ministère des Affaires étrangères, Paris. Diplomatic and consular correspondence and reports, 1856–66 (*passim*).

Bloomfield Papers, Public Record Office, London.

Foreign Office Papers, Public Record Office, London. Diplomatic and consular correspondence and reports, 1856–66 (*passim*).

Kriegsarchiv, Vienna. Official Acts, 1856, 1866, and miscellaneous papers, 1866.

Layard Papers, British Museum.

Reichsarchiv, Berlin. Diplomatic and consular correspondence and reports, 1866 (*passim*).

Royal Archives, Windsor. Letter of Clarendon to the Queen, August 10, 1857.

Russell Papers, Public Record Office.

Staatsarchiv, Vienna. Diplomatic and consular correspondence and reports, 1856–66 (*passim*).

Stratford Papers, Public Record Office.

Published
CONTEMPORARY BROCHURES

Anon., *L'Autriche et le prince roumain*, Paris, 1859.

Anon., *L'Empereur Napoléon et les Principautés roumaines*, Paris, 1858.

Anon., *Mémoire sur les conditions d'existence des Principautés danubiennes*, Paris, 1854.

Anon., *Les Principautés-Unies devant la conférence, mars, 1866*, Paris, 1866.

Anon. (Balcescu, N.), *Question économique des Principautés danubiennes*, Paris, 1850.

B. (Bolintineanu, D.), *L'Autriche, la Turquie, et la Moldo-Valachie*, Paris, 1856.

Bataillard, Paul, *La Moldo-Valachie dans la manifestation de ses efforts et ses vœux*, Paris, 1856.

Bengesco, G., *Mémorandum sur les églises, les monastères, les biens conventuels et spécialement sur les monastères dédiés de la principauté de Valachie*, Bucharest, 1858.

Boeresco, B., *Examen de la Convention rélative à l'organisation des Principautés danubiennes*, Paris, 1858.

Le Firman turc pour la convocation des divans ad hoc des principautés du Danube, Paris, 1857.

Mémoire relative à la question politique et économique de la Moldo-Valachie, Paris, 1856.

Boeresco, C., *Amélioration de l'état des paysans roumains*, Paris, 1861.

Bratiano, J-C., *Mémoire sur la situation de la Moldo-Valachie depuis le traité de Paris*, Paris, 1857.

---

[1] Confined to works cited in the foregoing work.

Castille, Hippolyte, *Portraits politiques et historiques au dix-neuvième siècle: Le prince Alexandre Ghika IX, caimacam de Valachie, et Nicolas Conaki-Vogorides, Caimacam de Moldavie*, Paris, 1857.

Chainoi, G. (pseud. for Ghika, John), *Dernière occupation des Principautés par la Russie*, Paris, 1853.

Cretzulesco, E. M., *La Roumanie en 1859*, Paris, 1859.

Texier, Edmond, *Appel au congrès en faveur des roumains*, Paris, 1856.

CONTEMPORARY TREATIES, MEMOIRS, CORRESPONDENCE, ETC.

Actes et documents relatifs à l'histoire de la régénération de la Roumanie, ed. Sturdza, D. A. *et al.*, 10 vols., Bucharest, 1900–9.

Acte și legiuiri privitoare la chestia tărăneasca, seria I (vol. iv, *Broșuri si extrase Românești și străine*), 4 vols., Bucharest, 1908.

Archives diplomatiques: recueil de diplomatie et d'histoire, Paris, 1860– .

Ashley, Evelyn, *The Life of Henry John Temple, Viscount Palmerston, with Selections from his Speeches and Correspondence*, 2 vols., London, 1877.

Bismarck: Die gesammelten Werke, ed. Petersdorff, H. von, 13 vols., Berlin, 1924–30.

Bolintineanu, D., *Viată lui Cuza-Vodă (Alexandru Joan I) și Calatoria la Constantinople*, Jassy, 1868.

British and Foreign State Papers, London, 1841– .

'Câtera farâme din correspondenta lui Alexandru Vodă Ghika' in *Analele Academiei Române*, seria II, tomul xxix, Bucharest.

Il Carteggio: Cavour-Nigra dal 1858 al 1861, Piano delle pubblicazioni della R. commissione editrice de' carteggi Cavouriani, 3 vols., Bologna, 1926–8.

Cavour, Lettere edite ed inedite (di) Camillo di, ed. Chiala, L., 4 vols., Turin, 1883–5.

Cavour, La Politique du Comte Camille de, 1852–61: Lettres inédites, ed. Bianchi, N., Turin, 1885.

Chalemal-Lacour, M. P., 'Les Hommes d'état de la Turquie' in *Revue des deux mondes*, 2nd per., vol. lxxiii.

(Charles I), *Aus dem Leben König Karls von Rumänien; Aufzeichnungen eines Augenzeugen*, 4 vols., Stuttgart, 1894–1900.

Charles Ier, Roi de Roumanie; Chronique, actes, documents, ed. Sturdza, D. A., 2 vols., Bucharest, 1899–1904.

Collectiune de tratatele si conventiunile romaniei ou puterile străine de la annulŭ 1368 pânĕ în ḑilele nóstre, ed. Mitilineu, M., Bucharest, 1874.

Correspondence diplomatique roumaine sous le roi Charles Ier, 1866–1880, ed. Iorga, N., Paris, 1923.

Desprez, H., 'La Moldo-Valachie et le mouvement roumain' in *Revue des deux mondes*, nouv. sér., vol. xxi.

Documents diplomatiques (Ministère des Affaires étrangères), 1861, 1864, 1866.

East, W. G., 'The Osborne Conference and Memorandum of August, 1857', in *English Historical Review*, vol. xliii.

Ernest II, Duke of Saxe-Coburg-Gotha, Memoirs of, tr. Andreae, P., 4 vols., London, 1888–90.

The European Concert in the Eastern Question: A Collection of Treaties and Other Public Acts, ed. Holland, T. E., Oxford, 1885.

Forester, Thomas, *The Danube and the Black Sea: A Memoir of their Junction by a Railway between Tchornavoda and Kustendji*, London, 1857.

Girardin, Saint-Marc, *Souvenirs de voyage et d'études*, Paris, 1852.

Gourdon, Édouard, *Histoire du Congrès de Paris*, Paris, 1857.

Greville, C. C. F., *A Journal of the Reign of Queen Victoria from 1852 to 1860*, 2 vols., London, 1887.

Hérocque-Melleville, E. N., *Six Mois en Valachie*, Paris, 1859.

Hübner, Count Joseph Alexander von, *Neuf Ans de souvenirs d'un ambassadeur d'Autriche à Paris sous le Second Empire*, 2 vols., Paris, 1904.

Iorga, N., *Mihail Kogălniceanu: scriitorul, omul politic şi Românul*, Bucharest.

'L'Italie libérée: Lettres et dépêches du roi Victor Emmanuel II et du Comte de Cavour au Prince Napoléon' in *Revue des deux mondes*, ser. 7, vol. xiv.

Kogălniceanu, Mihail, *Scrisori, 1834–1849*, Bucharest, 1913.

Kossuth, Louis, *Souvenirs et écrits de mon exil*, Paris, 1880.

La Marmora, A. F., *Un peu plus de lumière*, Paris, 1874.

Le Cler, G., *La Moldo-Valachie—ce qu'elle a été, ce qu'elle est, ce qu'elle pourrait être*, Paris, 1866.

Loftus, *The Diplomatic Reminiscences of Lord Augustus, 1837–1862*, 2 vols., London, 1892.

Malmesbury, Earl of, *Memoirs of an ex-Minister*, 2 vols., London, 1884.

Map of Europe by Treaty, The, ed. Hertslet, E., 4 vols., London, 1875.

Mars, V. de, 'L'Occupation russe dans les Principautés du Danube' in *Revue des deux mondes*, 2nd ser., vol. iv.

Maxwell, Sir Herbert, *The Life and Letters of George William Frederick, Fourth Earl of Clarendon*, 2 vols., London, 1913.

Negri, Costache, *Versuri, Proză, Scrisori*, ed. Gârleanu, E., Bucharest, 1909.

Newton, Lord, *Lord Lyons: A Record of British Diplomacy*, 2 vols., London, 1913.

Nouveau Recueil de traités, conventions, et autres transactions remarquables, servant à la connaissance des relations étrangères des puissances et états dans leurs rapports mutuels: continuation du grand recueil de G. Fr. de Martens, ed. Samner and Hopf, 35 vols., Göttingen, 1876–1908.

Ollivier, Émile, *L'Empire libérale: études, récits, souvenirs*, 17 vols., Paris, 1895–1915.

[1]Oncken, Hermann, *Die Rheinpolitik Kaiser Napoleons III. von 1863 bis 1870 und der Ursprung des Krieges von 1870–71*, 3 vols., Stuttgart, 1926.

Les Origines diplomatiques de la guerre de 1870–1871: recueil des documents publié par le ministre des affaires étrangerès, Paris, 1910– .

---

[1] Chiefly made up of dispatches.

Parliamentary Debates, pub. Hansard, T. C., third ser., 356 vols., London, 1830–91.

Parliamentary Papers, 1854–55, vol. lv, London, 1855.

Recueil d'actes internationaux de l'Empire ottoman, ed. Noradounghian, G., 4 vols., Paris, 1897–1903.

Rothan, G., *Les Origines de la guerre de 1870 : Politique française en 1866*, Paris, 1884.

Russell, *The Later Correspondence of Lord John, 1840–1878*, ed. Gooch, G. P., London, 1925.

Saint Marc-Girondin, *Souvenirs de voyage et d'études*, Paris, 1852.

Sayn-Wittgenstein-Berlebourg, Prince Émile, Souvenirs et correspondance (de), 2 vols., Paris, 1888.

Schickler, Fernand, *En orient: souvenirs de voyage, 1858–1861*, Paris, 1863.

Schlözer, Kurd von, Petersburger Briefe, 1858–1862, nebst einem Anhang, ed. Schlözer, L. von, Berlin, 1923.

Second Empire and its Downfall, The: Correspondence of the Emperor Napoleon III and his Cousin, Prince Napoleon, ed. Hauterive, Ernest d', tr., Wilson, H., London, 1927.

Senior, N. W., *Conversations with M. Thiers, M. Guizot, and Other Distinguished Persons during the Second Empire*, ed. Simpson, M. C. M., 2 vols., London, 1878.

Soutzo, *Mémoires du Prince Nicolas, 1798–1871*, Vienna, 1899.

Tacmelile agricole in România: legi și proiecte insoțite de expuneri de motive și rapoarte, 1859–1907, Bucharest, 1907.

Thouvenel, E., 'La Valachie en 1839' in *Revue des deux mondes*, nouv. sér., vol. xviii.

Thouvenel, L., *Pages de l'histoire du Second Empire d'après les papiers de M. Thouvenel*, Paris, 1903.

Le Secret de l'Empereur: Correspondance confidentielle et inédite échangée entre M. Thouvenel, le duc de Gramont, et le général comte de Flahaut, 1860–1863, Paris, 1889.

Trois Années de la question d'orient, 1856–1859, d'après les papiers inédits de M. Thouvenel, Paris, 1897.

Thun, Gräfin Leopoldine, *Erinnerungen aus meinem Leben*, Innsbruck, 1926.

Ubicini, M., *Valachie et Moldavie* (part 2 of Chopin, M., and Ubicini, M., *Provinces danubiennes*), Paris, 1856.

Urquhart, David, *The Mystery of the Danube*, London, 1851.

Vaillant, J. A., *La Romanie, ou histoire, langue, littérature, orographie, statistique des Romans*, 4 vols., Paris, 1844–5.

Vielcastel, Horace, Memoirs of : A Chronicle of the Principal Events, Political and Social, during the Reign of Napoleon III from 1851 to 1864, ed. and tr., Bousfield, C., London, 1888.

Victoria, Letters of Queen: A Selection from Her Majesty's Correspondence between the Years 1837 and 1861, ed. Benson, A. C., and Esher, Viscount, London, 1907.

Vitzthum von Eckstädt, St. Petersburg and London, 1852–1864, Reminiscences of Count Charles Frederick, ed. Reeve, H., 2 vols., London, 1887.

Wilkinson, William, *An Account of the Principalities of Wallachia and Moldavia, with Various Political Observations relative to them*, London, 1820.

Wilhelms des Grossen, Briefe, Reden und Schriften, ed. Berner, E., 2 vols., Berlin, 1906.

MISCELLANEOUS

Almanach de Gotha, 1860.

Annual Register, 1857, 1858.

Annuaire des deux mondes, 1856, 1866.

Arhivă: Organul societatiĭ ştiintifice şi literare din Jaşi (passim).

Newspapers and journals cited: *The Press, The Saturday Review, The Times, Le Constitutionel, Le Moniteur, Le Moniteur du soir, Le Journal des débats, La Nation, La Patrie, Le Siècle, Le Journal de St. Péters-bourg, Süddeutsches Monatsheft, Dimineaţă* (Bucharest).

SECONDARY AUTHORITIES

Arion, Charles C., *La Situation économique et sociale du paysan en Roumanie*, Paris, 1895.

Bamberg, Felix, *Geschichte der orientalischen Angelegenheit im Zeitraume des Paris und des Berliner Friedens*, Berlin, 1892.

Bengesco, Georges, *Bibliographie franco-roumaine depuis le commencement du XIXᵉ siècle jusqu'à nos jours*, Paris, 1907.

Bibesco, Prince Georges, *Règne de Bibesco*, 2 vols., Paris, 1893.

Blaramberg, N., *Essai comparé sur les institutions et les lois de la Roumanie depuis les temps les plus reculés jusqu'à nos jours*, Bucharest, 1885.

Ciroceanu, Georges D., *La Roumanie économique et ses rapports avec l'étranger de 1860–1915*, Paris, 1928.

Charles-Roux, F., *Alexandre II, Gortchakoff, et Napoléon III*, Paris, 1913.

Damé, Frédéric, *Histoire de la Roumanie contemporaine, depuis l'avènement des princes indigènes jusqu'à nos jours*, Paris, 1900.

Débidour, A., *Histoire diplomatique de l'Europe depuis l'ouverture du congrès de Vienne jusqu'à la fermeture du congrès de Berlin, 1814–1878*, 2 vols., Paris, 1891.

East, W. G., *The Union of Moldavia and Wallachia*, Cambridge, 1929.

Engel-Janosi, Friedrich, *Graf Rechberg: vier Capitel zu seiner und Österreichs Geschichte*, Munich, 1927.

Evans, Ifor L., *The Agrarian Revolution in Roumania*, Cambridge, 1924.

Filitti, Jean-C., *Les Principautés roumaines sous l'occupation russe, 1828–1834: le Règlement organique*, Bucharest, 1904.

Friedjung, Heinrich, *Der Krimkrieg und die Oesterreichische Politik*, Stuttgart, 1911, Bucharest, 1914.

Ghibănescu, Gh., *Cuzeştii*, Bucharest, 1912.

Iorga, N., *Geschichte des rumänischen Volkes im Rahmen seiner Staatsbildungen*, 2 vols., Gotha, 1905.

Histoire des relations russo-roumaines, Jassy, 1917.

La Gorce, Pierre de, *Histoire du Second Empire*, 7 vols., Paris, 1908–11.

Lane-Poole, Stanley, *The Life of the Right Honourable Stratford Canning, Viscount Stratford de Redcliffe, from his memoirs and private and official papers*, 2 vols., London, 1888.

Lindenberg, Paul, *König Karl von Rumänien: Ein Lebensbild dargestellt unter Mitarbeit des Königs*, Berlin, 1923.

Martin, Theodore, *The Life of His Royal Highness, the Prince Consort*, 4 vols., London, 1879.

Monicault, Gaston de, *La Question d'orient: le traité de Paris et ses suites*, 1856–71, Paris, 1898.

Pélissié du Rousas, G., *Le Régime des capitulations dans l'Empire ottoman*, 2 vols., Paris, 1910–11.

Riker, T. W., 'The Concert of Europe and Moldavia in 1857' in *English Historical Review*, vol. xliii.

'The Pact of Osborne' in *American Historical Review*, vol. xxxiv.

Robertson, C. Grant, *Bismarck*, London, 1918.

Rosetti, R., *Pentru ce s'au râsculat ţăranii*, Bucharest, 1907.

Satow, Sir Ernest, *An Austrian Diplomatist in the Fifties*.

Simpson, F. A., *Louis Napoleon and the Recovery of France, 1848–1856*, London, 1923.

Wambaugh, Sarah, *A Monograph on Plebiscites*, New York, 1920.

Witte, Jehan de, *Quinze Ans d'histoire, 1866–1881, d'après les mémoires du roi de Roumanie et les témoignages contemporains*, Paris, 1905.

Xénopol, A. D., *Domnia lui Cuza-Vodă*, 2 vols., Jassy, 1903.

Histoire des Roumains de la Dacie trajane depuis les origines jusqu'à l'union des principautés en 1859, 2 vols., Paris, 1896.

Xénopol, 'Nicolae Kretzulescu' in *Anatele Academiei Romăne*, seria II, tomul xxiv.

INDEX

Abd-ul-Aziz, Sultan, 323, 453, 557, 564–5.
Abd-ul-Medjid, Sultan, 77, 120, 150–1, 264, 304, 323.
Acte additionel, l', adopted, 455–6; making of constitution legal under, 523, 538.
Adrianople, Peace of, 2, 10, 259.
Adriatic, The, 274, 284.
Afif Bey, 186, 192.
Akkerman, 394; Convention of, 12–13.
Albert, Prince, 132.
Alexander, Prince, 467.
Alexander II, Tsar, at Stuttgart, 142; at Weimar, 143; threatens war, 513; cool to Charles, 552.
Alexandri, John, 237, 240–1, 252, 266.
Alexandri, Vasili, 69, 196.
Ali Pasha, at Congress of Paris, 43–4; character of, 55–6; at Vienna, 58; prohibits discussion of union by divans *ad hoc*, 58–9; precipitates resignation of hospodars, 68; yields on rights of divans *ad hoc*, 74; fall of, 77; refuses to take office, 78; ready to knife Reshid, 120; returns to ministry, 127, 151; explains circular, 145; French pressure upon, 155, 162; objects to hereditary hospodars, 168; and question of double election, 199, 217; fears Rouman independence, 236; in arms imbroglio, 274–6, 281, 284; in negotiations over union, 306–7, 312, 322, 324–5, 330–3; fears dismissal, 331; transferred to foreign office, 339; in controversy over dedicated monasteries, 360–1, 366–7, 369, 371–2, 431; requests sequestration of arms, 387; opposes sending commissioner to Principalities, 408; attitude towards projected dictatorship of Couza, 421, 424; and Couza's *coup d'état*, 449–51, 454–5; invites Powers to consider case of Couza, 486; invokes Protocol of 1859, 507–8; threatens withdrawal from Conference, 526; menaces Principalities, 544, 549, 551; explains armaments, 554; negotiates with Charles, 557, 560, 562–4. *See also* Porte; Turkey; Turks.
Alison, R., mission of, to Principalities, 34; wanted for commissioner, 83; mission of, to Jassy, 117; reported boasts of, 125.
Allied Powers, 24, 48.
Anthony (von Hohenzollern), Prince,

past career of, 527–8; works for son's candidature, 531–2, 534, 537.
Apponyi, Count, 133–4.
Arsaki, A., 26 n.4, 336–7, 345, 383–4, 390.
Aspromonte, Battle of, 384.
Austria, occupies Principalities, 24; interests of, in Principalities, 25, 27, 47 n.2; attitude of, towards union, 26–7, 41, 44, 92, 100, 230, 339, 516–17; invites delegates of Principalities to Vienna Conference, 29; under suspicion, 32–4; designs of, against plebiscite of 1857, 46, 58, 68–9, 71, 74, 87, 92, 95–6, 101, 105–7; and question of evacuating Principalities, 47–9, 52–4, 76; signs treaty of guarantee, 50; covets control of Danube, 65; connives at hospodars' fall, 68; on question of conference over Bolgrad, 75; wants intervention in Wallachia, 92–3; connexion of, with Pact of Osborne, 133; presses Porte, 145, 150, 162; at Conference of Paris (1858), 158, 160, 163–4, 170, 173–4; connexion of, with Capitulations, 177, 232, 353, 468; with caimacamie quarrel, 185, 187, 191, 200; in question of *de facto* recognition of Couza, 213, 231, 277; attitude of, towards double election, 215, 218, 220, 227–8, 247; fears conspiracy against her, 272; intervention of, in arms imbroglio, 275–6, 282–4; opposed to moving central commission, 295; opposed to changing Convention, 300, 312; in negotiations over union, 321–3, 325, 329–30, 339; criticized by Bulwer, 325; opposes title, 'Roumania', 348–9; and question of dedicated monasteries, 368, 431–2, 435 n.3; protests to Michael, 378; proposes conference over Servia, 379; accused of prodding Porte, 389; invokes Protocol, 397; menaces frontiers of Principalities, 438; and Couza, 449, 454; opposes national bank, 469; charged with fomenting revolution, 474; and question of Venetia-Principalities exchange, 476, 510–13; value to Principalities of annexation to, 480; alleged views of, 514; policy of, at Conference of Paris (1866), 516–17; Bismarck's design against, 536; question of importance of, 557; reassured regarding Charles, 565;